W9-BKQ-444

HANDBOOK OF PROGRAMMING LANGUAGES, VOLUME I

Object-Oriented Programming Languages

Peter H. Salus, Series Editor in Chief

Handbook of Programming Languages, Volume I: Object-Oriented Programming Languages

Peter H. Salus, Series Editor in Chief

FIRST EDITION

International Standard Book Number: 1-57870-008-6

Library of Congress Catalog Card Number: 97-81204

01 00 99 4 3 2

Interpretation of the printing code: The rightmost double-digit number is the year of the book's printing; the rightmost single-digit, the number of the book's printing. For example, the printing code 98-1 shows that the first printing of the book occurred in 1998.

Composed in Sabon and MCPdigital by Macmillan Technical Publishing

Printed in the United States of America

Warning and Disclaimer

Permissions

Associate Publisher
Jim LeValley

Managing Editor
Caroline Roop

Executive Editors
Linda Engelman
Tom Stone

Acquisitions Editors
Jane K. Brownlow
Karen Wachs

Development Editor
Kitty Wilson Jarrett

Project Editor
Brad Herriman

Copy Editor
Kristine Simmons

Indexers
Chris Cleveland
Bront Davis

Team Coordinator
Amy Lewis

Manufacturing Coordinator
Brook Farling

Book Designer
Gary Adair

Cover Designer
Karen Ruggles

Production Team Supervisor
Daniela Raderstorf

Production
Mary Hunt
Laura A. Knox

Overview

Table of Contents

Foreword to the *Handbook of Programming Languages*

The aim of the *Handbook of Programming Languages* is to provide a single, comprehensive source of information concerning a variety of individual programming languages and methodologies for computing professionals. The *Handbook* is published in multiple volumes and covers a wide range of languages, organized by type and functionality.

The *Handbook* includes four volumes:

Volume I: Object-Oriented Programming Languages

This volume contains chapters on Smalltalk, C++, Eiffel, Ada95, Modula-3, and Java.

Volume II: Imperative Programming Languages

This volume contains chapters on Fortran, Pascal, Icon, and C, as well as a chapter on intermediate languages by Ron Cytron.

Volume III: Little Languages and Tools

This volume contains chapters on little languages and domain-specific languages, such as troff, awk, sed, Perl, Tcl and Tk, Python, and SQL. It also contains seminal work by Brian Kernighan and Lorinda Cherry as well as Jon Bentley and essays by Paul Hudak and Peter Langston.

Volume IV: Functional and Logic Programming Languages

This volume contains chapters on functional (Lisp, Scheme, Guile, and Emacs Lisp) and logic (Prolog) programming languages.

Natural, or human, languages appear to be about 10,000 years old. Symbolic, or formal, languages began in Sumer (a civilization of southern Iraq from about 3800 to 2300 BCE), where we find the oldest writing system, cuneiform. It was followed by Egyptian hieroglyphics (about 3000 BCE), the language of the Harappa in the Indus valley, the Chinese shell and bone inscriptions, and (in the Western hemisphere) the language of the Maya.

Writing systems abstract from speech and formalize that abstraction in their symbols. This may be done semantically (for example, hieroglyphs, English numerals, and symbols such as &) or phonologically (for example, alphabetic spelling).

In more recent times, further abstractions have become necessary: warning beacons, flags on sailing vessels, railway telegraph/semaphore, Morse code, and so forth.

Mechanical methods for calculating are very old, but they all involve symbolic abstraction. The abacus is probably the oldest of such constructions. The Chinese and Egyptians had this device nearly four millennia ago. The Mayans possessed it when the Spanish arrived. It was only a few years after Napier's discovery of logarithms (1614), and the use of his "bones" (marked ivory rods) for multiplication, that the slide rule was invented.

In 1642, at the age of 18, Blaise Pascal invented a calculator that could add and carry to aid his father, a tax collector. Almost 30 years later, in 1671, Leibniz took Pascal's machine a step further and built a prototype machine that could multiply using an ingenious device called the *stepped wheel*, which was still in use in mechanical calculators manufactured in the late 1940s. Leibniz demonstrated his calculator to the Royal Society in London in 1676.

The first commercially successful calculator was invented by Charles Xavier Thomas in 1820. By 1878, an astounding 1,500 had been sold—nearly 30 per year. They were still being manufactured by Darras in Paris after World War I. The Brunsviga adding machine, based on an 1875 patent by Frank Stephen Baldwin, which substituted a wheel with a variable number of protruding teeth for the Leibniz stepped wheel, sold an incredible 20,000 machines between 1892 and 1912—1,000 per year.

The first keyboard-driven calculator was patented in 1850 by D. D. Parmalee, and Dorr Eugene Felt's Comptometer—the first successful key-driven, multiple-order calculating machine—was patented in 1887.

In 1812, Charles Babbage came up with a notion for a different type of calculator, which he termed a *difference engine*. He was granted support by the British government in 1823. Work stopped in 1833, and the project was abandoned in 1842, the government having decided the cost was too great. From 1833 on, though, Babbage devoted himself to a different sort of machine, an analytical engine, that would automatically evaluate any mathematical formula. The various operations of the analytical engine were to be controlled by punched cards of the type used in the Jacquard loom. Though only a fraction of the construction appears to have been effected, Babbage's notes, drawings, and portions of the engine are in the Victoria and Albert Museum (as is the set of Napier's bones that belonged to Babbage).

The Jacquard loom, a successful attempt at increasing production through automation, was itself the result of several prior innovations: In 1725 Bouchon substituted an endless paper tape with perforations for the bunches of looped string. In 1728 Falcon substituted perforated cards, but attached them to strings, and in 1748, Jacques de Vaucanson combined the bands of perforated paper and the cards. The patterns on the cards were perforated by machines that cut on designs painted on by stencils. The programmed machine was born.

Over 100 years later, Herman Hollerith, a graduate of Columbia College in New York, recalled the existence of those perforated cards. Hollerith had just started work at the Census Bureau at a generous salary of $600 per year. There he was put to work on a survey of power and machinery used in manufacturing. But he also met John Shaw Billings, who was in charge of "vital statistics." One night at dinner, Billings complained about the recently invented but inadequate tabulating device of Charles Seaton, which had been used for the census of 1870. Billings felt that given the increased population, the 1880 census might not be completed in less than seven or eight years, and the 1890 census would still be incomplete in 1900. "There ought to be a machine for doing the purely mechanical work of tabulating population and similar statistics," Billings said. "We talked it over," Hollerith recalled 30 years later, "and I remember...he thought of using cards with the description of the individual shown by notches punched in the edge of the card." Hollerith thought about constructing a device to record and read such information and asked Billings to go into business with him. Billings was a cautious man and said no.

In 1882 Hollerith went to MIT as an instructor in mechanical engineering (he was then 22). Teaching at MIT gave him the time to work on his machine. He first considered putting the information on long strips of paper, but this proved impractical. In the summer of 1883, Hollerith took a train trip west. On the train he saw the "punch photograph," a way for conductors to punch passengers' descriptions onto tickets so they could check that the same individual was using the ticket throughout the trip; in this system things like gender and hair and eye color were encoded.

Hollerith patented his first machine in 1884 and an improved design in 1886, when he performed a trial by conducting the Baltimore census. On the basis of reports of the trial, New Jersey and New York placed orders for machines (to tally mortality rates). Hollerith and some business colleagues bid for the contract for the 1890 census and won it. The government of Austria ordered machines in 1890. Canada ordered five the next year. Italy and Norway followed, and then Russia. The machines were a clear success. Hollerith incorporated his Hollerith Electric Tabulating System as the Tabulating Machine Company in 1896; he reincorporated it in 1905.

Nearly 80 years passed before the computer industry moved beyond several of Hollerith's insights. First, so that operators would have no problem orienting the cards, he cut a corner from the upper right. Second, he *rented* the machines at a reasonable rate (the rental fees for the 1890 census were $750,000; the labor cost in 1880 had been $5 million), but *sold* the patented cards (more than 100 million between 1890 and 1895). Third, he adapted the census-counting to tally freight and passenger data for railroads. Hollerith effectively invented reusability.

Despite the fact that Thomas Watson said (in 1945), "I think there is a world market for about five computers," the first completed was one he had funded. Howard Aiken of Harvard, along with a small team, began in 1939 to put together a machine that exploited Babbage's principles. It consisted, when completed in 1944, of a 51-foot by 8-foot panel on which tape readers, relays, and rotary switches were mounted. Nearly all of the operations of the Harvard Mark I Calculator were controlled by mechanical switches, driven by a 4-horsepower motor.

The first all-electronic computer was the Electronic Numerical Integrator and Calculator. Completed by J. W. Mauchly and J. P. Eckert of the University of Pennsylvania in late 1945 and installed in 1946, it was commissioned by the Ballistics Research Laboratory (BRL) at the Aberdeen (Maryland) Proving Ground. It was—and will remain, I expect—the largest computing machine ever built: It was made up of 18,000 tubes and 1,500 relays. ENIAC was the electronic analogue of the Mark I, but ran several hundred times faster.

ENIAC had offspring in England, too. Maurice V. Wilkes and his group began planning their Electronic Delay Storage Automatic Calculator (EDSAC) in late 1946, on Wilkes's return from Pennsylvania, and began work at the University Mathematical Laboratory in Cambridge early in the new year. It was one fifth the size of ENIAC and based on ideas that John von Neumann had presented in a paper. When it performed its first fully automatic calculation in May 1949, EDSAC became the first electronic machine to be put into operation that had a high-speed memory (store) and I/O (input/output) devices. Within a few years, EDSAC's library contained more than 150 subroutines, according to Wilkes.

At virtually the same time, in Manchester, a team under M. H. A. Newman began work on a machine that was to embody the EDVAC concepts. F. C. Williams, who invented cathode ray tube storage, I. J. Good, who had worked on the Colossus code-breaking machine with Alan M. Turing, and Turing himself, joined the team. The Manchester Automatic Digital Machine prototype was built in 1948, and the definitive machine ran its first program in June 1949. MADM introduced to computing both the index register and pagination.

In the meantime, IBM had begun work on its Selective-Sequence Electronic Calculator (SSEC). It is important to remember that while EDSAC was the first electronic computer, the SSEC was the first *computer*—it combined computation with a stored program. It was put into operation at IBM headquarters in Manhattan early in 1948, cleverly placed behind plate glass windows at street level so that pedestrians could see it operate. It was a large machine with 13,000 tubes and 23,000 relays. Because all the arithmetic calculations were carried out by the tubes, it was more than 100 times as fast as the Mark I. It also had three different types of memory: a high-speed tube store, a larger capacity in relays, and a vastly larger store on 80-column paper tape. Instructions and input were punched on tape and there were 66 heads arranged so that control was transferred automatically from one to the other. "It was probably the first machine to have a conditional transfer of control instruction in the sense that Babbage and Lady [Ada] Lovelace recommended," wrote B. W. Bowden in 1953. It did work for, among other things, the Atomic Energy Commission, before being dismantled in August 1952.

That very June, von Neumann and his colleagues completed Maniac at the Institute for Advanced Studies in Princeton, New Jersey. It employed the electrostatic memory invented by F. C. Williams and T. Kilburn, which required a single cathode ray tube, instead of special storage tubes.

The next advance in hardware came at MIT's Whirlwind project, begun by Jay Forrester in 1944. Whirlwind performed 20,000 single-address operations per second on 16-digit words, employing a new type of electrostatic store in which 16 tubes each contained 256 binary digits. The Algebraic Interpreter for the Whirlwind and A-2—developed by Grace Murray Hopper for the UNIVAC—are likely the most important of the machine-oriented languages.

The 704, originally the 701A, was released in 1954. It was the logical successor to the IBM 701 (1952, 1953). The evolution of the 701 into the 704 was headed up by Gene Amdahl. The direct result of the 701/704 was the beginning of work on Fortran (which stands for *formula translator*) by John Backus at IBM in 1953. Work on the Fortran translator (we would call it a compiler) began in 1955 and was completed in 1957. Fortran was, without a doubt, the first programming language.

In December 1959, at the Eastern Joint Computer Conference at the Statler Hotel in Boston, the three-year-old DEC unveiled the prototype of its PDP-1 (Programmed Data Processor-1). It was priced at $120,000 and deliveries began in November 1960.

The PDP-1 was an 18-bit machine with a memory capacity between 4,096 and 32,768 words. The PDP-1 had a memory cycle of 5 microseconds and a computing speed of 100,000 computations per second. It was the result of a project led by Benjamin Gurley and was composed of 3,500 transistors and 4,300 diodes. It had an editor, a macroassembler, and an ALGOL compiler, DECAL. It employed a paper tape reader for input and an IBM typewriter for output. The PDP-1 had the best cost/performance of any real-time computer of its generation. It was also the first commercial computer to come with a graphical display screen.

Just over 40 years ago there were no programming languages. In 1954 programming was still a function of hardware. Fortran was invented in 1957. It was soon being taught. By 1960, not only had COBOL and Lisp joined the roster, but so had others, many now thankfully forgotten. Over the past 40 years, nearly 4,000 computer languages have been produced. Only a tithe of these are in use today, but the growth and development of them has been progressive and organic.

There are a number of ways such languages can be taxonomized. One frequent classification is into machine languages (the natural language of a given device), assembly languages (in which common English words and abbreviations are used as input to the appropriate machine language), and high-level languages (which permit instructions that more closely resemble English instructions). Assembly languages are translators; high-level languages require conversion into machine language: These translators are called *compilers*. Among the high-level languages currently in use are C, C++, Eiffel, and Java.

Yet there is no guide for the overwhelmed programmer, who merely wants to get her job done. This *Handbook of Programming Languages* is intended to serve as an instant reference, a life-preserver, providing information to enable that programmer to make intelligent choices as to which languages to employ, enough information to enable him to program at a basic level, and references to further, more detailed information.

Peter H. Salus

Boston, February 1998

General Bibliography

Histories of Programming Languages

Bergin, T. J., and R. G. Gibson (Eds.). 1996. *History of programming languages*. Reading, MA: Addison-Wesley. Proceedings of ACM's Second History of Programming Languages Conference.

Sammet, J. A. 1969. *Programming languages: History and fundamentals.* Englewood Cliffs, NJ: Prentice Hall. An indispensable work.

Wexelblat, R. L. (Ed.). 1981. *History of programming languages.* New York: Academic Press. The proceedings of ACM's First History of Programming Languages Conference.

Reader on Programming Languages

Horowitz, E. 1987. *Programming languages: A grand tour* (3rd ed.). Rockville, MD: Computer Science Press.

Surveys and Guides to Programming Languages

Appleby, D. 1991. *Programming languages: Paradigm and practice.* New York: McGraw-Hill.

Bal, H. E., and D. Grune. 1994. *Programming language essentials.* Wokingham, England: Addison-Wesley.

Cezzar, R. 1995. *A guide to programming languages.* Norwood, MA: Artech House.

Sethi, R. 1996. *Programming languages: Concepts & constructs* (2nd ed.). Reading, MA: Addison-Wesley.

Stansifer, R. 1995. *The study of programming languages.* Englewood Cliffs, NJ: Prentice Hall.

Foreword to This Volume: Object-Oriented Programming Languages

Programming languages are just 40 years old. Programming with objects is less than 30 years old. SIMULA 67 was the first example of using classes of objects. The first truly object-oriented programming language was Smalltalk, named in 1971. But it was Smalltalk-80 that first drew attention. At AT&T Bell Labs, Bjarne Stroustrup was also influenced by SIMULA—he added classes to C in a compiler preprocessor. From this effort came C++, released in 1982–1985. At almost the same time (1982), Bertrand Meyer came out with Eiffel.

Ada, created by a U.S. government committee, was originally imperative. The most recent release is, however, clearly object oriented, and I have decided to place it in this volume of the *Handbook of Programming Languages*. I have made a similar decision about Modula-3. Modula-2 was a straightforward imperative language; however, Modula-3 is object oriented.

With CLOS, I made the opposite decision: I put it in Volume IV, "Functional and Logic Programming Languages," together with Emacs Lisp, Scheme, and Guile, rather than among the object-oriented languages.

Finally, I have included in this volume a lengthy section on Java, created only a few years ago by James Gosling and his group at Sun Microsystems.

Tim Budd (Oregon State University) and Doug Schmidt (Washington University) have written introductory essays on object-oriented languages; these are included at the beginning of this volume.

Throughout this volume, I have attempted to allow the authors to retain their own flavor, avoiding homogenization of their contributions.

Peter H. Salus

Boston, February 1998

Trademark Acknowledgments

All terms mentioned in this book that are known to be trademarks or service marks have been appropriately capitalized. Macmillan Technical Publishing cannot attest to the accuracy of this information. Use of a term in this book should not be regarded as affecting the validity of any trademark or service mark.

Dedication

This *Handbook* is dedicated to John Backus, James Gosling, Adele Goldberg, Ralph Griswold, Brian Kernighan, John McCarthy, Bertrand Meyer, Dennis Ritchie, Bjarne Stroustrup, and the memory of Joe Ossanna, without whose efforts most of these languages wouldn't exist.

Acknowledgments

Many individuals deserve mention where this enormous *Handbook* is concerned. First of all, Tom Stone, who abetted my thinking and then effected a contract prior to deserting me for another publisher; next, Jim LeValley and Don Fowley at Macmillan, for being willing to take a chance on this project. I'd also like to thank Linda Engelman, Tracy Hughes, Amy Lewis, Jane Brownlow, Karen Wachs, and Kitty Jarrett at Macmillan.

In addition to the many authors, I'd like to thank Lou Katz, Stuart McRobert, Len Tower, and Brent Welch for their advice, patience, and friendship.

My gratitude to the ACM, to Addison-Wesley Longman, to MIT Press, to O'Reilly & Associates, and to the Waite Group for permissions to reprint various materials is enormous.

The errors and omissions are mine.

About the Series Editor

Peter H. Salus

Peter H. Salus is the author of *A Quarter Century of UNIX* (1994) and *Casting the Net: From ARPANET to Internet and Beyond* (1995). He is an internationally recognized expert and has been the keynote speaker at Uniforum Canada, the UKUUG, the NLUUG, and the OTA (Belgium) in the past few years. He has been executive director of the USENIX Association and of the Sun User Group and vice president of the Free Software Foundation. He was the managing editor of *Computing Systems* (MIT Press) from 1987 to 1996. He writes on a variety of computing topics in a number of magazines. His Ph.D. in linguistics (New York University, 1963) has led him from natural languages to computer languages.

About the Authors

Ken Arnold

Ken Arnold is a leading expert in object-oriented design and implementation, and has written extensively on C and C++ topics for *UNIX Review*. He is the co-author of *A C User's Guide to ANSI C*. He is also the co-author, with James Gosling, of *The Java Programming Language*, part of the official Sun series of books on the Java language, packages, and environment. Ken is a senior staff engineer with Sun Microsystems, previously in Sun Labs, and now in JavaSoft. His is currently part of the team using the JavaSoft Remote Messaging Interface (RMI) to write distributed Java applications. Before coming to Sun, Ken's experience includes being part of the original Hewlett-Packard architectural team designing CORBA, several user interface and UNIX projects at Apollo Computers, and molecular graphics at UC-San Francisco. In the olden days, he was part of the 4BSD team at UC-Berkeley, where he created the curses library package for terminal-independent screen-oriented programs, and was co-author, with Mike Toy and Glen Wichman, of the computer game Rogue. He received his A.B. in computer science from UC-Berkeley in 1985.

Timothy A. Budd

Timothy A. Budd is an associate professor of computer science at Oregon State University. His major areas of interest include programming language design and implementation and the combination of multiple language paradigms. He is the author of several books on programming languages, including *A Little Smalltalk*, *Introduction to Object-Oriented Programming*, *APL Compiler*, and *Multi-Paradigm Programming in Leda*.

Michael B. Feldman

Michael B. Feldman received a B.S.E. in electrical engineering in 1966 from Princeton University, and M.S. and Ph.D. degrees in computer and information sciences from University of Pennsylvania in 1970 and 1973, respectively.

Dr. Feldman's interest in computer software was kindled by a junior-level course in which Fortran was used for solving numerical engineering problems. Dr. Feldman was back in Princeton from 1970 to 1974, employed as a computer scientist by Educational Testing Service. He then spent a year in Europe, as staff consultant to the managing director of Samsom Automatisering, a data-processing company in the Netherlands.

In 1975, Dr. Feldman joined the Department of Electrical Engineering and Computer Science at The George Washington University, where he now holds the rank of full professor. He is responsible for the CS majors-oriented introductory programming course, the undergraduate data structures and file structures courses, and a graduate course in concurrent programming. He received the Eta Kappa Nu Teacher of the Year Award in 1985.

He is the author of a number of popular textbooks. The most recent, *Ada 95 Problem Solving and Program Design* (Addison-Wesley, 1996) and *Software Construction and Data Structures* (Addison-Wesley, 1996) are best-sellers in their respective markets in the United States and abroad.

He and his students have developed educational software development environments with special features for studying Ada tasking. These systems, known as GW-Ada/Ed-DOS and GW-Ada/Ed-Mac, are available free on the Internet and are currently in use in hundreds of academic, government, and industrial sites around the world. More recently, the group has been responsible for a packaged version of the GNU Ada 95 (GNAT) compiler. Commonly referred to as ez2load, this distribution has been copied thousands of times from a number of Internet servers.

David Flanagan

David Flanagan is a consulting computer programmer, user interface designer, and trainer. He has a degree in computer science and engineering from Massachusetts Institute of Technology. David has written many books, including *Java in a Nutshell: A Desktop Quick Reference*, *JavaScript: The Definitive Guide*, *X Toolkit Intrinsics Reference Manual*, and *Motif Tools: Streamlined GUI Design and Programming with the Xmt Library*.

Adele Goldberg

Adele Goldberg is a founder of Neometron, Inc., a Texas-based company working toward Intranet-based dynamic knowledge management. She is also leading the development of LearningWorks, a freely available system for creating and delivering curriculum about software construction. She was a founder of ParcPlace Systems, Inc. (which created application development environments based on object-oriented technology that were sold to corporate development teams) and served variously as the company's CEO until 1991 and chairman of the board until April 1996. Dr. Goldberg received a Ph.D. in information science from the University of Chicago and spent 14 years as researcher and laboratory manager at the Xerox Palo Alto Research Center. From 1984 to 1986, Adele served as president of the ACM, having previously served as national secretary and editor-in-chief of *Computing Surveys*. Solely and with others, Dr. Goldberg wrote the definitive books on the Smalltalk-80 programming system and has authored numerous papers on project management and analysis methodology using object-oriented technology. She edited *The History of Personal Workstations*, published jointly by the ACM and Addison-Wesley in 1988 as part of the ACM Press Book Series on the History of Computing, which she organized; she also co-edited *Visual Object-Oriented Programming* with Margaret Burnett and Ted Lewis. Her latest book, with Kenneth S. Rubin, is on software engineering and is titled *Succeeding with Objects: Decision Frameworks for Project Management.*

Dr. Goldberg received the ACM Systems Software Award in 1987 along with Dan Ingalls and Alan Kay, as well as *PC Magazine*'s 1990 Lifetime Achievement Award for her significant contributions to the personal computer industry. She is a Fellow of the ACM, and was honored in 1995 with the Reed College Howard Vollum Award for contributions to science and technology. She is currently a member of the scientific advisory board of the German National Research Centers, is a director of The San Francisco Exploratorium, and is on the board of directors of two private technology companies.

James Gosling

James Gosling is a fellow and vice president at Sun Microsystems and the key architect of the Java programming language. Gosling received a Ph.D. from Carnegie Mellon University. After developing the initial versions of the Andrew toolkit at Carnegie Mellon, he joined Sun Microsystems in 1984, where he has worked on window systems, user interfaces, toolkits, and general system architecture. His research interests include both the intersection of computer science and graphics, and the design of user interfaces. He wrote an early version of Emacs and was the principal developer of NeWS, Sun's network-extensible windowing system. He was the 1996 recipient of Software Development's Programming Excellence Award.

Bill Joy

Bill Joy received his master's degree in electrical engineering from the University of California at Berkeley, where he was the principal designer of Berkeley UNIX. He wrote both ex and vi. He was one of the founders of Sun Microsystems and is now Sun's vice president of research and development. He designed Sun's Network File System (NFS), and worked on Sun's Scalable RISC Processor (SPARC). Joy received the ACM's Grace Murray Hopper Award in 1986 and the USENIX Association's Lifetime Achievement Award in 1993.

Andrew Koenig

Andrew Koenig is a member of the Large-Scale Programming Research Department at AT&T Research, which was once part of Bell Laboratories. He has been working mostly on C++ since 1986.

He joined Bell Labs in 1977 from Columbia University (New York). Aside from C++, his work has included programming language design and implementation, security, automatic software distribution, online transaction processing, and computer chess. He is the author of more than 100 articles and the book *C Traps and Pitfalls*, and coauthor of the book *Ruminations on C++*. He has taught courses at Columbia and Princeton Universities and Stevens Institute of Technology, given tutorials for USENIX Association, Stanford University, Boston University, Lund Institute of Technology, SIGS Conferences, the Federal Open Systems Conference Board, and the Federal Reserve Bank, and given invited talks for IBM, Syracuse University, ACM, IEEE, Miller-Freeman, and AT&T in Tokyo. He is the project editor of the ISO/ANSI C++ committee and a member of five airline frequent flyer clubs.

Bertrand Meyer

Bertrand Meyer is president of Interactive Software Engineering. He was the initial designer of the Eiffel method and language and has continued to participate in its evolution. He also directed the development of the ISE Eiffel environment, compiler, tools, and libraries through their successive versions. Some of his other activities include chairman of the TOOLS conference series, editor of Prentice Hall's *Object-Oriented* series, co-editor of the magazine *L'OBJET*, consulting editor of Addison-Wesley's *Eiffel in Practice* series, and associate member of the Applications Council of the French Academy of Sciences (CADAS). He is also active as a consultant (object-oriented system design, architectural reviews, technology assessment), trainer in object technology and other software topics, and conference speaker.

Farshad Nayeri

Farshad Nayeri is the director of product development at Critical Mass, Inc. (`http://www.cmass.com`), where he leads the development of systems programming language products for Modula-3 and Java. Before Critical Mass, he was a senior member of the technical staff at GTE Laboratories, where he conducted research in distributed object technology. Farshad has been a happy Modula-3 user since 1989.

Jonathan and Victoria Pletzke

Jonathan and Victoria Pletzke have been consulting on Smalltalk projects for a number of years and met on one such project. Jonathan wrote *Advanced Smalltalk* (with lots of help, of course) for people learning Smalltalk who wanted to learn more than just the basics. The Pletzkes' interests include graphical user interfaces (GUIs), objects, hardware interfaces, product creation, and peaceful coexistence. They live and work in Morristown, New Jersey, and can be reached at The Technical Expertise Corporation or via email at `jpletzke@sprynet.com` or `72603.563@compuserve.com`.

Douglas C. Schmidt

Douglas C. Schmidt is an assistant professor in the Department of Computer Science and in the Department of Radiology at Washington University in St. Louis. His research focuses on design patterns, implementation, and experimental analysis of object-oriented techniques that facilitate the development of high-performance, real-time distributed object computing systems on parallel processing platforms running over high-speed ATM networks. Dr. Schmidt is an internationally recognized expert on distributed object computing and has published widely in top IEEE, ACM, IFIP, and USENIX technical conferences and journals.

Dr. Schmidt has served as guest editor for feature topic issues on distributed object computing for the *IEEE Communications Magazine* and the *USENIX Computing Systems Journal*, and served as co-guest editor for the *Communications of the ACM* special issue on design patterns and the special issue on object-oriented frameworks. In addition, he has co-edited the book *Pattern Languages of Program Design* with James O. Coplien of Lucent Bell Labs and is co-editing another book on object-oriented application frameworks with Ralph E. Johnson and Mohamed Fayad. Dr. Schmidt has also served as the editor-in-chief of the *C++ Report* magazine. He is currently editing the *Patterns++* section of *C++ Report*, where he co-authors a column on distributed object computing with Steve Vinoski, senior architect for U.S. product development of IONA Technologies' Orbix object request broker. Dr. Schmidt is writing a book for Addison-Wesley on the topic of distributed object programming for a series edited by Brian Kernighan.

Dr. Schmidt served as the program chair for the 1996 USENIX Conference on Object-Oriented Technologies and Systems (COOTS) and the 1996 Pattern Languages of Programming conference. He has presented keynote addresses and tutorials on reusable design patterns, concurrent object-oriented network programming, and distributed object systems at many conferences including OOPSLA, the USENIX general technical conference, USENIX COOTS, ECOOP, IEEE Local Computer Networks, ACM PODC, IEEE ICNP, IEEE GLOBECOM, Object Expo, Component Users Conference, and C++ World.

In addition to his academic research, Dr. Schmidt has over a decade of experience building object-oriented communication systems. He is the chief architect and developer of the ADAPTIVE Communication Environment (ACE). Dr. Schmidt has successfully used ACE on large-scale projects at Ericsson, Siemens, Motorola, Kodak, Lucent, Lockheed Martin, Boeing, and SAIC. He and the members of his distributed object computing research group are currently using ACE to develop a high-performance, real-time CORBA ORB endsystem called TAO (The ACE ORB). TAO is the first real-time ORB endsystem to support end-to-end quality of service guarantees over ATM networks.

Dr. Schmidt received B.S. and M.A. degrees in sociology from the College of William and Mary in Williamsburg, Virginia, and an M.S. and a Ph.D. in computer science from the University of California, Irvine in 1984, 1986, 1990, and 1994, respectively.

Guy L. Steele, Jr.

Guy L. Steele, Jr., was the co-author of Scheme and has co-authored works on C and Lisp. Steele received the ACM's Grace Murray Hopper Award in 1988 and was named an ACM Fellow in 1994. He received his B.A. in applied mathematics from Harvard College in 1975 and his M.S. and Ph.D. in computer science and artificial intelligence in 1977 and 1980, respectively, from Massachusetts Institute of Technology. He currently is a senior scientist at Thinking Machines Corporation, where he is responsible for the design and implementation of parallel programming languages and other systems software for the Connection Machine computer system.

Bjarne Stroustrup

Bjarne Stroustrup was born in Aarhus, Denmark, in 1950. He received a Cand.Scient. (mathematics and computer science) in 1975 from University of Aarhus, Denmark, and a Ph.D. (computer science) in 1979 from Cambridge University, England.

Stroustrup is the designer and original implementor of C++ and the author of *The C++ Programming Language* and *The Design and Evolution of* C++. His research interests include distributed systems, operating systems, simulation, design, and programming.

Dr. Stroustrup is the head of AT&T Labs's Large-Scale Programming Research Department, he is an AT&T Bell Laboratories fellow, and he is an AT&T fellow. He is actively involved in the ANSI/ISO standardization of C++. He was the recipient of the 1993 ACM Grace Murray Hopper award and is an ACM fellow.

His non-research interests include general history, light literature, photography, hiking and running, travel, and music. He lives in Watchung, New Jersey, with his wife, daughter, and son.

Allen Wirfs-Brock

Allen Wirfs-Brock has been a leader in the industrialization and commercialization of Smalltalk since 1980. He was the architect of the Tektronix 4404 Smalltalk system, the first widely used Smalltalk-80 implementation. He founded Instantiations Inc., he was vice president of technology for Digitalk Inc., and he was chief scientist at ParcPlace-Digitalk. He has been an active participant in the X3J20 Smalltalk standardization effort since its inception and chairs its language specification subcommittee.

PART I
Object-Oriented Programming

CHAPTER 1

Object-Oriented Programming

by Timothy A. Budd

My first exposure to the concept of object-oriented programming came in 1983, soon after the publication of the famous "Blue Book" (*Smalltalk-80: The Language and Its Implementation*) by Adele Goldberg and David Robson (Goldberg & Robson, 1983). At the time, I was ignorant of the programming language Smalltalk-80, but I soon learned that a few of my colleagues at the University of Arizona—and more than a few of my students—had at least heard of the language from a series of articles that appeared in 1981 in *Byte* magazine. Some could even recall the earlier 1977 article by Alan Kay in *Scientific American* (Kay, 1977).

Despite my rather late start, I quickly became entranced with the ideas I found discussed in the Goldberg and Robson book, and determined that my students and I should explore them further. At that time, the computing facilities available to us were common for university laboratories. We had a small room full of VT-100–type terminals (24 columns of 80 characters of ASCII text), and we had only recently replaced our PDP-11/70 (128K memory, divided into a 64K data space and 64K code space) with a state-of-the-art VAX computer.

Clearly, using the Xerox PARC Smalltalk-80 system—which required a personal workstation with more computing power than our VAX, as well as a bitmapped display and an exotic new pointing device called the mouse—was out of the question. Not to be daunted by adversity, my students and I resolved to create a system to experiment with the Smalltalk *language*, even if we could not experience the full Smalltalk programming *environment*. In the 1984–1985 academic year, we created the system we christened "Little Smalltalk," an ASCII-based, non-graphical, non-event–driven implementation of a subset of the Smalltalk-80 language.

About this same time, Gary Levin—my colleague at the University of Arizona who is now at BellCore—was starting to experiment with a system developed at Bell Laboratories called *Classes: An Abstract Data Type Facility for the C Language* (Stroustrup, 1982). This was an interesting collection of C language macros that later evolved into the C++ programming language. Although the system had an annoying habit of using huge amounts of memory and regularly crashing the machine, it nevertheless contained some intriguing new features. Over lunches, Gary and I compared the ideas found in the C language extensions promulgated by Bell Laboratories with the concepts my students and I dealt with in Smalltalk.

Over the course of the next two years, I massaged my course lecture notes into a book format. The result was *A Little Smalltalk* (Budd, 1987). I distinctly recall thinking during this period that I better move fast to write and publish this book. Not only was tenure a very pressing concern, but many fads had come and gone in the recent history of computer science, and object-oriented programming could be just another fad. If I wanted to catch the wave, I needed to move quickly. If anybody had tried to tell me then that a decade later object-oriented programming would still be a hot topic, I would have thought they were crazy.

But here we are a dozen years later, and object-oriented programming is still being discussed and shows no sign of disappearing. What has become clear in the meantime is that, in fact, object-oriented techniques force a fundamental reevaluation of almost all aspects of computer programming.

This chapter introduces the basic ideas of object-oriented programming in a fashion that is independent of any particular programming language and is applicable to a wide number of different languages. The following sections first illustrate these ideas by depicting how problems are solved in the real world. The chapter then puts object-oriented programming in the context of a wider history of abstraction techniques that have been developed in computer programming. In short, this chapter explores the validity of the following two statements:

- OOP is a revolutionary idea, totally unlike anything that has come before in programming.
- OOP is an evolutionary step, following naturally on the heels of earlier programming abstractions.

1.1. Object-Oriented Programming: A Revolutionary Approach

The fundamental concept in understanding object-oriented programming has nothing to do with programming languages. Instead the key involves thinking about how one goes about structuring the solution to problems. This approach can easily be described without reference to any particular programming language, and even without reference to programming at all. My book *An Introduction to Object-Oriented Programming* (Budd, 1997) offers the following scenario:

> Suppose I wish to send some flowers to a friend for her birthday. She lives in a city many miles away, so my picking the flowers and carrying them to her door myself is out of the question. Nevertheless, sending her the flowers is an easy enough task; I merely go down to my local florist (who happens to be named Flo), tell her the variety or number of flowers I want sent and my friend's address, and I can be assured the flowers will be delivered expediently and automatically.

1.1.1. Agents and Messages

All the fundamental features of object-oriented programming can be identified in this simple and common situation. The mechanism used to solve the previous problem involved finding an appropriate agent (in object-oriented terms, an *object*) and giving to this agent a *message* that describes the request. In this scenario, the agent is the florist Flo, and the message is the selection of flowers desired and the addresses of the person to which the flowers should be sent. The sender does not know—nor does he need or want to know—the exact details concerning how the request will be carried out. Of course, the florist might well deliver a slightly different message to another florist in another city, who has earlier communicated with a flower wholesaler, and who now must communicate with a delivery person, and so on. Thus, an entire community of individuals must cooperate with each other to satisfy my request.

If we rephrase this approach to problem solving in more technical terms, it produces a situation that applies to object-oriented programming. In this case, action is initiated by the transmission of a *message* to an agent (an *object*) that is responsible for the action. The message encodes the request for an action and is accompanied by any additional information (arguments) needed to carry out the request. The receiver is the agent to whom the message is sent. If the *receiver* accepts the message, it accepts the responsibility to carry out the indicated action. In response to a message, the receiver performs some *method* to satisfy the request.

There is an ironic twist to viewing programming in these client/server terms. People are generally accustomed to depending on others for the advancement of their own goals. It is very much human nature that when a person is faced with a new problem to solve, one of the first questions he asks himself is who he can call on to help him with the problem at hand. Programmers, on the other hand, tend to be a fiercely independent lot. They most often are distrustful of any code they did not themselves have a hand in creating. Thus, although the object-oriented perspective of structuring a problem as a cooperating community of interacting agents might seem natural to novices, long-time expert programmers sometimes have a much more difficult time. Programmers must consciously work to resist the temptation to write everything from scratch and must be continually encouraged to make use of existing components and existing solutions to common problems.

1.1.2. Responsibilities and Information Hiding

In considering the scenario describing my interaction with the local florist, an important feature to note is that the florist is described by the services she provides, not by the actions she takes in the performance of her duties. In computer terms, this is called *information hiding*. I don't really know how my request will be processed, I don't really care to know. All I know is that my florist has agreed to the responsibility for providing this service, and that, having accepted my message, the florist will take the necessary actions.

The link between message and action in both the real world and in the object-oriented world is less binding than, for example, the link between a function name and a function implementation in a conventional programming language. This is because a message is transmitted to a *receiver*, and the interpretation of the message (that is, the actions to be performed) is determined entirely by the receiver. As a result, different objects might understand the same messages but might react differently. For example, an executive can give the same message to his secretary that he gave to the florist (namely, the address of the friend, the type of flowers desired, and the credit card number for payment) and will expect that the desired outcome will be achieved. But the actions that the secretary performs might be very different from those of the local florist. Thus the same message can elicit two entirely different behaviors.

Thus, the idea of messages in object-oriented programming is intimately tied to the concept of information hiding. The difference between viewing software in traditional, structured terms and viewing it from an object-oriented perspective can be summarized by a twist on a well-known quote:

> Ask not what you can do *to* your data structures, but rather ask what your data structures can do *for* you.

1.1.3. Classes and Instances

Although I have dealt with Flo the florist only a few times, I have a rough idea of the behavior I can expect when I go into her shop and present her with my request. I am able to make certain assumptions because I have some information about florists in general, and I expect that Flo, being an instance of this category, will fit the general pattern. We can use `Florist` to represent the category (or *class*) of all florists. Let us incorporate these notions into our next principle of object-oriented programming:

> All objects are *instances* of a *class*. The method invoked by an object in response to a message is determined by the class of the receiver. All objects of a given class use the same method in response to similar messages.

The same idea is incorporated in object-oriented programming languages. In a painting application, for example, I might have several instances of a general class `Rectangle` being displayed in a window. Each rectangle is in a sense different; each might have a different color or shape, for example. Yet each is also similar to the others; each could be, for example, moved or resized using the same commands. The notion of a class lets me describe the common features of the concept, while still allowing each object to have some sense of individuality.

1.1.4. Inheritance

I have more information about Flo—not necessarily because she is a florist, but because she is a shopkeeper. I know, for example, that I probably will be asked for money as part of the transaction, and that in return for payment I will be given a receipt. These actions are true of grocers, stationers, and other shopkeepers. Because the category `Florist` is a more specialized form of the category `Shopkeeper`, any knowledge I have of `Shopkeepers` is also true of `Florists` and hence of Flo.

The principle that knowledge of a more general category is also applicable to a more specific category is called *inheritance*. We say that the class `Florist` inherits attributes of the class (or category) `Shopkeeper`.

Classes can be organized into a hierarchical *inheritance* structure. A *child class* (or *subclass*) inherits attributes from a *parent class* higher in the tree. An *abstract parent class* is a class (such as `Mammal`) for which there are no direct instances; it is used only to create subclasses.

In programming languages, inheritance applies both to data values and to functions (that is, behavior). Both data fields and functions associated with a parent class become associated with child classes and are available for use when instances of a child class are created.

1.1.5. Method Binding and Overriding

The concept of an inheritance hierarchy is the key to understanding not only how separate concepts can share common features, but also how ideas can override, or hide, their inherited attributes.

The search for a method to invoke in response to a given message begins with the *class* of the receiver. If no appropriate method is found, the search is conducted in the *parent class* of this class. The search continues up the parent class chain until either a method is found or the parent class chain is exhausted. In the former case, the method is executed; in the latter case, an error message is issued. If methods with the same name can be found higher in the class hierarchy, the method executed is said to *override* the inherited behavior.

Overriding occurs in everyday life as well as in the object-oriented world. We know that mammals, for example, give birth to live young. Yet the category `Platypus` inherits from class `Mammal`, and platypuses lay eggs. In our mental model of the universe, the concept of giving birth to live young is associated at the `Mammal` level of Figure 1.1, while the concept of laying eggs at level `Platypus` overrides the inherited behavior. When we search for information concerning the breeding habits of a specific animal, we search the most specific category before progressing to the more general.

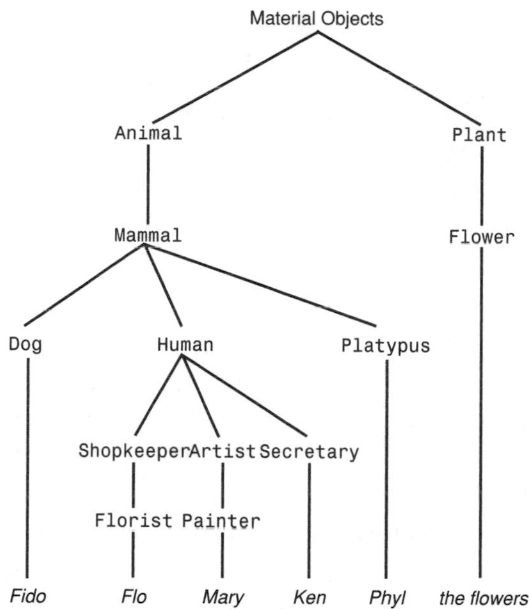

FIGURE 1.1. *A class hierarchy helps define characteristics of various material objects.*

1.1.6. Polymorphism

In a sense, it doesn't really matter whether I give my message to my florist directly, or to my secretary, as long as the resulting actions are satisfactory. Objects can be characterized by their behavior, and as long as the behavior is acceptable for certain problems, the particular characteristics of the object should be unimportant. In object-oriented languages, the inheritance hierarchy often is used not only for sharing code but also for describing characteristics.[1] For example, the class `Mammal` can be viewed as both a convenient handle (or storage container) for holding our general information about Mammals, and, as well, a defining constraint. If I tell you, for example, that a certain animal is a `Mammal`, you immediately know a lot of information about it.

[1] It has been noted that these two goals are not always coincident, and should not necessarily be handled by the same mechanism. This brief overview does not permit me to discuss the subclass/subtype distinction, or introduce some of the techniques used to separate these concepts. Interested readers should consult my book *An Introduction to Object-Oriented Programming,* 2nd Ed.

In programming languages this simple idea becomes manifest in the notion that we can separate the declared *type* of a variable from the *value* that it holds at any particular time. Imagine that we have a class hierarchy that mirrors that shown in Figure 1.1. We might have a variable that is declared as `Mammal`. In fact, it could be holding a value that is of type `Dog`. Since a Dog *is* a `Mammal` (by which we mean that the category `Dog` inherits from the category `Mammal`), any behavior that we expect from the more general class should certainly be exhibited by an instance of the child class.

The term *polymorphism* is often used to describe this idea. Polymorphism means roughly "many forms"; the variable that is declared as `Mammal` can, during the course of execution, take on many different forms—perhaps holding at one instance a cat, and another time a dog, at still another instance a human being.

This is an extremely simple idea with many powerful and subtle implications. It is the feature that permits the development of software frameworks, for example. A *framework* is a skeleton application that provides the structure, but no specific information, for solutions to a set of similar problems. The most common type of framework is a graphical user interface framework, or GUI. A GUI can be written so that it deals with a general class `Window`, for example (see Figure 1.2). A window has general characteristics, such as a rectangular shape, a height and width, the ability to be resized, moved around on the display surface, hidden, restored, made into an icon, and so on.

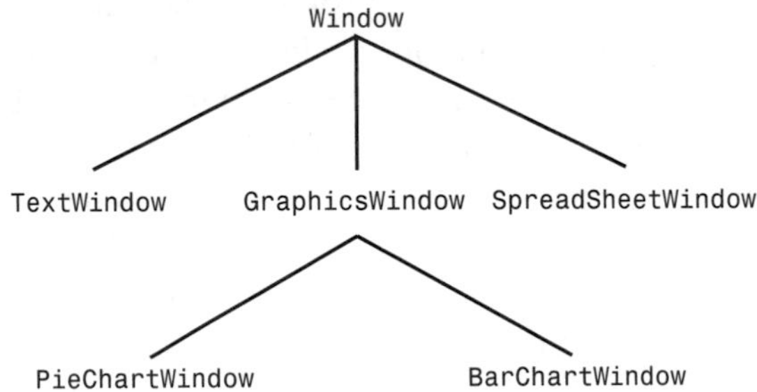

FIGURE 1.2. *An inheritance hierarchy for windows.*

All these general characteristics can be defined without reference to the particular contents of the window, in just the same way that we can discuss the characteristics of mammals without reference to a particular type of animal. The programmer using a framework then develops a new type of window by creating a subclass from the class `Window` (for example, `GraphicsWindow`). Features that are particular to the new application, such as the display of the contents of the window, are defined in this new class. Because the framework holds the window value in a polymorphic variable, the framework thinks the window is an instance of the class `Window`, whereas the programmer knows the actual value is an instance of the class `GraphicsWindow`.

1.1.7. Object-Oriented Computer Programming

Although object-oriented techniques may be easy to apply in real life, they can be frustratingly difficult to discover in computer programs. In real life the boundaries between objects are obvious and clear-cut. People are different from and interact with each other, balls bounce, birds fly, trees grow. The interfaces between physical objects are sharp and definable. When pondering the interaction between a baseball and the bat that hits it, we do not ask which object has the responsibility for determining that a collision has taken place or which object should control the change of state that occurs when they intersect.

But such decisions are the heart and soul of object-oriented design. In this respect, the process of object-oriented design is closer to the smooth functioning of an organization, such as a committee or club. Here the separation of responsibilities between, for example, the president and the vice-president may not be so clear-cut as the separation of responsibilities between a ball and a bat. Tracing the flow of interactions so that all necessary tasks are performed, all contingencies are predicted, and no one person (or object) is overburdened by too much work can be frustratingly difficult, both in real life and in object-oriented programming.

Much of the recent work in object-oriented design, such as the unified modeling language, as well as work in object-oriented structuring, such as the design patterns movement, can be seen as an attempt to provide guidelines that help determine how to divide responsibilities between many agents.

1.1.8. Summary of Object-Oriented Concepts

Alan Kay, considered by many to be the father of object-oriented programming, identified the following characteristics as fundamental to OOP (Kay, 1993):

- Everything is an *object*.
- Computation is performed by objects communicating with each other, requesting that other objects perform actions. Objects communicate by sending and receiving messages. A *message* is a request for action bundled with whatever arguments may be necessary to complete the task.
- Each object has its own *memory*, which consists of other objects.
- Every object is an *instance* of a *class*. A class simply represents a grouping of similar objects, such as integers or lists.
- The class is the repository for *behavior* associated with an object. That is, all objects that are instances of the same class can perform the same actions.
- Classes are organized into a singly rooted tree structure, called the *inheritance hierarchy*. Memory and behavior associated with instances of a class are automatically available to any class associated with a descendant in this tree structure.

1.2. OOP: An Evolutionary Idea

Having tried to convince the reader that object-oriented programming is a revolutionary idea, totally unlike anything that has come before, I will now endeavor to show that it is really evolutionary, clearly following on the heels of a long tradition of previous abstraction techniques.

From the beginnings of computer science it has been clear that the major difficulty in the development of large systems is not algorithmic, but is, rather, communication. Fred Brooks, in 1975, expressed it this way:

> Since software construction is inherently a systems effort—an exercise in complex interrelationships—communication effort is great, and it quickly dominates the decrease in individual task time brought about by partitioning. Adding more men then lengthens, not shortens, the schedule. (Brooks, 1975)

Over the years, programmers and language designers have developed a number of abstraction techniques to help control the flow of information between various parts of a large software system, as well as between the various members of a software development team. Symbolic assembly languages, for example, enabled the programmer to think about operations by name, rather than by numerical address. High-level languages freed the programmer from tasks such as register allocation and management. Procedures separated the naming of a task to be performed from the steps used in the achievement of the task, and started the long progression of information hiding mechanisms. Procedures by themselves cannot be used to hide information that must be shared between two or more routines. Block-scoped languages, such as Algol, were one attempt to solve this problem; modules were a slightly later and more successful mechanism.

David Parnas (1972), who popularized the notion of modules, described the following two principles for their proper use:

- One must provide the intended user with all the information needed to use a module correctly, and *nothing more.*
- One must provide the implementor with all the information needed to complete a module, and *nothing more.*

This philosophy is much like the military doctrine of "need to know," and should be etched on the inside of the eyelids of every good object-oriented programmer. When objects interact with each other, they should be tied together with the weakest strings possible.

Although modules provided an adequate mechanism for information hiding, they did nothing to deal with the problem of object creation. Imagine a module for manipulating complex numbers, for example, with the limitation that only one location can hold a number. Such a system would hardly be useful. A natural next step, therefore, was the development of the idea of an abstract data type. An abstract structure type (AST) provides the data-hiding benefits of a module and extends it with the ability to stamp out multiple copies of values. In a certain sense, an object is simply an abstract data type. People have said, for example, that Smalltalk programmers write the most "structured" of all programs because they cannot write anything but definitions of abstract data types. It is true that an object definition is an abstract data type, but the notions of object-oriented programming build on the ideas of abstract data types and add to them important innovations in code sharing and reusability.

As noted in the earlier parts of this chapter, object-oriented programming adds several important new ideas to the concept of the abstract data type. Foremost among these is *message passing*. Activity is initiated by a *request* to a specific object, not by the invoking of a function. In large part, this is merely a change of emphasis; the conventional view places primary emphasis on the operation, whereas the object-oriented view emphasizes the value itself. (Do you call the `push` routine with a stack and a data value, or do you ask a `stack` to push a value onto itself?) If this were all there is to object-oriented programming, the technique would not be considered a major innovation. But added to message passing are powerful mechanisms for overloading names and reusing software.

Implicit in message passing is the idea that the *interpretation* of a message can vary with different objects. That is, the behavior and response that the message elicit will depend on the object receiving it. Thus, `push` can mean one thing to a stack and a very different thing to a mechanical-arm controller. Because names for operations need not be unique, simple and direct forms can be used, leading to more readable and understandable code.

Finally, object-oriented programming adds the mechanisms of inheritance and polymorphism. *Inheritance* allows different data types to share the same code, leading to a reduction in code size and an increase in functionality. *Polymorphism* allows this shared code to be tailored to fit the specific circumstances of individual data types. The emphasis on the independence of individual components permits an incremental development process in which individual software units are designed, programmed, and tested before being combined into a large system.

1.3. Combining Revolution and Evolution

The history of object-oriented programming is full of ironies. Not so long ago, the 25th anniversary of OOP was celebrated, making object-oriented concepts about half the age of computer science as a whole. Although I earlier credited Alan Kay as being the father of object-oriented programming, Kay states clearly that all the basic ideas of object-oriented programming can be found in the programming language Simula 67 (Dahl & Nygaard, 1966), which was developed in the 1960s. However, had not Kay popularized object-oriented ideas with Smalltalk, Simula would probably have become little more than an interesting footnote in the discussion of programming languages. Thus, object-oriented concepts are, in computer science years (which, like dog years, run many times faster than the calendar), almost ancient history. Yet many people are just now discovering the concepts of object-oriented programming, making it one of the newest and fastest-growing ideas in the computer world today. The best programmers have always emphasized encapsulation, working in a more-or-less object-oriented fashion; yet programmers with years of experience in an imperative style of software development often have the most difficult time switching to an object-oriented way of thinking. It is this tug and pull of revolution and evolution, of new ideas being created and old ideas being seen in a new light, that makes object-oriented programming one of the most exciting areas of computer science today.

1.4. References

Brooks, F. P., Jr. 1975. *The mythical man-month: Essays on software engineering*. Reading, MA: Addison-Wesley.

Budd, T. A. 1987. *A little Smalltalk*. Reading, MA: Addison-Wesley.

Budd, T. A. 1997. *An introduction to object-oriented programming* (2nd ed.). Reading, MA: Addison-Wesley.

Dahl, O.-J., and K. Nygaard. 1966. Simula, an Algol-based simulation language. *Communications of the ACM* 9(9):671–678.

Goldberg, A., and D. Robson. 1983. *Smalltalk-80: The language and its implementation*. Reading, MA: Addison-Wesley.

Kay, A. C. 1977. Microelectronics and the personal computer. *Scientific American* 237(3):230–244.

Kay, A. C. 1993. The early history of Smalltalk. The Second ACM SIGPLAN history of programming languages conference (HOPL-II), *ACM SIGPLAN Notices* 28(3):69–75.

Parnas, D. L. 1972. On the criteria to be used in decomposing systems into modules. *Communications of the ACM* 15(12):1059–1062.

Stroustrup, B. 1982. Classes: An abstract data type facility for the C language. *ACM Sigplan Notices*, 17(1):42–51.

CHAPTER 2

Applying Design Patterns and Frameworks to Develop Object-Oriented Communication Software

by Douglas C. Schmidt

2.1. Understanding Object-Oriented Communication Software

Communication software for next-generation distributed applications must be flexible to support a growing range of multimedia datatypes, traffic patterns, and end-to-end quality of service (QoS) requirements. Moreover, communication software must be efficient to provide both low latency to delay-sensitive applications (such as avionics, simulation, and call processing) and high performance to bandwidth-intensive applications (such as medical imaging, satellite surveillance, and teleconferencing) over high-speed and mobile networks.

Despite dramatic increases in computing power and network bandwidth, however, the cost of developing communication software remains high and the quality remains relatively low. Across the industry, this situation has produced a communication software crisis, with computing hardware and networks getting smaller, faster, and cheaper while communication software gets larger, slower, and more expensive to develop and maintain.

The challenges of communication software arise from inherent and accidental complexities (Brooks, 1975). Inherent complexities stem from fundamental challenges of developing communication software. Chief among these are detecting and recovering from network and host failures, minimizing the impact of communication latency, and determining an optimal partitioning of application service components and workload onto processing elements throughout a network.

The accidental complexities associated with communication software stem from limitations with conventional tools and techniques. For instance, low-level network programming interfaces, such as sockets, are tedious and error prone. Likewise, higher-level distributed object computing toolkits such as CORBA, DCOM, and Java RMI lack key features (such as asynchronous I/O and end-to-end QoS guarantees) and are not yet optimized for applications with stringent performance requirements (Schmidt, Gokhale, Harrison, & Parulkar, 1997).

Another source of accidental complexity arises from the widespread use of algorithmic design techniques (Booch, 1993) to develop communication software. Although graphical user interfaces (GUIs) are largely built using object-oriented techniques, communication software has traditionally been developed with algorithmic techniques. However, algorithmic design yields non-extensible software architectures that cannot be customized rapidly to meet changing application requirements. Therefore, in an era of deregulation and stiff global competition, it is prohibitively expensive and time-consuming to repeatedly develop applications from scratch using algorithmic design techniques.

The examples in this chapter focus on developing high-performance concurrent Web servers using the ACE framework (Schmidt & Suda, 1994). ACE is an object-oriented framework that provides core concurrency and distribution patterns (Schmidt, 1996a) related to the domain of communication software. The framework and patterns in this chapter are representative of solutions that have been successfully applied to communication systems ranging from telecommunication system management (Schmidt, 1996a) to enterprise medical imaging (Pyarali, Harrison, & Schmidt, 1996) and real-time avionics (Harrison, Levine, & Schmidt, 1997).

This paper is organized as follows: The first section presents an overview of patterns and frameworks, discussing the need for the type of communication software framework provided by ACE. Subsequent sections outline the structure of the ACE framework and illustrate how patterns and components in ACE can be applied to develop high-performance Web servers.

2.2. Applying Patterns and Frameworks to Communication Software

Object-oriented (OO) techniques provide principles, methods, and tools that significantly reduce the complexity and cost of developing communication software. The primary benefits of OO stem from its emphasis on modularity and extensibility, which encapsulate volatile implementation details behind stable interfaces and enhance software reuse by factoring out common object structures and functionality. This chapter illustrates how to produce flexible and efficient communication software using OO application frameworks and design patterns.

A *framework* is a reusable, semi-complete application that can be specialized to produce custom applications. A *pattern* represents a recurring solution to a software development problem within a particular context. Patterns and frameworks can be applied synergistically to improve the quality of communication software by capturing successful software development strategies. Patterns capture abstract designs and software architectures in a systematic and comprehensible format, whereas frameworks capture concrete designs, algorithms, and implementations in particular programming languages.

2.2.1. Common Pitfalls of Developing Communication Software

Developers of communication software confront recurring challenges that are largely independent of specific application requirements. For instance, applications such as network file systems, electronic mail routers, remote login daemons, and Web servers all perform tasks related to connection establishment and service initialization, event demultiplexing and event handler dispatching, interprocess communication and shared memory management, static and dynamic component configuration, concurrency and synchronization, and persistence. Traditionally, these tasks have been implemented in an ad hoc manner using native operating system (OS) application programming interfaces (APIs)—such as the Win32 or POSIX—that are written in C.

Unfortunately, OS APIs do not represent an effective way to develop communication software. The following list details common problems associated with programming applications using OS APIs:

- *Excessive low-level details.* Developers must have detailed knowledge of low-level OS details, which diverts their attention from the strategic application-related semantics and structure of their programs. For instance, developers must carefully track which error codes are returned by each system call to handle OS-specific problems in their applications.

- *Continuous reinvention of incompatible higher-level programming abstractions.* The common remedy for the excessive level of detail with OS APIs involves defining higher-level programming abstractions. However, these abstractions are typically reinvented in an ad hoc manner by each developer or project; this hampers productivity and creates incompatible components throughout projects in large software organizations.

- *High potential for errors.* Low-level OS APIs are error-prone due to their lack of type-safety. For example, endpoints of communication in the Socket API are represented as untyped handles that increase the potential for subtle programming mistakes and runtime errors (Schmidt, Harrison, & Al-Shaer, 1995).
- *Steep learning curve.* Due to the excessive level of detail, the effort required to master OS-level APIs is very great. For instance, it is hard to learn how to program the thread cancellation mechanisms correctly in POSIX Pthreads applications.
- *Inability to scale up.* OS APIs define basic interfaces that do not scale up gracefully as applications grow in size and complexity. For instance, Win32 processes contain a limit of 64 thread local storage (TLS) keys, which is inadequate for large-scale application servers that utilize many DLLs and thread local objects.
- *Lack of portability.* Low-level OS APIs are notoriously nonportable, even across releases of the same operating system. For instance, implementations of the WinSock socket API on different versions of Windows NT possess incompatible timing-related bugs that occur sporadically when performing non-blocking connections.

It is possible to alleviate some of these problems by using higher-level distributed object computing (DOC) toolkits such as CORBA, DCOM, and Java RMI. However, this is only a partial solution, for the following reasons:

- *Lack of portability.* DOC toolkits are not widely portable. For instance, the Basic Object Adapter component in the CORBA 2.0 specification is woefully underspecified, which means that servers written in CORBA are not portable among ORB products from different vendors.
- *Lack of features.* DOC toolkits focus primarily on communication and therefore do not cover other key issues associated with developing distributed applications. For instance, DOC toolkits do not specify important aspects of high-performance and real-time distributed server development, such as shared memory, asynchronous I/O, multithreading, and synchronization (Schmidt et al., 1997).

- *Lack of performance.* Conventional DOC toolkits incur significant throughput and latency overhead. These overheads stem from excessive data copying, non-optimized presentation-layer conversions, internal message buffering strategies that produce non-uniform behavior for different message sizes, inefficient demultiplexing algorithms, long chains of intra-ORB virtual method calls, and lack of integration with underlying real-time OS and network QoS mechanisms.

2.2.2. Solutions in Patterns and Frameworks

Successful developers overcome the problems outlined previously by identifying the design patterns that underly proven solutions and by reifying these patterns in application frameworks. Patterns and frameworks help alleviate the continual rediscovery and re-invention of communication software concepts and components by capturing solutions to standard communication software development problems (Gamma, Helm, Johnson, & Vlissides, 1995). For instance, patterns are useful for documenting the structure and participants in common micro-architectures such as Reactors (Schmidt, 1995) and active objects (Lavender & Schmidt, 1996). These patterns are generalizations of object-structures that have proven useful in building flexible and efficient event-driven and concurrent communication software frameworks and applications.

Traditionally, communication software patterns have either been locked in the heads of the expert developers or buried deep within the source code. Allowing this valuable information to reside only in these locations is risky and expensive, however. For instance, the insights of experienced designers will be lost over time if they are not documented. Likewise, substantial effort could be necessary to reverse engineer patterns from existing source code. Therefore, capturing and documenting communication software patterns explicitly is essential in preserving design information for developers who enhance and maintain existing software. Moreover, knowledge of domain-specific patterns helps guide the design decisions of developers building new applications.

Although knowledge of patterns helps to reduce development effort and maintenance costs, reuse of patterns alone is not sufficient to create flexible and efficient communication software. Although patterns enable reuse of abstract design and architecture knowledge, abstractions documented as patterns do not directly yield reusable code. Therefore, it is essential to augment the study of patterns with the creation and use of application frameworks. Families of frameworks help developers avoid costly reinvention of standard communication software components by implementing common design patterns and factoring out common implementation roles.

Frameworks provide reusable software components for applications by integrating sets of abstract classes and defining standard ways that instances of these classes collaborate (Johnson & Foote, 1988). The resulting application skeletons can be customized by inheriting and instantiating from reusable components in the frameworks. The scope of reuse in a framework can be significantly larger than using traditional function libraries or conventional OO class libraries because frameworks are tightly integrated with key communication software tasks (such as service initialization, error handling, flow control, event processing, and concurrency control). In general, frameworks enhance class libraries in the following ways:

- Frameworks define semi-complete applications that embody domain-specific object structures and functionality. Class libraries provide a relatively small granularity of reuse. For instance, the classes in Figure 2.1(A) are typically low-level, relatively independent, and general components such as strings, complex numbers, arrays, and bitsets. In contrast, components in a framework collaborate to provide a customizable architectural skeleton for a family of related applications. Complete applications can be composed by inheriting from and/or instantiating framework components. As shown in Figure 2.1(B), this reduces the amount of application-specific code because much of the domain-specific processing is factored into the generic components in the framework.

- Frameworks are active and exhibit inversion of control at runtime. Class libraries are typically passive, i.e., they perform their processing by borrowing threads of control from self-directed application objects. This is illustrated in Figure 2.1(A), where the application-specific logic manages the event loop. In contrast, frameworks are active; i.e., they manage the flow of control within an application via event dispatching patterns such as Reactor (Schmidt, 1995) and Observer (Gamma et al., 1995). Figure 2.1(B) illustrates the callback-driven run-time architecture of a framework. This inversion of control is referred to as The Hollywood Principle (Vlissides, 1996), i.e., "Don't call us; we'll call you."

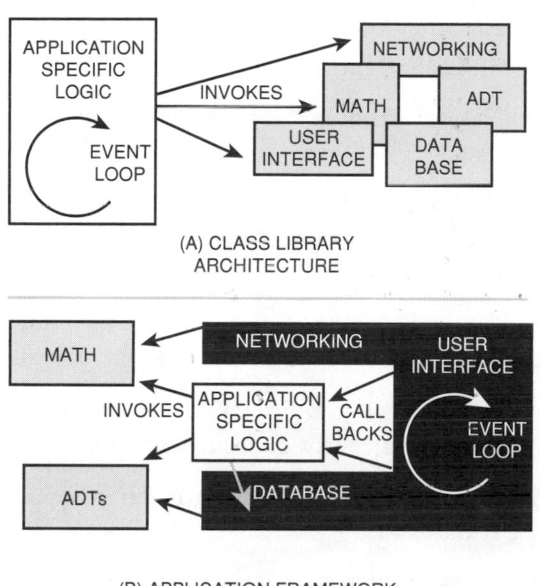

FIGURE 2.1. *Differences between class libraries and object-oriented frameworks.*

In practice, frameworks and class libraries are complementary technologies. Frameworks often utilize class libraries internally to simplify the development of the framework. For instance, portions of ACE use the string and vector containers provided by the C++ Standard Template Library (Stepanov & Lee, 1994) to manage connection maps and other search structures. In addition, application-specific callbacks invoked by framework event handlers frequently use class library components to perform basic tasks such as string processing, file management, and numerical analysis.

To illustrate how OO patterns and frameworks are being successfully applied to communication software, the remainder of this chapter examines the structure and use of the ACE framework (Schmidt & Suda, 1994).

2.3. Understanding ACE

ACE is an object-oriented framework that implements core concurrency and distribution patterns (Schmidt, 1996a) for communication software. ACE provides a rich set of reusable C++ wrappers and framework components that are targeted for developers of high-performance, real-time services and applications across a wide range of OS platforms. The components in ACE provide reusable implementations of the following communication software tasks:

- Connection establishment and service initialization (Schmidt, 1996b)
- Event demultiplexing and event handler dispatching (Harrison, Pyarali, Schmidt, & Jordan, 1997; Schmidt, 1995; Schmidt & Cranor, 1996)
- Interprocess communication (Schmidt et al., 1995) and shared memory management
- Static and dynamic configuration (Jain & Schmidt, 1997; Schmidt & Suda, 1994) of distributed communication services
- Concurrency and synchronization (Lavendar & Schmidt, 1996; Schmidt & Cranor, 1996)
- Distributed services, such as naming, event routing (Harrison, Levine, et al., 1997), logging, time synchronization, and network locking
- Middleware applications, such as high-performance Web servers (Hu, Pyarali, & Schmidt, 1997) and object request brokers (ORBs; Schmidt et al., 1997)

This section outlines the structure of the ACE framework. Section 2.4 illustrates how components and patterns in ACE can be applied to build high-performance, concurrent Web servers.

2.3.1. The Structure of ACE

ACE is a large framework, containing more than 100,000 lines of C++ code divided into about 250 classes. To separate concerns and to reduce the complexity of the frameworks, ACE is designed using a layered architecture. Figure 2.2 illustrates the vertical and horizontal relationships between ACE components.

The lower layers of ACE are C++ *wrappers* that encapsulate core OS communication and concurrency services. The higher layers of ACE extend the C++ wrappers to provide reusable *frameworks*, *self-contained distributed service components*, and *middleware applications* that simplify the creation, composition, and configuration of large-scale communication systems.

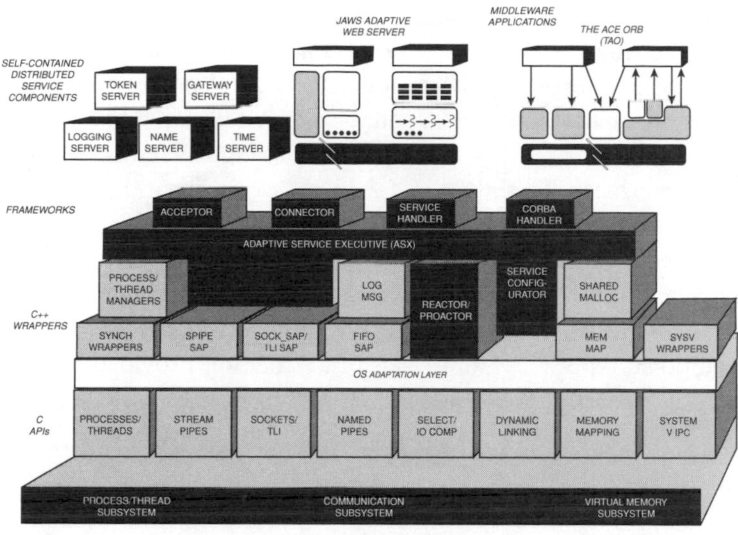

FIGURE 2.2. *The structure of the components in ACE.*

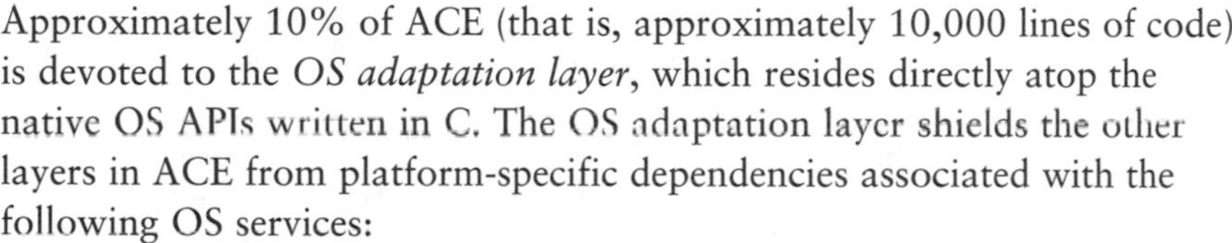

2.3.1.1. The ACE C++ Wrapper Layer

Approximately 10% of ACE (that is, approximately 10,000 lines of code) is devoted to the *OS adaptation layer*, which resides directly atop the native OS APIs written in C. The OS adaptation layer shields the other layers in ACE from platform-specific dependencies associated with the following OS services:

- *Concurrency and synchronization.* The adaptation layer encapsulates OS concurrency mechanisms for multithreading, multiprocessing, and synchronization.
- *Interprocess communication (IPC) and shared memory.* The adaptation layer encapsulates common OS mechanisms for local and remote IPC and shared memory.
- *Event demultiplexing mechanisms.* The adaptation layer encapsulates standard OS mechanisms for demultiplexing I/O-based, timer-based, signal-based, and synchronization-based events.
- *Explicit dynamic linking.* The adaptation layer encapsulates OS mechanisms for explicit dynamic linking, which allows application services to be configured at installation time or runtime.

The portability provided by the OS adaptation layer enables ACE to run on a wide range of operating systems, including most versions of UNIX, Win32, OpenEdition MVS, and embedded platforms such as VxWorks.

Although it is possible to program directly to the OS adaptation layer, most applications use the C++ wrappers layer, shown in Figure 2.2. ACE C++ wrappers improve application robustness by encapsulating and enhancing the native OS concurrency, communication, memory management, event demultiplexing, and dynamic linking mechanisms with type-safe OO interfaces. This alleviates the need for applications to directly access the underlying OS libraries, which are written using weakly typed C interfaces. Therefore, C++ compilers can detect type system violations at compile time rather than at runtime. ACE uses inlining extensively to eliminate performance penalties that would otherwise be incurred from the additional type-safety and levels of abstraction provided by the OS adaptation layer and the C++ wrappers.

The C++ wrappers provided by ACE are quite extensive, constituting about 50% of the source code. Applications can combine and compose these wrappers by selectively inheriting, aggregating, and/or instantiating the following components:

- *Concurrency and synchronization components.* ACE abstracts native OS multithreading and multiprocessing mechanisms—such as mutexes and semaphores—to create higher-level OO concurrency abstractions—such as active objects (Lavender & Schmidt, 1996) and polymorphic futures (Halstead, 1985).
- *IPC components.* These components encapsulate local and/or remote IPC mechanisms (Schmidt et al., 1995) such as sockets, TLI, UNIX FIFOs and STREAM pipes, and Win32 Named Pipes.
- *Memory management components.* The ACE memory management components provide a flexible and extensible abstraction for managing dynamic allocation and deallocation of shared memory and local memory.

2.3.1.2. The ACE Framework Components

Around 40% of ACE consists of communication software framework components that integrate and enhance the C++ wrappers. These framework components support the flexible configuration of concurrent communication applications and services. The framework layer in ACE contains the following components:

- *Event demultiplexing components.* The ACE Reactor (Schmidt, 1995) and Proactor (Harrison, Pyarali, et al., 1997) are extensible, object-oriented demultiplexers that dispatch application-specific handlers in response to various types of I/O-based, timer-based, signal-based, and synchronization-based events.

- *Service initialization components.* The ACE Connector and Acceptor components (Schmidt, 1996b) decouple the active and passive initialization roles, respectively, from tasks that communication services perform once initialization is complete.
- *Service configuration components.* The ACE Service Configurator (Jain & Schmidt, 1997) supports the configuration of applications whose services can be assembled dynamically at installation time and/or runtime.
- *Layered service stream components.* The ACE Streams components (Schmidt & Suda, 1994) simplify the development of concurrent communication software applications (such as protocol stacks) composed of hierarchically layered services.
- *ORB adapter components.* ACE can be integrated seamlessly with single-threaded and multithreaded CORBA implementations via ORB adapters (Pyarali et al., 1996).

When combined with the use of C++ language features (such as templates, inheritance, and dynamic binding) and design patterns (such as Abstract Factory, Builder, and Service Configurator), the ACE framework components facilitate the development of communication software that can be updated and extended without modifying, recompiling, relinking, or even restarting running systems (Schmidt & Suda, 1994).

2.3.1.3. Self-Contained Distributed Service Components

ACE provides a standard library of distributed services that are packaged as self-contained components. Although these service components are not strictly part of the ACE framework, they play two important roles:

- *Factoring out reusable distributed application building blocks.* These service components provide reusable implementations of common distributed application tasks such as naming, event routing, logging, time synchronization, and network locking.
- *Demonstrating common-use cases of ACE.* These distributed services also demonstrate how ACE components (such as Reactors, Service Configurators, Acceptors and Connectors, active objects, and IPC wrappers) can be used effectively to develop flexible and efficient communication software.

2.3.1.4. Middleware Applications

ACE has been used in research and development projects at many universities and companies. For instance, it has been used to build avionics systems at McDonnell Douglas (Schmidt et al., 1997); telecommunication systems at Bellcore (Schmidt, 1995), Ericsson (Schmidt & Stephenson, 1995), and Motorola (Schmidt, 1996a); and medical imaging systems at Siemens (Jain & Schmidt, June 1997) and Kodak (Pyarali et al., 1996). In addition, ACE has been the subject of many academic research projects. Two examples of middleware applications provided with the ACE release are

- The ACE ORB (TAO; Schmidt et al., 1997), which is a real-time implementation of CORBA built using the framework components and patterns provided by ACE
- JAWS (Hu et al., 1997), which is a high-performance, adaptive Web server built using the components in ACE

2.4. Developing High-Performance Web Servers with Patterns and Framework Components

The benefits of applying frameworks and patterns to communication software are best introduced by example. This section describes the structure and functionality of high-performance Web servers developed using the patterns and framework components in ACE. Many error-handling details are omitted to keep the code examples concise. In addition, the examples focus on features that are portable across multiple OS platforms, although noteworthy platform-specific features of ACE (such as asynchronous I/O and I/O completion ports) are described where appropriate.

2.4.1. An Overview of a Web System

Figure 2.3 illustrates the general architecture of a Web system. The diagram provides a layered view of the architectural components required for an HTTP client to retrieve an HTML file from an HTTP server (Fielding, Gettys, Mogul, Frystyk, & Berners-Lee, 1997). Through GUI interactions, the client application user instructs the HTTP client to retrieve a file. The *requester* is the active component of the client that communicates over the network. It issues a request for the file to the server with the appropriate syntax of the transfer protocol—in this case, HTTP. Incoming requests to the HTTP server are received by the *dispatcher,* which is the request demultiplexing engine of the server. It is responsible for creating new threads or processes (for concurrent Web servers) or managing sets of socket handles (for single-threaded concurrent servers). Each request is processed by a *handler,* which goes through a life cycle of parsing the request, logging the request, fetching file status information, updating the cache, sending the file, and cleaning up after the request is done. When the response returns to the client with the requested file, it is parsed by an HTML parser so that the file can be rendered. At this stage, the requester can issue other requests on behalf of the client (e.g., in order to maintain a client-side cache).

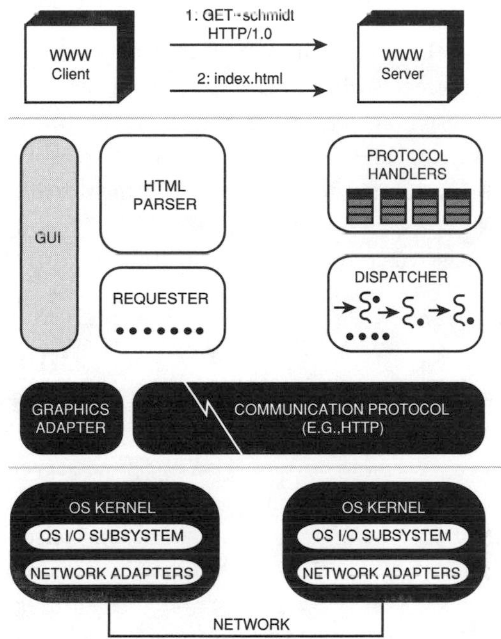

FIGURE 2.3. *The general architecture of a Web system.*

2.4.2. An Overview of an OO Web Server Communication Software Architecture

Figure 2.4 illustrates the general object-oriented communication software architecture for the Web servers covered in this section. The roles performed by the components in this architecture include the following:

- The *Event Dispatcher* encapsulates the Web server's concurrency strategies (such as Thread-per-Request or Thread Pool) and request dispatching strategies (such as synchronous Reactive or asynchronous Proactive dispatching). The ACE framework allows these strategies to be customized according to platform characteristics such as user-level versus kernel-level threading in the OS, the number of CPUs in the end system, and the existence of special-purpose OS support for HTTP processing, such as the Windows NT `TransmitFile` system call (Hu et al., 1997).

- An *HTTP Handler* is created for each client HTTP connection (e.g., from a Web browser). It parses HTTP requests and performs the work specified by the requests (e.g., retrieving Web pages). An HTTP Handler contains an ACE SOCK Stream, which encapsulates the data transmission capabilities of TCP/IP sockets.
- The *HTTP Acceptor* is a factory that accepts connections from clients and creates HTTP Handlers to process the requests from clients. There is typically one HTTP Acceptor per server, although certain concurrency strategies (such as Thread Pool) allocate multiple HTTP Acceptors to leverage OS multithreading capabilities. An HTTP Acceptor contains an ACE SOCK Acceptor, which encapsulates the passive connection establishment capabilities of TCP/IP sockets.

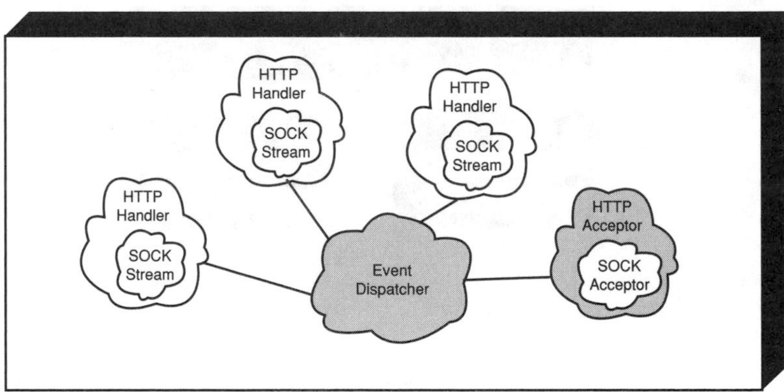

FIGURE 2.4. *The object-oriented communication software architecture for a Web server.*

The SOCK Acceptor and SOCK Stream are C++ wrappers provided by ACE. They shield applications from nonportable, tedious, and error-prone aspects of developing communication software using the native OS socket interfaces written in C. Other ACE components are introduced throughout this section as well.

2.4.3. Design Patterns for Web Server Communication Software

The communication software architecture diagram in Figure 2.4 explains how the Web server is structured but not why it is structured in this particular way. To understand why the Web server contains roles such as Event Dispatcher, Acceptor, and Handler requires a deeper understanding of the design patterns underlying the domain of communication software in general and Web servers in particular. Figure 2.5 illustrates the strategic and tactical patterns related to Web servers.

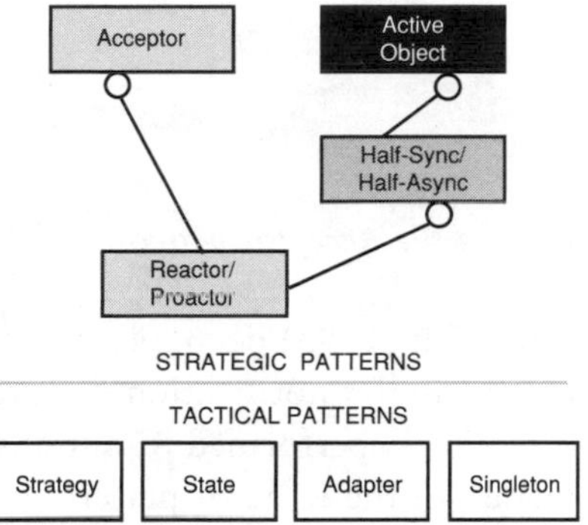

FIGURE 2.5. *Common design patterns in Web servers.*

2.4.3.1. Strategic Patterns

Certain patterns are strategic because they are ubiquitous to the domain of communication software. Therefore, these patterns significantly influence the software architecture of Web servers. The following list details the strategic patterns involved in communication software:

- Acceptor pattern
- Reactor pattern
- Proactor pattern
- Active object pattern
- Half-sync/Half-async pattern

The Acceptor pattern (Schmidt, 1996b) decouples passive connection establishment from the service performed once the connection is established. Figure 2.6 illustrates the structure of the Acceptor pattern in the context of Web servers. The HTTP Acceptor is a factory that creates, accepts, and activates a new HTTP Handler whenever the Event

Dispatcher notifies it that a connection has arrived from a client. All the Web server implementations described here use the Acceptor pattern to decouple connection establishment from HTTP protocol processing.

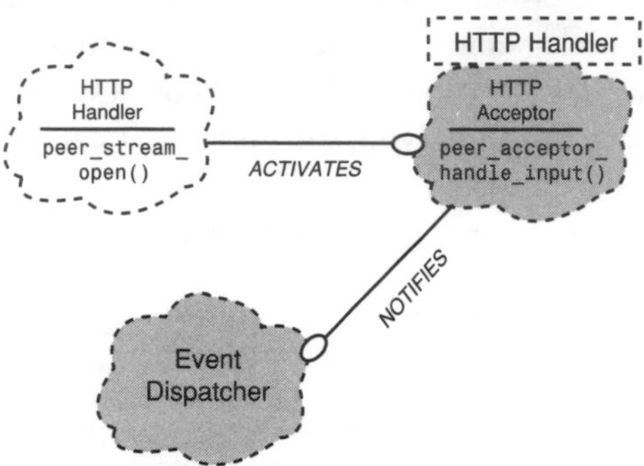

FIGURE 2.6. *The structure of the Acceptor pattern.*

The Reactor pattern (Schmidt, 1995) decouples the synchronous event demultiplexing and event handler notification dispatching logic of server applications from the service(s) performed in response to events. Figure 2.7 illustrates the structure of the Reactor pattern in the context of Web servers. Both the HTTP Acceptor and HTTP Handler inherit from the abstract Event Handler interface and register themselves with the Initiation Dispatcher for input events (i.e., connections and HTTP requests), respectively. The Initiation Dispatcher invokes the `handle_input` notification hook method of these Event Handler subclass objects when their associated events occur. The Reactor pattern is used by most of the Web server concurrency models presented in section 2.4.4.

The Proactor pattern (Harrison, Pyarali, et al., 1997) decouples the asynchronous event demultiplexing and event handler completion dispatching logic of server applications from the service(s) performed in response to events. Figure 2.8 illustrates the structure of the Proactor pattern in the context of Web servers. As before, both the HTTP Acceptor and HTTP Handler inherit from the abstract Event Handler interface. The difference is that this Event Handler defines completion hooks rather than initiation hooks. Therefore, when asynchronous invoked accept and read operations complete, the Completion Dispatcher invokes the appropriate completion hook method of these Event Handler subclass objects. The Proactor pattern is used in the asynchronous variant of the Thread Pool in section 2.4.4.3.

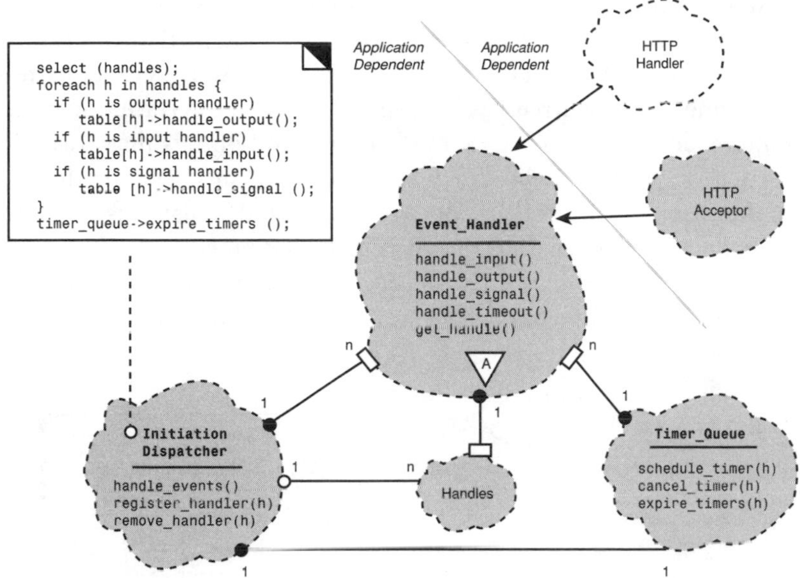

FIGURE 2.7. *The structure of the Reactor pattern.*

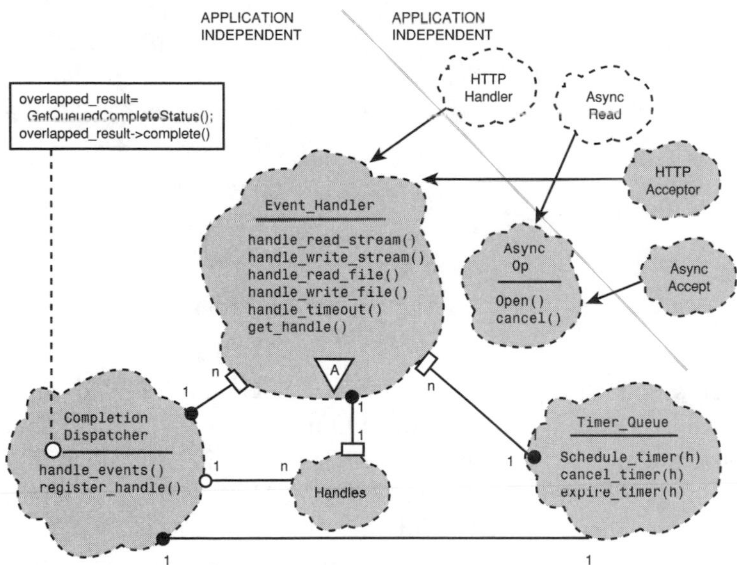

FIGURE 2.8. *The structure of the Proactor pattern.*

The Active Object pattern (Lavender & Schmidt, 1996) decouples method invocation from method execution, allowing methods to run concurrently. Figure 2.9 illustrates the structure of the Active Object pattern in the context of concurrent Web servers. The client interface transforms method requests (such as `get_request`) into method objects that are stored on an activation queue. The scheduler, which runs in a separate thread from the client, dequeues these method objects and transforms them back into method calls to perform the specified HTTP processing. The Active Object pattern is used in the Thread-per-Request model in section 2.4.4.2, the Thread Pool models in section 2.4.4.3, and the Thread-per-Session model in section 2.4.4.4.

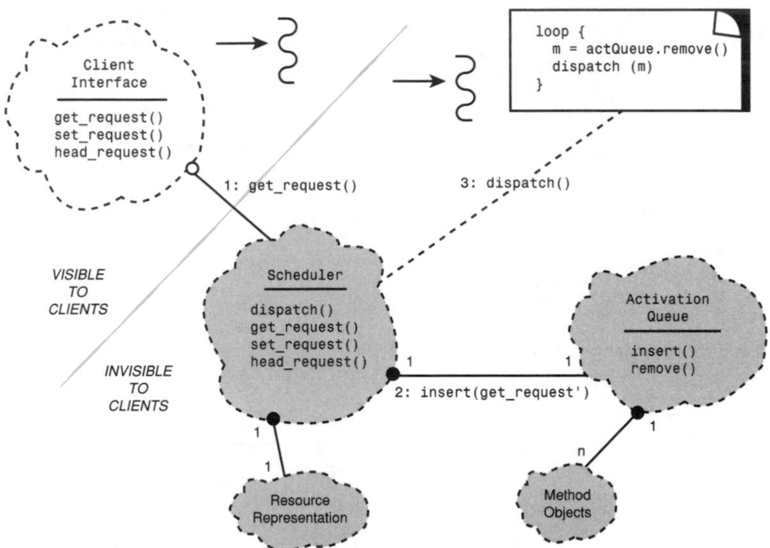

FIGURE 2.9. *The structure of the Active Object pattern.*

The Half-sync/Half-async pattern (Schmidt & Cranor, 1996) decouples synchronous I/O from asynchronous I/O in a system to simplify concurrent programming effort without degrading execution efficiency. Figure 2.10 illustrates the structure of the Half-sync/Half-async pattern in the context of the queue-based Thread Pool model in section 2.4.4.3. In this design, the Reactor is responsible for reading HTTP requests from clients and enqueueing valid requests on a message queue. This message queue feeds the pool of active objects that process the requests concurrently.

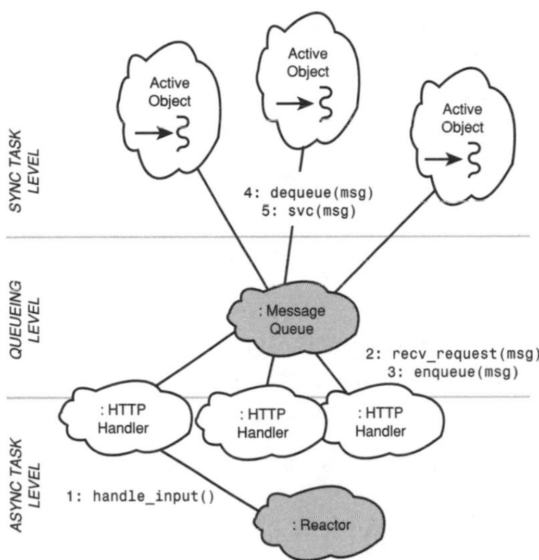

FIGURE 2.10. *The structure of the Half-sync/Half-async pattern.*

2.4.3.2. Tactical Patterns

Web servers also utilize many *tactical* patterns. In contrast to the strategic patterns described earlier, tactical patterns are domain independent and have a relatively localized impact on a software design. For instance, Singleton is a tactical pattern that often is used to consolidate all option processing used to configure a Web server. Although this pattern is domain independent and thus widely applicable, the problem it addresses does not affect Web server software architecture as pervasively as strategic patterns such as the Active Object and Reactor patterns. A thorough understanding of tactical patterns is essential, however, to implement highly flexible software that is resilient to changes in application requirements and platform environments.

The following tactical patterns are widely used in ACE and JAWS:

- The Strategy pattern defines a family of algorithms, encapsulates each one, and makes them interchangeable. JAWS uses this pattern extensively to configure different concurrency and event dispatching strategies without affecting the core software architecture of the Web server.

- The Adapter pattern transforms a nonconforming interface into one that can be used by a client. ACE uses this pattern in its OS adaptation layer to encapsulate the accidental complexity of the myriad native OS APIs in a uniform manner.
- The State pattern defines a composite object whose behavior depends on its state. The event dispatcher in JAWS uses the State pattern to seamlessly support both synchronous and asynchronous I/O.
- The Singleton pattern ensures that a class has only one instance and provides a global point of access to it. JAWS uses a Singleton to ensure that only one copy of its caching virtual filesystem exists in the Web server.

2.4.4. Implementing Web Server Concurrency Models with ACE

Existing Web servers use a wide range of concurrency strategies to implement the role of the event dispatcher. These strategies include single-threaded concurrency (e.g., Roxen), multiprocess concurrency (e.g., Apache), and multithread concurrency (e.g., PHTTPD, Zeus, JAWS). This section examines common Web concurrency models, including *single-threaded Reactive, Thread-per-Request, Thread Pool,* and *Thread-per-Session.* Each of these models is discussed below, focusing on the patterns they use and outlining how they can be implemented using ACE components.

Note how each concurrency model reuses most of the same patterns (e.g., Reactor, Acceptor, and Active Object) and ACE components (e.g., ACE Reactor, HTTP Acceptor, and HTTP Handler) simply by restructuring these core architectural building blocks in different configurations. This high degree of consistency is common in applications and frameworks that are explicitly built using patterns. When patterns are used to structure and document applications and frameworks, nearly every class plays a well-defined role and collaborates effectively with its related classes.

2.4.4.1. The Single-Threaded Reactive Web Server Model

In the Single-Threaded Reactive model, all connections and HTTP requests are handled by the same thread of control. This thread is responsible for demultiplexing requests from different clients and dispatching event handlers to perform HTTP processing. If each request is processed in its entirety, the Reactive Web server is deemed *iterative*. If the processing of each request is split into chunks that are performed separately, the Reactive Web server is deemed a *single-threaded concurrent* server.

The Single-Threaded Reactive model is a highly portable model for implementing the event dispatcher role in a Web server. This model runs on any OS platform that supports event demultiplexing mechanisms such as `select` or `WaitForMultipleObjects`. The structure of a Reactive Web server based on the ACE Reactor is shown in Figure 2.11. The ACE Reactor is an OO implementation of the Reactor pattern that waits synchronously in a single thread of control for the occurrence of various types of events (such as socket data, signals, or timeouts). When these events occur, the ACE Reactor demultiplexes the event to a pre-registered ACE Event Handler object and then dispatches the appropriate upcall method (e.g., `handle_input`, `handle_signal`, `handle_timeout`) on the object.

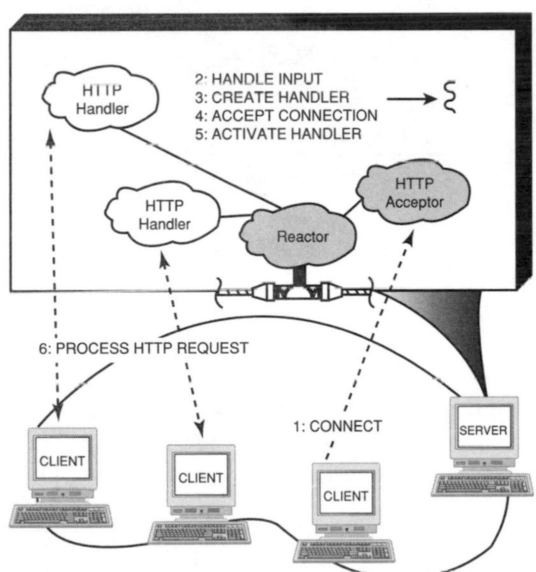

FIGURE 2.11. *The Single-Threaded Reactive Web server model.*

Figure 2.12 illustrates how the Reactor pattern is used to trigger the acceptance of HTTP connections from clients. When a connection event arrives from a client, the ACE Reactor invokes the `handle_input` factory method hook on the HTTP Acceptor. This hook accepts the connection and creates a new HTTP Handler object that processes the client request. Because this model is single-threaded and driven entirely by reactive I/O, each HTTP Handler must register with the ACE Reactor. The Reactor can then trigger the processing of HTTP requests from clients. When an HTTP `GET` request arrives, the ACE Reactor invokes the `handle_input` hook method on the HTTP handler. This hook processes the request by retrieving the URI from the HTTP GET request and transferring the specified file to the client.

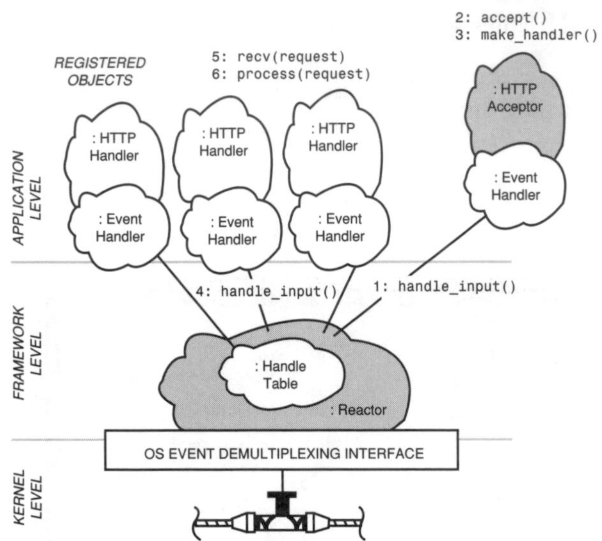

FIGURE 2.12. *Accepting connections and processing HTTP requests with the Reactor.*

To avoid blocking the server for extended periods of time, each I/O request can be broken into small chunks and sent separately. Therefore, the State pattern is typically used to maintain each HTTP handler's state (e.g., awaiting the GET request, transmitting the *n*th chunk, closing down). Likewise, the timer queue capabilities of the ACE Reactor can be used to prevent denial of service attacks where erroneous or malicious clients establish connections and consume Web server resources (e.g., socket handles) but never send data to or receive data from the server.

The main advantages of the Single-Threaded Reactive model are its portability and its low overhead for processing very small files. It is not suitable for high-performance Web servers, however, because it does not utilize parallelism effectively. In particular, all HTTP processing is serialized at the OS event demultiplexing level. This prevents Web servers from leveraging the parallelism available in the OS (e.g., asynchronous I/O) and hardware (e.g., DMA to intelligent I/O peripherals).

2.4.4.2. The Thread-per-Request Web Server Model

In the Thread-per-Request model, a new thread is spawned to handle each incoming request. Only one thread blocks on the acceptor socket. This acceptor thread is a factory that creates a new handler thread to process HTTP requests from each client.

The Thread-per-Request model is a widely used model for implementing multithreaded Web servers. This model runs on any OS platform that supports preemptive multithreading. The structure of a Thread-per-Request Web server based on the ACE Reactor and ACE Active Objects is shown in Figure 2.13.

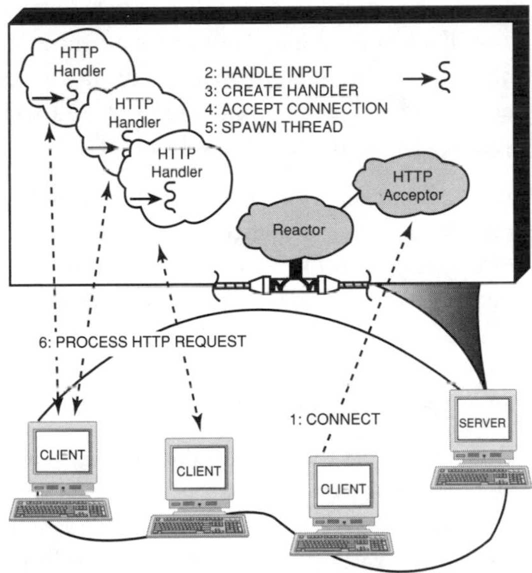

FIGURE 2.13. *The Thread-per-Request Web server model.*

Figure 2.13 illustrates how the ACE Reactor and HTTP Acceptor components can be reused for the Thread-per-Request model, i.e., the ACE Reactor blocks in the main thread waiting for connection events. When a connection event occurs it notifies the HTTP Acceptor factory, which creates a new HTTP Handler.

The primary difference between the Thread-per-Request model and the Single-Threaded Reactive model is that a new thread is spawned in each HTTP Handler to process every client request concurrently. Thus, the HTTP Handler plays the role of an active object—i.e., the ACE Reactor thread that accepts the connection and invokes the HTTP Handler executes concurrently with the threads that perform HTTP processing. In HTTP 1.0, the life cycle of an HTTP Handler active object is complete when the file transfer operation is finished.

The Thread-per-Request model is useful for handling requests for large files from multiple clients. It is less useful for small files from a single client due to the overhead of creating a new thread for each request. In addition, Thread-per-Request model can consume a large number of OS resources if many clients perform requests simultaneously during periods of peak load.

2.4.4.3. The Thread Pool Web Server Model

In the Thread Pool model, a group of threads is prespawned during Web server initialization. Each thread blocks on the same acceptor socket, waiting for connections to arrive from clients. Prespawning eliminates the overhead of creating a new thread for each request. It also bounds the number of OS resources consumed by a Web server.

The Thread Pool model is generally the most efficient way to implement the event dispatcher in high-performance Web servers (Hu, et al., 1997). This model is most effective on OS platforms (e.g., Windows NT, Solaris 2.6) that permit simultaneous calls to the accept function on the same acceptor socket. On platforms that do not allow this (e.g., most SVR4 implementations of UNIX), it is necessary to explicitly serialize accept with an ACE Mutex synchronization object.

There are several variations of the Thread Pool model. Figures 2.14 and 2.15 illustrate the *handle-based* and *queue-based* synchronous Thread Pool models, respectively. Figure 2.16 illustrates the asynchronous Thread Pool model. Each of these variants is outlined in the following text.

The *handle-based synchronous Thread Pool model* shown in Figure 2.14 does not use a Reactor. Instead, each thread in the pool directly invokes the `handle_input` method of the HTTP Acceptor, which blocks awaiting client connections on the acceptor socket handle. When clients connect, the OS selects a thread from the pool of HTTP Acceptors to accept the connection. After a connection is established, the acceptor "morphs" into an HTTP Handler, which performs a synchronous read on the newly connected handle. After the HTTP request has been read, the thread performs the necessary computation and file system operations to service the request. The requested file is then transmitted synchronously to the client. After the data transmission completes, the thread returns to the pool and reinvokes HTTP Acceptor's `handle_input` method.

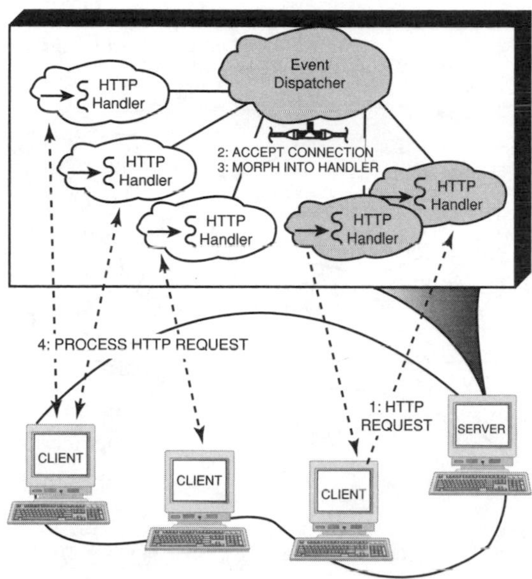

FIGURE 2.14. *The handle-based synchronous Thread Pool Web server model.*

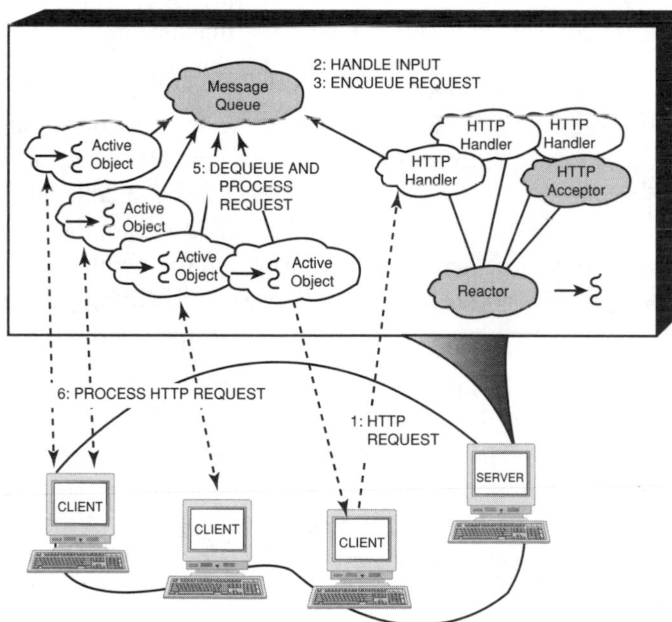

FIGURE 2.15. *The queue-based synchronous Thread Pool Web server model.*

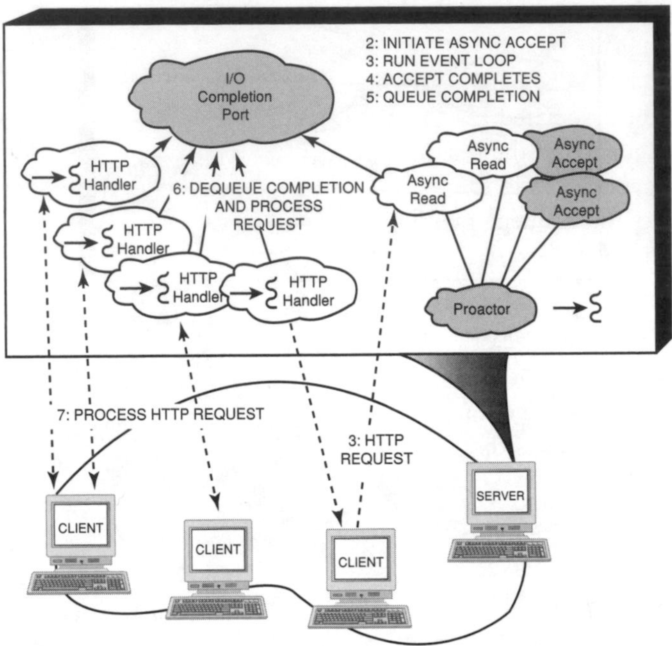

FIGURE 2.16. *The asynchronous Thread Pool Web Server model.*

Client requests can execute concurrently until the number of simultaneous requests exceeds the number of threads in the pool. At this point, additional requests are queued in the kernel's socket listen queue until a thread in the pool finishes its processing and becomes available. To reduce latency, the Thread Pool model can be configured to always have threads available to service new requests. However, the number of threads needed to support this policy can be very high during peak loads as threads block in long-duration synchronous I/O operations.

One drawback with the handle-based Thread Pool model is that the size of the socket listen queue is relatively small (around 8 to 10 connections on most OS platforms). Therefore, high-volume servers that receive hundreds of Web hits per second might not be able to accept connections fast enough to keep the kernel from rejecting clients. Moreover, it is not possible to prioritize which connections are dropped because the kernel does not distinguish among different clients.

The *queue-based synchronous Thread Pool* shown in Figure 2.15 uses the Half-sync/Half-async pattern, which combines the Reactor and Active

Object patterns. In this model, the ACE Reactor thread accepts connections from clients (via the HTTP Acceptor) and manages all the HTTP handlers. When HTTP requests arrive from clients, they are validated briefly by the associated HTTP Handler in the ACE Reactor thread and then are enqueued in the thread-safe ACE message queue that joins the async and sync layers in the Web server. Each active object in the thread pool invokes the dequeue method of the request queue, which blocks awaiting client requests.

After an HTTP request has been dequeued by a thread in the pool, this thread performs the necessary computation and file system operations to service the request. The requested data is then transmitted synchronously to the client. After the data transmission completes, the thread returns to the pool and reinvokes the dequeue method to retrieve another HTTP request.

In contrast with the handle-based Thread Pool model, the queue-based Thread Pool design makes it possible to accept (or reject) all incoming connections rapidly and prioritize how each client is processed. The primary drawback stems from the extra context switching and synchronization required to manage the queue in the Web server.

The *asynchronous Thread Pool model*, shown in Figure 2.16, uses the ACE Proactor, which manages an I/O completion port. An *I/O completion port* is a thread-safe queue of I/O completion notifications that resides in the OS kernel (in contrast, the queue-based Thread Pool managed the thread in user space). Each I/O operation is initiated and handed off to the kernel, where it runs to completion. Therefore, the initiating thread does not block. When these operations complete asynchronously, the kernel queues the resulting notifications at the appropriate I/O completion port.

As with the synchronous Thread Pool model, the asynchronous Thread Pool model is created during Web server initialization. Unlike in the synchronous model, however, the threads wait on an I/O completion port rather than waiting on `accept`. The OS queues up results from all asynchronous operations (e.g., asynchronous accepts, reads, writes) on the I/O completion port. The result of each asynchronous operation is handled by a thread selected by the OS from the pool of threads waiting on the completion port. The thread that dequeues the completion notification need not be the same one that initiated the operation.

The asynchronous Thread Pool model is typically less resource intensive and provides more uniform latency under heavy workloads than synchronous Thread Pool models (Hu et al., 1997). It is also more scalable because the same programming model works for a single thread as well as multiple threads. The primary drawback with the asynchronous Thread Pool model is that it is not portable to platforms that lack asynchronous I/O and proactive event dispatching. Windows NT 4.0 is the main contemporary operating system that supports I/O completion ports in its OS API. The ACE Proactor encapsulates the Windows NT 4.0 I/O completion port asynchronous demultiplexing mechanism within a type-safe C++ wrapper.

2.4.4.4. The Thread-per-Session Web Server Model

In the Thread-per-Session model, the newly created handler thread is responsible for the lifetime of the entire client session rather than just a single request from the client. As with the Thread-per-Request model, only one thread blocks on the acceptor socket. This acceptor thread is a factory that creates a new handler thread to interact with each client for the duration of the session. Therefore, the new thread can serve multiple requests from a client before terminating.

The Thread-per-Session model is not appropriate for HTTP 1.0 because the protocol establishes a new connection for each request. Thus, Thread-per-Session is equivalent to Thread-per-Request in HTTP 1.0. The Thread-per-Session model is applicable in HTTP 1.1, however, because it supports persistent connections (Fielding, Gettys, Mogul, Frystyk, & Berners-Lee, 1997; Mogul, 1995). Figure 2.17 illustrates the Thread-per-Session model.

The Thread-per-Session model provides good support for prioritization of client requests. For instance, higher-priority clients can be associated with higher-priority threads. Thus, a request from a higher-priority client is served ahead of requests from lower-priority clients because the OS can preempt lower-priority threads. One drawback to Thread-per-Session is that connections receiving considerably more requests than others can become a performance bottleneck. In contrast, the Thread-per-Request and Thread Pool models provide better support for load balancing.

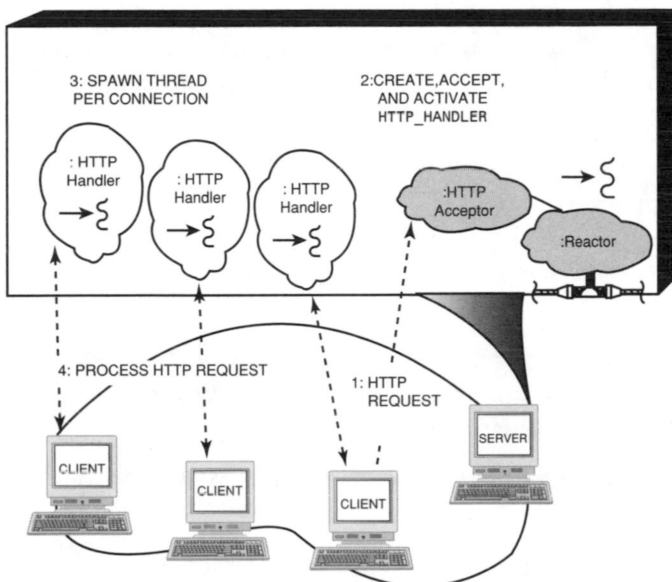

FIGURE 2.17. *The Thread-per-Session Web server model.*

2.5. Summary

Computing power and network bandwidth have increased dramatically over the past decade. However, the design and implementation of communication software remain expensive and error prone. Much of the cost and effort stem from the continual rediscovery and reinvention of fundamental design patterns and framework components across the software industry. Moreover, the growing heterogeneity of hardware architectures and diversity of OS and network platforms makes it hard to build correct, portable, and efficient applications from scratch.

Object-oriented application frameworks and design patterns help to reduce the cost and improve the quality of software by leveraging proven software designs and implementations to produce reusable components that can be customized to meet new application requirements. The ACE framework described in this chapter illustrates how the development of communication software, such as high-performance Web servers, can be simplified and unified. The key to the success of ACE is its ability to capture common communication software design patterns and consolidate these patterns into flexible framework components that efficiently encapsulate and enhance low-level OS mechanisms for interprocess communication, event demultiplexing, dynamic configuration, concurrency, and synchronization.

The ACE C++ wrappers, framework components, distributed services, and middleware applications are freely available at `www.cs.wustl.edu/~schmidt/ACE.html`. This URL contains complete source code, documentation, and sample applications, including JAWS.

2.6. References

Booch, G. 1993. *Object oriented analysis and design with applications*, 2d ed. Redwood City, CA: Benjamin/Cummings.

Brooks, F. P. 1975. *The mythical man-month*. Reading, MA: Addison-Wesley.

Fielding, R., J. Gettys, J. Mogul, H. Frystyk, and T. Berners-Lee. 1997. Hypertext Transfer Protocol—HTTP/1.1. *Standards Track RFC 2068: Network Working Group*. Available from `http://www.w3.org/`.

Gamma, E., R. Helm, R. Johnson, and J. Vlissides. 1995. *Design patterns: Elements of reusable object-oriented software*. Reading, MA: Addison-Wesley.

Halstead, R. H., Jr. 1985. Multilisp: A language for concurrent symbolic computation. *ACM Trans. Programming Languages and Systems* 7:501–538.

Harrison, T., D. Levine, and D. C. Schmidt. October 1997. The design and performance of a real-time CORBA event service. *Proceedings of OOPSLA '97*. Atlanta, GA: ACM.

Harrison, T., I. Pyarali, D. C. Schmidt, and T. Jordan. September 1997. Proactor—An object behavioral pattern for dispatching asynchronous event handlers. *The 4th Pattern Languages of Programming Conference*.

Hu, J., I. Pyarali, and D. C. Schmidt. November 1997. Measuring the impact of event dispatching and concurrency models on Web server performance over high-speed networks. *Submitted to the 2nd Global Internet Conference, IEEE*.

Jain, P., and D. C. Schmidt. June 1997. Service configurator: A pattern for dynamic configuration of services. *Proceedings of the 3rd Conference on Object-Oriented Technologies and Systems.* USENIX.

Johnson, R., and B. Foote. 1988. Designing reusable classes. *Journal of Object-Oriented Programming* 1:22–35.

Lavender, R. G., and D. C. Schmidt. 1996. Active object: An object behavioral pattern for concurrent programming. In J. O. Coplien, J. Vlissides, and N. Kerth (Eds.), *Pattern Languages of Program Design.* Reading, MA: Addison-Wesley.

Mogul, J. C. August 1995. The case for persistent connection HTTP. Proceedings of the ACM SIGcomm '95 Conference in Computer Communication Review, Boston.

Pyarali, I., T. H. Harrison, and D. C. Schmidt. 1996. Design and performance of an object-oriented framework for high-performance electronic medical imaging. *Computing Systems* 9:331–375.

Schmidt, D. C. 1995. Reactor: An object behavioral pattern for concurrent event demultiplexing and event handler dispatching. In J. O. Coplien and D. C. Schmidt (Eds.), *Pattern Languages of Program Design.* Reading, MA: Addison-Wesley.

Schmidt, D. C. 1996a. A family of design patterns for application-level gateways. *The Theory and Practice of Object Systems (Special issue on patterns and pattern languages)* 2(1).

Schmidt, D. C. 1996b. Acceptor and connector: Design patterns for initializing communication services. In R. Martin, F. Buschmann, and D. Riehle (Eds.), *Pattern Languages of Program Design.* Reading, MA: Addison-Wesley.

Schmidt, D. C., and C. D. Cranor. 1996. Half-sync/half-async: An architectural pattern for efficient and well-structured concurrent I/O. In J. O. Coplien, J. Vlissides, and N. Kerth (Eds.), *Pattern Languages of Program Design.* Reading, MA: Addison-Wesley.

Schmidt, D. C., A. Gokhale, T. Harrison, and G. Parulkar. 1997. A high-performance endsystem architecture for real-time CORBA. *IEEE Communications Magazine* 14.

Schmidt, D. C., T. H. Harrison, and E. Al-Shaer. 1995. Object oriented components for high-speed network programming. In *Proceedings of the 1st Conference on Object-Oriented Technologies and Systems.* Monterey, CA: USENIX.

Schmidt, D. C., and P. Stephenson. 1995. Experiences using design patterns to evolve system software across diverse OS platforms. In *Proceedings of the 9th European Conference on Object-Oriented Programming*. Aarhus, Denmark: ACM.

Schmidt, D. C., and T. Suda. 1994. An object-oriented framework for dynamically configuring extensible distributed communication systems. *IEE/BCS Distributed Systems Engineering Journal (Special issue on configurable distributed systems)* 2:280–293.

Stepanov, A., and M. Lee. 1994. The standard template library. Tech. Rep. HPL-94-93, Hewlett-Packard Laboratories.

Vlissides, J. 1996. The Hollywood principle. *C++ Report* 8.

PART II
Smalltalk

CHAPTER 3

The Community of Smalltalk

by Adele Goldberg

3.1. The Smalltalk Vision

Alan Kay had a vision of computer technology. Everyone, regardless of age, social background, or profession, would be able to use technology to access everyone else. Everyone, regardless of interest, education, or skills with computer technology, would be able to use a computer to access textual, graphical, audible, static, and dynamic information. Everyone would be able to use this information to test personal models of the world.

When Kay included the idea of modeling in his dream of everyone's computer technology, the realization of his vision changed. The vision of accessibility was formulated in terms of a small, affordable computer with network access to information from other computers. This vision he called the *Dynabook*. But the vision of modeling added the need to include programming support with the Dynabook. Someone had to program the Dynabook with models: models of physical and social processes, models of gaming techniques, models of businesses. Kay thought that everyone should be able to program the Dynabook. The vision of programming was understood as the ability to create simulations. These simulations are complex systems that should be created using modular designs that hide details when appropriate and expose them as needed. Kay called this programming language for everyone *Smalltalk*.

The design history of the Smalltalk family of programming languages is intrinsically interleaved with the history of personal computing at Xerox's Palo Alto Research Center (PARC). Each iteration of the programming language design involved new language specification, implementation on next-generation personal computer hardware, exploration of information access and manipulation applications, and trials with people who were not computer professionals. The implementation and application experiences necessarily influenced the software and hardware designs for the next iteration. This research cycle started in 1971 and ended around 1983 with the first public release of the language from Xerox. By 1984 the language had entered a commercialization stage, where the major changes were in class libraries and tools to support large system development. By 1996 the language's growing popularity waned in the face of poor business practice and the marketing skills of the Java proponents. The enthusiasm of the community of Smalltalk users, however, continues undaunted as they view the various commercial and free Smalltalk language systems (including Squeak, LearningWorks, GNU Smalltalk, and Little Smalltalk)[1] to be the most productive work environments available. Users measure the success of the language as much on its impact on rapidly and effectively building and maintaining business systems as on the extent to which it influences their own thinking processes.

3.2. Smalltalk-71: First Efforts

In 1971 Alan Kay joined the recently founded Xerox PARC to explore his vision of computer technology. His vision was the Dynabook, best described in the 1977 *IEEE Computer* paper about "personal dynamic media" (Kay & Goldberg, 1977). The vision expressed by Kay was a remarkable synthesis of ideas gleaned from very early ideas of Vannevar Bush (Bush, 1945), including the design of the Burroughs 220 and B5000 (Ivan Sutherland's Sketchpad graphical object manipulation and windows to a virtual computer world [Sutherland, 1963]), various programming languages (JOSS [Shaw, 1964], EULER [Wirth & Weber, 1966], LISP [McCarthy, 1960], and SIMULA [Dahl & Nygaard, 1966]), and personal learning experiences acquired while studying mathematics, biology, and computer science in the U.S. Air Force. Members of Kay's original research group (the Learning Research Group) were forever stimulated by his presentations of old films and slides, as he cajoled them to learn from the past while creating the future.[2]

---

[1] Both GNU Smalltalk and Little Smalltalk are public domain versions of Smalltalk available on a CD-ROM packaged with a book (Pletzke, 1997) that also provides public class libraries and comparisons of commercial systems. Squeak and LearningWorks can be found on their respective Web sites on the Internet.

[2] The community that invented and reinvented Smalltalk over more than two decades is large, too large to name each individual and their contributions. See Alan Kay's own history for a list of early contributors (Kay, 1996) as well as the acknowledgments in the original Smalltalk-80 book (Goldberg & Robson, 1983). Inclusion of references here is done only to support the telling of the history and is not necessarily a statement of relative importance.

The fundamental idea found in these related designs and experiences was the use of master descriptions that could create instances, each of which was an independent entity controlled either by a system of constraints or by a procedural programming language. Kay observed that this idea could be described as a complex computer system with a collection of smaller computers, each an independent simulation endowed with the power of a whole computer. Herbert Simon, too, argued that systems can best be understood by separating description from implementation (Simon, 1969). The description, defined as the interface of each system part to an outer environment, states the goals or role of the part. The details of implementation, or the inner mechanisms, can differ among parts with otherwise similar goals.

The first language Kay called Smalltalk was Smalltalk-71,[3] but this language was never actually implemented. Although it was the first Smalltalk, Smalltalk-71 was the third design for a Smalltalk language. The first design was for the FLEX machine (Kay, 1968), which consisted of object structures for a master and its instances, a syntax-directed compiler, an I/O handler, and a simple display editor for text and graphics. Kay worked on the FLEX machine with Ed Cheadle, influenced by the "human-oriented" interface work of Doug Engelbart at the Stanford Research Institute Center for the Augmentation of the Human Intellect (Engelbart & English, 1968). Engelbart's own vision of collaborative work encouraged Kay to think that the Dynabook needed a system that could be extended or tailored by its user.

The second Smalltalk, again designed in the context of the FLEX machine (Kay, 1969), was based on ideas from the language IMP (Irons, 1970) in which every procedure in the system defined its own syntax. This Smalltalk treated each object as its own syntax-directed interpreter of messages or requests to carry out function. The designs for Smalltalk-71 and Smalltalk-72 retained this object-defining syntax. The single fundamental representation, the object, tied function to the information needed to carry out that function. To use the function of an object, you send the object a message; the object then accesses and modifies its private memory to formulate an appropriate message response. No user has direct access to the private memory of the object. Thus, the notion of an

[3]Note that the numbers in the language version, such as 71, represent the year of design, not necessarily the year that the version of the language was fully implemented or the sequential version number.

object is like that of any well-defined system component. An object consists of an external aspect, defined as the message interface or set of functions that the object can be called on to perform. And it consists of an internal aspect, defined as the implementation of the messages and the description of a set of properties whose values persist over the object's lifetime. The Smalltalk/FLEX processing model involves synchronous messaging. An object sends a message and waits for a response.

The actual semantics of a Smalltalk-71 message expression were not known until runtime. At runtime, the interpreter determined which object was to receive a message. The object then parsed the input stream to identify the next message, searched the object definition for a method associated with that message, and then gave control to that method. In Smalltalk-71, the method could continue to parse the input stream for additional information and then compute a return value. This value was itself an object that could take control of the parsing process. Identifying tokens as object and message names, and identifying the meaning of these names, was thus determined dynamically at runtime. Multiple and independently defined objects could be sent the same message, with each independent type of object responding differently.

3.3. Smalltalk-72: Inventing Personal Workstations

The history of the design of Smalltalk is also the history of the invention of personal workstations at Xerox PARC.

Kay designed the FLEX machine while he was a graduate student at the University of Utah. He then worked at Stanford, where, in anticipation of joining Xerox PARC, he refined his ideas into a machine called the KiddiKomp, running a simulation language based on the language LOGO (Papert, 1980). This machine in turn evolved into the design of the miniCOM, complete with a bitmapped display, a pointing device, external storage, and the first language that was formally called Smalltalk. Kay's own history of this period contains interesting sketches of these early Dynabook designs (Kay, 1996).

A favorite folk tale in PARC history retells the birth of the Alto, PARC's first personal workstation. As Smalltalk was to be the basis for programming on a Dynabook, the test of its usefulness relied on its availability on a Dynabook, or at least on the Dynabook's closest approximation given known packaging and display technologies. At the outset of its creation, PARC consisted of several research laboratories, two of which focused on computing science. Kay's Learning Research Group (LRG) was in the System Science Laboratory (SSL), whereas most of the hardware designers resided in the Computer Science Laboratory (CSL). The decision to create two laboratories was made on the conjecture that two labs could muster more resources from Xerox than just one. The decision was made without the wisdom of hindsight that two labs would have to fight a zero-sum game for the same resources, should funding become tight (as it did around 1976).

In 1972 at Xerox PARC, there was not general agreement that everyone needed a personal workstation. Much of the successful computing science work had been carried out on time-sharing systems, systems whose users appeared satisfied to move textual information over telephone lines at 300 baud. But the Dynabook vision required that each individual have more than an illusion of access to computing capability. Because each Dynabook user was to be able to draw in full color, create and view Disney-quality animations, orchestrate and play back symphonies, and so on, individual ownership of computing power was essential. Kay's first request to get resources to build a few miniCOMs was turned down by the then CSL manager. Disappointed, LRG created demo simulations of painting, animation, gesture recognition, text and font editing, and music capture on a Data General NOVA with an experimental character generator.

Fortunately, as the folklore goes, the head of CSL was assigned to a three-month corporate task force and was therefore not present to stop the transfer of LRG funds to CSL to design and build the first Alto workstations (Thacker 1988). The full design was completed in one month and was well on its way to implementation by the time the CSL manager returned. By 1973 LRG had in its possession three Altos and was able to simulate the Dynabook idea. The (606×808) bitmapped display screen of the Alto was, in fact, supposed to be a transient phenomenon, used to simulate the interaction with flat-paneled display technology.

The Smalltalk implemented on the first Altos was Smalltalk-72. The first implementation experiment was coded in BASIC by Dan Ingalls on the

NOVA. Ingalls's goal was to check out the semantics of the proposed language. Ingalls then created a BCPL version for the NOVA, which he bootstrapped to the Alto in the spring of 1973. It was an interpreter with a simple reference-counting scheme for automatically managing the allocation and deallocation of objects in main memory. The kernel interpreter was simple because most useful data structures, control, and literals were realized as instances of classes with escapes to lower-level code for those object messages needing special primitive handling. Smalltalk-72 was available for use by both PARC researchers and invited visitors by the summer of 1973.[4] The display screen for the first Smalltalk-72 system was divided into two parts, called windows. Text editing of program code was done in the lower scrollable dialog window, and the graphical results were displayed in the upper window. As Smalltalk-72 evolved, LRG experimented with the first user interface based on overlapping windows.

The language itself mixed objects with functions (Goldberg & Kay, 1976). The following are some sample expressions:

```
3+4
☺ go 100 turn 90
do 4 (☺ go 100 turn 90)
for i ← 1 to 200 do (☺ go i*2 turn 89)
repeat 4 (☺ go 100 turn 90)
☞ size ← 100.
```

As you can see, Smalltalk-72 used a number of special iconic characters, such as a pointing finger preceding a name to signify the literal symbol rather than its value, and the smiling face to denote the line-drawing turtle named *smiley* (graphics using turtles was adopted from LOGO). Control structures were represented as functions (such as repeat [...], done, done with <value>, again, for, and do n [..]). The following symbols were used to denote the special ways in which an object could parse a message stream:

[4]I joined LRG at this time, in June 1973, having completed my Ph.D. from the University of Chicago and research program at the Institute for Mathematical Studies in the Social Sciences at Stanford University. My special interest was educational technology, teaching about and with computers.

◁	*Eyeball.* Answer not-false if a specific word appears as the next word in the message.
⚬⚬	*Open colon or uneval bind.* Receive the next literal token (single word or words enclosed in parentheses) from the message.
:	*Closed colon or eval bind.* Receive the next value from the message.
⚷	*Keyhole.* Same as uneval bind, except the current place in the message stream is retained (a kind of "peek ahead").
⇨	*Right arrow.* The conditional of the form *if-clause ⇨ (then-clause) else-clause.*

Smalltalk-72 had classes and instances but no class hierarchy. You use the following syntax to create a class:

```
to <class name> <temporary variables> | <instance variables> | <class
variables>
     (messages and responses)
```

You create an instance of a class with an expression in this form:

```
☞ <name> ← <value>
```

where <value> refers to a class. Classes implemented `isnew` to specify what to do when first creating an instance. Classes implemented `'s` (apostrophe+s) to access an instance variable value or to assign a new value to that variable. Classes implemented `is` to answer whether an instance is a member of a class. The name SELF referred to the current object in control of parsing the message stream (the message receiver). When the programmer wanted to force a new message receiver, sequences of message expressions were separated by a period. For example, a partial implementation of a class that describes a graphical box follows (using a turtle as the drawing pen, and assuming a single window in which the turtle draws):

```
To box var | turt size
(isnew  ⇨  (☞ turt ← turtle. ☞ size ← 50.
            turt place 100 150.
            SELF draw.)
 ◁ draw    ⇨    (do 4 (turt go size turn 90))
 ◁ redraw  ⇨    (SELF undraw.   : .  SELF draw.)
 ◁ move    ⇨    (SELF redraw turt penup go ( :  ) pendn) )
```

So, if we make joe a box

```
☞ joe ← box.
```

then

```
joe draw move 50
```

is interpreted as joe sees draw and so tells its turtle to draw a square with each side *size* long. The method for draw defaults to returning joe, so joe still has control and with its eyeball sees move. The method for move asks joe to redraw. The closed colon (:) symbol in the method for redraw denotes a request to evaluate the next expression, which in this case is the rest of the move method turt penup go (:) pendn. That is, the method for redraw parses the rest of the message stream found in the method for move. So evaluating the expression has the box's turtle lift up its pen to go some distance without marking the display surface, and then put down the pen. The closed colon in the method for move evaluates the number 50 in the original message stream.[5]

The two consequences of the Smalltalk-72 model for dynamic binding and syntax-directed interpretation made Smalltalk-72 (and Smalltalk-71 as well) both clever and somewhat incomprehensible. First, the method invoked when a message was sent to an object could itself describe changes to an object definition, thereby dynamically altering the meaning of an expression in the language. Second, an expression that was well formed syntactically might not be well defined semantically. From the syntactic elements alone, it was not possible to infer the type of the object and therefore how it would or could respond to the message. Robust run-time exception handling was consequently a significant requirement if the system was to be used by everyone.

In this fourth iteration of the Smalltalk invention, LRG researchers implemented applications for text editing, free-hand drawing, animation, and music editing. The goal was to write as much as possible in Smalltalk itself. The more code that was written in Smalltalk, the more the Dynabook owner could directly control. Probably the most innovative of these applications was Mighty Mouse, a first-of-its-kind direct-manipulation text editor created by Larry Tesler.

---

[5]I have to confess that I was not excited about Smalltalk-72 as a language for everyone. The idea that everyone could be taught how to write parsers, with nested stacking of the "current" message stream, was frightening.

The LRG research goal was to find the best combination of language definition, tools, and existing objects that could be combined by Smalltalkers to create information-manipulation kinds of applications. The mantra was that simple things should be easy to create, and hard things should still be feasible. This vision was to be realized more by creating a language whereby its users could create their own tools than by providing a finished toolbox. The compelling research question, though, was, Simple for whom? Feasible by whom? The target audience for Smalltalk was everyone, and everyone included young children as well as adults not interested in becoming programming professionals. With the availability of the Altos, it was now possible to begin research on whether children could learn to program in Smalltalk and how they could benefit from this knowledge.

3.3.1. Smalltalk-74: FastTalk

Smalltalk-74 was an effort to improve the performance of Smalltalk-72. It introduced an object representing a message, message dictionaries for classes, `bitblt` (the 2D graphics operator for bitmap graphics), and a better window interface. Another key innovation in Smalltalk-74 was OOZE (object-oriented zoned environment) as the new virtual memory system (Kaehler, 1981). The Alto included a 2.4MB model 30 disk drive for external storage. OOZE capitalized on the object-oriented nature of Smalltalk to allow 16-bit pointers to address 65KB objects so that a 96KB Alto could act as though its main memory were as big as its disk. Purging was done in the background, attempting not to interfere with the interactive nature of the Smalltalk system. Also, OOZE had a checkpointing scheme that ensured that the disk contained a recoverable image of Smalltalk objects no more than a few seconds old.

3.4. Smalltalk-76: Contributing to Educational Technology

The history of Smalltalk is also the history of educational technology research at Xerox PARC.

Computer-assisted instruction (CAI) was in vogue in the late '60s and early '70s. A number of programming languages for authoring courseware had been invented, including IBM's Coursewriter, PLATO from the University of Illinois, and TICCIT from Brigham Young University. The Stanford CAI project relied on courses developed using PDP-10 machine code. In all of these large NSF-funded projects, the educational philosophy was fundamentally drill-and-practice. The computer was not, in fact, the teacher but rather the monitor of self-paced, self-test curricula. The biggest beneficiaries of these CAI efforts were clearly the curriculum authors. Despite the poor ratio of preparation time to course time per student (sometimes estimated as 40 to 1), authors were enthusiastic to discover how the requirement to prepare detailed course materials for computer delivery helped them to understand and organize their own materials.

Researchers at BBN, MIT, the University of Pittsburgh, and Stanford were not surprised by the positive reception of authoring languages. After all, as they hypothesized, one learns by trying to explain. But what better way to explain than through a programming language instructing a computer? With BASIC and with LOGO, these researchers pursued their interest in teaching young children to program as a way to teach about mathematics and effective problem solving.

3.4.1. Smalltalk: A Programming Language of Educational Interest?

Alan Kay, too, was encouraged by reports from Seymour Papert's MIT laboratory in which children were taught LOGO and Turtle Geometry (Abelson & diSessa, 1981). He positioned Smalltalk as a modeling language for children and the Dynabook minimally as an electronic book in which book elements could be directly manipulated. Kay also measured the success of each Smalltalk design as much on its capability to be learned by kids as on the extent to which the language and tools simplified the development of complex information-handling applications. Children were the special instances of everyone. The real beneficiary of linking pedagogy with language design was the computer industry because the educational emphasis kept the research focused on user interface design. Windows with multiple views of information, context-dependent menus, and the extensive use of direct pointing devices (the mouse for text and large object control, tablet and pen for drawing and character recognition) were all inventions driven by the necessity of creating a programming environment usable by everyone.

From a systems perspective, Smalltalk-76 was designed for speed and efficiency, as well as to support large system development. The design was based on the requirement to make a language that could be compiled without giving up the flexibility of being able to implement (simulation) languages within the language. From a user perspective, the design was influenced by the desire to have children as the users. Early efforts by education researchers to match the MIT LOGO claims were disappointing. It seemed that the MIT experience was more a function of Papert's charisma than a property of LOGO and Turtle Geometry. The absence of a well-defined curriculum left researchers perplexed at what was really being accomplished with young children because no one could replicate the LOGO group's claims that children were inventing mathematics. The Smalltalk group suffered the same disenchantment and vowed to have a better-defined set of objectives and curriculum.

This vow motivated two important changes to Smalltalk: addition of a class hierarchy and a human-readable syntax. Happily, the two goals of creating a language that could be understood by humans and by computers (so that the compiler could be written) were compatible.

Traditional approaches to teaching how to program introduce abstract concepts about algorithms, data structures, and programming tools. LRG rejected these traditional approaches because they were not consistent with the Piagetian theory that young children learn best by starting with concrete examples from which they can eventually come to understand the more abstract basic concepts. Our Smalltalk curriculum idea was to give students concrete examples to explore, through object use and customization (Goldberg & Kay, 1977). Customization had to be safe so that students could be encouraged to explore any ideas that occurred to them. Existing examples could be provided by defining a class of objects and having the student explore the behavior of instances of the class. But directly changing the implementation of a class was not sufficiently safe. Thus, class hierarchies were born of the necessity to have students create objects just like ones they were using—except for a difference in behavior or properties, all definable in a subclass and therefore guaranteed not to break the existing uses of instances of the superclass.

The students had to be able to read existing code in order to make intelligent modifications. The ability to read code implied that the syntax had to be easily interpretable by a human being. This requirement to be able to read code, not just write it, encouraged the invention of programming tools in Smalltalk based on the ability to query the system about existing object definitions and their relations to one another (Goldberg, 1984). The paper called "Programmer as Reader" (Goldberg, 1986) describes how the Smalltalk programming environment evolved on the principle that you learn to write by reading and you learn to read by writing. The intimate relation between decoding and encoding must be supported by the programming tools.

Smalltalk-76 was initially implemented on Altos. The Altos were robust machines, holding up to use by Xerox PARC administrators, secretaries, and researchers, as well as the large number of children and other visitors PARC hosted. LRG did a number of projects in Smalltalk-76 to test the breadth of applications that could be expressed easily with Smalltalk. One of these was an application to manage the book catalog of the PARC library. The application was actively used for a number of years. Most of the educational experimentation was done with specially conducted classes of students ages 12–13. These classes were held in cooperation with a local junior high school's mentally gifted minors program. The students were driven to PARC during the school day. Saturday classes were held for the children of PARC employees.

These classes were productive in formulating a curriculum that led students from learning about line drawing, freehand painting and animation, to describing simple simulations and even tools (Goldberg & Ross, 1981). One student invented her own painting tools (remember, this is the mid-1970s, long before Apple introduced the Macintosh). Two students wrote papers, published in *Creative Computing Magazine,* about their experiences.

To broaden the school experience and to avoid the time spent transporting students, LRG planned to take several Altos to the junior high school. The plan was carried out, but not without a clash with SSL and PARC management on the topic of removing equipment from the PARC building. (The actual problem was likely whether Xerox had protected its proprietary interests in the hardware and software and had sufficient insurance, but was presented mostly as bureaucratic hesitation.) The school experience was delightful; it demonstrated the robustness of the Smalltalk-76 system under use in an open resource center of a public school. The system's flexibility allowed the students to explore a wide range of simulation ideas. They wrote interactive games (Pong and various war-like games were typical), variations on the painting tool, and animations.

3.4.2. Smalltalk-76: The Language Definition

The primary designer of Smalltalk-76 was Dan Ingalls (Ingalls, 1978). The system was implemented in the Alto microcode as a byte-coded interpreter. Everything in Smalltalk-76 was an object, as everything in UNIX is a file, although some tricks were played to allow this metaphor to extend right down to the level of integer arithmetic. A class was created as an instance of the system class `Class`. You sent a class the message `new` to create an instance. Classes were objects, with a structure that encoded the inheritance hierarchy and a protocol that supported the creation and maintenance of their instances. The library contained about 50 classes representing all the operating system functions, files, network services, basic data structures, printing, editing applications, graphics, and user interface windowing system.

Because Smalltalk-76 provided a class hierarchy, the language included special variables `self` and `super`, each referring to the receiver of a message. The variable `self` indicated that the search for the appropriate method to execute should start in the class of the current receiver, and `super` indicated that the search should start in the message dictionary of the superclass. As part of eliminating the capability of objects to parse the message stream, Ingalls introduced the syntactic convention whereby message selectors consisted of a series of keywords, each ending with a colon to indicate that a value corresponding to a formal parameter was required. The colon was an obvious choice because it kept the familiar way in which parsing for the next argument to evaluate was done in Smalltalk-72. The up arrow continued to denote a return with value from the method, with the return value defaulted to `self`. The right arrow token (right arrow) continued to indicate a conditional expression, whereas `repeat`⸰ announced repetition. The open colon on a keyword allowed arguments to be passed unevaluated; blocks of code in square brackets could be passed in this manner for later evaluation. This syntax enabled users to create new control structures.

As a basis for comparing the syntax, the description of a `Box` class is shown here (note that Smalltalk-76 retained the use of an iconic font):

```
Class new title:  'Box';
        subclassof: Object;
        fields:   'size turt ;
        asFollows!
initialization
        setValues          size ←   50. turt ←  Turtle new.
accessing
        position           ^ turt position
        position: aPoint   turt position: aPoint
        direction          ^turt direction
        size               ^size
action
        move: dist         turt penup. turt go: dist. turt pendown.
display
        hide               (turt color = #black) ⇨ [turt white] turtblack.
                           self showBox.
                           (turt color = #black) ⇨ [turt white] turtblack.
        show               super show. self showBox.
        showBox            1 to: 4 do: [turt go: size. turt turn: 90]
```

If `joe` is a variable name, then

```
joe ← Box new.
joe position: 10 @ 50.
joe move: 10.
```

creates a new box, positions it at coordinates (10,50), and then moves the box by 10.

Notice that for the purposes of this example we continued to rely on turtle line drawing, although Smalltalk-76 provided a number of other drawing techniques, and we assumed that the turtle knew the window in which to draw.

3.4.3. Browsers, Inspectors, and Debuggers

Like the last version of Smalltalk-72, the Smalltalk-76 system supported overlapping windows. Ingalls had produced an early version of code browsing, which was essentially an editing window open on a file containing the textual representation of a class and providing the ability to (re)compile the full class. Larry Tesler produced the first code browsers with subviews as a structured way to examine a class. His method views let the programmer call on the compiler to compile just one method at a time. These programming tools introduced a new interactive and incremental approach to software development. The tools were based on three ideas: display the structure of the software (parts and relations), provide techniques for asking questions about that structure, and handle an incremental cycle for edit-compile-test at the method level. A browser displays the class description in terms of attribute structure, the message interface, and the methods that implement messages. An inspector displays the current values of an instance's attributes. A debugger—which really serves as a process inspector—displays the sequence of message sends interrupted once an exception occurs. Browsers, inspectors, and debuggers do more than display the descriptions and current values; they allow the user to change methods and values in the middle of an execution and then continue.

When programmers started writing class descriptions in these browsers, a new era of design began. The average size of a method tended to correspond to the screen space available for typing the method text (which consisted of around seven message expressions in addition to the method header information).[6] Software evolved (actually it felt like software was molded like clay). The programmer could write a partial class description, create an instance to try out its partial capabilities, add more messages or modify existing methods, and try these changes out on that same instance. The programmer could change the behavior of software describing an instance while the instance continued to exist.

[6]Although some programmers could argue that the per-message breakdown leads to these small method sizes (and undoubtedly it is an important factor), the claim about the impact of the screen space allotted by the browser is based on code comparisons that Steve Putz and I performed as part of a project to design a visual syntax for methods.

3.4.4. Using Smalltalk-76: Some PARC Folklore

3.4.4.1. Smalltalk Supports Rapid Development

In 1977 Bob Taylor (then acting head of CSL) came up with an interesting idea for a PARC seminar. He proposed to invite the president and chairman of the Xerox Corporation, along with Xerox's highest ranked officers, to spend two days at PARC. During that time, they would be presented with two important ideas: Computers of the future would be general-purpose devices customized by the addition of software to create business systems, and software would be created as a composition of otherwise independent components. As an example of the second idea, Taylor proposed that the researchers in CSL explain how their text editor (BRAVO) was both a standalone application and the text editor for an electronic mail system (a perfectly reasonable idea, if, in fact, it was not altogether available in the software in CSL at the time). Taylor further proposed that LRG create a hands-on laboratory in which the Xerox executives could experience the idea of component-based system creation, up close and personal.

LRG had nine weeks in which to design and implement a framework and a curriculum. The framework had to be customizable by various software components to produce different applications. The curriculum had to guarantee that each seminar participant would create a usable application. The framework created was a general one for specifying discrete, event-driven simulations, complete with a set of probability distributions for scheduling the arrival times and service times of customers and workers. The design was based on earlier work in SIMULA by Graham Birtwistle, called DEMOS (Birtwistle, 1979). The user interface consisted of an object browser that was a filter to display only four kinds of objects: `Simulations`, `Stations`, `Workers`, and `Customers` (rather than the entire Smalltalk library). By selecting one of the four classes of object, the user requested a list of all existing examples. Selecting `Simulation` displayed a list, such as `CarWash`, `Ferry`, `ComputerNetwork`, `new`. By selecting the item `new`, the user could specify another simulation, such as `ProductionLine` or `CopierCenter`. The user then selected one of the existing simulations and was shown the two important messages to simulations that had to be implemented (`arrivalSchedule` and `availableResources`). Similarly, selecting `Station` or `Worker` or `Customer` gave the user access only to those messages that had to be implemented in order to create a particular simulation. Built into the browser was some visual programming capability to draw images of simulation components and to specify the screen layout of stations. When the composed simulation was run, an animation appeared on the screen, along with a window in which statistics accumulated.

The simulation kit offers an interesting example of the kind of uses for which Smalltalk is best suited. Smalltalk systems contain a model of how types of components interact, here a model of event-driven simulations. There is also a set of components for specializing that model, a set of viewing and interacting components for constructing specializations, and a set of tools with which to create new components, modify the model, and design new views and ways to interact. The simulation framework is abstract in that it provides a set of interacting objects that describes a general class of application but does not describe a specific application until the components are attached to the framework at appropriate points of customization.

The seminar for the Xerox executives was successful, but not without some cost.[7] Nine weeks was hardly sufficient time to invent and implement the simulation kit, design and document five different customizations (all based on actual Xerox business experience and chosen so that the seminar participants could see the possible variety), and train mentors so that every participant's success was guaranteed. But the real story happened a week before show time. The design of the simulation kit assumed that the class/subclass approach to specialization was the right one. Creating a new worker meant creating a new subclass of class `Worker`. Running the simulation with this new worker meant creating instances as needed. The Smalltalk-76 approach to object reference and automatic reclamation continued to use OOZE. But OOZE was designed with assumptions about the relative numbers of classes, instances, and subclasses. One week before the seminar, OOZE had to be redesigned and reimplemented to account for an increased demand on managing subclasses rather than instances. It was like pulling a support beam out of a completed house and replacing it, while the house was still being used, and expecting no new cracks to show up. It worked.

[7]I had given birth to my second daughter just before the seminar preparation began. As project leader, I was given an Alto to use at home, but towards the end spent many late nights at PARC. Terry Winograd kindly walked the corridors with a crying two-month-old Rachel. On the day of the seminar, my babysitter became sick, so Rachel attended the seminar as well!

3.4.4.2. Smalltalk Supports Rapid Change

One of the most interesting applications in Smalltalk-76 was a multimedia document galley editor written by Diana Merry. It incorporated text and graphics into a general framework for managing document elements. Upon hearing of a visit by an influential Xerox executive, LRG agreed to demonstrate Smalltalk and various applications, including the galley editor. The demonstration was performed on a new PARC workstation, the Dorado, another Smalltalk-76 microcoded byte-code interpreter. We defined a filmstrip as a sequence of images and added a filmstrip as a document element. The task was easy because a small number of messages was sent by the document to any element and therefore to which a filmstrip had to respond. The demo was a page duplicated from a Xerox copier manual that displayed a sequence of text and pictures depicting the flow of paper through the copier. As if on cue, the executive wondered out loud whether the paper could really flow, and we selected the run command.

The demo then turned to the Smalltalk programming environment to explain the cross-referencing capability of the class browser. Again, the executive demonstrated his understanding by asking whether the particular pathway to a retrieved class method could be remembered. Tesler immediately said yes (after all, a computer scientist was asked whether he could do something with software—the answer is always yes). But the then head of PARC, escorting his corporate colleague, admonished that we indeed could not. Tesler left in a silent huff. By the time the demo completed, he was back, loaded some code, and gave the demonstration of bookmarking class method access.

A similar story of the rapid change of system software written in Smalltalk was told the day LRG entertained distinguished visitors from Siemens. Glenn Krasner gave the demo that day, carefully explaining the concepts and mechanisms behind the query interface to the Smalltalk system. But it was clear that the visitors were not pleased. Indeed, they were scowling. "Is there a problem?" we asked. "Indeed, there is," they answered. "Selected text should not be highlighted that way." We had been using the well-accepted technique of highlighting text by complementing the color of the text from black on white background to white on black. "And what should it be?" we asked. "You should put a box around the text," they answered—and so Glenn did. Without engaging in the usual human factors arguments that these gentlemen were prepared to hear, Glenn simply demonstrated how to discover the code that highlighted text and replace it with code that created the box. In fact, what Glenn did was interrupt the process of text selection by typing Ctrl+C to open the Smalltalk debugger as an inspector of the activation stack at the point of interruption. In the debugger, Glenn browsed to the method that highlights text and replaced it with a method to draw a box. He then pressed the `proceed` command and continued the demo.

3.4.5. Smalltalk-78: Portability Matters

The Dorado was not a Dynabook. A Dynabook is something you can take with you wherever you go. Weighing in at less than 15 pounds, a Dynabook is something you can put on your lap and work with for several hours, and your legs stay awake. A Dynabook is small and weighs less, has a lot of battery power, has a good quality display screen, and runs Smalltalk.

The NoteTaker was a step in the Dynabook direction. It was a computer about the size of a small suitcase. It could fit under your airplane seat if you flew coach. A NoteTaker had three 8086 processors, one for the bitmapped display screen, one to run the Smalltalk interpreter, and one to handle I/O. The battery pack could last several hours. Furthermore, Doug Fairbairn's planned redesign of the NoteTaker packaging represented a significant decrease in size.

The name *NoteTaker* came from a proposed educational use for the system. Suppose you were teaching a history or social studies course. The class is studying the history of England and France, noticing the intrigue in the two aristocratic circles. Some students hypothesize that the intrigue was fostered by gossip among the servants during official visits. Suppose you could formulate this hypothesis as a formal model of communications and its effect on government decision making. To test the theory, the students could gather information from the library, "taking notes" about patterns of communication and decision making. Suppose that the model was implemented as a computer system and that the students, while in the library, typed their notes directly into the computer as data to test the model. Would such a modeling tool be feasible? Would such a note-taking tool contribute to the students' ability to learn about and from history?

Xerox had another interesting problem. The Xerox technicians were not doing an excellent job of servicing customers. The documentation they used was large and filled the trunk of a car. Technicians did not carry that documentation into the customer's office; technicians did not go down to their cars to read out-of-date documentation. LRG proposed that the corporate documentation team consider using the NoteTaker as a new medium for publishing their materials. Technicians could take the computer into the customer office and search in real time for up-to-date information when any questions arose. The documents could be kept up-to-date by frequent downloads over telephone wires.

The year was 1978. People did not carry computers around with them. Not in a library. Not to customer offices.

And so the then head of PARC canceled the NoteTaker project. "No one wants portability," he said.

3.4.6. 1979: Steve Jobs, Sun, and Standard Microprocessors

Research is about taking risks. Research is permission to fail, as long as you learn and can report on the reasons for failure. A corporation that funds major research efforts has two responsibilities. The first is to monitor the work of its researchers and to understand how that work can be leveraged. The second is to monitor the work of others and to understand how that work can be leveraged.

1979 was a year of ominous events. It was the year Kay did not return. He had gone on sabbatical, visiting Information Sciences Institute, USC. He left Xerox to join Atari. Eventually he went to Apple and then in 1997 joined Disney.

Steve Jobs, then head of the fledgling Apple Corporation, visited PARC. He actually visited PARC twice. The first visit was hosted as a courtesy to the Xerox Venture Group, which had a significant investment in Apple. The visit involved a management demo, orchestrated in the foyer of the entrance to PARC and presented to Jobs, John Couch, and Jeff Raskin (who had visited PARC earlier when he was a UC professor and had encouraged Jobs to see for himself). Ingalls and Tesler gave the demos.[8] Then Jobs came back for a second demo. He came back with the entire Lisa programming team. (Lisa was the predecessor office workstation to the Macintosh and the competitor to the Xerox Star Workstation of the same time period.) Jobs sat with the Apple programmers in a conference room and waited. He waited three hours while I, as current LRG

[8]Tesler left PARC that year to join Apple, followed by Ingalls a year later.

manager, argued in vain that a demo for the programming team was an inappropriate give-away of Xerox research results. Worse, Jobs insisted that I give the demo, knowing I was the group's teacher. My manager at the time was head of the PARC Science Center (PARC was split into two while the Corporation sought a new PARC manager who could do a better job of handling the disagreements between CSL and most of the rest of PARC). My manager ordered me to give the demo, claiming later that he was ordered to do so from corporate. It is doubtful that corporate understood enough to be giving any such orders. The plans for Lisa were revised.

By 1979 standard microprocessors were sufficiently powerful to run a language system such as Smalltalk. The NoteTaker ran Smalltalk on Intel 8086 processors. At Stanford, the Sun workstation, part of the larger Stanford University Network project, had been designed using the Motorola 68000 family of microprocessors. The Sun workstation appeared to be the perfect vehicle for Smalltalk. As Peter Deutsch noted, the 68000 was the first commercial microprocessor with a powerful enough architecture (specifically a flat address space of more than 16 bits) to run Smalltalk.

When PARC first started, there was no capital equipment. MAXC (Multi-Access Xerox Computer, a microcoded emulation of a DEC PDP-10) had been built because the request to buy a PDP-10—and thereby be compatible with the ARPA community from which most of the research staff came—had been denied. The Altos were built and spread throughout PARC and the rest of the Xerox research community. Then the Dolphins (Xerox 1100) and the Dorados were built. Each time a new machine appeared, battle lines were drawn on whether funding would be provided to recapitalize researchers who appeared already rich in computing power. LRG managed to stay ahead of the funding game by selling old machines to buy new ones (first Altos for Dolphins, then Dolphins for Dorados). Sales were restricted to other Xerox groups, although both the U.S. White House and the CIA (via Xerox Special Interest Systems) were Dolphin users.

Now we wanted Sun boards. We started by borrowing from Fairchild Schlumberger. We borrowed a Sun board and one of Schlumberger's best developers, Alan Schiffman. He and Peter Deutsch set out to design PS (as in "Peter's Smalltalk," "Peter and Schiffman," or "Portable Smalltalk"). The next step was to sell Dorados to buy workstations from the new Sun Microsystems Corporation. My new manager, the new head of PARC, told me later that CSL was shocked that we were permitted to buy non-Xerox machines. But he supported my argument that someone at PARC needed to understand what the rest of the world was doing.

The PS work needs special mention here because it demonstrated why Smalltalk is so interesting. Smalltalk is a system in which to describe systems. The Smalltalk compiler and development tools were written in Smalltalk itself, lending the system to changeability at all levels. Deutsch designed a 68000 assembler language development environment by writing a 68000 emulator in Smalltalk and using the standard Smalltalk browsers and inspectors to access 68000 code (Deutsch, 1983). Resulting 68000 code was then cross-assembled from the Dorado to the 68000 Sun board. This 68000 development environment was the only example we knew of where one used a combination of subclassing and class parameterization to achieve reusability of an entire development environment as a framework whose concrete completions were themselves environments for different languages. More than half the PS project effort was spent building this highly productive development environment. A similar approach was used to develop 8086 code for the NoteTaker.

PS convinced us that Smalltalk would run well on standard microprocessors. We no longer needed to rely on microcoding Xerox proprietary machines, so we decided it was time to expand the audience for Smalltalk. We decided to create a Smalltalk that the rest of the world could use.

In 1979 we asked Xerox for the right to publish Smalltalk, the language and its implementation and the applications we had built to test the Smalltalk model of computing. Xerox officially gave this permission, remarking that no one inside Xerox wanted Smalltalk. With that simple statement, Xerox officially ignored the increasing demands from a key Xerox customer, the CIA, for Smalltalk and Smalltalk-capable workstations.

3.5. Smalltalk-80: Creating the Smalltalk Community

The history of Smalltalk is also the history of the formation of a community of software developers, many of whom formed commercial enterprises and bet their careers on the business of being Smalltalk designers, implementers, and trainers.

Smalltalk-80 was created for the explicit purpose of having a version of the language that could be distributed outside Xerox along with its tools and library. Broad distribution required a portable implementation specification. LRG transformed itself into SCG (the Systems Concepts Group). We were done doing learning research (or learning to do research). We were, in fact, temporarily done doing research and were intent on getting closure to the 10 years of work. We expected to accomplish two goals by creating Smalltalk-80. First, we hoped to influence the next generation of hardware designers, to challenge them to consider whether there was any special hardware assist for processing languages such as Smalltalk. Second, we hoped to create a larger community of Smalltalkers who could help invent subsequent versions. As it turned out, the first goal was not necessary, as demonstrated by the Smalltalk On A RISC work at UC Berkeley (Samples et al., 1986). This was a great research project and a result that probably saved us a lot of time and money. But the second goal was necessary, as the problems we were hoping to tackle next required more people, more ideas, and more users.[9] As it turned out, we underestimated the scope of the work we would need to do, taking 3 years rather than the expected 1 year to complete the language, tools, and class library revisions, and to write comprehensive documentation.

3.5.1. Smalltalk-80: The Language and Its Implementation

The Xerox Smalltalk systems all consisted of two primary layers: a virtual machine and a virtual image.[10] The virtual machine makes the hardware system friendly to the Smalltalk object model. Early implementations were microcoded interpreters; starting with the NoteTaker and then PS, the virtual machine was written in assembly code, C, or another high-level language. The virtual image consists of everything else, written in Smalltalk.

The compiler, written in Smalltalk, translates Smalltalk expressions and methods into the virtual machine's machine language. This machine language is byte coded. The virtual machine implementation executes these byte codes. Initial virtual machine implementations executed the byte codes through interpretation. Later implementations, beginning with PS, compiled the byte codes to machine code. SCG took seriously Butler Lampson's observation that any interpreter can be turned into a compiler by running the interpreter and capturing the execution stream.

---

[9]After the Smalltalk-80 publications, SCG was elevated to SCL, a research laboratory, and turned its interest to how technology can help groups work together when team members work at geographic distances. In 1985 videoconferencing and video editors were added to Smalltalk-80 as a part of this research effort. The research was later reported on (Bly et al., 1993).

[10]I am using the standard terminology here, although there was nothing really "virtual" about these system layers. The virtual machine is really a virtual machine implementation, and the virtual image is a real file containing all the objects in the language system not represented in the machine implementation.

Although it took a circuitous path, this approach is quite similar to many so-called normal compilers that use a two-phase approach to compilation. The first phase is to translate the source language into intermediate representation; the second phase translates that intermediate representation into machine code. In the case of Smalltalk, the intermediate representation is the virtual machine's byte codes (and associated data structures). Then, for the Xerox implementations, the code generation is performed at execution time.

What distinguishes Smalltalk from most other languages at the time is that other languages discard the intermediate representation and only save the machine code, whereas Smalltalk saves only the intermediate representation. In this way, Smalltalk applications could be fully portable across a wide range of processors, able to store code in very compact form, and still retain much of the speed of machine code. In order to make this space/speed tradeoff, Xerox Smalltalk implementations generated code on demand and kept a relatively small cache of machine code.

The Smalltalk-80 class library in the virtual image was created by rewriting Smalltalk-76 *in situ*. We kept the system running at all times and rewrote major system classes by category (such as magnitudes, arithmetic objects, strings, and collections). With each category of revision, we invoked what we called a "junta." We took advantage of the Smalltalk capability of metamorphasizing objects—as though time stood still, all instances of one class could become instances of another class. For example, all existing strings in the system could become instances of the new string class. We changed the syntax so that the character set corresponded to a standard ASCII character set, removing the requirement that target Smalltalk machines be capable of handling pictorial fonts.

One of the most interesting changes to Smalltalk was to finally create a system in which everything truly was an object with all processing done as messages to an object. Thus control structures were implemented as messages to an `Integer`, `Interval`, `Block`, or `Collection` object, as shown in the following list (note that := denotes assignment):

Simple repetition
```
10 timesRepeat:
    [joe turnBy: 10].
```

Conditional
```
(number \\ 2) = 0
    ifTrue: [parity := 0]
    ifFalse: [parity := 1].
```

Enumerated iteration
```
5 to: 25 by: 2
    do: [:arg|joe growBy: arg].
#(joe mary sam)
    do: [:arg|arg print].
```

`while` loop
```
[joe direction < 180]
whileTrue: [joe turnBy: 5].
```

```
index := 1.
[index > list size]  whileFalse:
  [list at: index put: 0.
  index := index + 1.].
```

Other enumerations create new collections

Answers `#(4 9 25 49 121)`	`#(2 3 5 7 11) collect: [:prime|prime*prime]`
Answers `4`	`letters := #(a B d a F G q S a A). (letters select: [:each| each asLowercase==$a]) size.`
Answers `6`	`(letters reject: [:each| each asLowercase~~$a]) size.`

For everything to be an object, a class itself must be an object. As every object is an instance of a class, then a class must be an instance of a class. In Smalltalk-80, we called the class of the class a *metaclass*.[11] The class of a metaclass must be a metaclass as well. In Smalltalk-76, the structure was simpler. Every object was an instance of a class. Every class was an object and therefore had to be an instance of a class as well; we called that class simply `Class`. Class `Class`, by necessity, was an instance of itself. All classes in the system formed a single class hierarchy, with the topmost superclass called `Object`. Class `Class` was a subclass of class `Object`; class `Object` was an instance of class `Class`. This relationship is shown in Figure 3.1.

The Smalltalk-76 class hierarchy supported differentiating behavior for instances of different classes. It did not support the capability to define behavior specific to different classes, in particular, initialization behavior. Creation of a metaclass hierarchy allowed us to solve the instance creation problem without mixing in the use of functions, as we had done in Smalltalk-76. But it also caused us to create a complex set of relations, which is hard for beginning Smalltalk programmers to understand. Figure 3.2 is a diagram of the top of the Smalltalk-80 hierarchy; it shows how metaclasses, classes, and instances are related. The particular problem we solved was how to handle the creation message as a proper message to an object, and how to force proper initialization of instance variables. You send the message `new` (or some other appropriate message) to the class object to create an instance of itself. The class object then sends that newly created instance a message, such as `initialize`. Every class then can implement its own `initialize` message to provide default values for instance variables. The metaclass hierarchy provides the objects that can know these initialization behaviors.

[11]See Kiczales et al. (1991) for a full treatment of the use of metaclass protocols.

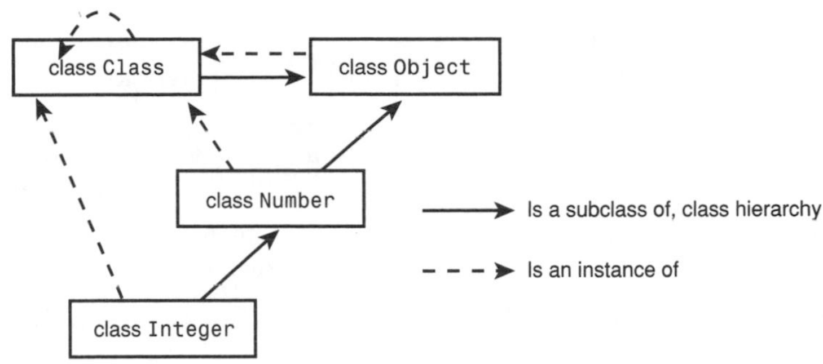

FIGURE 3.1. *Smalltalk-76 class relations.*

Existence of the class as an object, however, opened the door to having any number of initialization messages sent to the class and then passed on to a newly created instance. The class could now have its own behavior—for example, `Date` could respond to `today` with the current day and year. Beginning Smalltalk programmers are often confused by the notion of a class as both an object capable of responding to arbitrary messages and as a special kind of object creating instances of itself. The confusion is highlighted by the design of the typical Smalltalk browser, which makes no effort to display classes as ordinary objects yet simultaneously presents methods to the class itself as well as to its instances. The system is further confused because this capability of a metaclass to have instance-specific behavior (as defined in the class) is not shared by a class to have its own instance-specific behavior (as defined in the metaclass).

Similar treatment is given to the properties of objects. A class describes the property structure of its instances. These are called *instance variables*. A class as an object can have its own properties, and these are the class's instance variables. Instance variables are accessible only by methods defined in the context of the object's class. But there are also variables accessible by all instances of a class—these are called *class variables*. Variables can also be shared across multiple classes that are not part of the same class hierarchy subtree. These variables are called *pool variables*. The special dictionary *Smalltalk* contains global name/value pairs for all classes and pool dictionaries.

The Smalltalk-80 class hierarchy factors descriptions of objects into various levels of detail, anticipating further research into kinds of classes. The important point to remember is that the choice of class hierarchy, including how metaclasses work, is part of the runtime environment and not inherent in the language semantics. The irony is that in an effort to simplify the system, we managed to produce a more complex class library.

Moreover, because the tools did not reflect the flexibility that the metaclass protocol offered, some interesting opportunities were lost. In fact, having class `Class` as an instance of `Metaclass` demonstrates that Smalltalk-80 supported instance-specific behavior. No tools made it obvious, but other instances of `Metaclass` could have been created offering alternative instance-specific behavior.

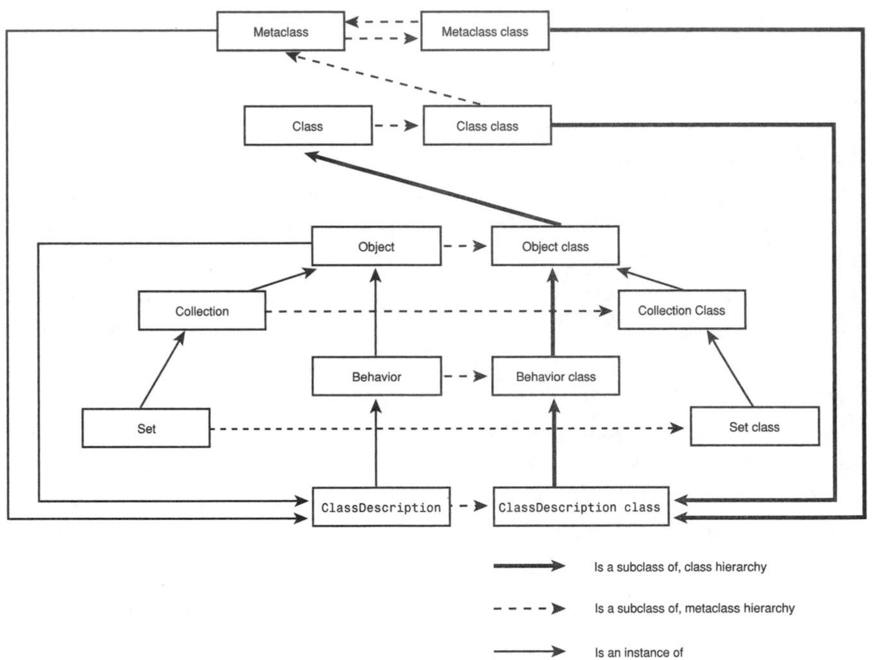

FIGURE 3.2. *Smalltalk-80 class relations.*

The definition for the Smalltalk-80 language system has not changed much since its first publication in the *Byte Magazine* of August 1981. The only major change was in creating full closure for blocks, which is basically a Smalltalk version of lambda expressions. This addition has proven useful to Smalltalk developers creating systems that dynamically create and bind behavior to objects. The full definition for Smalltalk-80, including changes proposed by the Smalltalk ANSI group, is provided in Chapter 4, "Programming with Smalltalk."

Here we revisit the `Box` class example, this time written in Smalltalk-80:

```
Model subclass: #Box
     instanceVariableNames: 'size direction position '
     classVariableNames: ''
```

```
Box methodsFor: 'initialization'!
    initialize              super initialize.
                            size := 50. position := 0 @ 0. direction := 0.
Box methodsFor: 'accessing'!
    position                ^position
    position: aPoint        position := aPoint
    direction               ^direction
    size                    ^size
    graphicsContext         ^Screen default
Box methodsFor: 'action'!
    move: dist
          rad x y |
          rad := self direction degreesToRadians.
          x := self position x. y := self position y.
          self position: x + (dist * rad sin) rounded @ (y - (dist *
          rad cos)) rounded.
Box methodsFor: 'display'!
    hide                    self graphicsContext clear.
    show                    self displayOn: self graphicsContext
    displayOn: surface      surface displayPolygon: self relativeVertices
                            at: self position
Box methodsFor: 'private'!
    relativeVertices
          "A box is drawn by computing the coordinates of its four vertices
          relative to the actual position of the box."
          | arr angle rad p |
          p := 0 @ 0.
          angle := self direction + 270.
          arr := OrderedCollection new.
          arr add: p.
          3 timesRepeat:  [ angle := angle + 90.
             rad := angle degreesToRadians.
             p := p + (self size * rad sin @ (self size * rad cos negated)).
             arr add: p rounded].
          ^arr asArray
```

The only unusual part of this code is that we assume a version of Smalltalk-80 with a drawing window on the display screen accessed by asking a class object `Screen` for its current graphics display context (`Screen default`). Note that the example is presented in a stylized form because (as with Smalltalk-76) there is no Smalltalk-80 syntax for linear presentation of a class description (except of course for the file format, full of exclamation points as used in the example).

For virtual memory, one of the Smalltalk-80 implementations used a new design called LOOM (large object-oriented memory). OOZE was limited by its ability to handle only 64KB objccts and only 245 classes. LOOM was Ted Kaehler's design for a faster virtual memory system (Kaehler, 1986; Kaehler & Krasner, 1984). LOOM accesses objects that are in memory by indexing a table (similar to how the language interpreter works) rather than hashing into the resident object table, the way OOZE worked. As with OOZE, LOOM swaps objects to the disk and operates without assistance from the programmer.

3.5.2. Composition Architectures

Another invention of Smalltalk-80 was derived from earlier work done in Smalltalk-76. In Smalltalk-76, the programming tools were done with what Ingalls called "pluggable interfaces." The idea was to create a framework with which an application was formed by composition of components. A class acting as a kind of scaffold for the framework demands that a precise set of messages be implemented in order to participate in the composition. The basic composition idea is simple and much like that used by the earlier Smalltalk galley editor. But pluggable interfaces were made harder to understand by allowing the programmer to declare alternative message names to fulfill the required component behaviors. Declaration was done at the time a component instance was created, written as literal symbols and therefore not easy to cross reference with the typical Smalltalk browsers. This design is in contrast to the subclassing approach, whereby the scaffolding class provides default behavior for an application. Subclasses then reimplement inherited messages to create alternative application behavior. And of course, the cross-reference tools can find and display these subclass refinements.

The work on pluggable interfaces represents one of several efforts in the Smalltalk research to create an architectural style for how objects with particular roles should relate to one another. Probably the most widely known delete style is MVC (which stands for "model, view, controller"), having gained most recent fame as one of the few design patterns with any real use history (Krasner & Pope, 1988).[12] The MVC idea came from several sources; it was recommended by Trygve Reenskaug for his application work in Smalltalk-76 (Reenskaug, 1981) and used by the database community as a style for handling multiple viewer interest in a shared database. MVC was implemented in Smalltalk-76 by Steve Putz and created for the original Smalltalk-80 by Jim Althoff. Althoff and I were interested in factoring the roles of objects in a way that would support inheritance of roles among three players in any user interface design: the model, its views, and the possible ways in which the user might control or interact with the model and the views. The MVC architecture provides a protocol with which a view or controller declares itself as a dependent of a model and specifies which changes to the model are of particular interest. The MVC framework provides the mechanisms by which change is broadcast to all interested dependents.

[12]MVC is also documented in the design patterns book (Gamma et al., 1995).

The power of the MVC framework lies in its ability to describe a model without knowledge of particular users of the model, while still allowing the model to be shared among a diverse user community. We were disappointed that the computer science community has focused its attention on whether this should be the trio MVC or just the pair M and V, rather than discussing the value of the proffered factoring. At first, these technologists argued about speed, focusing on control that centered on pointing to and changing graphical views of graphical models, and forgetting that models are not always graphical and might be "viewed" with sound or touch. Second, the technologists argued that for any view, only one preferred controller exists. We provided three parts to the architecture because we believed that more work should be done on different kinds of controllers for different kinds of people, especially for people with visual or hand-skill disabilities that detracted from their ability to use graphical interactive systems.

3.5.3. First Licenses

In 1980, in order to publish the Smalltalk system, we organized a joint project with four other companies: HP, DEC, Apple, and Tektronix. These companies met our requirements for participation: They were hardware vendors with in-house software development teams that could port the Smalltalk-80 system to their companies' own computers. The deal was simple. The companies received a license to provide Smalltalk-80 version 1.0 on their computers in exchange for commenting on drafts of our book about Smalltalk and porting the virtual machine to test the implementation specification for this book.

It is possible that the decision maker at Xerox agreed to this licensing arrangement because he received advice from a former PARC employee that there was no internal interest. Certainly, such advice was given because we were privy to the written documentation. Seven years later this same decision maker would be instrumental in helping us form an independent company to sell systems based on Smalltalk. Also, seven years later, we had to resolve the paranoia in the growing Smalltalk community that Xerox would sue other vendors of Smalltalk. To create maximum legal comfort and to ensure that Smalltalk was generally available, our commercial company offered licenses for the language itself as well as the class library interface design. Although we tried to provide free licenses, we discovered that we had to charge $1 to create the desired comfort. With the exception of a check from IBM that was never cashed, all licenses were paid in cash, signed by company officers, and framed for my office wall.

In May 1983 the first of three Smalltalk-80 books (Goldberg & Robson, 1983) was published, followed shortly after by two others (Krasner, 1984; Goldberg, 1984). The first book introduced the language and its implementation, as reviewed by developers in the four participating companies. The second was a collection of papers written about the porting experience and included the primary documentation on the LOOM object-reclamation system. The third detailed the programming environment tools and user interface. The publisher announced a fourth book about building applications, although no such book was contracted and no further writing energy could be found.

The then head of the Xerox Office Systems Group and inventors and sellers of the Star Workstation belatedly decided that the Smalltalk publication plans were a potential problem. How should they answer a customer request for Smalltalk on the Star Workstation? Xerox had agreed to distribution of the system to universities, but withheld commercial distribution for a year. During that time, we were obligated to port Smalltalk-80 to the Star Workstation. Because the Star office software was written in Mesa (Mitchell, 1979), and because Mesa was the language of choice for the Star, we were also obligated to write the virtual machine using Mesa. We were fortunate to hire two very good developers (Paul McCullough and Frank Zdybel), whose Smalltalk/Mesa we named Molasses in honor of the speed with which it ran. The implementation marks the first time we had created the Smalltalk programming environment as embedded in another programming environment, so we ultimately found the exercise interesting, albeit a waste of skilled manpower. We were relieved that no Star workstation customer ever requested a Smalltalk system.

The Star experience offered us another opportunity to present Smalltalk as a business solution for Xerox. Sales of the Star did not meet expectation, despite a very successful initial Star launch that certainly stunned the computer industry with the sophistication of its design and function. The then head of the PARC Systems Center (the half of a temporarily divided PARC that contained CSL) cooperated with the Dallas-based management team of the Office Systems Group in brainstorming potential cures for the Star sales problem. Four PARC researchers were invited to Dallas, two from CSL and two from SCG (Ingalls and me), to discuss the problem. The CSL recommendation was to design and build a new workstation that was cheaper and faster. SCG suggested that the problem was that the initial buy-in to the Star required too much know-how and expense (the Star initial configuration consisted of three workstations, a printer, and an Ethernet, at a time when people did not understand how to drive a mouse or scan a display screen). As a result, SCG designed Twinkle, a 68010-based personal workstation, with simple text editing and freehand graphics (Smalltalk applications), and submitted the design with intention to build and deliver in 1983. The Twinkle idea was also interesting because it would have given Xerox a pathway to ride the Motorola and Intel technology performance curves.

We never received a response to our proposal (likely changes in management in Dallas left our recommendation in the "unanswered mail" box; also, we were also politically incorrect in offering freehand graphics to the Star designers, who demonstrated deep religious convictions about structured graphics). Given the success in 1984 of the Macintosh launch, we believe Twinkle would indeed have been a constructive solution.

3.5.4. The CIA Analyst and Joshua

Why were we so confident that we could build a Smalltalk-based Twinkle solution in just over a year? Our plan was to leverage work already in progress in the Xerox Dallas Development Center, motivated largely by interest from the CIA.

Smalltalk-80 was implemented on the Xerox 1100 (Dolphin), making the Smalltalk system more generally available within Xerox. In particular, the 1100 implementation gave the Pasadena-based XSIS group its first access to Smalltalk.[13] Several early large Smalltalk-80 applications were produced by XSIS, notably a layout system for the *New York Times Book Review*. XSIS primarily sold into the U.S. intelligence community with a charter to do advanced designs based on research goals directed from within the intelligence community. The CIA was no stranger to PARC. A group of AI researchers from BBN had joined PARC SSL, bringing their government relations with them. As this folk tale is recalled, two very astute technology managers from the CIA saw the Smalltalk demos on a visit to PARC and requested that their new ideas for an Analyst Workstation be built using the language system. By the time we discovered this activity, a first prototype was completed and in use at NPIC, where a professional photographer was using Smalltalk to design new graphical interfaces for managing his desktop information. All this preceded the release of the Smalltalk-80 books. As a result, this photographer figured out how to hack together Smalltalk code by reading our code to see how our tools were implemented.

[13]XSIS engineers also ported Smalltalk-80 to the follow-on Star Workstation, code named Dandilion.

Fear set in. As far as we could tell, XSIS was building a product—the Analyst—using a research result. No matter how good we were as system developers, we fell short of finishing our work to product level. We clearly had not stopped short enough. The XSIS Analyst was built on an unsupported programming language and development environment. Even though we were just researchers, we knew that this behavior was a formula for disaster.

Then we discovered the group in Dallas. A small group of very good system developers had decided that Smalltalk was worth their attention. Encouraged by interest from the CIA, they designed a 68000 add-on board for the Xerox 800 (an 8086-based personal computer built by Olivetti and sold successfully by Xerox). The add-on board, code named Joshua, had 1MB of RAM and ran Smalltalk adequately. Another design was based on the 68010 with 4MB of RAM, which improved performance. The Dallas team worked with SCG to learn about the PS virtual machine and make use of Deutsch's 68000 development environment. Our hope was that we could transfer the research results to Dallas, and they would take ownership of product creation and support for the CIA and other future customers. Unfortunately and despite a large order already in place (we were told that the CIA alone wanted 10,000 Smalltalk boards), Xerox's pricing caused the order to be canceled and then Xerox canceled Joshua.

Instead of our sending research results to Dallas, Dallas came to PARC, and we formed ParcPlace Systems.

3.5.5. The Commercialization Experience

Actually, we formed ParcPlace Holders, a corporation with the mission of creating a business plan for a software company. This corporation negotiated with Xerox, and later with Xerox and a group of venture capitalists, to form a company called ParcPlace Systems. The final papers were completed March 18, 1988.[14]

[14]Within 24 hours of the formation of ParcPlace Systems, Apple filed its lawsuit against Microsoft and Hewlett-Packard, claiming violation of Apple's graphical interface design. ParcPlace's formation was announced in the *Wall Street Journal*, reporting the general opinion that Apple's claim was without merit because most of the key graphical user interface (GUI) elements appeared first in the Xerox Smalltalk system. The lawsuit was even more peculiar because, by the mid–1980s, most of the original Xerox Smalltalk team was employed at Apple.

Although the politics of how we reached this point might be interesting to the curious historian, it takes us far afield from our Smalltalk technology story. The commercialization story is interesting inasmuch as it sets the context for further language and language system invention. Suffice it to say that the first release by Xerox[15] of a commercial Smalltalk-80 system, named Smalltalk 2.1, occurred in the fall of 1986. The key developers were David Leibs, Russ Pencin, Ron Carter, Stephen Pope, Peter Deutsch, and Glenn Krasner. This system, along with systems from two other Smalltalk vendors on personal computers and the team from Tektronix, was exhibited at the first ACM OOPSLA (Object-Oriented Programming Systems, Languages, and Applications) conference in Portland, Oregon.[16]

The ParcPlace Systems (PPS) mission was to create a Smalltalk development environment that enabled programmers to create applications that were portable across all standard workstations, without recompilation yet with host system integration. The market tag line was "write once, run anywhere." PPS accomplished its mission first by inventing new implementation capability—a new C-based virtual machine called HPS and a faster, dynamic (just-in-time) compiler (Deutsch & Schiffman, 1984). Second, PPS created an operating system framework that could be specialized for each supported vendor system (Sun, HP, Apollo, Macintosh, and DOS personal computers). Third, PPS invented a user interface framework with specializations that emulated each of the standard windowing systems. PPS also improved on the performance and capability of the memory manager with the introduction of generation scavenging schemes (Ungar & Jackson, 1988). The consequence of this technology meant that from its first year, PPS sold and supported 11 different products, representing the 11 different configurations of processors, operating systems, and windowing systems that were popular on the market in the late 1980s. At a time when development costs were very high and target machine populations very diverse, the PPS portability story was well positioned, opening doors to major financial institutions as well as semiconductor and telecommunication companies.

---

[15]The ParcPlace team functioned under the Xerox umbrella for 19 months while negotiating with the Xerox lawyers for the technology transfer, so legally customers bought these first products from Xerox.

[16]OOPSLA was formed by researchers and company personnel from the Smalltalk, CLOS, Actor, and Eiffel communities, with seed funding from the discretionary budget of the then ACM president—me.

3.5.5.1. Extending the Use of Dynamic Binding for General Composition

The early ParcPlace commercial experience was an adventure in redesigning the virtual machine for portability, creating product-level documentation to update and complement the books, and building up a quality training and consulting organization. Certainly the portability capability was without precedent. HPS represented an advance in Smalltalk implementation technology with Deutsch's new code generation scheme that simultaneously achieved relatively easy machine portability, fast code generation, and good code quality. For business reasons, the scheme was not published. The object memory management in the virtual machine was significantly improved with a generation scavenger and weak finalization techniques that netted PPS its first patent. Deutsch worked on a new graphics model, investigating a model with full PostScript graphics contexts, coordinate transformations, and color space matching. Ultimately, Deutsch chose a graphics model for Smalltalk-80 that provided mappings for color capabilities and revealed pixel depth, color capabilities, and screen resolution to the programmer but was not fully resolution-dependent graphics like PostScript.[17]

Probably the most important contribution from PPS was the design architecture for the graphical application builder, known as VisualWorks. As early as 1988, David Leibs and I worked with the CIA to review and reconsider the requirements for the Analyst Workstation. We proposed a new concept for providing end user customization of knowledge management in the CIA, code named Sleeper. Buried in this work were the seed ideas for new ways to manage dependencies among system components and new ways to compose the viewing and controlling components of a GUI. When Kenneth Rubin, then manager of PPS training, convinced Leibs that his group needed a consultant's GUI toolkit, Leibs returned to the original Sleeper ideas. He then worked with Frank Zdybel to create the VisualWorks application model and GUI layout framework.

[17]Deutsch's opinion at the time was that the best graphics model for Smalltalk was one that would automatically convert colors to gray shades or halftones (later he added scaling for fonts), but that revealed pixel depth, color capabilities, and screen resolution to the programmer if desired. He strongly opposed integration with native user interface toolkits on the grounds that it would untowardly increase the maintenance burden from the platform fan out (that is, the need for different implementations for distinct operating system/user interface combinations). He advocated emulating the platform in Smalltalk using a framework approach, and then later endorsed using a framework whose concrete subclasses would link to the platform's toolkit. Allowing programs to invoke platform toolkit capabilities directly, he correctly predicted, would result in destruction of real portability.

The key idea was to take dynamic binding one step further than runtime method lookup by creating *value models*. A value model stores and retrieves a value using the messages `value:` and `value`. Any object in the system can become a dependent of a value model (consistent with the original MVC dependency and change broadcast mechanisms). Whenever it receives the message `value:`, a value model automatically broadcasts that a change has occurred to all objects that have registered interest. Additional protocol allowed an object to declare that its interest in the value model change should be served by sending itself or another object a particular message. Different kinds of value models provide various forms of communications about how system change should be channeled. The VisualWorks architecture is thus built on indirection and declarations of intentions (and therefore more in the design direction of Alan Kay's original ideas that programming should be done as an expression of goals and strategies for meeting those goals).

Other Smalltalk vendors created GUI builders as well, hoping to create visual programming mechanisms that would accommodate a larger consumer marketplace for their Smalltalk products. Parts Workbench from Digitalk represented an attempt to reflect similar work at Microsoft for Visual Basic. Like its IBM counterpart Visual Age, Visual Basic offers a direct manipulation-style interface by which the programmer can literally show the system which objects to use and how they can communicate. These systems suffer from the inability to scale. The programmer shows the system how objects relate by connecting the objects with labeled lines. The usual confusions arise when textual programming must be mixed with line drawing and the lines (often called wires) must be displayed on the screen for the direct manipulation. Inevitably, complex systems look like colored spaghetti (Burnett et al., 1995).

3.5.5.2. Early Vendors

At the time that ParcPlace Systems was formed, several other commercial endeavors existed, as either an outcome of the original licensing program (the commercial license available after the Star implementation was completed) or independent efforts based on published descriptions of the language. The first commercial license went to Tom Love at ITT. Love and Brad Cox later designed a Smalltalk-like preprocessor to C, called Objective C, which they sold through their company Productivity Products Inc. (Cox, 1986). The company changed its name to StepStone and licensed its Objective C to Steve Jobs's new company NeXT.

The earliest commercial Smalltalk was Rosetta Smalltalk, an implementation on small Z80 personal computers. Rosetta Smalltalk resembled Smalltalk-72 but used a pattern-matching approach to parsing message expressions. The developers published their version of Smalltalk at an ACM symposium in 1979 (Warren & Abbe, 1979) and exhibited the running system at the Personal Computing Faire held in association with that year's NCC. The developers presented their work as exploratory and claim (on their Web site in 1997) that they did not pursue their product plans because PARC started to give Smalltalk away for free. Most likely, the developers referred to the special arrangement with the reviewers, which they knew about as consultants to Intel on how Smalltalk might be implemented on the 432. Intel was not an official part of the release process because it could not meet our requirement to assign an internal software team to the project.

Another early design for Smalltalk on small personal computers was achieved by Tim Budd and his students at the University of Arizona in 1984. Based on the published Smalltalk-80, the group called its language Little Smalltalk (Budd, 1987). Budd published his version of the language as a book and offered the software for free, providing an early learning experience for university computer science students. Little Smalltalk is written in C and runs under UNIX operating systems. The language is still available and in use today.

A few technologists from Computer Sciences Corporation were working in Italy for Olivetti when they noticed the Smalltalk description in the August 1981 *Byte Magazine*. They set out to implement a textual version of the language that they called Methods. Olivetti transferred the ownership of their work to a new company they formed, called Digitalk. At one point, the founders of Digitalk visited PARC to learn more about Smalltalk. They were certain that an example in the magazine (of block contexts) was in error and were looking for the correct syntax (the example was not in error). Because it was a text-based language, Methods did not try to leverage the library of the Xerox Smalltalk system. In 1986 Digitalk abandoned Methods to market Smalltalk V, a version with a graphical interface. Both of these products were available on PCs and the Apple Macintosh. Unlike Xerox Smalltalk, the compiler and most of the lower-level system functions were not written in Smalltalk itself, which allowed Digitalk to protect what was considered to be the company's special intellectual property. Digitalk did not offer application portability, preferring instead to adhere to the different GUI rules for Mac and Windows.

In contrast, a group from the Linus Pauling Institute in Palo Alto, California, formed a company called Softsmarts and created a PC version of Smalltalk based on the book specification of the virtual machine. The group licensed the virtual image from Xerox. Unfortunately, they were not successful because the Xerox pricing policy targeted the workstation market, not PCs. Later, the founder joined Apple, and then went to a Smalltalk-based training and consulting company called Knowledge Systems Corporation in North Carolina before eventually joining IBM.

Tektronix also went into the Smalltalk business, delivering an extremely well-designed implementation on the Tektronix 4400 (the Magnolia). This workstation included graphics capability that made Smalltalk look very special. The core team, including the marketing manager, formed a training and consulting company called Instantiations, which was later bought by Digitalk. In 1995, with both companies fighting the sales and marketing capability of an IBM Smalltalk entry, ParcPlace Systems and Digitalk merged. (Later sections discuss this in more detail.) Eventually, as a consequence of a business downturn, the company formed from the merger permitted the original Instantiations group to re-create the company to sell the Digitalk Visual Smalltalk technology.

Europe was represented in the Smalltalk community as well. In Germany, Georg Heeg proved to be one of the most active distributors of Smalltalk and object-oriented databases. Small distribution companies started in France, Belgium, Italy, Czechoslovakia (later Slovakia), the United Kingdom, and Scandinavia. Both PPS and Digitalk distributed products as well in Japan, Australia, Mexico, and South America. Fuji Xerox, PPS's partner in Japan, arranged to have the Smalltalk books translated into Japanese while also organizing seminars and courses and creating commercial applications.

3.5.5.3. University Activity

Researchers at universities around the world actively explored Smalltalk. We licensed the virtual image free to all universities and gave access to our PS implementation to selected groups, notably at Dortmund in Germany, Yale, the University of Massachusetts, and the University of Washington. The earliest UNIX implementations were done at the University of Washington, with funding SCG obtained by licensing Smalltalk-80. Alan Borning's Ph.D. thesis centered on ThingLab, a constraint system that introduced one of the earliest multiple inheritance systems for Smalltalk (Borning, 1979; Borning & Ingalls, 1982). Eliot Moss at the University of Massachusetts (Moss et al., 1987) worked on new implementation schemes using Apollo's version of UNIX. Eliot Miranda from Queen Mary College, University of London, developed BrouHaHa, a portable implementation of the Smalltalk-80 virtual machine interpreter. Written almost entirely in C, BrouHaHa is portable among 32-bit machines with C compilers (Miranda, 1987). The Dortmund group, headed by Georg Heeg, formed a commercial company and became an early distributor in Germany for PPS. The Berkeley Smalltalk implementation was also made freely available and was a significant factor in increasing the awareness and use of Smalltalk-80 at universities.

Ralph Johnson at the University of Illinois has been instrumental as an educator, a researcher, and a consultant. His early work was the Typed Smalltalk project, whose goal was to provide an optimizing compiler for Smalltalk applications (Johnson, 1986). Others worked on type inferencing, with the earliest work done by Nori Suzuki, a researcher at PARC and later at the University of Tokyo (but most recently a high-level manager with Sony). UC Berkeley students and faculty, led by Dave Patterson, investigated implementation architectures and the possibility of special hardware designs in the Smalltalk on a RISC project mentioned earlier (Ungar & Patterson, 1983). Notable among these students was David Ungar, whose work on generation scavenging proved significant in the redesigns for the PPS products (Ungar, 1986). Ungar then worked on the language SELF (first at Stanford and then at Sun Microsystems), whose compiler design influenced David Griswold. Griswold initially created StrongTalk (Griswold, 1993), a typechecker for a downward-compatible subset of Smalltalk. He then combined the StrongTalk designs with that of the SELF compiler to create a small and fast virtual machine kernel, one for Smalltalk and another for Java. Griswold's company, Horizon Technologies, was acquired in 1997 by Sun Microsystems.

3.5.5.4. A Period of Acquisitions

Meanwhile, in Ottawa, Canada, at Carlton College, Dave Thomas, John Pugh, and Wilf LaLonde decided to revolutionize the computer science department by revamping their courses to focus on object technology. Their programming language of choice was Smalltalk because they had designed a new team tool for Smalltalk developers published under the name Orwell (Thomas & Johnson, 1988). By their own report, they were able to make this transition because they were willing to do the detailed curriculum work themselves and because the implications of the decision were not well understood at the time. Pugh and LaLonde formed The Object People, a training and consulting company, and Thomas formed Object Technology, Inc. (OTI), to carry out contract work with the

Canadian intelligence community and productize the Orwellian team tool (product named ENVY). Educating Carlton students and then having the first pick for their companies represented smart business practice. OTI built the first real-time embedded Smalltalk systems. Later, OTI worked with Tektronix to create a commercial embedded Smalltalk system for oscilloscopes. OTI also wrote its own virtual machine for the Macintosh, which was the Mac product sold by Digitalk. The relationship between OTI and Digitalk was not always friendly; it grew worse when Jim Anderson (Digitalk chairman and a founder) mishandled the relationship with IBM that Thomas had helped form. IBM used the Digitalk Smalltalk to create a new visual programming interface but found it could not partner well with Digitalk and turned to OTI for more support. OTI created a Smalltalk front end to the IBM AS400 and implemented Smalltalk on IBM's mainframe systems under MVS. IBM then announced Visual Age, which was based on the OTI Smalltalk implementations and was a direct competitor to Digitalk's own component-based Parts Workbench. It was no surprise to the Smalltalk community when, in 1995, OTI was acquired by IBM.

On entering the Smalltalk market, IBM set out to create a standard. For the first time since his earlier visit to PARC, Jim Anderson of Digitalk asked to talk with me. He specifically wanted us to team up to drive the standard, essentially not cooperating with IBM. Because PPS had already signed an agreement with IBM to cooperate in setting the standard through proper ANSI channels, we did not respond to Jim's proposition. The initial analysis by the IBMers showed that Digitalk would have to make considerable changes, not the least of which was the update to full block closure, which Digitalk had agreed to in 1986 but never carried out.

In 1991 I stepped down as PPS CEO to focus on technical work I had started on object analysis (Rubin & Goldberg, 1992) and project management (Goldberg & Rubin, 1995). The replacement I hired was Bill Lyons. PPS then made a number of ill-considered acquisitions, ignored the successful strategy that built the company to qualify for an IPO, and eventually lost customer and investor confidence. Lyons orchestrated a merger with Digitalk in 1995 (forming ParcPlace-Digitalk, or PPD), and bought ObjectShare and Polymorphic Systems (two firms whose success depended on the success of PPD). The merger and formation of PPD was confusing to the Smalltalk community as the company delayed putting in place a combined technology direction. Adding to the confusion, Jim Anderson, pre-merger chairman of Digitalk, stated publicly that he had lost faith in Smalltalk in the face of the Java juggernaut. Lyons resigned in 1997, and the company was reconstituted under the new name ObjectShare. The apparent winner, because of PPD problems, has surely been the OTI/IBM team, which has been able to maintain and expand on the commercial Smalltalk opportunity. I resigned in 1995, although I stayed until the spring of 1996 to complete the first release of LearningWorks (a new Smalltalk development environment designed for developing and delivering educational curriculum).

Despite this unfortunate outcome for Smalltalk commercial efforts, the two decades of Smalltalk contribution to research and commercial support for developing innovative software systems has left a lasting impact on the computer industry. The original Dynabook and Smalltalk vision, however, has still not been realized. The last iteration of Smalltalk invention offers a significant solution for professional software system developers. The Smalltalk object model and interactive development environment are copied by all modern language systems. But the Smalltalk Dynabook goal was and still is to create an accessible information modeling system for everyone. Fortunately, Kay's vision is strong and the computer industry young.

3.6. Acknowledgments

This history of Smalltalk was created by a community of some of the brightest and most dedicated people the computer industry has experienced. Their dedication to the advancement of technology and the value the technology brings to businesses and individuals has left me with remarkable personal memories of the past 25 years. Special acknowledgment to those who helped me accurately recall some of those memories: Dennis Allison, Ron Carter, Peter Deutsch, Dan Ingalls, Glenn Krasner, David Leibs, Eliott Miranda, Russ Pencin, and Bill Shauck. Of course the opinions and any errors are all mine.

3.7. References

Abelson, H., and A. diSessa. 1981. *Turtle geometry: The computer as a medium for exploring mathematics*. Cambridge, MA: MIT Press.

Birtwistle, G. M. 1979. *DEMOS: A system for discrete event modeling on SIMULA*. London: Macmillan.

Bly, S., S. Harrison, and S. Irwin. 1993. Media spaces: Bringing people together in a video, audio, and computing environment. *Communications of the ACM* 36(1):28–46.

Borning, A. 1979. *ThingLab, A constraint-oriented simulation laboratory*. Palo Alto, CA: Xerox PARC.

Borning, A., and D. Ingalls. 1982. Multiple inheritance in Smalltalk-80. *Proceedings of the AAAI International Conference on Artificial Intelligence*. Pittsburgh.

Budd, T. 1987. *A little Smalltalk*. Reading, MA: Addison-Wesley.

Burnett, M. M., A. Goldberg, and T. Lewis (Eds.). 1995. *Visual object-oriented programming*. Greenwich, CT: Manning.

Bush, V. 1945. As we may think. *Atlantic Monthly* 176:101–108.

Cox, B. 1986. *Object-oriented programming: An evolutionary approach*. Reading, MA: Addison-Wesley.

Dahl, O.-J., and K. Nygaard. 1966. SIMULA—An ALGOL-based simulation language. *Communications of the ACM* 9:671–678.

Deutsch, L. P. 1983. Reusability in the Smalltalk-80 programming system. *ITT Workshop on Software Reusability, Newport, RI.*

Deutsch, L. P., and A. Schiffman. January 1984. Efficient implementation of the Smalltalk-80 system. *11th Annual Symposium on Principles of Programming Languages.*

Engelbart, D. C., and W. K. English. 1968. A research center for augmenting human intellect. *Proceedings of the FJCC* 33:395–410.

Gamma, E., R. Helm, R. Johnson, and J. Vlissides. 1995. *Design patterns: Elements of reusable object-oriented software*. Reading, MA: Addison-Wesley.

Goldberg, A. 1984. *Smalltalk-80: The graphical programming environment*. Reading, MA: Addison-Wesley.

Goldberg, A. 1987. Programmer as reader. *Proceedings of IFIP 86*, H. J. Kugler (Ed.), Amsterdam: North-Holland.

Goldberg, A., and A. Kay (eds). 1976. *Smalltalk-72 instruction manual.* Palo Alto, CA: Xerox PARC.

Goldberg, A., and A. Kay. 1977. *Methods for teaching the programming language Smalltalk*. Palo Alto, CA: Xerox PARC.

Goldberg, A., and J. Ross. 1981. Is the Smalltalk-80 system for children? *Byte Magazine* 6(8):348–368.

Goldberg, A., and D. Robson. 1983. *Smalltalk-80: The language and its implementation*. Reading, MA: Addison-Wesley. (Later revised as Goldberg, A., and D. Robson. 1986. *Smalltalk-80: The language*. Reading, MA: Addison-Wesley.)

Goldberg, A., and K. S. Rubin. 1995. *Succeeding with objects: decision frameworks for project management*. Reading, MA: Addison-Wesley.

Griswold, D. 1993. StrongTalk: Typechecking Smalltalk in a production environment. *Proceedings of the ACM OOPSLA 93 Conference.*

Ingalls, D. January 1978. The Smalltalk-76 programming system: Design and implementation. *Proceedings of the ACM Symposium on Principles of Programming Languages.*

Irons, E. T. 1970. Experience with an extensible language. *Communications of the ACM* 13(1):31–40.

Johnson, R. 1986. Type-checking Smalltalk. *Proceedings of the ACM OOPSLA 86 Conference, Special Issue of SIGPLAN Notices* 21(11):315–321.

Kaehler, T. 1981. Virtual memory for an object-oriented language. *Byte Magazine* 6(9):378–387.

Kaehler, T. 1986. Virtual memory on a narrow machine for an object-oriented language. *Proceedings of the ACM OOPSLA 86 Conference, Special Issue of SIGPLAN Notices* 21(11):87–106.

Kaehler, T., and G. Krasner. 1983. LOOM: Large object-oriented memory for Smalltalk-80 systems. In Glenn Krasner (Ed.), *Smalltalk-80: Bits of History, Words of Advice* (pp. 251–270). Reading, MA: Addison-Wesley.

Kay, A. C. 1968. FLEX: A flexible extensible language. Master's thesis, University of Utah.

Kay, A. C. 1969. The reactive engine. Doctoral dissertation, University of Utah.

Kay, A. C. 1996. The early history of Smalltalk. In T. J. Bergin and R. G.

Gibson (Eds.), *The History of Programming Languages II* (pp. 511–578). Reading, MA: ACM Press, Addison-Wesley.

Kay, A. C., and A. Goldberg. 1988. Personal dynamic media. In A. Goldberg (Ed.), *A history of personal workstations.* New York: ACM Press.

Kiczales, G., J. Des Rivieres, and D. Bobrow. 1991. *The art of the Metaobject Protocol.* Cambridge, MA: MIT Press.

Krasner, G. (Ed.). 1983. *Smalltalk-80: Bits of history, words of advice.* Reading, MA: Addison-Wesley.

Krasner, G., and S. Pope. 1988. A cookbook for using the model-view-controller user interface paradigm in Smalltalk-80. *Journal of Object-Oriented Programming* 1(3):26–49.

McCarthy, J. P. 1960. Part I, Recursive functions of symbolic expressions and their computation by machine. *Communications of the ACM* 3(4):184–195.

Miranda, E. 1987. BrouHaHa: A portable Smalltalk interpreter. *Proceedings of the ACM OOPSLA 87 Conference, Special Issue of SIGPLAN Notices* 22(12):354–365.

Mitchell, J. G., W. Maybury, and R. Sweet. 1979. *Mesa language manual (version 5.0).* Palo Alto, CA: Xerox PARC.

Moss, E., et al. Managing stack frames in Smalltalk, SIGPLAN Symposium on Interpreters and Interpretive Techniques. *ACM SIGPLAN Notices* 22(7).

Papert, S. 1980. *Mindstorms: Children, computers, and powerful ideas.* New York: Basic Books.

Pletzke, J. 1997. *Advanced Smalltalk.* New York: Wiley.

Reenskaug, T. 1981. User-oriented descriptions of Smalltalk systems. *Byte Magazine* 6(9):147–166.

Rubin, K. S., and A. Goldberg. 1992. Object behavior analysis. *Communications of the ACM.* 35(9):45–62.

Samples, A. D., D. Ungar, and P. Hilfinger. 1986. SOAR: Smalltalk without bytecodes. *Proceedings of the ACM OOPSLA 86 Conference, Special Issue of SIGPLAN Notices* 21(11):107–118.

Shaw, J. C. 1964. *JOSS: A designer's view of an experimental online computer system*. Santa Monica, CA: RAND.

Simon, H. A. 1969. *The Sciences of the Artificial.* Cambridge, MA: MIT Press.

Sutherland, I. C. 1963. Sketchpad: A man–machine graphical communication system. *Proceedings of the SJCC* 23:329–346.

Thacker, C. P. 1988. Personal distributed computing: The ALTO and Ethernet hardware. In A. Goldberg (Ed.), *A History of Personal Workstations* (pp. 267–290). New York: ACM Press.

Thomas, D., and K. Johnson. 1988. Orwell: A configuration management system for team programming. *Proceedings of the ACM OOPSLA 88 Conference, Special Issue of SIGPLAN Notices* 23(11): 135–141.

Ungar, D. 1986. The design and evaluation of a high-performance Smalltalk system. Doctoral thesis, University of California, Berkeley.

Ungar, D., and F. Jackson. 1988. Tenuring policies for generation-based storage reclamation. *Proceedings of the ACM OOPSLA 88 Conference, Special Issue of SIGPLAN Notices* 23(11):18–26.

Ungar, D., and D. Patterson. 1983. Berkeley Smalltalk: Who knows where the time goes? In G. Krasner (Ed.), *Smalltalk-80: Bits of History, Words of Advice* (pp. 189–206). Reading, MA: Addison-Wesley.

Warren, S., and D. Abbe. October 1979. Rosetta Smalltalk: A conversational, extensible microcomputer language. *Proceedings of the Second Symposium on Small Systems*, Dallas, TX.

Wirth, N. K., and H. Weber. 1966. EULER: A generalization of ALGOL and its formal definition: Part I. *Communications of the ACM* 9(1):13–25.

CHAPTER 4

Programming with Smalltalk

by Allen Wirfs-Brock

This chapter is an introduction to programming in Smalltalk. It explains the basic concepts and constructs of the Smalltalk programming language and class libraries. The reader is assumed to be an experienced programmer who ideally has some exposure to object-oriented concepts and programming languages.

Early development of Smalltalk (Kay, 1996) took place at the Xerox Palo Alto Research Center during the 1970s. The development of Smalltalk at Xerox culminated with the release of Smalltalk-80 (Goldberg, 1993) in 1983. Since that time, a number of commercial and experimental implementations of Smalltalk have been created by companies and individuals. Most modern Smalltalk systems are either derived from or modeled after Smalltalk-80. However, substantial variation exists among Smalltalk implementations. X3J20 is a technical committee of the National Committee for Information Technology Standards that is chartered to produce an ANSI standard for the Smalltalk programming language. At the time of this writing (mid-1997), X3J20 is in the final stages of the development of this standard. The description of Smalltalk presented in this chapter is based on the most current X3J20 working drafts (X3J20, 1997) and should closely reflect the contents of the final standard. In this chapter, the phrase *standard Smalltalk* is used to specifically refer to Smalltalk as defined by the X3J20 committee.

4.1. Objects

Smalltalk is called an *object-oriented programming language* because a Smalltalk programmer is primarily concerned with defining and manipulating *objects*. A Smalltalk object is an entity within a program that has certain distinguishing characteristics:

- An object has *identity*. Each object is distinguishable.
- An object can store data.
- An object can respond to requests to perform computations.

All data within a Smalltalk program are represented as objects, and all computations are performed as manipulations of objects. Unlike many other object-oriented languages, Smalltalk does not distinguish between objects and more primitive non-object data types. Every datum, including integers and characters, within a Smalltalk program is uniformly treated as an object.

4.1.1. Objects Referenced as Literals

For a program to manipulate an object, it must be able to refer to that object. Within the text of a Smalltalk program, objects are referenced either as literals or as the values of variables. In Smalltalk, a literal is a syntactic form that defines an object. The most commonly used literals define objects that are numeric or string constants.

Decimal integer literals are sequences of decimal characters that define an object representing an integer numeric value. Nondecimal radices can be specified by preceding the digits of the literal with a radix specifier consisting of a decimal number followed by the letter `r`. A floating-point literal is a sequence of decimal digits with an embedded decimal point and an optional exponent specifier. Floating-point literals define objects that represent floating-point computational values. A decimal number can be optionally preceded by a hyphen to indicate a negative value. Some examples are listed here:

```
0
1024
-10000000000000
16rFFFF
8r177777
3.1416
1.0e10
1.0e-10
```

A character literal defines an object that represent an individual code point in a character set. A character literal is written by preceding a character with a dollar sign. A string literal defines an object that represents some fixed sequence of characters. A string literal is written as a sequence of characters enclosed within single quotes. For example, consider the following lines:

```
$x         "the character x"
$$         "the character $"
'a Smalltalk string literal'
'Alan''s language'
```

Within the text of a Smalltalk program, a comment is represented by a sequence of characters enclosed in quotation marks. This chapter occasionally uses such comments in examples to clarify their meaning.

A reserved identifier is used as the literal representation of objects that represent the boolean truth values and for the unique object that is the initial value of all variables that are not explicitly initialized. The following represent reserved identifiers:

```
true
false
nil
```

An *array literal* defines an object that is a data structure aggregating other literal objects. An array literal consists of a hash symbol (#) followed by list of literals in parentheses. For example, consider the following lines:

```
#(1 -2 3 -4)                "an array of four small integers"
#(1 1.0 $1 'one')           "a heterogeneous array"
#( #(1 true) #(0 false))    "an array of arrays"
```

4.1.2. Objects Referenced as Variables

Most objects do not have a literal syntax that can be used to reference them. Variables are used within the text of a Smalltalk program to reference arbitrary objects. Identifiers are used to name variables. Within Smalltalk identifiers, upper- and lowercase letters are considered to be distinct characters. By convention, variables with a limited scope of visibility are written with an initial lowercase letter, and variables with a relatively global scope are written with an initial uppercase letter. Standard Smalltalk permits the underscore character to be used within an identifier, but Smalltalk's historic convention is to use embedded uppercase letters within an identifier to distinguish the individual words of a phrase. Some examples of Smalltalk variable names include the following:

```
temp1                    "a local variable"
Transcript               "a well-known global variable"
lastUpdateTime           "a variable with a descriptive name"
last_update_time         "a legal but non-idiomatic name"
```

At any time, a variable references a single object. The object that a variable references is called the *value* of the variable. Unless it is explicitly initialized, a variable initially references the object that is the value of the literal identifier nil. The value of a variable is modified by using the assignment operator. The assignment operator is written as a colon immediately followed by an equal sign (:=). The assignment operator is the only true operator in the Smalltalk language. It replaces the value of the variable to the left of the assignment operator with the value of the expression to the right of the assignment operator. Individual statements in Smalltalk programs are separated using periods. Some examples are listed here:

```
temp1 := 'this is a string'.
temp2 := temp1.
          "both variables now reference the same string object"
temp1 := nil. "restore temp1 to its original value,
          temp2 still references the string"
temp1 := temp2 := #(1 2 3 4). "multiple assignment"
```

Smalltalk variables store references to objects, not the objects themselves. If the value of one variable is assigned to another variable, then both variables reference the same object. Any change to an object's state made through a reference from a variable is visible through all other variables that reference the same object. Assignment to a variable does not modify the state of the object previously referenced by the variable; it only changes which object the variable references.

Smalltalk variables are untyped. A reference to any object can be assigned to any Smalltalk variable. An individual variable can reference many different types of objects over the course of its existence. The fact that Smalltalk variables are untyped does not mean that Smalltalk is not a type-safe language. Smalltalk is dynamically typed. Whenever an operation is applied to an object, Smalltalk dynamically verifies that the operation is defined for that particular type of object and signals an error condition if it is not.

4.2. Behavior and Messages

Any state (data) that a Smalltalk object can store is *encapsulated*. This means that the data are not directly accessible by those parts of a program that are not directly related to the definition of the object. Generally, a Smalltalk programmer cannot access and thus does not need to be aware of the specific implementation of an object's encapsulated state. An object's *behavior* is the set of publicly callable operations that are defined for the object. Smalltalk programmers usually characterize an object by its behavior rather than its state. They think about what the object can do, not how its data are structured.

A *message* is a request to an object to do something. What an object does in response to a message is invoke one of the operations that make up the object's behavior. The majority of code in a Smalltalk program consists of *message expressions*, which cause messages to be sent to objects. In fact, except for variable assignments, all computations in a Smalltalk program are expressed in terms of message expressions.

A message expression specifies an object that is the *receiver* of the message, a *selector* that names the operation to be invoked by the message, and optionally, a set of objects that serve as *arguments* for the message. Several syntactic variants of message expressions exist, but they all have the same general structure, which reads from left to right as follows:

```
receiver    selector    arguments
```

The objects that serve as the receiver or arguments of a message expression can be identified by variables or literals, or as the value of other message expressions. There are three specific syntactic forms for selectors and three corresponding variants of message expression syntax. The following sections address unary messages, binary messages, and keyword messages.

4.2.1. Unary Messages

A *unary message* expression defines a message that has no arguments. The selector of a unary message is an identifier. Here are some examples of unary expressions:

```
12345 negated
        ⇨ -12345
'abc' reverse
        ⇨ 'cba'
#(1 2 3) last
        ⇨ 3
```

A Smalltalk message expression always computes and returns a value as the result of the expression. The value of a message expression is a reference to an object. In these and other examples we use the symbol ⇨ on the line following the expression to identify a printable description of the object that is the result of the expression. This is a typographical convention and is not part of the Smalltalk language.

In the first expression, the integer object represented by the literal object 12345 is the receiver of the message. The selector is the identifier negated. The message invokes an operation that computes the negated value of the receiver.

Because message expressions have a value, they can be used to directly specify the receiver (or arguments) of other message expressions. For example, consider these lines:

```
#(1 2 3) last negated
         ⇨ -3
```

This is a compound message expression consisting of two unary messages. The first message expression sends the message with the selector `last` to the literal array, and the result is the integer object `3`. That object then becomes the receiver of a message whose selector is negated. This message returns `-3`, which is the value of the compound expression. In general, the individual messages composing a compound sequence of unary messages are evaluated left to right.

In Smalltalk programs, the receiver of a message is most frequently specified using a variable. Hence, an expression such as the one shown previously might actually appear as follows:

```
list last negated
```

In this case, the first identifier, `list`, is a variable, and the remaining two identifiers are selectors. For the most part, this should not be a source of confusion. Simply read expressions from left to right.

4.2.2. Binary Messages

The second syntactic form for message expressions is a *binary message* expression. Each binary message expression has exactly one argument. In standard Smalltalk, the selector of a binary message is composed of one or more characters from the following set:

```
! % & * + -, / < = > ? @ \ ~ ¦
```

These characters include the symbols most commonly used in algebraic notation for numeric expressions. This is not a coincidence. Binary selectors are most commonly used for messages that perform arithmetic operations or comparisons between the receiver and the argument. The use of binary selectors results in message expressions that appear similar to conventional algebraic expressions. Consider the following expressions, for example:

```
123 + 456                "addition"
         ⇨ 579
9 >= 10                  "greater than or equal to"
         ⇨ false
true & false             "boolean and"
         ⇨ false
'abc' , 'xyz'            "string concatenation"
         ⇨ 'abcxyz'
```

When multiple binary messages are used to compose a compound message expression, the individual binary messages are evaluated strictly left to right. All binary selectors have the same precedence. Fortran-style operator precedence rules are not used. Consider the following example:

```
1 + 2 * 3
         ⇨ 9    "Fortran or C would yield 7"
```

Parentheses can be used to alter the strict left-to-right evaluation order, as in this example:

```
1 + (2 * 3)
         ⇨ 7
```

Even though binary selectors look like and are used as arithmetic operators, they are in fact regular message sends. The meaning of a selector, such as +, is dependent on the message receiver. Programmers can define new types of objects in which + or any other binary selector has meanings other than arithmetic addition.

Compound message expressions can also be formed from combinations of unary and binary message expressions. Unary selectors have higher precedence than binary selectors. Consider this line, for example:

```
x squared + y squared
```

This code computes the sum of squares. Parentheses can also be used in such expressions:

```
(x squared + y squared) sqrt
```

If this expression had not included parentheses, the receiver of the `sqrt` (square root) message would have been the result of squaring `y`, not the result of the addition of the squares.

4.2.3. Keyword Messages

The third syntactic form for message expressions is a *keyword message expression*. A keyword message expression has one or more arguments. Each argument is preceded by a *keyword*, which is an identifier immediately followed by a colon. The selector of a keyword message is formed by concatenating the keywords from left to right. Here are some examples of keyword message expressions:

```
2 raisedTo: 16
        ⇒ 65536

'abcdef' copyFrom: 3 to: 4
        ⇒ 'cd'

#(12 13 14 15) copyReplaceFrom: 1 to: 3 with: #($a $b)
        ⇒ #($a $b 15)
```

The first example has only one keyword and argument. Its selector is `raisedTo:`. The second example is a message with two arguments; its selector is formed by combining the keywords into `copyFrom:to:`. The last example's selector is `copyReplaceFrom:to:with:`.

The order of the keywords is important because changing the order of keywords produces a different selector. Similarly, removing a keyword produces a different selector. A particular object could be a valid receiver for each of the following messages:

```
anObject from: 1.
anObject from: 1 to: 5.
anObject to: 5 from: 1.
anObject to: 5.
```

However, each of these messages has a distinct selector and would invoke a separate and distinct operation on the receiver.

Keyword messages can be combined with unary messages and binary messages to form a compound message expression. A simple, nonparenthesized expression can contain only a single keyword message. The keyword message has lowest precedence. The expressions defining the arguments are evaluated from left to right, and the keyword message itself is evaluated last. Here is an example of such a complex statement:

```
aString copyFrom: aString size // 2 + 1 to: aString size
```

If a keyword message had been used in the subexpression for one of the arguments, parentheses would have been required:

```
aString copyFrom: (aString size quo:2) + 1 to: aString size
```

Occasionally, the need arises to direct a series of individual messages to the same receiver. Smalltalk provides a syntactic construct called a *cascade* that facilitates this. If a message expression is immediately followed by a semicolon, then a message expression without an explicit receiver must immediately follow the semicolon. The receiver of the message to the left of the semicolon is also used as the receiver of the message expression to the right of the semicolon. For example, this code:

```
anArray last
        start;
        continue;
        stop.
```

has the same meaning as this code:

```
temp := anArray last.
temp start.
temp continue.
temp stop.
```

An object's behavior is defined by a set of methods. A *method* is essentially a function that consists of a sequence of Smalltalk message expressions. Each method also has an associated method selector. When a message expression is evaluated, its selector is used to find the method with a matching selector from the behavior of the object that is the receiver of the message. That method is then evaluated, and its result is used as the value of the original message expression.

4.2.4. Polymorphism with Identical Messages

Different Smalltalk objects can respond to identical messages in differing ways. This is called *polymorphism*. Polymorphism is possible because different objects can have different methods that match a particular message selector. The determination of which method is executed depends on the actual object that is the receiver of the message when the message is evaluated. Repeated evaluations of a particular message expression in the text of a Smalltalk program can result in the execution of different methods if each evaluation uses a different object as the receiver of the message.

4.3. Relationships Among Classes

An object encapsulates a set of variables and a set of methods that can operate on those variables. A *class* is a common specification of variables and methods that is shared in common by a set of related objects. Objects that share a common class definition are called *instances* of the class. A class definition is a template that describes the common characteristics shared by all instances of a class. Various Smalltalk implementations use differing means for specifying class definitions. For now, we will ignore these differences and use a fill-in-the-blank style of form to describe classes. The basic template for a class looks like this:

Class Name	`<identifier that is the class's global name>`
Superclass	`<global name of another class>`
Instance Variables	`<list of identifiers>`
Instance Methods	
`<source code of individual methods>`	

Following is the partial definition of a simple class whose instances might represent individual customers in a customer information system:

Class Name	`Customer`
Superclass	`Object`
Instance Variables	`name address customerNumber`
Instance Methods	
`<source code of individual methods>`	

A *class name* is an identifier that is used to refer to a class within a Smalltalk program. By convention, class names should be capitalized. Class names have global scope within a Smalltalk program. They also must be unique. Class names can be used as read-only variables within Smalltalk expressions. A class name cannot be the target of an assignment operator. The value of such a variable is a *class object*. Messages to class objects are most commonly used to create new instances of the class.

Consider these lines, for example:

```
Customer new
        ⇨ "a new instance of Customer"
Array new: 5
        ⇨ #(nil nil nil nil nil) "new 5-element, uninitialized array"
```

The message selector `new` is most frequently used to create new instances of a class. The selector `new:` is used to create instances that can vary in size. The argument to `new:` specifies the size of the variable-sized part of the new object.

Although most objects are explicitly created by sending messages such as new, there are no messages for explicitly destroying objects. Smalltalk is a *garbage-collected* language. It is the responsibility of a Smalltalk implementation to automatically release any storage or other resources used by an object when the object is no longer accessible from any variable or statement of the program.

4.3.1. Instance Variables

The variables encapsulated by an object are called *instance variables*. A class definition specifies the number of instance variables and specifies a name for each variable. Instances of the class `Customer`, defined in the preceding example, have three instance variables: `name`, `address`, and `customerNumber`. The instance variables of an object are directly accessible only by that object's methods. This is accomplished by limiting the scope of the instance variable names to those methods.

The instance variables of multiple instance of a class are separate and distinct. If two instances of `Customer` are created, then each instance has distinct instance variables corresponding to `name`, `address`, and `customerNumber`. When a method is selected for execution as the result of a message send, the instance variable names in the method are bound to the actual instance variables of the object that is the receiver of the message.

The default value of all instance variables of a newly created object is nil. Typically, a programmer will want to initialize the values of some or all of the instance variables to more useful values. This cannot be done by direct assignment because instance variables are encapsulated and cannot be directly accessed outside of the object's methods. To initialize the instance variables, a method is needed. Consider these lines, for example:

```
name:    initName address: initAddr customerNumber: initNumber
         "initialize the state of the receiver to the argument values"
         name := initName.
         address := initAddr.
         customerNumber := initNumber
```

This is a simple method definition. The first line of the method is called the *message pattern*. It specifies the selector of the method and declares names for the arguments to the method.

4.3.2. Method Definition

Within the body of a method, argument names can be used as read-only variables. The second line of the method is a comment. Conventionally, a comment is placed here to describe the purpose of the method. The rest of the method is the method body, which consists of a sequence of Smalltalk expressions that are executed when this method is evaluated by a message send. In this example, the body simply consists of a set of assignments of argument values to instance variables. When the method is evaluated, the argument names are bound to the actual arguments of the invoking message, and the instance variable names are bound to the actual instance variables of the receiver of the message.

Methods always return some value. The return value can be explicitly specified using a *return statement*. A return statement is a Smalltalk expression immediately preceded by a carat (`^`). The value of the expression becomes the returned value of the method. Here are examples of some return statements:

```
^42             "return the literal integer object, 42"
^name           "return the current value of an instance variable"
^Customer new   "return a new Customer object"
```

Many methods, such as the one above, are not written with a return statement. If a method does not end with an explicit return statement, the method implicitly returns the object that was the receiver of the message that activated the method. Within the body of a method, the identifier (`self`) is bound to the receiver of the message. Thus, the following method definition is exactly equivalent to that given previously:

```
name: initName address: initAddr customerNumber: initNumber
      "initialize the state of the receiver to the argument values"
      name := initName.
      address := initAddr.
      customerNumber := initNumber.
      ^self
```

Using this method, a new `Customer` object might be created and assigned to a temporary variable by this expression:

```
temp := Customer new name:'Joe' address:'Any City' customerNumber: 1.
```

This expression first sends a message with the selector `new` to the class object named `Customer`. The result of that message send is a new instance of `Customer`, which becomes the receiver for the message with the selector `name:address:customerNumber:`. This message invokes the method that assigns the arguments to the receiver's instance variables and then returns the receiver. Finally, the new customer object, which is the returned value, is assigned to the variable named `temp`.

Users of the `Customer` class are likely to want to retrieve the values stored in its instance variables. Because of the encapsulation of instance variables, this requires the use of methods such as the following:

```
name
        "return the name of the customer"
        ^name

address
        "return the current address from the receiver"
        ^address
```

Methods such as these that simply return the value of an instance variable are called *accessor methods*. Note that a programmer need not provide accessor methods for all the instance variables defined by a class. Some instance variables can be considered completely private to the implementation of the class. If an accessor method is not provided for such an instance variable, it is accessible only to the class's methods.

Instead of thinking about accessor methods as retrieving the value of an instance variable, it is better to think about them as retrieving the value of an abstract attribute of the object. The implementation of this attribute might initially be as an instance variable, but as the definition of the class evolves, the implementation of the attribute might change to become some sort of computation. The use of accessor methods shields client code from such changes. Smalltalk's uniformity of reference greatly facilitates this type of abstraction. All accesses to an object, outside of the object's class definition, must be expressed as message sends.

Now that we have defined some methods for `Customer`, we can complete its class definition template:

Class Name	`Customer`
Superclass	`Object`
Instance Variables	`name address customerNumber`
Instance Methods	

```
name: initName address: initAddr customerNumber: initNumber
  "initialize the state of the receiver to the argument values"
  name := initName.
  Address := initAddr.
  customerNumber := initNumber
```

```
name
  "return the name of the customer"
  ^name
```

```
address
  "return the current address from the receiver"
  ^address
```

The one part of the basic class definition template that remains to be discussed is the superclass. Most classes are defined as refinements of an existing class. The class from which a new class is derived is called the *superclass* of the new class. The derived class is called a *subclass* of its superclass.

A class can have exactly one *immediate* superclass. The superclass field of a class definition is used to specify the immediate superclass. The immediate superclass can itself be a subclass of another class. Thus, each class can have a chain of superclasses that starts with its immediate superclass and continues through the superclasses of the immediate superclass. The final class of this chain is usually the class named `Object`. `Object` does not have a superclass.

4.3.3. Inheritance Among Classes

The relationship between a class and its superclasses is called *inheritance*. A subclass inherits the instance variable and method definitions of its superclasses. Because Smalltalk only allows an object to have a single immediate superclass, it is said to support *single inheritance*. This is in contrast to languages such as C++ and Eiffel that allow a class to have multiple immediate superclasses. Such languages are said to support *multiple inheritance*.

Through the mechanisms of inheritance, all the instance variables and methods defined by the superclasses are also defined for the subclass. The instance variables and methods explicitly defined by the subclass augment those that are inherited from its superclasses.

The encapsulated state of an instance of a class includes instance variables corresponding to each of the instance variables of its superclasses in addition to the instance variables it explicitly defines. The names of each instance variable must be unique for the class, regardless of whether the variable is defined by the class or by one of its superclasses.

The behavior of an instance of a subclass includes all the instance methods defined by its superclasses, augmented by the methods explicitly defined in the subclass definition. If the selector of a method in a subclass is the same as the selector of a method that is inherited from a superclass, the subclass's method *overrides* (replaces) the inherited method in the subclass's behavior. Thus, a subclass can extend the inherited behavior of its superclass by defining new methods or can modify the inherited behavior by overriding methods. Smalltalk does not provide a mechanism for excluding an inherited method from the behavior of a subclass.

4.3.4. Subclasses and Inheritance

Much of the power of object-oriented programming comes from the use of inheritance to build families of related classes. Subclasses can build on an abstraction defined by a superclass and can change it in many different ways. Some common uses of subclassing include:

- *Specialization.* The subclass represents a specialization of its superclass that adds additional attributes and behavior. An example is a `CreditorCardCustomer` that extends the `Customer` class by adding behavior to record and access credit card–related information.
- *Alternative state representation.* The subclass can maintain the same public interface but optimize its internal representation of state for some purpose. An example would be classes such as `LinearSearchList`, `BinarySearchList`, and `HashedSearchList` that inherit from a `SearchableList` class. Each subclass would use a different internal list representation and search algorithm.
- *Implementation sharing.* The subclass can use an inherited implementation structure but define new public behavior that presents the class as an abstraction that is totally different from the superclass. An example would be a class named `CardDeck` that inherited from a `SearchableList` class and added protocol that related to playing card games.

By carefully structuring a class hierarchy, inheritance can be used to share and reuse code among a number of classes. In a well-designed class hierarchy, each class should add or replace the minimal amount of code needed to distinguish it from its superclass. However, a subclass can replace inherited code only in method-sized units. This means that the structure of a superclass's methods has a great impact on how easy it is to subclass it.

One goal in designing a Smalltalk subclass is to minimize the amount of code that must be physically copied from the superclass. Copied code is the antithesis of code reuse and makes programs significantly more difficult to maintain. Large, complex methods in a superclass are difficult to override without significant textual code copying. Consider a 60-line method and a subclass that needs to change 1 line in the middle of that method. Because of the method-level granularity of subclass code replacement, the programmer of the subclass would have to duplicate 59 lines of code in order to replace that single line. To avoid this problems, most Smalltalk programmers use procedural decomposition to split complex methods into a number of short, simple submethods. Any individual submethod can then, if necessary, be overridden by a subclass without the need for duplicating or overriding other submethods.

4.3.4.1. The `self` Identifier

Procedural decomposition in Smalltalk requires the use of the reserved identifier `self`. Within a method, the value of `self` is the actual object that was the receiver of the message that activated the method. `self` can be used in any context in which a literal is allowed, including as an argument or a receiver of a message. Procedural decomposition is accomplished within a method by using self as the receiver of messages. Consider these lines, for example:

```
someMethodThatPerformsAComplexComputation
    "The algorithm used by this method requires pre- and post-
    conditioning of its data."
    self preConditionData.
    self complexAlgorithm.
    self postConditionData
```

The class also defines methods named `preConditionData`, `complexAlgorithm`, and `postConditionData` that implemented the details of the three parts of the computation. A subclass could override any of the three methods without having to override or duplicate the other two methods.

4.3.4.2. The `super` Identifier

Sometimes in creating a subclass, the need arises to extend rather than replace an inherited method. For example, some additional code might need to be added at the beginning or end of an inherited method. This can be accomplished using the reserved identifier *super*. This identifier can be used only as the receiver of a message. `super` is like `self` in that it is a reference to the object that was the receiver for the message that activated the current method. However, a message send with `super` as its receiver invokes the method for the message's selector from the behavior of the superclass of the class that defines the method containing the message expression. If the selector of the send to `super` is the same as the selector of the current method, the send will invoke the method that is overridden by the current method.

A subclass can extend a method with additional code by overriding the superclass's method and including within the body of the new method a message send to `super` using the method's selector. Consider the following, for example:

```
someExtensibleThing:arg
    "Override the inherited method to do additional computations
    before and after the inherited method"
    self beforeAction.
    super someExtensibleThing:arg.
    self afterAction.
```

4.3.5. Class Definitions

In section 4.3, we mentioned that the value associated with a class name is a class object and that new instances are typically created by sending messages to a class object. Where are the methods that implement these messages defined? The following sections address class methods, class instance variables, and class variables.

The implementation for standard methods such as `new` and `new:` are inherited from the definition of `Object` and are available to all classes that are direct or indirect subclasses of `Object`. However, it is occasionally useful to define additional methods for class objects. For example, instead of using a sequence of messages to create and initialize an object such as this one:

```
Customer new name:'Joe' address:'Any City' customerNumber: 1
```

we might prefer to use a single message that both creates and initializes a new instances:

```
Customer name:'Joe' address:'Any City' customerNumber: 1
```

This line is more concise and has the advantage that a programmer cannot inadvertently forget to initialize the new instance. Such a message can be implemented by using a *class method.* Class methods are similar to instance methods, but instead of extending the behavior of a class's instances, they extend the behavior of the class object itself. Class methods are defined in a separate section of the class definition template:

Class Name	Customer
Super Class	Object
Instance Variables	name address customerNumber
Instance Methods	
name: initName address: initAddr: customerNumber: initNumber "initialize the state of the receiver to the argument values" name := initName. Address := initAddr. customerNumber := initNumber	
name "return the name of the customer" ^name	
address "return the current address from the receiver" ^address	
Class Methods	
name: initName address: initAddr customerNumber: initNumber "create and initialize a new instance using the argument values" | c | c := self new. ^c name: initName address: initAddr customerNumber: initNumber	

The `new` method just defined essentially encapsulates the compound message sequence used to create and initialize a new instance. However, in this example we choose to use a sequence of expression and a temporary variable instead of a compound message expression. This line:

```
| c |
```

is a declaration of a method temporary variable named `c`. A method can have an arbitrary number of temporary variables that are declared by listing them between vertical bars immediately before the first statement of the method. The scope of a method temporary variable is limited to the method in which it is declared. Each time a method is activated, a new set of temporary variables is created and initialized to nil for use by that activation of the method.

This method first creates an uninitialized customer instance by sending the message `new` to `self`. Within a class method, `self` is bound to the class object. In this case, the value of `self` is the class object, `Customer`, so the new message creates a new instance of that class. This object is assigned to the temporary variable c. Finally, the message name:address:customerNumber: is sent to the value of c. This message invokes the instance method whose selector is name:address:customerNumber: and which initializes its receiver, the new instance.

Note that an instance method is still needed to initialize the instance variables of the new instance. This is because the instance variable names are accessible only to instance methods. A class method cannot directly access the instance variables of instances of the class. Like any other object, a class object must use messages to access the state of other objects, including its instances.

This example also illustrates a use of polymorphism. Different methods with the same selector (name:address:customerNumber:) are defined for both the instance behavior and the class behavior. A message expression using that selector invokes one or the other of the methods, depending on what object was the actual receiver of the message. Looking at an expression such as the following out of context, it is impossible to determine which method would be executed:

```
c name:'Joe' address:'Any City' customerNumber: 1
```

If the actual receiver (the value of c) is the class object, the class method is invoked. If the actual receiver is an instance of Customer, then the instance method is invoked.

Just as it is useful to define state variables for instance objects, it is also useful to be able to define state variables for class objects. Consider, for example, the situation in which we needed to count the number of Customer objects that were created. One way to do this would be to extend the class method name:address:customerNumber: to maintain a counter:

```
name: initName address: initAddr customerNumber: initNumber
    "create and initialize a new instance using the argument values"
    | c |
    c := self new.
    customerCount := customerCount + 1.
    ^c name:initName address:initAddr customerNumber: initNumber
```

The remaining issue is how to declare the variable customerCount. Declaring it as a method temporary would not work because new temporary variables are created and initialized to nil each time a method is executed. Instead, customerCount can be made a class instance variable. Class instance variables are declared in a separate section of the class definition template. A *class instance variable* is an instance variable of a class object. As such, a class instance variable is accessible from the class methods, but because it is part of the state of the class object, it retains its value across multiple method invocations.

Just as instance variables cannot be accessed by class methods, class instance variables cannot be accessed by instance methods. Occasionally, it is useful to have a variable that is shared by all instances of a class, and possibly with the class object itself. For example, we might need to enhance our customer object to include an instance variable that records the customers personal credit limit. However, because we have already written code using the original definition of `Customer`, we would prefer to make this change in a way that did not require us to change every place we have already coded `name:address:customerNumber:` to create or initialize a new instance. One way to accomplish this would be to redefine the instance method for this selector so that it initializes the credit limit instance variable to a default value. Doing this, the instance method might be rewritten as follows:

```
name: initName address: initAddr customerNumber: initNumber
    "initialize the state of the receiver to the argument values"
    name := initName.
    address  := initAddr.
    customerNumber := initNumber.
    creditLimit := 500. "set credit limit to default value"
```

This version has the disadvantage that it uses a hard-coded constant for the default value. Clearly, such constants should be avoided to improve both readability and maintainability of code. Preferably, we would use a symbolic constant such as this one:

```
creditLimit := DefaultCreditLimit. "set to default value"
```

This can be accomplished by declaring `DefaultCreditLimit` as a class variable of `Customer`. A *class variable* is a variable that is shared by all the instances of a class and by the class object. A class variable is also shared by the instances and class objects of any subclasses. A name of a class variable is globally visible to all instance and class methods of a class and its superclass. Because class variables have a relatively global scope, their names are, by convention, usually capitalized.

One remaining issue is the initialization of `customerCount` and `DefaultCreditLimit`. For the methods `name:address:customerNumber:` to work properly, these variables must be initialized to some appropriate numeric objects. By convention, class objects are usually initialized by a class method with the selector named `initialize`. Such a method for `Customer` might be as follows:

```
initialize
    "Initialize class and class instance variables"
    DefaultCreditLimit := 500.
    customerCount := 0.
```

This method would be invoked by an expressions such as this one:

```
Customer initialize.
```

This expression would need to be executed before the first usage of `Customer` within a program.

Using class methods, class instance variables, and class variables, the definition of `Customer` now has this complete template:

Class Name	Customer
Super Class	Object
Instance Variables	name address customerNumber creditLimit
Instance Methods	

```
name: initName address: initAddr: customerNumber: initNumber
   "initialize the state of the receiver to the argument values"
   name := initName.
   Address := initAddr.
   customerNumber := initNumber
```

```
name
   "return the name of the customer"
   ^name
```

```
address
   "return the current address from the receiver"
   ^address
```

Class Instance Variables	customerCount
Class Methods	

```
initialize
   "Initialize class and class instance variables"
   DefaultCreditLimit := 500.
   CustomerCount := 0
```

```
name: initName address: initAddr customerNumber: initNumber
   "create and initialize a new instance using the argument values"
   | c |
   c := self new.
   ^ c name: initName address: initAddr customerNumber: initNumber
```

4.4. Control Structures

A Smalltalk program consists of a set of class definitions that define the objects that will be sent messages to perform the function of the program. The actual computational logic of the program is encoded in the objects' methods and is expressed as sequences of message sends. Pure sequential execution of message sends is insufficiently powerful for solving all but the simplest programming problems. Most interesting algorithms require the capability to conditionally or iteratively execute code. Programming languages usually support this by providing specialized statements for specifying conditional and iterative execution. Smalltalk does not use such statements, however. In Smalltalk, all computation except assignment is expressed using message sends. Even conditional and iterative execution is accomplished using message sends. This is possible because of the power of polymorphism.

4.4.1. Conditional Execution

In Smalltalk, a conditional is usually expressed using a message with the selector `ifTrue:ifFalse:`. The receiver of this message should be one of the boolean objects, true or false. The arguments must be objects that implement the message value. For example, a simple conditional might be

```
booleanValue ifTrue: trueAction ifFalse: falseAction.
```

In this example, `booleanValue` is assumed to be a variable whose value is one of the boolean objects. `trueAction` and `falseAction` are assumed to be objects that respond to the message value. More commonly such an expression would be written as a compound message expression in which the receiver of `ifTrue:ifFalse:` is an expression that evaluates to `true` or `false`. Consider the following line, for example:

```
A>B ifTrue: trueAction ifFalse: falseAction.
```

If the receiver of `ifTrue:ifFalse:` is `true`, the message value is sent to the first argument, and the result of that message is returned as the result of the `ifTrue:ifFalse:` message. If the receiver is `false`, the value is sent to the second argument, and its result is returned as the value of `ifTrue:ifFalse:`.

A conditional message such as `ifTrue:ifFalse:` can be implemented solely using polymorphism without requiring any other special language constructs. The key to this is to implement `true` and `false` as instances of different classes with different methods for the selector `ifTrue:ifFalse:`. If `true` is an instance of the class named `True` and `false` is an instance of the class named `False`, the definitions of the methods `ifTrue:ifFalse:` would be as follows:

Class **`True`** Instance Method
`ifTrue:` trueAction **`ifFalse:`** ignoredAction "Because the receiver is known to be true, return the result of evaluating the first argument. The second argument is ignored." ^trueAction value

Class `False` Instance Method

`ifTrue:` `ignoredAction` **`ifFalse:`** `falseAction`
`"Because the receiver is known to be false, evaluating the second argument. The first argument is ignored`
`^falseAction value`

Thus, by using polymorphic message sends, we can construct an expression that will conditionally perform one of two possible actions. However, how can we easily express these actions? Based on what we have described to this point, the only possible way would be to define a separate class and value method for each possible action. For example, we might define the following:

Class `Action1` Instance Method

```
value
   "Subtract B from A."

   ^A-B
```

Class `Action2` Instance Method

```
value
   "Subtract A from B."

   ^B-A
```

Using these definitions, we could write the example expressions as follows:

```
A>B ifTrue: Action1 new ifFalse: Action2 new.
```

The argument expressions create new objects that respond appropriately to the `value` message. These objects are created and passed as the arguments of `ifTrue:ifFalse:`. If the expression `A>B` evaluates to `true`, then the `ifTrue:ifFalse:` method in class `True` is invoked and the message value is sent to the instance of `Action1`. `Action1` responds by returning the result of `A-B`. Otherwise, the `ifTrue:ifFalse:` method in class `False` is invoked and the message value is sent to the instance of `Action2`. `Action2` responds by returning the result of `B-A`.

It would be very cumbersome to have to create a new class every time we needed to express a conditional within a program. Large programs would require thousands of these classes, which would be difficult to manage and difficult to read. Note that we capitalized the variables `A` and `B`, indicating that they are global variables. We did this because we needed to directly access them from code fragments in at least three different classes.

Smalltalk avoids these problems by providing a syntactic construct called a *block constructor* that creates objects that uniquely respond to the message value. A block constructor is a sequence of expressions enclosed in square brackets. For example, `[a+b]` is a simple block constructor. The object that is created by a block constructor is called a *block*. The term *block closure* is sometimes used to describe these objects. When a block is sent the message value, it evaluates the expressions enclosed by the brackets of the block constructor. The value of the last of these expressions is returned as the result of the `value` message. Using blocks, our example can be written without defining any auxiliary classes:

```
A>B ifTrue: [A-B] ifFalse: [B-A].
```

The code within a block has access to the same variable scopes to which it would have access if the block brackets were not present. Thus, we do not need to use global variables in our example. The block can access the same method argument, temporaries, and instance variables as any neighboring code that is outside the block. So the final form of our example conditional expression is

```
a>b ifTrue: [a-b] ifFalse: [b-a].
```

Strictly by using polymorphic message sends and block constructors, Smalltalk can provide the equivalent of `if-then-else` statements. Smalltalk also includes the following short-hand variants:

`ifTrue:`	No `else` clause
`ifFalse:`	No `then` clause
`ifFalse:ifTrue:`	Reversed order

4.4.2. Iterative Execution

Blocks are also used by Smalltalk to specify iteration. `While` loops are coded in Smalltalk using the message selectors `whileTrue:` and `whileFalse:`. Consider this line, for example:

```
[temp < 10] whileTrue: [temp := temp + 1]
```

These messages are sent to a block that evaluates to a boolean object. The receiver block is repetitively evaluated, and each time it evaluates to the boolean object identified by the message selector (`true` for `whileTrue:`, `false` for `whileFalse:`), the argument block is evaluated. The first time the receiver block does not evaluate to the matching value, iteration terminates and execution continues with the next statement.

Blocks can accept one or more arguments. The formal parameter names for a block's arguments are listed immediately following the opening bracket of the block. Each parameter name is preceded by a colon, and the final parameter name is followed by a vertical bar. Here are examples of blocks that take one, two, and three arguments:

```
block1 := [:argument | someArray at: argument put: 0]

block2 := [:arg1 :arg2 | someArray at: arg1 put: arg2]

block3 := [:target :index :value | target at: index put: value]
```

Blocks that accept arguments are evaluated using variants of the `value:` message. One `value:` keyword is used to correspond to each formal parameter of the block. The value of each keyword argument is associated with the corresponding parameter, according to its position. The preceding blocks might be evaluated using the following expressions:

```
block1 value: 5.  "the value of the argument is 5"

block2 value: 9 value: 'pickle'. "store 'pickle' in element 9"

block3 value: (Array new: 5) value: 1 value: Customer new.
```

By using blocks with arguments, more complex control structures can be constructed. A classic `do` loop is created using a block with one argument:

```
1 to: 10 by: 2 do: [:i| someArray at: i put: 0]
```

A variant form of this message (whose selector is `to:do:`) implicitly uses an increment (the `by:` argument) of `1`. Although most Smalltalk compilers optimize the implementation of `to:do:by:` and `to:do:`, it is possible to implement them strictly using `whileTrue:`. Here is an example of such an implementation:

Class `Number` Instance Method

```
to: endValue by: increment do: aBlock
    "iterate from the value of the receiver to the endValue.
    On each iteration, evaluate aBlock with the induction variable
    as the argument. For this example the increment is assumed to be
    positive."

    |i|
    i := self.
    [i <= endValue] whileTrue: [aBlock value: i. i := i + increment]
```

Using blocks, it is easy to construct methods that implement more specialized control constructs. For this reason, the actual use of conventional `do` loops is fairly rare in Smalltalk programs. Instead, programmers typically use messages that invoke more specialized forms of iteration. For example, the message do: is used to iterate over each element on an array or any other type of data collection that supports it via polymorphism. This includes strings because they are defined as collections of characters. The message do: evaluates its argument block once for each element in the data collection that is the receiver of the message. The data elements are successively passed as the argument to the block. The following illustrates some examples that use do:. The first example simply sends a message to each element of an array. The second code fragment shows how do: can be used to count the number of occurrences of a specific character within a string:

```
customerArray do: [:each| each  printMonthlyStatement].
n := 0.
'This is a test' do: [:c| c = $s ifTrue: [n := n + 1]].
^n
        ⇒ 3  "the character $s occurred three times"
```

The message collect: is similar to do: in that it evaluates a block for each element of a data collection. However, unlike do:, collect: returns a new collection that is the same size as the original collection. Each element of the new collection is the object that is the result of evaluating the argument block using the corresponding element of the receiver collection as the argument. For example, the following expression creates an array containing the names of each customer from an array of customer objects:

```
nameArray := customerArray collect: [:element| element name]
```

The messages select: and reject: are used to create new collections consisting of those elements from the receiver collection that pass or fail a test that is specified by the argument block. The message select: includes in the result collection only those elements for which the argument block evaluates to true. The message reject: excludes elements for which the argument block evaluates to true. Consider these lines, for example:

```
'John Q Public' select: [:c| c isUppercase]
        ⇒ 'JQP'
#(1 2 3 4 5 6 7 8 9) reject: [:n| n odd]
        ⇒ #(2 4 6 8)
```

4.4.3. Combined Conditional and Iterative Execution

Multiple blocks can also be used to create control structures that combine iterative and conditional operations. For example, the message detect:ifNone: is used to search a collection for the first element that passes a test defined by the first argument block. However, if a matching element is not found, the second block argument is evaluated and its result is returned. This is used to provide a default value for situations where searches fail. Consider these lines, for example:

```
customerJohn := customerArray
                  detect: [:cust| cust name = 'John Q Public']
                  ifNone: [Customer "create a default customer"
                                name: 'John Q Public'
                                address: 'Any Town'
                                customerNumber: 1].
```

Messages such as `do:`, `select:`, `reject:`, and `collect:` are reminiscent of Lisp map functions. *Map functions* typically take a list and a function as arguments and apply the function to each element of the list. Similarly, in Smalltalk the common iteration messages are sent to a collection and take a block as an argument. In modern Lisp dialects such as Scheme, the function argument to a map function is a lexical closure. A *lexical closure* is a function whose free variables have been bound within an active environment of variables. Smalltalk blocks are semantically equivalent to Scheme closures. This is the reason that blocks are sometimes also called block closures. It is important to understand that each evaluation of a block constructor creates a new and distinct block closure object with distinct variable bindings. When a block closure is created, the bindings of any references from the block to variables or arguments in the surrounding method (or any surrounding blocks) are fixed such that the block still references the current activation of those variables whenever the block closure is evaluated. The following method returns a block as its result:

Class `Something` Instance Method

```
capture: arg
    "return a block that remembers the value passed into capture:"
    |temp|
    temp:=arg.
    ^[temp]
```

This method accepts an arbitrary object and returns a block that at some later time can be evaluated to return the original argument object. Consider these expressions, for example:

```
block1 := Something new capture: 'a string to capture in block 1'.
block1 value
        ⇨ 'a string to capture in block 1'
```

Additional invocations of the `capture:` method create additional block objects, each of which can return different values. The additional method invocations and block creations do not affect the values that were captured by any previously existing blocks, even though they were created by the same block constructor:

```
block2 := Something new capture: 'captured by block 2'.
block3 := Something new capture: 'block 3 holds me'.
block2 value
        ⇨ 'captured by block 2'
block1 value
        ⇨ 'a string to capture in block 1'
block3 value
        ⇨ 'block 3 holds me'
```

Each time the method `capture:` is invoked, a new local variable is created and bound to the name `temp`. The reference to `temp` from within the block is bound to that specific local variable. When the block object is returned from the method, its reference to the local variable causes the variable to continue to exist, even though the method invocation that created the variable has terminated. Because each block in the preceding example is created by a separate method invocation, each block references a different local variable named `temp`. In fact, the use of a temporary variable is not necessary in this example. The block could be code to directly return the value of the method argument, as its binding is also uniquely captured each time a block is created.

The life cycle of a Smalltalk temporary variable or argument does not necessarily follow the normal FIFO pattern of ALGOL-like block-structured languages. Because a block closure can capture a reference to a temporary variable or argument, such variables must continue to exist as long as the block closure exists. This period can extend after the return from the method or block invocation that created the variable or argument.

Just as methods can declare temporary variables, blocks can also declare local temporary variables. The syntax is similar to that used for methods. The local variables names for a block immediately follow the block arguments and are enclosed in vertical bars. Consider this code, for example:

```
[:each |
    | temp |
    temp := each size + 15.
    Array new: temp].

[| size tempArray| " a no argument block with temps"
    size := 10.
    tempArray := Array new: size.
    1 to: size do: [:i| tempArray at: i put: 'initial string']].
```

4.5. Computed Message Selectors

In all the examples used to this point, the message selector for each message send has been specified as part of the syntax of a message send expression.

In some situations, it is useful to dynamically change the message selector that will be used at some point in a program. Consider the case of a class that represents menus in a graphical user interface. Each instance of the class would represent a particular menu, which consists of a number of labeled items. A message to the menu object would cause a graphic representation of the labels to be displayed and would accept user input to select one of the items. Upon selection of an item, the menu object would send a message to some object indicating which item was selected. The following partial class definition presents the skeleton of the definition of such a class:

Class Name	`Menu`
Superclass	`Object`
Instance Variables	`labels`
Instance Methods	

```
label: anArray
  "Initialize a menu object. The argument is an array of strings that
  specify the labels of the menu."
  | c |
  labels size > 5 ifTrue: [self error: "Too many items for menu'].
  labels := anArray
```

```
selectNotifying: agent
  "display the menu, get the users selection, and notify the agent
  according to which item was selected"
  | item |
  self display.
  item := self getSelection.
  self hide.
  item > 0 ifTrue: [self notify: agent with: item]
```

```
display
  "Private - Present a graphic display of the menu items"
  ...
```

```
getSelection
  "Private - Interact with the use to determine which item is
  selected. Return the index of the selected label. Return 0 if
  no selection was made."
  ...
```

```
hide
  "Private - Remove the graphic display of the menu items"
  ...
```

```
notify: agent with: labelIndex
  "Private - Send a message to the agent object that identifies the
  item that was selected"
  labelIndex = 1 ifTrue: [^agent item1Selected].
  labelIndex = 2 ifTrue: [^agent item2Selected].
  labelIndex = 3 ifTrue: [^agent item3Selected].
  labelIndex = 4 ifTrue: [^agent item4Selected].
  labelIndex = 5 ifTrue: [^agent item5Selected].
```

A programmer would create an instance of this class by using an expression such as the following:

```
editMenu := Menu new labels: #('cut' 'copy' 'paste').
```

At the point in the program where this menu should be presented to the user, the programmer might code this line:

```
editMenu selectNotifying: editorObject.
```

The object that was the value of `editorObject` would then be sent an `item n Selected` message that indicated which menu item was actually selected.

There are several undesirable properties of `this` class. The most obvious problem is that its menus can have only a fixed number of items. This limitation comes from the need to use a separate message expression to send each of the possible item-selected messages. This requirement, in turn, arises from the manner in which message selectors are syntactically specified in a message expression.

Another undesirable property is that the `editorObject` that is notified of the selection must have been written such that it implements methods named `item1Selected`, `item2Selected`, and `item3Selected`. This closely couples the implementation of the `editorObject` and the `Menu` class. Such coupling would make it difficult to modify the method of selection used by the program or to reuse the `editor` object in a different program. It would be more desirable for the `editor` object to receive messages with names such as cut, copy, and paste when a menu item is selected. Of course, other instances of `Menu` that notified other types of objects would prefer to use other problem-specific message selectors to notify of selection.

What is needed to solve these problems is a means to parameterize the method selector that is sent to notify the agent of the selection. This can be accomplished through the use of blocks or message selector objects.

A block is an object that represents the capability to send the message `cut` to an arbitrary object that is passed as an argument when the block is evaluated. Consider the following block:

```
[:obj| obj cut]
```

This type of block is much more flexible than a simple message expression. As an object, it can be assigned to variables and aggregated into data structures. For example, three such blocks could be collected into an array such as this one:

```
selectionMessages := Array new: 3.
selectionMessages
     at: 1 put: [:obj| obj cut];
     at: 2 put: [:obj| obj copy];
     at: 3 put: [:obj| obj paste].
```

Based on this paradigm, the `Menu` class could be modified such that it encapsulates an additional instance variable named `blocks` that holds an array of blocks. Each block in the array would provide the message expression used to indicate that the corresponding label item had been selected. The implementation of the `notify:with:` method would change to the following:

```
notify: agent with: labelIndex
    "Private - Send a message to the agent object that identifies the
    item that was selected"
    ^(blocks at: labelIndex) value: agent
```

Although this design now accommodates an arbitrary number of labels in a menu and allows arbitrary messages for signaling selection, it requires a much more complex sequences of expressions to create a menu object. The original expression:

```
editMenu := Menu new labels: #('cut' 'copy' 'paste').
```

must be replaced with something like this:

```
selectionMessages := Array new: 3.
selectionMessages
    at: 1 put: [:obj| obj cut];
    at: 2 put: [:obj| obj copy];
    at: 3 put: [:obj| obj paste].
editMenu := Menu new
            labels: #('cut' 'copy' 'paste')
            blocks: selectionMessages.
```

Smalltalk is able to avoid such complexity by providing a mechanism to directly parameterize the selector of a message send without using blocks. This mechanism depends on the capability to directly manipulate message selectors as objects. Smalltalk syntax provides a literal notation for such objects. A message selector immediately preceded by a `#` is a selector literal. Examples of such literals include the following:

```
#new
#detect:ifNone:
#>=
```

The value of a selector literal is a message selector object. Selector objects can be assigned to variables, passed as arguments, and compared for equality. Their most important property is their use as the argument to the `perform` family of messages. Via inheritance from class `Object`, all Smalltalk objects are able to respond to the following set of messages:

```
perform:
perform: with:
perform: with:with:
perform: withArguments:
```

The first argument to the `perform` messages must be a message selector object. The effect of a `perform` message is to send a new message using the argument message selector to the original receiver of the `perform` message. The `with` arguments to a `perform` message provide the arguments for the new message. For example, the following pairs of expressions are equivalent:

```
aCustomer name              aCustomer perform: #name
3 + 4                       3 perform: #+ with: 4
```

By using `perform:`, we can modify our sample menu class to use an array of message selectors to specify the selection actions. The implementation of the `notify:with:` method would change to this:

```
notify: agent with: labelIndex
     "Private - Send a message to the agent object that identifies the
      item that was selected"
     ^agent perform: (selectors at: labelIndex)
```

Similarly, an instance-creation expression for the example would be as follows:

```
editMenu := Menu new
                 labels: #('cut' 'copy' 'paste')
                 selectors: #(#cut #copy #paste).
```

4.6. Exception Handling

Exceptions are unusual or unexpected events that can occur during the execution of a Smalltalk program. When one of these exceptional events occurs, the program must take some special action. Some exceptional conditions are frequent enough that provisions for dealing with them are made an explicit part of a class's message protocol. For example, the message `at:ifAbsent:` is used to access an object from a collection. This message explicitly deals with the situation when the object is not found. A block is used to allow the programmer to specify the exceptional action:

```
result := aCollection at: key ifAbsent: [self defaultValue]
```

Other exceptional conditions are less localized or more difficult to anticipate. A more general mechanism is needed that can deal with exceptional occurrences that might occur during the entire scope of a computation. For these situations, standard Smalltalk provides a generalized exception-handling mechanism.

In the standard Smalltalk exception system, exceptions are represented as objects. Different kinds of exceptions are defined using different Smalltalk classes. Each exception class defines a default action that is performed upon occurrence of the exception if the programmer has not taken explicit action in anticipation of the exception.

The following are some commonly used exception classes; indentation indicates a subclass relationship:

`Error`	Any program error
`ZeroDivide`	Attempt to divide by zero
`MessageNotUnderstood`	Receiver of a message does not have method for it
`Notification`	An event that usually can be ignored
`Warning`	The user of the program should be informed

4.6.1. Exception Handlers

A programmer can do something other than the default action associated with an exception by associating an *exception handler* with the execution of a block. Exception handlers are established by sending the message `on:do:` to a block:

```
[x / y]
     on: ZeroDivide
     do: [:ex| Transcript show: 'zero divide detected'.]
```

This expression causes its receiver (the block containing `x / y`) to be evaluated as if the message value had been sent to it. If a `ZeroDivide` exception occurs while executing the block, the *handler block* (the argument `to do:`) is evaluated. In this example, the handler block causes a message to be displayed to the program user.

The handler block is passed a single argument (`ex` in this example), which is an instance of the actual class of exception that occurred. This object can be used to obtain additional information about the exception or to control what program action occurs when the exception block is completed. In many cases, the argument is not used and can be ignored.

An exception handler usually completes by returning the value of the handler block in place of the value of the receiver block. (Note that the previous example would return the value of the `show:` message.) If instead of displaying a message the programmer wanted to return the value `1` when a division by zero occurred, we would rewrite the previous expressions as follows:

```
[x / y] on: ZeroDivide do: [:ex| ex resume:1]
```

This might be used as follows:

```
fudgeFactor := [x / y] on: ZeroDivide do: [:ex|ex resume: 1].
```

If instead of returning a value we want to exit the current method, we can place an explicit return within the handler block:

```
fudgeFactor := [x / y] on: Error do: [:ex| ^'not computable'].
```

Note that in the last example, we specified `Error`, instead of `ZeroDivide`, as the exception to be handled. When we specify an exception to be handled, we are really saying that we want to handle the named exception and also any exceptions that are subclasses of the named exception. Because `ZeroDivide` is a subclass of `Error`, an attempt to divide by zero or any other error that occurs while evaluating `x / y` causes the enclosing method to return the string `'not computable'`.

An exception is signaled by sending the message signal to the class that defines the exception. For example, the following creates an error exception:

```
Error signal
```

If there is an active handler that deals with the `Error` exception, it will be executed. Otherwise, the default action for the exception will be executed. It is often useful to provide a textual description when signaling an exception. This is accomplished by sending the message `signal:` to an exception class:

```
Warning signal:  'the disk is almost full'
```

4.6.2. Exception Resumability

A handler block usually completes by executing the final statement of the block. The value of the final statement is then used as the value returned by the exception handler to the sender of the `on:do:` message. The *resumability* attribute of an exception determines whether a handler block can return control to the signaler of an exception. A *resumable exception* can return the message that signaled the exception. A *nonresumable* exception never returns to the signaler of the exception. For example, the following expression returns `5` as the value of the `on:do:` message:

```
([Error signal] on: Error do: [:ex| 5]) "returns 5 here"
```

The next expression returns `5` as the value of the signal message:

```
([Notification signal "returns 5 here"]
    on: Notification do: [:ex| ex resume: 5]).
```

Resumability is an attribute of an exception, not of the exception handler. An instance of an exception can be explicitly tested to determine whether it is resumable. This is accomplished by sending it the message `isResumable`. In the following example, the exception handler either returns `5` to the signaler or `10` from the `on:do:` message, depending on whether the exception class defines a resumable or nonresumable exception:

```
[someExceptionClass signal ] on: Error
     do: [:theException|
                  theException isResumable
                       ifTrue: [theException resume: 5]
                       ifFalse: [10]]
```

4.6.3. Methods of Exiting a Handler Block

Occasionally, it is desirable to conclude processing of a handler block before reaching the final statement of the blocks. This can be accomplished in several ways by sending appropriate messages to the argument of a handler block.

The message `exit:` causes its argument to be returned as if it were the value of the final statement of the handler blocks. The following two handlers have exactly the same behavior:

```
[Error signal] on: Error do: [:ex| 5].
[Error signal]
     on: Error
     do: [:theException| theException exit: 5].
```

The most common use of `exit:` is in a conditional expression of a complex handler block. If the argument of a handler block is a resumable exception, the message `resume:` can be used in place of `exit:`. It is an error to send `resume:` to a nonresumable exception. Doing so causes an exception to be signaled.

Another way to exit a handler block is with the `retry` message. This message terminates the handler block and retries the evaluation of the receiver of the `on:do:` block. Any `ensure:` or `ifCurtailed:` clean-up blocks created by the original evaluation of the receiver block or by the handler block are executed before the evaluation is retried:

```
[^ x / y]
     on: ZeroDivide
     do: [:ex|
          y := 0.000001. " make the divisor very small but > 0"
          ex retry]
```

The message `retryUsing:` is similar to `retry`, but instead of evaluating the original receiver block, the argument to `retryUsing:` is evaluated in its place:

```
[self doSomeTaskTheFastWay]
     on: LowMemory
     do: [:ex|
         ex retryUsing: [self  doSomeTaskTheSpaceEfficientWay]]
```

The occurrence of an exception most frequently causes Smalltalk to discard the block evaluation currently in progress. Sometimes a method does something that requires a subsequent action, regardless of whether an exception occurs. A good example is a method that places a lock on an external file. As long as the lock is in place, other users cannot access the file. Such a lock must be released even if an exception occurs. The following is an example of a method that might be written in a class that supports file access to implement such behavior:

```
whileLockedDo: aBlock
    "Lock the receiving file.  Process the argument block while the
    file is locked, then unlock the file.  Return the value of the
    argument block. Be sure to release the lock if an exception
    occurs."
    self lock.  "set the lock"
    ^aBlock ensure: [self unlock "clear the lock"]
```

When sent to a block, the message `ensure:` causes the receiver to be evaluated just as if the message value had been sent to the block. The value returned is the result of evaluating the receiver. The argument to the `ensure:` method is a block called the *clean-up block*. After evaluating the receiver, the clean-up block is also evaluated. The clean-up block is also automatically evaluated if for any reason the receiver block does not return normally. In particular, if an exception occurs while evaluating the receiver, the clean-up block is executed if the exception handler does not resume execution within the receiver block. Executing an explicit return that goes outside the receiver block is another situation that causes execution of the clean-up block. This is illustrated by the following example:

```
myFile whileLockedDo:
    [myFile atEnd
        ifTrue: [^nil]
        ifFalse: [myFile next]]
```

The clean-up block within `whileLockedDo:` is executed even if the argument block encounters an end of file and explicitly returns nil.

The message `ifCurtailed:` is similar to `ensure:`. Its receiver is a block and its argument is a clean-up block. The message `ifCurtailed:` differs in that its clean-up block is evaluated only if the receiver block does not complete normally.

4.7. Class Libraries and Protocols

We have now covered most of the essential features of the Smalltalk programming language. The language is quite simple and primarily provides a means for defining new classes of objects and for orchestrating message interaction between objects.

All Smalltalk systems include a large library of predefined classes. Familiarity with and use of these classes is a key part of successful Smalltalk programming. A Smalltalk program never starts out as a blank sheet of paper that the programmer fills with newly written classes. Instead, Smalltalk programmers start with the predefined class library and choose which of the classes can be reused to implement the current programming task.

Modern commercial Smalltalk development environments provide more than a thousand classes in their class libraries. Such libraries provide classes that support all aspects of modern applications, including graphical user interfaces, relational database access, and distributed computing. The standard Smalltalk class library consists of a subset of the classes found in such libraries. The class library of standard Smalltalk is focused on classes that have nearly universal applicability. This class library provides classes that are likely to be useful for all types of applications operating in any computing environment. In addition to the basic behavior for all objects, the areas of functionality addressed by the standard library include numeric computations, string manipulation, data collections and structures, and basic file I/O.

Smalltalk programmers generally do not need to be aware of the implementation details of a class in order to use it. Instead, Smalltalk programmers must understand the public behavior of a class's instances. We have seen how, through the use of polymorphism, different classes of objects can support identical behaviors. For these reasons, the standard Smalltalk class library is not defined as a strict implementation hierarchy of concrete classes. Instead, the standard Smalltalk class library is defined by sets of *protocols*. Informally, a protocol is a set of related messages that an object can support. Through the use of polymorphism, a particular protocol can be supported by many different classes, including classes that are not related through inheritance.

The definition of standard Smalltalk includes a notation for describing protocols. However, protocols are not a formal part of the Smalltalk programming language. Protocol specification can only occur embedded within comments in the text of a Smalltalk program.

A protocol is a named specification for a group of messages. A protocol specifies for each of its message selectors the function performed by the message. It also specifies what types of objects are allowed as arguments for each message and what type of object is returned as the result of the message. The types of argument and result objects are specified using protocol names and indicate that the argument or result must be an object that supports the named protocol.

The name of a protocol is one or more Smalltalk identifiers surrounded by angle brackets. Some valid protocol names include the following:

```
<Object>
<collection class>
<exceptionSignaler>
```

The individual messages in a protocol are each described by their *signature*. The signature of a message specifies a protocol that must be supported by each argument object and a protocol that is supported by the object returned by the message. The syntax of a signature specification is similar to the message pattern of a method. However, instead of argument names, a signature specifies the protocol name for each argument. A signature specifies the result type of a message with a return symbol (^) followed by the protocol name of the object returned by the message. Here are some signatures:

```
negated ^ <number>
& <boolean> ^ <boolean>
detect: <object> ifNone: <block0> ^ <object>
```

Some messages are used exclusively for their side effects. The result object is usually ignored for such messages and is excluded from its signature.

A protocol specification can also specify the names of one or more protocols to which the specified protocol is said to *conform*. Protocol conformance is essentially inheritance of signatures. If protocol `<a>` conforms to protocol `<b>`, then all message signatures of `<b>` are implicitly also part of protocol `<a>`. In addition, protocol `<a>` can refine the argument and result types and the semantic specification of any message signature from `<b>`.

As an introduction to the standard Smalltalk class library, the following section describes some of its most important protocols. These include the protocols that all objects support and the protocols for the most commonly used objects, such as numbers and boolean values. The following section also describes the principal protocols for collections, which are the objects most commonly used to create data structures. Some of the protocols that are not described include streams, which are used primarily for file access, and the protocols for objects representing dates and times. The descriptions of the protocols follow the terminology and structure developed for standard Smalltalk by the X3J20 committee. In a few cases, the protocols have been slightly simplified or abridged.

4.7.1. Protocols for Common Objects

The <Object> protocol specifies the messages that all Smalltalk objects support. The majority of messages in this protocol relate to comparing and testing objects. There are also messages for message sends with computed selectors and for producing textual descriptions of objects:

Protocol <Object>	
Messages:	
== <Object> ^ <boolean>	Tests for object identity
~~ <Object> ^ <boolean>	Negated test for object identity
= <Object> ^ <boolean>	Tests equality
~= <Object> ^ <boolean>	Negated test for equality
class ^ <classDescription>	Gets an object's class object
copy ^ <Object>	Creates a copy of an object
error: <string>	Signals that an error condition has been detected
hash ^ <integer>	Gets an object's equality hash code
identityHash ^ <integer>	Gets an object's identity hash code
isKindOf: <classDescription> ^<boolean>	Tests if within a class hierarchy
isMemberOf: <classDescription> ^ <boolean>	Tests whether an instance is of a particular class
isNil ^ <boolean>	Tests for nil
notNil ^ <boolean>	Performs a negated test for nil
perform: <selector>	Indicates a unary message send with computed selector
perform: <selector> with: <Object>	Indicates message send with computed selector
perform: <selector> with: <Object> with: <Object>	Indicates message send with computed selector
perform: <selector> withArguments: <Array>	Indicates message send with computed selector
printOn: <writeStream>	Writes textual description of an object to a stream
printString ^ <string>	Gets a textual description of an object
respondsTo: <selector> ^ <boolean>	Tests whether receiver's behavior includes a selector
yourself ^ <Object>	Indicates no-op, return the receiver

Identity is one of the fundamental traits of Smalltalk objects. Identity means that any two distinct objects can be distinguished from each other. The == message is used to test for object identity. == returns true if and only if its receiver and argument are the same object. The message `~~` is the logical negation of `==`. The messages `isNil` and `notNil` are short-hand tests for identity with the object `nil`:

```
a := Object new.
b := a.
a == b "test two references to the same object"
     ⇨ true
Object new == Object new "two new objects must be distinct"
     ⇨ false
a isNil    "a was a newly created object"
     ⇨ false
b := nil.
b notNil
     ⇨ false
```

In addition to testing for identity, two objects can also be tested for equality using the messages `=` and `~=`. Equality is a much more elusive concept than identity. In general, two objects are considered equal if they may be used interchangeably in most contexts. For example, it seems reasonable to consider two numeric objects that have the same mathematical value to be equal or two strings containing identical character sequences to be equal. For other classes, it is less obvious what should constitute a definition of equality. The default definition of equality implemented by class `Object` is to define equality the same as identity. Two objects are equal if they are the same object. Many classes refine this definition to provide more specific and useful meanings:

```
(3+4) = (3.0+4.0)
     ⇨ true
Object new ~= Object new
     ⇨ true
```

Hash tables are frequently used in the creation of Smalltalk data structures. The messages `hash` and `identityHash` both return integer values that can be used to index hash tables. If a hash table uses object identity (`==`) to distinguish elements, then `identityHash` is used as the hash function when indexing the table. If a hash table uses equality (`=`) to distinguish elements then `hash` is used as the hash function. Any two object that compare equal using the `=` message must return equal values for the `hash` message.

The message `copy` is used to create a new object that shares most essential characteristics with the receiver of the copied object. Like equality, the exact semantics of copying an object should be defined by each class. The default implementation that is inherited from class `Object` is to create a new object whose encapsulated state is the same as the receiver's.

The message `class` when sent to an instance of a class returns the class object for that class. Here's an example:

```
c := Customer new.
c class
    ⇒ Customer
```

The `isMemberOf:` message is used to determine if its receiver is an instance of a specific class. The `isKindOf:` message determines if its receiver is an instance of the argument class or an instance of any of the subclasses of the argument class. The message `respondsTo:` is used to determine if a message with the argument selector is included in the receiver's behavior:

```
c isMemberOf: Customer
    ⇒ true
c isMemberOf: Object
    ⇒ false
c isKindOf: Object "Customer is a subclass of Object"
    ⇒ true
c respondsTo: #respondsTo:
    ⇒ true
'abc' respondsTo: #customerNumber
    ⇒ false
```

The message `printString` is used to produce a string that contains a textual description of its receiver. The exact contents of the string is determined by the class of the receiver and some classes may provide elaborate descriptions of their instances. The description of an object, such as a number, that has a literal representation is the literal. The default description of other objects is to state that it is an instance of its class name. The message `printOn:` produces the same description as `printString`, but the description is appended to the `<writableStram>` argument:

```
Customer new printString
    ⇒ 'a Customer'
(3+4) printString
    ⇒ '7'
```

The message `yourself` simply returns its receiver. This message is most commonly used at the end of a sequence of cascaded messages to access the cascaded receiver. Here's an example:

```
a := (Array new: 2)
        at: 1 put: 'a';
        at: 2 put: 'b';
        yourself.
```

The protocol `<classDescription>` defines the essential behavior of all class objects. It is also the protocol supported by the object that is the result of sending the message `class` to any object. It primarily provides messages that identify a class's position in a class hierarchy. <classDescription> conforms to the <Object> protocol. Thus any object that conforms to <classDescription> also support all the messages specified in <Object>.

The protocol named <instantiator> defines the most common message for creating a new instance of a class. The standard class object with the global name Object conforms to <classDescription> and <instantiator>. Instances of Object conform to <Object>:

Protocol <classDescription>	Conforms to: <Object>
Messages:	
allSubclasses^<sequencedReadableCollection>	Returns all subclasses of a class
allSuperclasses^<sequencedReadableCollection>	Returns all superclasses of a class
name^<string>	Returns class name of the receiver class
subclasses^<sequencedReadableCollection>	Performs a negated test for equality
superclass^<classDescription>	Returns the immediate superclass

Protocol <instantiator>	
Messages:	
new^<Object>	Creates a new object

Protocol <Object class>	Conforms to: <Object>, <instantiator>

The message name is used to obtain a textual description of a <classDescription>. If the receiver is a class object (or the result of sending class to an instance of a class), the description is the global name of the class. If the receiver is the result of sending the message class to a class object, the description is the global name of the class followed by the word class:

```
Object name
    ⇒ 'Object'
Array class name
    ⇒ 'Array class'
```

Any <classDescription> identifies a position in the class hierarchy. The message superclass returns a <classDescription> of the class from which objects described by the receiver directly inherit. The message allSuperclasses returns a collection of all superclasses of the receiver. The message subclasses returns a list of all the immediate subclasses of a class while `allSubclasses` returns a collection of all classes that inherit from the receiver, either directly and indirectly:

```
Object superclass
    ⇒ nil "Object does not inherit from anything"
Object allSuperclasses
    ⇒ #( )    "an empty collection"
Customer superclass
    ⇒ Object
```

The protocol `<boolean>` specifies the behavior of the objects `true` and `false`. If defines the basic operations of boolean algebra as well as "short-circuited" boolean operations. `<boolean>` also defines the conditional execution messages. `<boolean>` conforms to `<Object>`, so all the `<Object>` message can also be sent to `<boolean>` objects:

Protocol `<boolean>`	Conforms to: `<Object>`
Messages:	
`& <boolean> ^ <boolean>`	Logical and
`| <boolean> ^ <boolean>`	Logical or
`and: <block0> ^ <boolean>`	Short-circuited and
`eqv: <boolean> ^ <boolean>`	Logical equivalence
`ifFalse: <block0> ^<Object>`	False conditional execution
`ifFalse: <block0> ifTrue: <block0> ^<Object>`	Reversed-order conditional
`ifTrue: <block0> ^<Object>`	True conditional
`ifTrue: <block0> ifFalse: <block0> ^<Object>`	Normal conditional
`not ^ <boolean>`	Logical negation
`or: <block0> ^ <boolean>`	Short-circuited and
`xor: <boolean> ^ <boolean>`	Exclusive or

The logical operations all have their conventional meanings. The conditional messages were explained earlier in the discussion of control structures. The short-circuited boolean operations make use of blocks to defer execution of their second arguments. The argument blocks should return `<boolean>` objects:

```
(a size >= 4) and: [(a at: 4) = something]
obj fastTestwithFalseNegatives  or: [obj slowerAcurateTest]
```

The instances of some classes represent ordered values. The protocol `<magnitude>` defines a set of messages for testing the ordering of such objects:

Protocol `<magnitude>`	Conforms to: `<Object>`
Messages:	
`< <magnitude> ^ <boolean>`	Tests whether receiver less than the argument
`<= <magnitude> ^ <boolean>`	Tests whether receiver less than or equal to the argument
`> <magnitude> ^ <boolean>`	Tests whether receiver is greater than the argument
`>= <magnitude> ^ <boolean>`	Tests whether receiver is greater than or equal to the argument
`between: <magnitude> and:`	Tests whether within a range
`<magnitude> ^ <boolean>` `max: <magnitude> ^ <magnitude>`	Determines the larger of the receiver and the argument
`min: <magnitude> ^ <magnitude>`	Determines the smaller of the receiver and the argument

Because `<magnitude>` conforms to `<object>`, any object that supports the `<magnitude>` protocol supports the messages `#=` and `#~=`. Classes of objects that polymorphically support the `<magnitude>` protocol include the numeric objects as well as characters. The receiver and argument of these messages must be comparable values. Any two numeric objects may be compared, even if they are instances of difference classes. Similarly, any two characters can be compared. However, a numeric object cannot be compared to a character object.

Character objects make up the individual elements of strings and can be expressed using character literals. Character objects conform to the protocol `<Character>`:

Protocol `<Character>`	Conforms to: `<magnitude>`
Messages:	
`asLowercase ^ <Character>`	If the receiver is an uppercase letter, returns its lowercase equivalent
`asString ^ <string>`	Creates a string object containing only the receiver
`asUppercase ^ <Character>`	If the receiver is a lowercase letter, returns its uppercase equivalent
`codePoint ^ <integer>`	Returns the encoding of the receiver in the implementation-dependent character set
`isAlphaNumeric ^ <boolean>`	Tests whether receiver is either a letter or a digit
`isDigit ^ <boolean>`	Tests whether the receiver is a numeric character
`isLetter ^ <boolean>`	Tests whether the receiver is an alphabetic character
`isLowercase ^ <boolean>`	Tests whether the receiver is a lowercase letter
`isUppercase ^ <boolean>`	Tests whether the receiver is an uppercase letter

Character objects represent individual entries in an implementation-dependent character set. ASCII and Unicode are the character sets most commonly used by Smalltalk implementations. The elements of a character set are integers that are called *code points*. The message codePoint, when sent to a character object, returns the corresponds code point. A character object that corresponds to a particular code point can be accessed by sending the message codePoint: to the class object named Character:

Protocol <Character class>	Conforms to: <classDescription>
Messages:	
codePoint: <integer> ^ <Character>	Returns the character object corresponding to a code point

Blocks were discussed in section 4.4. They are objects that represent Smalltalk code in a bound to a specific variable environment. The messages for all blocks are defined by <block>. The applicability of other messages depends on the number of arguments defined for the block:

Protocol <block>	Conforms to: <Object>
Messages:	
argumentCount^<integer>	Number of arguments required by the block
valuewithArguments: <Array>^<Object>	Evaluates the block using the arguments

Protocol <block0>	Conforms to: <block>
Messages:	
ensure: <block0> ^ <Object>	Evaluates the receiver, then the cleanup block
ifCurtailed: <block0> ^ <Object>	Evaluates the receiver protected by a cleanup block
on: <exceptionSelector> do: <block1> ^ <Object>	Evaluates the receiver in the context of an exception handler
value ^ <Object>	Evaluates the receiver
whileFalse	Repetitively evaluates the receiver until it returns true
whileFalse: <block0>	Repetitively evaluates the receiver until it returns true; after each evaluation, except the last, evaluates the argument
whileTrue	Repetitively evaluates the receiver until it returns false
whileTrue: <block0>	Repetitively evaluates the receiver until it returns false; after each evaluation except the last, evaluate the argument

Protocol `<block1>`	Conforms to: `<block>`
Messages:	
`value: <Object> ^ <Object>`	Evaluates the receiver

Protocol `<block2>`	Conforms to: `<block>`
Messages:	
`value: <Object> value: <Object> ^ <Object>`	Evaluates the receiver

Exception classes and exception object were discussed previously in the chapter. Exception classes conform to the protocol `<exceptionSelector>`, `whereas` their instances conform to `<signaledException>`. These protocols are not described here, but examples of their usage can be found section 4.6.

4.7.2. Numeric Protocols

Standard Smalltalk supports four basic types of numeric objects: integers, fractions, floating-point objects (also called *floats*), and scaled decimal objects. One or more classes can be used to implement each type of number. All numeric classes conform to the protocol `<number>`. Generally, the arguments to numeric messages can be instances of any class of number. Thus, mixed-mode arithmetic expressions are supported. When an arithmetic message involves different classes of numbers, the result is usually a number object of the more general type. The generality of the numeric types, in descending order is

Float

Scaled decimal

Fraction

Integer

Thus, an operation that involves a float and scaled decimal usually produces a floating-point result, and an operation involving a fraction and an integer usually produces a fraction as a result. Messages are also provided for the explicit conversion of numbers to the various numeric types:

Protocol <number>	Conforms to: <magnitude>
Messages:	
* <number> ^ <number>	Multiplication
+ <number> ^ <number>	Addition
- <number> ^ <number>	Subtraction
/ <number> ^ <number>	Division
// <number> ^ <integer>	Division truncated toward negative infinity
\\ <number> ^ <number>	Remainder of // division
abs ^ <number>	Absolute value
asFloat ^ <float>	Convert to floating point number
asFraction ^ <fraction>	Convert to fraction number
asInteger ^ <integer>	Convert to integer number (rounded)
asScaledDecimal ^ <scaledDecimal>	Convert to scaled decimal number
ceiling ^ <integer>	Smallest integer >= receiver
floor ^ <integer>	Largest integer <= receiver
negated ^ <number>	Negation
negative ^ <boolean>	Tests whether receiver is less than 0
positive ^ <boolean>	Tests whether receiver is greater than or equal to 0
quo: <number> ^ <integer>	Division truncated toward zero
raisedToInteger: <integer> ^ <number>	Receiver raised to the argument power
reciprocal ^ <number>	1 divided by the receiver
rem: <number> ^ <number>	Remainder of rem: division
rounded ^ <integer>	Round receiver to nearest integer
roundedTo: <number> ^ <number>	Round to nearest multiple of argument
sign ^ <integer>	Encode receiver's sign as an integer (-1,0,+1)
sqrt ^ <float>	Positive square root
squared ^ <number>	Square of the receiver
strictlyPositive ^ <boolean>	Tests whether receiver is greater than zero
to: <number> ^ <Interval>	Creates an interval whose step is one
to: <number> by: <number> ^ <Interval>	Creates an interval
to: <number> by: <number> do: <block1> ^ <Object>	Evaluates block for each member of an interval
to: <number> do: <block1> ^ <Object>	Evaluates block for each member of an interval
truncated ^ <integer>	Truncates to nearest integer toward zero
truncateTo: <number> ^ <number>	Truncates to a multiple of the argument

Integers have arbitrary precision. The number of digits in an integer object is limited only by the available memory of the computer. It is common for a Smalltalk implementation to use several different classes and encodings for integer objects, depending on the size and sign of the integer value. Regardless of their class, bit manipulation operations are valid only for positive integers and operate as if their values were encoded using binary notation. All integer classes conform to the protocol `<integer>`:

Protocol `<integer>`	Conforms to: `<number>`
Messages:	
`allMask: <integer> ^ <boolean>`	Tests if all masked bits are set
`anyMask: <integer> ^ <boolean>`	Tests if any masked bit is set
`bitAnd: <integer> ^ <integer>`	Bitwise logical and
`bitAt: <integer> ^ <integer>`	Value of bit at the indexed position
`bitOr: <integer> ^ <integer>`	Bitwise logical or
`bitShift: <integer> ^ <integer>`	Shifts the bits right or left
`bitXor: <integer> ^ <integer>`	Bitwise logical exclusive or
`clearBit: <integer> ^ <integer>`	Clears the bit at the indexed position
`even ^ <boolean>`	Tests if evenly divisible by 2
`factorial ^ <integer>`	Computes factorial of the receiver
`gcd: <integer> ^ <integer>`	Computes greatest common divisor
`highBit ^ <integer>`	Index position of most significant non-zero bit
`isBitSet: <integer> ^ <boolean>`	Tests state of bit at the indexed position
`lcm: <integer> ^ <integer>`	Computes least common multiple
`noMask: <integer> ^ <boolean>`	Tests if no masked bits are set
`odd ^ <boolean>`	Tests if not evenly divisible by 2
`printOn: <writeStream> base: <integer>`	Writes text of number to a stream in a specified base
`printStringRadix: <integer>`	Returns the text of number in specified base

Because `<integer>` conforms to `<number>`, all the arithmetic messages are available for integer objects. When an arithmetic message is sent to an integer receiver and has an integer argument, the resulting value is also an integer object in all cases except for the `#/` message. If the receiver is evenly divisible by the argument, the result is an integer, but if the receiver is not evenly divisible, the result is a fraction object:

```
8 / 4
    ⇒ 2
4 / 8
    ⇒ (1/2)    "a fraction"
```

A fraction object is an exact representation of a rational number. It is characterized by its numerator and denominator. Fraction objects implement the protocol `<fraction>`:

Protocol `<fraction>`	Conforms to: `<number>`
Messages:	
`denominator ^ <integer>`	Returns the fraction's denominator
`numerator ^ <integer>`	Returns the fraction's numerator

The arithmetic message, when used with fractions or with an integer and a fraction, produces a fraction as a result unless the denominator of the result would be 1. In this case, the result is an integer. Unlike floating-point numbers, calculation using fractions is always exact. Here's an example:

```
(1/3)+(1/3)
     ⇨ (2/3)
(1.0/3.0)+(1.0/3.0)
     ⇨ 0.666667
```

A floating-point object is a limited-precision approximation of a real number. Floating-point objects may have limited precision, and they may also have a performance advantage because they are typically implemented using hardware floating-point operations. A standard Smalltalk implementation may provide classes that implement several different precisions for floating-point numbers. All floating-point classes conform to the protocol `<float>`. `<float>` defines messages that support the common mathematical functions:

Protocol `<float>`	Conforms to: `<realNumber>`
Messages:	
`arcCos ^ <float>`	Inverse cosine of receiver
`arcSin ^ <float>`	Inverse sine of receiver
`arcTan ^ <float>`	Inverse tangent of receiver
`cos ^ <float>`	Cosine in radian of receiver
`degreesToRadians ^ <float>`	Convert from degrees to radians
`exp ^ <float>`	Exponential function of receiver
`fractionPart ^ <float>`	Fractional part of the receiver
`floorLog: <number> ^ <integer>`	Largest integer ≤ log (receiver) to the argument base
`integerPart ^ <float>`	Integer part of the receiver
`ln ^ <float>`	Natural logarithm of receiver
`log: <number> ^ <float>`	Logarithm to the argument base of the receiver
`radiansToDegrees ^ <float>`	Converts from radians to degrees
`raisedTo: <number> ^ <float>`	Receiver raised to the argument power
`sin ^ <float>`	Sine in radian of receiver
`tan ^ <float>`	Tangent of receiver in radians

Standard Smalltalk allows for an implementation to have up to three different precisions of floating-point number objects. The precision of a floating-point literal is specified by the exponent character in the literal. Valid exponent characters are `e`, `d`, and `q`. Here's an example:

```
1.234e3
3.1415926535898d0
6.9314718055994530941723212145817657q-1
```

Standard Smalltalk does not specify the actual precision of floating-point objects, nor does it require that an implementation support multiple floating-point precisions. However, it does specify that if an implementation supports multiple precisions, then the following rule must be followed:

precision(`e`)<precision(`d`)<precision(`q`)

Scaled decimal numbers have arbitrary precision to the left of the decimal point and limited precision to the right of the decimal point. The number of decimal digits to the right of the decimal point is called the *scale* of the number. Scaled decimal numbers are particularly useful for representing currency amounts:

Protocol `<scaledDecimal>`	Conforms to: `<number>`
Messages:	
`fractionPart ^ <scaledDecimal>`	Fractional part of the receiver
`integerPart ^ <scaledDecimal>`	Integer part of the receiver
`scale ^ <integer>`	Number of digits to the right of the decimal, including trailing 0s
`significantDigits ^ <integer>`	Total digits to right and left of decimal point

Scaled decimal literals are decimal numbers followed by the letter `s`. The `s` may be followed by decimal digits that specify an explicit scale for the number. Here's an example:

```
12s   "scale is 0"
12.34s "scale is 2"
12.34s4 "12.3400 scale is 4"
```

4.7.3. Collection Protocols

Almost all programs have the need to organize data into aggregates or data structures. Smalltalk provides a rich set of classes, called the *collection classes*, that support the organization of data. The core collection classes are `Array`, `Bag`, `ByteArray`, `Dictionary`, `Interval`, `OrderedCollection`, `Set`,

`SortedCollection`, and `String`. Each of these classes has specific distinguishing characteristics:

- `Array`—Fixed size, accessed via numeric indexes.
- `Bag`—Variable size, unordered elements, may have duplicate elements, accessed by element value.
- `ByteArray`—Fixed size, accessed via numeric indexes, elements are integers in the range 0–255.
- `Dictionary`—Variable size, keyed access, unordered.
- `Interval`—Fixed size, accessed via numeric index, numeric elements in an arithmetic progression.
- `OrderedCollection`—Variable size, ordered, extensible at either end, accessed via numeric index.
- `Set`—Variable size, unordered, no duplicate elements, accessed by element value.
- `SortedCollection`—Variable sized, ordered by sort function, accessed via numeric index.
- `String`—Fixed size, accessed via numeric indexes, elements must be character objects.

Generally, collections are heterogeneous. The elements they store may be any class of object and the elements of an individual collection may be of different classes. `ByteArray`, `Interval`, and `String` are exceptions in that their elements are restricted to types of objects.

All types of collections except intervals may be created using the protocol named `<collection class>`:

Protocol `<collection class>`	Conforms to: `<Object class>`
Messages:	
`new: <integer> ^ <collection>`	Creates a new collection big enough to hold the specified number of elements

The message `new:` sent to a collection class object creates a new instance of the class that is capable of holding at least the number of elements specified by the argument. Here's an example:

```
a := Array new: 10.
s := Set new: 256.
t := SortedCollection new:15.
a size
    ⇒ 10
t size
    ⇒ 0
```

Instances of `Array`, `ByteArray`, and `String` have a fixed size that is specified when the collection is created. The array created in the above expression will have exactly 10 elements, each of which will initially contain the value `nil`. Most other types of collections may be dynamically sized. For these collections, the message `new:` creates an empty collection. That is why the message `size` sent to `t` in the above expression returns `0`. The newly created `SortedCollection` is empty. For this type of collection the argument to `new:` is used to specify an anticipated number of elements that will be stored in the collection. This may be used to optimize the internal representation of the collection instance.

Because `<collection class>` conforms to `<Object class>`, objects that support this protocol also implement the message `new`. When the message `new` is sent to a collection class object, a new empty collection is created. Instances of `Array`, `ByteArray`, and `String` have a fixed size of zero elements:

```
OrderedCollection new.
Dictionary new.
String new.     "A null String has not elements"
```

All types of collection class objects except for dictionaries and intervals also implement the protocol `<initializeableCollection class>`. This protocol provides messages that create new collection instances that are initialized to contain specific elements:

Protocol `<initializeableCollection class>`	Conforms to: `<collection class>`
Messages:	
`with: <Object> ^ <collection>`	Creates a new collection initialized with 1 element
`with: <Object> with: <Object> ^ <collection>`	Creates a new collection initialized with 2 elements
`with: <Object> with: <Object> with: <Object> ^ <collection>`	Creates a new collection initialized with 3 elements
`with: <Object> with: <Object> with: <Object> with: <Object> with: <Object> ^ <collection>`	Creates a new collection initialized with 4 elements
`withAll: <collection> ^ <collection>`	Creates a new collection initialized with the elements of the argument collection

The `with:` messages create new collections that are instances of the receiver class and that contain the arguments as their elements. Here's an example:

```
a := Array with: Customer new.
o := OrderedCollection with: 'abc' with: 'def'.
```

The message withAll: creates a new collection containing the same elements as an argument collection. The class of the argument collection need not be the same as that of the new collection:

```
noDups := Set withAll: #('xyz' 'abc' 'qwer' 'abc').
ordered := SortedCollection withAll: noDups.
Array withAll: ordered
     ⇒ #('abc' 'qwer' xyz')
```

This example uses withAll: messages along with different collection classes to produce an ordered array of strings with duplicates eliminated. The first line creates a Set whose contents is initialized from a literal array of string objects. Because instances of Set do not have duplicate elements one of the 'abc' strings is discarded. The second line creates a SortedCollection from the contents of the Set. The SortedCollection uses the default sort function, which sorts the strings into ascending order. Finally, the last expression creates an array whose contents are the sorted strings from the SortedCollection.

Dictionaries do not implement the <initializeableCollection class> protocol because they require the association of a key with each element. <SortedCollection class> extents the protocol of <initializeableCollection class> to allow the explicit specification of a sort function for the collection.

Protocol <SortedCollection class>	Conforms to: <initializeableCollection class>
Messages:	
sortBlock: <block2> ^ <SortedCollection>	Creates an empty SortedCollection that uses the specified sort block

The message sortBlock: is used to specify a function for ordering elements as they are added to the collection. The function is specified using a block, called a *sort block*. The block must be a two-argument block that returns a boolean object. For example, a SortedCollection that orders its elements in descending order of their sizes would be created using

```
SortedCollection sortBlock: [:e1 :e2| e1 size > e2 size]
```

A sort block should be defined such that it returns true if the object passed as its first argument should come before the argument passed as the second argument. If a SortedCollection is created without the explicit specification of a sort block, then the following default sort block is used:

```
[:e1 :e2| e1 < e2]
```

This block will result in the elements being sorted in ascending order, as defined for them using the < message.

All collection objects share a fundamental set of messages, regardless of their class or how they were created. The protocol <collection> defines this set of messages:

Protocol <collection>	Conforms to: <Object>
Messages:	
asArray ^ <Array>	Returns an Array containing the receiver's contents
asBag ^ <Bag>	Returns a Bag containing the receiver's contents
asOrderedCollection ^ <OrderedCollection>	Returns a OrderedCollection containing the receiver's contents
asSet ^ <Set>	Returns a Set containing the receiver's contents
asSortedCollection ^ <SortedCollection>	Returns a SortedCollection containing the receiver's contents
asSortedCollection: <block2> ^<SortedCollection>	Returns a SortedCollection containing the receiver's contents, using the argument block to specify the sort order
collect: <block1> ^ <collection>	Returns a new collection that is the result of applying the argument block to each element of the receiver
detect: <block1> ^ <Object>	Returns an element of the receiver for which the argument block evaluates to true
detect: <block1> ifNone: <block0> ^ <Object>	Returns an element of the receiver for which the first argument evaluates to true: if there are none, evaluates the second block
do: <block1>	Evaluates the argument block for each element of the receiver
includes: <Object> ^ <boolean>	Tests if any element of the receiver equals the argument
inject: <Object> into: <block2> ^ <Object>	Evaluates the argument block using each element and the succeeding result; returns the final value
isEmpty ^ <boolean>	Tests if the receiver contains no elements
notEmpty ^ <boolean>	Performs an inverted test whether receiver contains no elements
occurencesOf: <Object> ^ <integer>	Determines how many elements equal the argument
reject: <block1> ^ <collection>	Returns a new collection containing the elements of the receiver for which the argument block evaluates to false
select: <block1> ^ <collection>	Returns a new collection containing the elements of the receiver for which the argument block evaluates to true
size ^ <integer>	Returns the number of elements in the receiver

The protocol <collection> defines three groups of messages: conversion messages, query messages, and mapping messages. The conversion messages all have selectors that begin with the characters as. They are used to create different types of collection that contains the same elements as the receiver of the message. They are also used to guarantee that a collection is of a particular type. For example, a method that is willing to accept any type of collection as an argument but that needs to use an array for its internal processing might begin like this:

```
someComputationOn: aCollection
    |tempCollection|
    tempCollection := aCollection asArray.
    "the rest of the method uses"
    ...
```

The conversion messages do not necessarily create a new object. If the receiver of a conversion message is already an instance of the class that is the target of the conversion, the receiver may be returned as the value of the message. In the preceding example, if the object that is the value of aCollection is already an array, then that same object may be returned from asArray and assigned to tempCollection. If a program requires the creation of a new object, then it should either use the copy message or the withAll: class message instead of one of the conversion messages.

The message asSortedCollection: allows the specification of a sort block for the SortedCollection. This sort block contains the elements of the receiver collection; asSortedCollection uses the default sort block.

The query messages provide information about the contents of the collection. For example, size, isEmpty, and notEmpty provide information on the number of elements in a collection. The message includes: is used to determine whether a particular object is in a collection, and occurencesOf: is used to determine how many times a particular object is in a collection. These messages and most other messages that test for particular objects within collections use the message = to compare objects. For the purposes of these messages, any two objects that answer true when compared using = are considered equivalent:

```
#( 1 1.0 1.000s) occurencesOf: 2/2
    ⇒ 3    "These different number objects are all = to 2/2"
```

Most of the mapping messages are discussed in section 4.4. One additional mapping message is inject:into:. This message evaluates a block for each element of a collection while permitting a value to be passed from the evaluation for one element to the evaluation for the next element. For example, this expression will return the total length of all the strings in the receiver collection:

```
#('abc' 'a string' 'qwer')
        inject: 0 into: [:subtotal :element | subtotal + element size]
          ⇒ 15
```

When this expression is executed, the block is first evaluated with `0` (the `inject:` argument) as its first argument and `'abc'` as its second argument. The block computes the size of `'abc'`, adds it to `0`, and returns `3` as the result of the block. `3` is then passed as the first argument of the second evaluation of the block, and `'a string'` is passed as the second argument. This computes `11`, which is returned from the block and passed to the next block evaluation, along with `'qwer'`. This time `15` is returned and because all the elements of the receiver have been exhausted, that value is returned as the result of the `inject:into:` message.

Although `<collection>` provides messages for iterating over the elements of a collection, it does not provide any messages for adding, removing, or accessing individual objects in a collection. This is because the applicability of these operations and the appropriate messages for performing them depends on the characteristics of the collection. Several different protocols are used to define these sets of messages.

The protocol `<extensibleCollection>` defines the messages that can be used to add and remove elements from non-keyed, variable-sized collection:

Protocol `<extensibleCollection>`	Conforms to: `<collection>`
Messages:	
`add: <Object>`	Adds the argument to the receiver
`addAll: <collection>`	Adds all elements of the argument to the receiver
`remove: <Object> ^ <Object>`	Removes the argument from the receiver
`remove: <Object> ifAbsent: <block0>^ <Object>`	Removes the argument from the receiver or evaluate the block
`removeAll: <collection>`	Removes all elements of the argument from the receiver

Instances of `Bag`, `Set`, `OrderedCollection`, and `SortedCollection` all support the `<extensibleCollection>` protocol. The message `add:` is used to add individual elements, and addAll: is used to add a group of elements. How the elements are processed by the collection depends on the class of the collection. The remove: messages deletes objects from collections. Here's an example:

```
b := Bag new.
b addAll: #( 6 4 2 2 4 6).
^b
     ⇒ Bag(2 2 4 4 6 6) "ordering is implementation dependent"
s := Set new.
s addAll: #( 6 4 2 2 4 6).
^s
     ⇒ Set(2 4 6) "ordering is implementation dependent"
b remove: 4.0
     ⇒ Bag(2 2 4 6 6)
```

How the elements are processed by the collection depends on the class of the collection. Adding duplicate elements to a Bag adds the elements, whereas adding them to a Set ignores the duplicates. Objects are selected using = as an equality test. In the last example, the integer object 4 is removed from the Bag because it compares equal to the floating-point object 4.0.

Set and Bag are classes whose protocols conform precisely to <extensibleCollection>:

Protocol <Bag>	Conforms to: <extensibleCollection>

Protocol <Set>	Conforms to: <extensibleCollection>

Both Bag and Set are unordered collections, which means that there is no natural ordering of their elements. Any observed ordering is an implementation artifact on which programmers should not depend. Bag and Set differ only in how they deal with duplicate elements. Interestingly, Set does not provide protocols for set theoretic operations and does not have messages for union, intersection, or other functions on mathematical sets.

Dictionaries are also unordered collections. Dictionaries differ from bags and sets in that each element of a dictionary has an associated *key* that identifies it. The key is an object that is associated with an element when it is added to a dictionary and is used to subsequently access or delete the element. <abstractDictionary> defines the common protocol for all dictionaries:

Protocol `<abstractDictionary>`	Conforms to: `<Collection>`
Messages:	
`addAll: <abstractDictionary>`	Adds each key/value pair in the argument to the receiver
`at: <Object> ^ <Object>`	Returns the value associated with the argument key
`at: <Object> ifAbsent: <block0> ^ <Object>`	Returns the value associated with the argument key; if there is no such key in the collection, evaluates the block
`at: <Object> ifAbsentPut: <block0> ^ <Object>`	Returns the value associated with the argument key; if there is no such key, evaluates the block and puts it into the dictionary using the key
`at: <Object> put: <Object> ^ <Object>`	The second argument is stored using the first argument as its key
`includesKey: <Object> ^ <boolean>`	Tests if the receiver contains an element with this key
`keyAtValue: <Object> ^ <Object>`	If the argument is an element of the dictionary, returns its key
`keyAtValue: <Object> ifAbsent: <block0> ^ <Object>`	If the argument is an element of the dictionary, returns its key; if not, evaluates the block and returns its value
`keys ^ <collection>`	Returns a collection containing all the keys in the receiver
`keysAndValuesDo: <block2>`	The argument is a two-argument block; for each element of the receiver, evaluates the block using its key as the first argument and the element as the second's argument
`keysDo: <block1>`	Evaluates the block using each key as its argument
`removeKey: <Object> ^ <Object>`	Removes the element whose key is the argument
`removeKey: <Object> ifAbsent: <block0> ^ <Object>`	Removes the element whose key is the argument; if no such key exists, evaluates the block
`values ^ <collection>`	Returns a collection of all elements in the receiver

Elements are normally added to a dictionary using the message `at:put:`. The argument for the `at:` keyword is the key, and the argument for the `put:` keyword is the element that is associated with the key. Elements are retrieved using the `at:` message and a key. The message `includesKey:` can be used to test whether the collection includes an element with a specific key. Elements are removed using `removeKey:`:

```
d := Dictionary new.
obj := Object new.
d at: 'abc' put: 'xyz'. "keys and value may be any class of objects"
d at: 123 put: #('one' 'two' 'three').
d at: obj: put: [self doIt].        "even blocks may be stored"
s size
    ⇨ 3
d includes: obj
    ⇨ true
d includes: Object new
    ⇨ false        "not the same key as used earlier"
d removeKey: obj.
d size
    ⇨ 2
```

Standard Smalltalk defines two specific classes of dictionaries: `Dictionary` and `IdentityDictionary`. Their behavior differs only in the manner in which they compare keys. An instance of `Dictionary` considers two objects to be the same key if an `=` comparison of the objects returns `true`. An instance of `IdentityDictionary` uses `==` to compare keys:

```
normalDictionary := Dictionary new.
identityDictionary := IdentityDictionary new.
identityDictionary
    at: 1 put: 'integer';
    at: 1.0 put: 'float';
    at: 1s put: 'scaled'.
 identityDictionary size
    ⇨ 3
normalDictionary addAll: identityDictionary.
normalDictionary size
    ⇨ 1
```

In this example, three different number objects, each with a value equal to `1`, are first used as keys to `IdentityDictionary`. Because `IdentityDictionary` uses object identity to distinguish keys, the three objects are three different keys. `IdentityDictionary` has three elements. These keys and elements are then added to an instance of `Dictionary` that uses equality to distinguish keys. Because the three numeric objects all compare as equal to one another, they are considered the same key. Each element that is added replaces the preceding element with the same key, and ultimately the dictionary contains only one element.

Whereas dictionaries are unordered and their elements are accessed using arbitrary objects as keys, several other types of collections impose an ordering on their elements and allow access to elements by their ordinal position. In essence, the integer ordinal position, or *index,* of an element serves as a key for accessing the element. Such collections are sometimes referred to as *indexable collections*. The root protocol for indexable collections is named <sequencedReadableCollection>. Several commonly used classes including arrays and strings support this protocol:

Protocol <sequencedReadableCollection> abbreviated <sRC>	Conforms to: <collection>
Messages:	
<sRC> ^ <sRC>	Concatenates collections
after: <Object> ^ <Object>	Returns the element that follows the argument element
at: <integer> ^ <Object>	Returns the element at the position specified by the argument
before: <Object> ^ <Object>	Returns the element that precedes the argument element
copyFrom: <integer> to: <integer> ^ <sRC>	Creates a new collection from a subsequence of elements
copyReplaceAll: <sRC> with: <sRC> ^ <sRC>	Creates a new collection with one subsequence replaced by another
copyReplaceFrom: <integer> to: <integer> with: <sRC> ^ <sRC>	Creates a new collection from the receiver with a subsequence of elements replaced from another collection
copyReplaceFrom: <integer> to: <integer> withObject: <Object> ^ <sRC>	Creates a new collection from the receiver with a subsequence of elements replaced with a specific object
copyWith: <Object> ^ <sRC>	Copies receiver with the argument appended
copyWithout: <Object> ^ <sRC>	Copies receiver without any elements equal to the argument
findFirst: <block1> ^ index	Index of first element for which the block evaluates to true
findLast: <block1> ^ index	Index of last element for which the block evaluates to true
first ^ <Object>	Retrieves the first element of the collection
indexOf: <Object> ^ <number>	Index of first element equal to argument
indexOf: <Object> ifAbsent: <block0> ^ <number>	Index of first element equal to argument; evaluates block if none
indexOfSubCollection: <sRC> startingAt: <integer> ^ <number>	Starting at the specified position find the index of the first subsequence that is equal to the argument collection
indexOfSubCollection: <sRC> startingAt: <integer> ifAbsent: <block0> ^ <number>	Starting at the specified position find the index of the first subsequence that is equal to the argument collection; if not found, evaluates the argument block
last ^ <Object>	Retrieves the last element of the collection
reverse ^ <sRC>	Creates a new collection with the receiver's elements reversed
reverseDo: <block1>	In reverse order, evaluates the block for each receiver element
with: <sRC> do: <block2>	Evaluates the block using pairs of elements from the receiver and argument collections

The basic message for accessing an element according to its position is `at:`. The numbering of element position starts at 1:

```
#('alpha' 'beta' 'gamma') at: 2
     ⇨ 'beta'
'abcdefghijklmnopqrstuvwxyz' at: 14
     ⇨ $n
```

The first and last elements may be directly requested. Elements can be accessed based on the location relative to other elements or based on search criteria specified using a block:

```
'abcdefghijklmnopqrstuvwxyz' last
     ⇨ $z
#('alpha' 'beta' 'gamma') before: 'gamma'
     ⇨ 'beta'
#('alpha' 'beta' 'gamma') findFirst: [:elem| elem size = 5]
     ⇨ 'alpha'
#('alpha' 'beta' 'gamma') findLast: [:elem| elem size = 5]
     ⇨ 'gamma'
```

The `index of` messages support searching for the index position of specific objects or subsequences of objects. If the desired object or subsequence is not found, an index of `0` is returned. Alternative forms allow the specification of a block that is evaluated if the search is not successful:

```
#('alpha' 'beta' 'gamma') indexOf: 'gamma' startingAt: 1
     ⇨ 3
#('alpha' 'beta' 'gamma') indexOf: 'alpha startingAt: 2
     ⇨ 0
'abcdefghijklmnopqrstuvwxyz'
         indexOfSubCollection: 'xyz'
         startingAt: 1
         ifAbsent: [self error: 'not found']
     ⇨ 24
```

The comma binary selector is used to concatenate one named `<sequencedReadableCollection>` with another, producing a new collection. `copyFrom:to:` is used to create a new collection containing a subsequence of the values. `reverse` creates a new collection of the elements in reverse order:

```
'abc' , '123'
     ⇨ 'abc123'
'abc123' copyFrom: 2 to: 5
     ⇨ 'bc12'
#('alpha' 'beta' 'gamma') reverse
     ⇨ #('gamma' 'beta' 'alpha')
```

The messages `copyWith:` is used to create a new collection that appends a single element. `copyWithout:` copies the elements of its receiver to a new collection and excludes a particular element. `copyReplaceFrom:to:with:` makes a copy while replacing a specific subsequence, and `copyReplaceAll:with:` makes a copy that replaces one subsequence of elements with another:

```
#('alpha' 'beta' 'gamma') copyWith: 'delta'
    ⇒ #('alpha' 'beta' 'gamma' 'delta')
'remove blanks from this string' copyWithout: Character blank
    ⇒ 'removeblanksfromthisstring'
'abc123' copyReplaceFrom: 2 to: 5 with: 'XX'
    ⇒ 'aXX3'
', <sequenceReadableCollection> ^  <sequenceReadableCollection>'
        copyReplaceAll: '<sequenceReadableCollection>'
        with: '<sRC>'
    ⇒ ', <sRC> ^ <sRC>'
```

`<sequencedReadableCollection>` defines several additional iteration messages in addition to the iterators defined by `<collection>`. `reverseDo:` operates just like `do:`, but the elements are processed in reverse order. `with:do:` is used to iterative over corresponding elements of two equal-sized collections:

```
#('cut' 'copy' 'paste')
        with: #(#cut #copy #paste)
        do: [:label :selector |
            label = selectedLabel ifTrue: [^self perform: selector]]
```

Some indexable collections such as literal arrays are read-only and support only the `<sequencedReadableCollection>` protocol. Most indexable collections, however, can be written to and modified in place. The `<sequencedReadableCollection>` protocol (abbreviated as `<sC>`) is extended by the protocol `<sequencedCollection>` with the messages that can be used to modify the state of such collections:

Protocol `<sequencedReadableCollection>` abbreviated `<sC>`	Conforms to: `<collection>`
Messages:	
`at: <integer> put: <Object> ^ <Object>`	Replaces the element at the specified index with the argument object
`atAll: <collection> put: <Object> ^ <sC>`	Replaces all the elements whose indices are specified by the argument collection with the argument object
`atAllPut: <Object> ^ <sC>`	Replaces all elements of the receiver with the argument
`replaceFrom: <integer> to: <integer> with: <sRC> ^ <sC>`	Replaces the identified subsequence of the receiver with the elements of the argument collection
`replaceFrom: <integer> to: <integer> with: <sRC> startingAt: <integer> ^ <sC>`	Replaces the identified subsequence of the receiver with the elements of the argument collection starting at a specified index
`replaceFrom: <integer> to: <integer> withObject: <Object> ^ <sC>`	Replaces each element of the identified subsequence of the receiver with the argument object

We have already seen an example of the use of the at:put: message to insert elements into arrays. atAll:put: is used to store a single value at multiple indices, and atAllPut: stores a single value at all indices:

```
a := Array withAll: #(1 2 3 4 5 6).
a atAll: #(2 4) put: 'inserted'.
    ⇒ Array(1 'inserted' 3 'inserted' 5 6)
(String new: 5) atAllPut: $x
    ⇒ 'xxxxx'
```

The replace messages work much like the corresponding copyReplace message defined by <sequencedReadableCollection> except that instead of creating a new collection with substituted elements, they update the receiver collection in place.

Array and ByteArray are classes whose protocols conform to <sequencedCollection>. They differ only in the type of objects that may be stored as their elements. The elements of Array may be any object, whereas the elements of ByteArray are restricted to integer objects whose values are in the range of 0 to 255. Array literals are not modifiable, so they conform to <sequencedReadableCollection>. Interval is a class whose elements are numbers that form an arithmetic progression:

Protocol <Array>	Conforms to: <sequencedCollection>

Protocol <ByteArray>	Conforms to: <sequencedCollection>

Protocol <Interval>	Conforms to: <sequencedReadableCollection>

Strings are indexable collections whose elements are restricted to being character objects. Most of the unique behavior of strings is defined in the protocol <readableString>. One of the important characteristics of strings is that they may be ordered according to an implementation-dependent collating sequence. Therefore, <readableString> conforms to <magnitude> as well as <sequencedReadableCollection>:

Protocol <readableString>	Conforms to: <sequencedReadableCollection>, <magnitude>
Messages:	
asLowercase ^ <String>	Creates a new string with all uppercase letters converted to lowercase
asString ^ <String>	Returns an instance of String containing the same characters as the receiver
asSymbol ^ <Symbol>	Returns an instance of Symbol containing the same characters as the receiver
asUppercase ^ <String>	Creates a new string with all lowercase letters converted to uppercase
match:<readableString> ^ <boolean>	Tests if the string pattern argument matches the receiver
sameAs: <readableString> ^ <boolean>	Tests if the receiver and argument are identical except for case differences

The messages asLowercase and asUppercase are used to produce new strings containing the same characters except for case conversions. Except for = and ~=, the magnitude comparison operations (<, <=, >, >=) perform case-insensitive comparisons. The message sameAs: is used to perform an equality test for strings that ignores case differences. The argument to the message match: is a pattern for a simple regular expression pattern matcher. The message returns true or false, depending on whether the receiver matches the pattern. The character # in the pattern matches any single character, and the character * matches any sequence of zero or more characters. Case differences are ignored when matching patterns:

```
'This Is A Test' asLowercase
    ⇒ 'this is a test'
'this is a test'
    ⇒ 'THIS IS A TEST'
'This Is A Test' = 'this is a test'
    ⇒ false
'This Is A Test' sameAs: 'this is a test'
    ⇒ true
'This Is A Test' match: '#his*tes#'
    ⇒ true
```

Symbol is a special class of strings that has a single unique instance for each possible sequence of characters. This allows object identity to be used to test whether two symbol values are equal. A special literal syntax is used for to symbols. A symbol literal is a quoted string preceded by a hash symbol (#). Although Smalltalk does not require symbol literals, most implementations also treat message selectors as symbols:

```
str1 := String withAll: 'abc'.
str2 := String withAll: 'abc'. "make two distinct strings"
str1 == str2
     ⇨ false
str1 asSymbol == #'abc' "a literal symbol"
     ⇨ true
str1 asSymbol = str2 asSymbol "identity test performed"
     ⇨ true
```

String literals conform to the protocol of `<readableString>`. Symbol literals and dynamically created symbols conform to `<Symbol>`, which is a refinement of `<readableString>`. All other strings (which are all mutable strings) conform to `<String>`, which is a refinement of both `<readableString>` and `<sequencedCollection>`:

Protocol `<Symbol>`	Conforms to: `<readableString>`

Protocol `<String>`	Conforms to: `<readableString> <sequencedCollection>`

Arrays, strings, and intervals are indexable but are also fixed size. When one of these objects is created, the number of elements it contains is unchangeable. The remaining types of collections are also indexable, but their sizes may change dynamically. The protocol `<sequencedContractibleCollection>` defines the behavior for indexable collections from which elements may be removed:

Protocol `<sequencedContractibleCollection>`	Conforms to: `<sequencedCollection>`
Messages:	
`removeAtIndex: <integer> ^ <Object>`	Removes and returns the element at the indexed position
`removeFirst ^ <Object>`	Removes and returns the first element of in receiver
`removeFirstIfAbsent: <block0> ^ <Object>`	Removes and returns the first element of in receiver; evaluates the block if the collection is empty before removing the element
`removeLast ^ <Object>`	Removes and returns the last element of in receiver
`removeFirstIfAbsent: <block0> ^ <Object>`	Removes and returns the last element of in receiver, evaluates the block if the collection is empty before removing the element

A `SortedCollection`, as discussed previously, is a collection that supports the removal of elements based on their index within the collection but does not allow an index to be specified when elements are added. This is necessary because the index of an item in a `SortedCollection` represents its position in the sort order of all the elements in a collection. It is not possible to determine an item's sort position in the sort order until it is actually added. `SortedCollection` supports the protocol `<extensibleCollection>` for adding and remove elements without specifying an index and `<sequencedContractibleCollection>` for removing elements based on their index position. `SortedCollection` also defines the protocol for accessing and changing the sort blocks that determine the collection sort order:

Protocol `<SortedCollection>`	Conforms to: `<extensibleCollection>`, `<sequencedContractibleCollection>`
Messages:	
`sortBlock ^ <block2>`	Returns the sort block that determines the order of the collection
`sortBlock: <block2>`	Installs a new sort block and reorders the elements using it

An `OrderedCollection` is a dynamically sized, indexable collection that supports both the removal and the insertion of elements based on index positions. Like `SortedCollection`, the protocol for `OrderedCollection` conforms to <extensibleCollection> and <sequencedContractibleCollection>. It adds messages for inserting elements based on index positions:

Protocol <OrderedCollection>	Conforms to: <extensibleCollection>, <sequencedContractibleCollection>
Messages:	
add: <Object> after: <Object> ^ <Object>	Adds an object immediately after the first occurrence of another
add: <Object> afterIndex: <integer> ^ <Object>	Adds an object immediately after a specified index position
add: <Object> before: <Object> ^ <Object>	Adds an object immediately before the first occurrence of another
add: <Object> beforeIndex: <integer> ^ <Object>	Adds an object immediately before a specified index position
addAll: <collection> after: <Object> ^ <collection>	Adds all elements of the argument collection immediate after the first occurrence of the argument object
addAll: <collection> afterIndex: <integer> ^ <collection>	Adds all elements of the argument collection immediate after the specified index position
addAll: <collection> before: <Object> ^ <collection>	Adds all elements of the argument collection immediate before the first occurrence of the argument object
addAll: <collection> beforeIndex: <integer> ^ <Collection>	Adds all elements of the argument collection immediate before the specified index position
addAllFirst: <collection> ^ <collection>	Adds all elements of the argument collection to the front
addAllLast: <collection> ^ <collection>	Adds all elements of the argument collection to the back
addFirst: <Object> ^ <Object>	Adds an object to the front of the receiver collection
addLast: <Object> ^ <Object>	Adds an object to the back of the receiver collection

OrderedCollection can be thought of as a double-ended queue with interior access. When viewed as a queue, the message addLast: adds an element at the back of the queue and the message removeLast removes elements from the front of the queue. OrderedCollections can also be used as a stack. In this case, addLast: serves as the push operation and removeLast serves as the pop operation.

4.8. Smalltalk Program Structure

We have now described the nature of Smalltalk objects and classes, the syntax of the Smalltalk language, and some of the predefined classes that are available to Smalltalk programmers. What remains to be described is how these elements are organized to support complete programs that are implemented using Smalltalk.

Smalltalk implementations that are modeled after Smalltalk-80 are structured around a *virtual image*. We will use the term *classic Smalltalk* to refer to such implementations. A virtual image is a persistent collection of dynamic Smalltalk objects. It includes the object's executable behavior. A virtual image is used in conjunction with a *virtual machine,* which is a Smalltalk execution engine implemented as a systems program on some computer platform. When a virtual image is loaded onto a running virtual machine, a predetermined Smalltalk method is selected for execution. The virtual machine executes this method, and the method can then send messages that propagate execution throughout the methods of the objects within the virtual image. At any point, the state of the executing virtual image can be saved to a file in a persistent external form. A saved virtual image can be subsequently reloaded onto a virtual machine, and execution will continue from the point at which it was suspended when the virtual image was saved.

Using classic Smalltalk, an application program is usually distributed as a saved virtual image that contains all the classes, methods, and objects necessary to represent the program. A user executes such a program by loading it onto an appropriate virtual machine.

The contents of a classic Smalltalk virtual image include the classes that make up the standard, predefined Smalltalk class library. The contents also includes objects that provide the implementation mechanisms for all elements of the Smalltalk language, including class definitions, methods, variables, and blocks. These objects implement protocols that support the dynamic creation and modification of Smalltalk program elements within the virtual image. Using these protocols, Smalltalk code can be written that cause new classes and methods to be dynamically created. This process of using Smalltalk code within a running image to dynamically modify and extend itself is called *reflection*. Typically a Smalltalk programmer does not need to manually write the code to create new classes and methods because the virtual image also contains classes that implement high-level, interactive programming tools. It is the implementation of these tools that most commonly make use of reflection. Normally a programmer interacts with these tools to create new classes and methods.

When we discussed class definitions earlier, we mentioned that different Smalltalk implementations use various forms for describing classes. One of these forms is that which is presented by the interactive programming tools. Classic Smalltalk systems include a tool called a *browser* that presents class definitions in the context of a highly structured user interface. Another form used by classic Smalltalk for describing a class is a message that causes a new class to be created. Using reflection, a class can be created by a message such as this:

```
Object subclass: #NewClassName
        instanceVariables: 'x y z'
        classVariableNames: ''
        poolDictionaries: ''.
```

The message is sent to the intended superclass of the new class. This example would create a new class named `NewClassName` that is a subclass of `Object` and whose instances contain instance variables named `x`, `y`, and `z`. Additional messages would then be directed to the class object, `NewClassName`, in order to create instance and class methods. Although this general mechanism is provided by all classic Smalltalk implementations, the exact message selectors used for these operations vary among implementations.

Program creation through the use of reflection within a virtual image is a powerful implementation technique. However, it introduces complications into the software development process. One of these complications is the issue of how to prepare a virtual image containing a completed application for deployment to the users of the application. In most cases, it is not desirable for the deliverable application to contain the interactive tools that are used for Smalltalk programming. In addition, most programs only make use of some subset of all the predefined classes in the Smalltalk class library. Any unused classes within the deployed virtual image potentially waste system resources. Finally, most deployed applications do not require the use of reflection during execution of the application, yet its existence can have negative effects on application performance. Classic Smalltalk systems address these issues by providing various tools that are aids in removing development tools and unused classes from a virtual image in preparation for deployment.

Some recent Smalltalk implementations attempt to address these issues by treating the Smalltalk language in a more conventional manner. These implementations do not use reflection to implement a development environment that operates within the same virtual image as the application under development. Instead, they implement the development environment as an independent program that is separate and distinct from the application under development. In such implementations, a Smalltalk "program" is simply a set of class definitions that may be compiled into an executable program file. Whether this compilation process takes place incrementally or in batch mode, or whether it makes use of some form of reflection, is considered to be a characteristic of an implementation not a characteristic of the Smalltalk language itself.

Standard Smalltalk defines the Smalltalk language in a manner that can accommodate both the classic and the newer style of Smalltalk implementation. Standard Smalltalk defines the attributes that must be specified when creating Smalltalk language elements and the required semantics of language elements. In does not, however, mandate a particular syntax for writing complete Smalltalk programs. It does define the execution semantics of a complete Smalltalk program. A implementation of standard Smalltalk may choose to map the definition of language elements into a concrete syntax, reflective message, or the user interface of an incremental programming environment. These are all valid, as long as the required execution semantics are followed. To facilitate the interchange of code between implementations, standard Smalltalk also defines a program interchange file format. This format is not intended to be directly read or written by human programmers. Instead, it is designed such that any standard Smalltalk implementation, regardless of whether it is based on reflection or uses a virtual image, can translate its internal representation of a Smalltalk program to and from the interchange format.

4.9. Source Material

Goldberg, A., and D. Robson. 1983. *Smalltalk-80: The language and its implementation*. Reading, MA: Addison-Wesley.

Kay, A. C. 1996. The early history of Smalltalk. In T. J. Bergin and R. G. Gibson (Eds.), *History of programming languages* (pp. 511–579). New York: ACM Press.

The X3J20 Committee. 1997. *Draft American national standard for information systems—Programming languages—Smalltalk: Working draft*. Washington, DC: National Committee for Information Technology Standards.

CHAPTER 5

Smalltalk: A Developer's Perspective

by Jonathan Pletzke and Victoria Pletzke

This chapter is primarily targeted to all computer programmers, who may know something or nothing about Smalltalk. Although the typical reader of this chapter may know about other programming languages and some features of programming languages, this chapter is presented and written in a manner for all who are interested in learning about Smalltalk. Specifically, this chapter shares what makes Smalltalk different, what it's like to program in Smalltalk, how Smalltalk has been successfully applied, and where to find out more about this programming language. Ultimately, the goal of this chapter is to provide a feel of what it is like to use Smalltalk and to offer an understanding for why programmers like to use Smalltalk.

In this chapter, `code in this typeface`, represents Smalltalk source code. The Smalltalk source code is mixed in with regular text, as Smalltalk tends to follow the English (or other) language of the developers, and is quite readable and self-documenting.

As with most technologies, the marketers have sold Smalltalk as the "silver bullet" (Brooks, 1995) capable of solving all the ills of the development world. Although Smalltalk is good for many types of applications, it is also a poor choice for others, so success in Smalltalk is more a matter of good management than a choice of technology.

The tools industry is abuzz with the virtues of Java, but most of the features present in Java have been a part of Smalltalk for more than 25 years. Furthermore, in stark contrast to Java, Smalltalk has grown slowly and steadily in popularity and success during its long presence as a development language. Because the tools manufacturers make money only on the sale of development tools, training, and upgrades, the stagnation of the C++ market to date has launched the Java market into the forefront of the media's attention. A few years ago, when C++ was touted as the solution to the world's development woes, Smalltalk was supposed to fall by the wayside as yet another abandoned technology. But in 1996, IBM posted a 225% increase in sales of the VisualAge/Smalltalk product, and new Smalltalk products were announced and delivered by entrepreneurial companies such as Intuitive, Object Connect SARL, and QKS.

In addition to new commercial ventures, Apple Computer released a free version of Smalltalk, nicknamed 'Squeak' (`http://www.research.apple.com/research/proj/Learning_Concepts/squeak/intro.html`), that has been ported to many platforms, includes the virtual machine source code in 'C' (which is generated in part from Smalltalk code), and was created by some of the early Xerox PARC researchers, who now work at Apple and more recently at Disney. Another free version of Smalltalk, SmalltalkExpress (released by ObjectShare), was derived from a commercial development tool called Smalltalk/V (now Visual Smalltalk) and is available free on the Internet (`http://www.objectshare.com`). LearningWorks, a derivative of the VisualWorks product, has also been released as free software (`http://learningworks.neometron.com`). LearningWorks includes a reduced set of functionality aimed at teaching new Smalltalk programmers techniques and extensive Smalltalk class libraries by gradually revealing more classes and methods as the student progresses.

Many programmers enjoy working with Smalltalk and swear they will never program in anything else again. This chapter covers the history and some of the main advantages (and disadvantages) of embarking on a Smalltalk development journey. The simplicity of the one-page language is revealed, and some of the key features of the Smalltalk runtime and development environments are detailed. The chapter also illustrates the culture of the language, the people and how they work together as a community, and some projects that have met with success in Smalltalk.

5.1. The History of Smalltalk

Smalltalk got its start in the early 1970s in the Xerox Palo Alto Research Center (PARC; Bergin & Gibson, 1996). The team that invented the Smalltalk language and development environment was headed by Alan Kay.

Smalltalk was born as a simulation language, along the lines of Simula (a specialized enhancement to ALGOL). Many versions of Smalltalk came out of Xerox PARC—from 1971 to 1980 (the final version was called Smalltalk-80). In these years, Smalltalk was the operating system for the Dynabook and other computers.

When the folks at Apple Computer stopped by Xerox to see Smalltalk, they were impressed. They took the ideas of a GUI, and scalable typefaces with them, but didn't grasp the power of object-oriented programming at the time. The ex-Xerox PARC people who founded Adobe Systems came from Smalltalk, where the concept of scalable typefaces was prototyped. It seems as though many of the innovations in desktop computing today are technologies that started in Smalltalk at Xerox PARC. This leads one to the question of whether the current developers of Smalltalk software are also inventing the future of computing.

5.1.1. Early Smalltalk Commercialization

The widespread introduction of Smalltalk happened when Smalltalk, along with a colorful balloon, appeared on the cover of *Byte Magazine*'s August 1981 issue (*Byte Magazine*, 1981). The issue focused on Smalltalk and included articles from some of the researchers at Xerox PARC. At the time of the issue, no easily obtainable versions of Smalltalk were in existence.

In the few years following the *Byte Magazine* articles and the publication of a series of books covering Smalltalk (Goldberg & Robson, 1989), commercial versions of Smalltalk became available. These versions were reported to be slow (running on an IBM-AT) and required lots of memory (more than 640K). These versions were also slow due to interpreted execution.

5.1.2. Current Smalltalk Commercialization

The current versions of Smalltalk bear little resemblance to the original implementations. Although the development environment includes some of the same types of code browsers, the environment has turned into a complete team development environment to be envied by most other development environments. The Smalltalk environment runs across almost every platform and provides easy, if not immediate, portability between these platforms. Smalltalk systems also integrate with legacy code and external features easily, regardless of whether these features are written in COBOL, C, C++, assembly, or any other language. Smalltalk can now be packaged as a unit that can be called by other languages, as is done in ObjectStudio version 5.

If the notion of a ubiquitous virtual machine takes off, then a virtual machine will be available on every machine, and that virtual machine could be capable of running both Java and Smalltalk. Smalltalk vendors have created technology to allow some portions of Java code to be generated from Smalltalk programs. Others have created virtual machines that run Java and Smalltalk. Regardless of the approach, the current Java craze enhances the ability of the existing Smalltalk vendors to deliver Smalltalk—as well as the subset of Smalltalk technology found in Java—to more users on more platforms than ever before.

5.2. Smalltalk Features

Smalltalk provides the developer with some unique core functionality. In addition, the Smalltalk library provides built-in features that can be used as they are or extended to suit the needs of the application.

5.2.1. Core Features

Smalltalk is unlike many languages in that it is compiled to virtual machine byte codes. A virtual machine is a program, usually written in C or assembly language, that provides a primitive set of functions that are translated into actions on the native host platform. A virtual machine is similar to micro-code in construction of computers, and hardware can be created based on the definition of a virtual machine. For example, Java hardware is now being created based on the Java virtual machine.

Smalltalk can be totally platform independent, depending on how many platforms the virtual machine has been localized to support, as well as the generalization of the differing operating system services in the class library. Typically, the GUI, file system, and printing services have been abstracted for all available platforms. Platform-dependent functionality is available but is usually marked as such to prevent platform-specific code from being written by application developers.

A significant feature of Smalltalk for developers is incremental compilation. Because the Smalltalk development tools are tightly integrated with the language and class libraries, Smalltalk code is always written in small pieces, called *methods*. These methods are edited and saved independently of the entire class, so when a method is saved, it is also compiled into the virtual machine byte codes. Optimizations—including in-lining of function calls that return static values or values of variables—are performed at this time as well. Each method save takes less than a second, allowing the application developer to resume his or her work. The methods can even be edited, saved (forcing a recompile), and then executed from within the debugger of an active application.

One of the most elegant features of Smalltalk is that, by definition, everything in it is an object. This includes the classes (which are instances of `Class`) and `MetaClass`, if present. Some versions of Smalltalk make special consideration in internal storage for certain data types, such as `Strings`, `Symbols`, and `Integers`, and store them in a different internal format for performance reasons. However, inside Smalltalk, these data types appear as objects because the storage method is encapsulated and therefore is hidden from the application developer.

Smalltalk is a dynamically bound language, which means that the exact execution path of the program is not known at compile time. One favorite practice (which has its pros and cons) is to respond to messages that are not defined for a class by overriding the `doesNotUnderstand: aMessage` method. This method is sent to any object in Smalltalk if the virtual machine is unable to find an appropriate method for a message. In this method, many tricks can be played, including changing the receiver of the message (`anotherObject perform: aMessage`), changing the message into one that is understood (`self perform: (aMessage selector: #aDefinedSelector; yourself)`), or accessing a variable or external feature (`self oleInterface performActionFor: (aMessage selector)`). Anything that can be done in code can also be done to change the receiver, the form of the message, or any of the arguments, including the number of arguments.

Garbage collection has freed the Smalltalk developer from worrying about the allocation and deallocation of memory resources. Through the magic of the virtual machine, all requests for storage space are tracked, and when an object is no longer referenced by any other object in Smalltalk, it is deallocated and the memory returns to the application to be used again. A significant performance problem can occur if the Smalltalk developer inadvertently creates large amounts of garbage through inefficient coding. When this happens, the allocation and deallocation of memory (garbage collection) consumes a significant portion of the execution time of the program and leads to poor response. Thus, the programmer must still be aware of the creation of garbage and reduce the consumption. One favorite technique often seen when iterating through a set of values is recycling—when an object is created, it is reused and then discarded at the end.

The garbage collection algorithms are different from one implementation to the next, but all offer some level of control that can improve application performance. The frequency with which garbage collection is executed, as well as the capability to manually force garbage collection, is available to the application developer. Most implementations also allow the developer to control the memory size of the "new space" for newly created objects, the memory size of the "old space" for objects that have been "tenured," and the quantity of time required to achieve tenure.

5.2.2. Class Library Features

An extensive and mature class library accompanies all Smalltalk development environments. The libraries vary across versions on implementation of the GUI and external interfacing, but overall they share a significant number of common features. These features are unique to Smalltalk and provide a powerful environment that lends itself to many types of applications. Included in class libraries are multiprocess frameworks, external code interfacing (to C, COBOL, or another), external resource interfacing (such as OLE and OCXs), exception handling, dependency and event frameworks, and reflective capabilities (such as modifying the executing program and querying the structure of an application).

Smalltalk has always been a multiprocess environment. Even on operating systems that don't support simultaneously executing tasks, Smalltalk provides it's own internal process framework. As shown in Figure 5.1, an operating system process may contain one or more threads, with one of these threads handling the Smalltalk language processing. The Smalltalk language processing is split among as many Smalltalk processes as the application requires. The scheduling of these processes differs between versions, as does the number of operating system threads. A Smalltalk process is similar to an operating system thread in that it is contained entirely within Smalltalk. However, on platforms that support threads, Smalltalk processes do not become operating system threads. There are some exceptions to this rule:

- The ObjectStudio version of Smalltalk that does offer multiple threads
- An add-in to VisualWorks that provides operating system threads through a different set of calls
- IBM Smalltalk's coroutine calls, which use a separate operating system thread to make external system calls

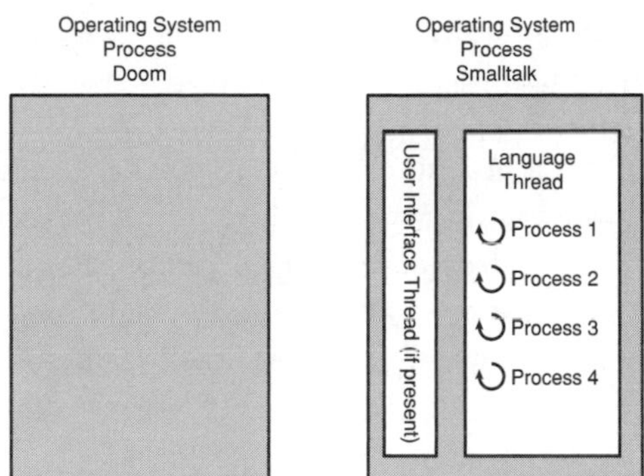

FIGURE 5.1. *Smalltalk supports multiple processes, even when the host platform does not.*

Often, Smalltalk applications are required to interface with C DLLs, COBOL programs, or other external code modules. Many options are available to interface with these modules, and Smalltalk programmers make use of the facilities to call these external programs. Because most Smalltalk development is done on PCs or workstations, the most common interface of external code is through a C dynamic link library or C shared library. The C interface is the most common external interface supported in Smalltalk, although Smalltalk MVS for IBM mainframes calls external COBOL modules and fits well in that environment.

Smalltalk programs take advantage of many of the same features that other languages use on the host platforms. This can include OCXs for custom GUI controls and OLE for interaction with email and desktop applications under Microsoft operating systems. These features are available in the base Smalltalk products, as well as toolkits from third-party developers. People have interfaced Smalltalk to hardware for communications and control, music and graphics systems, and every conceivable type of other system. Often, an application in Smalltalk is the GUI front end and the "glue" that holds together other separate technologies developed in other languages.

5.2.2.1. Exception Handling

Smalltalk systems include an extremely powerful exception-handling framework. Although the Smalltalk versions differ in syntax and implementation, the common function is to signal errors that occur many layers deep in code, and to respond to those errors in the best layer of application code. For example, in an engineering application, the divide-by-zero error must be handled in any situation in which it might occur. The five possible paths for dealing with an error are shown in Figure 5.2. Choices 4 and 5 create a new stack frame to further execute the other handlers registered previously, while options 1 and 3 drop back one stack frame, and option 2 may drop several. Experienced Smalltalk programmers realize that they must reset any state information changed before the error was encountered when dropping stack frames.

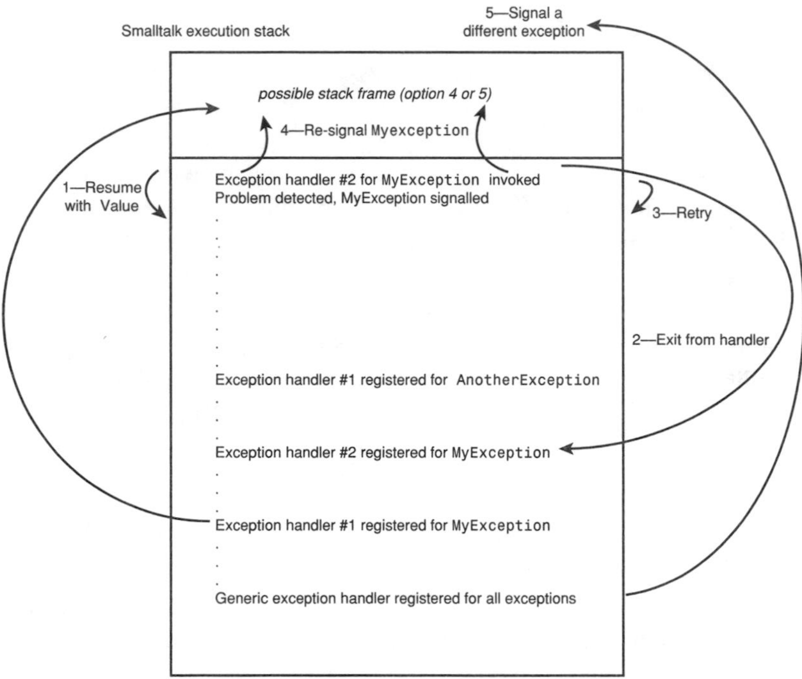

FIGURE 5.2. *Exception handling in Smalltalk provides complex strategies for dealing with errors.*

In Smalltalk, you have several options that are implemented based on the code that is executed:

- *Resume execution, with a different value, where the error occurred.* Sometimes in an engineering calculation, you might want to divide by zero to get an extremely high number (approaching infinity). In other cases, you might want a different equation to be invoked. For example, the following:

```
[ (a + b) / c ]
    when: self divideByZeroException
    do: [:signal ¦ signal resumeWith: 99999 ]
```

replaces the value in the block with 99999, and

```
[ (a + b) / c ]
    when: self divideByZeroException
    do: [: signal ¦ signal resumeWith: (a + b) ]
```

continues execution with the result of a added to b in the stack frame where the error occurred. The use of exception handling does not need to occur within the same set of code or the same class. It can go through many layers of methods and classes and then jump to the exception-handling block elsewhere on the stack when an error is detected.

- *Resume execution after the exception-handler block.* The expression

```
[ (a + b) / c ]
    when: self divideByZeroException
    do: [:signal ¦ signal exitWith: 1 ]
```

continues execution in the current method with the value of 1 for the expression (a + b) / c.

- *Retry execution of the protected code.* The expression

```
[ (a + b) / c ]
    when: self divideByZeroException
    do: [:signal ¦ signal retry ]
```

is a poor code example because a divide-by-zero error will not be resolved unless the variables are changing during execution or c is a random number. A retry operation is much more useful when the problem could be due to an external resource that might become available again, such as a file or a network connection that can experience transient disruptions during the normal course of application execution.

- *Re-signal the exception for another handler further up the stack.* The expression

```
[ (a + b) / c ]
    when: self divideByZeroException
    do: [:signal ¦ signal signal]
```

signals `divideByZeroException` again and looks for another handler that is further down the stack. If none is found, then the default handler is invoked, which could open the debugger or give the user an error message. This action is usually taken after some logic in the exception handler is unable to resolve the problem.

- *Signal a different type of exception.* The expression

```
[ (a + b) / c ]
    when: self divideByZeroException
    do: [:signal ¦ self badMathError signalWith: signal
exception ]
```

provides a new type of signal that is searched for down the stack. Turning one type of exception into another is not frequently done, but it can be useful when creating layers of software that provide a common application programming interface (API) independent of the components used. An example of this is an object translation/brokering mechanism that provides a consistent API and exception interface to the developer while also accommodating an interchangeable database interface with varying API and exception interfaces.

Exception handling is a powerful framework that should be used to deal with unexpected system errors that could happen in your application. It is not good practice to go overboard with this mechanism and create exception handlers for nonexceptional cases (such as application logic). In such a case, the code might become cluttered, less readable, and much harder to maintain.

5.2.2.2. Dependencies and Event Frameworks

Exceptions are part of the API that an object in Smalltalk provides; events and dependencies are another. The concept of dependencies has been in Smalltalk for some time, and the event frameworks that are a logical extension of the dependency mechanism have become very popular in the past few years.

The dependency mechanism allows for a loose coupling between two or more objects. When one object changes, it does not have to include specific processing to notify other programs about the change. Instead, the object can simply declare, "I've changed," and the mechanism notifies all the objects that have registered interest in the change.

For example, a class `Person` has an instance variable called `lastName`. When `lastName` changes in an instance of `Person`, an instance of `GovernmentAgency` might be interested. The instance of `GovernmentAgency` might express interest in the changes to `Person` by sending the message `addDependent:` to `Person` with an argument of `self` (the `GovernmentAgency`). When `Person` has a change to the `lastName`, it sends the message `changed: anAspect` to `self` (`Person` now), and then `GovernmentAgency` is notified. An example of a dependency relationship between Jonathan and Victoria is shown in Figure 5.3. In the example, Jonathan and Victoria are both dependents of each other. They want to know about all the events that occur with each other. They are also dependents of the publisher, and they want to know about the progress of the book.

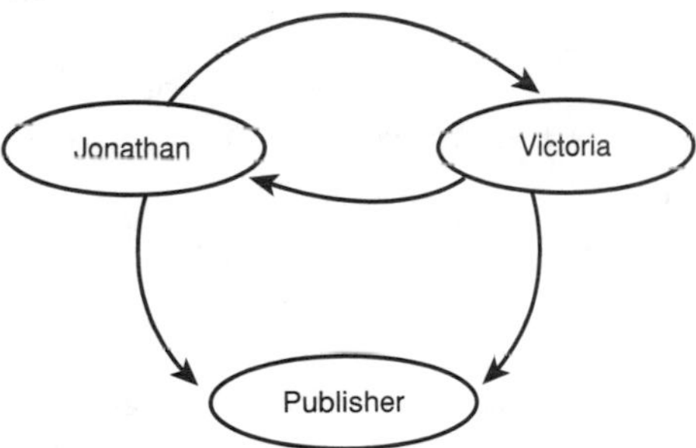

FIGURE 5.3. *Jonathan and Victoria are dependents of each other and the publisher, and they want to know about the progress of the book.*

Another example of this mechanism at work is two views of the same object. One can be a data entry screen, and the other a graph. When changes are made on one screen, those changes are made to a common model object. This model object then says, "I've changed," and all the views that are interested are notified. This is model, view, controller (MVC) in action.

The MVC paradigm was born in Smalltalk and deals with the GUI (also born in Smalltalk). As shown in Figure 5.4, the model refers to a data object that holds information (such as `Person`). The view is the graphical representation of this information that is presented to the user. The controller is the combination of the mouse (another Smalltalk concept) position and state of buttons that takes input from the user and sends messages to the model and view objects. In essence, the view displays information to the user, the controller responds to user input, and the model is the functional part of the application.

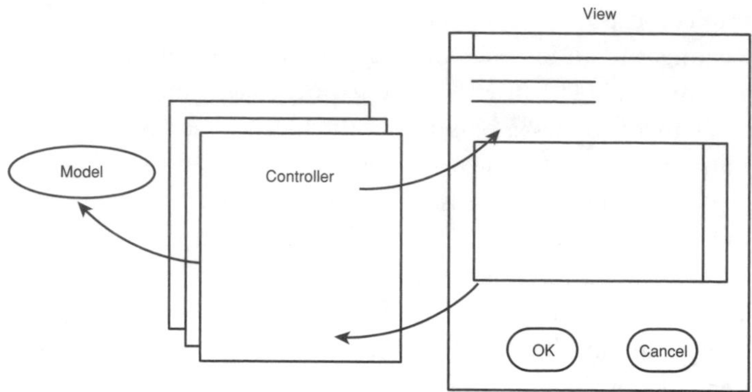

FIGURE 5.4. *In the original MVC, the view and controller know about each other and the model, but the model does not know about either of them.*

This paradigm does not exist in the popular modern GUIs today. The view and controller have been merged into one entity, known as a *control* or *widget*. In VisualWorks, the paradigm is still present and is applied to single controls as well as entire windows. A new twist to the MVC paradigm that is gaining popularity involves the model as it is in Figure 5.4, but in which the view encompasses both the view and controller, and in which a new definition of controller allows a single view to be reused with different behavior. An example of this is a window that appears the same to a user at all times but has drastically different code behind it based on any criteria desired by the system designers. One common use is for one controller that allows editing and stores to a database, whereas another simply allows browsing of the information. The definition of the word *controller* varies in implementations of Smalltalk, although it is really just a general term. Because the native GUIs today combine the original view and controller into one item, the word *controller* represents an interfacing mechanism that allows the same view to behave differently in some circumstances. This is illustrated in Figure 5.5.

The event framework is a logical extension of the dependency mechanism. Each use of the event framework includes an aspect of interest as well as a receiver object and selector. When an object changes, it can execute code such as

```
self signalEvent: #lastName with: self lastName
```

which causes all registered handlers to be called. This contrasts with the simpler dependency model of any `changed` message from an object, causing the dependent's `update` method to be called for every reason (not just the aspect of interest). The event framework can be useful in directing specific behavior between the two loosely coupled objects without a lot of conditional logic in the `update` method to determine what aspect changed and how to deal with it.

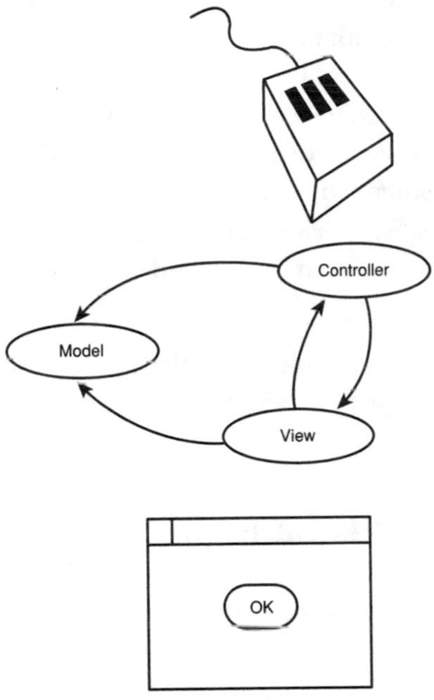

FIGURE 5.5. *GUIs today combine the original view and controller into one item.*

5.2.2.3. Reflective Capabilities of Smalltalk

One of the greatest features of working with Smalltalk is the ability to write programs that analyze and can create other programs. Most Smalltalk development environments include the capability to generate some portion of source code of a Smalltalk application, most commonly the GUI source code from an editor, but also mappings between objects and relational databases.

Other development environments and languages also include the capability to generate source code, but few include the capability to query the running application about program structure. For example, you can ask any object for its class by sending the message `class` to the object. Because classes are themselves instances of `MetaClass`, you also can send messages to the class to find out things such as the superclass, the entire superclass chain, the instance variables, the class variables, the class instance variables, each or any of the compiled methods, the selectors for each of the methods (method names), or anything else.

You also can create new types of system services—such as conversions between objects and relational data sets—and use these properties to break encapsulation to insert information into an instance of a class. For example, you can use system services to check the validity of certain types of methods, check the stack for previously selected methods, and create new types of development tools, as discussed in section 5.2.2. You can even create programs that create additional programs (classes or methods) as they run, provided that you include the compiler in the deployed application.

The numerous features available in Smalltalk (combined with what is provided by vendors, third parties, and freeware) make Smalltalk a continual learning experience.

5.3. The Smalltalk Language

The Smalltalk language is simple—so simple, in fact, that it can be written on one page. The concepts are also simple:

- Everything is an object.
- Objects send messages to each other.
- A message causes the execution of a method.
- A single value (object) is answered as the result of any message send. (This object might be an array of objects or the default value, which is the recipient of the message.)
- Common variables and methods are organized into classes, and similar classes can inherit from a single superclass, which can also inherit.

5.3.1. One-Page Syntax

So few language constructs exist in Smalltalk that the syntax can be written in one page. Although the original one-page syntax of Smalltalk (written one night to win a bet at Xerox PARC) has never been published, the following table provides our one-page summary of the syntax and some of the common constructs.

TABLE 5.1. *Smalltalk syntax.*

Element	*Description*
`"Public - Answer result"`	A comment
`'String'`	A string literal
`$X`	A character literal
`[ ]`	A block
`;`	Cascade messages to same receiver
`.`	End of statement
`#symbol`	A symbol literal
`^returnValue`	Return of a method
`:=`	Assign to variable on left
`self`	Object of method
`super`	Skip self and look to the superclass for the message to follow
`true`	Single instance of class `True`
`false`	Single instance of class `False`
`nil`	Single instance of class `UndefinedObject`
`value ifTrue: [] ifFalse: []`	Conditional based on value
`10 timesRepeat: []`	Repeat 10 times
`1 to: 10 do: [:i ¦ ]`	Go through interval of 1–10, passing value into block
`[] whileTrue: []`	Evaluate second block repeatedly until first block evaluates to `false`
`anObject aMessage`	A message send with no argument (all message sends return one object)
`anObject aMessage: anArgument`	A message send including an argument (more arguments are added with additional keywords that include a colon and an argument name)
`¦ temporary ¦`	A temporary variable at the start of any method

Because Smalltalk is weakly typed (meaning that there is only one type, an object), the declarations of variables cannot make any distinction between types of classes. The message `isKindOf: aClass` can be sent to any object to determine the class of which it is an instance, and code can proceed from there. The drawback to this type of coding is that it defeats some polymorphism, but it does reduce the number of extraneous methods in commonly used classes such as `String` and `Integer`. It is also worth noting that because the developer has total control over Smalltalk, additional rigor can be placed on the declaration of variables, including typing variables by class if necessary.

5.4. Some Simple Smalltalk Code

To better understand the syntax, the following sections show some examples of what Smalltalk code looks like. The examples range from simple to slightly more complex. Any one of the introductory Smalltalk books or online tutorials can provide more detailed examples in the context of a simple application, and more complex examples can be found in *Advanced Smalltalk* (Pletzke, 1997).

A class in Smalltalk is defined and edited in any of the numerous code browsers or in the debugger. The definition of a simple class, `Person`, with four instance variables is shown here:

```
Object subclass: #Person
        instanceVariableNames: 'firstName lastName middleInitial
birthDate'
        classVariableNames: ''
        poolDictionaries: ''
```

Notice that the instance variables are not declared with any type or size information. Any variable can contain any value because the type held by each variable is an object, and everything is an object.

One of the simplest types of methods in Smalltalk is an accessor, which provides access to an instance variable for setting the value or getting the value. Most Smalltalk code includes accessors for all variables, and the private or public distinction is made in the method comment. `>>` is used to denote a method of the class `Person`, but does not appear in code anywhere. The code is simply entered into a browser opened on the `Person` class:

```
Person>>birthDate
        "Public - Answer the birthDate instance variable"

        ^birthDate



Person>>birthDate: aDate
        "Public - Set the birthDate instance variable."

        birthDate := aDate
```

A more complex method than the accessor is one that actually does something, although accessors can be modified to provide initialization on demand of variables as well as undergo database searches. A simple method that returns a person's age as of today makes use of the class `Person` (called `self` in the method) and the `Date` class, which understands the message `today`:

```
Person>>age
        "Public - Answer the age of self as of today"

        ^Date today year - self birthDate year
```

In this method, the message `today` is sent to the class `Date`, which answers an instance of `Date` containing the current day, month, and year. The message `year` is sent to that instance of `Date`, which answers an instance of `Integer`. The `-` is sent to that `Integer` after evaluating the argument for the `-` message, an `Integer` obtained by sending the message `year` as the result of the message `birthDate` sent to `self`.

Typical Smalltalk coding creates simple methods that are approximately this complex to slightly more complex, and then assembles these methods into comparably simple methods. This results in a lot of methods generated, but the complexity of problems, methods, and solutions is reduced considerably, and similar operations can share common sets of code. Any time a Smalltalk programmer finds that he or she is copying code, he or she can instead create a new method that contains the common code and can refer to it from both (or many) other methods.

5.4.1. Blocks

Blocks are pieces of Smalltalk code that are portable between methods and classes. A block is compiled in a method within a class, just as with all the other code, but it is not executed when it is encountered. Instead, execution is deferred until the block is sent the message `value`. For this reason, blocks can be passed as arguments between classes and are an extremely powerful and useful mechanism. The following are some examples of blocks:

- `[ :a :b ¦ a firstName > b firstName ]`—A block that could be answered by the `Person` class for a particular type of sort.
- `[ :each ¦ each isNil ]`—A block that can be used for removing nil elements from a collection.

- `[ self draw ]`—A block that can be passed as an argument to another object and will not be executed until it is sent the message `value`. `self` in the block represents the object in which the method was compiled and does not necessarily refer to the object that will value the block.

5.4.2. ANSI Standard Smalltalk

The ANSI standard committee has been meeting on the topic of a standard for Smalltalk for some years now, and drafts have come out. Smalltalk programmers have always enjoyed a simple syntax that is portable among all vendors' versions of Smalltalk. However much they have in common, though, the class libraries have some differences that can make the moving of the GUI or the external interface code difficult. These differences are being worked on in the committee and might never be completely resolved. It is a tall order to try to make the entire class library compatible, as most other libraries (especially C++ libraries) differ significantly from one vendor to another.

5.5. The Smalltalk Development Environment

Perhaps the greatest draw for developers is the nicely integrated development environment that Smalltalk offers. From any text pane in the environment, you can type in Smalltalk code, execute it, display the result as a string, or open an interactive inspector of the resulting object.

5.5.1. Browsers and Team Development Tools

Smalltalk development environments include many more powerful tools than any other environment the authors have encountered. You cannot only edit the code in the code editor, but you also can do so in the debugger during execution of a program. You can inspect the values of the objects, see the types of classes, change the values, or execute code that modifies the values of an object. You can browse the code class by class and look at the inheritance of a class. You can also find all the senders of a certain method (everywhere that the method is mentioned in source code), all implementors of a certain method (so that the polymorphism of a message can be understood), references to variables, and so on. Another powerful feature is to browse the messages sent in a method (the functions that are referenced in the method) and then see all the other senders or implementors of a message. In this way, you have instant access to plenty of examples of how a method is used, including the code that you are adding to the system, which appears in all the browsers in the system.

With all this code-control power and the banishment of the source code file as the unit of coding, a new way to manage the Smalltalk source code is desirable. Several products have been created; the most popular one is ENVY, which appears in all the IBM Smalltalk and Java professional development products. This development tool allows the management of Smalltalk source code at the finest level of granularity (the method) to be grouped into classes and applications, assigned to users, and organized into subsystems. Standard file-based version-control systems pale in comparison to ENVY's sophistication and ease of use.

5.5.2. Smalltalk Development Tools

Regardless of the technology or language, a specific need might emerge for a development tool. In Smalltalk, this need is easily met through customization of the existing development tools, extensions to those tools, and entirely new tools that share the same interface to the stored source code and compiler. This means that the development tools can be customized to adapt to any process and can be improved by the developers to increase their satisfaction and productivity. One drawback to this is that some developers spend more time monkeying around with the development tools than creating their application code. Some people recommend that a person like this be assigned as the "toolsmith" to a development effort and be responsible for developing tools to improve the productivity of the whole group. One true test of the addiction of a Smalltalk developer to the language is to query the number of class browsers a developer has written to replace the standard class browser.

Smalltalk offers one of the richest sets of libraries available in any development system. This includes classes and frameworks for GUIs (including many custom and extensible widgets), collections, streams, magnitude, file, database, communications, Web, and distributed applications. These class libraries and frameworks have evolved for many years and they enable an experienced Smalltalk developer to create powerful applications in a fraction of the time that it might take in another language.

Most of the Smalltalk development environments sold today also include a visual programming environment. This environment allows novice Smalltalkers to begin their Smalltalk experience by "wiring" together parts visually, and it similarly saves the experienced programmer hours of work on building the GUI. Some of these visual programming parts include capabilities to access external databases, communicate with other computers, and create complex Web applications. The visual programming environment can also be extended to include new features, or it can be used to divide work among various groups of developers.

One unique thing about Smalltalk is that you are customizing an already running, debugged, stable, and mature application. All Smalltalk development environments include the necessary components to run as a standalone application. In fact, you add your application logical and user interface, then strip out the development tools, and voilá—you have your running application. This differs from most other programming languages in that time is spent either redoing the basic shell of the application each time a new project is started, or a previous project is gutted for code with which to begin development.

All Smalltalk application development work is stored in a file called the "image." The image contains the binary executable code for every method, as well as instances of objects. The top-level, global object in Smalltalk is called `Smalltalk` and is an instance of `SystemDictionary`. This is where all the global objects, pool dictionaries (such as shared dictionaries), and classes are stored. When an object is removed from the dictionary, it is garbage collected if it isn't referenced by any other object. Conversely, if junk accumulates in globals or class variables, then the image will grow in size and you will be faced with "image creep." This isn't a problem if the image is never saved, but common practice is to save the image often. When saving the image, everything that is in the image (all of which is currently in RAM) is stored to disk into an image file. Source code is usually stored automatically in either a text file or a shared source code repository and is not part of the image. This image is a snapshot of the entire development (or runtime) environment at a point in time.

One approach that has been taken with Smalltalk is the encapsulation of the level and the type of work. The tool vendor (the producer of a Smalltalk development environment) creates a virtual machine and a basic class library. In addition to the basics (that is, magnitude, collections, file system, streams, GUIs), the tool vendor can create additional frameworks that can be used for such processes as communications, distributed processing, Web servers, transaction processing, database interfaces, and conversion of database records to objects. These frameworks are components developed by experts within a certain domain, which eliminates the need for this expertise within the application development group. For example, communications using TCP/IP need not be understood well, or at all, by an application developer who desires to write a distributed application. Instead, the developer can utilize a framework already designed and built by a communications expert and can use that framework to accomplish the application development goals.

A development team that uses Smalltalk can consist of the following components: expert low-level people (operating system and platform experts) who fashion system components, GUI experts who fashion widgets, domain experts who engineer industry solutions, and corporate gurus who engineer corporatewide solutions. Finally, application developers can use components built by others (who have expertise in the given component area) to create end-user software, as well as create their own components.

5.6. Advantages and Disadvantages to Smalltalk

As with any other development tool, there are pros and cons to the use of Smalltalk. Smalltalk is well suited for simulations and modeling of complex situations. It is overkill for simple GUI on mainframe, unless the interaction with the mainframe system is extremely complex, involving combinations of many transactions.

Smalltalk fails when the expectations of the organization do not match what is known about Smalltalk and the development of systems in Smalltalk. The syntax of Smalltalk is easy to learn and can be well understood in a day. It is essential that a developer master the concepts of object-oriented development, although not unique to Smalltalk, to succeed in Smalltalk programming. Other object-oriented languages can be used as procedural solutions, but Smalltalk requires the understanding and use of object orientation in order to have success.

With the depth and richness of the class libraries that come with Smalltalk, and with the add-on libraries from the vendors and the third parties, significant time must be allowed to learn and master these libraries. Although it takes about a day to learn the syntax, it takes a lifetime to learn the libraries, especially when there is always something new available or a new way to do an old thing. When you have an understanding of object-oriented concepts and have some good experience with the vast class libraries, your resulting applications can be developed more quickly and are more robust, more reusable, and easier to change quickly.

5.7. The Smalltalk Culture

Smalltalk has a strong culture of extremely enthusiastic developers, zealots, and visionaries. One important aspect is the active third-party development tools vendors, which complement the Smalltalk development tools with powerful general and specialized components. Many of these third parties charge a fraction of what it would cost (in time and money) an application developer to create the component and immediately deliver a debugged, running component.

Third parties also provide services such as consulting and training. These services range in price, quality, and area of expertise, as well as locality. A great number of Smalltalk vendors and service providers are located in North Carolina, New York, New Jersey, California, Toronto, and most large cities. Outside North America, products are being created in Europe and Asia, and the services markets are equally active.

The Smalltalk Industry Council (STIC), a cooperative industry association for Smalltalk, is dedicated to promoting the value of Smalltalk to all industries. STIC members include the larger Smalltalk vendors and service providers. For more information about STIC and Smalltalk, visit the STIC Web site at `http://www.stic.org`.

5.7.1. Frameworks and Patterns

Several strong players in Smalltalk are involved in the latest frameworks and patterns research and discovery. The creation of frameworks (reusable structured classes to solve specific problems) for sale and for use within an organization is quite popular. Smalltalk makes it easy to create them by providing the object orientation necessary, as well as source code management tools to help control the deployment of the frameworks. Patterns (practices that have been discovered to be useful and applicable to many situations) have been applied to many Smalltalk applications, and discussions on the discovery of various patterns can be found in most Smalltalk user groups, conferences, books, and articles.

5.7.2. Object Technology Centers

One of the most recent additions to the Smalltalk culture is object technology centers (OTCs). Although they are not exclusive to Smalltalk, OTCs seem to be a part of companies with multiple Smalltalk efforts in progress.

The definition of an OTC and the role it plays in relationship to ongoing projects vary among corporations. The OTC can be established as an object support group consisting of experienced developers offering all projects guidance throughout their development lifecycle, from analysis to deployment. The OTC can also be established as the center for reuse, driving projects to not only develop reusable objects, components, or frameworks, but also to use the components developed by others, both within and outside the corporation. On the other hand, instead of just policing the practice of reuse, the OTC can be responsible for developing reusable objects, components, and frameworks. The OTC can also play the role of researcher and support personnel of development tools. A somewhat simpler OTC role is collection of in-house consultants/mentors loaned out to development efforts for stated periods of time to perform pre-defined functions for the project. The various roles and responsibilities of running an OTC and coordinating object projects can be found in *Succeeding with Objects: Decision Frameworks for Project Management*, by Adele Goldberg and Kenneth S. Rubin (1995).

Regardless of the definition and role the OTC plays, the most crucial element of its success within a corporation is senior management support and belief in its existence. This support ensures necessary department and corporate buy-in. Without support, the group will not have the "teeth" to achieve the intended purpose for its foundation.

5.7.3. The Smalltalk Development Lifecycle

The development lifecycle of Smalltalk can be a very different experience for different organizations and individuals. Frequently, Smalltalk applications are developed iteratively, and the developers are active players in gathering requirements through use cases, analysis and design of object models, development of code, creation of test cases, and deployment of applications. Many claims have been made about how quickly Smalltalk development can be done, but those are true only when the requirements are clear and the developers are experienced with both Smalltalk and the type of problem that the software will solve. With the right combination of Smalltalk and domain experience, proven methodology—such as Objectory (Jacobson, 1992)—and good management, organizations are creating quality software that is a corporate investment and asset, not just an expense.

5.7.4. The Vendors

Currently, IBM dominates the sales of Smalltalk development environments. Some of the smaller entrepreneurial companies offer interesting technology that can play a larger role in the future. (See Table 5.2.)

TABLE 5.2. *Emerging Smalltalk environment products.*

Vendor	*Product*	*Description*
IBM	VisualAge/Smalltalk	Currently, this is the top-selling product. It runs on OS/2, Windows 3.1, Windows 95, Windows NT, AIX, SunOS, and HP/UX. (`http://www.software.ibm.com/ad`)
ObjectShare (formerly ParcPlace-Digitalk)	VisualWorks	The Xerox PARC spin-off product still bears great resemblance to the original Smalltalk. It is available on the widest range of platforms but provides a mostly emulated user interface and polled execution of the GUI (although both can be changed in the pack age). (`http://www.parcplace.com`)
ObjectShare (formerly ParcPlace-Digitalk)	Visual Smalltalk (Smalltalk/V)	The fate of this product is currently unknown because ParcPlace-Digitalk has put any work on the product on hold. It might be sold off to another vendor. The product runs on Windows and OS/2, but the user interface is not completely portable between the two. (`http://www.parcplace.com`)
QKS	SmalltalkAgents	Although originally available only for the Macintosh this product will be available on the Windows platform. It provides an innovative

Vendor	*Product*	*Description*
		set of development tools and many useful extensions to the language, along with fast execution. (`http://www.smalltalkagents.com`)
VMark (Cincom)	ObjectStudio/Enfin	This product has been passed from one company to the next and is currently being developed by Cincom. It provides some unique features, but the development tools are more like those in a C development environment. (`http://www.vmark.com`)
Intuitive	Dolphin Smalltalk	An innovative product from England, it provides a small footprint product that integrates well with the Microsoft operating systems. The demo includes Web functionality which parallels that of Java. (`http://www.intuitive.co.uk`)
ObjectConnect SARL	Smalltalk MT	This version is for the newest Microsoft operating systems and features a small footprint and fast runtime. (`http://www.objectconnect.com`)
eXept Software AG	Smalltalk X	ST/X has been around for a while in beta and is now available commercially for UNIX X Window–based computers. (`http://www.informatik.uni-stuttgard.de/stx/stx.html`)

5.7.5. Freeware and Shareware

Numerous free versions of Smalltalk are available to play with and learn Smalltalk. These products can also be used for real applications, but don't expect perfection in features or technical support on these versions.

5.7.5.1. Apple Computer: Squeak

The Squeak technology is available from Apple Research (`http://www.research.apple.com/research/proj/Learning_Concepts/squeak/intro.html`) and is a free version of Smalltalk. It is being worked on by some of the early Xerox PARC researchers and authors (Kaehler & Patterson, 1986) and has been ported to several operating systems. Squeak generates C source code that can be compiled for each of the target platforms and includes full source for the classes and the virtual machine.

5.7.5.2. LearningWorks

LearningWorks (`http://learningworks.neometron.com`) is a limited version of the VisualWorks product. It is intended for learning and research and includes a restricted set of tools rather than the full-blown development environment. Adele Goldberg started working on this project while she was at ParcPlace with the goal of creating a tool that provides progressively more classes and methods in the Smalltalk class hierarchy. This tool is intended to assist people learning the language and libraries by presenting the basics first and providing progressively more exposure to classes and methods as the learner progresses. LearningWorks runs on a number of platforms, including Windows, Macintosh, and UNIX flavors.

5.7.5.3. ObjectShare: SmalltalkExpress

In SmalltalkExpress a souped-up version of an older Digitalk product is combined with a GUI builder. This product is free on the Web (`http://www.objectshare.com`) and also has documentation available online. It runs as a 16-bit application under Windows.

5.7.5.4. Little Smalltalk

Little Smalltalk is a simplified Smalltalk, created by students led by Dr. Timothy Budd. Little Smalltalk is discussed in Budd's book (Budd, 1987), and the original command-line version has been enhanced with a GUI for Windows and Macintosh. Full source code is available from `ftp://ftp.cs.orst.edu/pub/budd/little/readme.html`.

5.7.5.5. GNU Smalltalk

GNU Smalltalk is a simple, command-line version of Smalltalk that is slowly being worked on as a volunteer effort. As part of GNU, it includes full source code and can be used for simple projects as well as to learn the internal workings of a virtual machine.

5.8. Projects That Use Smalltalk

Many types of projects have been deployed successfully using Smalltalk as the development tool. These projects vary greatly in scope, but most are not trivial. The majority of Smalltalk applications tend to be complex applications that do more than just provide a GUI to a database or an old mainframe system. They often incorporate complex rules, behaviors, and interfaces to external systems. Many industry groups are creating reusable object-oriented components for use in Smalltalk and other object-oriented languages.

5.8.1. Smalltalk as a Web Server

A premiere information provider was one of the first to develop Internet commerce using Smalltalk as the vehicle. An application was built that provides an interface to customers on the Web, takes credit card orders, gathers information from mainframe systems, and provides the reports to the customers. Other organizations have developed intranet applications for purposes such as scheduling meetings and information dissemination. One great advantage that Smalltalk has here is that all the clients (Web browsers) require less RAM and CPU than Smalltalk clients, so they can run on existing, inexpensive PCs. The Smalltalk application serves many clients as it runs on a high-end PC or workstation.

5.8.2. Trading in Smalltalk

Wall Street was another early adopter of Smalltalk, modeling complex, constantly changing financial algorithms in Smalltalk. The financial sector made use of the quick turn-around time on changes to the application to tune financial forecasting and tracking tools to provide better return on investment to customers.

5.8.3. Banking in Smalltalk

Banks of all types have also used Smalltalk to interface to their numerous back-end systems. In many cases, Smalltalk developers have had to code to mainframe "CICS" transactions for the financial institution to maintain their high level of data integrity.

5.8.4. Insurance and Smalltalk

The insurance industry has a large number of companies developing applications in Smalltalk. These applications cover all aspects of the insurance business, including underwriting tools, policy issuance systems, rating systems, accounting systems, decision support systems, and claims systems. Many applications interface to their existing mainframe applications, legacy data stores, and desktop applications. The insurance companies are beginning to work together to create industry-standard solutions built in Smalltalk.

5.8.5. Telecommunications and Smalltalk

Telecommunications applications in Smalltalk have varied from real-time Smalltalk systems for switching and teleconferences to order entry systems for telephony products, service, and equipment. A complex compensation system was written in Smalltalk at one of the largest telecommunications companies. Television networks are also using Smalltalk to develop their internal information systems technology, as well as to coordinate their network feeds through Smalltalk-powered communications equipment.

5.8.6. Manufacturing, Utility, Pharmaceuticals, and Transportation with Smalltalk

Some of the larger Smalltalk development efforts have gone on in the United States, Canada, and Europe for manufacturing support systems. Utilities have created massive information management systems using Smalltalk and object databases such as Gemstone (which uses Smalltalk as its query language). Pharmaceutical companies are starting to use Smalltalk in limited ways as well, and airlines have also used Smalltalk to develop their internal applications. Furthermore, electronic test equipment has been created using Smalltalk as the development language. The "Network Vehicle" that appeared at the COMDEX conference in 1997 was a highly computerized minivan that featured Smalltalk for its command and control system.

5.8.7. The Government and Smalltalk

The government has been an early and quiet consumer of the Smalltalk technology. Information-processing applications and rapid development of custom applications have been accomplished in various government agencies. Some of the early Smalltalk-developed technologies, including the Analyst product from Xerox, have been deployed in the U.S. government. More recently, the U.S. Department of Defense selected Smalltalk for the production phase of the Joint Warfare System (JWARS).

5.9. Conclusion

The future of Smalltalk is one of slow, steady growth. Although there is currently great publicity for Java, this languages is a long way from providing the stable solutions that Smalltalk has been providing for years. The overly optimistic prediction of the International Data Corporation in the report titled "Smalltalk Market Accelerates" (McClure, 1995)(commissioned by the Smalltalk Industry Council) predicted an exponential growth in Smalltalk sales, but the reality has been closer to linear growth over the last few years. A more recent report from International Data Corporation titled "Smalltalk Strengths Stand Out" (McClure, 1997) reports that the predicted exponential growth was incorrect, but that Smalltalk will continue its 20% annual growth. The existing applications in Smalltalk will continue to be enhanced and extended, and as more developers become knowledgeable about object-oriented concepts, they will choose object-oriented development tools such as Smalltalk for their applications. The role of Smalltalk as a server will increase as the need for complex application servers to provide content to the Internet and intranet clients skyrockets. Smalltalk has the maturity and current assets to provide this functionality, but it still commands a premium price (although the prices are dropping). The individual must weed through the various claims about development tools and products. One fact that probably isn't mentioned often is that most Smalltalk developers really enjoy Smalltalk and wouldn't trade it for another language unless it offered everything that Smalltalk offers and has at least one great advantage over Smalltalk.

5.10. Smalltalk Places of Interest

The following Web sites offer additional information for those who wish to learn more about Smalltalk and the Smalltalk environment.

`http://home.sprynet.com/sprynet/jpletzke` (The authors' Web page)

`http://st-www.cs.uiuc.edu/` (Smalltalk Archive)

`http://www.stic.org` (Smalltalk Industry Council)

`http://www.oti.com` (OTI)

`http://www.qks.com` (QKS-SmalltalkAgents)

`http://www.intuitive.co.uk` (Intutive-Dolphin Smalltalk)

`http://www.objectconnect.com` (Object Connect-Smalltalk MT) `http://www.sigs.com` (SIGS, publisher of *Object Magazine*, and *The Smalltalk Report*. Organizer of the Smalltalk Solutions Conference)

`http://www.smalltalksystems.com` (Former Digitalk and ObjectShare people and products)

5.11. References

Bergin, T., and R. Gibson (Eds.). 1996. *History of programming language, Volume 2*. New York: ACM Press, pp. 511–598.

Brooks, F. 1995. *The mythical man-month*. Reading, MA: Addison-Wesley.

Budd, T. 1987. *A little Smalltalk*. Reading, MA: Addison-Wesley.

Byte Magazine. 1981. Volume 6, Number 8.

Goldberg, A., and D. Robson. 1989. *Smalltalk-80: The language*. Reading, MA: Addison-Wesley.

Goldberg, A., and K. S. Rubin. 1995. *Succeeding with objects: Decision frameworks for project management*. Reading, MA: Addison-Wesley.

Jacobson, I. 1992. *Object-oriented software engineering: A use case approach*. New York: ACM Press.

Kaehler, T., and D. Patterson. 1986. *A taste of Smalltalk*. New York: Norton.

McClure, S. 1995. *Smalltalk market accelerates*. Framingham, MA: International Data Corporation. IDC #9818

McClure, S. 1997. *Smalltalk strengths stand out*. Framingham, MA: International Data Corporation. IDC #9818

Pletzke, J. 1997. *Advanced Smalltalk*. New York: Wiley.

PART III

C++

CHAPTER 6

A History of C++

by Bjarne Stroustrup

This chapter outlines the history of the C++ programming language from 1979 to 1997. The emphasis is on the ideas, constraints, and people that shaped the language, rather than the minutiae of language features. Key design decisions relating to language features are discussed, but the focus is on the overall design goals and practical constraints. The evolution of C++ is traced from C with Classes to the ISO standards effort and the explosion of use, interest, commercial activity, compilers, tools, environments, and libraries.

This chapter is a revised and extended version *of History of C++*: 1979–1991 (Stroustrup, 1996).

6.1. Introduction to C++

C++ was designed to provide imula's facilities for program organization together with C's efficiency and flexibility for systems programming. It was intended to deliver that to real projects within six months of when the idea was conceived. It succeeded.

At the time, I realized neither the modesty nor the preposterousness of that goal. The goal was modest in that it did not involve innovation and preposterous in both its time scale and its Draconian demands on efficiency and flexibility. Although a modest amount of innovation did emerge over the years, efficiency and flexibility have been maintained without compromise. Although the goals for C++ have been refined, elaborated, and made more explicit over the years, C++ as used today directly reflects its original aims.

This chapter is organized in roughly chronological order:

- Section 6.2, "C with Classes: 1979–1983." This section describes the fundamental design decisions for C++ as they were made for C++'s immediate predecessor.
- Section 6.3, "From C with Classes to C++: 1982–1985." This section describes how C++ evolved from C with Classes until the first commercial release and the printing of the book that defined C++ in October 1985.
- Section 6.4, "C++ Release 2.0: 1985–1988." This section describes how C++ evolved during the early years of commercial availability.
- Section 6.5, "Standardization: 1988–1998." This section describes the way C++ evolved under the pressures of heavy use in diverse application areas and how the C++ community handled this challenge through formal ISO standardization.
- Section 6.6, "The Standard Library." This section presents the quest for a standard C++ library.
- Section 6.7, "The Explosion in Interest and Use: 1987–the Present." This section deals with non-language factors, such as the growth of a C++ tools and library industry. It also tries to estimate the impact of commercial competition on the development of C++.
- Section 6.8, "Retrospective." This section considers how C++ met its design goals, how it might have been a better language, and how it might become an even more useful tool.

Most of this chapter is on the early years because the design decisions made early determined the further development of the language. It is also easier to maintain a historical perspective because I have had many years to observe the consequences of decisions.

Essential language features are presented to make this chapter approachable by a non-C++ specialist. However, the emphasis is on the people, ideas, and constraints that shaped C++ rather than on detailed descriptions of those language features or their use. For a description of what C++ is today and how to use it, see *The C++ Programming Language*, Third Edition (Stroustrup, 1997). For more details on the design and evolution of C++, see *The Design and Evolution of C++* (Stroustrup, 1994).

6.2. C with Classes: 1979–1983

C++ evolved from an earlier version of C called C with Classes. The work and experience with C with Classes from 1979 to 1983 determined the shape of C++.

6.2.1. Prehistory of C++

The prehistory of C++—the couple of years before the idea of adding Simula-like features to C occurred to me—is important because during this time the criteria and ideals that later shaped C++ emerged. I was working on my Ph.D. thesis in the Computing Laboratory of Cambridge University in England. My aim was to study alternatives for the organization of system software for a distributed system. The conceptual framework was provided by the capability-based Cambridge CAP computer and its experimental and continuously evolving operating system (Wilkes & Needham, 1979). The details of this work and its outcome (Stroustrup, 1979a) are of little relevance to C++. What is relevant, however, was the focus on composing software out of well-delimited modules and that the main experimental tool was a relatively large and detailed simulator I wrote for simulating software running on a distributed system.

The initial version of this simulator was written in Simula and ran on the Cambridge University computer center's IBM 360/165 mainframe. It was a pleasure to write that simulator. The features of Simula were almost ideal for the purpose, and I was particularly impressed by the way the concepts of the language helped me think about the problems in my application. The class concept allowed me to map my application concepts into the language constructs in a direct way that made my code more readable than I had seen in any other language. The way Simula classes can act as co-routines made the inherent concurrency of my application easy to express. For example, an object of class `computer` could trivially be made to work in pseudo-parallel with other objects of class `computer`. Class hierarchies were used to express variants of application-level concepts. For example, different types of computers could be expressed as classes derived from class `computer`, and different types of inter-module communication mechanisms could be expressed as classes derived from class `IPC`. The use of class hierarchies was not heavy, however; the use of classes to express concurrency was much more important in the organization of my simulator.

During writing and initial debugging, I acquired a great respect for the expressiveness of Simula's type system and its compiler's ability to catch type errors. The observation was that a type error almost invariably reflected either a silly programming error or a conceptual flaw in the design. The latter was by far the most significant and a help that I had not experienced in the use of more primitive "strong" type systems. In contrast, I had found Pascal's type system worse than useless—a strait-jacket that caused more problems than it solved by forcing me to warp my designs to suit an implementation-oriented artifact. The perceived contrast between the rigidity of Pascal and the flexibility of Simula was essential for the development of C++. Simula's class concept was seen as the key difference, and ever since, I have seen classes as the proper primary focus of program design.

I had used Simula before (during my studies at the University of Aarhus in Denmark) but was very pleasantly surprised by the way the mechanisms of the Simula language became increasingly helpful as the size of the program increased. The class and co-routine mechanisms of Simula and the comprehensive type-checking mechanisms ensured that problems and errors did not (as I—and I guess most people—would have expected) grow linearly or more than linearly with the size of the program. Instead, the total program acted more like a collection of small (and therefore easy to write, comprehend, and debug) programs rather than a single large program.

The implementation of Simula, however, did not scale in the same way, and as a result, the whole project came close to disaster. My conclusion at the time was that the Simula implementation (as opposed to the Simula language) was geared to relatively small programs and was inherently unsuited for larger programs (Stroustrup, 1979a). Link times for separately compiled classes were abysmal: It took longer to compile 1/30 of the program and link it to a precompiled version of the rest than it took to compile and link the program as a monolith. This I believe to be more a problem with the mainframe linker than with Simula, but it was still a burden. On top of that, the runtime performance was such that there was no hope of using the simulator to obtain real data. The poor runtime characteristics were a function of the language and its implementation rather than a function of the application. The overhead problems were fundamental to Simula and could not be remedied. The cost arose from several language features and their interactions: runtime type checking, guaranteed initialization of variables, concurrency support, and garbage collection of both user-allocated objects and procedure activation records.

For example, measurements showed that more than 80% of the time was spent in the garbage collector despite the fact that resource management was part of the simulated system so that no garbage was ever produced. Simula implementations improved, but the order-of-magnitude improvement relative to systems programming languages did not (to the best of my knowledge) materialize.

To avoid terminating the project, I rewrote the simulator in BCPL and ran it on the experimental CAP computer. The experience of coding and debugging the simulator in BCPL was horrible. BCPL makes C look like a very high-level language and provides absolutely no type checking or runtime support. The resulting simulator did, however, run suitably fast and gave a whole range of useful results that clarified many issues for me and provided the basis for several papers on operating system issues (Stroustrup, 1978, 1979b, 1981b).

Upon leaving Cambridge, I swore never again to attack a problem with tools as unsuitable as those I had suffered while designing and implementing the simulator. The significance of this to C++ was the notion I had evolved of what constituted a "suitable tool" for projects such as the writing of a significant simulator, an operating system, and similar systems programming tasks:

- A good tool would have Simula's support for program organization—that is, classes, some form of class hierarchies, some form of support for concurrency, and strong (that is, static) checking of a type system based on classes. This I saw as support for the process of inventing programs, as support for design rather than just support for implementation.
- A good tool would produce programs that ran as fast as BCPL programs and share BCPL's ability to easily combine separately compiled units into a program. A simple linkage convention is essential for combining units written in languages such as C, Algol68, Fortran, BCPL, and assembler into a single program and thus not get caught by inherent limitations in a single language.
- A good tool should also allow for highly portable implementations. My experience was that the "good" implementation I needed would typically not be available until "next year" and only on a machine I couldn't afford. This implied that a tool must have multiple sources of implementations (no monopoly would be sufficiently responsive to users of "unusual" machines and to poor graduate students), that

there should be no complicated runtime support system to port, and that there should be only very limited integration between the tool and its host operating system.

Not all of these criteria were fully formed when I left Cambridge, but several were and more matured on further reflection on my experience with the simulator, on programs written over the next couple of years, and on the experiences of others as learned through discussions and reading code. C++ as defined at the time of Release 2.0 strictly fulfills these criteria. The fundamental tensions in the effort to design templates and exception-handling mechanisms for C++ arise from the need to depart from some aspects of these criteria. I think the most important aspect of these criteria is that they are only loosely connected with specific programming language features. They do not specify solutions to specific problems. Rather, they specify constraints on solutions. Over the years, the initial criteria developed into a more comprehensive set that guided the design and evolution of C++ (Stroustrup, 1994).

My background in operating systems work and my interest in modularization and communication had permanent effects on C++. The C++ model of protection, for example, is based on the notion of granting and transferring access rights, the distinction between initialization and assignment has its root in thoughts about transferring capabilities, and the design of C++'s exception-handling mechanism was influenced by work on fault-tolerant systems done by Brian Randell's group in Newcastle in the 1970s.

6.2.2. The Birth of C with Classes

The work on what eventually became C++ started with an attempt to analyze the UNIX kernel to determine to what extent it could be distributed over a network of computers connected by a local area network. This work started in April 1979 in the Computing Science Research Center of Bell Laboratories in Murray Hill, New Jersey. Two subproblems soon emerged: how to analyze the network traffic that would result from the kernel distribution and how to modularize the kernel. Both required a way to express the module structure of a complex system and the communication pattern of the modules. This was exactly the kind of problem that I had become determined never to attack again without proper tools. Consequently, I set about developing a proper tool according to the criteria I had formed in Cambridge.

In October 1979, I had a preprocessor called Cpre that added Simula-like classes to C running, and in March 1980, this preprocessor had been refined to the point where it supported one real project and several experiments. My records show the preprocessor in use on 16 systems by then. The first key C++ library, the task system supporting a co-routine style of programming (Shopiro, 1987; Stroustrup, 1980b, 1987b), was crucial to the usefulness of C with Classes (as the language accepted by the preprocessor was called) in these projects.

During the April to October period, the transition from thinking about a tool to thinking about a language had occurred, but C with Classes was still thought of primarily as an extension to C for expressing modularity and concurrency. A crucial decision had been made, however. Even though support of concurrency and Simula-style simulations was a primary aim of C with Classes, the language contained no primitives for expressing concurrency; rather, a combination of inheritance (class hierarchies) and the ability to define class member functions with special meanings recognized by the preprocessor was used to write the library that supported the desired styles of concurrency. Please note that "styles" is plural. I considered it crucial—as I still do—that more than one notion of concurrency should be expressible in the language. This decision has been reconfirmed repeatedly by me and my colleagues, by other C++ users, and by the C++ standards committee. There are many applications for which support for concurrency is essential, but there is no one dominant model for concurrency support; thus, when support is needed, it should be provided through a library or a special-purpose extension so that a particular form of concurrency support does not preclude other forms.

Thus, the language provided general mechanisms for organizing programs rather than support for specific application areas. This was what made C with Classes and later C++ a general-purpose language rather than a C variant with extensions to support specialized applications. Later, the choice between providing support for specialized applications or general abstraction mechanisms came up repeatedly. Each time, the decision was to improve the abstraction mechanisms.

An early description of C with Classes was published as a Bell Labs technical report in April 1980 (Stroustrup, 1980a) and later in *SIGPLAN Notices*. The SIGPLAN paper was followed in April 1982 by a more detailed Bell Labs technical report *Adding Classes to the C Language: An Exercise in Language Evolution* (Stroustrup, 1982) that was later published in *Software: Practice and Experience*. These papers set a good example by describing only features that were fully implemented and had been used. This was in accordance with a long-standing tradition of Bell Labs Computing Science Research Center. That policy was modified only where more openness about the future of C++ became necessary to ensure a free and open debate over the evolution of C++ among its many non-AT&T users.

C with Classes was explicitly designed to allow better organization of programs; computation was considered a problem solved by C. I was very concerned that improved program structure was not achieved at the expense of runtime overheads compared to C. The explicit aim was to match C in terms of runtime, code compactness, and data compactness. To wit: Someone once demonstrated a 3% systematic decrease in overall runtime efficiency compared with C. This was considered unacceptable, and the overhead was promptly removed by compiler improvements. Similarly, to ensure layout compatibility with C and thereby avoid space overheads, no housekeeping data was placed in class objects.

Another major concern was to avoid restrictions on the domain where C with Classes could be used. The ideal—which was achieved—was that C with Classes could be used for whatever C could be used for. This implied that in addition to matching C in efficiency, C with Classes could not provide benefits at the expense of removing dangerous or ugly features of C. This observation or principle had to be repeated often to people (rarely C with Classes users) who wanted C with Classes made safer by increasing static type checking along the lines of early Pascal. The alternative way of providing safety, inserting runtime checks for all unsafe operations, was (and is) considered reasonable for debugging environments, but the language could not guarantee such checks without leaving C with a large advantage in runtime and space efficiency. Consequently, such checks were not provided for C with Classes, although C++ environments exist that provide such checks for debugging. In addition, users can and do insert runtime checks (assertions; Stroustrup, 1997) where needed and affordable.

C allows quite low-level operations such as bit manipulation and choosing between different sizes of integers. There are also facilities, such as explicit unchecked type conversions, for deliberately breaking the type system. C with Classes, and later C++, follow this path by retaining the low-level and unsafe features of C. In contrast to C, C++ systematically eliminates the need to use such features except where they are essential.

C++ provides facilities that allow a programmer to avoid unsafe operations except through explicit requests. I strongly felt then, as I still do, that there is no one right way of writing every program and a language designer has no business trying to *force* programmers to use a particular style. The language designer does, on the other hand, have an obligation to encourage and support a variety of styles and practices that have been proven effective and to provide language features and tools to help programmers avoid the well-known traps and pitfalls.

6.2.3. C with Classes Feature Overview

The features provided in the initial 1980 implementation can be summarized as follows:

- Classes
- Derived classes
- Public/private access control
- Constructors and destructors
- Call and return functions (see section 6.2.4.8)
- Friend classes
- Type checking and conversion of function arguments

During 1981, three more features were added

- Inline functions
- Default arguments
- Overloading of the assignment operator

Because a preprocessor was used for the implementation of C with Classes: only new features—that is, features not present in C—needed to be described and the full power of C was directly available to users. Both of these aspects were appreciated at the time. Having C as a subset dramatically reduced the support and documentation work needed. This was most important because for several years I handled all the C with Classes and later C++ documentation and support in addition to doing the experimentation, design, and implementation. Having all C features available further ensured that no limitations introduced through prejudice or lack of foresight on my part would deprive a user of features already available in C. Naturally, portability to machines supporting C was ensured.

Initially, C with Classes was implemented and used on a DEC PDP/11, but soon, it was ported to machines such as DEC VAX and Motorola 68000–based machines.

C with Classes was still seen as a dialect of C. Furthermore, classes were referred to as "An Abstract Data Type Facility for the C Language" (Stroustrup, 1980a). Support for object-oriented programming was not claimed until the provision of virtual functions in C++ in 1983 (Stroustrup, 1984a).

6.2.4. C with Classes Feature Details

Clearly, the most important aspect of C with Classes—and later of C++—was the class concept. Many aspects of the C with Classes class concept can be observed by examining a simple example from *Classes: An Abstract Data Type Facility for the C Language* (Stroustrup, 1980a):

```
class stack {
    char    s[SIZE];      /* array of characters */
    char *  min;          /* pointer to bottom of stack */
    char *  top;          /* pointer to top of stack */
    char *  max;          /* pointer to top of allocated space */
    void    new();        /* initialization function (constructor) */
public:
    void push(char);
    char pop();
};
```

A class is a user-defined data type. A class specifies the type of the class members that define the representation of a variable of the type (an object of the class), specifies the set of operations (functions) that manipulate such objects, and specifies the access users have to these members. Member functions are typically defined elsewhere:

```
char stack.pop()
{
    if (top <= min) error("stack underflow");
    return *(--top);
}
```

Objects of class `stack` can now be defined and used:

```
class stack s1, s2;             /* two variables of class stack */
class stack * p1 = &s2;         /* p1 points to s2 */
class stack * p2 = new stack;   /* p2 points to stack object allocated
                                   on free store */
s1.push('h');                   /* use object directly */
p1->push('s');                  /* use object through pointer */
```

Several key design decisions are reflected here:

- C with Classes follows Simula in letting the programmer specify types from which variables (objects) can be created, rather than, say, the Modula approach of specifying a module as a collection of objects and functions. In C with Classes (as in C++), a class is a type. This is a key notion in C++. When *class* means user-defined type in C++, why didn't I call it *type*? I chose *class* primarily because I dislike inventing new terminology and found Simula's quite adequate in most cases.
- The representation of objects of the user-defined type is part of the class declaration. This has far-reaching implications. For example, it means that true local variables can be implemented without the use of free store (heap store, dynamic store) or garbage collection. It also means that a function must be recompiled if the representation of an object it uses directly is changed. See section 6.4.3 for C++ facilities for expressing interfaces that avoid such recompilation.
- Compile-time access control is used to restrict access to the representation. By default, only the functions mentioned in the class declaration can use names of class members. Members (usually function members) specified in the public interface—the declarations after the `public:` label—can be used by other code.
- The full type (including both the return type and the argument types) of a function is specified for function members. Static (compile-time) type checking is based on this type specification. This differed from C at the time, where function argument types were neither specified in interfaces nor checked in calls.
- Function definitions are typically specified elsewhere to make a class more like an interface specification than a lexical mechanism for organizing source code. This implies that separate compilation for class member functions and their users is easy and the linker technology traditionally used for C is sufficient to support C++.
- The function `new()` `a constructor,` is a constructor, a function with a special meaning to the compiler. Such functions provided guarantees about
  classes. In this case, the guarantee is that the constructor—known somewhat confusingly as a `new` function at the time—is guaranteed to be called to initialize every object of its class before the first use of the object.
- Both pointers and non-pointer types are provided (as in both C and Simula).

Much of the further development of C with Classes and C++ can be seen as exploring the consequences of these design choices, exploiting their good sides, and compensating for the problems caused by their bad sides. Many, but by no means all, of the implications of these design choices were understood at the time *Classes: An Abstract Data Type Facility for the C Language* was written (dated April 3, 1980). This section tries to explain what was understood at the time and give pointers to sections explaining later consequences and realizations.

6.2.4.1. Runtime Efficiency

In Simula, it is not possible to have local or global variables of class types; that is, every object of a class must be allocated on the free store using the `new` operator. Measurements of my Cambridge simulator had convinced me that this was a major source of inefficiency. Later, Karel Babcisky (1984) from the Norwegian Computer Centre presented data on Simula runtime performance that confirmed my conjecture. For that reason alone, I wanted global and local variables of class types.

In addition, having different rules for the creation and scope of built-in and user-defined types is inelegant, and I felt that on occasion, my programming style had been cramped by absence of local and global class variables in Simula. Similarly, I had on occasion missed the ability to have pointers to built-in types in Simula, so I wanted the C notion of pointers to apply uniformly over user-defined and built-in types. This is the origin of the notion that over the years grew into a principle for C++: User-defined and built-in types should behave the same relative to the language rules and receive the same degree of support from the language and its associated tools. When the ideal was formulated, built-in types received by far the best support, but C++ has overshot that target so that built-in types now receive slightly inferior support compared to user-defined types.

The initial version of C with Classes did not provide inline functions to take further advantage of the availability of the representation. Inline functions were soon provided, though. The general reason for the introduction of inline functions was concern that the cost of crossing a protection barrier would cause people to refrain from using classes to hide representation. In particular, *Adding Classes to the C Language: An Exercise in Language Evolution* observes that people had made data members public to avoid the function call overhead incurred by a constructor for simple classes where only one or two assignments are needed for initialization. The immediate cause for the inclusion of inline functions into C with Classes was a project that couldn't afford function call overhead for some classes involved in real-time processing.

Over the years, considerations along these lines grew into the C++ principle that it was not sufficient to provide a feature; it had to be provided in an affordable form. Most definitely, *affordable* was seen as meaning "affordable on hardware common among developers" as opposed to "affordable to researchers with high-end equipment" or "affordable in a couple years when hardware is cheaper." C with Classes was always considered something to be used *now* or *next month* rather than simply a research project to deliver something a couple of years hence.

Inlining was considered important for the utility of classes, and therefore the issue was more *how* to provide it than *whether* to provide it. Two arguments won the day for the notion of having the programmer select which functions the compiler should try to inline. First, I had poor experiences with languages that left the job of inlining to compilers "because clearly the compiler knows best." The compiler knows best only if it has been programmed to inline and it has a notion of time and space optimization that agrees with mine. My experience with other languages was that only "the next release" would actually inline, and it would do so according to an internal logic that a programmer couldn't effectively control. To make matters worse, C (and therefore C with Classes and later C++) has genuine separate compilation so that a compiler never has access to more than a small part of the program (section 6.2.4.2). Inlining a function for which you don't know the source appears feasible given advanced linker and optimizer technology, but such technology wasn't available at the time (10 years later, it still wasn't in most environments). Furthermore, extensive global analysis and optimization easily become unaffordable for large systems—where optimizations are most critical. C with Classes was designed to deliver efficient code given a simple portable implementation on traditional systems. Given that, the programmer had to help. Even today, the choice seems right.

6.2.4.2. The Linkage Model

The issue of how separately compiled programs are linked together is critical for any programming language and to some extent determines the features the language can provide. One of the critical influences on the development of C with Classes and C++ was the decision that

- Separate compilation should be possible with traditional C/Fortran UNIX/DOS style linkers.
- In principle, linkage should be type safe.
- Linkage should not require any form of database (although one could be used to improve a given implementation).
- Linkage to program fragments written in other languages such as C, assembler, and Fortran should be easy and efficient.

C uses header files to ensure consistent separate compilation. Declarations of data structure layouts, functions, variables, and constants are placed in header files that typically are textually included into every source file that needs the declarations. Consistency is ensured by placing adequate information in the header files and ensuring that the header files are consistently included. C++ follows this model up to a point.

The reason that layout information can be present in a C++ class declaration (although it doesn't *have* to be; see section 6.4.3) is to ensure that the declaration and use of true local variables are easy and efficient. Here's an example:

```
void f()
{
      stack s;
      int c;
      s.push('h');
      c = s.pop();
}
```

Using the `stack` declaration from section 6.2.4, even a simplistic C with Classes implementation can ensure that no use is made of free store for this example, that the call of `pop()` is inlined so that no function call overhead is incurred, and that the non-inlined call of `push()` can invoke a separately compiled function `pop()`. In this, C++ resembles Ada (Ichbiah, 1979).

At the time, I felt that there was a tradeoff between having separate interface and implementation declarations (as in Modula-2) plus a tool (linker) for matching them up and having a single class declaration, plus a tool (a dependency analyzer) that considered the interface part separately from the implementation details for the purposes of recompilation. It appears that I underestimated the complexity of the latter and also that the proponents of the former approach underestimate the cost (in terms of porting problems and runtime overheads) of the former.

The concern for simplistic implementations was partly a necessity caused by the lack of resources for developing C with Classes and partly a distrust of languages and mechanisms that required clever techniques. An early formulation of a design goal was that C with Classes "should be implementable without using an algorithm more complicated than a linear search." Wherever that rule of thumb was violated—as in the case of function overloading (section 6.3.3.3)—it led to semantics that were more complicated than anyone felt comfortable with and typically also led to implementation complications.

The aim—based on my Simula experience—was to design a language that would be easy enough to understand to attract users and easy enough to implement to attract implementers. For C with Classes, and later C++, to survive in competition with C, a relatively simple implementation used by a relatively novice user in a relatively unsupportive programming environment would have to deliver code that compared favorably with C code in development time, correctness, runtime speed, and code size.

This was part of a philosophy of fostering self-sufficiency among users. The aim was always—and explicitly—to develop local expertise in all aspects of using C++. Most programming language and tools purveyors must follow the exact opposite strategy. They keep users dependent on services that generate revenue for a central support organization and consultants. In my opinion, this contrast is a deep reason for some of the differences between C++ and many other languages.

The decision to work in the relatively primitive—and almost universally available—framework of the C linking facilities caused the fundamental problem that a C++ compiler must always work with only partial information about a program. An assumption made about a program could possibly be violated by a program written tomorrow in some other language (such as C, Fortran, or assembler) and linked in—possibly after the program has started executing. This problem surfaces in many contexts. It is hard for an implementation to guarantee

- That something is unique
- That (type) information is consistent
- That something is initialized

In addition, C provides only the feeblest support for the notion of separate namespaces so that avoiding namespace pollution by separately written program segments becomes a problem (see section 6.5.7). Over the years, C++ has tried to face all these challenges without departing from the fundamental model and technology that give portability, but in the C with Classes days, we simply relied on the C technique of header files.

Through the acceptance of the C linker came another principle for the development of C++: that C++ is just one language in a system and not a complete system. In other words, C++ accepts the role of a traditional programming language with a fundamental distinction between the language, the operating system, and other important parts of the programmer's world. This delimits the role of the language in a way that is hard to do for a language, such as Smalltalk or Lisp, that is conceived as a complete system or environment. It makes it essential that a C++ program fragment can call program fragments written in other languages and that a C++ program fragment can itself be called by program fragments written in other languages. Being "just a language" also allows C++ implementations to benefit directly from tools written for other languages.

The need for a programming language and the code written in it to be just a cog in a much larger machine is of utmost importance to most industrial users, yet such coexistence with other languages and systems was apparently not a major concern to most theoreticians, would-be perfectionists, and academic users. I believe this to be one of the main reasons for C++'s success.

6.2.4.3. Static Type Checking

I have no recollection of discussions, no design notes, and no recollection of any implementation problems with the introduction of static (*strong*) type checking into C with Classes. The C with Classes syntax and rules, the ones subsequently adopted for the ANSI C standard, simply appeared fully formed in the first C with Classes implementation. After that, a minor series of experiments led to the current (stricter) C++ rules. Static type checking was to me, after my experience with Simula and Algol68, a simple *must*, and the only question was exactly how it was to be added.

To avoid breaking C code, it was decided to allow the call of an undeclared function and not perform type checking on such undeclared functions. This was of course a major hole in the type system and several attempts were made to decrease its importance as the major source of programming errors before finally—in C++—the hole was closed by making a call of an undeclared function illegal. One simple observation defeated all attempts to compromise and thus maintain a greater degree of C compatibility: As programmers learned C with Classes, they lost the ability to find runtime errors caused by simple type errors. Having come to rely on the type checking and type conversion provided by C with Classes or C++, they lost the ability to quickly find the silly errors that creep into C programs through the lack of checking. Further, they failed to take the precautions against such silly errors that good C programmers take as a matter of course. After all, "such errors don't happen in C with Classes." Thus, as the frequency of runtime errors caused by uncaught argument type errors goes down, their seriousness and the time needed to find them goes up. The result was seriously annoyed programmers demanding further tightening of the type system.

The most interesting experiment with "incomplete static checking" was the technique of allowing calls of undeclared functions but noting the type of the arguments used so that a consistency check could be done when further calls were seen. Many years later, when Walter Bright independently discovered this trick, he named it "autoprototyping," using the ANSI C term *prototype* for a function declaration. The experience was that autoprototyping caught many errors and initially increased a programmer's confidence in the type system. However, because consistent errors and errors in a function called only once in a compilation were not caught, autoprototyping ultimately destroyed programmer confidence in the type checker and induced a sense of paranoia even worse than I have seen in C or BCPL programmers.

C with Classes introduced the notation `f(void)` for a function `f` that takes no arguments as a contrast to `f()` that in C declares a function that can take any number of arguments of any type without any type check. My users soon convinced me, however, that the `f(void)` notation wasn't very elegant and that having functions declared `f()` accept arguments wasn't very intuitive. Consequently, the result of the experiment was to have `f()` mean a function `f` that takes no arguments, as any novice would expect. It took support from both Doug McIlroy and Dennis Ritchie for me to build up courage to make this break from C. Only after they used the word *abomination* about `f(void)` did I dare give `f()` the obvious meaning. However, to this day, C's type rules are much more lax than C++'s and any use of `f()` as a function declaration is incompatible between the two languages.

Another early attempt to tighten C with Classes's type rules was to disallow "information destroying" implicit conversions. Like others, I had been badly bitten by implicit `long` to `int` and `int` to `char` conversions. I decided to try to ban all implicit conversions that were not value preserving—that is, to require an explicit conversion operator wherever a larger object was stored into a smaller. The experiment failed miserably. Every C program I looked at contained large numbers of assignments of `int` variables to `char` variables. Naturally, because these were working programs, most of these assignments were perfectly safe. That is, either the value was small enough not to become truncated or the truncation was expected or at least harmless in that particular context. There was no willingness in the C with Classes community to make such a break from C. I'm still looking for ways to compensate for these problems.

6.2.4.4. Why C?

A common question at C with Classes presentations was "Why use C? Why didn't you build on, say, Pascal?" One version of my answer can be found in *The C++ Programming Language* (Stroustrup, 1986a):

C is clearly neither the cleanest language ever designed nor the easiest to use, so why do so many people use it?

- C is *flexible*: It is possible to apply C to most application areas and to use most programming techniques with C. The language has no inherent limitations that preclude particular kinds of programs from being written.
- C is *efficient*: The semantics of C are "low level"—that is, the fundamental concepts of C mirror the fundamental concepts of a traditional computer. Consequently, it is relatively easy for a compiler or a programmer to efficiently utilize hardware resources for a C program.
- C is *available*: Given a computer, whether the tiniest micro or the largest super-computer, the chance is that there is an acceptable quality C compiler available and that that C compiler supports an acceptably complete and standard C language and library. There are also libraries and support tools available so that a programmer rarely needs to design a new system from scratch.
- C is *portable*: A C program is not automatically portable from one machine (and operating system) to another nor is such a port necessarily easy to do. It is, however, usually possible and the level of difficulty is such that porting even major pieces of software with inherent machine dependencies is typically technically and economically feasible.

> Compared with these first-order advantages, the second-order drawbacks such as the curious C declarator syntax and the lack of safety of some language constructs become less important. Designing "a better C" implies compensating for the major problems involved in writing, debugging, and maintaining C programs *without compromising the advantages of C*. C++ preserves all these advantages and compatibility with C at the cost of abandoning claims to perfection and of some compiler and language complexity. However, designing a language "from scratch" does not ensure perfection and the C++ compilers compare favorably in runtime, have better error detection and reporting, and equal the C compilers in code quality.

This formulation is more polished than I could have managed in the early C with Classes days, but it does capture the essence of what I considered important about C and that I did not want to lose in C with Classes. Pascal was considered a toy language (Kernighan, 1981), so it seemed easier and safer to add type checking to C than to add the features considered necessary for systems programming to Pascal. At the time, I had a positive dread of making mistakes of the sort where the designer, out of misguided paternalism or plain ignorance, makes the language unusable for real work in important areas. The 10 years that followed clearly showed that choosing C as a base left me in the mainstream of systems programming where I intended to be. The cost in language complexity has been considerable, but manageable.

At the time, I considered Modula-2, Ada, Smalltalk, Mesa, and Clu as alternatives to C and as sources for ideas for C++ (Stroustrup, 1984b), so there was no shortage of inspiration. However, only C, Simula, Algol68, and (in one case) BCPL left noticeable traces in C++ as released in 1985. Simula gave classes, Algol68 operator overloading (section 6.3.3.3), references (section 6.3.3.4), and the ability to declare variables anywhere in a block (section 6.3.3.1), and BCPL gave `//` comments (section 6.3.3.1).

There were several reasons for avoiding major departures from C style. I saw the merging of C's strengths as a systems programming language with Simula's strengths for organizing programs as a significant challenge in itself. Adding significant features from other languages could easily lead to a "shopping list" language and destroy the integrity of the resulting language. To quote from *The C++ Programming Language* (Stroustrup, 1986a):

> A programming language serves two related purposes: It provides a vehicle for the programmer to specify actions to be executed and a set of concepts for the programmer to use when thinking about what can be done. The first aspect ideally requires a language that is "close to the machine" so that all important aspects of a machine are handled simply and efficiently in a way that is reasonably obvious to the programmer. The C language was primarily designed with this in mind. The second aspect ideally requires a language that is "close to the problem to be solved" so that the concepts of a solution can be expressed directly and concisely. The facilities added to C to create C++ were primarily designed with this in mind.

Again this formulation is more polished than I could have managed during the early stages of the design of C with Classes, but the general idea was clear. Departures from the known and proven techniques of C and Simula would have to wait for further experience with C with Classes and C++ and further experiments. I firmly believe—and believed then—that language design is not just design from first principles but also an art that requires experience, experiments, and sound engineering tradeoffs. Adding a major feature or concept to a language should not be a leap of faith but a deliberate action based on experience and fitting into a framework of other features and ideas of how the resulting language can be used. The post-1985 evolution of C++ shows the influence of ideas from Ada, Clu, and ML.

6.2.4.5. Syntax Problems

Could I have "fixed" the most annoying deficiencies of the C syntax and semantics at some point before C++ was made generally available? Could I have done so without removing useful features (to C with Classes's users in their environments—as opposed to an ideal world) or introducing incompatibilities that were unacceptable to C programmers wanting to migrate to C with Classes? I think not. In some cases, I tried, but I backed out my changes after complaints from outraged users. The part of the C syntax I disliked most was the declaration syntax. Having both prefix and postfix declarator operators cause a fair amount of confusion. So does allowing the type specifier to be left out (meaning `int` by default). In 1995, the C++ standards committee finally banned implicit `int` in declarations. However, the unfortunate declarator syntax remains unchanged.

My eventual rationale for leaving things as they were was that any new syntax would (temporarily at least) add complexity to a known mess. Also, even though the old style is a boon to teachers of trivia and to people wanting to ridicule C, it is not a significant problem for C programmers. In this case, I'm not sure if I did the right thing, however. The agony to me and other C++ implementers, documenters, and tool builders caused by the perversities of syntax has been significant. Users can—and do—of course insulate themselves from such problems by writing in a small and easily understood subset of the C/C++ declaration syntax.

A significant syntactic simplification for the benefit of users was introduced into C++ at the cost of some extra work to implementers and some C compatibility problems. In C, the name of a structure, a "structure tag," must always be preceded by the keyword `struct`. Here's an example:

```
struct buffer a;     /* 'struct' is necessary in C */
```

In the context of C with Classes, this had annoyed me for some time because it made user-defined types second-class citizens syntactically. Given my lack of success with other attempts to clean up the syntax, I was reluctant and only made the change—at the time where C with Classes was mutated into C++—at the urging of Tom Cargill. The name of a `struct` or a `class` is now a type name and requires no special syntactic identification:

```
buffer a;     // C++
```

The resulting fights over C compatibility lasted for years (see also section 6.3.4).

6.2.4.6. Derived Classes

The derived class concept is C++'s version of Simula's prefixed class notion and thus a sibling of Smalltalk's subclass concept. The names *derived* class and *base* class were chosen because I never could remember what was *sub* and what was *super* and observed that I was not the only one with this particular problem. It was also noted that many people found it counterintuitive that a subclass typically has *more* information than its superclass. In inventing the terms derived class and base class, I departed from my usual principle of not inventing new names where old ones exist. In my defense, I note that I have never observed any confusion about what is base and what is derived among C++ programmers and that the terms are trivially easy to learn, even for people without a grounding in mathematics.

The C with Classes concept was provided without any form of runtime support. In particular, the Simula (and C++) concept of a virtual function was missing. The reason for this was that I—with reason I think—doubted my ability to teach people how to use them and even more my ability to convince people that a virtual function is as efficient in time and space as an ordinary function as typically used. Often, people with Simula and Smalltalk experience still don't quite believe that until they have had the C++ implementation explained to them in detail—and many still harbor irrational doubts after that.

Even without virtual functions, derived classes in C with Classes were useful for building new data structures out of old ones and for associating operations with the resulting types. In particular, as explained in *Classes: An Abstract Data Type Facility for the C Language* (Stroustrup, 1980a) and *Adding Classes to the C Language: An Exercise in Language Evolution* (Stroustrup, 1982), they allowed list classes to be defined and also task classes (that is, concurrency-support classes).

In the absence of virtual functions, a user could use objects of a derived class and treat base classes as implementation details (only). Alternatively, an explicit type field could be introduced in a base class and used together with explicit type casts. The former strategy was used for tasks where the user sees only specific derived task classes and "the system" sees only the task base classes. The latter strategy was used for various application classes where, in effect, a base class was used to implement a variant record for a set of derived classes. Much of the effort in C with Classes and later C++ has been to ensure that programmers needn't write such code. Most important in my thinking at the time and in my own code was the combination of base classes, explicit type conversions, and (occasionally) macros to provide generic container classes. Eventually, these techniques matured into C++'s template facility and the techniques for using templates together with base classes to express commonality among instantiated templates (section 6.6.3).

6.2.4.7. The Protection Model

Before starting work on C with Classes, I worked with operating systems. The notions of protection from the Cambridge CAP computer and similar systems—rather than any work in programming languages—inspired the C++ protection mechanisms. The class is the unit of protection and the fundamental rule is that you cannot grant yourself access to a class; only the declarations placed in the class declaration (supposedly by its owner) can grant access. By default, all information is private.

Access is granted by declaring a function in the public part of a class declaration or by specifying a function or a class as a *friend*. Initially, only classes could be friends, thus granting access to all member functions of the friend class, but later it was found convenient to be able to grant access (friendship) to individual functions. In particular, it was found useful to be able to grant access to global functions.

A friendship declaration was seen as a mechanism similar to that of one protection domain granting a read/write capability to another.

Even in the first version of C with Classes, the protection model applied to base classes as well as members. Thus a class could be either publicly or privately derived from another. The private/public distinction for base classes predates by about five years the debate on implementation inheritance versus interface inheritance (Liskov, 1987; Snyder, 1986). If you want to inherit an implementation only, you use private derivation in C++. Public derivation gives users of the derived class access to the interface provided by the base class. Private derivation leaves the base as an implementation detail; even the public members of the private base class are inaccessible except through the interface explicitly provided for the derived class.

To provide semi-transparent scopes, a mechanism was provided to allow individual public names from a private base class to be made public (Stroustrup, 1982).

6.2.4.8. Runtime Guarantees

The access control mechanisms described previously simply prevent unauthorized access. A second kind of guarantee was provided by special member functions, such as constructors, that were recognized and implicitly invoked by the compiler. The idea was to allow the programmer to establish guarantees, sometimes called invariants, that other member function could rely on. For example, *Classes: An Abstract Data Type Facility for the C Language* (Stroustrup, 1980a) presented this refinement of class `stack` (section 6.2.4):

> All stacks created using the definition above have the size `SIZE`. This is not ideal, so let us try again:

```
class stack
{
        void        new(short);
        void        delete(void);
        char *      min;
        char *      top;
        char *      max;
public:
        void        push(char);
        char        pop(void);
};
```

This `class stack` declaration does not specify the amount of store to be allocated for the stack itself. Instead it is specified that an argument of type `short` must be provided for `stack.new()`. Arguments to a `new()` function are provided as part of the declaration of a class object. Here's an example:

```
class stack s1(SIZE), s2(200);
```

The `new()` function then provides the interpretation of them:

```
void stack.new(int size)
{
        top = min = new char[size];
        max = min+size-1;
}
```

A vector of `size` characters is allocated on the free store. This, however, creates a new problem. Because we cannot (in general) assume that a garbage collector is available, we must clean up after ourselves. That is, in this case we must deallocate the vector pointed to by `min` when an object of `class stack` is deleted. This is done by defining a parameterless function called `delete`:

```
void stack.delete()
{
        delete min;
}
```

If a function of this name is mentioned in the class declaration, it is guaranteed to be the last function accessing an object of that class before it is deleted.

The initial syntax for constructors and destructors was revised during the revision that yielded the initial C++ (section 6.3.3.1) so that the example looks like this:

```
class stack {
        char* min;
        char* top;
        char* max;
public:
        stack(int);             // constructor
        ~stack();               // destructor

        void  push(char);
        char  pop();
};

void stack::stack(int size)
{
     top = min = new char[size];     // allocate space for elements
     max = min+size-1;
```

```
}

void stack::~stack()
{
    delete[] min;       // delete array of elements
}
```

Constructors and destructors proved immensely valuable and are the basis for many C++ programming styles (for example, see section 6.5.6).

Curiously enough, the initial implementation of C with Classes contained a feature that is not provided by C++ but is often requested. In C with Classes, it was possible to define a function that would implicitly be called before every call of every member function (except the constructor) and another that would be implicitly called before every return from every member function. They were called call and return functions. They were used to provide synchronization for the monitor class in the original task library (Stroustrup, 1980b):

```
class monitor : object {
    /* ... */
    call() { /* grab lock */ }
    return() { /* release lock */ }
};
```

These are similar in intent to the `CLOS` `:before` and `:after` methods. Call and return functions were removed from the language because nobody (but me) used them and because I seemed to have completely failed to convince people that `call()` and `return()` had important uses. In 1987, Mike Tiemann suggested an alternative solution called "wrappers" (Tiemann, 1987), but at the USENIX implementors' workshop in Estes Park, this idea was deemed to have too many problems to be accepted into C++.

6.2.4.9. Features Considered but Not Provided

In the early days, many the features were considered that later appeared in C++ or are still discussed. These included virtual functions, *static* members, templates, and multiple inheritance. However, "All of these generalizations have their uses, but every feature of a language takes time and effort to design, implement, document, and learn....The base class concept is an engineering compromise, like the C class concept" (Stroustrup, 1982). I just wish I had explicitly mentioned the need for experience. With that, the case against featurism and for a pragmatic approach would have been complete.

The possibility of automatic garbage collection was considered on several occasions before 1985 and deemed unsuitable for a language already in use for real-time processing and hard-core systems tasks such as device drivers. In those days, garbage collectors were less sophisticated than they are today, and the processing power and memory capacity of the average computer were small fractions of what today's systems offer. My personal experience with Simula and reports of other GC-based systems convinced me that GC was unaffordable by me and my colleagues for the kind of applications we were writing. Had C with Classes (or even C++) been defined to require automatic garbage collection, it would have been more elegant but stillborn.

Direct support for concurrency was also considered but rejected in favor of a library-based approach (see section 6.2.2).

6.2.5. The C with Classes Work Environment

I designed and implemented C with Classes as a research project in the Computing Science Research Center of Bell Labs. This center provided a possibly unique environment for such work. When I joined, I was basically told to "do something interesting," given suitable computer resources, encouraged to talk to interesting and competent people, and given a year before having to formally present my work for evaluation.

There was a cultural bias against "grand projects" requiring many people, against "grand plans" such as untested paper designs for others to implement, and against a class distinction between designers and implementers. If you liked such things, Bell Labs and others have many places where you could indulge such preferences. However, in the Computing Science Research Center, it was almost a requirement that you—if you were not into theory—(personally) implement something embodying your ideas and find users who could benefit from what you built. The environment was very supportive of such work and the Labs provided a large pool of people with ideas and problems to challenge and test anything built. Thus I could write in *The C++ Programming Language* (Stroustrup, 1986a):

> There never was a C++ paper design; design, documentation, and implementation went on simultaneously. Naturally, the C++ front end is written in C++. There never was a C++ project either, or a C++ design committee. Throughout, C++ evolved, and continues to

> evolve, to cope with problems encountered by users and through discussions between the author and his friends and colleagues.

Only after C++ was an established language did more conventional organizational structures emerge. And even then I was officially in charge of the reference manual and had the final say over what went into it until that task was handed over to the ANSI C++ committee in early 1990. On the other hand, after the first few months I never had the freedom to design just for the sake of designing something beautiful or to make arbitrary changes in the language as it stood at any given time. Whatever I considered a language feature required an implementation to make it real. Furthermore, any change or extension required the concurrence and usually the enthusiasm of key C with Classes and later C++ users.

Because there was no guaranteed user population, the language and its implementations could survive only by serving the needs of its users well enough to counteract the organizational pull of established languages and the marketing hype of newer languages.

C with Classes grew through discussions with people in the Computing Science Research Center and early users there and elsewhere in the Labs. Most of C with Classes and later C++ was designed on somebody else's blackboard and the rest on mine. Most ideas were rejected as too elaborate, too limited in usefulness, too hard to implement, too hard to teach for use in real projects, not efficient enough in time or space, too incompatible with C, or simply too weird. The few ideas that made it through this filter—invariably involving discussions among at least two people—I then implemented. Typically, the idea mutated through the effort of implementation, testing, and early use by me and one or two others. The resulting version was tried on a larger audience and would often mutate a bit further before finding its way into the "official" version of C with Classes as shipped by me. Usually, a tutorial was written somewhere along the way. I considered a tutorial an essential design tool because if a feature cannot be explained simply, the burden of supporting it will be too great. This point was never far from my mind because during the early years, I *was* the support organization.

In the early days, Sandy Fraser, my department head at the time, was very influential. For example, I believe he was the one who encouraged me to break from the Simula style of class definition, where the complete function definition is included, and adopt the style where function definitions are typically elsewhere, thus emphasizing the class declaration's role as an interface. Much of C with Classes was designed to allow simulators to be built that could be used in Sandy Fraser's work in network design.

The first real application of C with Classes was such network simulators. Sudhir Agrawal was another early user who influenced the development of C with Classes through his work with network simulations. Jonathan Shopiro provided much feedback of the C with Classes design and implementation based on his simulation of a "dataflow database machine."

For more general discussionson programming language issues, as opposed to looking at applications to determine which problems needed to be solved, I turned to Dennis Ritchie, Steve Johnson, and, in particular, Doug McIlroy. Doug McIlroy's influence on the development of both C and C++ cannot be overestimated. I cannot remember a single critical design decision in C++ that I have not discussed at length with Doug. Naturally, we didn't always agree, but I still have a strong reluctance to make a decision that goes against Doug's opinion. He has a knack for being right and an apparently infinite amount of experience and patience.

Because the main design work for C with Classes and C++ was done on blackboards, the thinking tended to focus on solutions to "archetypical" problems: small examples that are considered characteristic for a large class of problems. Thus, a good solution to the small example provides significant help in writing programs dealing with real problems of that class. Many of these problems have entered the C++ literature and folklore through my use of them as examples in my papers, books, and talks. For C with Classes, the example considered most critical was the `task` class that was the basis of the task-library supporting Simula-style simulation. Other key classes were `queue`, `list`, and `histogram` classes. The `queue` and `list` classes were based on the idea—borrowed from Simula—of providing a `link` class from which users derived their own classes.

The danger inherent in this approach is creating a language and tools that provide elegant solutions to small selected examples, yet don't scale to building complete systems or large programs. This was counteracted by the simple fact that C with Classes (and later C++) had to pay for itself during its early years. This ensured that C with Classes couldn't evolve into something that was elegant but useless.

6.3. From C with Classes to C++: 1982–1985

During 1982, it became clear to me that C with Classes was a "medium success" and would remain so until it died. I defined a medium success as something so useful that it easily paid for itself and its developer, but not so attractive and useful that it would pay for a support and development organization. Thus, continuing with C with Classes and its C preprocessor implementation would condemn me to support C with Classes use indefinitely. I was convinced that there were only two ways out of this dilemma:

- Stop supporting C with Classes so that the users would have to go elsewhere (freeing me to do something else).
- Develop a new and better language based on my experience with C with Classes that would serve a set of users large enough to pay for a support and development organization (thus freeing me to do something else). At the time, I estimated that 5,000 industrial users was the necessary minimum.

The third alternative, increasing the user population through marketing (hype), never occurred to me. What actually happened was that the explosive growth of C++, as the new language was eventually named, kept me so busy that to this day, I haven't managed to get sufficiently detached to do something else of significance.

The success of C with Classes was, I think, a simple consequence of meeting its design aim: C with Classes did help organize a large class of programs significantly better than C without the loss of runtime efficiency and without requiring enough cultural changes to make its use infeasible in organizations that were unwilling to undergo major changes. The factors limiting its success were partly the limited set of new facilities offered over C and partly the preprocessor technology used to implement C with Classes. There simply wasn't enough support in C with Classes for people who *were* willing to invest significant efforts to reap matching benefits; C with Classes was an important step in the right direction, but only one small step. As a result of this analysis, I began designing a cleaned-up and extended successor to C with Classes and implementing it using traditional compiler technology.

The resulting language was at first still called C with Classes, but after a polite request from management, it was given the name C84. The reason for the naming was that people had taken to calling C with Classes "new C" and then C. This last abbreviation led to C being called "plain C," "straight C," and "old C." The name C84 was used only for a few months, partly because it was ugly and institutional, partly because there would still be confusion if people dropped the "84". I asked for ideas for a new name and picked C++ because it was short, had nice interpretations, and wasn't of the form "*adjective* C." C++ can, depending on context, be read as "next," "successor," or "increment," although it is always pronounced "plus plus." The name C++ and its runner-up ++C are fertile sources for jokes and puns—almost all of which were known and appreciated before the name was chosen. The name C++ was suggested by Rick Mascitti. It was first used in *Data Abstraction in* C (Stroustrup, 1984b), where it was edited into the final copy in December 1983.

6.3.1. Aims

During the 1982-1984 period, the aims for C++ gradually became more ambitious and more definite. I had come to see C++ as a language separate from C, and libraries and tools had emerged as areas of work. Because of that, because tools developers within Bell Labs were beginning to show interest in C++, and because I had embarked on a completely new implementation that would become the C++ compiler front end, Cfront, I had to answer key questions:

- Who will the users be?
- What kind of systems will they use?
- How will I get out of the business of providing tools?
- How should the answers to the first three questions affect the language definition?

My answer to Who will the users be? was that first my friends within Bell Labs and I would use it; then more widespread use within AT&T would provide more experience; then some universities would pick up the ideas and the tools; and finally AT&T and others would be able to make some money by selling the set of tools that had evolved. At some point, the initial and somewhat experimental implementation done by me would be phased out in favor of more "industrial strength" implementations by AT&T and others.

This made practical and economic sense; the initial (Cfront) implementation would be tool-poor, portable, and cheap because that was what I, my colleagues, and many university users needed and could afford. Later, there would be ample scope for AT&T and others to provide better tools for more specialized environments. Such better tools aimed primarily at industrial users needn't be cheap and thus would be able to pay for the support organizations necessary for large-scale use of the language. That was my answer to How will I get out of the business of providing tools? Basically, the strategy worked. However, just about every detail actually happened in an unforeseen way.

To get an answer to What kind of systems will they use? I simply looked around to see what kind of systems the C with Classes users actually did use. They used everything from boxes that were so small that they couldn't run a compiler, to mainframes. They used more operating systems than I had heard of. Consequently, I concluded that extreme portability and the ability to do cross compilation were necessities and that I could make no assumption about the size and speed of the machines running generated code. To build a compiler, however, I would have to make assumptions about the kind of system people would develop their programs on. I assumed that 1MIPS plus 1MB would be available. That assumption I considered a bit risky because most of my prospective users at the time had at most part of a PDP11 or some other relatively low-powered or timeshared system available.

I did not predict the PC revolution, but by overshooting my performance target for Cfront, I happened to build a compiler that could run (barely) on an IBM PC/AT, thus providing proof that C++ could be an effective language on a PC and thereby spurring commercial software developers to beat it.

As the answer to How does all this affect the language definition? I concluded that no feature must require really sophisticated compiler or runtime support, that available linkers must be used, and that the code generated would have to be efficient (comparable to C) even initially.

6.3.2. Cfront

I designed and implemented the Cfront compiler front end for the C84 language between spring 1982 and summer 1983. The first user outside the Computer Science Research Center, Jim Coplien, received his copy in July 1983. Jim was in a group that had been doing experimental switching work with C with Classes in Bell Labs in Naperville, Illinois, for some time.

In that same time period, I designed C84, drafted the reference manual published January 1, 1984 (Stroustrup, 1984a), designed the `complex` number library and implemented it together with Leonie Rose (Rose & Stroustrup, 1984), designed and implemented the first `string` class together with Jonathan Shopiro, maintained and ported the C with Classes implementation, and supported the C with Classes users and helped them become C84 users. That was a busy year and a half.

Cfront was a traditional compiler front end performing a complete check of the syntax and semantics of the language, building an internal representation of its input, analyzing and rearranging that representation, and finally producing output suitable for some code generator. The internal representation was a graph with one symbol table per scope. The general strategy is to read a source file one global declaration at a time and produce output only when a complete global declaration has been completely analyzed.

The organization of Cfront was fairly traditional except maybe for the use of many symbol tables instead of just one. Cfront was originally written in C with Classes (what else?) and soon transcribed into C84 so that the very first working C++ compiler was done in C++. Even the first version of Cfront used classes heavily but no virtual functions because they were not available at the start of the project.

The most unusual—for its time—aspect of Cfront was that it generated C code. This has caused no end of confusion. Cfront generated C because I needed extreme portability for an initial implementation and I considered C the most portable assembler around. I could easily have generated some internal back-end format or assembler from Cfront, but that was not what my users needed. No assembler or compiler back-end served more than maybe a quarter of my user community and there was no way that I could produce the, say, six back ends needed to serve just 90% of that community. In response to this need, I concluded that using C as a common input format to a large number of code generators was the only reasonable choice. The strategy of building a compiler as a C generator later became quite popular so that languages such as Ada, CLOS, Eiffel, Modula-3, and Smalltalk have been implemented that way. I got a high degree of portability at a modest cost in compile-time overhead. Over the years, I have measured this overhead on various systems and found it to be between 25% and 100% of the "necessary" parts of a compilation.

Please note that the C compiler is used as a code generator *only*. Any error message from the C compiler reflects an error in the C compiler or in Cfront, but not in the C++ source text. Every syntactic and semantic error is in principle caught by Cfront, the C++ compiler front-end. I stress this because there has been a long history of confusion about what Cfront is. It has been called a preprocessor because it generates C, and for people in the C community (and elsewhere), that has been taken as proof that Cfront was a rather simple program—something like a macro preprocessor. People have thus deduced (wrongly) that a line-for-line translation from C++ to C is possible, that symbolic debugging at the C++ level is impossible when Cfront is used, that code generated by Cfront must be inferior to code generated by "real compilers," that C++ wasn't a "real language," and so on. Naturally, I have found such unfounded claims most annoying—especially when they were leveled as criticisms of the C++ language. Several C++ compilers used Cfront together with local code generators without going through a C front end. To the user, the only obvious difference is faster compile times.

Cfront was only a compiler front end and could never be used for real programming by itself. It needed a driver to run the source file through the C preprocessor, Cpp, and then run the output of Cpp through Cfront and the output from Cfront through a C compiler:

In addition, the driver must ensure that dynamic (runtime) initialization is done. In Cfront 3.0, the driver becomes yet more elaborate as automatic template instantiation (section 6.6.3) is implemented (McClusky, 1992).

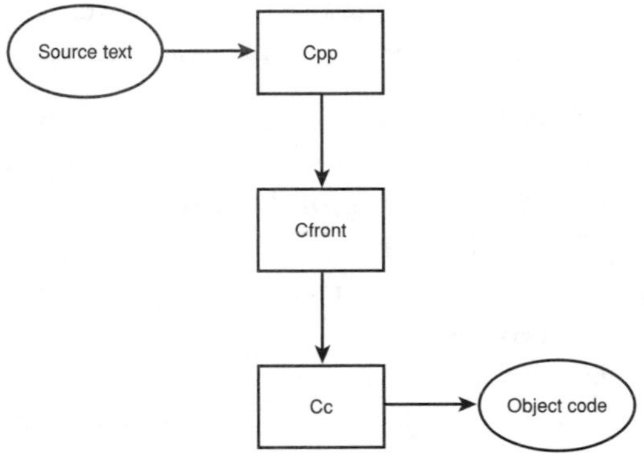

As mentioned, I decided to live within the constraints of traditional linkers. However, there was one constraint that I felt was too difficult to live with, yet so silly that I had a chance of fighting it if I had sufficient patience: Most traditional linkers had a very low limit on the number of characters that can be used in external names. A limit of 8 characters was common, and 6 characters and one case only are guaranteed to work as external names in Classical C; ANSI/ISO C accepts that limit also. Given that the name of a member function includes the name of its class and that the type of an overloaded function has to be reflected in the linkage process somehow or other, I had little choice. Consequently, I started (in 1982) lobbying for longer names in linkers. I don't know if my efforts actually had any effect, but these days, most linkers do give me the much larger number of characters I need. Cfront uses encodings to implement type-safe linkage in a way that makes a limit of 32 characters too low for comfort and even 256 is a bit tight at times (see section 6.3.3.3). In the interim, systems of hash coding of long identifiers have been used with archaic linkers, but that was never completely satisfactory.

Versions of C++ were often named by Cfront release numbers. Release 1.0 was the language as defined in *The C++ Programming Language* (Stroustrup, 1986a).

Releases 1.1 (June 1986) and 1.2 (February 1987) were primarily bug fix releases but also added pointers to members and protected members (section 6.4.1). Release 2.0 was a major cleanup that also introduced multiple inheritance (section 6.4.2) in June 1989. Release 2.1 (April 1990) was primarily a bug fix release that brought Cfront into line (almost) with the definition in *The Annotated C++ Reference Manual* (ARM) (Ellis & Stroustrup, 1990; see section 6.6.1). Release 3.0 (September 1991) added templates (section 6.6.3) as specified in the ARM. Release 4.0 from HP added exception handling (section 6.6.4) as specified in the ARM.

I wrote the first versions of Cfront (1.0, 1.1, 1.2) and maintained them; Steve Dewhurst worked on it with me for a few months before Release 1.0 in 1985. Laura Eaves did much of the work on the Cfront parser for Releases 1.0, 1.1, 2.1, and 3.0. I also did the lion's share of the programming for Releases 1.2 and 2.0, but starting with Release 1.2, Stan Lippman also spent most of his time on Cfront. George Logothetis, Judy Ward, Nancy Wilkinson, and Stan Lippman did most of the work for Releases 2.1 and 3.0. The work on 2.0 was coordinated by Barbara Moo, and Andrew Koenig organized Cfront testing. Barbara also coordinated Releases 1.2, 2.1, and 3.0. Sam Haradhvala from Object Design Inc. did an initial implementation of templates in 1989 that Stan Lippman extended and completed for Release 3.0 in 1991. The initial implementation of exception handling in Cfront was done by Hewlett-Packard in 1992. In addition to these people who have produced code that has found its way into the main version of Cfront, many people have built local C++ compilers from it. Apple, Centerline (formerly Saber), ParcPlace, Sun, HP, and others shipped products that contained locally modified versions of Cfront.

As late as 1997—15 years after its initial design—tens of thousands of copies of Cfront were in daily use.

6.3.3. Language Feature Details

The major additions to C with Classes introduced to produce C++ were

- Virtual functions
- Function name and operator overloading
- References

- Constants (`const`)
- User-controlled free-store memory control
- Improved type checking

In addition, the notion of call and return functions (section 6.2.4.8) was dropped due to lack of use, and many minor details were changed to produce a cleaner language.

6.3.3.1. Minor Changes to C++

The most visible minor change to C++ was the introduction of BCPL-style comments:

```
int a; /* C-style explicitly terminated comment */
int b; // BCPL-style comment terminated by end-of-line
```

Because both styles of comments are allowed, people can simply use the style they like best.

The name `new` function for constructors had been a source of confusion, so the name constructor was introduced (section 6.2.4.8).

In C with Classes, a dot was used to express membership of a class as well as express selection of a member of a particular object. This had been the cause of some minor confusion and could also be used to construct ambiguous examples. To alleviate this, `::` was introduced to mean membership of class, and `.` was retained exclusively for membership of object.

I borrowed the Algol68 notion that a declaration can be introduced wherever it is needed (and not just at the top of some block). Thus, I enabled an initialize-only or single-assignment style of programming that is less error prone than traditional styles. This style is essential for references and constants that cannot be assigned and inherently more efficient for types where default initialization is expensive.

6.3.3.2. Virtual Functions

The most obvious new feature in C++ compared to C with Classes—and certainly the one that had the greatest impact on the style of programming you could use for the language—was virtual functions. The idea was borrowed from Simula and presented in a form that was intended to make a simple and efficient implementation easy. The rationale for virtual functions was presented in *The C++ Programming Language* (Stroustrup, 1986a) and *What Is Object-Oriented Programming?* (Stroustrup, 1986c).

To emphasize the central role of virtual functions in C++ programming, I quote the latter (Stroustrup, 1986c) in detail here:

> An abstract data type defines a sort of black box. Once it has been defined, it does not really interact with the rest of the program. There is no way of adapting it to new uses except by modifying its definition. This can lead to severe inflexibility. Consider defining a type `shape` for use in a graphics system. Assume for the moment that the system has to support circles, triangles, and squares. Assume also that you have some classes:
>
> ```
> class point{ /* ... */ };
> class color{ /* ... */ };
> ```
>
> You might define a shape like this:
>
> ```
> enum kind { circle, triangle, square };
>
> class shape {
>     point center;
>     color col;
>     kind k;
>     // representation of shape
> public:
>     point where() { return center; }
>     void move(point to) { center = to; draw(); }
>     void draw();
>     void rotate(int);
>     // more operations
> };
> ```
>
> The type field `k` is necessary to allow operations such as `draw()` and `rotate()` to determine what kind of shape they are dealing with (in a Pascal-like language, one might use a variant record with tag `k`). The function `draw()` might be defined like this:
>
> ```
> void shape::draw()
> {
>     switch (k) {
>     case circle:
>         // draw a circle
>         break;
>     case triangle:
>         // draw a triangle
>         break;
>     case square:
>         // draw a square
>     }
> }
> ```

This is a mess. Functions such as `draw()` must know about all the kinds of shapes there are. Therefore, the code for any such function grows each time a new shape is added to the system. If you define a new shape, every operation on a shape must be examined and (possibly) modified. You are not able to add a new shape to a system unless you have access to the source code for every operation. Because adding a new shape involves touching the code of every important operation on shapes, it requires great skill and potentially introduces bugs into the code handling other (older) shapes. The choice of representation of particular shapes can get severely cramped by the requirement that (at least some of) their representation must fit into the typically fixed-size framework presented by the definition of the general type `shape`.

The problem is that there is no distinction between the general properties of any shape (a shape has a color, it can be drawn, and so on) and the properties of a specific shape (a circle is a shape that has a radius, is drawn by a circle-drawing function, and so on). Expressing this distinction and taking advantage of it define object-oriented programming. A language with constructs that allows this distinction to be expressed and used supports object-oriented programming; other languages don't.

The Simula inheritance mechanism provides a solution. First, specify a class that defines the general properties of all shapes:

```
class shape {
    point center;
    color col;
    // ...
public:
    point where() { return center; }
    void move(point to) { center = to; draw(); }
    virtual void draw();
    virtual void rotate(int);
    // ...
};
```

The functions for which the calling interface can be defined, but where the implementation cannot be defined except for a specific shape, have been marked "virtual" (the Simula and C++ term for "may be redefined later in a class derived from this one"). Given this definition, we can write general functions manipulating shapes:

```
void rotate_all(shape** v, int size, int angle)
// rotate all members of vector "v" of size "size" "angle" degrees
{
    for (int i = 0; i < size; i++) v[i]->rotate(angle);
}
```

To define a particular shape, we must say that it is a shape and specify its particular properties (including the virtual functions):

```
class circle : public shape {
    int radius;
public:
    void draw() { /* ... */ };
    void rotate(int) {}    // yes, the null function
};
```

In C++, class `circle` is said to be *derived* from class `shape`, and class `shape` is said to be a *base* of class `circle`. An alternative terminology calls `circle` and `shape` subclass and superclass, respectively.

For further discussion of virtual functions and object-oriented programming, see section 6.3.7 and section 6.4.3.

The key implementation idea was that the set of virtual functions in a class defines an array of pointers to functions so that a call of a virtual function is simply an indirect function call through that array. There is one array per class and one pointer to such an array in each object of a class that has virtual functions.

I don't remember much interest in virtual functions at the time. It may be that I didn't explain the concepts involved well. But the main reactions I received from people in my immediate vicinity were indifference and skepticism. A common opinion was that virtual functions were simply a kind of crippled pointer to function and thus redundant. Worse, it was sometimes argued that a well-designed program wouldn't need the extensibility and openness provided by virtual functions so that proper analysis would show which non-virtual functions could be called directly. Therefore, the argument went, virtual functions were simply a form of inefficiency. Clearly I disagreed and added virtual functions anyway.

6.3.3.3. Overloading

Several people had asked for the ability to overload operators. Operator overloading "looked neat" and I knew from experience with Algol68 how the idea could be made to work. However, I was reluctant to introduce the notion of overloading into C++ for the following reasons:

- Overloading was reputed to be hard to implement so that compilers would grow to monstrous size.
- Overloading was reputed to be hard to teach and hard to define precisely so that manuals and tutorials would grow to monstrous size.
- Code written using operator overloading was reputed to be inherently inefficient.
- Overloading was reputed to make code incomprehensible.

If the last two reasons were true, then C++ would be better off without overloading. If the first two were true, then I didn't have the resources to provide overloading.

However, if all these conjectures were false, then overloading would solve some real problems for C++ users. There were people who would like to have complex numbers, matrices, and APL-like vectors in C++. There were people who would like range-checked arrays, multidimensional arrays, and strings in C++. There were at least two separate applications for which people wanted to overload logical operators such as `|` (or), `&` (and), and `^` (exclusive or). The way I saw it, the list was long and would grow with the size and the diversity of the C++ user population. My answer to the potential problem of making code obscure was that several of my friends, whose opinions I valued and whose experience was measured in decades, claimed that their code would become cleaner if they had overloading. So what if one can write obscure code with overloading? It is possible to write obscure code in any language. It matters more how a feature can be used well than how it can be misused.

Next, I convinced myself that overloading wasn't inherently inefficient (Ellis & Stroustrup, 1990; Stroustrup, 1984c). The details of the overloading mechanism were mostly worked out on my blackboard and those of Stu Feldman, Doug McIlroy, and Jonathan Shopiro.

Thus, having worked out a solution to the efficiency problem, I needed to concern myself with the issues of compiler and language complexity. I first observed that use of classes with overloaded operators, such as `complex` and `string`, was quite easy and didn't put a major burden on the programmer. Next, I wrote the manual sections to prove that the added complexity wasn't a serious issue; the manual needed less than a page and a half extra (out of a 42-page manual). Finally, I did the first implementation in 2 hours using only 18 lines of extra code in Cfront, and I felt I had demonstrated that the fears about definition and implementation complexity were somewhat exaggerated.

Naturally, all these issues were not really tackled in this strict sequential order. However, the emphasis of the work did start with utility issues and slowly drifted to implementation issues. The overloading mechanisms were described in detail in "Operator Overloading in C++" (Stroustrup, 1984c) and examples of classes using the mechanisms were written up (Rose & Stroustrup, 1984; Shopiro, 1985).

In retrospect, I underestimated the complexity of the definition and implementation issues and compounded these problems by trying to isolate overloading mechanisms from the rest of the language semantics. The latter was done out of misguided fear of confusing users. In particular, I required that a declaration

```
overload print;
```

should precede declarations of an overloaded function `print`, such as

```
void print(int);
void print(const char*);
```

I also insisted that ambiguity control should happen in two stages so that resolutions involving built-in operators and conversions would always take precedence over resolutions involving user-defined operations. Maybe the latter was inevitable given the concern for C compatibility and the chaotic nature of the C conversion rules for built-in types. These conversions do *not* constitute a directed acyclic graph; for example, implicit conversions are allowed both from `int` to `float` and from `float` to `int`. However, the rules for ambiguity resolution were too complicated, caused surprises, and had to be revised for Release 2.0. I still consider these rules too complex but do not see scope for more than minor adjustments.

Requiring explicit `overload` declarations was plain wrong and the requirement was dropped in Release 2.0.

6.3.3.4. C++ References

References were introduced primarily to support operator overloading. C passes every function argument by value, and where passing an object by value would be inefficient or inappropriate, the user can pass a pointer.

This strategy doesn't work where operator overloading is used. In that case, notational convenience is essential so that a user cannot be expected to insert address-of operators if the objects are large.

Problems with debugging Algol68 convinced me that having references that didn't change what object they referred to after initialization was a good thing. If you want to do more complicated pointer manipulation in C++, you can use pointers. Because C++ has both pointers and references, it does not need operations for distinguishing operations on the reference itself from operations on the object referred to (like Simula) or the kind of deductive mechanism employed by Algol68.

It is important that `const` references can be initialized by both non-lvalues and lvalues of types that require conversion. In particular, this is what allows a Fortran function to be called with a constant:

```
extern "Fortran" float sqrt(const float&);    // '&' means reference

void f()
{
     // ...
     sqrt(2);                           // call by reference
     // ...
}
```

Jonathan Shopiro was deeply involved in the discussions that led to the introduction of references. In addition to the obvious uses of references, such as argument, passing we considered the ability to use references as return types important. This allowed us to have a very simple index operator for a string class:

```
class String {
     // ...
     char& operator[](int index);  // subscript operator; return a reference
};

void f(String& s)
{
     char c1 = ...
     s[i] = c1;       // assign to operator[]'s result
     // ...
     char c2 = s[i]; // assign operator[]'s result
}
```

We considered allowing separate functions for left-hand and right-hand side use of a function but considered using references the simpler alternative even though this implies that we need to introduce additional "helper classes" to solve some problems where returning a simple reference isn't enough. In retrospect, some way of defining separate functions for left-hand and right-hand side use would have been useful in many cases.

6.3.3.5. Constants (`const`)

In operating systems, it is common to have access to some piece of memory controlled directly or indirectly by two bits: one that indicates whether a user can write to it and one that indicates whether a user can read it. This idea seemed to me directly applicable to C++, and I considered allowing every type to be specified `readonly` or `writeonly` (Stroustrup, 1981a). The proposal was focused on specifying interfaces rather than on providing symbolic constants for C. Clearly, a `readonly` value is a symbolic constant, but the scope of the proposal was far greater. Initially, I proposed pointers to `readonly` but not `readonly` pointers. A brief discussion with Dennis Ritchie evolved the idea into the `readonly`/`writeonly` mechanism that I implemented and proposed to an internal Bell Labs C standards group chaired by Larry Rosler. There, I had my first experience with standards work. I came away from a meeting with an agreement (that is, a vote) that `readonly` would be introduced into C—yes C, not C with Classes or C++—provided it was renamed `const`. Unfortunately, a vote isn't executable, so nothing happened to our C compilers. A while later, the ANSI C committee (X3J11) was formed, and the `const` proposal resurfaced there and became part of ANSI/ISO C.

In the meantime, however, I had experimented further with `const` in C with Classes and found that `const` was a useful alternative to macros for representing constants only if a global `const`s were implicitly local to their compilation unit. Only in that case could the compiler easily deduce that their value really didn't change and allow simple `const`s in constant evaluations and thus avoid allocating space for such constants and use them in constant expressions. C did not adopt this rule. This makes `const`s far less useful in C than in C++ and leaves C dependent on the preprocessor, whereas C++ programmers can use properly typed and scoped `const`s.

6.3.3.6. Memory Management

Long before the first C with Classes program was written, I knew that free store (dynamic memory) would be used more heavily in a language with classes than in traditional C programs. This was the reason for the introduction of the `new` and `delete` operators in C with Classes. The `new` operator that both allocates memory from the free store and invokes a constructor to ensure initialization was borrowed from Simula. The `delete` operator was a necessary complement because I did not want C with Classes to depend on a garbage collector (section 6.8.2.1). The reasons for that included poor experience with the overhead of garbage collectors, a need to coexist with programs written in C, use of C with Classes in low-level and performance-critical software (such as device drivers), and use of C with Classes in systems where predictability of service was important (such as real-time control software).

The argument for the `new` operator can be summarized like this. Would you rather write this:

```
X* p = new X(2);
```

or this:

```
struct X * p = (struct X *) malloc(sizeof(struct X));
if (p == 0) error("memory exhausted");
p->init(2);
```

In which version are you most likely to make a mistake? The arguments against—which were voiced quite a lot at the time—were "but we don't *really* need it," and "but someone will have used `new` as an identifier." Both observations are correct, of course.

Introducing operator `new` thus made the use of free store more convenient and less error prone. This increased its use even further so that the C free-store allocation routine `malloc()` used to implement `new` became the most common performance bottleneck in real systems. This was no real surprise either; the only problem was what to do about it. Having real programs spend 50% or more of their time in `malloc()` wasn't acceptable.

I found per-class allocators and deallocators very effective. The fundamental idea is that free-store memory usage is dominated by the allocation and deallocation of a lot of small objects from very few classes. Take over the allocation of those objects in a separate allocator, and you can save both time and space for those objects and also reduce the amount of fragmentation of the general free store. The mechanism provided for 1.0, "assignment to `this`," was too low level and error prone and was replaced by a cleaner solution in Release 2.0 (section 6.4.1).

Note that static and automatic (stack allocated) objects were always possible and that the most effective memory-management techniques relied heavily on such objects. The string class was a typical example: Here `String` objects are typically on the stack so that they require no explicit memory management, and the free store they rely on is managed exclusively and invisibly to the user by the `String` member functions.

6.3.3.7. Type Checking

The C++ type-checking rules were the result of experiments with C with Classes. All function calls are checked at compile time. The checking of trailing arguments can be suppressed by explicit specification in a function declaration. This is essential to allow C's `printf()`:

```
int printf(const char* ...); // accept any argument
                             // after the initial character string

// ...

printf("date: %s %d 19%d\n",month,day,year); // maybe right
```

Several mechanisms were provided to alleviate the withdrawal symptoms that many C programmers feel when they first experience strict checking. Overriding type checking using the ellipsis was the most drastic and least recommended of those. Function name overloading (section 6.3.3.3) and default arguments (Stroustrup, 1986a) made it possible to give the appearance of a single function taking a variety of argument lists without compromising type safety. The stream I/O system demonstrates that the weak checking wasn't necessary even for I/O (see section 6.5.3.1).

6.3.4. C++'s Relationship to Classic C

With the introduction of a separate name, C++, and the writing of a C++ reference manual (Stroustrup, 1984a), compatibility with C became an issue of major importance and a point of controversy.

Also, in late 1983, the branch of Bell Labs that developed and supported UNIX and produced AT&T's 3B series of computers became interested in C++ to the point where it was willing to put resources into the development of C++ tools. Such development was necessary for the evolution of C++ from a one-man show to a language on which a corporation could base critical projects. Unfortunately, it also implied that development management needed to consider C++.

The first demand to emerge from development management was that of 100% compatibility with C. The ideal of C compatibility is quite obvious and reasonable, but the reality of programming isn't that simple. For starters, with which C should C++ be compatible? C dialects abounded, and although ANSI C was emerging, it was still years from having a stable definition, and its definition allowed many dialects. Naturally, the average user who wanted C compatibility insisted that C++ should be compatible with the local C dialect. This was an important practical problem and a great concern to me and my friends. It seemed far less of a concern to business-oriented managers and salespeople who either didn't quite understand the technical details or wanted to use C++ to tie users into their software or hardware.

Another side of the compatibility issue was more critical: "In which ways must C++ differ from C to meet its fundamental goals?" and also "In which ways must C++ be compatible with C to meet its fundamental goals?" Both sides of the issue are important and revisions were made in both directions during the transition from C with Classes to C++ as shipped as Release 1.0. Slowly and painfully, an agreement emerged that there would be no gratuitous incompatibilities between C++ and ANSI C (when it became a standard; Stroustrup, 1986a), but that there was such a thing as an incompatibility that was not gratuitous. Naturally, the concept of "gratuitous incompatibilities" was a topic of much debate and took up a disproportional part of my time and effort. This principle has lately been known as "C++: As Close to C as Possible—But No Closer," after the title of a paper by Andrew Koenig and me (Koenig & Stroustrup, 1989a).

Some conclusions about modularity and how a program is composed out of separately compiled parts were explicitly reflected in the original C++ reference manual (Stroustrup, 1984a):

- Names are private unless they are explicitly declared public.
- Names are local to their file unless explicitly exported from it.
- Static type is checked unless explicitly suppressed.
- A class is a scope (implying that classes nest properly).

The first point doesn't affect C compatibility, but the other three imply incompatibilities:

- The name of a non-local C function or object is by default accessible from other compilation units.
- C functions need not be declared before use and by default calls are not type checked.
- C structure names don't nest (even when they are lexically nested).
- C++ has a single namespace whereas C had a separate namespace for "structure tags" (section 6.2.4.5).

The "compatibility wars" now seem petty and boring, but some of the underlying issues are still unresolved and caused problems for the ANSI/ISO committee. I strongly suspect that the reason the compatibility wars were drawn out and curiously inconclusive was that we never quite faced the deeper issues related to the differing goals of C and C++. Instead we saw compatibility as a set of separate issues to be resolved individually.

Typically, the least fundamental issue, namespaces, took the most effort but was eventually resolved (Ellis & Stroustrup, 1990).

I had to compromise the notion of a class as a scope and accept the C "solution" in order to be allowed to ship Release 1.0. One practical problem was that I had never realized that a C `struct` didn't constitute a scope so that examples like this are legal C:

```
struct outer {
    struct inner {
        int i;
    };
    int j;
};

struct inner a = { 1 };
```

When the issue came up toward the end of the compatibility wars, I didn't have time to fathom the implications of the C solution, and it was much easier to agree than to fight the issue. Later, after many technical problems and much discontent from users, nested class scopes were reintroduced into C++ in 1989 (Ellis & Stroustrup, 1990).

After much hassle, C++'s stronger type checking of function calls was accepted (unmodified). An implicit violation of the static type system is the original example of a C/C++ incompatibility that is not gratuitous. As it happens, the ANSI C committee adopted a slightly weaker version of C++'s rules and notation on this point and declared uses that don't conform to the C++ rules obsolete.

I had to accept the C rule that global names are by default accessible from other compilation units. There simply wasn't any support for the more restrictive C++ rule. This meant that C++, like C, lacked an effective mechanism for expressing modularity above the level of the class and the file. This led to a series of complaints, and in 1994, the C++ standard committee accepted a proposal for a mechanism to avoid namespace pollution (section 6.5.7) (Stroustrup, 1994). However, people—such as Doug McIlroy—who argued that C programmers would not accept a language in which every object and function meant to be accessible from another compilation unit had to be explicitly declared as such, were probably right at the time and saved me from making a serious mistake. I am now convinced that the original C++ solution wasn't elegant enough anyway.

6.3.5. Tools for Language Design

Theory and tools more advanced than a blackboard have not been given much space in the description of the history of C++. I tried to use yacc (an LALR(1) parser generator) for the grammar work and was defeated by C's syntax (section 6.2.4.5). I looked at denotational semantics but was again defeated by quirks in C. Ravi Sethi had looked into that problem and found that he couldn't express the C semantics that way (Sethi, 1980). The main problem was the irregularity of C and the number of implementation-dependent and undefined aspects of a C implementation.

Much later, the ANSI/ISO C++ committee had a stream of formal definition experts explain their techniques and tools and give their opinion of the extent to which a genuine formal approach to the definition of C++ would help us in the standards effort. My conclusion is that with the current state of the art, and certainly with the state of the art in the early 1980s, a formal definition of a language that is not designed together with a formal definition method is beyond the ability of all but a handful of experts in formal definition.

This confirms my conclusion at the time. However, that left us at the mercy of imprecise and insufficient terminology. Given that, what could I do to compensate? I tried to reason about new features both on my own and with others to check my logic. However, I soon developed a healthy disrespect for arguments (definitely including my own) because I found that it is possible to construct a plausible logical argument for just about any feature. On the other hand, you simply don't get a useful language by accepting every feature that makes life better for someone. There are far too many reasonable features and no language could provide them all and stay coherent. Consequently, wherever possible, I tried to experiment.

My impression was and is that many programming languages and tools represent solutions looking for problems, and I was determined that my work should not fall into that category. Thus, I follow the literature on programming language and the debates about programming languages, primarily looking for ideas for solutions to problems my colleagues and I have encountered in real applications. Other programming languages constitute a mountain of ideas and inspiration—but it has to be mined carefully to avoid featurism and inconsistencies. The main sources for ideas for C++ were Simula, Algol68, and later Clu, Ada, and ML. The key to good design is insight into problems, not the provision of the most advanced features.

6.3.6. *The C++ Programming Language* (First Edition)

In fall 1983, my next door neighbor at work, Al Aho, suggested that I write a book on C++ structured along the lines of Brian Kernighan and Dennis Ritchie's *The C Programming Language* and base it on my published papers, internal memoranda, and the C++ reference manual (Kernighan & Ritchie, 1978). Completing the book took nine months.

The preface mentions the people who had by then contributed most to C++: Tom Cargill, Jim Coplien, Stu Feldman, Sandy Fraser, Steve Johnson, Brian Kernighan, Bart Locanthi, Doug McIlroy, Dennis Ritchie,

Larry Rosler, Jerry Schwarz, and Jon Shopiro. My criterion for adding a person to that list was that I was able to identify a specific C++ feature that he or she caused to be added.

The book's opening line "C++ is a general-purpose programming language designed to make programming more enjoyable for the serious programmer" was deleted twice by reviewers who refused to believe that the purpose of programming-language design could be anything but some serious mutterings about productivity, management, and software engineering. However, "C++ was designed primarily so that the author and his friends would not have to program in assembler, C, or various modern high-level languages. Its main purpose is to make writing good programs easier and more pleasant for the individual programmer" (Stroustrup, 1991). This was the case whether those reviewers were willing to believe it or not. The focus of my work is the person, the individual (whether part of a group or not), the programmer. This line of reasoning has been strengthened over the years and is even more prominent in the Second Edition (Stroustrup, 1991).

The C++ Programming Language (Stroustrup, 1986a) was the definition of C++ and the introduction to C++ for an unknown number of programmers, and its presentation techniques and organization (borrowed with acknowledgments if not always sufficient skill from *The C Programming Language*) have become the basis for an almost embarrassingly large number of articles and books. It was written with a fierce determination not to preach any particular programming technique. In the same way as I feared to build limitations into the language out of ignorance and misguided paternalism, I didn't want the book to turn into a "manifesto" for my personal preferences.

6.3.7. The "What Is?" Paper

Having shipped Release 1.0 and sent the camera-ready copy of the book to the printers, I finally found time to reconsider larger issues and to document overall design issues. Just then Karel Babcisky (the chairman of the Association of Simula Users) phoned from Oslo with an invitation to give a talk on C++ at the 1986 ASU conference in Stockholm. Naturally, I wanted to go, but I was worried that presenting C++ at a Simula conference would be seen as a vulgar example of self advertisement and an attempt to steal users away from Simula. After all, I said, C++ is not Simula, so why would Simula users want to hear about it?

Karel replied "Ah, we are not hung up on syntax." This provided me with an opportunity to write not only about what C++ was, but what it was supposed to be and where it didn't measure up to those ideals. The result was the paper *What Is Object-Oriented Programming?* (Stroustrup, 1986c) that I presented to the ASU conference in Stockholm.

The significance of this paper is that it is the first exposition of the set of techniques that C++ was aiming to support. All previous presentations, to avoid dishonesty and hype, had been restricted to describe what features were already implemented and in use. The "What Is?" paper defined the set of problems I thought a language supporting data abstraction and object-oriented programming ought to solve and gave examples of language features needed.

The result was an affirmation of the importance of the multiparadigm nature of C++ (Stroustrup, 1986c):

> Object-oriented programming is programming using inheritance. Data abstraction is programming using user-defined types. With few exceptions, object-oriented programming can and ought to be a superset of data abstraction. These techniques need proper support to be effective. Data abstraction primarily needs support in the form of language features, and object-oriented programming needs further support from a programming environment. To be general purpose, a language supporting data abstraction or object-oriented programming must enable effective use of traditional hardware.

The importance of static type checking was also strongly emphasized. In other words, C++ follows the Simula rather than the Smalltalk model of inheritance and type checking (Stroustrup, 1986):

> A Simula or C++ class specifies a fixed interface to a set of objects (of any derived class), whereas a Smalltalk class specifies an initial set of operations for objects (of any subclass). In other words, a Smalltalk class is a minimal specification and the user is free to try operations not specified, whereas a C++ class is an exact specification and the user is guaranteed that only operations specified in the class declaration will be accepted by the compiler.

This has deep implications for the way you design systems and for what language facilities are needed. A dynamically typed language such as

Smalltalk simplifies the design and implementation of libraries by postponing type checking to runtime. Here's an example (using C++ syntax):

```
stack cs;
cs.push(new Saab900);
cs.pop()->takeoff();      // Oops! Run time error:
                          // a car does not have a takeoff method.
```

This delayed type-error detection was considered unacceptable for C++, yet there had to be a way of matching the notational convenience and the standard libraries of a dynamically typed language. The notion of parameterized types was presented as the (future) solution for that problem in C++:

```
stack(plane*) cs;

cs.push(new Saab37b);      // ok a Saab37b is a plane
cs.push(new Saab900);      // error, type mismatch: car passed, plane*
                           // expected

cs.pop()->takeoff();       // no run-time check needed
cs.pop()->takeoff();       // no run-time check needed
```

The key reason for considering compile-time detection of such problems essential was the observation that C++ is often used for programs executing where no programmer is present. Fundamentally, the notion of static type checking was seen as the best way of providing the strongest guarantees possible for a program rather than merely a way of gaining runtime efficiency.

The "What Is?" paper lists three aspects in which C++ was deficient:

> *Parameterized types (templates)*: Ada, Clu, and ML support parameterized types. C++ does not; the syntax used here is simply devised as an illustration. Where needed, parameterized classes are "faked" using macros. Parameterized classes would clearly be extremely useful in C++. They could easily be handled by the compiler, but the current C++ programming environment is not sophisticated enough to support them without significant overhead and inconvenience. There need not be any runtime overheads compared with a type specified directly.
>
> *Exception handling*: As programs grow, and especially when libraries are used extensively, standards for handling errors (or more generally, "exceptional circumstances") become important. Ada, Algol68, and Clu each support a standard way of handling exceptions. Unfortunately, C++ does not. Where needed, exceptions are "faked" using pointers to functions, exception objects, error states, and the C library `signal` and `longjmp` facilities. In general, this is not satisfactory and fails even to provide a standard framework for error handling.

> *Multiple inheritance*: Given this explanation, it seems obvious that it might be useful to have a class B inherit from two base classes A1 and A2. This is called multiple inheritance. (Stroustrup, 1986c)

All three facilities were linked to the need to provide better (that is, more general, more flexible) libraries. All are now available in C++. Note that adding multiple inheritance and templates was considered as early as 1982 (Stroustrup, 1982).

6.4. C++ Release 2.0: 1985–1988

By mid-1986, the course for C++ was set for all who cared to see. The key design decisions were made. The direction of the future evolution was set with the aim for parameterized types, multiple inheritance, and exception handling. Much experimentation and adjustment based on experience was needed, but the glory days were over. C++ had never been silly putty, but there was now no real possibility for radical change. For good and bad, what was done was done. What was left was an incredible amount of solid work. At this point, C++ had about 2,000 users worldwide.

This was the point where the plan—as originally conceived by Steve Johnson and me—was for a development and support organization to take over the day-to-day work on the tools (primarily Cfront), thus freeing me to work on the new features and the libraries that were expected to depend on them. This was also the point where I expected that first AT&T and then others would start to build compilers and other tools to eventually make Cfront redundant.

Actually, they had already started, but the good plan was soon derailed due to management indecisiveness, ineptness, and lack of focus. A project to develop a brand-new C++ compiler diverted attention and resources from Cfront maintenance and development. A plan to ship a Release 1.3 in early 1988 completely fell through the cracks. The net effect was that we had to wait until June 1989 for Release 2.0, and that even though 2.0 was significantly better than Release 1.2 in almost all ways, 2.0 did not provide the language features outlined in the "What Is?" paper. Consequently, a significantly improved and extended library wasn't part of it.

Many of the people who influenced C with Classes and the original C++ continued to help with the evolution in various ways. Phil Brown, Tom Cargill, Jim Coplien, Steve Dewhurst, Laura Eaves, Keith Gorlen, Bob Kelley, Brian Kernighan, Andy Koenig, Archie Lachner, Stan Lippman, Larry Mayka, Doug McIlroy, Pat Philip, Dave Prosser, Peggy Quinn,

Jerry Schwarz, Roger Scott, Jonathan Shopiro, and Kathy Stark were explicitly acknowledged in *Exception Handling for C++* (Stroustrup, 1989b).

Stability of the language definition and its implementation was considered essential. The features of 2.0 were fairly simple modifications of the language based on experience with the 1.* releases. The most important aspect of Release 2.0 was that it increased the generality of the individual language features and improved their integration into the language.

6.4.1. C++ 2.0 Feature Overview

The main features of 2.0 were first presented in "The Evolution of C++: 1985–1987" (Stroustrup, 1987a) and summarized in the revised version of that paper (Stroustrup, 1989b), which accompanied 2.0 as part of its documentation:

- Multiple inheritance
- Type-safe linkage
- Better resolution of overloaded functions
- Recursive definition of assignment and initialization
- Better facilities for user-defined memory management
- Abstract classes
- Static member functions
- `const` member functions
- `protected` members (first provided in Release 1.2)
- Overloading of operator `->`
- Pointers to members (first provided in Release 1.2)

Most of these extensions and refinements represented experience gained with C++ and couldn't have been added earlier without more foresight than I possessed. Naturally, integrating these features involved significant work, but it was most unfortunate that this was allowed to take priority over the completion of the language as outlined in the "What Is?" paper.

Most features enhanced the safety of the language in some way or other. Cfront 2.0 checked the consistency of function types across separate compilation units (type-safe linkage), made the overload resolution rules order independent, and also ensured that more calls were considered ambiguous. The notion of `const` was made more comprehensive, pointers to members closed a loophole in the type system, and explicit class-specific memory allocation and deallocation operations were provided to make the error-prone "assignment to `this`" technique redundant.

To some people, the most important feature of Release 2.0 wasn't a feature at all but a simple space optimization. From the beginning, the code generated by Cfront tended to be pretty good. As late as 1992, Cfront generated the fastest-running code in a benchmark used to evaluate C++ compilers on a Sparc. There have been no significant improvements in Cfront's code generation since Release 1.0. However, Release 1.* was wasteful because each compilation unit generated its own set of virtual function tables for all the classes used in that unit. This could lead to megabytes of waste. At the time (about 1984), I considered the waste necessary in the absence of linker support and asked for such linker support. By 1987, that linker support hadn't materialized. Consequently, I re-thought the problem and solved it by the simple heuristic of laying down the virtual function table of a class right next to its first non-virtual non-inline function.

6.4.2. Multiple Inheritance

In many people's minds, multiple inheritance—the ability to have two or more direct base classes—is *the* feature of 2.0. I disagreed at the time because I felt that the sum of the improvements to the type system was of far greater practical importance. Also, adding multiple inheritance in 2.0 was a mistake. Multiple inheritance belongs in C++ but is far less important than parameterized types. As it happened, parameterized types in the form of templates appeared only in Release 3.0. There were a couple of reasons for choosing to work on multiple inheritance at the time: The design was further advanced and the implementation could be done within Cfront. Another factor was purely irrational: Nobody doubted that I could implement templates efficiently. Multiple inheritance, on the other hand, was widely supposed to be very difficult to implement efficiently. Thus, multiple inheritance seemed more of a challenge, and because I had considered it as early as 1982 and found a simple and efficient implementation technique in 1984, I couldn't resist the challenge. I suspect that this is the only case where fashion affected the sequence of events.

In September 1984, I presented the C++ operator overloading mechanism at the IFIP WG2.4 conference in Canterbury (Stroustrup, 1984c). There, I met Stein Krogdahl from the University of Oslo, who was just finishing a proposal for adding multiple inheritance to Simula (Krogdahl, 1984). His ideas became the basis for the implementation of ordinary multiple base classes in C++. He and I later found out that the proposal was almost identical to an idea for providing multiple inheritance in Simula that had been considered by Ole-Johan Dahl in 1966 and rejected because it would have complicated the Simula garbage collector (personal communication, 1988).

The original and fundamental reason for considering multiple inheritance was simply to allow two classes to be combined into one in such a way that objects of the resulting class would behave as objects of either base class (Stroustrup, 1986c):

> A fairly standard example of the use of multiple inheritance would be to provide two library classes `displayed` and `task` for representing objects under the control of a display manager and co-routines under the control of a scheduler, respectively. A programmer could then create classes such as

```
class my_displayed_task : public displayed, public task {
    // ...
};

class my_task : public task {  // not displayed
    // ...
};

class my_displayed : public displayed  {   // not a task
    // ...
};
```

> Using (only) single inheritance, only two of these three choices would be open to the programmer.

The implementation requires little more than remembering the relative offsets of the `task` and `displayed` objects in a `my_displayed_task` object. All the gory implementation details were explained in "Multiple Inheritance for C++" (Stroustrup, 1987b). In addition, the language design must specify how ambiguities are handled and what to do if a class is specified as a base class more than once in a derived class (Stroustrup, 1987b):

> Ambiguities are handled at compile time:

```
class A { public: void f(); /* ... */ };
class B { public: void f(); /* ... */ };
class C : public A, public B {  /* no f() ... */ };
```

```
    void g()
    {
        C* p;
        p->f();      // error: ambiguous
}
```

In this, C++ differs from the object-oriented Lisp dialects that support multiple inheritance.

Basically, I rejected all forms of dynamic resolution beyond the use of virtual functions as unsuitable for a statically typed language under severe efficiency constraints. Maybe I should at this point have revived the notion of call and return functions (section 6.2.4.8) to mimic the CLOS `:before` and `:after` methods. However, people were already worrying about the complexity of the multiple inheritance mechanisms, and I am always reluctant to reopen old wounds.

Multiple inheritance in C++ became controversial (Cargill, 1991; Carroll, 1991; Sakkinen, 1992; Waldo, 1991) for several reasons. The arguments against it centered on the real and imaginary complexity of the concept, the utility of the concept, and the impact of multiple inheritance on other extensions and tool building. In addition, proponents of multiple inheritance can and do argue over exactly what multiple inheritance is supposed to be and how it is best supported in a language. I think—as I did then—that the fundamental flaw in these arguments is that they take multiple inheritance far too seriously. Multiple inheritance doesn't solve all your problems, but it doesn't need to because it is quite cheap, and sometimes it is very convenient to have. Grady Booch (1991) expressed a slightly stronger sentiment: "Multiple inheritance is like a parachute; you don't need it very often, but when you do, it is essential."

Over the years, the use of multiple inheritance has grown steadily and a number of programming techniques that rely on it have evolved. By now (1998), I consider multiple inheritance important for any language that has both static type checking and inheritance.

6.4.3. Abstract Classes

The very last feature added to 2.0 before it shipped was abstract classes. Late modifications to releases are never popular, and late changes to the definition of what will be shipped are even less so. I remember that several members of management thought I had lost contact with the real world when I insisted on this feature.

A common complaint about C++ was (and is) that private data is visible and that when private data is changed, code using that class must be recompiled. Often, this complaint is expressed as "abstract types in C++ aren't really abstract." What I hadn't realized was that many people thought that because they *could* put the representation of an object in the private section of a class declaration, they actually *had to* put it there. This is clearly wrong (and that is how I failed to spot the problem for years). If you don't want a representation in a class, thus making the class an interface only, you simply delay the specification of the representation to some derived class and define only virtual functions. For example, you can define a `set` of `T` pointers like this:

```
class set {
public:
     virtual void insert(T*);
     virtual void remove(T*);

     virtual int is_member(T*);

     virtual T* first();
     virtual T* next();

     virtual ~set() { }
};
```

This provides all the information people need to use `set` except that whoever actually creates the `set` must know something about how some particular kind of `set` is represented. For example, given the following, we can create `slist_set` objects that can be used as `sets` by users that have never heard of a `slist_set`:

```
class slist_set : public set, private slist {
     slink* current_elem;
public:
     void insert(T*);
     void remove(T*);

     int is_member(T*);

              T* first();
              T* next();

     slist_set() : slist(), current_elem(0) { }
};
```

The only problem was that in C++ as defined before 2.0, there was no explicit way of saying "The `set` class is just an interface: Its functions need not be defined, it is an error to create objects of class `set`, and anyone who derives a class from `set` must define the virtual functions specified in `set`."

Release 2.0 allowed a class to be declared explicitly `abstract` by declaring one or more of its virtual functions "pure" using the syntax `=0`:

```
class set {     // abstract class
public:
    virtual void insert(T*) = 0;     // pure virtual function
    virtual void remove(T*) = 0;

    // ...
};
```

The `=0` syntax wasn't exactly brilliant, but it expresses the desired notion of a pure virtual function in a way that is terse and fits the use of `0` to mean "nothing" or "not there" in C and C++. The alternative, introducing a new keyword such as `pure`, wasn't an option. Given the opposition to abstract classes as a "late and unimportant change," I would never simultaneously have overcome the traditional, strong, widespread, and emotional opposition to new keywords in parts of the C and C++ community.

The importance of the abstract class concept is that it allows a cleaner separation between a user and an implementor than is possible without it. This limits the amount of recompilation necessary after a change and also the amount of information necessary to compile an average piece of code. By decreasing the coupling between a user and an implementor, abstract classes provide an answer to people complaining about long compile times and also serve library providers who must worry about the impact to users of changes to a library implementation. I had unsuccessfully tried to explain these notions in *The C++ Programming Language* (Stroustrup, 1986a). With an explicit language feature supporting abstract classes, I was much more successful (Stroustrup, 1991).

6.5. Standardization: 1988–1998

Sometime in 1988, it became clear that C++ would eventually have to be standardized (Stroustrup, 1989). There was now a handful of independent implementations in use or being produced, and clearly an effort had to be made to write a more precise and comprehensive definition of the language and also to gain wide acceptance for that definition. At first, formal standardization wasn't considered an option. Many people involved with C++ considered—and still consider—standardization abhorrent before genuine experience is gained. However, making an improved reference manual wasn't something that could be done by one person (me) in private. Input and feedback from the C++ community were needed. Thus I came upon the idea of rewriting the C++ reference manual and circulating its draft among important and insightful members of the C++ community worldwide.

6.5.1. The Annotated Reference Manual

At about the same time, the part of AT&T that sold C++ commercially wanted a new and improved C++ reference manual and gave Margaret Ellis the task of writing it. It seemed only reasonable to combine the efforts and produce a single, externally reviewed reference manual. It also seemed obvious to me that publishing this manual with some additional information would hasten the acceptance of the new definition and make C++ more widely understood. Thus, the *Annotated C++ Reference Manual* (Ellis & Stroustrup, 1990) was written "to provide a firm basis for the further evolution of C++ … (and) to serve as a starting point for the formal standardization of C++."

As Ellis and Stroustrup (1990) pointed out:

> The C++ reference manual alone provides a complete definition of C++, but the terse reference manual style leaves many reasonable questions unanswered. Discussions of what is *not* in the language, *why* certain features are defined as they are, and *how* one might implement some particular feature have no place in a reference manual but are nevertheless of interest to most users. Such discussions are presented as annotations and in the commentary sections.
>
> The commentary also helps the reader appreciate the relationships among different parts of the language and emphasizes points and implications that might have been overlooked in the reference manual itself. Examples and comparisons with C also make this book more approachable than the bare reference manual.

After some minor squabbling with the product people, it was agreed that we'd write the ARM (as *The Annotated C++ Reference Manual* came to be popularly called) describing the whole of C++, that is with templates and exception handling, rather than as a manual for the subset implemented by the most recent AT&T release. This was important because it clearly established the language itself as different from any one implementation of it. This principle had been present from the very beginning but needs to be restated often because users and implementors seem to have difficulty remembering it.

I wrote every word of the reference manual proper except the section on the preprocessor that Margaret Ellis adopted from the C Standard. The annotations were jointly written and partly based on my earlier papers (Stroustrup, 1987a, 1987c, 1988a, 1988b).

The reference manual proper of the ARM was reviewed by about a hundred people from two dozen organizations. Most are named in the acknowledgment section of the ARM. In addition, many contributed to the whole of the ARM. The contributions of Brian Kernighan, Andrew Koenig, and Doug McIlroy were specifically noted. The reference manual proper from the ARM was accepted as the basis for the ANSI standardization of C++ in March 1990.

The ARM doesn't attempt to explain the techniques that the language features support. That essential job was left for the second edition of *The C++ Programming Language* (Stroustrup, 1991).

6.5.2. ANSI and ISO

The initiative toinitiative formal (ANSI) standardization of C++ was taken by HP in conjunction with AT&T, DEC, and IBM. Larry Rosler from HP was important in this initiative. The proposal for ANSI standardization was written by Dmitry Lenkov (1989). Lenkov's proposal cites several reasons for immediate standardization of C++:

- "C++ is going through a much faster public acceptance than most other languages."
- "Delay will lead to dialects."
- "Requires a careful and detailed definition providing full semantics... for each language feature."
- "C++ lacks some important features... exception handling, aspects of multiple inheritance, features supporting parametric polymorphism, and standard libraries."

The proposal also stressed the need for compatibility with ANSI C. The organizational meeting of the ANSI C++ committee X3J16 took place in December 1989 in Washington, D.C., and was attended by about 40 people, including people who took part in the C standardization, people who by now were old-time C++ programmers, and others. Dmitry Lenkov became its chairman and Jonathan Shopiro its editor.

At the height of its work, the committee had more than 250 members, out of which between 50 and 100 turned up at meetings. The aim of the committee was a draft standard for public review in late 1993 or early 1994 with the hope of an official standard about two years later. A first public review happened in 1995 and a second in 1997. The C++ ISO standard is expected in 1998.

This was an ambitious schedule for the standardization of a general-purpose programming language. To compare, the standardization of C took seven years. The rules for what a standard is and the process by which it is supposed to be produced were repeatedly changed, and different national standards bodies appeared to have quite different interpretations of the ISO rules.

Naturally, standardization of C++ wasn't just an American (ANSI) concern. From the start, representatives from other countries attended the ANSI C++ meetings. And in Lund, Sweden, in June 1991, the ISO C++ committee WG21 was convened and the two C++ standards committees decided to hold joint meetings—starting immediately in Lund. Representatives from Canada, Denmark, France, Japan, Sweden, the UK, and the U.S. were present. Notably, the vast majority of these national representatives were actually long-time C++ programmers. The C++ committee had a difficult mission:

- The definition of the language must be precise and comprehensive.
- C/C++ compatibility had to be addressed.
- Extensions beyond current C++ practice had to be considered.
- Libraries had to be considered.

On top of that, the C++ community was *very* diverse and totally unorganized so that the standards committee naturally became an important focal point of that community. In the short run, that is the most important role for the committee.

C compatibility was the first major controversial issue we had to face. After some—occasionally heated—debate it was decided that 100% C/C++ compatibility wasn't an option. Neither was significantly decreasing C compatibility. C++ was a separate language and not a strict superset of ANSI C and couldn't be changed to be such a superset without breaking the C++ type system and without breaking millions of lines of C++ code. This decision, often referred to as "As Close to C as Possible—but no closer" after a paper written by Andrew Koenig and me (Koenig & Stroustrup, 1989a), is the same one that has been reached over and over again by individuals and groups considering C++ and the direction of its evolution (section 6.3.4).

6.5.3. C++ 2.1 Feature Overview

The ARM presented a few minor features that were not implemented until 2.1 releases from AT&T and other C++ compiler vendors:

- Nested classes
- Separate overloading of prefix and suffix `++` and `--`
- `volatile` (as introduced into C by the ANSI C committee)

- Local static arrays (as introduced into C by the ANSI C committee)

The most obvious of these were nested classes. I was strongly encouraged to revert to the original definition of nested class scopes by comments from external reviewers of the reference manual. I also despaired over ever getting the scope rules of C++ coherent while the C rule was in place (section 6.3.4). Having classes be proper scopes for their members has proven invaluable in library design.

The main impetus to allow people to overload prefix and postfix increment (`++`) independently came from people who wanted "smart pointers" that behaved exactly like ordinary pointers except for some added work done "behind the scenes." The specific problem that convinced me came from Brian Kernighan.

During the standards process, many more minor features were added:

- European character set representation of C++.
- Relaxing the rule for return types for overriding functions.
- Declarations in conditions.
- Overloading based on enumerations.
- User-defined allocation and deallocation operators for arrays.
- Forward declaration of nested classes.
- Mutable.
- More explicit conversion operators (`static_cast`, `reinterpret_cast`, and `const_cast`).
- A Boolean type (`bool`).
- Optional explicit template instantiation.
- Explicit template argument specification in template function calls.
- Member templates.
- Class templates as template arguments.
- A `const` *static* member of integral type can be initialized by a `constant`-*expression* within a class declaration.
- Use of extended character sets in identifiers.
- Partial specialization of templates.
- `explicit` constructors.

I deem a feature minor if its use primarily affects the clarity of individual statements and localized pieces of code. The design of C++ was centered on major features. I consider a language feature *major* if it affects the way we think about programming and the way we organize our code. The ARM and the standardization process introduced four major features:

- Templates (section 6.5.4)
- Exception handling (section 6.5.5)
- Namespaces (section 6.5.6)
- Runtime type identification (section 6.5.7)

Both minor and major features are described from a historical and design perspective in *The Design and Evolution of* C++ (Stroustrup, 1994) and from a programmer's perspective in *The C++ Programming Language*, Third Edition (Stroustrup, 1997).

6.5.4. Some Minor Features

By definition, minor features don't affect the way we can design a C++ program. They can, however, have a strong impact on the clarity of a code fragment. A minor feature can also help overall code quality by eliminating some error-prone aspect of programming. Thus, the compound effect of minor features on programs and on programmers' confidence in their code can be significant. Otherwise, why bother with minor features at all? Here I give a few examples. Interestingly enough, programmers seem to be spending far more time discussing minor issues than thinking about and discussing major ones.

6.5.4.1. Explicit Constructors

By default, a constructor taking a single argument defines a conversion from its argument type. Here's an example:

```
class String {
    String(const char*); // constructor from C-style string;
                         // defines conversion from C-style string to String
    // ...
};

void f()
{
    String s("explicit construction");
    s = String("new string");
    s = "Implicit conversions can be very convenient";
    // ...
}
```

However, this implicit conversion is not always ideal. For example, the stack from section 6.2.4.8 takes an integer size. Consequently, it also defines conversion from int to stack:

```
void g()
{
    stack s(10);        // stack of 10 elements
    stack s2 = 20;      // stack of 20 elements (surprising?)

    s2 = 30;            // surprise: means "s2 = stack(30);"
                        // assign a stack of 30 elements to s2
    // ...
};
```

The obvious solution—allowing the user to specify which constructors define implicit conversions in addition to defining ways of explicitly constructing objects—was adopted as the result of a proposal from Nathan Myers with a syntax proposed by me:

```
class Stack {
public:
    explicit Stack(int); // "explicit" means:
                         // don't define an implicit conversion
    // ...
};

Stack s1(10);            // ok
Stack s2 = 10;           // error: no implicit conversion from int to
                            Stack
```

It can be argued that by default, constructors ought not to define implicit conversions and that what's needed is an implicit or conversion keyword to allow the programmer to indicate that a constructor should define an implicit conversion. However, after 15 years of active use of C++, such arguments are academic.

6.5.4.2. A More Explicit Notation for Type Conversion

In C and badly written C++, explicit type conversion—often called casting—is frequent and a major source of errors. Most explicit type conversions are also inherently low-level and unsafe operations, so it has been my long-term goal to eliminate their use. In well-designed C++ code, explicit type conversions are very rare. For example, *The C++ Programming Language*, Third Edition (Stroustrup, 1997) uses only five casts in realistic examples.

The traditional, C-style, cast is syntactically unobtrusive and can perform a variety of logically unrelated conversions:

```
struct Derived : public Base { /* ... */ };

void f(int i, double d, char* p, Base* pb, Derived* pd, const char* p)
```

```
{
    i = (int)d;           // truncating arithmetic conversion
    d = (double)i;        // arithmetic conversion
    i = (int)p;           // unsafe, implementation
                          // dependent pointer-to-int conversion
    p = (char*)i;         // unsafe, implementation
                          // dependent int-to-pointer conversion
    pd = (Derived*)pb;    // class hierarchy navigation
    p = (char*)pc;        // remove const protection
}
```

Few programmers can consistently explain what such conversions do and whether the semantics of one is well-defined, implementation-defined, or undefined.

After a proposal by me, supported by an analysis of millions of lines of code by Dag Bruck and Sean Corfield, and other evidence of problems related to the use of casts, the standards committee adopted a set of less error-prone conversion operators:

```
void g(int i, double d, char* p, Base* pb, Derived* pd, const char* p)
{
    i = static_cast<int>(d);
    d = static_cast<double>(i);
    i = reinterpret_cast<int>(p);
    p = reinterpret_cast<char*>(i);
    pd = static_cast<Derived*>(pb);     // a runtime checked
                                        // dynamic_cast (section 6.5.8)
                                        // might be preferable
    p = const_cast<char*>(pc);
}
```

Each of these operators can perform only a specific subset of all possible conversion operations. This enables some compile-time checking, encourages the programmer to think about what kind of conversion is needed, and gives the reader a clue about the intended meaning. For example, a `static_cast` can perform only relatively well-behaved conversions; if you need to do a conversion that is so nasty that a conversion back to the original type is required for reasonably safe use, a `reinterpret_cast` is required. The names of the conversion operators were deliberately chosen to be long and ugly to remind people of the nature of the operations they perform.

Unfortunately, the committee was not able to decide to deprecate C-style casts, so individual programmers and organizations must find ways to avoid them.

6.5.4.3. Declarations in Conditions

Where people conscientiously try to avoid uninitialized variables, they are left with one of the following:

- Variables used for input:

```
int i;
cin>>i;
```

- Variables used in conditions:

```
Tok* ct;
if (ct = gettok()) { /* ... */ }
```

During the design of the runtime type identification mechanism in 1991 (section 6.5.8), I realized that the latter cause of uninitialized variables could be eliminated by allowing declarations to be used as conditions:

```
if (Tok* ct = gettok()) {
    // ct is in scope here
}

// ct is not in scope here
```

This feature is not merely a cute trick to save typing. It is a direct consequence of the ideal of locality. By joining the declaration of a variable, its initialization, and the test on the result of that initialization, we achieve a compactness of expression that helps eliminate errors arising from variables being used before they are initialized. By limiting their scope to the statement controlled by the condition, we also eliminate the problem of variables being "reused" for other purposes or accidentally used after they were supposed to have outlived their usefulness. This eliminated a further minor source of errors.

The inspiration for allowing declarations in expressions came from expression languages—in particular from Algol68. I "remembered" that Algol68 declarations yielded values and based my design on that. Later, I found my memory had failed me: Declarations are one of the very few constructs in Algol68 that do not yield values! I asked Charles Lindsey about this and received the answer, "Even Algol68 has a few blemishes where it isn't completely orthogonal." I guess this just proves that a language doesn't have to live up to its own ideals to provide inspiration.

If I were to design a language from scratch, I would follow the Algol68 path and make every statement and declaration an expression that yields a value. I would probably also ban uninitialized variables and abandon the idea of declaring more than one name in a declaration. However, these ideas are clearly far beyond what would be acceptable for C++.

6.5.5. Templates

In the original design of C++, parameterized types (templates) were considered but postponed because there wasn't time to do a thorough job of exploring the design and implementation issues. I first presented templates at the 1988 USENIX C++ conference in Denver (Stroustrup, 1988a):

> For many people, the largest single problem using C++ is the lack of an extensive standard library. A major problem in producing such a library is that C++ does not provide a sufficiently general facility for defining "container classes" such as lists, vectors, and associative arrays.

There are two approaches for providing such classes/types: You can either rely on dynamic typing and inheritance as Smalltalk does, or you can rely on static typing and a facility for arguments of type `type`. The former is very flexible but carries a high runtime cost and, more importantly, defies attempts to use static type checking to catch interface errors. I chose the most flexible variant of the latter approach that I could devise. It was an important design aim for templates to be able to use them to define vector and list types that could compete with the built-in, but error-prone, array type. This implied that it had to be possible to perform operations on types specified using templates without function call overhead. Furthermore, it had to be possible to specify templates that put no restrictions on their parameters.

A C++ parameterized type is called a *class template*. A class template specifies how individual classes can be constructed much like the way a class specifies how individual objects can be constructed. A vector class template might be declared like this:

```
template<class T> class vector {
    T* v;
    int sz;
public:
    vector(int);
    T& operator[](int);
    T& elem(int i) { return v[i]; }
    // ...
};
```

The `template<class T>` prefix specifies that a template is being declared and that an argument `T` of type `I` will be used in the declaration. After its introduction, T is used exactly like other type names within the scope of the template declaration. Vectors can then be used like this:

```
vector<int> v1(20);
vector<complex> v2(30);

typedef vector<complex> cvec;    // make cvec a synonym for vector<complex>

cvec v3(40);                     // v2 and v3 are of the same type

v1[3] = 7;
v2[3] = v3.elem(4) = complex(7,8);
```

C++ does not require the user to explicitly instantiate (that is, specify which version of a template needs to be generated for particular sets of template arguments) a template. The most fundamental reason is that only when the program is complete can it be known what templates need to be instantiated. Many templates will be defined in libraries and many instantiations will be directly and indirectly caused by users who don't even know of the existence of those templates. It therefore seemed unreasonable to require the user to request instantiations (say, by using something such as Ada's new operator). Requiring explicit instantiation of template functions would also have seriously hampered generic programming.

Avoiding unnecessary space overheads caused by too many instantiations of template functions was considered a first order—that is, language-level—problem rather than an implementation detail. I considered it unlikely that early (or even late) implementations would be able to look at instantiations of a class for different template arguments and deduce that all or part of the instantiated code could be shared. The solution to this problem was to use the derived class mechanism to ensure code sharing among derived template instances.

The template mechanism is completely a compile-time and link-time mechanism. No part of the template mechanism needs runtime support. This leaves the problem of how to get the classes and functions generated (instantiated) from templates to depend on information known only at runtime. The answer was, as ever in C++, to use virtual functions and abstract classes. Abstract classes used in connection with templates also have the effect of providing better information hiding and better separation of programs into independently compiled units.

6.5.5.1. Template Refinements

The standards committee didn't change anything fundamental in the template design. It did, however, make more minor refinements and extensions to templates than to any other part of the language. I suspect that the fundamental reason for that was that I hadn't personally implemented templates. Consequently, there were more weak spots in the template design and in the description of that design than in any other part of C++. Curiously enough, part of the reason for the changes was the strength of the initial design. Templates proved far more useful than most people had expected, and styles of usage that I had anticipated only in the most general sense became popular. The result was a persistent demand for generality and flexibility beyond the ARM specification, which I had made somewhat restrictive in the hope of minimizing implementation problems.

The two most important extensions to the template concept were partial specialization and member templates. The most difficult template issue addressed by the committee was whether it would be a good idea to require that a template be defined in every translation unit in which it was used.

In addition, the overload resolution rules were revised to bring template functions into line with ordinary (non-template) functions. This revision closely mirrors the revision of the overload resolution rules for ordinary functions that was done in connection with Releases 2.0 and 2.1 of Cfront. In both cases, it took serious use of the initial facilities to determine the right rules.

6.5.5.2. Specialization

Specialization was provided in the ARM to allow a separate implementation of a template for a given template argument:

```
template<class T> void sort(vector<T>);  // sort vectors using T's <
                                         // operator

void sort<char*>(vector<char*>);        // sort vectors using strcmp()

void f(vector<int>& vi, vector<char*>& vcs)
{
     sort(vi);      // sort using integer <
     sort(vcs);     // sort using strcmp()
}
```

The primary use of specialization is to provide separate implementations for "irregular types" such as C-style strings and arrays. I noticed that a generalization of this idea would be

```
template<class T> class vector { /* ... */ };       // vector of
                                                    // arbitrary T

template<class T> class vector<T*> { /* ... */ }; // vector of pointer
                                                    // to T

vector<complex> vc;        // implement using general template
```

```
vector<Shape*> vps;          // implement using pointer specialization
vector<Record*> vpr;         // implement using pointer specialization
```

The importance of specialization is that it provides great flexibility in an orderly and declarative manner without complicating the interface presented to users. Thus, the writer of a template can provide significant optimizations without the intervention of users of the template. For example, all `vectors` of pointers can be implemented without replication of the code for `vector` operations. Often, specialization allows us to simplify the interface to a concept by providing separate implementations for types that would otherwise have forced us to make an irregularity visible to users. The `sort()` template is an example of that. Without the specialization, the comparison criteria would have had to be passed as an argument.

6.5.5.3. Member Templates

By default, you would expect to be able to declare a template as a member of a class. However, while writing the ARM, I couldn't prove to myself that member templates wouldn't cause serious implementation problems so I didn't allow them. This caution proved warranted. Consider this promising idea for a more elegant variant of double dispatch:

```
class Shape {
    // ...
    template<class T> virtual Bool intersect(const T&) const =0;
};

class Rectangle : public Shape {
    // ...
    template<class T> virtual Bool intersect(const T& s) const;
};
```

This would generate a new intersect function each time a user used `intersect()` with a new argument type. From a user's point of view, this is an elegant solution to a hard problem. Unfortunately, it breaks C++ object model by requiring the virtual function table to be arbitrarily extended based on use. This would imply postponing calculating the layout of the virtual function table until link time or—in the presence of dynamic linking—until runtime. By implication, the traditional ways of implementing virtual function calls could not be used.

Consequently, only nonvirtual member templates are allowed. The particular problem that prompted the acceptance of member templates was the need to provide conversions between templates that represent "smart pointers":

```
template<class T> class Ptr { // pointer to T
    T* p;
public:
    Ptr(T*);
    template<class T2> operator Ptr<T2> ()
    {
        return Ptr<T2>(p);     // works if p can be converted to a T2*
    }
    // ...
};

void f(Ptr<Shape*> ps, Ptr<Circle*> pc, Ptr<Record*> pr)
{
    ps = pc;    // ok a Circle* can be converted to a Shape*
    pc = ps;    // error: a Shape* cannot be converted to a Circle*
    pc = pr;    // error: a Record* cannot be converted to a Circle*
}
```

The use of member templates to address the need for smart pointer conversions was first discovered when David Jordan, Andrew Koenig, and I were trying to find a way to specify pointers for the Object Data Management Group's effort to standardize a C++ interface to object-oriented databases.

6.5.5.4. Template Instantiation

Unfortunately, the ARM was not sufficiently specific about how a definition of a template function was to be presented to a compilation system. My intent was to maintain the usual C and C++ model of compilation where a function can be called given only a declaration specifying its calling interface as long as its definition is supplied in some compilation unit. This is sometimes called the separation model of template compilation. The first (Cfront-based) implementation of templates provided that. However, separate compilation of template functions is hard, and it was possible to misread the ARM text so as not to require it. Furthermore, to encourage experimentation with alternative implementation strategies, the ARM specifically allowed implementors to impose constraints on the way template definitions were presented to the compilation system. The first PC implementation of templates, provided in Borland's Release 4.0, simply required the definition of a template function to be in scope wherever the template was called.

Requiring a programmer to supply the definition of a template everywhere it is used (called the inclusion model of template compilation) simplified the compilation process so much that John Spicer of the C++ compiler company Edison Design Group started a long campaign to make this model the only one required by the standard. I considered the option of including a template definition with every use acceptable and in the spirit of the way a programmer can request inlining for a function.

However, I considered a requirement to include a template definition with every use unacceptable because this forces a programmer to merge the source text of unrelated modules into a single compilation. Such merging can cause surprising changes of meaning by changing the context of a definition. In particular, there is no effective way of protecting a definition from having its meaning changed by unexpected macros. For a long time, these two views proved irreconcilable and the standards committee basically separated into two opposing camps over the template compilation model issue. Neither camp had the massive majority necessary to settle the issue in a way that satisfied the ANSI and ISO requirement for a consensus.

Fortunately, the stalemate was broken by a clever and innovative proposal from a group of people from SGI, including Matt Austern, Jim Denert, and John Wilcox. That proposal focused on the ways that names in a template definition were resolved. The idea was to formulate those rules in such a way that the meaning of a use of a template would in most cases be independent of how a programmer presented it to the compilation system. The technique simplifies separate compilation of template functions to the point where a function can be generated from a template at link time from partially compiled source code. This implies that generation of new functions from a template at runtime is possible for systems with runtime linking. In addition, the technique provides a degree of protection against interference between code from different logical modules included in a single compilation unit.

The fundamental idea is to bind a name used within a template definition at the definition point unless the name depends on a template argument. If a name depends on a template argument, it is looked up in scopes related to its actual template parameters in a way that minimizes dependence of the location of the use and the location of the template definition. If different name bindings can result from lookups at different points of use of a template given the same template arguments, such uses of the template are illegal (Stroustrup, 1997).

6.5.6. Exception Handling

Exceptions were considered in the original design of C++ but were postponed because there wasn't time to do a thorough job of exploring the design and implementation issues. Exceptions were considered essential for error handling in programs composed out of separately designed libraries.

The actual design of the C++ exception mechanism stretched from 1984 to 1989. Andrew Koenig was closely involved in the later iterations and is the coauthor (with me) of the published papers (Koenig & Stroustrup, 1989a, 1990). I also had meetings at Apple, DEC, Microsoft, IBM, Sun, and other places where I presented draft versions of the design and received valuable input. In particular, I searched out people with actual experience with systems providing exception handling to compensate for my personal inexperience in that area. Throughout the design effort, there was an increasing influence of systems designers of all sorts and a decrease of input from the language design community. In retrospect, the greatest influence on the C++ exception-handling design was the work on fault-tolerant systems started at the University of Newcastle in England by Brian Randell and his colleagues, and continued in many places since.

The following assumptions were made for the design:

- Exceptions are used primarily for error handling.
- Exception handlers are rare compared to function definitions.
- Exceptions occur infrequently compared to function calls.

These assumptions, together with the requirement that C++ with exceptions should cooperate smoothly with languages without exceptions, such as C and Fortran, led to a design with multilevel propagation. The view is that not every function should be a firewall and that the best error-handling strategies are those in which only designated major interfaces are concerned with non-local error-handling issues. By allowing multilevel propagation of exceptions, C++ loses one aspect of static checking. One cannot simply look at a function to determine which exceptions it may throw. C++ compensates by providing a mechanism for specifying a list of exceptions that a function may throw.

I concluded that the ability to define groups of exceptions is essential. For example, a user must be able to catch any I/O library exception without knowing exactly which exceptions those are. Many people, including Ted Goldstein and Peter Deutsch, noticed that most such groups were equivalent to class hierarchies. We therefore adopted a scheme inspired by ML where you throw an object and catch it by a handler declared to accept objects of that type. This scheme naturally provides for type-safe transmission of arbitrary amounts of information from a throw point to a handler. Here's an example:

```
class Matherr { /* ... */ };
class Overflow : public Matherr { /* ... */ };
class Underflow : public Matherr { /* ... */ };
```

```
class Zerodivide : public Matherr { /* ... */ };
class Int_add_overflow : public Overflow { /* ... */ };

void f()
{
    // ...

    try {
        f();
    }
    catch (Overflow& over) {
        // handle Overflow or anything derived from Overflow
    }
    catch (Matherr& math) {
        // handle any Matherr
    }

    // ...
}
```

Thus `f()` might be written like this:

```
void f() throw(Matherr&) // f() can throw Matherr&
                         // exceptions (and only Matherr& exceptions)
{
    // ...
    if (d == 0) throw Zerodivide();
    // ...
    if (check(x,y)) throw Int_add_overflow(x,y);
    // ...
}
```

`Zerodivide` is caught by the `Matherr&` handler, and `Int_add_overflow` is caught by the `Overflow&` handler that might access the operand values `x` and `y` passed by `f()` in the object thrown.

The central point in the exception-handling design was the management of resources. In particular, if a function grabs a resource, how can the language help the user to ensure that the resource is correctly released upon exit even if an exception occurs? The problem with most solutions are that they are verbose, tedious, potentially expensive, and therefore error prone. However, I noticed that many resources are released in the reverse order of their acquisition. This strongly resembles the behavior of local objects created by constructors and destroyed by destructors (section 6.2.4.8). Thus we can handle such resource acquisition and release problems by a suitable use of objects of classes with constructors and destructors. Here's an example:

```
void f(const char* file_name, Lock& lck)
{
    File_ptr p(file_name,"r");    // open file and use through "p"
    Lock_ref r(lck);              // acquire lck

    // code using p relying on lck being held
}
```

The file is implicitly closed by `p`'s destructor and the lock is implicitly released by `r`'s destructor.

I named this technique "resource acquisition is initialization." It provides a systematic and declarative way of dealing with cleanup problems that have traditionally been addressed by ad hoc techniques relying on explicitly catching every exception to gain control at the return from a function (called `catch(...)` in C++ and `finally` in some other languages). The ad hoc techniques are error prone in that they rely on programmers consistently adding code to deal with error conditions—and avoiding such reliance is one of the main reasons to use exceptions. The "resource acquisition is initialization" technique extends to partially constructed objects and thus addresses the otherwise difficult issue of what to do when an error is encountered in a constructor.

During the design, the most contentious issue turned out to be whether the exception-handling mechanism should support termination semantics or resumption semantics—that is, whether it should be possible for an exception handler to require execution to resume from the point where the exception was thrown. The main resumption-versus-termination debate took place in the ANSI C++ committee. After a discussion that lasted for about a year, the exception-handling proposal as presented in the ARM (that is, with termination semantics) was voted into C++ by an overwhelming majority. The key to that consensus was presentations of experience data based on decades of use of systems that supported both resumption and termination semantics by representatives of DEC, Sun, Texas Instruments, IBM, and others. Basically, every use of resumption had represented a failure to keep separate levels of abstraction disjointed.

The C++ exception-handling mechanism is explicitly *not* for handling asynchronous events directly. This view precludes the direct use of exceptions to represent something like hitting a Del key and the replacement of UNIX signals with exceptions. In such cases, a low-level interrupt routine must somehow do its minimal job and possibly map into something that could trigger an exception at a well-defined point in a program's execution.

As ever, efficiency was a major concern. The C++ exception-handling mechanism can be implemented without any runtime overhead to a program that doesn't throw an exception (Stroustrup, 1988a). It is also possible to limit space overhead, but it is hard simultaneously to avoid runtime overhead and code size increases.

6.5.7. Namespaces

C++ followed C in having a single global namespace. This caused name clashes in larger programs and left the class as C++'s only language mechanism for directly supporting grouping of declarations. However, classes are designed to support the declaration and use of objects, and the support for objects gets in the way of (mis)using classes as modules. I regret not providing C++ with some form of namespace control early on when that could have been done without debate and when experimentation was easy. However, the resolution mechanisms I looked at, such as Ada packages and Modula-2 modules, had too great an overlap with the C++ class mechanism and thus didn't fit. Furthermore, separate compilation alleviated the problem—and thus postponed its proper solution.

After several false starts, a facility for defining and using namespaces was introduced into C++ in 1994. In the standards committee, the initial impetus came from a proposal written by Keith Rowe from Microsoft. By early 1993, I had—with the help of multimegabyte email exchanges and discussions at the standards meetings—synthesized a coherent proposal. I recall technical contributions on namespaces from Dag Bruck, John Bruns, Steve Dovich, Bill Gibbons, Philippe Gautron, Tony Hansen, Peter Juhl, Andrew Koenig, Eric Krohn, Doug McIlroy, Richard Minner, Martin O'Riordan, John Skaller, Jerry Schwarz, Mark Terribile, and Mike Vilot.

The basic idea is simple: A name can be declared in a named scope—called a namespace—and to use a name from outside its namespace, some explicit action is needed. By default, this eliminates name clashes. The problem is to make access so convenient that people do not reject namespaces as not worth the effort to use them.

For example, here are some facilities for dealing with time that have been defined in their own namespace `Chrono` to establish the fact that they constitute a logical explicit unit and to avoid name clashes:

```
namespace Chrono { // facilities for dealing with time

    class Date {
        // ...
    };

    int operator-(Date a, Date b);
    bool leapyear(int y);
    Date next_weekday(Date d);
    Date next_saturday(Date d);

    class Time {
        // ...
    };

    // ...
}
```

A programmer can refer to a name from a namespace by explicit qualification:

```
void f(Chrono::Date d)
{

     Chrono::Date monday = Chrono::next_saturday(d).add_day(2);
     // ...
}
```

However, I saw no hope of programmers accepting a notation that verbose and redundant. In particular, there would be no way of gradually introducing namespaces into existing programs. Consequently, we provided mechanisms for making a namespace name implicit. A `using` declaration introduces a local synonym into a scope:

```
using Chrono::Date; // Date is Chrono::Date

void f(Date d)
{
     Date monday = Chrono::next_saturday(d).add_day(2);
     // ...
}
```

A `using` directive is a somewhat more powerful and therefore potentially more dangerous mechanism that makes every name from a namespace available in a scope:

```
void g(Chrono::Date d)
{
     using namespace Chrono; // make Chrono names available

     Date monday = next_saturday(d).add_day(2);
}
```

The `using` directive is intended primarily to smooth the introduction of namespaces into existing programs where there is no explicit mention of namespaces.

Andrew Koenig observed that in many cases, no explicit resolution mechanism was needed if we resolved a function call or the use of an operator based on the namespace (or namespaces) of the operands. Here's an example:

```
void f(Chrono::Date d)
{
     Chrono::Date monday = next_saturday(d).add_day(2);
     if (monday-d < 2) {
          // ...
     }
     // ...
}
```

Here, `next_saturday()` and the operator defined in `Chrono` are used because those are the ones logically connected with the operands by being declared in `Chrono`. For further details, see *The Design and Evolution of C++* (Stroustrup, 1994) and *The C++ Programming Language*, Third Edition (Stroustrup, 1997).

6.5.8. Runtime Type Identification

In the original C++ design, I deliberately didn't include the Simula mechanisms for runtime type identification (`QUA` and `INSPECT`). In my experience, they were almost always misused so that the benefits from having the mechanism would be outweighed by the disadvantages. However, in large systems composed of separately developed parts, it is often unavoidable that information is passed around in ways that renders their exact type unknown. Thus, I reluctantly accepted that the time to introduce a mechanism for runtime type identification had come. The immediate impetus was work by Dmitry Lenkov and his colleagues at HP (Lenkov, Mehta, & Unni, 1991). Lenkov and I developed a proposal for a standard mechanism for runtime type identification where the primary operation is a runtime-checked pointer conversion. Here's an example:

```
void my_fct(Dialog_box* bp)
{
    if (My_dbox* dbp = dynamic_cast<My_dbox*>(bp)) {

        // use dbp
    }
    else {

        // treat *pb as a "plain" dialog box
    }
}
```

The `dynamic_cast<My_dbox*>(bp)` operator converts its operand `bp` to the desired type `My_dbox*` if `*bp` really is a `My_dbox` or a class derived from `My_dbox`; otherwise, the value of `dynamic_cast<My_dbox*>(bp)` is `0`.

Thus, the `dynamic_cast` operator combines a test of the actual type of the object taking inheritance into account (like Smalltalk's `isKindOf`) with a pointer conversion. For a language that relies on static type checking, the conversion is necessary, and not taking inheritance into account would render the operation clumsy and error-prone. The use of an "ugly" conversion notation and the absence of a type-switch statement (like Simula's `INSPECT`) is intended to minimize (mis)use of runtime type information to write programs that violate modularity by centralizing information about otherwise unrelated types in type switches.

For further details, see *The Design and Evolution of* C++ (Stroustrup, 1994) and *The* C++ *Programming Language*, Third Edition (Stroustrup, 1997).

6.5.9. Rampant Featurism?

A critical issue for the standards committee was how to handle the constant stream of proposals for language changes and extensions. The focus of that effort was the extensions working group of which I was the chairman. It is much easier to accept a proposal than to reject it. You win friends this way and people praise the language for having so many "neat features." Unfortunately, a language made as a shopping list of features without coherence will die, so there is no way we could accept even most of the features that would be of genuine help to some section of the C++ community.

How did the committee do? Only four major new features were accepted: the "mandated" extensions (exception handling and templates), namespaces, and runtime type information. In addition, about two dozen minor features and clarifications were approved.

As I write this (1998), the chance of any significant additions to the C++ language by the standards committee is zero. Many minor extensions were added, but I think that C++ is now a significantly more powerful, pleasant, and coherent language than it was when the standards process started. See also *The Design and Evolution of* C++ (Stroustrup, 1994) and *The* C++ *Programming Language*, Third Edition (Stroustrup, 1997).

6.6. The Standard Library

To a programmer, the distinction between the language proper and its most fundamental libraries is academic. Essentially, no real code is written in the language itself without the use of libraries, and learning to use the language involves essential library features long before the more advanced and intricate language features are mastered. Consequently, a good standard library is a great asset to a language, and the absence thereof is a liability.

The search for a good set of libraries to include with every C with Classes implementation started even before the completion of the first implementation of the language, and much of the evolution of C++ was driven by a desire to provide better support for library building. Unfortunately, this quest for a good standard library did not yield acceptable results fast enough, and the absence of a large and solid standard library was a liability to C with Classes and C++.

6.6.1. Early Foundation Libraries

The very first real code to be written in C with Classes was the task library (Stroustrup, 1980b), providing Simula-like concurrency for simulation. The first real programs were simulations of network traffic, circuit board layout, and so on, using the task library. The task library was still heavily used in the mid-1990s. The task library was the first of many attempts to provide support for concurrency in C++ (Wilson & Lu, 1996). Many of these attempts were successful, but the extreme diversity of user needs has (at least so far) defeated all attempts to establish a standard model for concurrency for C++. Instead, a variety of system-dependent concurrency facilities are used.

The standard C library was available from C++—without overhead or complication compared with C—from day one. So were all other C libraries. Classical data types such as character strings, range-checked arrays, dynamic arrays, and lists were among the examples used to design C++ and test its early implementations.

The early work with container classes such as `list` and `array` were severely hampered by the lack of support for a way of expressing parameterized types. In the absence of proper language support, we had to make do with macros. The best that can be said for the C preprocessor's macro facilities is that they allowed us to gain experience with parameterized types and support individual and small group use.

Much of the work on early libraries was done in cooperation with Jonathan Shopiro, who in 1983 produced list and string classes that saw wide use within AT&T. These list and string classes are the basis for the classes found in the Standard Components library that was developed in AT&T Bell Labs and later sold by UNIX Systems Laboratories.

The development of these early libraries gave us much valuable experience with C++ and with library design. However, my conclusion at the time was that in the absence of parameterized types, C++ wasn't capable of supporting a sufficiently good standard library and that we did not understand enough to build a widely acceptable standard library for C++. In retrospect, I was probably right about the technical problems, but I underestimated our ability to provide something (barely) acceptable to users.

The design of these early libraries interacted directly with the design of the language and in particular with the design of the overloading mechanisms.

6.6.2. The Stream I/O Library

C's `printf` family of functions is an effective and often convenient I/O mechanism. It is not, however, type safe or extensible to user-defined types (classes). Consequently, I started looking for a type-safe, terse, extensible, and efficient alternative to the `printf` family. Part of the inspiration came from the last page and a half of the Ada rationale (Ichbiah, 1979), which is an argument that you cannot have a terse and type-safe I/O library without special language features to support it. I took that as a challenge. The result was the stream I/O library that was first implemented in 1984 and presented in *Strings and Lists for C++* (Stroustrup, 1985). Soon after, Dave Presotto reimplemented the stream library without changing the interfaces.

To introduce stream I/O, this example was considered:

```
fprintf(stderr,"x = %s\n",x);
```

Because `fprintf()` relies on unchecked arguments that are handled according to the format string at runtime, this is not type safe. Had `x` been a user-defined type like `complex`, there would have been no way of specifying the output format of `x` in the convenient way used for types "known to `printf()`" (for example, `%s` and `%d`). The programmer would typically have defined a separate function for printing complex numbers and then written something like this:

```
fprintf(stderr,"x = ");
put_complex(stderr,x);
fprintf(stderr,"\n");
```

This is inelegant. It would have been a major annoyance in C++ programs that use many user-defined types to represent entities that are interesting and critical to an application.

Type security and uniform treatment can be achieved by using a single overloaded function name for a set of output functions:

```
put(stderr,"x = ");
put(stderr,x);
put(stderr,"\n");
```

The type of the argument determines which `put` function is invoked for each argument. However, this is too verbose. The C++ solution, using an output stream for which `<<` has been defined as a `put` to operator, looks like this:

```
cerr << "x = " << x << "\n";
```

where cerr is the standard error output stream (equivalent to the C stderr). If x is an int with the value 123, this statement prints

```
x = 123
```

followed by a newline onto the standard error output stream.

This style can be used as long as x is a type for which operator << is defined, and a user can trivially define operator << for a new type. If x is the user-defined type complex with the value (1,2.4), the statement prints the following on cerr:

```
x = (1,2.4)
```

The stream I/O facility is implemented exclusively using language features available to every C++ programmer. Like C, C++ does not have any I/O facilities built into the language. The stream I/O facility is provided in a library and contains no "extra-linguistic magic."

The idea of providing an output operator rather than a named output function was suggested by Doug McIlroy. This requires operators to return their left-hand operand for use by further operations.

In connection with Release 2.0, Jerry Schwarz reimplemented and partially redesigned the streams library to serve a larger class of applications and to be more efficient for file I/O. A significant improvement was the use of Andrew Koenig's idea of manipulators (Stroustrup, 1991) to control formatting details such as the precision used for floating-point output. Experience with streams was a major reason for the change to the basic type system and to the overloading rules to allow char values to be treated as characters rather than small integers the way they are in C:

```
char ch = 'b';
cout << 'a' << ch;
```

In Release 1.*, this code would output a string of digits reflecting the integer values of the characters a and b; whereas Release 2.* outputs ab as one would expect.

The iostreams library was further revised during the standards process. The most visible change was that the streams are now parameterized on the type used to communicate with lower-level I/O systems. This change was made to ensure that languages that require multibyte encodings, notably Japanese and Chinese, would be handled on an equal footing with single-byte characters. Similarly, the standard string type is parameterized on its character type.

6.6.3. The Standard Template Library

For about a decade, Alexander Stepanov had been searching for a way to write uncompromisingly generic algorithms. For example, he wanted to write a `find()`—that is, a linear search—for a given value in a container in such a way that it

- Worked for elements of arbitrary type (such as `int`, `string`, and `Payroll_record`)
- Worked on any type of container (such as built-in array, `list`, and `map`)
- Was as efficient as a similar search anyone could write for a value of a specific type on a specific type of container

This work led to libraries written in Scheme, CLOS, and Ada86 (Musser & Stepanov, 1989), which failed to meet the stringent criteria set by Stepanov and his collaborators (notably David Musser from Rensselaer Institute of Technology). During a dinner with Andrew Koenig and Barbara Moo in August 1993, Stepanov explained that he had completed a C++ library that met his criteria. Koenig took an interest in that library—ambitiously called the STL (the Standard Template Library)—and managed to get me interested also.

To my surprise, the STL met almost all the criteria for a set of containers suitable for a standard that I had formulated over the years. Years earlier, Stepanov had in AT&T Bell Labs worked on the Standard Components Library and had taken part in some of the early discussion about the design of templates. However, I had lost contact with him, and the STL went beyond any library that I had seen for C++ (Stepanov & Lee, 1994). In style and contents, it differed from existing C++ libraries. In fact, its style was closer to what you see in functional programming languages than to any of the commonly used C++ foundation libraries.

After some thought, Koenig invited Stepanov to give a technical presentation of the STL at a C++ standards meeting in November 1993. This presentation led to some enthusiasm, some thoughts about how the STL `vector`s, `set`s, `map`s, and so on might serve as standard containers for C++, and eventually to a detailed proposal to make a set of templates closely resembling part of the STL part of the C++ standard library. An initial outline of this proposal was worked out at a meeting of committee members (Tom Keffer, Nathan Meyer, Larry Podmolik, Mike Vilot, Richard Wilhelm, and me) hosted by Stepanov at HP in spring 1994 and completed by Stepanov and his coworker at HP, Meng Lee. This proposal, strongly supported by Koenig and me, was accepted by the standards committee in July 1994.

In *The C++ Programming Language*, Third Edition (Stroustrup, 1997), I summarized the criteria for a standard library facility like this:

The facilities offered by the C++ standard library are designed to be

- Invaluable and affordable to essentially every student and professional programmer, including the builders of other libraries.
- Used directly or indirectly by every programmer for everything within the scope of the library.
- Efficient enough to provide genuine alternatives to hand-coded functions, classes, and templates in the implementation of further libraries.
- Either policy free or giving the user the option to supply policies as arguments.
- Primitive in the mathematical sense. That is, a component that serves two weakly related roles will almost certainly suffer overhead compared to individual components designed to perform only a single role.
- Convenient, efficient, and reasonably safe for common uses.
- Complete at what they do. The standard library may leave major functions to other libraries, but if it takes on a task, it must provide enough functionality so that individual users or implementors need not replace it to get the basic job done.
- Able to blend well with and augment built-in types and operations.
- Type safe by default.
- Supportive of commonly accepted programming styles.
- Extensible to deal with user-defined types in ways similar to the way built-in types and standard-library types are handled.

  For example, building the comparison criteria into a sort function is unacceptable because the same data can be sorted according to different criteria. This is why the C standard library `qsort()` takes a comparison function as an argument rather than rely on something fixed, say, the < operator. On the other hand, the overhead imposed by a function call for each comparison compromises `qsort()` as a building block for further library building. For almost every data type, it is easy to do a comparison without imposing the overhead of a function call.

The STL manages to meet most of these criteria by formalizing the notion of a sequence of elements, by providing containers that support that notion, and by having functions operate on sequences through an abstraction of a pointer to an element of a sequence (called an *iterator*). In addition to offering the most common types of containers (such as `list`, `vector`, `set`, and `map`), the STL provides the most common algorithms on containers (such as `find`, `sort`, and `merge`).

From a language point of view, the key to the STL is the use of overload resolution to determine what template specializations are to be generated for a specific call:

```
template<class Iterator> void sort(Iterator,Iterator);
template<class Iterator, class Cmp> void sort(Iterator,Iterator,Cmp);

void f(vector<int>&vi, list<string>&lst)
{
     sort(vi.begin(),vi.end());
     sort(lst.begin(),lst.end());
     sort(lst.begin(),lst.end(),my_string_compare);
}
```

Here, `vi.begin()` and `vi.end()` produce iterators for the beginning and the end of the `vector<int>` called `vi`. Then a version of the generic `sort()` is called for two iterators pointing to `int`s in a `vector`. Similarly, `lst.begin()` and `lst.end()` produce iterators for the beginning and the end of the `list<string>` called `lst`. Then a version of the generic `sort()` is called for two iterators pointing to strings in a list.

Because all information is available, the only reason to produce less than optimal code is a poor compiler. In practice, C++ compilers are pretty good at generating code for calls like these. In particular, critical operations such as comparisons are trivially inlined. Where the default operation is unsuitable, the user can supply a suitable one. In the preceding case, I provided an alternative to the default < operator as a third argument. Again, the overload resolution and template instantiation mechanisms resolve the call into close to optimal code.

The STL relies heavily on function objects to provide flexibility and efficiency. For example, consider finding the first element in a list with a value less than some integer `i`:

```
void f(list<int>& m, int i)
{
     list<int>::iterator p = find_if(m.begin(),m.end(),less_than(i));
     // ...
}
```

Note the use of the nested type `iterator` to ensure that the programmer doesn't have to know the actual mechanism used to iterate through a `list`. Every standard container has an `iterator` type.

How would I define `less_than`? It cannot be an ordinary function because it needs to be initialized with a value that it later uses to compare against a sequence of values from the `list`. As used, `less_than` must be a function that returns an object that can be invoked to do a comparison:

```
template<class T> class Less_than {
    T val;
public:
    Less_than(const T& v) val(v) { }                    // store value
    bool operator()(const T& v) { return v<val; }       // compare against
value
};

template<class T> Less_than<T> less_than(const T& v)
{
    return Less_than<T>(v);  // create and return Less_than object for v
}
```

This style was inspired by the use of higher-order functions (that is, functions that return functions) in functional programming languages.

Note that the function object `Less_than` and the function `less_than()` were defined as templates so that they could be used for a variety of types:

```
void g(vector<string>& m, string s)
{
    vector<string>::iterator p = find_if(m.begin(),m.end(),less_than(s));
    // ...
}
```

The `find_if` algorithm might be expressed like this:

```
template<class Iter, class Pred> Iter find_if(Iter first, Iter last, Pred p)
{
    while (first!=last && !p(*first)) first++;
    return first;
}
```

The part of the STL that was accepted into the standard did not include a hash table. This was an obvious disadvantage and several people—notably Javier Barreiro, Robert Fraley, and David R. Musser—promptly proceeded to produce hash tables that fitted into the STL framework. Unfortunately, these implementations and their specifications reached the committee so late in the standards process that they were not accepted into the standard. Instead, these hash table implementations were made publicly available.

The standard library containers store copies of objects given as arguments to insertion functions. That is, the critical requirement on an element type of a standard container is that it can be copied. There is no requirement that an element type has to be derived from a particular class. Thus, the standard library containers are non-intrusive. This is essential to allow standard containers to hold built-in types, such as `int` and `char*`, and types that were not defined with the containers in mind, such as types from older code and data structures shared with C programs. For applications where it is essential, a programmer can provide optimized intrusive implementations as specializations. To preserve polymorphic behavior of contained objects, we can insert pointers or handle objects into containers. The standard library provides function objects that allow the standard algorithms to operate on containers of pointers. These member function adapters were my main technical contribution to the STL.

The actual algorithms of the STL were chosen to be a significant subset of the fundamental algorithms described by Knuth (1973). In particular, the STL provided a superset of what AT&T's Standard Components offered, most of what CLOS offered, and most of what Ada offered in the area of fundamental algorithms.

6.6.4. Standard Library Facilities

In *The C++ Programming Language*, Third Edition (Stroustrup, 1997), I summarize the standard library as shown in the following list.

The facilities provided by the standard library can be classified like this:

- Basic runtime language support (such as for allocation and runtime type information).
- The C standard library (with very minor modifications to minimize violations of the type system).
- Strings and I/O streams (with support for international character sets and localization).
- A framework of containers (such as `vector`, `list`, and `map`) and algorithms using containers (such as general traversals, sorts, and merges).
- Support for numerical computation (complex numbers plus vectors with arithmetic operations, BLAS-like and generalized slices, and semantics designed to ease optimization).

Thus, C++ finally has a standard library that covers the fundamental data structures and their basic algorithms. A programmer will of course want more facilities. Graphics is an obvious example. However, I saw the job of a standard to support library building and a library industry. There is little point in a small group of people—however well-meaning—trying to supply every need of an enormous user population. Consequently, the standards committee sensibly restricted its activities to a relatively small set of library facilities. That set of facilities was partially determined by history and partly by the criterion that the standard library should provide what separately developed libraries needed to communicate. Thus, the standard library provides complex arithmetic because C++ implementations always did. The standard library provides `string` and `list` because if it didn't, every major library would have to provide its own `string` and `list` and still be forced to communicate with other libraries using only built-in types.

The standard `string` type is the result of the efforts of many people in the library working group of the standard committee. Its distinguishing feature is that it is a template that can be used to represent strings of characters in essentially any character set.

The standard library provides a vector type with associated operations to support numeric calculations, called `valarray`, based on the work of Ken Budge (Budge, Perry, & Robinson, 1992).

6.7. The Explosion in Interest and Use: 1987–The Present

C++ was designed to serve users. It was not an academic experiment to design the perfect programming language, nor was it a commercial product meant to enrich its developers. Thus to fulfill its purpose, C++ had to have users—and it did (see Table 6.1).

TABLE 6.1. C++ *use.*

Date	*Estimated Number of Users*
October 1979	1
October 1980	16
October 1981	38
October 1982	85
October 1983	??+2 (no Cpre count)
October 1984	??+50 (no Cpre count)

continues

TABLE 6.1. *Continued.*

Date	*Estimated Number of Users*
October 1985	500
October 1986	2,000
October 1987	4,000
October 1988	15,000
October 1989	50,000
October 1990	150,000
October 1991	400,000

In other words, the C++ user population doubled every 7.5 months or so. These are conservative figures. The actual number of C++ users has never been easy to count. First, there were implementations such as GNU's G++ and Cfront shipped to universities for which no meaningful records could be kept. Second, many companies, both tools suppliers and end users, treat the number of their users and the kind of work they do like state secrets. However, I always had many friends, colleagues, contacts, and many compiler suppliers who were willing to trust me with figures as long as I used them in a responsible manner. This enabled me to estimate the number of C++ users. These estimates are created by taking the number of users reported to me or estimated based on personal experience, rounding them all down, adding them, and then rounding down again. These numbers are the estimates made at the time and not adjusted in any way. To support the claim that these figures are conservative, I can mention that Borland, the largest single C++ compiler supplier at the time, publicly stated that it had shipped 500,000 compilers by October 1991. In 1996 alone, more than a million C++ implementations were sold (International Data Corporation study, 1997).

Early users had to be gained without the benefit of traditional marketing. Various forms of electronic communication played a crucial role in this. In the early years, most distribution and all support were done using email, and relatively early, newsgroups dedicated to C++ were created (*not* at the initiative of AT&T marketing) that allowed a wider dissemination of information about the language, techniques, and the current state of tools. These days this is fairly ordinary, but in 1981 it was relatively new. I think that only the spread of Interlisp over the ARPAnet provides a contemporary parallel.

Later, more conventional forms of communication and marketing arose. After AT&T released Cfront 1.0, some resellers, notably Glockenspiel in Ireland and its U.S. distributor Oasys (later part of Green Hills) started some minimal advertising in 1986. When independently developed C++ compilers such as Oregon Software's C++ Compiler (developed by Mike Ball at TauMetric Software in San Diego) and Zortech's C++ Compiler (developed by Walter Bright in Seattle) appeared, C++ became a common sight in ads (from about 1988).

6.7.1. Conferences

In 1987, USENIX, the UNIX users' association, took the initiative to hold the first conference specifically devoted to C++. Thirty papers were presented to 214 people in Santa Fe, New Mexico, in November 1987.

The Santa Fe conference set a good example for future conferences with a mix of papers on applications, programming and teaching techniques, ideas for improvements to the language, libraries, and implementation techniques. Notably for a USENIX conference, there were papers on C++ on the Apple Macintosh, OS/2, the Connection machine, and for implementing non-UNIX operating systems (for example, CLAM [Call, 1987] and Choices [Campbell, 1987]). The NIH library (Gorlen, Orlow, & Plexico, 1987) and the Interviews library (Linton & Calder, 1987) also made their public debut in Santa Fe. An early version of what became Cfront 2.0 was demonstrated, and I gave the first public presentation of its features. The USENIX conferences continue as a technically and academically oriented forum for C++ and programming in general. The proceedings from USENIX C++ conferences are among the best reading about C++ and its use. In addition, many commercial and semi-commercial conferences cover C++.

6.7.2. Journals and Books

By 1991, there were more than 60 books on C++ available in English, along with both translations and locally written books available in languages such as Chinese, Danish, French, German, and Japanese. By 1996, several hundred books on C++ had appeared. Naturally, the quality varied enormously.

The first journal devoted to C++, *The C++ Report* from SIGS publications, began in January 1989 with Rob Murray as its editor. A larger and glossier quarterly, *The C++ Journal*, appeared in spring 1991. In addition, there are several newsletters controlled by C++ tools suppliers, and many journals such as *Computer Language*, *The Journal of Object-Oriented*

Programming, *Dr. Dobbs' Journal*, *The C Users' Journal*, and *.EXE* run regular columns or features on C++. Andrew Koenig's column in *The Journal of Object-Oriented Programming* was particularly consistent in its quality and lack of hype.

Newsgroups and bulletin boards such as `comp.lang.c++` on Usenet and `c.plus.plus` on BIX also produced hundreds of thousands of messages over the years to the delight and despair of their readers. Keeping up with what was written about C++ was more than a full-time job.

6.7.3. Compilers

The Santa Fe conference marked the announcement of the second wave of C++ implementations. Steve Dewhurst described the architecture of a compiler he and others were building in AT&T's Summit facility, Mike Ball presented some ideas for what became the TauMetric C++ compiler (more often known as the Oregon Software C++ compiler), and Mike Tiemann gave an animated and interesting presentation of how the GNU G++ he was building would do just about everything and put all other C++ compiler writers out of business. The new AT&T C++ compiler never materialized; GNU C++ Version 1.13 was first released in December 1987; and TauMetric C++ first shipped in January 1988.

Until June 1988, all C++ compilers on PCs were Cfront ports. Then Zortech started shipping its compiler. The appearance of Walter Bright's compiler made C++ "real" for many PC-oriented people for the first time. More conservative people reserved their judgment until the Borland C++ compiler in May 1990 or even Microsoft's C++ compiler in March 1992. DEC released its first independently developed C++ compiler in February 1992, and IBM released its first independently developed C++ compiler in May 1992. By the mid-1990s, more than a dozen C++ compilers had been independently developed.

In addition to these compilers, Cfront ports were everywhere. In particular, Sun, HP, Centerline, ParcPlace, Glockenspiel, and Comeau Computing shipped Cfront-based products on just about any platform. In the late 1990s, a compiler front end from the Edison Design Group seemed to occupy the ecological niche for a highly portable C++ analyzer carved out by Cfront.

6.7.4. Tools and Environments

C++ was designed to be a viable language in a tool-poor environment. This was partly a necessity because of the almost complete lack of resources in the early years and the relative poverty later. It was also a conscious decision to allow simple implementations and, in particular, simple porting of implementations.

Later, C++ programming environments emerged that are a match for the environments habitually supplied with other object-oriented languages. For example, ObjectWorks for C++ from ParcPlace was essentially the best Smalltalk program development environment adapted for C++, and Centerline C++ (formerly Saber C++) was an interpreter-based C++ environment inspired by the Interlisp environment. This gave C++ programmers the option of using the more whizzy, more expensive, and often more productive environments that have previously only been available for other languages or as research toys. An environment is a framework in which tools can cooperate. Later, a host of such environments for C++ appeared. Most C++ implementations on PCs are compilers embedded in a framework of editors, tools, file systems, standard libraries, and so on. MacApp and the Mac MPW were the Apple Macintosh versions of that; ET++ was a public domain version in the style of the MacApp. Lucid's Energize, HP's Softbench, and IBM's VisualWorks were yet other examples.

6.7.4.1. Early Libraries

There were and are many significant C++ libraries. Most were domain specific or even application specific, such as a library for building systems controlling a telephone operator's console. However, some were foundation libraries that acted as a kind of standard library for a particular implementation or platform. These are mentioned only briefly here because even though they were essential to their users, they did not affect the development of C++ significantly.

The most significant early libraries were Keith Gorlen's (Gorlen, 1990) NIH class library that provides a Smalltalk-like set of classes and Mark Linton's Interviews library (Linton & Calder, 1987) that makes use of the X Window system convenient from C++. GNU C++ (G++) came with a library designed by Doug Lea that was distinguished by heavy use of abstract base classes. Rogue Wave and Dyad supplied large sets of libraries primarily aimed at scientific uses. Rogue Wave and the Irish company Glockenspiel for years supplied libraries for various commercial uses. Rational shipped a C++ version of "The Booch Components" that was originally designed for and implemented in Ada86 by Grady Booch. Grady Booch and Mike Vilot designed and implemented the C++ version. The Ada86 version was 150,000 non-commented source lines compared to the C++ version's 10,000 lines; inheritance—combined with templates and constructors and destructors—can be a very powerful mechanism for organizing libraries without loss of performance or clarity.

This is only a very short list of early libraries to indicate the diversity of C++ libraries. Many more libraries exist. In particular, most tools suppliers provide foundation libraries for their users. It seems that the "software components" industry that pundits have promised for years—and bemoaned the lack of—has finally come into existence.

6.7.5. Commercial Competition

Commercial competitors were largely ignored and the C++ language was developed according to the original plan, its own internal logic, and the experience of its users. There was (and is) always much discussion among programmers, in the press, at conferences, and on the electronic bulletin boards about which language is best and which language will win some sort of competition for users. Personally, I consider much of that debate misguided and uninformed, but that doesn't make the issues less real to a programmer, manager, or professor who has to choose a programming language for his or her next project. For good and bad, people debate programming languages with an almost religious fervor and often consider the choice of programming language the most important choice of a project or organization.

In the early years, Modula-2 (Wirth, 1982) was by many considered a competitor to C++. However, until the commercial release of C++ in 1985, C++ could hardly be considered a competitor to any language, and by then Modula-2 seemed to me to have been largely outcompeted by C. Later, it was popular to speculate about whether C++ or Objective C (Cox, 1986) was to be "*the* Object-Oriented C." Ada (Ichbiah, 1979) was often a possible choice of organizations who might use C++. In addition, Smalltalk (Goldberg & Robson, 1983) and some object-oriented variant of Lisp (Kiczales, des Rivieres, & Bobrow, 1992) would often be considered for applications that did not require hard-core systems work or maximum performance. Lately, some people have been comparing C++ with Eiffel (Meyer, 1988) and Modula-3 (Nelson, 1991) for some uses.

My personal view is different. The main competitor to C++ was C. The reason that C++ is the most widely used object-oriented language today is that it was and is the only one that could consistently match C on C's own turf and that allows a transition path from C to a style of system design and implementation based on a more direct mapping between application-level concepts and language concepts (usually called data abstraction or object-oriented programming). Secondarily, many organizations that consider a new programming language have a tradition for the use of an in-house language (usually a Pascal variant) or Fortran.

Except for serious scientific computation, these languages can be considered roughly equivalent to C when compared with C++.

In the secondary competition between C++ and other newer languages supporting abstraction mechanisms (object-oriented programming languages, languages supporting data abstraction), C++ was during the early years (1984 to 1989) consistently the underdog as far as marketing was concerned. In particular, AT&T's marketing budget during that period was usually empty, and AT&T's total spending on C++ advertising was about $3,000. To this day, most of AT&T's visibility in the C++ arena relies on Bell Labs's traditional policy of encouraging developers and researchers to give talks, write papers, and attend conferences rather than on any deliberate policy to promote C++. Within AT&T, C++ was also a grass-roots movement without money or management clout. Naturally, coming from AT&T Bell Labs helps C++, but that help is earned the hard way by surviving in a large-company environment.

In competition, C++'s fundamental strength is its ability to operate in a traditional environment (social and computer-wise), its runtime and space efficiency, the flexibility of its class concept, its low price, and its nonproprietary nature. Its weaknesses compared to newer languages are some of the uglier parts inherited from C—its lack of spectacular new features (such as built-in data base support), its lack of spectacular program development environments (only lately have C++ environments of the sort people have taken for granted for Smalltalk and Lisp become available for C++), its lack of standard libraries (only years after C++'s initial appearance did major libraries become widely available for C++—and there wasn't a significant standard library until 1996), and its lack of salespeople to balance the efforts of richer competitors. With C++'s recent dominance in the market, the last factor disappeared. Some C++ salespeople will undoubtedly embarrass the C++ community by emulating some of the sleazy tricks and unscrupulous practices that salespeople and advertising folks have used to attempt to derail C++'s progress.

An important factor, both for and against C++, was the willingness of the C++ community to acknowledge C++'s many imperfections. This openness is reassuring to many who have become cynics from years of experience with the people and products of the software tools industry but also infuriating to perfectionists and a fertile source for fair and not-so-fair criticism of C++. On balance, I think that tradition of throwing rocks at C++ within the C++ community has been a major advantage. It kept us honest, kept us busy improving the language and its tools, and kept the expectations of C++ users and would-be users realistic.

In competition with traditional languages, C++'s inheritance mechanism was a major plus. In competition with languages with inheritance, C++'s static type checking was a major plus. Of the languages mentioned, only Eiffel, Modula-3, and Ada95 (Tucker, 1992) combined the two in a way similar to C++.

In 1995, Java burst upon the programming scene with an unprecedented style of and amount of marketing. This was the first time that the resources of a large corporation had been thrown squarely into a programming language debate. Sun's corporate marketing ran prime-time television and whole-page newspaper ads proclaiming the virtues of using nothing but Java ("100% pure. No non-Java code") aimed at non-programmers. Sun apparently saw Java as a means of survival by harnessing the widespread anti-Microsoft feeling. In this context, language-technical issues were strictly secondary to corporate strategy. The Sun "white paper" launching Java set the tone by claiming Java superior in all ways to essentially all modern general-purpose programming languages, including C++, Smalltalk, and Eiffel.

Superficially, Java resembles C++. The Java syntax is very similar to C++'s, the Java inheritance mechanism is basically a subset of C++'s, Java's built-in data types are a subset of C's, and Java's exception-handling mechanism is almost identical to C++'s. This inevitably led to comparisons between Java and C++ for real-world projects. However, Java's model of objects is much more similar to Smalltalk's than it is to C++'s, and in some ways it resembles Simula's. As usual, C++'s raw speed and ability to manipulate low-level resources directly placed it in a strong position. So did C++'s ability to directly and efficiently use the immense amounts of existing code in C, C++, Fortran, and so on. In addition, Java did not have a mechanism for expression parameterized types and classes, nor ways of defining user-defined types that can be used exactly as built-in types. Instead, Java offered type safety, guaranteed (as opposed to C++'s optional) garbage collection, and a concurrency mechanism. This adds up to fundamental differences in programming style and efficiency.

Only time will tell to what extent Java and C++ are really competitors in the significant application areas. Java is advertised as simpler than C++ and accessible to less-skilled programmers. I doubt the claim about simplicity—especially as the Java language is still growing and massive libraries are an integral part of a programmer's world—and less-skilled programmers are simply not going to succeed at the more ambitious projects at which C++ excels. It remains to be seen how Java evolves, how it scales to larger projects, and whether the Java community is able to maintain a common set of libraries that is large enough to allow significant systems to remain portable in the face of the inevitable attempts of platform suppliers to lock in their users through incompatibilities and extensions.

C++ was designed to be a systems programming language and a language for applications that had a large systems-like component. This was the area that my friends and I knew well. The decision not to compromise C++'s strengths in this area to broaden its appeal has been crucial in its success. Only time will tell if this has also compromised its ability to appeal to an even larger audience. I would not consider that a tragedy because I am not among those who think that a single language should be all things to all people; and C++ already serves the community it was designed for well. However, I suspect that through the design of libraries, C++'s appeal will be very wide.

6.8. Retrospective

It is often claimed that hindsight is an exact science. It is not. The claim is based on the false assumptions that we know all relevant facts about what happened in the past, that we know the current state of affairs, and that we have a suitably detached point of view from which to judge the past. Typically, none of these conditions holds. This makes a retrospective on something as large, complex, and dynamic as a programming language in large scale use hazardous. Anyway, let me try to stand back and answer some hard questions:

- Did C++ succeed at what it was designed for?
- Is C++ a coherent language?
- What was the biggest mistake?

Naturally, the replies to these questions are related. The basic answers are yes, yes, and not shipping a larger library with Release 1.0.

6.8.1. Did C++ Succeed at What It Was Designed For?

"C++ is a general purpose programming language designed to make programming more enjoyable for the serious programmer" (Stroustrup, 1986a). In this, it clearly succeeded, especially in the more specific aim of letting reasonably educated and experienced programmers write programs at a higher level of abstraction (as in Simula) without loss of efficiency compared to C for applications that were demanding in time, space, inherent complexity, and constraints from the execution environment.

More generally, C++ made object-oriented programming and data abstraction available to the community of software developers that until then had considered such techniques and the languages that supported them such as Smalltalk, Clu, Simula, Ada, and OO Lisp dialects, with disdain and even scorn: "expensive toys unfit for real problems." C++ did three things to overcome this formidable barrier:

- It produced code with runtime and space characteristics that competed head-on with the perceived leader in that field: C. Anything that matched or beat C *must* be fast enough. Anything that didn't could and would—out of need or mere prejudice—be ignored.
- It allowed such code to be integrated into conventional systems and produced on traditional systems. A conventional degree of portability, the ability to coexist with existing code, and the ability to coexist with traditional tools, such as debuggers and editors, were essential.
- It allowed a gradual transition to these new programming techniques. It takes time to learn new techniques. Companies simply cannot afford to have significant numbers of programmers unproductive while they are learning. Nor can they afford the cost of failed projects caused by programmers poorly trained and inexperienced in the new techniques failing by overenthusiastically misapplying ideas.

In other words, C++ made object-oriented programming and data abstraction cheap and accessible.

In succeeding, C++ didn't just help itself and the C++ programmers. It also provided a major impetus to languages that provided different aspects of object-oriented programming and data abstraction. C++ wasn't everything to all people and didn't deliver on every promise ever made about some language or other. It did deliver on its own promises often enough to break down the wall of disbelief that stood in the way of all languages that allowed programmers to work at a higher level of abstraction.

6.8.2. Is C++ a Coherent Language?

C++ was successful in its own terms and is an effective vehicle for systems development, but is it a good language? Does C++ have an ecological niche now that the barriers of ignorance and prejudice against abstraction techniques have been broken?

Basically, I am happy with the language and quite a few users agree. There are many details I'd like to improve if I could, but the fundamental concept of a statically typed language using classes with virtual functions as the inheritance mechanism and facilities for low-level programming is sound.

6.8.2.1. What Should and Could Have Been Different?

Given a clean slate, what would be a better language than C++ for the things C++ is meant for? Consider the first-order decisions: use of static type checking, clean separation between language and environment, no direct support for concurrency, ability to match the layout of objects and call sequences for languages such as C and Fortran, and C compatibility.

First, I considered, and still consider, static type checking essential both as a support for good design and secondarily for delivering acceptable runtime efficiency. Were I to design a new language for what C++ is used for today, I would again follow the Simula model of type checking and inheritance, *not* the Smalltalk or Lisp models. As I have said many times, "Had I wanted an imitation Smalltalk, I would have built a much better imitation. Smalltalk is the best Smalltalk around. If you want Smalltalk, use it" (Stroustrup, 1990). Having both static type checking and dynamic type identification (for example, in the form of virtual function calls) implies some difficult tradeoffs compared to languages with only static or only dynamic type checking. The static type model and the dynamic type model cannot be identical and thus there will be some complexity and inelegance that can be avoided by supporting only one type model. However, I wouldn't want to write programs with only one model.

I also still consider a separation between the environment and the language essential. I do not want to use only one language, only one set of tools, and only one operating system. To offer a choice, separation is necessary. However, once the separation exists, one can provide different environments to suit different tastes and different requirements for supportiveness, resource consumption, and portability.

We never have a clean slate. Whatever new things we do, we must also make it possible for people to make a transition from old tools and ideas to new. Thus, if C hadn't been there for C++ to be almost compatible with, then I would have chosen to be almost compatible with some other language.

Should a new language support garbage collection directly, say, as Modula-3, Smalltalk, and Java do? If so, could C++ have met its goals had it provided garbage collection? Garbage collection is great when you can afford it. Therefore, the option of having garbage collection is clearly desirable. However, garbage collection can be costly in terms of runtime, real-time response, and porting effort (exactly how costly is the topic of much confused debate). Therefore, being forced to pay for garbage collection at all times isn't necessarily a blessing. C++ allows *optional* garbage collection (Ellis & Stroustrup, 1990), and I expect to see many experiments with garbage-collecting C++ implementations in the near future. However, I am convinced (after reviewing the issue many times over the years) that had C++ depended on garbage collection, it would have been stillborn. By the mid-1990s, very effective garbage collectors were available for C++. Thus, garbage-collected C++ is an option for both experimental and production systems.

Should a language have reference semantics for variables (that is, a name is really a pointer to an object allocated elsewhere) like Smalltalk, Java, or Clu or true local variables like C and Pascal? This question relates to several issues such as coexistence with other languages, compatibility, and garbage collection. Simula and Java dodged the question by having references to class objects (only) and true variables for objects of built-in types (only). Again, I consider it an open issue whether a language could be designed that provided the benefits of both references and true local variables without ugliness. Given a choice between elegance and the benefits of having both references and true local variables, I'll take the references plus true local variables.

6.8.2.2. What Should Have Been Left Out?

Even *Classes: An Abstract Data Type Facility for the C Language* (Stroustrup, 1980a) voiced concern that C with Classes might have become too large. I think a smaller language is number one on any wish list for C++, yet people deluge me and the standards committee with extension proposals. The fundamental reason for the size of C++ is that it supports more than one way of writing programs, more than one programming paradigm. From one point of view, C++ is really four languages in one: a C-like language plus an Ada-like language, plus a Simula-like language, plus a language for generic programming, plus what it takes to integrate those features into a coherent whole.

Brian Kernighan observed that in C, there is usually about one way of solving a given problem, whereas in C++, there are more ways. I conjecture that there typically is more than one way in C but that people don't see them. In C++, there are typically at least three alternatives and experienced people have quite a hard time not seeing them. There always is a design choice, but in most languages the language designer has made the choice for you. For C++ I did not; the choice is yours. This is naturally abhorrent to people who believe that there is exactly one right way of doing things. It can also scare beginners and teachers who feel that a good language is one that you can completely understand in a week. C++ is not such a language. It was designed to provide a tool set for a professional, and complaining that there are too many features is like the layman looking into an upholsterer's tool chest and exclaiming that there couldn't possibly be a need for all those little hammers.

People sometimes point to C compatibility, overloading, and multiple inheritance as features that C++ would have been better without. My estimate is that C compatibility was and remains essential, that overloading is critical for many techniques (especially in libraries) so that C++ wouldn't have succeeded without it, and that multiple inheritance was useful and has steadily increased in importance over the years as people more directly model their ideas using inheritance.

6.8.2.3. What Should Have Been Added?

As ever, the principle is to add as little as possible. A letter published on behalf of the extensions working group of the C++ standards committee puts it this way (Stroustrup, 1992):

> First, let us try to dissuade you from proposing an extension to the C++ language. C++ is already too large and complicated for our taste, and there are millions of lines of C++ code out there that we endeavor not to break. All changes to the language must undergo tremendous consideration. Additions to it are undertaken with great trepidation. Wherever possible, we prefer to see programming techniques and library functions used as alternatives to language extensions.
>
> Many communities of programmers want to see their favorite language construct or library class propagated into C++. Unfortunately, adding useful features from diverse communities could turn C++ into a set of incoherent features. C++ is not perfect, but adding features could easily make it worse instead of better.

Given that, what features have caused trouble by their absence? Or more precisely, what could have been added given our knowledge at the time, given the capabilities of the programmers and systems at the time, and without changing the nature of C++ in a way that I considered undesirable?

I considered many minor features, such as nested functions and the overloading of the . (dot) operator (Stroustrup, 1994). Over the years, C++ acquired enough such little features that minor deletions would probably have benefited the language and its users more than any minor addition. I cannot think of a specific minor feature that would have made a major difference to the majority of C++ programmers without having significant complementary negative side effects.

Of the major features, garbage collection and some support for concurrency featured most prominently in my thinking. As mentioned, I considered requiring garbage collection infeasible and favored optional garbage collection. Similarly, I favored the support of concurrency through machine-specific extensions and libraries. I do harbor a small hope that one day we might develop a close-to-universally acceptable form of concurrency support (see my foreword to *Parallel Programming Using C++* [Wilson & Lu, 1996]). However, the support provided by current languages such as Ada95 and Java seems primarily to show how far we still have to go before reaching a sufficiently general and acceptable form of concurrency support.

If I had known how to do so efficiently, I would have added a way of resolving a virtual function call based on the dynamic type of more than one operand. That is, I suspect I would have added a form of multimethods (Kiczales, des Rivieres, & Bobrow, 1992). However, I never worked out a system for that which satisfied me.

6.8.3. What Was the Biggest Mistake?

To my mind, there really is only one contender for the title of "worst mistake." Release 1.0 and my first edition (Stroustrup, 1986a) should have been delayed until a larger library, including some simple classes such as singly and doubly linked lists, an associative array class, a range checked array class, and a simple string class, could have been included. The absence of those led to everybody reinventing the wheel and to an unnecessary diversity in the most fundamental classes. However, could I have done that? In a sense, I obviously could. The original plan for my book included three library chapters—one on the stream library, one on the container classes, and one on the task library—so I knew roughly what I wanted. Unfortunately, I was too tired and couldn't do container classes without some form of templates.

In retrospect, I also regret not having been able to keep working on an implementation to have a proper environment in which to conduct experiments and be able to set a standard for correctness, quality of error messages, quality of code, and so on, that the commercial implementations would have to exceed to be regarded as acceptable. However, the amount of work and the amount of money required to keep such a standards-setting implementation viable were prohibitive. The availability of test suites has not been sufficient to keep the commercial implementations to as high a standard as I would have liked to see. The commercial competition has often focused on programming and execution environments to the detriment of the core language implementations. The standard ought to help, but achieving quality on a large scale is far harder than it appears.

6.8.4. Hopes for the Future

My hope is that C++ may serve its user community well. The language and its standard library are now good enough to be a stable base for tools, environments, and libraries. I expect such supporting facilities to emerge even more rapidly than before. I hope the completeness of the language and the stability of its definition will lead to a new level of stability and quality of implementations. I also expect to see an improvement in compiler speeds and the quality of generated code.

The key is for the C++ community to develop appropriate design and programming techniques and to spread understanding of successful techniques—new and old—much more widely than is currently the case. There are immense gains to be had by using the language more effectively than has been done in most places so far. Standard C++ has the features and the maturity to support techniques that are far more effective than what has been the norm in the industry during the early 1990s. The best has yet to come.

6.9. Acknowledgments

It is clear that given the number of people who have contributed to C++ in some form or other over the last 12 years or so, I must have left most unmentioned. Some have been mentioned in this chapter; more can be found in section 1.2c of the ARM and other acknowledgment sections of my books and papers. Here I just mention Doug McIlroy, Brian Kernighan, Andrew Koenig, and Jonathan Shopiro, who have provided constant help, ideas, and encouragement to me and others for a decade.

I'd also like to mention the people who have done much of the hard but usually unnoticed and unacknowledged work of developing and supporting Cfront through the years when we were always short of resources: Steve Dewhurst, Laura Eaves, Andrew Koenig, Stan Lippman, George

Logothetis, Glen McClusky, Judy Ward, Nancy Wilkinson, and Barbara Moo, who managed AT&T Bell Labs's C++ development and support group during the years when the work got done.

Also thanks to C++ compiler writers, library writers, and so on, who sent me information about their compilers and tools—most of which went beyond what could be presented in a paper: Mike Ball, Walter Bright, Keith Gorlen, Steve Johnson, Kim Knuttilla, Archie Lachner, Doug Lea, Mark Linton, Aron Insinga, Doug Lea, Dmitri Lenkov, Jerry Schwarz, Michael Tiemann, and Mike Vilot.

In addition, thanks to people who read drafts of this chapter and provided many constructive comments: Dag Bruck, Steve Buroff, Peter Juhl, Brian Kernighan, Andrew Koenig, Stan Lippmann, Barbara Moo, Jerry Schwarz, and Jonathan Shopiro.

Most comments on the various versions of this chapter were of the form "This chapter is too long...please add information about X, Y, and Z...also be more detailed about A, B, and C." I have tried to follow the first part of that advice, although the constraints of the second part have ensured that this did not become a short chapter. Without Brian Kernighan's help, this chapter would have been much longer. See *The Design and Evolution of C++* (Stroustrup, 1994) for a longer and less historically oriented discussion of the design of C++.

Thanks to Peter Salus for encouraging me to bring this story from 1991 up toward the end of the standards process.

6.10. References

Babcisky, K. September 1984. *Simula performance assessment.* Conference on System Implementation Languages: Experience and Assessment. Canterbury, Kent, UK.

Birtwistle, G., O.-J. Dahl, B. Myrhaug, and K. Nygaard. 1979. *Simula begin.* Lund, Sweden: Studentlitteratur..

Booch, G. 1991. *Object-oriented design.* Benjamin Cummings.

Booch, G., and M. M. Vilot. 1990. *The design of the C++ Booch components.* The OOPSLA'90 conference.

Budge, K., J. S. Perry, and A. C. Robinson. August 1992. *High-performance scientific computation using C++.* USENIX C++ conference. Portland, Oregon.

Call, L. A., et al. November 1987. *An open system for graphical user interfaces*. USENIX C++ conference. Santa Fe, NM.

Campbell, R., et al. November 1987. *The design of a multiprocessor operating system*. USENIX C++ conference. Santa Fe, NM.

Cargill, T. A. 1991. The case against multiple inheritance in C++. *Computing Systems* 4(1).

Carroll, M. April 1991. Using multiple inheritance to implement abstract data types. *The C++ Report*.

Cristian, F. 1989. Exception handling. In T. Anderson (Ed.), *Dependability of resilient computers*. Blackwell Scientific Publications.

Cox, B. 1986. *Object-oriented programming: An evolutionary approach*. Reading, MA: Addison-Wesley.

Ellis, M. A., and B. Stroustrup. 1990. *The annotated C++ reference manual*. Reading, MA: Addison-Wesley.

Goldberg, A., and D. Robson. 1983. *Smalltalk-80, The language and its implementation*. Reading, MA: Addison-Wesley.

Goodenough, J. December 1975. Exception handling: Issues and a proposed notation. *CACM*.

Gorlen, K. E. November 1987. *An object-oriented class library for C++ programs*. Proceedings of the USENIX C++ conference. Santa Fe, NM.

Gorlen, K. E., S. M. Orlow, and P. S. Plexico. 1990. *Data abstraction and object-oriented programming in C++*. West Sussex, England: Wiley.

Ichbiah, J. D., et al. 1979. Rationale for the design of the ADA programming language. *SIGPLAN Notices* 14(6):Part B.

International Data Corporation study. 1997. Quoted by Mike Riciutti in a C|net report, May 15, 1997.

Johnson, R. E. 1989. The importance of being abstract. *The C++ Report* 1(3).

Kernighan, B. July 1981. *Why Pascal is not my favorite programming language*. AT&T Bell Labs Computer Science Technical Report No. 100.

Kernighan, B., and D. Ritchie. 1978. *The C programming language*. Englewood Cliffs, NJ: Prentice Hall.

Kernighan, B., and D. Ritchie. 1988. *The C programming language* (2nd ed.). Englewood Cliffs, NJ: Prentice Hall.

Kiczales, G., J. des Rivieres, and D. G. Bobrow. 1991. *The art of the Metaobject Protocol.* Cambridge, MA: MIT Press.

Knuth, D. 1973. *The art of computer programming* (Vol. 3). Reading, MA: Addison-Wesley.

Koenig, A. June 1988. *Associative arrays in* C++. Proceedings of the USENIX conference. San Francisco, CA.

Koenig, A., and B. Stroustrup. 1989a. C++: As close to C as possible—But no closer. *The C++ Report.* 1(7).

Koenig, A., and B. Stroustrup. November 1989b. *Exception handling for* C++. Proceedings of the C++ at Work conference..

Koenig, A., and B. Stroustrup. 1990. Exception handling for C++. *Journal of Object-Oriented Programming* 3(2):16–33.

Krogdahl, S. 1984. *An efficient implementation of Simula classes with multiple prefixing*. Research Report No. 83. University of Oslo, Institute of Informatics.

Lenkov, D. 1989. *C++ standardization proposal.* ANSI standard no. X3J11/89-016.

Lenkov, D., M. Mehta, and S. Unni. April 1991. *Type identification in* C++. Proceedings of the USENIX C++ conference. Washington, DC.

Linton, M. A., and P. R. Calder. November 1987. *The design and implementation of interviews*. Proceedings of the USENIX C++ conference. Santa Fe, NM.

Liskov, B. October 1987. *Data abstraction and hierarchy*. Addendum to Proceedings of OOPSLA'87.

McCluskey, G. 1992. An environment for template instantiation. *The C++ Report.*

Meyer, B. 1988. *Object-oriented software construction*. Englewood Cliffs, NJ: Prentice Hall.

Musser, D. R., and A. A. Stepanov. 1989. *The Ada generic library*. Berlin: Springer-Verlag.

Nelson, G. (Ed.). 1991. *Systems programming with Modula-3.* Englewood Cliffs, NJ: Prentice Hall.

Rose, L. V., and B. Stroustrup. January 1984. *Complex arithmetic in* C++. Internal AT&T Bell Labs Technical Memorandum. (Reprinted in *AT&T C++ Translator Release Notes*, November 1985.)

Sakkinen, M. 1992. A critique of the inheritance principles of C++. *Computing Systems* 5(1).

Sethi, R. January 1980. *A case study in specifying the semantics of a programming language*. Seventh annual ACM symposium on principles of programming languages.

Shopiro, J. E. July 1985. *Strings and lists for C++*. AT&T Bell Labs Internal Technical Memorandum.

Shopiro, J. E. November 1987. *Extending the C++ task system for real-time control*. Proceedings of the USENIX C++ conference. Santa Fe, NM.

Snyder, A. September 1986. *Encapsulation and inheritance in object-oriented programming languages*. Proceedings of OOPSLA'86.

Stepanov, A., and M. Lee. 1994. *The standard template library*. HP Labs Technical Report HPL-94-34.

Stroustrup, B. 1978. On unifying module interfaces. *ACM Operating Systems Review* 12(1):90–98.

Stroustrup, B. 1979a. *Communication and control in distributed computer systems*. Ph.D. thesis, Cambridge University, England.

Stroustrup, B. October 1979b. *An inter-module communication system for a distributed computer system*. First International Conference on Distributed Computing Systems..

Stroustrup, B. 1980a. *Classes: An abstract data type facility for the C language*. Bell Laboratories Computer Science Technical Report CSTR-84.

Stroustrup, B. 1980b. *A set of C classes for co-routine style programming*. Bell Laboratories Computer Science Technical Report CSTR-90.

Stroustrup, B. January 1981a. *Extensions of the C language type concept*. Bell Labs Internal Memorandum.

Stroustrup, B. 1981b. Long return: A technique for improving the efficiency of inter-module communication. *Software Practice and Experience*, pp. 131–143.

Stroustrup, B. April 1982. *Adding classes to C: An exercise in language evolution*. Bell Laboratories Computer Science internal document.

Stroustrup, B. 1984a. *The C++ reference manual*. AT&T Bell Labs Computer Science Technical Report No. 108.

Stroustrup, B. 1984b. Data abstraction in C. *Bell Labs Technical Journal* 63(8):1701–1732.

Stroustrup, B. September 1984c. *Operator overloading in* C++. IFIP WG2.4 Conference on System Implementation Languages: Experience & Assessment. Canterbury, England.

Stroustrup, B. June 1985. *An extensible I/O facility for* C++. Summer 1985 USENIX Conference..

Stroustrup, B. 1986a. *The* C++ *programming language*. Reading, MA: Addison-Wesley.

Stroustrup, B. 1986b. An overview of C++. *ACM SIGPLAN Notices*, pp. 7–18.

Stroustrup, B. August 1986c. *What is object-oriented programming*? 14th ASU Conference.

Stroustrup, B. November 1987a. *The evolution of* C++: *1985–1987.* USENIX C++ conference. Santa Fe, NM.

Stroustrup, B. May 1987b. *Multiple inheritance for* C++. EUUG spring conference, May 1987.

Stroustrup, B. 1988b. Type-safe linkage for C++. *Computing Systems* 1(4).

Stroustrup, B. 1988a. *Parameterized types for* C++. USENIX C++ conference, Denver, CO.

Stroustrup, B. 1989b. Standardizing C++. *The* C++ *Report* 1(1).

Stroustrup, B. 1989a. The evolution of C++: 1985–1989. *USENIX Computing Systems* 2(3).

Stroustrup, B. 1990. On language wars. *Hotline on Object-Oriented Technology*. 1(3).

Stroustrup, B. 1991. *The* C++ *programming language* (2nd ed.). Reading, MA: Addison-Wesley.

Stroustrup, B. 1992. How to write a C++ language extension proposal. *The* C++ *Report*.

Stroustrup, B. 1994. *The design and evolution of* C++. Reading, MA: Addison-Wesley.

Stroustrup, B. 1996. A history of C++: 1979–1991 (pp. 699–754). In T. J. Bergin and R. G. Gibson (Eds.), *The history of programming languages*. Reading, MA: Addison-Wesley.

Stroustrup, B. 1997. *The C++ programming language* (3rd ed.). Reading, MA: Addison-Wesley.

Stroustrup, B., and D. Lenkov. 1992. Runtime type identification for C++. *The C++ Report*.

Stroustrup, B., and J. Shopiro. 1987. *A set of C classes for co-routine style programming*. USENIX C++ conference. Santa Fe, NM.

Taft, S. T. 1992. Ada 9X: A technical summary. *CACM*.

Tiemann, M. November 1987. *Wrappers*. Proceedings of the USENIX C++ conference. Santa Fe, NM..

Waldo, J. 1991. Controversy: The case for multiple inheritance in C++. *Computing Systems* 4(2).

Wilkes, M. V., and R. M. Needham. 1979. *The Cambridge CAP computer and its operating system*. North Holland, NY: Elsevier.

Wilson, G. V., and P. Lu (Eds.). 1996. *Parallel programming using C++*. Cambridge, MA: The MIT Press.

Wirth, N. 1982. *Programming in Modula-2*. New York: Springer-Verlag.

CHAPTER 7

A Detailed Introduction to C++

by Andrew Koenig

C++ is the result of an unusual strategy in programming language design: It is intended to allow programmers to express high-level solutions to problems without compromising their ability to get at low-level machine facilities efficiently. For example, although many programming languages allow direct access to the machine's memory, and many programming languages support a variable-length string type, few languages support both at once. Not only does C++ support both, but it does so by making it possible to implement variable-length strings efficiently in the library, rather than by building them into the compiler. As another example, although C++ does not offer garbage collection as a standard part of the language, it is possible to use C++ to implement flexible data structures that are almost as easy to use as their garbage-collected counterparts are.

This chapter assumes that the reader is an experienced programmer, preferably one who knows more than one programming language thoroughly, but it does not assume any knowledge of C or C++. It uses examples of C++ programs in several styles to give enough of a feel for the language to make it possible to understand substantial C++ programs, and perhaps even to write them. To that end, we will emphasize the parts of the language that are most important in practical use; other sources cover the language in exhaustive detail.

Although this chapter discusses the most important concepts in the C++ standard library, it emphasizes the core language. With a thorough understanding of the core language and an overview of the key ideas behind the library, it is possible to find appropriate library facilities in a more detailed reference. Moreover, because the standard library is not aimed at any particular application area, and because the library is a more recent development than the core language, many C++ programs are written in terms of application-specific libraries, rather than relying exclusively on the standard library.

7.1. C++ Overview

Section 7.1 describes the most common styles for using C++ and explains a small, but complete, C++ program that solves an interesting problem. Section 7.2 describes the most fundamental parts of the language, on which the rest of C++ is built. The descriptions in section 7.2 do not assume a prior knowledge of C.

Section 7.3 covers the facilities that C++ uses to support data abstraction, with an emphasis on programs that deal with objects of types that are known at the time the program is written. Section 7.4 covers programs whose knowledge of types is deferred until the time the program is compiled. Such programs are often called "generic programs," and the C++ template facility is the fundamental tool for supporting them.

Section 7.5 discusses object-oriented programming, which is a technique for writing programs that deal with types that are not completely known until the program actually runs. The discussion includes a complete example program, which manipulates expression trees.

Finally, Section 7.6 gives a high-level overview of the standard library.

Of course, a chapter of this size cannot convey everything there is to know about C++. However, it is intended to give enough information that it can serve as a basis for future study. Section 7.7 recommends books that are likely to be useful for such study. Of course, the way to learn a skill is to use it, so any study of C++ should include writing programs.

7.1.1. A Multiparadigm Language

In addition to supporting programs written with different degrees of abstraction, C++ also supports programs written with different kinds of abstraction.

For example, many C++ programs are what might be called "bread and-butter programs." They may use library facilities—even sophisticated ones—but they don't do much in the way of defining their own abstractions. Prosaic though they might be, such programs constitute many of the most productive applications of any programming language.

Another important programming style that C++ supports well is classical data abstraction. This phrase refers to programs that define individual abstract data types that other parts of the program—or other programs—then use. The best known example of this style in C++ is using the language to define a data type that represents variable-length character strings. Although such strings are part of the standard library, we can reimplement them without relying on the library, which makes their construction a useful subject for study.

A kind of abstraction that has become associated with C++ in recent years is generic programming. We talk about programs as being generic if they deliberately try to ignore as much as possible about the data types they use. For example, we might talk about a generic sorting algorithm, referring to one that is capable of sorting the elements of any sequence, regardless of the specific structure of the sequence or the types of the elements.

Finally, there is object-oriented programming, which is programming with inheritance and dynamic binding. This style is particularly useful for simulation—either of things that exist or things that do not. For example, we can think of the buttons, icons, and other elements of a graphical user interface as simulating an imaginary reality. The point of object-oriented programming is to be able to ignore the differences between the types of the objects in a system, but only when it is useful to do so. So, for example, when we move a graphical element around, we would like not to have to care what kind of element it is, but when it comes time to display it, the details become crucially important.

7.1.2. Elementary C++ Examples

The classic example of a small C++ program announces its presence and then exits:

```
/* A small C++ program */

#include <iostream>
using namespace std;        // Access the standard library

int main()
{
    cout << "Hello, world!" << endl;
    return 0;
}
```

This program begins with a comment. Comments in C++ programs either begin with `/*` and end with the next `*/`, or begin with `//` and end at the end of the line. Comments do not nest.

The next line of this program tells the compiler to use the standard I/O library. We can think of it as a request to copy the contents of a file that contains appropriate declarations into the program in place of the `#include` directive itself. The third line departs slightly from pedantically recommended practice and tells the compiler to make all the names from the standard library available to the program without further formality. Without that third line, the references to `cout` and `endl` would need to be spelled `std::cout` and `std::endl`.

On the next line begins the definition of a function called `main`, which returns a value of type `int`. Then comes a request to print on the file `cout` (which represents the standard output stream for the program) the string `Hello, world!`, followed by a special value `endl` called a *manipulator.*

This manipulator does two things: It causes the output stream to begin a new line, and it also forces out any characters that might have been buffered as a result of previous output. Finally, the program returns a value of `0` to the operating system, which value represents successful completion.

The reason that we can use `<<` to print on `cout` is that `cout` has an appropriately defined type. Part of that definition says that when the `<<` operator uses objects of that type as its left argument, the effect is to write a representation of the operator's right argument into the output stream that the left argument denotes. Thus, for example, we can print the value of $\sqrt{2}$ by writing

```
#include <iostream>
#include <math>
using namespace std;

int main()
{
     cout << "The square root of 2 is " << sqrt(2.0) << endl;
     return 0;
}
```

This program prints values of three different types: a string literal, a real number, and a manipulator. We shall see later how the C++ language facilities make it possible for the library to contain enough information to let the compiler decide, with no execution-time overhead at all, which library services are appropriate for printing each of these values.

As a more abstract example, here is a program that reads its standard input and counts how many times each distinct word appears in that input:

```
#include <iostream>
#include <iomanip>
#include <map>
#include <string>
using namespace std;

int main()
{
     string s;
     map<string, int> m;

     while (cin >> s)
          ++m[s];
     map<string, int>::const_iterator it;
```

```
    for (it = m.begin(); it != m.end(); ++it)
          cout << setw(8) << it->second << " " << it->first << endl;

    return 0;
}
```

The four `#include` directives tell the compiler about our intent to use various library facilities: `<iostream>` gives us `cin`, `cout`, and the associated `<<` and `>>` operators; `<iomanip>` gives us the `setw` manipulator; and `<string>` and `<map>` give us the types with those names. As before, `using namespace std;` makes it unnecessary to identify the individual names that we use from the standard library.

This program uses a library data structure called a `map`, which is also sometimes called an associative array. It may be useful to think of it as a kind of array whose "subscripts" are not necessarily integers. In this particular example, those subscripts are strings and the array elements themselves are integers.

The first thing the program does is to read its entire input and use an associative array to count words:

```
while (cin >> s)
      ++m[s];
```

This piece of code crams a lot into its two lines.

The expression `cin >> s` is a request to read from the standard input (identified by the library object `cin`) into a local variable, of type `string`, named `s`. In addition to reading from its input file, the `>>` operator returns a value that indicates whether the input attempt was successful. The `while` loop therefore executes its subject statement `++m[s]` repeatedly, as long as there is input to be read.

The statement

```
++m[s];
```

is essentially equivalent to

```
m[s] = m[s] + 1;
```

so it adds `1` to the value of `m[s]`. Here, we can think of `m[s]` as being the element of `m` that has index `s`, but with the added—and essential—wrinkle that if such an element does not already exist, it will be created, with value `0`, immediately before we try to increment it. All this behavior is defined as part of the `map` type.

The other knowledge we need in order to understand this fragment is that the `string` type represents a variable-length character string, and that the normal behavior of the `>>` operator when presented with a string is to read the next word from the input and store the value of that word in the string.

In short, because of the abstractions provided by the `cin` object and the `string` and `map` types from the standard library, our two-line loop does a lot of useful work.

Once we have our data stored in the map, we must retrieve it. To that end, the library supplies a type called a map iterator. We can think of an object of such a type as behaving somewhat like a pointer: It identifies a location in the map and lets us step through the map one element at a time.

When we say

```
map<string, int>::const_iterator it;
```

we are defining a local variable named `it` whose type is appropriate for a constant iterator (i.e. an iterator that does not have permission to change the values of the map over which it iterates) over a map from `string` to `int`. We are not intended to know the type of this object directly, but the library guarantees that we can do certain things with objects of that type.

The `for` statement that follows the definition of `it` could just as well have been written as

```
it = m.begin();
while (it != m.end()) {
        cout << setw(8) << it->second << " " << it->first << endl;
        ++it;
}
```

The `map` type defines `m.begin` and `m.end` as functions that return iterators that refer directly to the first element and "one past the last element" of `m`, respectively. The reason that `m.end()` does not refer to an element is that an empty map has no elements to which to refer. Instead, many C++ library facilities adopt the notion of asymmetric bounds by delimiting a range by its first element (if there is one) and one past its last element (or where its last element would be). This practice implies, for example, that `m.begin()` and `m.end()` are equal if and only if `m` has no elements.

Each time through the loop, we execute `++it`. Earlier, we noted that `++m[s]` added `1` to `m[s]`, but we could say that only because we knew that `m[s]` was an integer. Here, on the other hand, we do not know the type of `it`—so what does it mean to add `1` to `it`?

In fact, it might not mean anything at all. Instead, when we deal with iterators or other C++ abstract data types, we should think of `++` as a way to cause an object to take on the next value in the sequence of values that it might have. Fortunately,[1] that treatment does what we wanted, which is to cause `it` to refer to each of the elements of `m` in turn.

All we need to know, for now, about `it` is that if the value of `m[s]` is `i`, then at some point `it` will take on a value such that `it->first` is `s` and `it->second` is `i`. We shall see later how such things are possible. For now, our knowledge indicates that if we print the values of `it->second` and `it->first`, in that order, for each value of `it`, we will get the results we seek.

We have already seen how to use `cout` to print values. The one other new idea in this example is the use of `setw` to control the output format: Saying `cout << setw(8)` guarantees that the next value written on `cout` will occupy at least `8` characters in the output stream. Think of `setw` as meaning *set the width*.

If we run this program with

```
as I was going down the stair
I saw a man who wasn't there
he wasn't there again today
I wish that man would go away
```

as input, its output will be

```
3 I
1 a
1 again
1 as
1 away
1 down
1 go
1 going
1 he
2 man
1 saw
1 stair
1 that
1 the
2 there
1 today
1 was
2 wasn't
1 who
1 wish
1 would
```

[1]By design, actually.

If you were to conclude from this output that C++ associative arrays store their elements in increasing order by subscript, you would be quite correct.

7.1.3. Language Versus Library

It would have been possible to define C++ so that types like `map` were built into the compiler. Indeed, some languages, such as Awk (described in *The Awk Programming Language*, by Aho, Kernighan, and Weinberger [1988]), make it possible to write programs that look quite a bit like these C++ examples. C++, in contrast, takes a more general approach: The language includes facilities that make it possible for libraries to define these data types, as well as others.

The language needs a substantial amount of mechanism in order to allow the construction of libraries that make these examples possible. For example, consider just the input loop of our word-counting program:

```
string s;

while (cin >> s)
        ++m[s];
```

Even if we ignore, for the moment, the associative array that does the word counting, there is still a lot going on behind the scenes in

```
cin >> s
```

After we execute this expression, `s` contains a word that has been read from the standard input. Aside from the total amount of memory available, there is no limit on how long that word might be. Therefore, the library must allocate dynamic memory to contain that word, and must continue to allocate more memory as needed if the word turns out to be very long.

Similarly, if we were to say

```
string t = s;
```

the library would have to arrange to copy the characters stored in `s` into the newly created string `t`, again without knowing, until the statement is actually executed, how much memory the string might occupy. Note again that it is not sufficient that the language contain such mechanisms directly. Rather, it must contain mechanisms that allow such flexible strings to be implemented in the library, even though the language does not know about strings on its own account.

Sections 7.2 through 7.5 talk about these mechanisms. We will begin with an overview of the fundamental types, after which we will talk about classes, or user-defined abstract types. Next, we will discuss templates, which are the main mechanism for writing generic programs, and virtual functions, which are essential for writing object-oriented programs. Section 6 gives a brief overview of the key ideas behind the C++ standard library.

7.2. C++ Fundamentals

As its name suggests, C++ is based on C. This lineage is most easily seen in the fundamental facilities. The overall structure of a program, the built-in types (aside from the `bool` type), and the operators all come from C. C programmers will therefore find much that is familiar in this section, and may therefore wish to skim it and dwell only on those details that do not strike a familiar chord.

7.2.1. Program Structure

A C++ program consists of one or more translation units. Loosely speaking, a translation unit is a part of a program that can be compiled separately from other translation units. More precisely, a translation unit is the result of applying a preliminary compilation phase called preprocessing to a source file.

A source file usually begins with one or more `#include` directives, each of which causes the preprocessor to copy declarations of entities (functions, global variables, types, and so on) that are defined in other translation units.

As an example, let us return to our sample program from section 7.1.2:

```
#include <iostream>
using namespace std;

int main()
{
    cout << "Hello, world!" << endl;
    return 0;
}
```

Preprocessing this source file yields a translation unit that defines a single function named `main`. Every C++ program is required to define the `main` function in exactly one of its translation units; the C++ implementation executes the program by calling `main` as a subroutine.

We have already mentioned that the `#include` directive makes available an assortment of facilities that permit input/output. It can be useful to think of the way it does so as by copying appropriate declarations into the source text at the point of the `#include`. This way of viewing the behavior of `#include` is not fully accurate, however, because of the angle brackets (`< >`) surrounding the name `iostream`. These brackets are reserved for naming facilities that are built into the standard library, which means that the implementation is free to take advantage of knowledge of the nature of those facilities. So, for example, a compiler is permitted to recognize

```
#include <iostream>
```

as a special case and "turn on" access to an assortment of precompiled code.

Nevertheless, the notion of treating `#include` as a form of textual substitution is useful—and indeed it is common to use that textual substitution facility when putting source programs together. As a simple example, suppose that we have a program that consists of many translation units, each of which begins with

```
#include <iostream>
using namespace std;
```

Then we might want to put those two lines into a file called, say, `iolib`, after which we could rewrite our sample program to look like this:

```
#include "iolib"

int main()
{
     cout << "Hello, world!" << endl;
     return 0;
}
```

Notice that the `#include` directive now uses double quotes instead of angle brackets. This usage indicates that the string inside the quotes should be translated to the name of a file in an implementation-defined way, and a copy of the contents of the file inserted in the program in place of the `#include` directive.

To make this example a little less simplistic, suppose we wanted to rewrite our program so that the code to print `Hello, world!` did not have to appear directly in `main`. Then we might write a translation unit that looks like this:

```
// file greet.c

#include <iostream>

using namespace std;
```

```
void greet()
{
    cout << "Hello, world!" << endl;
}
```

We have changed the name of our routine from `main`, which the system knows is special, to `greet`, which has no magical properties. We have also changed the return type from `int` to `void`, because we don't really want the obligation to tell our caller anything about what we did.

At this point, the typical C++ implementation would let us compile the `greet.c` file, but we would not be able to execute it because there is no `main` function. To solve that problem, we will define a second translation unit:

```
// file main.c

void greet();

int main()
{
    greet();
    return 0;
}
```

Our `main.c` file contains a declaration of `greet`, but the file doesn't define `greet`. Because we did not define `greet`, in this file, the compiler assumes that `greet` is defined in a different translation unit.

We should now be able to compile `main.c`, but we still cannot execute it because there is no definition for `greet`. However, if we have already compiled `greet.c`, the typical C++ implementation will give us a way to combine the compiler output from `greet.c` and `main.c` and execute the resulting program.

There is one more important subtlety in constructing programs from source files: How can we tell that the declaration of `greet` (in `main.c`) and its definition (in `greet.c`) are consistent if the two files are compiled separately? The first step is to repeat the declaration in the file that contains the definition:

```
// file greet.c, revised version
#include <iostream>

using namespace std;

void greet();

void greet()
{
    cout << "Hello, world!" << endl;
}
```

There is no harm in declaring and defining `greet` in the same translation unit, and there is one significant benefit: It lets the compiler check consistency between the declaration and the definition. However, it is still conceivable that the declaration of `greet` in `main.c` might differ from the one in `greet.c`.

Fortunately, we can solve that problem, too—by moving the declaration into a separate file. We will then include that file in `greet.c`, and also in `main.c`, which will ensure that it has the same contents in both contexts.

We will therefore define a source file called `greet.h` that has only the declaration of `greet`:

```
// source file greet.h

void greet();
```

Then we use that file in both `greet.c` and `main.c`:

```
// file greet.c, final version

#include <iostream>
#include "greet.h"

using namespace std;

void greet()
{
     cout << "Hello, world!" << endl;
}

// file main.c, final version

#include "greet.h"

int main()
{
     greet();
     return 0;
}
```

Our small program has grown into three source files. The first, `greet.h`, exists only so that `#include` directives can copy it into other files. This ensures that if the declaration of `greet` ever changes, it is necessary to change it in only a single place. The next one is `greet.c`, which defines the `greet` function. By including `greet.h`, `greet.c` ensures that the definition (in `greet.c`) and the declaration (in `greet.h`) are consistent. The last file contains the main program, which needs the declaration of `greet` (from `greet.h`) but not its definition.

This kind of program structure is important for large projects, in which several people may be working on different source files independently, and in which multiple versions of source files may exist. However, it implies that there is not always a direct correspondence between what we think of as the key parts of a program and the physical manifestations of those parts. To see this, consider the `greet.h` file. Nothing in the C++ language requires that file to exist, or that there be only one such file. We could have written a declaration of the `greet` function in every translation unit that uses that function, and as long as all the declarations were mutually consistent, there would be nothing wrong. But we deliberately chose to put a single declaration for `greet` into a separate source file, and then used the preprocessor to cause that file to be copied into every translation unit. By doing so, we ensure that all the declarations are consistent with each other. Indeed, we effectively gain the right to talk about "the declaration of `greet`," because all the declarations come from a single piece of source code. This technique of splitting a program into source files so as to avoid having to duplicate declarations pervades C++ programs.

7.2.2. Numbers and Arithmetic

7.2.2.1. Integers

Because C++ is intended to be able to run efficiently on a wide variety of hardware, it leaves many of the details of its fundamental types up to the implementation rather than defining those types precisely. The idea is to allow compilers to choose the most natural representation for each of the arithmetic types, while still constraining the types enough to allow programmers to write useful programs. C++ offers an assortment of different ways of storing data because such choices can have a crucial effect on the efficiency—especially the space efficiency—of programs.

Accordingly, there are three distinct signed integer types and three distinct unsigned integer types. The signed types are `short int` (or just `short`), `int`, and `long int` (or just `long`); the unsigned types are `unsigned short int`, `unsigned int`, and `unsigned long int` (or `unsigned short`, `unsigned`, and `unsigned long`). The keywords, if there are more than one, can appear in any order. Compilers must implement each of the `short` types so as to contain at least 16 bits, as they must also for each of the plain `int` types. The `long` types must occupy at least 32 bits. Moreover, each `long` type must be at least as long as each plain `int` type, which must be at least as long as each `short` type. Compilers are allowed to use either one's- or two's-complement notation for the signed types.

In other words, a `short` or a plain `int` variable is guaranteed to hold any value between `-32767` and `32767`, inclusive, and implementations are permitted to allow a wider range. A `long` variable must be able to hold any value between `-2147483647` and `2147483647`, inclusive, and implementations might allow a wider range. Similarly, an `unsigned short` must be able to contain any value between `0` and `65535`, and so on.

Why bother with separate `int` and `short` types if they have the same requirements? Although the language definition doesn't actually say, the idea is that `short` variables will store only small integers, regardless of context; `int` variables will store values that are commensurate with the size of memory; and `long` variables can potentially store the largest integers that the implementation can handle. In particular, array indices have type `int`, so an implementation that restricts the magnitude of `int` values to 2^{15} will similarly restrict the sizes of arrays.

There are few surprises in the definition of integer arithmetic. The operators `+`, `-`, `*`, and `/` are defined with their usual meanings, and `%` is the remainder operator. Unsigned arithmetic is always modulo 2^n, where n is the number of bits in the particular unsigned values being used. Signed integer division is permitted to truncate the quotient toward zero or toward `-∞`, as long as the behavior of `/` is consistent with the behavior of `%`. In other words, it is required that `((a/b)*b)+(a%b)` be equal to `a` whenever `b` is nonzero.

Aside from the question of whether division truncates up or down, integer arithmetic is always either exactly defined, if the result of the operation will fit in an appropriately sized integer, or completely undefined, if the result will not fit. In particular, implementations are permitted, but not required, to check for integer overflow, so that implementers can choose the most effective strategy for their particular machines.

In addition to the five arithmetic operators, there are the six relational operators `<`, `>`, `<=`, `>=`, `==`, and `!=`, and the shift operators `<<` and `>>`. The right operand of a shift, which says by how many bits to shift the left operand, is required to be non-negative, and it is up to the implementation whether shifting a negative number to the right propagates the sign bit or introduces zeroes.

There are also four bitwise logical operations on integers: and (`&`), or (`|`), exclusive or (`^`), and not (`~`).

Finally, for all the arithmetic operators, there are corresponding compound assignment operators. For example, if `a` and `b` are integral variables, `a <<= b` is equivalent to `a = a << b` except that in the former case, `a` is evaluated only once.

7.2.2.2. Using Integer Arithmetic

Here is an example that uses several of the arithmetic operators, and also demonstrates a few other aspects of C++. It is a function that counts the number of 1-bits in the representation of a `long unsigned` value:

```
unsigned short count_bits(long unsigned n)
{
    int result = 0;

    while (n != 0){
          if ((n & 1) != 0)
            result += 1;
          n >>= 1;
    }

    return result;
}
```

This function has one parameter, which, when the function is called, will be initialized to a copy of the corresponding argument. There is therefore no harm in modifying the parameter, as we do later in the function.

Curly braces (`{ }`) are used for grouping, similarly to `begin` and `end` in Algol or Pascal. The `if` statement has no corresponding `then`; in C++, `then` is an ordinary identifier with no special properties.

Use of whitespace, including indentation, is generally neutral in C++, but can make programs easier—or harder—to read. Two important exceptions to that neutrality principle are that a newline cannot occur within a string literal, and that preprocessor directives (which begin with `#`) end at the end of the current line.

The statement

```
result += 1;
```

could have been written

```
++result;
```

with exactly the same effect. More generally, if `e` is an expression of built-in type, then `(++e)` is exactly equivalent to `((e)+=1)`, and similarly for `(--e)` and `((e)-=1)`.

Perhaps a more interesting phenomenon—and certainly one that is deeply ingrained in C++ programming—is the postfix `++` operator. Essentially, `(e++)` is equivalent to `((++e)-1)`, but this equivalence is not a terribly useful way to understand the operator. It is more useful to say that the value of `(e++)` is the same as the value of `e`, but it has the side effect of adding `1` to `e` after fetching the value of `e`.

Probably the most common use of postfix `++` is in manipulating array indices. In many languages it is common to say things like

```
n = a[i];
i = i + 1;
```

with the notion that after we have fetched `a[i]`, we are done with that value of `i` so we should increment it to the next value. In C++, the usual way to express such things is

```
n = a[i++];
```

After this explanation, the `count_bits` function should be easy enough to understand. We have counted all the bits in `n` if and only if all the (remaining) bits are zero, so we will continue counting until that is the case. Each iteration of the loop examines the low-order bit of `n`, by evaluating `n & 1`, and increments `result` if that bit is on. After looking at the low-order bit, the program discards the bit by shifting `n` right one bit.

7.2.2.3. Truth Values

Our `count_bits` example has a loop that repeatedly evaluates the condition `n != 0`. The type of that condition is `bool`; the possible values of type `bool` are `true` and `false`. It is possible to use a number as a truth value; in such contexts, zero is considered `false` and any other value is considered `true`. For that reason, we could have replaced

```
while (n != 0) { /* ... */ }
```

with

```
while (n) { /* ... */ }
```

However, the latter construction is marginally less clear, because it requires more special knowledge to understand, and what was written was less obviously what was intended.

When a `bool` value is used as a number, `false` is treated as `0` and `true` is treated as `1`. So, for example, it is possible to test whether `x` is between `y` and `z`, inclusive, by writing `((x>=y)>(z<=x))`.[2]

Three operators take `bool` arguments and yield `bool` results: logical `and` (`&&`), logical `or` (`||`), and logical not (`!`). The first two of these operators evaluate their right operands only if doing so is necessary to determine the result. So, for example, in an expression like `((x != 0) && ((y/x) > z))`, it is guaranteed that `y/x` will be evaluated only if `x` is nonzero.

[2] Why one would want to do this in practice, instead of saying `((x>=y)&&(x<=z))`, is beyond my understanding; but it makes a nice example.

7.2.2.4. Characters

In C++, characters are just tiny integers. In particular, they participate in arithmetic the same way as integers. Why bother, then, with a separate character type?

One reason is that characters are not required to contain more than 8 bits, which means that if characters were some kind of `int`, it would be necessary to find a separate name for the character type anyway. Another is notational convenience: By making characters a distinct type, it is possible to treat them differently from integers in overloading contexts, so that

```
cout << 'a' << endl;
```

prints the character `a` and not the corresponding integer value.

As is the case with integers, characters can be signed or not, so there are distinct `signed char` and `unsigned char` types. In addition, there is a plain `char` type, which is required to have the same representation as one of the other two types, but it is up to the implementation which of those types it should be. As usual, the choice is intended to reflect which representation is most natural for the machine.

There is also a "wide character" type called `wchar_t`, which must contain at least 16 bits, and which is intended to be used for representing characters in languages such as Japanese, which have many more characters than the Latin alphabet provides.

Character literals, such as `'a'`, are enclosed in single quotes. Certain nonprinting characters have special representations, such as `'\n'` for a newline character, `'\t'` for a tab, and `'\b'` for a backspace. This use of the `\` character implies that one must write `'\\'` to represent a single `\`, and `'\''` to represent a `'`.

It is also possible to write a character literal that represents the character corresponding to a particular integer, either in octal or hexadecimal. So, for instance, `'\40'` is the character equivalent to `32` (octal `40`), and is the same character as `'\x20'`. On implementations based on the ASCII character set, that character is the same as `' '`. The most common use of this notation is `'\0'`, or the null character, which, as we shall see, has a special conventional role in C++ programs.

7.2.2.5. Floating-Point Arithmetic

C++ has three floating-point types, called `float`, `double`, and `long double` in order of nondecreasing precision. The term "nondecreasing" is appropriate instead of "increasing" because the implementation can implement `float` with the same precision as `double` or `double` with the same precision as `long double`.

The `double` type is preferred, in the sense that ordinary floating-point literals such as `3.5` have type `double`. Literals in the other two types look like `3.5F` (or `3.5f`) and `3.5LF` (or `3.5lf`).

All the arithmetic operators that work with integers work with floating-point numbers as well, except for the shift operators. There is no exponentiation operator, but there is a library function called `pow` that has the equivalent effect.

7.2.3. Enumerated Types

It is often useful to be able to define a variable that can take on one of a set of values that are known during compilation. For example, we might want to record the state of a traffic light (or a collection of traffic lights). In C++, we call such types enumerated types:

```
enum TrafficLight { broken, red, yellow, green };
```

This declaration defines a type called `TrafficLight`. Variables of that type can have one of four values, called enumerators, namely `broken`, `red`, `yellow`, or `green`. We can then write, for example:

```
TrafficLight tl;

tl = yellow;
if (tl == green) {
     // something is wrong
}
```

Enumerated types are distinct from other numeric types, but they can be converted to integers. So, for example, if our traffic light is still `yellow`, executing

```
cout << tl << endl;
```

will print `2`. It will not print `yellow`, because C++ does not want to impose the overhead of storing the names of all enumerated types on programs that do not need those names.

As this example implies, the values of enumerated types correspond to consecutive integers, starting from zero. If a value of an enumerated type is used in a context that requires an integer, the value will be converted automatically.

It is also possible to state explicit values for the enumerators:

```
enum Operator { plus = '+', minus = '-', times = '*', divide = '/' };
```

The character literals are taken as the integers that correspond to those characters in the machine's character set. As this example implies, such usage provides a convenient way to ascribe names to characters when writing lexical analyzers and similar programs.

7.2.4. Numeric Conversions

Many rules govern the value of expressions that contain operands of several numeric types. Usually, the precise details of the rules are not important. Approximately, conversions happen as needed to bring the operands of each operator to a common type, and when there is a choice, conversions that preserve information are preferred over conversions that lose information. Moreover, conversion to unsigned types is preferred to conversion to signed types, and all arithmetic on `short` integers or characters implies conversion to `int` or longer.

Thus, for example, the value of `(3/5)+2.1` is `2.1` because both the operands of the `/` are already the same type. The result of `3/5` is `0` because integer division truncates toward zero (if the quotient were negative, the implementation would have been permitted to truncate the quotient zero or toward -∞, but both alternatives are equivalent for a positive quotient); that zero is then converted to `double` for addition to `2.1`. As another example, although

```
cout << 'a' << endl;
```

prints `a`,

```
cout << ('a' + 0) << endl;
```

prints the integer that corresponds to `a` in the machine's collating sequence, because addition converts its operands to `int` or longer.

7.2.5. Operator Precedence

With all the operators we have encountered, it is important to know how they group, both to make it easier to read other people's programs and to reduce the number of parentheses.

Unary operators have the highest precedence, and they group right to left. Usually it is meaningless to talk about associativity of unary operators, but in C++ it is crucially important because there are both prefix and postfix unary operators. So, for example, the expression `*p++` means the same as `*(p++)`, because unary operators are right associative. We shall discuss the meaning of these expressions later.

Another kind of unary operator is a `cast`, which is the name of a type enclosed in parentheses. An expression of the form `(T)e` is the value of `e` after conversion to type `T`. The precise nature of this conversion depends on the type of `e` and the type `T`; we will discuss some examples of such conversions later.

We shall also discuss later the meanings of the binary operators `.` and `->` and the subscripting and function call "operators" `[]` and `()`, which have the same precedence as the unary operators.

Next in precedence come the pointer-to-member operators `.*` and `->*`, which we shall discuss later.

All the arithmetic operators have lower precedence than the ones we have mentioned so far. The arithmetic operators that group the most tightly are `*`, `/`, and `%`, with `+` and `-` at the next level down.

Below the arithmetic operators are the shift operators, so that `x<<y+z` means `x<<(y+z)` and not `(x<<y)+z`.

Next come the relational operators, with the unusual property that `==` and `!=` have lower precedence than the other four. This implies that `x<y==y<z` means `(x<y)==(y<z)`, which is true if `x<y` and `y<z` are both true, or both false.

Next come the bitwise operators `&`, `|`, and `^`. Each of these has its own precedence, so that `a&b^c&d` means `(a&b)^(c&d)` and `a^b|c` means `(a^b)|c`. Lower still are the logical operators `&&` and `||`, with `&&` binding more tightly than `||`.

Next come the assignment operators `=`, `+=`, `-=`, and so on. They all have the same precedence and, uniquely among the binary operators, group from right to left.

Lower still is the only ternary operator, which we have not yet discussed. Expressions that use it take the form `e?e1:e2`. The expression `e` is evaluated and converted to `bool`; if `e` is true, the result is `e1`; otherwise it is `e2`. As you might expect, only one of `e1` or `e2` is evaluated—never both.

The operator with the lowest precedence is the comma operator. It evaluates its left operand, then discards it and evaluates its right operand, yielding that operand as its result. For example, if `i` and `j` are integer variables of the same type, we might say that `i++` is equivalent to `(j=i, ++i, j)` except for its effect on `j`.

It is important not to confuse precedence with order of evaluation. Most operators (the exceptions being `&&`, `||`, `?:`, and `,`) evaluate their operands in unspecified order, so that even though precedence demands a particular grouping, that may not say anything about side effects. For example, consider the following function:

```
int f(int n)
{
    cout << n << endl;
    return n;
}
```

This function prints its argument as a side effect, and then returns that argument. Suppose that we use it several times in an expression, such as

```
f(3) * f(4) + f(5)
```

There is no question as to the value of this expression: It has the same value as 3*4+5, or 17. But that says nothing about the order in which 3, 4, and 5 are printed, because + could evaluate its operands in either order, and so could *. Programs that depend on side effects in this way are ill advised.

7.2.6. Pointers, References, and Arrays

In keeping with its desire to allow its programs to get close to the hardware, C++ offers two different abstractions for the notion of a machine address. One of these abstractions, the pointer, treats an address as an object in its own right, and associates with each pointer the type of the object to which it (potentially) points. The other abstraction, the reference, treats an address solely as a way of remembering the location of a particular object and referring to that object again later. References are not objects, and the allowable operations on references are severely restricted. Nevertheless, they are useful in a variety of contexts, and absolutely essential in a few of them.

C++ arrays are so closely connected with pointers that it is difficult to describe them separately. Partly for that reason, arrays turn out to be most useful as an implementation medium for library classes. Once such classes exist (and the standard library does, indeed, support them), using built-in arrays directly becomes almost unnecessary. Nevertheless, it is important to describe arrays, because they are so fundamental,[3] and because understanding them is essential to understanding other C++ data structures and the structure of the standard library.

---

[3] Trenchard More has reportedly said that we know arrays to be the most fundamental data structure because every programmer has at one time or another asked management for arrays.

7.2.6.1. Pointers

For every object type `T`, there is a corresponding pointer type "pointer to `T`." This type is often written `T*`, even though referring to the type that way is potentially confusing.

Part of the confusion arises from the way pointer variables are declared. One does, indeed, write

```
T* p;
```

but some people also write

```
T *p;
```

and the latter form may be more accurate. The point is that each of these two definitions says that `*p` has type `T`, and therefore, by inference, that `p` has type "pointer to `T`."

This difference in treatment is not merely pedantic, as can be seen by the definition

```
T *p, q;
```

This definition says that `*p` and `q` both have type `T`, so that `p` is a pointer but `q` is not!

It should be obvious by now that if `p` is a pointer, `*p` is the object to which `p` points. Moreover, the result of unary `*` is what is called an *lvalue*, which means that it is permitted to appear on the left side of an assignment, or, equivalently, that it has an address.

If `v` is an lvalue, then `&v` is the address of `v`. The lvalue requirement keeps us from writing expressions such as `&3`, which are meaningless because `3` does not have a meaningful address. Thus, for instance, if we say

```
double x;
double* xp = &x;
```

then `*xp` is equivalent to `x`, and after executing

```
*xp = 3;
```

the value of `x` will be `3.0`. Here, the compiler knew that `*xp` was a `double`, because of the type of `xp`, and therefore converted `3` to `double` as part of the assignment.

Pointers are independent of the objects to which they point, which implies that those objects might go away before the pointers themselves do. C++ makes no attempt to defend against such eventualities. For example:

```
int main()
{
    int* p;
    {
        int x;

        p = &x;
    }

    *p = 42;        // error—dangling pointer
    return 0;
}
```

There was nothing wrong with setting `p` to the address of `x`, but once `x` went out of scope (at the `}` that was paired with the last `{` before `x`'s definition), any further use of `p`, other than to give `p` a new value, would be invalid. Examples such as this one show that pointers, despite their importance, are hazardous.

7.2.6.2. References

References are somewhat like pointers, but because they are much more restricted in what they can do, they are generally less hazardous. In particular, a reference is not an object, and once a reference has been created, it is not possible to make it refer to a different entity.

References are declared similarly to pointers. So, for instance, after saying

```
int x;
int* p = &x;
int& r = x;
```

we have established `p` as a pointer that points to `x` and `r` as a reference that refers to `x`. However, while the pointer declaration syntax has a clear analogy in the expression syntax (by saying that `*p` is an `int`), the reference declaration syntax does not. The most useful way to think about declarations of references is therefore probably to convert them mentally to declarations of pointers, by changing `&` to `*`, and parse them that way.

Because a reference cannot be rebound after it is created, one must bind a reference at the time one creates it. Therefore,

```
int& z;             // illegal
```

is prohibited, because `z` is not bound to anything.

Returning to the declaration of `r`, we find that `r` and `x` are now effectively two names for the same object:

```
r = 3;              // x is now 3
```

There is never any need—nor even any way—to dereference a reference explicitly, the way one dereferences a pointer.

References are most useful as function parameters, where they are used to implement call by reference. For example,

```
void int_assign(int& dest, int source)
{
    dest = source;
}
```

is a function that assigns its second operand to its first. We might use that function this way:

```
int n;
int_assign(n, 42);              // n = 42
```

with the same effect as assigning directly to `n`. Using references this way is, for example, what permits expressions like `cin >> n` to modify the value of `n`. Otherwise, it would be necessary to write `cin >> &n` in order to grant write access to `n`.

7.2.6.3. Arrays

In C++, as in early versions of Pascal, arrays have only a single dimension. Multidimensional arrays are written as arrays of arrays. Also as in early versions of Pascal, the size of a C++ array is part of its type. This implies that the size of an array must be known at compilation time, which would be a nearly insurmountable obstacle were it not for the useful properties of pointers and the way in which C++ treats dynamic memory. Having all arrays' sizes known during compilation dramatically simplifies compiler design, because it means that all stack frame sizes and layouts are known during compilation. Using dynamically allocated memory for all variable-sized data structures is not as much a hardship as it might appear, because those data structures can be wrapped in library classes and thereby made essentially as easy to use as built-in types.

As with pointers, the syntax for declaring arrays is derived from how the arrays are used. So, for example, if `T` is the name of a type,

```
T x[10];
```

declares an array of `T` objects with `10` elements. The initial element always has index `0`, so the indices of the elements of this array range from `0` through `9`, inclusive.

Suppose we try to use both arrays and pointers in a single declaration, such as

```
int *xx[10];
```

What does that mean? Again, we note that the declaration mirrors the use, so we are saying that `*xx[10]` has type `int`.[4] Next we note that unary operators, such as `*`, and subscripting, all have the same precedence and group right to left. That means that `*xx[10]` means the same as `*(xx[10])`, and indeed we could have written the declaration as

```
int *(xx[10]);
```

with the same meaning. If declaration mirrors use, then the declaration must mean that if we extract an element of `xx`, we can apply `*` to that element and obtain an `int`. In other words, we have declared `xx` as an array of pointers to `int`. In effect, the fact that unary operators group right to left in expressions implies that they group left to right in declarations. If we wanted to declare a pointer to an array, we would have written

```
int (*xp)[10];
```

7.2.6.4. Pointers and Arrays

On the surface, it appears that an expression enclosed in `[ ]` is a subscript, and that subscripting is a primitive operation. The truth is more subtle:

- Most uses of the name of an array automatically transform the array name into a pointer to its initial element.
- Pointer arithmetic is defined to be as convenient as indexing.
- The `[]` operator is actually defined in terms of pointer arithmetic.

We will consider each of these statements in turn.

There are very few operations on arrays directly: Essentially the only things you can do with a whole array is take its address or determine its size. So, for example, in

```
int x[10];
int* p = x;
int (*xp)[10] = &x;
```

we have used `x` to initialize `p` without explicitly taking the address of `x`. Whenever we do that, it implicitly takes the address of the initial element of `x`, so `p` now points to that initial element.

[4] We aren't quite saying that because `xx[10]` doesn't exist the indices stop at 9. But for appropriate values of `i`, we are saying that `*xx[i]` has type `int`.

On the other hand, when we write &x, we are taking the address of the entire array x, which, although it corresponds to the same memory location as the initial element, has a different type. We can then set xp to that address, because xp is a pointer to an array with the appropriate size and type.

It is important to realize that p and xp are not interchangeable in this context:

```
p = &x;                 // error
xp = x;                 // error
```

In each case, the error is that the types of the left-hand and right-hand sides of the assignment disagree, and there is no implicit conversion between those types.

The next important thing to realize about pointers is that if p points to an element of an array, then p+1 is defined to point to the next element and p-1 to the previous element, assuming that each element exists. In this particular example, we have set p to x, so p points to element 0 of the array x. That implies that p+5 points to element 5, and so on.

At an implementation level, computing p+n requires the machine to multiply n by the size of the object to which p points. This size can always be determined at compile time, so if n is a constant also (as it would be in p+1), the compiler can do that multiplication as it compiles the program.

Element n of the array x has address p+n, or, equivalently, x+n. From that, it should be easy to see that *(x+n) is the element itself, rather than the address, and that x[n] is therefore equivalent to *(x+n). Indeed, indexing is defined that way: x[n] means the same as *(x+n).

This definition has an amusing consequence: Because addition is commutative, x+n means the same as n+x, which means that x[n] means the same as n[x], provided only that x and n have built-in types. This property, however, is more amusing than useful.

The truly useful property is that not only can we refer to x[n], but we can also refer to p[n] where p is a pointer. This property implies that we can use a pointer to the initial element of an array as if it were the array itself. In fact, the pointer is more useful than the array for one important reason: It need not actually point to the initial element of the array. For example, consider

```
void int_clear(int* p, int n)
{
      while (--n >= 0)
              p[n] = 0;
}
```

This function clears (sets to zero) n array elements starting at the one addressed by p. We can use this function to clear an array of integers, as in

```
int table[100];
int_clear(table, 100);
```

but we can also use it to clear any subarray of such an array, as in

```
int_clear(table+23, 17);
```

This second call, which clears elements 23, 24, ...39 of the table, does something that would have been much more difficult without the correspondence between pointers and arrays.

Adding integers to pointers is straightforward, as is subtracting integers from pointers. If it is possible to add a negative integer to a pointer, it should also be possible to subtract a positive integer, and indeed it is. There are two other properties of pointer arithmetic that are also important, and which are less obvious.

One property is that it is possible to subtract two pointers and obtain an integer, provided that the pointers point to two elements of the same array. At the machine level, this subtraction involves address subtraction followed by division by the size of an element. The other property is more interesting, and is sometimes absolutely crucial: It is always possible to obtain a pointer one element beyond the last element of an array, provided that one does not actually try to use the element stored there. To see why this property is important, consider an alternative version of int_clear:

```
void int_clear(int* p, int n)
{
      int* limit = p + n;
      while (p < limit)
            *p++ = 0;
}
```

In principle, this version of int_clear should be faster than the previous one, because it changes only one variable each time through the loop instead of two. But in order to work, it must be able to form an address that points one element past the end of the array. For example, if we say

```
int table[100];
int_clear(table, 100);
```

the first thing int_clear does is to set limit to an address one element beyond the end of table. This technique is so widespread, and so important, that it is explicitly permitted, even though there is clearly not an actual element there.

7.2.6.5. Pointers and Dynamic Memory

Because we can use pointers almost as if they were arrays, the normal way to allocate dynamic memory returns a pointer to the initial element of that memory. For example, to allocate a dynamic array with `n` elements, we might say

```
int* dynamic_table = new int[n];
int_clear(dynamic_table, n);
```

We have not seen `new int[n]` before, but its behavior should be obvious: It allocates enough dynamic memory for an `n`-element array of integers and returns a pointer to the initial element. Once we have stored that pointer, here in `dynamic_table`, we can use it almost as if it were an array. For example, we can call `int_clear` to set the elements to `0`, we can refer to `dynamic_table[i]`, and so on.

When we are done with this memory, we can say

```
delete[] dynamic_table;
```

which returns the memory to the system. The `[ ]` indicate that we have asked to delete an array.

7.2.6.6. Pointers and Constants

If `T` is a type, we can have "pointer to `T`," "reference to `T`," and "array of `T`." We can also have "constant `T`," which is a type that is like `T` but whose objects are immutable during their lifetimes.

C++ uses the `const` modifier for that purpose. So, for example, we might say

```
const int N = 1000;
```

or, equivalently,

```
int const N = 1000;
```

with the idea that `N` might represent the size of some data structure, and we might want to ensure that `N` does not change during execution. Indeed, if a variable is declared `const`, and it is initialized with an expression that consists entirely of constants, then the compiler will treat the variable itself as a constant and allow its use as the size of an array. We can therefore say, for example,

```
int table[N];
```

Once we have the `const` modifier, it makes sense to think about how it might combine with other types. For example, if we write

```
const int *p;
```

we are saying, by analogy with use, that `*p` is a pointer to a `const int`, or, in other words, that `p` points to memory that we are not allowed to change. If, on the other hand, we wanted to define a pointer `cp` that was itself immutable, we might write

```
int x;
int *const cp = &x;
```

Here, the sequence `* const` always defines a pointer that does not change. Such a pointer must be initialized when it is declared, because there will be no opportunity to do so later.

Among the most common uses of `const` is in conjunction with references. For example:

```
double x = 4.1;
const double& y = x;
```

Now, `y` is another name for `x`, except that we are not allowed to use `y` to change the value of `x`:

```
x = 4.2;            // y is now 4.2
y = 4.2;            // error
```

One common use of references to `const` objects is as a way to avoid copying function arguments. Here's an example:

```
double abs(const double& x)
{
        double result = x;
        if (x < 0)
                result = -result;
        return result;
}
```

If `a` is a variable of type `double` and we call `abs(a)`, there is no need to copy `a` into the `abs` function, because the function does it itself when it assigns `x` to `result`. The `const double&` parameter is a way of saying "This parameter is a `double`, which need not be copied, because I promise not to change it."

We will see later that references to constants are absolutely essential as a tool for defining the semantics of abstract data types.

7.2.7. String Literals

Now that we understand characters, pointers, and arrays, we can discuss strings. The reason that so many preliminaries are needed to understand strings is that

- C++ does not have a built-in string type. Instead, strings are implemented as part of the library.
- However, it is obviously essential to be able to write string literals as part of a program.

This puts the language in an interesting dilemma: It doesn't make sense for built-in constructions such as string literals to know about specific library types, but if literals have a built-in type, then they won't have the same type as string variables.

C++ resolves this dilemma by choosing the second alternative: After executing

```
string s = "Hello, world!";
```

the variable `s` actually has a different type from the literal `"Hello, world!"`. Fortunately, this discrepancy does not cause much trouble in practice—but it is important to know about it.

A string literal is actually an array of `const` characters, which is initialized before the program executes. To make it possible to determine the length of the array, the compiler quietly inserts an extra, null character at the end of the string. As with any other array, a string literal is usually converted automatically into a pointer to the initial character of the array.

In other words, for example, the type of `"Hello, world!"` is "pointer to `const` character," and it evaluates to a pointer to an array of 14 characters. Indeed, when we write

```
cout << "Hello, world!" << endl;
```

we could have achieved the same effect, albeit more clumsily, by saying

```
const char Hello[14] = {
      'H', 'e', 'l', 'l', 'o', ',', ' ',
      'w', 'o', 'r', 'l', 'd', '!', '\0'
};

cout << Hello << endl;
```

In either case, the `<<` operator is presented with a pointer to the initial `H` of the string, and the library figures out how many characters to print by copying characters to the standard output one at a time until it is about to copy a `'\0'` character.

In contrast, if we were to say

```
string hello = "Hello, world!" << endl;

cout << hello << endl;
```

the library would be presented with an object of type string, whose properties we have yet to discuss, and would produce exactly the same output through completely different means.

As another illustration of how to use arrays, pointers, and numbers, here is one way to implement a standard C++ library function called strlen. This function takes a pointer to the initial element of a null-terminated array of characters and returns the number of characters in the array, excluding the null at the end:

```
int strlen(const char* p)
{
	int result = 0;

	while (*p != '\0') {
		++p;
		++result;
	}
	return result;
}
```

Note that although p points at immutable memory, that is no bar to changing the value of p itself.

Here is a somewhat terser way to achieve the same effect:

```
int strlen(const char* p)
{
	const char* q = p;

	while (*q++ != '\0') { }

	return q - p - 1;
}
```

To convince yourself that this function works, note that *q++ has the same value as *q but has the side effect of incrementing q. That means that when the loop exits, q will point one character beyond the '\0' terminator. Note also that this version depends on the ability to point one element beyond the end of any array.

7.2.8. Functions

C++ uses the term function to refer to all procedures, whether or not they have side effects or return a value. Every function has a definition and zero or more declarations, which will usually appear in different translation units. A typical function definition looks like

```
return-type    name (parameters)    block
```

although this description is too simple to cover, for example, functions that return pointers to functions. The parameters are a sequence of zero or more declarations, each of which declares a single variable. Because a block begins with `{` and ends with `}`, the last character of a function definition is always `}`. A function that does not return a value can be declared to return a value of type `void`.

Here is a function that computes the absolute value of its integer argument:

```
int abs(int x)
{
      if (x < 0)
            x = -x;
      return x;
}
```

From this example, we can see that the parameter `x` can be changed. This change does not affect the value of the argument, so that after

```
int n = -37;
int m = abs(n);
```

the value of `n` is still `-37`.

More specifically, the semantics of passing an argument to a function are the same as the semantics of using that argument to initialize the formal parameter. So calling `abs(n)` does not change the value of `n` for the same reason that saying

```
int x = n;
if (x < 0)
      x = -x;
```

does not change the value of `n`.

On the other hand, there is nothing to stop a parameter from having a reference type, in which case changing the parameter does change the argument:

```
void clobber(int& z)
{
      z = 0;
}
```

Now, the semantics of

```
clobber(n);
```

are the same as

```
int& z = n;
z = 0;
```

Both forms set the value of `n` to `0`.

A function can return a reference, too, so that

```
int& R(int& x)
{
      return x;
}
```

defines a function called `R` that accepts an integer lvalue and returns that same lvalue. Here,

```
R(n) = 0;
```

would have the same effect as

```
n = 0;
```

because calling `R(n)` executes `R` with its parameter `x` bound to the object `n`. When `R` returns, what it returns is therefore a reference to `n`, so assigning to `R(n)` has the same effect as assigning to `n`.

Functions can be recursive, but a function definition cannot physically appear inside another function definition. The restriction on nesting simplifies the implementation compared with Algol or Pascal, because it means that a function cannot ever reference the stack frame of any other function directly.

7.2.8.1. Default Arguments

It can be useful to allow the user of a function to omit one or more arguments when the omitted arguments have obvious, commonly used values. For example, consider a function that writes a newline character on a file:

```
void write_newline(ostream& s)
{
      s << "\n;
}
```

We might want to be able to say that calling

```
write_newline();
```

is equivalent to calling

```
write_newline(cout);
```

One way to tell the compiler about this abbreviation is

```
void write_newline(ostream& s = cout)
{
      s << "\n;
}
```

`= cout` is a *default argument*, which is a value to be used in place of an omitted argument. Only trailing arguments are permitted to be left out in this way.

7.2.8.2. Exiting from a Function

There are three ways for control to leave a function. The normal way is by executing a

```
return expression;
```

statement, which uses *expression* to initialize the value returned by the function. If the function returns `void`, *expression* must not appear. Moreover, control is allowed to flow off the end of a function that returns `void`; doing so is equivalent to saying

```
return;
```

immediately before the last `}` of the function.

The third way of leaving a function is by executing a `throw` statement. If there is no `try` statement in the function that catches the exception being thrown, control automatically propagates from the function to its caller, then to the caller of that function, and so on. For example:

```
void toss(int v)
{
      throw v;
}
```

is a function that always exits by throwing an exception. If we now write

```
void pass(int p)
{
      try {
            toss(p);
      } catch (char c) {
            return c+1;
      }
}
```

and then call `pass` in the following context:

```
int n = 0;

try {
      pass(1234);
} catch (int i) {
      n = i;
}
```

the effect will be to set `n` to `1234`. The reason is that we have called `pass(1234)`, which calls `toss(1234)`, which throws the value `1234`. Executing the throw terminates execution of toss and takes us back to pass. However, the catch clause in pass is looking for a char, not an int, so control passes through pass and back to the catch that expects an int value.

One of the most common ways to use exceptions is for the particular exceptions a function might throw to be part of its interface. One can imagine a description that says "This function returns the square root of its argument, except that if the argument is negative, it throws the following exception...." To make such specifications more explicit, a function definition can include an *exception specification*. Here's an example:

```
double sqrt(double x) throw(bad_sqrt) { /* ... */ }
```

Such a specification is a promise that the function will throw only the exception(s) named; a runtime check ensures that the promise is kept.

7.2.9. Statements

Like most programming languages, C++ distinguishes between declarations, expressions, and statements. In appropriate contexts, declarations and statements can be nested within other declarations and statements, but neither can be nested inside an expression. Every statement ultimately appears inside the definition of a function, where it forms part of what happens when that function is called.

Unless otherwise specified, the statements that constitute a function are executed in the order in which they appear. Exceptions include: loops; calls to functions; the goto, break, and continue statements; and the try and throw statements associated with exception handling.

Statements are written in free form, in the sense that beginning a new line in mid-statement does not affect the statement's meaning. Accordingly, most statements end with semicolons, the main exception being the block (which begins with { and ends with }).

7.2.9.1. The Null Statement

The simplest statement is the null statement, which is just a semicolon. We have already encountered a common use for a null statement, in this context:

```
int strlen(const char* p)
{
      const char* q = p;

      while (*q++ != '\0') { }

      return q - p - 1;
}
```

Here, the loop

```
while (*q++ != '\0') { }
```

could just as well have been written

```
while (*q++ != '\0');
```

where the semicolon is a null statement. However, that semicolon is so inconspicuous that it would be better to write

```
while (*q++ != '\0') ;
```

or even

```
while (*q++ != '\0')
        ;
```

to emphasize that there is something there.

7.2.9.2. The Expression Statement

Placing a semicolon after any expression turns it into a statement, which, when executed, evaluates the expression and discards the result. For that reason, most expression statements have useful side effects, either assigning a value to a variable, as in

```
x = 42;
```

or calling a function, as in

```
cout << "Hello, world!" << endl;
```

In this latter example, the function called is the second `<<` operator; its arguments are the subexpression

```
cout << "Hello, world!"
```

and the object `endl`.

7.2.9.3. Blocks

Enclosing zero or more statements in curly braces `{ }` turns them into a single statement. Declarations can be intermixed with those statements; such declarations define local variables that persist (only) until the `}`. Aside from defining local variables, the most common use of blocks is as the subject of an `if` or `while` statement. For example, if `x` and `y` are variables of type `int`, we might write

```
if (x < y) {
        int z = x;
        x = y;
        y = z;
}
```

to exchange `x` and `y` if `x<y`.

7.2.9.4. Conditionals

The C++ conditional statement takes one of the forms

```
if (expression) statement
if (expression) statement else statement
```

Note that `expression` must be surrounded by parentheses, and that `then` is not a keyword in C++. As with other languages with similar conditional statements, the ambiguity in

```
if (expression1) if (expression2) statement1 else statement2
```

is resolved by associating each `else` with the nearest unmatched `if`, so that this example is equivalent to

```
if (expression1) { if (expression2) statement1 else statement2 }
```

The `expression` in an `if` statement, as in other conditional contexts, is considered to be false if it evaluates to zero and true otherwise. It is common to use values of nonnumeric types, such as pointers, in `if` statements. For example, you might write

```
if (p)
        *p = 0;
```

instead of

```
if (p != 0)
        *p = 0;
```

7.2.9.5. Loops

The fundamental way to write a loop in C++ is the `while` statement, which is syntactically similar to the `if` statement:

```
while (expression) statement
```

To write a loop that must always be executed at least once, use the form

```
do statement while (expression);
```

tests the value of the expression at the end of the loop instead of at the beginning.

In addition, the common form

```
{
        statement1
        while (expression) {
              statement2
              expression2;
        }
}
```

can be abbreviated as

```
for(statement1 expression; expression2) statement2
```

There is no semicolon between `statement1` and `expression` because `statement1` will usually end with a semicolon. So, for example, if `a` is an array with 100 elements, we can set those elements to zero by writing

```
{
        int i = 0;
        while (i < 100) {
                a[i] = 0;
                ++i;
        }
}
```

where the outermost `{ }` are there to bound the scope of the local variable `i`. We can achieve the same effect by writing

```
for (int i = 0; i < 100; ++i)
        a[i] = 0;
```

Similarly, we can turn

```
i = 0;
j = 1;
while (i < 100) {
        a[i] = j;
        ++i;
        j += 7;
}
```

into

```
for ({ i = 0; j = 1; } i < 100; ++i, j += 7)
        a[i] = j;
```

by using the comma operator to combine the two expression statements

```
++i;
j += 7;
```

into the single expression statement

```
++i, j += 7;
```

and then using its constituent expression in the `for` statement. Note that there is no semicolon after the `}`.

7.2.9.6. Jumps

The `break`, `continue`, and `goto` statements provide for explicit transfer of control. Executing

```
break;
```

jumps to the point immediately after the end of the nearest enclosing `while`, `for`, `do`, or `switch` statement; executing

```
continue;
```

jumps back to the beginning of the next iteration (including the test) in the nearest enclosing `for`, `while`, or `do` statement. So, for example, if we want to do something to each of the nonzero elements of an `n`-element array `x`, we might write

```
for (int i = 0; i < n; ++i) {
        if (x[i] != 0) {
              // do something to x[i]
        }
}
```

Equivalently, we might write

```
for (int i = 0; i < n; ++i) {
        if (x[i])
              continue;
        // do something to x[i]
}
```

Here, the `continue` statement ends the current iteration and starts the next one. Similarly, if we wanted to find the index of the first nonzero element, if any, we might write

```
int i = 0;
while (i < n && x[i] == 0)
        ++i;
```

or we might write

```
int i;
for (i = 0; i < n; ++i)
        if (x[i])
               break;
```

In the latter example, `i` is defined outside the `for` statement to force its scope to include whatever might follow the `for` statement.

The `goto` statement behaves similarly to such statements in other languages. The target of a `goto` is a label, which is an identifier followed by a colon. Labels can have the same names as other entities without ambiguity, because the only place they can ever appear is before a colon or after a `goto` keyword. The scope of a label is the entire function in which it appears, which implies that it is possible to jump from outside a block to inside it. However, such a jump cannot bypass the initialization of a variable.

The last `goto` I wrote in a real program was in 1980 or so, where it was used to restart an iteration from inside a `switch` statement. To understand it, we must first understand the `switch` statement.

7.2.9.7. Switches

A `switch` is a way of doing a multiway jump based on the value of an integral expression (which, in practice, often yields a character or a value of enumerated type). Strictly speaking, the form is

```
switch (expression) statement
```

but in practice, the statement is almost always a block.

Within that block may appear labels of the form

```
case expression:
```

with the requirement that each of the expressions must be an integral expression whose value can be determined during compilation, and all the expressions must have distinct values.

In addition, the label

```
default:
```

may appear, but no more than once.

Executing a `switch` statement evaluates the parenthesized expression and jumps to the `case` label whose value matches it. If there is no match, control passes to the `default:` label, if any, or to the point immediately after the entire `switch` statement.

Because `case` labels are just labels, control will flow from one to the next unless the programmer takes explicit action to prevent it from doing so. The usual such action is to use a `break` statement before each `case` label after the first. For example:

```
int day;
char* day_name;

// ...

switch (day) {

case 0:
        day_name = "Sunday";
        break;

case 1:
        day_name = "Monday";
        break;
```

```
case 2:
        day_name = "Tuesday";
        break;

case 3:
        day_name = "Wednesday";
        break;

case 4:
        day_name = "Thursday";
        break;

case 5:
        day_name = "Friday";
        break;

case 6:
        day_name = "Saturday";
        break;

default:
        day_name = "???";
}
```

If `day` is negative, or greater than `6`, `day_name` will be set to (the address of the initial character of a null-terminated array initialized with) `???` by virtue of the `default` label. If that label, and its corresponding assignment, did not appear, `day_name` would have retained its previous value.

As another example, suppose that `p` points to an element of a character array, and that immediately following this element is the first of a (possibly empty) sequence of `+`, `-`, `#`, or space characters. Suppose further that you want to scan this sequence of characters and set one or more of the variables `plus`, `minus`, `sharp`, or `space` to `true`, depending on which of the characters appears in the sequence. You want to stop scanning as soon as you encounter a character that is not one of these, but not before—even if you encounter all four characters and therefore know that all four variables will be `true`—because the value of `p` after you're finished is important.

Here is one way to solve this problem:

```
while (true) {
        if (*++p == '+')
              plus = true;
        else if (*p = '-')
              minus = true;
        else if (*p = ' ')
              space = true;
        else if (*p = '#')
              sharp = true;
        else break;
}
```

However, most compilers implement this sequence of tests as written, where a `switch` might well generate faster code. We could write an appropriate `switch` statement this way:

```
while (true) {
        switch (*++p) {

        case '+': plus = true; continue;
        case '-': minus = true; continue;
        case ' ': space = true; continue;
        case '#': sharp = true; continue;
        default:
              break;       // Wrong!!
        }
}
```

but this strategy does not work because the `break` statement exits from the `switch` but not from the `while`. I believe that the least convoluted way to write this particular example efficiently is to use a `goto`:

```
top:
        switch(*++p) {

        case '+': plus = true; goto top;
        case '-': minus = true; goto top;
        case ' ': space = true; goto top;
        case '#': sharp = true; goto top;

        }
```

If the character is none of the four we care about, control passes to the statement after the `switch`.

7.2.9.8. Exceptions

A program that discovers a state of affairs with which it cannot cope may wish to give up and transfer control elsewhere. In principle, the program that found the problem does not need to know what is going to happen next, as long as it can say in enough detail what is wrong so as to allow some other part of the program to handle the problem.

Exceptions are the mechanism by which C++ handles such situations. A program indicates that it cannot continue by saying

```
throw expression;
```

Executing a `throw` statement either terminates the program or transfers control to a `try` statement whose execution is in progress, and that has allowed for the possibility of catching a value of the same type (or a type that is similar enough). If no appropriate `try` statement is presently being executed, the program terminates.

For example,

```
try {
      throw 123;
} catch (char c) {
      cout << "caught a character " << c << endl;
} catch (int n) {
      cout << "caught an integer " << n << endl;
}
```

prints

```
caught an integer 123
```

and then continues execution from after the last `}`. On the other hand, changing `123` to `123.0` would cause the program to terminate unless some other `try` statement was presently executing that can catch values of type `double`.

Exceptions are often class objects, and are usually thrown in one function and caught in another; so we will return to the discussion of exceptions after we have explored functions and classes.

7.2.9.9. Overloading

More than one function can have the same name, provided that the functions differ in type or number of parameters. Such a function is called *overloaded*. Calling an overloaded function implies a compile-time check: Is there a single function that is a better match for the arguments than any other? To be the best match, a function must be a better match than the others on one or more arguments and no worse in any argument. The notion of "better match" is somewhat complicated to describe precisely, but intuitively speaking, the less conversion that has to be done to get the argument to the type of the parameter, the better the match. So, for example, we can overload `abs`:

```
int abs(int x) { return x<0? -x: x; }
short abs(short x) { return x<0? -x: x; }
long abs(long x) { return x<0? -x: x; }
float abs(float x) { return x<0? -x: x; }
double abs(double x) { return x<0? -x: x; }
```

after which `abs(0)` will call the `int` version, `abs(-2.3)` will call the `double` version, and `abs('c')` will call the `int` version because converting a `char` to `int` is preferable to converting it to any other integral type.

7.2.9.10. Operators

Functions can have names such as `operator+` (or, equivalently, `operator +`); such functions define additional meanings for the operator symbols. To stop programmers from changing the well-established core language, C++

requires such functions to have at least one parameter of user-defined type. Moreover, programmers cannot invent new operator symbols; they are limited to the ones that are already there.

For example, if `s` is a variable of type `string`, and we write

```
cout << s
```

that expression is really equivalent to calling

```
operator<<(cout, s)
```

and we can define the function thus called as

```
ostream& operator<<(ostream& stream, const string& s)
{
        // ...
}
```

Two operators with the unusual names of `operator[]` and `operator()` figure prominently in C++ programs. They permit the definition of syntactic forms that would otherwise denote subscripting and function calls. So, if `x` has a user-defined type,

```
x(arg1, arg2, arg3)
```

is an abbreviation for

```
x.operator() (arg1, arg2, arg3)
```

and

```
x[arg]
```

is an abbreviation for

```
x.operator[] (arg)
```

These operators allow for user-defined types that look like arrays and functions.

7.2.10. Namespaces

We have seen program examples that define names like `abs` and `sqrt`, which are also part of the standard library. How can we avoid clashing with that library? C++ uses namespaces to answer this question.

A namespace is purely a syntactic notion: By enclosing one or more declarations in

```
namespace name { declarations }
```

the programmer can "attach" the given name to each name declared in the declarations. Such names are then considered different from the same names in other namespaces.

If `x` is defined in namespace `N`, the most direct way to refer to that `x` from outside `N` is as `N::x`. From inside `N`, no special pleading is necessary. For example:

```
namespace Mine {
        int x;

        void f()          // Mine::f
        {
                x = 0;    // Mine::x
        }
}

namespace Yours {
        int x;

        void f()          // Yours::f
        {
                x = 0;    // Yours::x
        }
}

int x;

void f()
{
        x = 0;            // global x
        Mine::x = 0;
        Yours::x = 0;
        Mine::f();
        Yours::f();
}
```

Alternatively, it is possible to make the contents of a namespace available in the current context in one of two ways. The safer of the two is to mention a single name:

```
using Mine::x;
```

says that `x` should refer to `Mine::x` within the current scope. Alternatively, one can obtain wholesale access to a namespace by writing

```
using namespace Yours;
```

after which all names from `Yours` are available without further ado.

Of course, making names available in quantity can give rise to ambiguity, so that after seeing the definitions of `Mine` and `Yours` above, saying

```
int x;

void g()
{
        using namespace Mine;

        x = 0;          // ambiguous
}
```

would fail because the compiler would not know whether to use `Mine::x` or the global `x`.

The standard library puts all its names in a namespace called `std`, to avoid clashes with user-defined names. It is therefore not uncommon for programs to begin by saying

```
using namespace std;
```

This strategy has the additional advantage that vendors can create alternative versions of the standard library, which can then be accessed by changing the name of a namespace in a single place only.

7.3. Data Abstraction

The fundamental notion of data abstraction is that it should be possible to define and implement a data structure without exposing the implementation details to the people who use that data structure. For a programming language to support data abstraction, then, it must offer a way of distinguishing the parts of the program that use a data structure from the parts of the program that implement it. Moreover, it must be able to prevent the users of the data structure from getting at the details that are rightfully revealed only to the implementation.

C++ supports data abstraction by allowing the programmer to define data structures that have some of their components identified as *private*. Private components, as parts of the implementation, are off limits to ordinary uses of the data structure.

7.3.1. Structures and Classes

The main tool for constructing user-defined data types is the class, which can be defined in one of two ways:

```
class { member definitions };

struct { member definitions };
```

The only difference between `struct` and `class` is in the visibility assumed by default for members of the structure: They are assumed to be public in a class defined by `struct`, and private in a class defined by `class`.

The member definitions look like other definitions, including both variables and functions. It is probably the most useful to think about member variables as describing the contents of each object of this particular class, and of member functions as describing the actions that it makes sense for such an object to perform.

As a simple example, consider the following definition:

```
struct Point {
        int x, y;
};
```

Here we have defined a new type, called `Point`, and said that every object of type `Point` has members `x` and `y`, each of which has type `int`. Thus, if we define a `Point` object, by saying

```
Point p;
```

we have implicitly said that the object `p` has members `x` and `y`, which we can refer to directly by mentioning `p.x` or `p.y`.

If we have a pointer to a `Point` object, such as

```
Point* pt;
```

then we can refer to the `x` and `y` components of the object to which `pt` points by writing `(*pt).x` or `(*pt).y`, respectively. These usages are sufficiently common that we can abbreviate them as `pt->x` and `pt->y`.

Once we have defined a structure, we can use it as if it were any other type. So, for example, we can create arrays of `Points`, pointers and references to `Points`, functions that take `Points` as arguments and return them as results, and so on.

In order to make it easier to use structures as parts of other structures, C++ ordinarily defines assignment and initialization on structures in terms of assignment and initialization of their elements. So, for example, if we write

```
Point p;
p.x = 7;
p.y = 3;
Point q = p;
```

we rely on being able to initialize the `Point` object called `q` from the `Point` object called `p`, which initialization is equivalent to initializing `p.x` and `p.y` independently. As another example, we can define

```
struct Box {
        Point origin;
        Point corner;
};
```

after which `Box` assignment and initialization will automatically be defined in terms of `Point` assignment and initialization, which in turn will automatically be defined in terms of the constituent `int`s.

Simple as they are, these structures are sufficient to define most kinds of classical data structures. However, as they stand, their structure is completely open. The fact that a `Point` is a pair of integers is available for the world to see. What we need is a way to hide how a `Point` is implemented, while still allowing `Point`s to be useful. That is, we would like to define a version of `Point` that lets us put integers into a `Point` object and take them out again, but does not reveal how those integers are stored. In C++, we do that by defining member functions that correspond to the actions an object can perform, and then using protection labels to bar access to the parts of the object that constitute the implementation.

7.3.2. Member Functions

On the surface, a member function is simple enough: It is a class member that happens to have function type. So, for example, we might change our `Point` class slightly:

```
struct Point {
     int xval, yval;
     int x() { return xval; }
     int y() { return yval; }
     void x(int newx) { xval = newx; }
     void y(int newy) { yval = newy; }
};
```

Here, we have changed the names of our `x` and `y` members to `xval` and `yval`, and added overloaded member functions `x` and `y` that get and set the x- and y-values. Then we can write code like this:

```
Point p;
p.x(42);            // p.xval is now 42
p.y(37);            // p.yval is now 37
int n = p.x();      // n is now 42
```

The ability to write such code relies on two subtleties of C++. We can see the first one by examining, say, the body of one of the `x` member functions of `Point`:

```
int x() { return xval; }
```

To what object does the name `xval` refer? To call this particular `x` function, we had to write an expression similar to `p.x()`, so the answer is the `xval` that is a member of `p`. That is, when we call a member function, we call it as a member of some object, just as we do when we refer to a data member.

The second subtlety stems from the first: Within the body of a member function, we can refer to other members of that same object without having to say what object we mean. We have just seen the reason: Calling a member function requires that it be a member of a particular object, so once we have said what object we mean, we know what object will contain the other members to which we might be referring.

Here is another way to look at it. When we call `p.x()`, we are apparently not passing any parameters to `x`. But appearances deceive, because while `x` is running, it knows that it is doing so on behalf of the object `p`. In effect, we can think of `p` as a hidden argument to `x` even though `p` does not actually appear in the argument list.

Indeed, we can carry this line of reasoning a little further, by noting that within the body of `x`, not only is the identity of `p` implicitly known, but it is made explicitly available to us through a "variable" called `this`. The idea is that while a member function is executing, the keyword `this` is the address of the object on behalf of which it is executing. We could, therefore, have written our `Point` structure as follows, without changing its behavior at all:

```
struct Point {
     int xval, yval;
     int x() { return this->xval; }
     int y() { return this->yval; }
     void x(int newx) { this->xval = newx; }
     void y(int newy) { this->yval = newy; }
};
```

We did not have to write `this->` explicitly because within the body of a member function, uttering the name of another member of the same class is equivalent to prefixing the name of that member by `this->`.

There is one more subtlety we must mention, which has to do with the type of `this`. At first it would seem that, within a member function of class `point`, the type of `this` would be `Point*`. A little reflection, though, should convince us that it should be `Point* const`, to prevent its value from being changed while a member function is running. That is, while a member function is executing, it is not allowed to say that it should suddenly start working on some other object instead.

But what about this case?

```
const Point q = p; q.x(36);
```

We have said that `q` is not supposed to change after we create it, and then we ask to change `q.xval` to be `36`. What should happen here?

The answer is that this program will not compile. While `q.x` is executing, the variable `this`, with type `Point* const`, would have to hold the address of `q`. But the address of `q` has type `const Point*`, and we cannot convert from that type to `Point* const`.

What we need is a way to say that it is permitted to call `q.x()`, because doing so will not change the value of `q`. Moreover, we must be able to do so without making a similar promise for `q.x(36)`, because that will change the value of `q`.

The way we make such a promise is to change the definition of `Point` yet again:

```
struct Point {
    int xval, yval;
    int x() const { return xval; }      // const added
    int y() const { return yval; }      // const added
    void x(int newx) { xval = newx; }
    void y(int newy) { yval = newy; }
};
```

We have changed the definitions of `x()` and `y()` by inserting `const` between the argument list and the function body. This says two things. First, it says that if `q` is a `const Point`, it is permitted to call `q.x()` because doing so will not change the value of `q`. Second, it says that within the body of `q.x`, the "variable" `this` has type `const Point* const`. That is, it is a pointer to a `const`, and neither the pointer nor the object to which it points is allowed to change.

So, for example, if we had changed the definition of the other overloaded `x` function to be

```
void x(int newx) const { xval = newx; }
```

the program would once again not compile because

```
xval = newx;
```

would be equivalent to

```
this->xval = newx;
```

and, because `this` had type `const Point* const`, `this->xval` would have type `const int` and therefore could not stand on the left-hand side of an assignment.

There is one more important point to mention about member functions, and that is how they affect program organization. In this little example, we have written the entire body of each member function out as part of the class definition. In practice, though, classes may have many member functions, and they may well be large. If a program has many translation units, we do not want to make the compiler read the definitions many times. Therefore, we need a way of separating the definition of the class from the definitions of its member functions, which we do along the following lines. First, we remove the bodies from the member functions, leaving only the type information. We can remove the names of the member function parameters (here `newx` and `newy`) as well. Once we have done this, we have a declaration that can appear in every translation unit that uses an object of type `Point`, so we put it in a separate file called, say, `Point.h`:

```
// file Point.h
struct Point {
     int xval, yval;
     int x() const;
     int y() const;
     void x(int);
     void y(int);
};
```

Next, we take the function bodies and compile them separately:

```
#include "Point.h"
int Point::x() const { return xval; }
int Point::y() const { return yval; }
void Point::x(int newx) { xval = x; }
void Point::y(int newy) { yval = y; }
```

When we do so, we will want to ensure that a copy of the definition of `Point` appears in the file that contains the function bodies—but we do that in only a single place.

Finally, there is an important implementation note. Most C++ compilers will treat a member function body that appears as part of the class definition as an implicit request to implement that member function by expanding its body inline instead of compiling a separate subroutine for it. It is therefore common practice to define classes that have tiny member functions, such as we have just seen, as part of the class definition. This strategy ensures that there is as little overhead as possible associated with using member functions; for the typical implementation, that overhead will be zero.

7.3.3. Protection

Once we have defined a `Point` class that has member functions to access and modify its coordinates, we might like to ensure that only those member functions are used for that purpose, and close off direct access to the `xval` and `yval` components. We can do so as follows:

```
class Point{
private
    int xval, yval;
public:
    int x() const { return xval; }
    int y() const { return yval; }
    void x(int newx) { xval = newx; }
    void y(int newy) { yval = newy; }
};
```

Because we are bringing protection into the picture, we emphasize that protection by using `class` rather than `struct` for our data structure.

The `private:` and `public:` labels say that everything that follows such a label, until the next label or the end of the class, is private or public. So in this case, if `p` is a `Point`, then any attempt to refer to `p.xval` or `p.yval` will evoke a diagnostic message from the compiler, unless that attempt is within the body of a member function of that class.

There is one other way to access private members of a class, and that is through a friend function. A friend is a function that is not a member, but has the same privileges as members. If a class has any friends, it must say what they are.

For example, we might write a function that computes the distance between two `Point`s as follows:

```
double sq(double d) { return d * d; }
double distance(const Point& p, const Point& q)
{
    return sqrt(sq(p.x()-q.x())+sq(p.y()-q.y()));
}
```

where the `sq` function is useful because C++ does not have an exponentiation operator. As written, the `distance` function uses only the public members of `Point`. However, we might want to rewrite it so that it accesses the internal representation of the `Point` objects directly:

```
double distance(const Point& p, const Point& q)
{
    return sqrt(sq(p.xval-q.xval)+sq(p.xval-q.xval));
}
```

As rewritten, this function would not compile because it uses private data in `p` and `q`. Moreover, it does not make sense to make `distance` a member of `Point`, because it acts on two `Point` objects and not just one. Instead, we should make it a friend:

```
class Point {
    friend double distance(const Point&, const Point&);
    // as before
};
```

A `friend` declaration can appear anywhere in a class definition, but it must appear somewhere—once for each friend function. It does not matter whether a `friend` declaration appears in the `private`, `public`, or `protected` section of a class definition; the effect is the same in each case.

7.3.4. Special Member Functions

So far, we have glossed over an important aspect of classes: What happens when variables of those classes are created and destroyed? For example, if we want to define a `Point` whose coordinates are `3` and `4`, it would be nice to be able to write something more compact than

```
Point p;
p.x(3);
p.y(4);
```

Moreover, copying and assigning a class object are potentially fundamental operations on such an object, and we will see how useful it can be for the definition of copying and assignment of objects of a particular class to be something other than simply copying or assigning their members.

To permit this kind of fine-grained control, C++ provides three kinds of special member functions: the constructor, the destructor, and the assignment operator.

7.3.4.1. Constructors

A constructor is a member function that is invoked automatically every time an object of the given class is created. The destructor is invoked automatically whenever an object is destroyed, and the assignment operator is used whenever such an object appears on the left-hand side of an assignment as part of an expression.

If we do not define any constructors at all for a class, the compiler creates one for us with no parameters. That constructor does nothing beyond constructing the members of the class in the ordinary way. In other words, the compiler actually created a constructor for our `Point` class that is as if we had written

```
Point() { }
```

One implication of this is that if we say

```
Point p;
```

then `p.x()` has no meaningful value, because we didn't give an initial value for `p.xval`.

Suppose, now, that we wanted to augment our `Point` class so that the coordinates of a `Point` would be zero by default, and so that we could explicitly specify the starting values if we wished. Then we might change our class as follows:

```
class Point {
public:
    Point(): xval(0), yval(0) { } Point(int x, int y): xval(x), yval(y)
{ }
    // ...
};
```

A constructor looks like any other member function, but there are a few differences:

- Its name is always the same as the name of its class; that is how we know it is a constructor.
- It can have constructor initializers that say how to create the members of its class as part of constructing the class object itself.
- It cannot be `const`, because it is necessary to modify an object in order to construct it.

In this particular example, we have defined two constructors. The first one says that if we construct a `Point` without saying what its coordinates are, they are set to zero. The second says that we can give the coordinates for a `Point` explicitly.

This definition would let us write

```
Point p(3, 4);
```

instead of

```
Point p;
p.x(3);
p.y(4);
```

Moreover, we can use expressions such as `Point(3, 4)` to denote otherwise anonymous `Point` objects that the compiler constructs automatically for the occasion. So, for example,

```
double d = distance(Point(), Point(3, 4));
```

would set `d` to `5.0`, within the precision of floating-point arithmetic.

7.3.4.2. Copy Constructors

Of the overloaded constructors that a class can have, one is special. That constructor is the one whose parameter is a reference to a constant object of the class type itself. So, for class `Point`, the special constructor is the one that takes a `const Point&` parameter.

Such a constructor is called a *copy constructor*; it describes how to copy an object of the given type. Copying an object is, after all, equivalent to constructing a new object of the same type and initializing it from the object that is being copied. So, for example, we would define an appropriate copy constructor for class `Point` as

```
class Point {
public:
    Point(const Point& p): xval(p.xval), yval(p.yval) { }
    // ...
};
```

This copy constructor initializes `xval` and `yval` from the corresponding members of the object that is being copied.

Copy constructors control almost every context in which objects are copied. For example, when we write a function that takes a `Point` argument:

```
void draw(Point p) { /* ... */ }
```

then every time we call `draw`, the C++ implementation will use the copy constructor of class `Point` to copy the argument into the local variable `p`. Similarly, if `p` is a `Point` and we write

```
Point q = p;
```

then the implementation will use the copy constructor to construct `q`. The copy constructor is even used to return an object from a function. In fact, the only context in which a copy of an object can be formed without using the copy constructor is when on object is assigned to another as part of an expression (rather than as part of a declaration). So, for example, although

```
Point q = p;
```

uses the copy constructor to form `q`, if we subsequently use

```
q = p;
```

then we will be assigning `p` to `q`, obliterating the prior value of `q`. Such assignments do not use the copy constructor; instead, they use the assignment operator.

It is important to realize that a copy constructor must take a reference parameter. Suppose, for example, that we had written

```
Point(Point p): xval(p.xval), yval(p.yval) { } // Wrong!
```

Then when we called this constructor, we would have to copy the argument to initialize p. How would we copy it? By using the copy constructor. But first we would have to copy the argument to initialize the parameter p. Evidently, the result of trying to define a copy constructor this way would be an infinite recursion.

By defining copy constructors to take references, we say that we do not want to copy the argument before copying it. In effect, the parameter p is bound directly to the argument object, which is just what we want if we are going to copy the argument.

The copy constructor we wrote in this example does just what the default definition of copying does: It copies the components of the object. As it happens, the compiler will generate a copy constructor for us if we don't write one, and the copy constructor it generates copies the components of the object. So we did not need this particular copy constructor at all—but we will see contexts later in which copy constructors are essential.

7.3.4.3. Assignment Operators

The next special member function to consider is the assignment operator. It is similar to a copy constructor, but instead of having the same name as the class itself, it is called operator=. By convention, the assignment operator should return a reference to its left-hand side—that is, a reference to *this. So, for example, we might define an assignment operator for our Point class as

```
class Point {
public:
     Point& operator=(const Point& p) {
          xval = p.xval;
          yval = p.yval;
          return *this;
     }
     // as before
};
```

Note that we do not use constructor initializers in the assignment operator, because xval and yval are being assigned, not initialized, and because the assignment operator is not a constructor.

As with the copy constructor, assignment operators should have reference parameters. However, an assignment operator that takes a Point rather than a Point& will merely cause needless calls to the copy constructor, rather than a catastrophic failure.

If a class does not have any assignment operator at all, the compiler will create one that assigns all the members of the class and returns a reference to the left-hand side.

7.3.4.4. Destructors

A destructor runs automatically whenever an object of its class is destroyed. Like constructors and assignment operators, destructors are distinguished by name: A destructor's name is the name of its class, preceded by a tilde (~). As with constructors and assignment operators, the compiler will generate a destructor if we do not write one. However, destructors behave slightly differently in this regard from the other special member functions, because whatever we write in our destructor will take place in addition to the default action, which is to destroy the data members. This makes sense because there is no way to escape the requirement to destroy the members of an object as part of destroying the object itself.

Our `Point` class does not need a destructor, but if it did, it would look like this:

```
class Point {
public:
    ~Point() { /* ... */ }
    // as before
};
```

7.3.5. Pointers to Members

A member of a class object is an object in its own right, so that it is possible to form a pointer to it:

```
struct Thing {
        int n;
        double x, y;
};

void f()
{
        Thing t;

        double* dp = &t.x;
}
```

Here, `dp` is caused to point to the `x` member of a particular `Thing` object.

It can be useful, however, to identify a member of a class without identifying a particular object of that class. We do that with a special type called a *pointer to member*. We might, for example, use `&Thing::x` to refer to "the member `x` of class `Thing`." The type of `&Thing::x` is "pointer to member of `Thing` of type `double`," and we can store such a value in a variable by writing

```
double Thing::*p;
```

This declaration says that `p` is a pointer to a member of class `Thing` that has type `double`; we can give `p` a value by writing

```
p = &Thing::x;
```

If `t` is a `Thing` object, we can then use the expression `t.*p` as another way of referring to `t.x`. Similarly, if `tp` is a pointer to `Thing`, `tp->*p` is another way to refer to `tp->x`.

7.3.6. A Data Abstraction Example

We have finally learned enough C++ so that we can define a class called `String` whose objects represent variable-length character strings. In particular, we will make it possible to say

```
String s = "Hello, world!";
cout << s << endl;
```

and have the program greet the world accordingly.

We will first note that, because arrays have fixed length, there is no way to store a variable-length string directly in a class object. Instead, we will represent a string as a pointer to the initial character of a dynamically allocated array of characters. To determine the length of the string, we will adopt the same convention that string literals use: The last significant character of the string will be followed by a null character `'\0'`.

As part of our implementation, we will use two simple functions from the standard library. We have already seen one of them: `strlen` takes a pointer to the initial character of a null-terminated array and returns the number of characters, not counting the null. The other library function that we will use is `strcpy`. It copies the null-terminated string given by its second argument—including the null character—into memory starting at the location given by its first argument. When it is done, it returns its first argument:

```
char* strcpy(char* p, const char* q)
{
        char* r = p;
        while ((*p++ = *q++) != '\0')
                ;
        return r;
}
```

Here, all the work is done inside the loop: We copy the character at which `q` points into the character at which `p` points, remember the character, increment `p` and `q`, and test whether the remembered character is zero. If so, then we have just copied the null terminator and we're done. Otherwise, we're done with this trip through the loop, and it's time to begin the next iteration.

We know how to move characters around; we know how we are going to store the characters of a `String`; what more do we need? When we design C++ classes, we will often encounter a close relationship between the copy constructor, destructor, and assignment operator. This relationship comes about because an assignment operator gets rid of the old value of the object and then gives it a new one, and those two operations are exactly what the destructor and copy constructor do. Newcomers to C++ therefore often ask if it is possible to call a constructor directly.

However, a constructor does not merely assign values to members; it creates those members as well. Therefore, the cleanest way to exploit the similarity between the constructors, destructor, and assignment operator is to define auxiliary member functions that will implement the more primitive operations.

In the case of a `String`, those operations turn out to be

- Given a pointer to the first character of a null-terminated character array,

  Allocate enough dynamic memory to contain a copy of the characters in that array.

  Copy the characters from the array into the new memory

  Set our pointer to point to the initial character of the new memory.

- Delete the memory to which our pointer points.

With the benefit of all this hindsight, then, we can start implementing our `String` class from the bottom up:

```
class String {
public:
    // The interface member functions go here
private:
    char* data;

    void init(const char* p) {
        data = new char[strlen(p) + 1];
        strcpy(data, p);
    }
    void destroy() {
        delete[] data;
    }
};
```

Once we have defined these primitive operations, we can write the constructors, destructor, and assignment operator in terms of them:

```
class String {
public:
    String() { init(""); }
    String(const char* p) { init(p); }
    String(const String& s) { init(s.data); }
    ~String() { destroy(); } String& operator=(const String& s) {
        if (this != &s) {
            destroy();
            init(s.data);
        }
        return *this;
```

```
    }
private:
    // as before
};
```

This code is all we need to capture the essentials of variable-length strings.

The first constructor says how to construct a string when we have not given an initial value:

```
String s;
```

Calling `init("")` is an easy way to cause `data` to point to a dynamically allocated null character, which is how we represent a string with no characters. The second constructor says how to construct a `String` from a string literal or other character array; the third is the copy constructor. The destructor is trivial; it just calls `destroy`. In fact, the only part of this class that is not trivial is the assignment operator.

The reason that the assignment operator is slightly tricky is that it has to cater to the possibility of assigning a string to itself:

```
String s("foo");
s = s;
```

Here we used the copy constructor to give `s` an initial value. There is no problem there. But when we execute `s = s`, we have a problem: The left- and right-hand sides of the assignment refer to the same object. If we are not careful, we will `destroy` the `data` and then try to copy the characters we have just destroyed.

We avoid this problem by checking for self-assignment explicitly, and doing nothing in that particular case. When we're done, we return `*this` as our value, whether or not we did any work.

Of course, as it stands, this class is useless because, although we can put characters into an object of that class, there is no way to get any data out of the object. To ensure that the class is not completely useless, we will make it possible to print `String` objects.

To do that, we must define an overloaded `operator<<` that will be executed when we write expressions such as

```
cout << s
```

where `s` is a `String` object. To do that, we need to know that the type of `cout` is `ostream`, and that an output operator `<<` must have a reference to `ostream` as its first parameter. We must also know that output operators are expected to return their left argument as their result, so that expressions such as

```
cout << s << endl
```

can work. With that knowledge, we can write

```
ostream& operator<<(ostream& ostrm, const String& s)
{
     ostrm << s.data;
     return ostrm;
}
```

To print a `String`, we print the pointer that the `String` contains. This must work in the same way that

```
cout << "Hello, world"
```

works, because the string literal is little more than a pointer. So we define printing our `String` class in terms of printing string literals, and we are done.

Well, we're almost done, anyway. The last thing we need to do is to give our `operator<<` permission to know about the representation of a `String` object, by saying

```
class String {
     friend ostream& operator<<(ostream&, const String&);
     // as before
};
```

Of course, this `String` class is much simpler than the version in the standard library. For example, for such a class to be useful in practice, it must support input as well as output. It also needs operations to manipulate the contents of `Strings`, such as fetching individual characters, concatenating `Strings`, and so on. Such complexities are beyond the scope of this chapter.

The important points to remember about C++ data abstraction are

- C++ supports data abstraction with classes.
- A class definition describes the contents of objects of that class.
- Class objects have members, which can be functions or data.
- Members can be public or private, depending on whether they are part of the interface or the implementation.
- Constructors, destructors, and assignment operators allow fine-grained control over how objects can be used.

- The data-abstraction facilities of C++ make it possible to define new types that are almost as easy to use as the built-in types. In particular, they make it unnecessary to have types such as variable-length strings built into the language. Instead, such types can be—and are—part of a library.

7.4. Generic Programming

Generic programming in C++ is based on an engineering compromise that is aimed at one of the oldest controversies in programming language design: When is the right time to bind decisions about types? One school of thought, which pervades languages such as Fortran, Algol, and Pascal, is that types should be fixed at the time the program is written. The other, which pervades languages such as Lisp and Smalltalk, is that types should be determined dynamically as the program executes.

One argument in favor of determining types early is that it allows earlier error detection, which should make software more reliable—at least in principle. Moreover, doing so enables the compiler to generate more efficient machine code, because it can take the types of variables into account. One argument in favor of determining types late is that programs can be more flexible, so late binding of types yields more expressive power.

The key idea behind C++ generic programming is that there is a third choice of when to fix the types in a program: when the program is compiled. This choice is particularly interesting in the context of libraries, because it permits programmers to write libraries without knowing the specific types of the objects with which those libraries will be used. When someone wants to use one of those libraries, that user will usually know the relevant types, so all the relevant information will still be available by the time the program is compiled.

7.4.1. Template Functions

As a typical example, consider the `abs` function that we used earlier as an example of overloading:

```
int abs(int x) { return x<0? -x: x; }
short abs(short x) { return x<0? -x: x; }
long abs(long x) { return x<0? -x: x; }
float abs(float x) { return x<0? -x: x; }
double abs(double x) { return x<0? -x: x; }
```

We had to define this function five times to cover even the most fundamental relevant types. What a nuisance! This is the kind of example that is often used to argue in favor of dynamic types.

In C++, we can abbreviate all these forms of `abs` by writing

```
template<class T>
T abs(T x) { return x<0? -x: x; }
```

The use of the word `class` in the context of a template definition is slightly misleading: It really means "any type," but templates are a relatively recent part of C++, and introducing `type` as a new keyword would have broken too many programs to introduce `type` as a new keyword. More recently, the usage

```
template<typename T>
T abs(T x) { return x<0? -x: x; }
```

was defined to be equivalent, but the older usage of `class` is much more popular at present.

It is reasonable to think of either of these function definitions as an abbreviation for a finite, but unbounded, set of overloaded functions. The compiler will instantiate this function as needed, once for each relevant type `T`, after which using this `abs` is as easy—and efficient—as using the other overloaded versions would be. Moreover, the generic `abs` function will work with any type that can be compared with zero and supports unary negation.

One might argue that this version of `abs` is too general. For example, if we have a class that represents complex numbers, this version of `abs` does the wrong thing. Indeed, it does a senseless thing, because it is meaningless to ask whether a complex number is less than zero. For this and similar reasons, C++ allows template functions to be specialized by writing functions that handle specific types, such as

```
double abs(const Complex& z)
{
    return sqrt(sq(z.re()) + sq(z.im()));
}
```

which we have defined in terms of the `sq` function that we defined earlier. In effect, the combination of templates and specializations lets us tell the compiler how to do a limited form of dynamic computation on types while it is compiling the program, while still avoiding any of the execution-time inefficiencies associated with dynamic types.

7.4.2. Template Classes

Templates come in two forms: functions and classes. When we use a template function, the compiler can usually figure out the type to use for instantiation by looking at the argument(s).

So, for example, it is clear that if we call `abs(3)`, we should instantiate `abs` with the type parameter `T` being `int`. When we use a template class, however, the "value" of the type parameter becomes part of the type itself.

The best way to make this distinction clear is with an example. Suppose, for instance, that we wanted to revise our `String` class to allow strings of any kind of character, not just plain `char`. We might begin by defining generic versions of `strlen` and `strcpy`:

```
template<class T>
int strlen(const T* p)
{
    int n = 0;
    while (*p++)
        ++n;
    return n;
}

template<class T>
T* strcpy(T* p, const T* q)
{
    T* r = p;
    while ((*p++ = *q++) != 0)
        ;
    return r;
}
```

The only change from the previous versions, aside from turning them into templates, is that we changed the character literal `'\0'` into plain `0` so as not to be biased in favor of any particular element type.

Then we could make our `String` class generic:

```
template <class T>
class String {
    friend ostream& operator<<(ostream&, const String&);
public:
    String() { init(null); }
    String(const T* p) { init(p); }
    String(const String& s) { init(s.data); }
    ~String() { destroy(); }
    String& operator=(const String& s) {
        if (this != &s) {
            destroy();
            init(s.data);
        }
        return *this;
}
```

```
private:
    static T null[1];
    T* data;

    void init(const T* p) {
        data = new T[strlen(p) + 1];
        strcpy(data, p);
    }
    void destroy() {
        delete[] data;
    }
};
template<class T> T String<T>::null[1];

template<class T>
ostream& operator<<(ostream& ostrm, const String<T>& s)
{
    ostrm << s.data;
    return ostrm;
}
```

Aside from making this class a template, and changing `char` to `T` where appropriate, the only change was to the constructor that did not take any argument. The reason for the change was to remove the dependency on the type of the string literal `""`, because it does not necessarily make sense to use `""`, which has type `char*`, to initialize a string of characters of arbitrary type. Instead, we defined a `static` data member, which is a member that has one instance for the entire class rather than one instance for each object.

In the case of a template class, there is one instance of the data member for each instantiation of the class. That is, `String<char>`, `String<unsigned char>`, and `String<wchar_t>` each has its own `null` member. In this example, the member is a single-element array, which we must define at one single point in the program as shown. This definition as a global object causes the element of that array to be initialized automatically by a default that is zero for all integral types, including character types. This array is therefore what we use to represent a single-element array, of unknown type, whose element is zero.

To use a template type that represents a container, such as our revised `String`, we must explicitly mention the element type. So, for example, we can write

```
String<char> sc;
String<unsigned char> uc;
String<wchar_t> kanji_name;
```

and so on.

7.4.3. Generic Algorithms

When we rewrote `strlen`, we did so to make it work with arrays of elements of any type that could be compared to zero. However, a further rewrite makes `strlen` even more general:

```
template<class T>
int strlen(T p)            // instead of const T* p
{
     int n = 0;
     while (*p++)
            ++n;
     return n;
}
```

Now, we do not even require `p` to be a pointer. We just require it to be an object of a type that gives a meaningful value to `*p++`. Because of operator overloading, `p` could be any class object that behaves enough like a pointer; all that `strlen` would require would be suitable definitions for `operator*` and `operator++`.

Indeed, the notion of defining a function that works with any type that supports the requisite operations is the source of a great deal of power in the C++ standard library, and offers more possibilities than can be described in detail in a single article. We can, however, offer a sample.

Consider how we might go about reversing the elements of an array. A fairly general way of describing an array is by a pair of pointers; typically one pointer will point to the first element and the other to one past the last element. We might write a function to reverse such an array as follows:

```
template<class T>
void reverse(T* begin, T* end)
{
     while (begin < end)
            swap(*begin++, *--end);
}
```

where `swap` might be defined as follows:

```
template<class T>
void swap(T& x, T& y)
{
     const T temp = x;
     x = y;
     y = temp;
}
```

The asymmetry between `*begin++` and `*--end` is necessary because `end` starts out pointing one element past the end of the array. We must therefore decrement `end` before we dereference it.

This definition of `reverse` is overspecified in two important respects: It assumes that `begin` and `end` are pointers, and that there is an order relation `<` defined on them. Imagine if `begin` and `end` were class objects that had `++`, `--`, and `*` defined appropriately, but did not have `<` defined. Such objects might, for example, represent locations in a doubly-linked list, whose elements might be arbitrarily scattered throughout memory. It would therefore make sense to use `==` and `!=` to compare such objects, even if `<` might not make sense.

It is possible to reverse a data structure defined by such objects, although it costs a small amount of extra overhead to do so:

```
template<class T>
void reverse(T begin, T end)
{
    while (begin != end)
        if (begin != --end)
            swap(*begin++, *end);
}
```

Here, as before, we loop as long as there is work to do. However, this time, we decrement `end` and compare it against `begin` a second time before swapping `*begin` and `*end` and then incrementing `begin`. This double test is necessary to ensure that `begin` and `end` do not cross.

What we have gained for this small overhead is the ability to use a single algorithm to reverse any data structure for which there exists a type that acts sufficiently like a pointer. Moreover, there exist much more sophisticated techniques that can remove even this small amount of extra overhead.

7.5. Object-Oriented Programming

Despite the benefits of determining types during compilation, rather than when the program is written or run, there are times when it can be useful to defer knowledge of the type of an object until the program looks at that particular object. The most common context for deferring such knowledge is when we have a collection of data structures that are similar to each other in some way. Then we may wish sometimes to consider only those properties that they have in common, and other times to take their differences into account.

For example, if we are writing a system that displays a variety of graphic symbols on a screen, we often might care only that an object represents something that we can potentially display. However, when it comes time to display it, we will care what particular kind of symbol it is, because different symbols will require different display algorithms.

C++ uses two separate mechanisms to make object-oriented programming possible. One is inheritance, which lets us describe a class by describing only the members that it has in addition to those provided by some other class. The other is the notion of a virtual function, which is a function that is selected at run time based on the type of an object.

7.5.1. Inheritance

A class can nominate one or more other classes as base classes. If a class `D` says that `B` is a base class, we say that `D` is derived from `B`. In that case, `D` will have all the members that `B` has, as well as any other members that `D` defines. For example, if we declare

```
struct B {
    int x;
    double y;
};
struct D: B {
    int z;
};
```

then class `D` has three members: an `int` called `z`, which `D` defined explicitly, and two other members called `x` and `y`, which `D` inherited from its base class `B`.

As a more complicated example, suppose that we wish to use the `String` class that we defined earlier to define a new class to represent colored strings, which might be strings that, when displayed, appear in a particular color. Such a class might look like this:

```
template<class T, class Color>
class ColorString: public String<T> {
public:
    // interface members go here
private:
    Color col;
};
```

where the phrase `public String<T>` says that the fact that `ColorString` (which is an abbreviation for `ColorString<T, Color>`) is derived from `String<T>` should be publicly known. This example shows two common techniques for building new types from existing ones: inheritance and composition. If we have a class `RGB` that describes a particular way of dealing with colors, we will note that `ColorString<char, RGB>` has `String<char>` as a base class, but does not have `RGB` as a base class. That means that every member of `String<char>` is also a member of `ColorString<char, RGB>`, but that members of `RGB` are not members of `ColorString<char, RGB>`.

Another way to look at it is that a `ColorString` is a kind of `String`, but it is not a kind of `Color`.

7.5.1.1. Inheritance and Constructors

It is not quite correct to say that every member of a base class is a member of the derived class, because that statement is not true for constructors, destructors, or the assignment operator. Derived class constructors must say how to construct the base class parts of their object. So, for example, if we were going to complete the definition of our `ColorString` class, we would have to give it a whole new set of constructors, each of which would have to construct the underlying `String` somehow. If `ColorString` inherited the constructors of `String`, then it would be possible to construct a `ColorString` without touching anything more than the underlying `String` part, merely by using one of the inherited `String` constructors.

What C++ does instead is to say that every constructor in a derived class can say how it wants to initialize the base class part with an appropriate base class constructor. It does this by using constructor initializers, which we have already seen, but saying that they should name the base class rather than just naming individual members.

To continue this example in the context of `ColorString`, imagine that we wanted the default constructor (i.e., the one with no parameters) of `ColorString` to construct a `String` with no characters, whose color was the default value of the type parameter `Color`. Then we might say

```
template<class T, class Color>
class ColorString: public String<T> {
public:
     ColorString() { }
     ColorString(const String<T>& s): String<T>(s) { }
     // ...
private:
     Color col;
};
```

The first constructor says nothing about how to initialize the components of a `ColorString<T, Color>`, so they will be initialized to their default values. The second constructor tells how to construct a `ColorString<T, Color>` from a `String<T>`. This constructor says that the `String<T>` part of the `ColorString<T, Color>` object should be initialized with the given `String<T>` value. Because it says nothing about how to initialize the member `col`, that member will start out with whatever default value an object of class `Color` ordinarily has. This particular `ColorString` constructor could also have been written as

```
ColorString(const String<T>& s): String<T>(s), col(Color()) { }
```

with the same effect.

In short, every class must describe all the ways in which an object of that class might potentially be constructed; it does not inherit constructors from its base class(es). Each derived class constructor can use the base class constructors to say how to initialize the part of the derived class object that it has in common with its base class.

7.5.1.2. Inheritance and Destructors

Destructors are cumulative, in the sense that anything a derived class destructor says to do will be in addition to whatever the base class destructors do. Therefore, destroying a derived class object executes both the derived class and base class destructors.

In general, that means that a derived class destructor needs to concern itself only with destroying things that were specifically constructed in the derived class destructor; the base class will take care of itself.

7.5.1.3. Inheritance and Assignment

Assignment is slightly unusual, in that the compiler will generate a derived class assignment operator that uses the base class assignment operator(s) if the user does not provide one explicitly. A user who defines a derived class assignment operator must explicitly assign the base class part if that is the desired effect.

7.5.2. Dynamic Binding

Deriving a class from another immediately establishes a hierarchy. We typically use such hierarchies to capture common ways of thinking about data. For example, we can imagine a hierarchy such as,

```
class Vehicle { /* ... */ };
class Aircraft: public Vehicle { /* ... */ };
class Airplane: public Aircraft { /* ... */ };
class Helicopter: public Aircraft { /* ... */ };
class RoadVehicle: public Vehicle { /* ... */ };
class Automobile: public RoadVehicle { /* ... */ };
class Truck: public RoadVehicle { /* ... */ };
```

and so on. If we were writing programs to deal with vehicles, we can imagine that sometimes we might care what a vehicle was, say, a `Helicopter`, because helicopters can hover and other kinds of aircraft cannot. Other times, we might care only that a vehicle was an `Aircraft`; and sometimes, it might interest us only that it was a `Vehicle`.

7.5.2.1. Virtual Functions

C++ allows us to look at objects in different levels of detail at different times by offering two facilities:

- If class D is publicly derived from class B, a pointer (or reference) to a D object can be converted into a pointer (or reference) to a B object. If we have a pointer to B that actually points to a D object, we can convert that pointer back into a pointer to D.
- If class B has a virtual function and we have a pointer to B that actually points to a D object, using that pointer to call the virtual function will actually call the function defined in class D.

Here is a simple example that illustrates both of these facilities. First, we define two simple classes, each of which has two member functions:

```
class B {
public:
    void f() { cout << "B::f" << endl; }
    virtual void g() { cout << "B::g" << endl; }
};
class D: public B {
public:
    void f() { cout << "D::f" << endl; }
    virtual void g() { cout << "D::g" << endl; }
};
```

Strictly speaking, we did not need to declare D::g to be virtual; once a function is declared as virtual in a base class, all functions with the same name and argument types in all derived classes are virtual also. Notice that we have defined functions in class D with the same name as functions in class B. This is no problem in general, because classes are scopes and names defined in derived classes hide the corresponding names in the base classes.

Now we define a B object and a D object and make a B pointer point to each one:

```
int main() {
    B b;
    D d;

    B* p1 = &b;
    B* p2 = &d;
    // ...
```

At this point, p1 and p2 are pointers, each of which nominally points at a B object. What happens if we use these pointers to call the f and g functions?

```
    // ...
    p1->f(); // B::f
    p1->g(); // B::g
    p2->f(); // B::f
    p2->g(); // D::g (!)
}
```

There should be no question about what the calls do that use `p1`, because `p1` is declared to point at a `B` object and actually does so. Indeed, we could remove the definition of class `D` entirely and the calls that use `p1` would still work the same way.

The interesting part is when we use `p2`, because although we said that the type of `p2` is a pointer to a `B` object, `p2` actually points at a `D` object. Because every `D` is a kind of `B`, we can ordinarily think of `p2` as pointing at "the `B` part of a `D` object." If we view it that way, it is not surprising that calling `p2->f()` should print `B::f`. However, when we declared `B::g` to be virtual, we said that we want the particular function that we call to be determined by the type of the object, not by the type of the pointer. The effect is therefore to call `D::g`.

In order for virtual function calls to work efficiently, the language imposes two requirements. First, the pointer must actually point at an object from the appropriate inheritance hierarchy (in this case, the hierarchy rooted in `B`). That is why it is possible to convert a pointer to `D` into a pointer to `B`, but similar conversions between other pointer types are not possible. Second, the argument and result types for virtual functions must match in the base and derived classes.[5] This allows the compiler to generate code that decides only which function to call, without having to generate, code to convert the arguments dynamically to appropriate types.

The C++ virtual function mechanism is designed to offer a useful compromise between speed and flexibility. The only context in which a virtual function call can take place is if it is being called through a pointer or a reference to a base class. This call can happen only after the compiler has seen the declaration of the base class, which means that the compiler knows all the virtual functions in that base class. Moreover, when the compiler is compiling each derived class, it also knows the definition of the base class, which means that it can match virtual functions in the derived class with the corresponding ones in the base class.

The effect of these requirements is to make it possible to call a virtual function without ever having to search an associative data structure during execution. A typical way of implementing virtual functions is to give each object that has any virtual functions at all a single pointer that points to a compiler-generated table that identifies the type of that object. That table will have one entry for each virtual function in that object's class. Because

[5]There is a fairly obscure exception to this rule: If `D` is derived from `B`, `D1` is derived from `B1`, and a virtual function in `B` returns a pointer or reference to `B1`, then the corresponding virtual function in `D` is allowed to return a pointer or reference to `D1`.

the compiler knows all the relevant virtual functions when it sees the class definition, it is possible to allocate entries in the table during compilation. That means that calling a virtual function is just a matter of fetching the pointer from the object, fetching the address of the virtual function from an offset into the table that has been predetermined at compile time, and jumping to the appropriate function. The additional cost of a virtual function call varies with the implementation, but will typically be about the same as calling an ordinary function with no arguments and no result.

7.5.2.2. Virtual Destructors

Because virtual functions are useful only when called through pointers or references, they are most interesting when used in conjunction with dynamically allocated objects. When an object is dynamically allocated, it is usually dynamically freed as well, and just as it may be useful to ignore the specific type of an object when using it, it may also be useful to ignore the specific type when freeing its memory.

For example, consider a dynamically allocated `Vehicle`:

```
Vehicle* vp = new Helicopter(args);
```

We declared `vp` as a pointer to `Vehicle` because we did not want to have to remember that we were dealing with a `Helicopter`. However, when we no longer need this particular `Helicopter`, there is trouble:

```
delete vp;        // Wrong!
```

The trouble is that we are trying to deallocate a `Vehicle`, but what we really have is a `Helicopter`.

In a case like this, we have to tell the compiler that when we delete something that is nominally a `Vehicle`, it might actually be an object of any type derived from `Vehicle`. The way to do this is to give class `Vehicle` a virtual destructor:

```
class Vehicle {
public:
     virtual ~Vehicle() { }
     // ...
};
```

Virtual destructors are usually empty, because they are typically nothing more than a signal to the compiler to do the right thing in the context of a `delete`.

7.5.2.3. Pure Virtual Functions

It is often useful to define a base class whose sole purpose is to be a base class; there will never be any objects of that class. So, for example, it is likely that we will never want to have an object that represents a vehicle without saying something about what kind of vehicle we have. In such a case, we have to define the virtual function in the base class, because it is part of the interface to the base class, but it is hard to know how to do so, because the virtual function is meaningful only for derived classes.

C++ offers us a way around this dilemma by letting us define a *pure virtual function* We do so by writing, for example:

```
class Vehicle {
public:
     void start() = 0;
     // ...
};
```

Here we have said that every `Vehicle` can be `start`ed somehow, but we don't know how until we know what kind of `Vehicle` we have.

A class that has one or more pure virtual functions is called an *abstract base class*. To ensure that these undefined functions are never called, the compiler prevents an object of an abstract base class from ever being created, except as part of an object of a derived class. Such derived classes must override, and define, every pure virtual function in the base class, or else they are considered abstract base classes themselves and cannot be used to create objects either.

Later, we will see an example of an abstract base class.

7.5.2.4. Dynamic Casts

Suppose we have a pointer to a `Vehicle` and we want to know whether the pointer actually points to a `Helicopter` (or some type derived from `Helicopter`). Why might we care? Usually the reason is that we wish to take some kind of action in the case of a `Helicopter` that is not appropriate for other kinds of `Vehicle`.

The most straightforward way to base an action on the specific type of an object is to define a virtual function in the base class, and then override it in the appropriate derived class with one that performs the appropriate action. However, this strategy is not always possible, because we do not always control the definition of our base classes.

To allow for type inquiry even for classes we did not define, C++ has a dynamic cast facility. Suppose, for example, that `vp` points to some kind of `Vehicle`. Then we might write:

```
Helicopter* hp = dynamic_cast<Helicopter*> (vp);
```

If vp actually did point to a Helicopter object or an object of a class derived from Helicopter, then hp will now point to the same object. Otherwise hp will be zero. A similar facility exists for references, but because a reference must always refer to an object, a dynamic cast on a reference will throw an exception if it fails.

There are other special-purpose casts available as well, but they are beyond the scope of this chapter.

7.5.2.5. Protection and Inheritance

When we have been defining our derived classes, we have always said things along the lines of

```
class D: public B { /* ... */ };
```

Here, the public means that it should be publicly known that D is derived from B. It is that fact that allows us to convert a D pointer into a B pointer.

We could also have said

```
class D: private B { /* ... */ };
```

or, equivalently,

```
class D: B { /* ... */ };
```

in which case B would be called a private base class of D. Private base classes are uncommon; conceptually they are classes where the inheritance is part of the implementation but not part of the interface.

In keeping with the open nature of classes derived with struct, public inheritance is the default there; so

```
struct D: B { /* ... */ };
```

is equivalent to

```
class D: public B { public: /* ... */ };
```

The presence of inheritance opens the possibility for one other kind of protection. In the absence of inheritance, an abstract data type has two aspects to its construction: those seen by its users and those seen as part of its implementation. With inheritance, however, comes a third possibility, namely members that derived classes see but general users do not.

To cater to inheritance this way, C++ has a third protection keyword, protected. If we write a class such as

```
class B {
public:
    // ...
```

```
protected:
    // ...
private:
    // ...
};
```

then anyone can access the members defined after the `public` label, only members and friends of `B` and members of classes derived from `B` can access members defined after the `protected` label, and only members and friends of `B` can access members defined after the `private` label.

7.5.3. An Extended Object-Oriented Programming Example

To give a clearer idea of the point of data abstraction and object-oriented programming, here is a complete program that uses data abstraction, inheritance, and dynamic binding. This example first appeared in the *Journal of Object-Oriented Programming*, and a somewhat different version appears in *Ruminations on* C++ (Koenig A. & Moo, 1997). This program shows a lot of ideas, despite its small size, and will repay careful study.

The program deals with trees that represent arithmetic expressions. For example, the expression `(-5)*(3+4)` corresponds to the following tree:

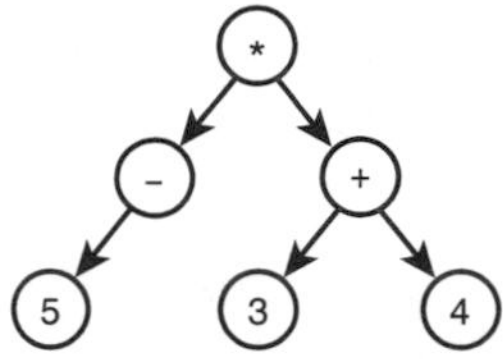

An expression tree contains nodes that represent constants, unary operators, and binary operators. Such a tree might be used in a compiler or a calculator program. Inheritance captures the similarities between the types of nodes. Dynamic binding allows nodes to "know" what type they are, making it unnecessary to incorporate this knowledge in every program that uses these trees. Together, inheritance and dynamic binding make it possible to add new kinds of nodes without incorporating this knowledge in every program that accesses a node. Data abstraction allows programmers to create and use these trees without worrying about their internal representation, and allows the people who implement the trees to change their representation without breaking the programs that use them.

The goal is to be able to write:

```
main()
{
    Tree t = Tree ("*", Tree ("-", 5), Tree ("+", 3, 4));
    cout << t << "\n";
    t = Tree ("*", t, t);
    cout << t << "\n";
}
```

and get

```
((-5)*(3+4))
(((-5)*(3+4))*((-5)*(3+4)))
```

as output, without having to worry about how a `Tree` is represented or about when or how to allocate and free memory for parts of a `Tree`.

This toy program does things that are typical of many larger programs such as compilers, editors, CAD/CAM systems, and others that deal with complicated input. Much of the effort in such programs is in manipulating trees, graphs, and similar data structures. Authors of such programs perennially face problems of memory allocation, flexibility, and efficiency. Object-oriented techniques allow the solutions of these problems to be localized so that each subsequent change does not require parallel changes all over the program.

7.5.3.1. The Node Class

The diagram contains two distinct kinds of objects: *nodes* (represented by circles) and *edges* (represented by arrows). Each node contains either an operand or an operator. Each edge can be thought of as representing the entire tree at the end of its arrow. Thus the natural way to represent a tree involves two classes: one, called `Node`, to represent nodes and the other, called `Tree`, to represent trees (or, equivalently, edges).

Here is the declaration of the `Node` class:

```
class Node {
    friend class Tree;
    friend ostream& operator<< (ostream&, const Tree&);
private:
    int use;
protected:
    Node() { use = 1; }
    virtual void print (ostream&) const = 0;
    virtual ~Node() { }
};
```

The `Node` constructor is declared as `protected` so that only members or friends of the `Node` class, or classes derived from `Node`, can create `Nodes`. The `Node` and `Tree` classes are interrelated, so the `Node` class definition nominates the `Tree` class as a friend. Recall that friends have the same privileges as members, but are not members. If two classes depend on each other's implementations, the right way to handle this in C++ is to use friend declarations.

The `Node` class definition also includes a declaration of the `<<` output operator for `Tree` objects so that the `Tree` output routine can access the private data of the associated `Node`. This operator should not be a member of `Node` because it acts on an `ostream`, not a `Node`. The `ostream` class has been defined elsewhere and this program cannot (and should not) change that definition! However, the program that prints a `Node` needs to know how a `Node` is represented and is therefore declared as a `friend`. This is another example of using a `friend` declaration to link two classes.

The `print` function is a pure virtual function. We are not ever actually going to have any objects of class `Node`, but only of classes derived from `Node`. Therefore, although we need to define `print` in the `Node` base class (because although there are no `Node` objects, we will nevertheless have pointers to `Node` and use those pointers to call the virtual `print` function), we do not need to say what it does. There are no objects of class `Node`, so we will always be executing the `print` function in a class derived from `Node`. Later declarations will derive several different kinds of nodes and the appropriate actions will be selected automatically during execution to print and deallocate them.

7.5.3.2. The `Tree` Abstract Base Class

If a `Node` contains the data, a `Tree` controls how a user accesses the data:

```
class Tree {
     friend class Node;
     friend ostream& operator<< (ostream&, const Tree&);
public:
     Tree(int);
     Tree(const char*, const Tree&);
     Tree(const char*, const Tree&, const Tree&);
     Tree(const Tree& t) { p = t.p; ++p->use; }
     ~Tree() { if (--p->use == 0) delete p; }
     Tree& operator=(const Tree& t);
private:
     Node* p;
};
```

The only datum in a `Tree` object is a pointer to a `Node`. The three constructors after the `public` label allow a `Tree` to be built from an integer, or from a string literal (which is really a character pointer) and one or two other `Tree`s.

Two function definitions and one declaration control memory allocation. The first of these is the copy constructor, which tells how to create a `Tree` from another `Tree`. It makes the newly created `Tree` point to the same `Node` as the `Tree` from which it is being created, and increments the use count to account for the fact that there is one more pointer to that `Node` than there was before. The `Tree` destructor just decrements the use count in the `Node` associated with the `Tree` being destroyed and frees the `Node` if the use count becomes zero. Although this particular program never assigns one `Tree` to another, the assignment operator is declared here for completeness. Its definition is deferred for later.

Using the `<<` output operator on a `Tree` calls the `print` function of the corresponding `Node`. The `print` function is `virtual`, so the call is dynamically bound:

```
ostream&
operator<<(ostream& o, const Tree& t)
{
    t.p->print(o); // virtual call
    return o;
}
```

7.5.3.3. Deriving Classes from Node

So far, `Node`s aren't good for much because they contain no data. Indeed, because a `Node` is an abstract base class, we cannot actually create objects of that class. So we have no choice to to derive classes from `Node`.

The first class we will derive is one that represents integers:

```
class IntNode: public Node {
    friend class Tree;
private:
    int n;
    IntNode (int k): n (k) { }
    void print (ostream& o) const { o << n; }
};
```

Strictly speaking, the `private` label is unnecessary because the members will be private anyway. The point is to ensure that ordinary users will not be able to create `IntNode` objects, because those objects are intended to be used only as part of the implementation of class `Tree`. For the same reason, we nominate class `Tree` as a friend.

Similarly, we define classes to represent unary and binary operators:

```
class UnaryNode: public Node {
    friend class Tree;
```

```
private:
    const char* op;
    Tree opnd;
    UnaryNode (const char* a, const Tree& b): op (a), opnd (b) { }
    void print (ostream& o) const
    {
        o << "(" << op << opnd << ")";
    }
};

class BinaryNode: public Node {
    friend class Tree;
private:
    const char* op;
    Tree left;
    Tree right;
    BinaryNode (const char* a, const Tree& b, const Tree& c):
        op (a), left (b), right (c) { }
    void print (ostream& o) const {
        o << "(" << left << op << right << ")";
    }
};
```

Each of these classes is a kind of `Node` that contains some extra information and has its own constructor and `print` function. Each class nominates `Tree` as a friend so that the `Tree` constructors can call the constructors for the corresponding types of nodes.

7.5.3.4. Constructing `Tree` Constructors

Here are the definitions of the `Tree` constructors:

```
Tree::Tree(int n): p(new IntNode(n)) { }

Tree::Tree(const char* op, const Tree& t):
    p(new UnaryNode(op, t)) { }

Tree::Tree(const char* op, const Tree& left, const Tree& right):
    p(new BinaryNode (op, left, right)) { }
```

The first of these constructors tells how to build a `Tree` from an `int`, which allows an `int` argument to be passed to a `Tree` parameter. Thus

```
Tree t = Tree("*", Tree("-", 5), Tree("+", 3, 4));
```

means the same thing as

```
Tree t = Tree("*",
    Tree("-", Tree(5)),
    Tree("+", Tree(3), Tree(4)));
```

but the former is easier to understand than the latter.

Each constructor uses `new` to allocate, in dynamic memory, an appropriate object of a class that is derived from `Node`, and stores the address of that object in the `Tree` it is constructing. The `Node` constructor automatically ensures that the use count starts out at `1`.

7.5.3.5. How the Data Structures Work

Consider what happens when the `main` program above executes the subexpression `cout << t`. Variable `t` is a `Tree`, so this subexpression calls

```
operator<<(ostream&, const Tree&)
```

which in turn extracts `t.p`. This is a pointer to a `Node` of some type—which type is not known until execution. When that pointer is used to call `t->print`, the type of node determines during execution which `print` function will be called.

Similarly, when it comes time to delete a `Node`, the destructor is virtual. Thus each of the `delete p;` statements in the `Tree` definition determines during execution what kind of `Node` is being deleted so that its constituent `Trees` can be (recursively) deleted.

The C++ compiler can check types in this program during compilation, despite the dynamic binding, because each use of dynamic binding is restricted to a single inheritance hierarchy. In practice, this restriction results in catching many errors during compilation that would otherwise go undetected until execution. The restriction also makes it possible for run-time selection to be extremely fast; in most applications the overhead for virtual functions is unmeasurably small.

We said earlier that dynamic binding makes it possible to add new kinds of nodes without changing all the code that uses nodes. Here's an example.

Suppose we want to add a `TernaryNode` to represent ternary operators such as `?:` (the if-then-else operator). First we declare `TernaryNode`:

```
class TernaryNode: public Node {
     friend class Tree;
private:
     const char* op;
     Tree left;
     Tree middle;
     Tree right;
     TernaryNode(const char* a, const Tree& b,
          const Tree& c, const Tree& d):
               op (a), left (b), middle (c), right (d) { }
     void print(ostream& o) const {
          o << op << "(" << left << "," <<
               middle << "," << right << ")";
     }
};
```

This declaration is similar to the declaration of `BinaryNode` and, in fact, started as a copy of it. Next we define a `Tree` constructor for a `TernaryNode`:

```
Tree::Tree(const char* op,
     const Tree& left, const Tree& middle, const Tree& right)
{
     p = new TernaryNode(op, left, middle, right);
}
```

We insert a declaration for this constructor into the class definition for `Tree`:

```
class Tree {
     friend class Node;
     friend ostream& operator<<(ostream&, const Tree&);
public:
     Tree(int);
     Tree(const char*, const Tree&);
     Tree(const char*, const Tree&, const Tree&);
     Tree(const char*, const Tree, const Tree&, const Tree&); // new
     Tree(const Tree& t) { p = t.p; ++p->use; }
     ~Tree() { if (—p->use == 0) delete p; }
     Tree& operator=(const Tree& t);
private:
     Node* p;
};
```

and we are done!

7.5.3.6. Assignment

Although we did not use `Tree` assignment in this example, we should define it anyway. Here is one way to do it:

```
Tree& Tree::operator=(const Tree& t)
{
     ++t.p->use;
     if (--p->use == 0)
          delete p;
     p = t.p;
     return *this;
}
```

Whenever we define an assignment operator, it is essential to be sure that the right thing happens when we assign an object to itself. In this case, the definition works because we are careful to increment `t.p->use` before we decrement `p->use` (which is equivalent to `this->p->use`). The reason is that if `this` points to the same object as the one to which `p` refers, incrementing `t.p->use` will ensure that `p->use` cannot be zero after it was decremented, so the object we are assigning is not going to be deleted while we are still using it.

7.6. The Standard Library

C++ comes with an extensive library—so extensive that there is not room here to describe it in detail. However, after acquiring a thorough knowledge of the base language, it is not hard to understand the library. The library does, however, rely on a few subtle concepts, so we will describe those concepts here.

What is the point of a standard library? It is impossible for a library to provide everything that every programmer might want, so a library must restrict its goals. In the case of C++, the main ideas are to offer facilities with the property that

- They cannot be expressed directly in the core language—such as input/output.
- They are otherwise reimplemented in virtually every application—such as variable-length character strings.
- Although they could be implemented in the language, they can be implemented more efficiently if the compiler knows how they are defined—such as the square root function.
- By being built on a single conceptual framework, they encourage users to use that same framework in their own programs—such as containers and algorithms.

Of course, the C++ library does not include every facility that meets one of these requirements, but most of the library is motivated by one or more of them.

Every part of the library has an associated header, which makes the relevant part of the library available to the user in namespace `std`. So, for example, if we want to use the I/O library, we must say

```
#include <iostream>
```

in each translation unit that uses it. There is no actual requirement that there be a file of source text that corresponds to `iostream`, but it is easiest to think of `iostream` as being a file that declares appropriate facilities and makes their definitions available to the compiler.

Because the library ordinarily lives in namespace `std`, it is necessary to say somehow that the program intends to use names from that namespace. So, for example, it is not sufficient to say

```
#include <iostream>
int main()
{
    cout << "Hello, world" << endl; // Wrong!
}
```

because there is no clue that `cout` is really `std::cout` and not some other variable named `cout`.

It is easy to make all the names from the standard library available by saying

```
using namespace std;
```

after including the relevant header files. Our example program could therefore be corrected either by saying

```
#include <iostream>
main()
{
     std::cout << "Hello, world!" << std::endl;
}
```

or

```
#include <iostream>
using namespace std;
main()
{
     cout << "Hello, world!" << endl;
}
```

In this chapter, we have consistently assumed that the programmer did the latter of these, and we shall continue to do so throughout this section. Moreover, we will not clutter up the exposition by naming the appropriate headers to use in each example, because the presentation is enough of an overview that we expect programmers to have to consult a more detailed description of the library in order to use it anyway. This section aims to introduce enough of the main ideas behind the library to make it possible to use a detailed library description without becoming hopelessly lost.

7.6.1. Input/Output

C++ actually has two I/O libraries: It inherited one of them from C, and acquired a new one along the way. Both libraries are part of the C++ standard, but the native C++ library is generally recommended over the C library.

The main reason to write a new library is extensibility. The most commonly used function in the C library is `printf`, which relies on a language facility that is used for almost no other purpose: the ability to define functions that take variable numbers of arguments. For example, using the C library, we might say

```
printf("The square root of 2 is %g\n", sqrt(2.0));
```

The first argument to `printf` is a string literal (or, more precisely, a pointer to the initial character of a null-terminated array of characters) that describes what `printf` is to print. Characters other than `%` stand for themselves; a `%` introduces a format specifier that corresponds to one or more of the succeeding arguments to `printf` and also says how those arguments are to affect the output. So, for example, `%g` means "take a `double` value from the argument list and print it in the most general form for floating-point values."

The form that `printf` uses is concise and easy to understand. However, it has three significant disadvantages:

- It is difficult to see how to extend the `printf` strategy to deal with objects of other types. Even if `printf` were extended with the ability to install additional format characters, it would still be necessary for authors of distinct types to coordinate the format characters they chose to use.
- There is no way for the compiler to verify that the values being printed have types that are compatible with the format string. It is possible, in principle, for the compiler to check the types against the format string if the format string is a literal, but the format string could be computed during execution.
- The decision about what types to print is based on the contents of the format string, which means that type decisions are being made during execution. At least in principle, it must be faster to make such decisions during compilation.

The native C++ I/O library uses overloading to deal with all these problems. The library class `ostream` has overloaded `operator<<` members for all the fundamental types, and the `istream` class has similarly overloaded `operator>>` members for input. Moreover, additional library classes, such as strings and complex numbers, define their own overloaded `operator<<` and `operator>>` functions as appropriate. Operator overloading therefore makes it possible for authors of other library classes to define I/O for those classes without interfering with each other.

The I/O library is so large that few people will ever use more than a small part of it. The most important classes are certainly `istream` and `ostream`, which represent input and output files respectively. From each of those classes is then derived a family of classes that represent particular kinds of files. For example, class `ifstream` is derived from class `istream` to represent an input file that is identified by its name. If, for example, we have a file named `foo`, we can prepare to read that file by creating an appropriate `ifstream` object:

```
ifstream ourfile("foo");
```

After that, saying

```
ourfile >> x;
```

will read a value from the file `foo` into `x`; the exact way in which it does so will depend on the type of `x`. The destructor for class `ifstream` will automatically release any resources that were acquired when we created `ourfile`, so it is generally not necessary to close files explicitly.

At the beginning of this article, we saw two manipulators called `setw` and `endl`. There are many more manipulators, all of which are based on a common idea. A manipulator is nothing more than a function that can act on an I/O stream. So, for example, `endl` is really a function defined along the following lines:

```
ostream& endl(ostream& o)
{
     // start a new line on output stream o
     // flush the output stream o
     return o;
}
```

The reason it is possible to say

```
cout << endl
```

is that among the definitions of overloaded `<<` in class `ostream` is one that accepts a (pointer to a) function. It "prints" that function by calling the function with the stream itself as its argument. In effect, we have

```
class ostream {
public:
     // ...
     ostream& operator<<(ostream& func(ostream&)) {
          return func(*this);
     }
     // ...
};
```

The effect of this is that saying

```
cout << endl
```

is equivalent to saying

```
endl(cout)
```

A function such as this version of `operator<<` is called an applicator because it applies its argument to the file it represents. The library has a large variety of manipulators that control various aspects of formatting.

This entire discussion of the I/O library is oversimplified in at least one important respect: All the I/O library functions are really templates so that they can work on different kinds of characters. So, for example, the name `ostream` is really an abbreviation for `basic_ostream<char>`. Similarly, the name `wostream` is an abbreviation for `basic_ostream<wchar_t>`, and if a system has some complicated notion of characters that includes font, size, and other magic, it should be possible to use the standard I/O library with those characters too.

Of course, not all I/O must be done with `<<` and `>>`; those operators are intended purely for human-readable I/O. The library also provides a wide selection of functions for doing I/O a character at a time, a line at a time, or in other units.

7.6.2. Strings

Strings are part of the standard library because otherwise every project would have its own way of defining them. Like the I/O library, the string library is really based on templates, so that the name `string` is really an abbreviation of `basic_string<char>`. The string library is mostly straightforward. Strings can vary in length, with the memory for them being dynamically allocated. It is fairly common to construct a string from a null-terminated character array, and there are several ways to pick the individual characters out of a string once the string has been constructed.

Operations on strings include assignment, concatenation, comparison, and assorted operations for finding characters within strings that have particular properties. For example, there is a fast operation to find the first character in a string that is also a character of some other string.

As a small example, here is a function that takes a string `s` and an unsigned integer `n` and replicates the string `n` times:

```
string repeat(const string& s, unsigned n)
{
    string result;
    while (n) {
            result += s;
            --n;
    }
    return result;
}
```

This function is remarkable in that it is unremarkable: The only part of it that might not be obvious is the use of `+=` for concatenation. By analogy with numbers,

```
result += s
```

is equivalent to

```
result = result + s
```

except that `result` is evaluated only once. This distinction is important here for efficiency reasons: If the library knows that the program is intending to concatenate `s` onto the end of `result`, it will be able to so do much more efficiently than if it had to form a brand new string to hold `result + s` and then copy that string into `result`.

If we are at all concerned about efficiency, however, there is one more thing we should do: After saying

```
string result;
```

we should say

```
result.reserve(s.size() * n);
```

This causes the library to preallocate enough memory for the `result` object to hold all the characters in the result. As far as the actual value of `result` goes, this call to `reserve` makes no difference. But by preallocating the memory, `reserve` guarantees that the successive calls to `+=` will not cause reallocation of the entire `result` string. The preallocation might therefore make the difference between a linear and a quadratic algorithm.

7.6.3. Numerics

C++ has an assortment of library functions, such as `sin`, `cos`, and `sqrt`, that are inherited from C. These functions are part of the library because it is hard to implement them both portably and efficiently. Moreover, if the compiler knows something about the standard library, it can detect when programs are using these functions and generate appropriate machine instructions directly.

In addition, C++ has two families of classes that are intended for more general numeric computation. One handles complex arithmetic; the other handles arrays in a style that can be efficiently implemented on supercomputers.

Complex arithmetic is not built into C++. Instead, there is a library template class `complex` that is instantiated with the appropriate element type. Thus we can refer to `complex<float>`, `complex<double>`, and so on.

Having complex arithmetic as part of the library is almost as convenient as it would be if complex arithmetic were built into the language. The main disadvantage is that there is no special form for complex constants. However, it is possible to write expressions such as `complex<double>(3, 4)`, which are not particularly inconvenient.

The numeric array class `valarray` is intended for high-performance numeric applications, particularly in the presence of optimizing compilers for special-purpose hardware. The idea is to restrict the operations on such arrays so that compilers can make plausible assumptions about how they will be used, and also to offer commonly used numeric array operations that might not generalize well to arrays of other types.

For example, if we say

```
valarray<double> v1, v2, v3;
```

and then subsequently give appropriate values to `v1` and `v2`, then

```
v3 = v1 + v2;
```

will add the corresponding elements of `v1` and `v2` and store each element of the result in `v3`.

The `valarray` classes offer only one-dimensional arrays. However, they have auxiliary classes that are intended to make it both easy and efficient to simulate the appearance of multidimensional arrays. For example, one of these auxiliary classes is called `slice`; among its constructors is one that takes three integers representing an initial value, a count, and a distance. The idea is that a slice represents a sequence of equally spaced elements within an array, which might be used to represent (part of) a row, column, or diagonal.

For example, suppose we have a `valarray` with 100 elements:

```
valarray<double> v(100);
```

Then we can view it as a one-dimensional array with 100 elements, but we can also view it as a matrix with ten rows and ten columns.

If we view `v` as a matrix, then the first row comprises elements 0, 1, ..., 9. We can use `v[slice(0, 10, 1)]` to refer to the elements of that row. Here `0` is the index of the initial element, `10` is the number of elements, and `1` is the distance between consecutive elements.

The first column of the matrix has elements 0, 10, 20, ..., 90; we can refer to that column as `v[slice(0, 10, 10)]`. More generally, we can use `v[slice(n, 10, 1)]` to refer to the nth row and `v[slice(n, 10, 10)]` to refer to the nth column. We can even refer to the two main diagonals as `v[slice(0, 10, 11)]` and `v[slice(9, 10, 9)]`.

If you are a numerical analyst, this description has probably whetted your appetite; in which case you are invited to refer to a more detailed description of the library.

7.6.4. Containers

There is no single best way to store a collection of related data, so the C++ library offers several choices. All of these choices are made available as templates that define types that hold values. So, for example, we can define an object of type `vector<int>`. If we do so, that object will contain a vector of integer values. We emphasize the notion of value here because putting something into a container copies it, and taking it out copies it again. In order to put objects into a container while preserving their identities, you should store pointers to the objects instead.

There are two kinds of containers in the standard library: sequential containers and associative containers. Although these containers are not related by inheritance, the containers of each kind have several operations in common with each other. We do not have room to enumerate all the container operations, but we can give an idea of the most important properties of the containers.

7.6.4.1. Sequential Containers

The sequential containers are `vector`, `list`, and `deque` (which stands for *double-ended queue*). All of them support the ability to append elements at the end of the sequence and remove them again efficiently. However, their capabilities vary beyond that.

For example, as its name suggests, a vector will typically store its elements in contiguous memory. This makes it possible to access the elements in random order, if necessary, but makes it somewhat more difficult to append elements efficiently.

The `list` class is intended to be an idealization of a doubly linked list. Accordingly, it is possible to insert elements efficiently into a list, not only at the end, but also at the beginning and between any pair of adjacent elements.

The deque class is more like a vector than like a list. The main difference between a vector and a deque is that the deque supports efficient insertion at either end, not just at one end.

As a simple example, we can create a vector that contains the squares of the integers from 0 through 99 as follows:

```
vector<int> squares(100);

for (int i = 0; i < 100; ++i)
    squares[i] = i * i;
```

This example, however, does not take advantage of the sequential nature of vectors. Instead, it preallocates memory and uses random-access indexing for something that could be done more directly. If we wanted to use vectors sequentially, we might write:

```
vector<int> squares;

for (int i = 0; i < 100; ++i)
    squares.push_back(i * i);
```

This version has the advantage that we now do not need to precompute how many elements the vector will have. However, it is somewhat slower than the first version because the library will have to reallocate the memory that the vector occupies several times.

We can avoid reallocation by giving the vector a hint about how much memory to occupy:

```
vector<int> squares;

squares.reserve(100);
for (int i = 0; i < 100; ++i)
    squares.push_back(i * i);
```

The call to reserve tells the library to allocate at least enough memory for 100 elements.

One advantage of using vectors sequentially is that the same code will work for lists:

```
list<int> squares;

for (int i = 0; i < 100; ++i)
    squares.push_back(i * i);
```

Now, however, there is no reason to reserve space in advance. Moreover, if we wanted, we could have used push_front to push the squares onto the beginning of the list (which would have reversed their order). We could have used a deque the same way.

7.6.4.2. Associative Containers

Associative containers keep their elements sorted, which makes it easy to determine quickly whether a particular element is in the container. Indeed, there are operations that do more than that, such as determining the first element that is greater than a particular value, less than a particular value, and so on.

Of course, this property carries with it the requirement that the elements in the container must have `<` appropriately defined on them. Most of the fundamental types have appropriate definitions of `<`; users who define their own types must define `<` themselves if they wish objects of those types to be held by associative containers.

The two main associative containers are `set` and `map`. A `set` is just that; any particular value appears in a `set` only once, and there are efficient operations to test if particular values are there, combine sets in various ways, and so on.

We have already seen the `map` class; we can think of a `map` as a set of key-value pairs, sorted by key, with the requirement that all the keys be distinct. Indeed, the library provides a template called `pair`, and it is possible to treat a `map<K, V>` object as a sequence of `pair<const K, V>` values.

In addition to `set` and `map`, there are `multiset` and `multimap`. The difference between the multi- and the other versions is that they allow multiple elements with the same value.

It should be easy to see why a `multimap` is useful. For example, we might keep track of student registration with a `multimap<Student, Course>` object. Such an object would store student-course pairs, so if a student was enrolled in `n` courses, there would be `n` distinct pairs for that student.

It is less obvious why a `multiset` should be useful. What does a `multiset<T>` buy us that a `map<T, int>` doesn't? We could, after all, associate a count with each `T` value; that count would represent "how many times" the value appears in the multiset.

It turns out, however, that there is an important distinction: Values that are equal might not be identical. For example, some operating systems do not distinguish between files that are equal except for the case of the letters in their names. On such an operating system, `FOO` and `foo` would be two names for the same file. If we were writing programs to run under such an operating system, we might want to define a class that represents file names. Such a class might plausibly have the property that two file names are equal even though the characters that constitute them are not.

In such a case, it might be important to keep track of several different files that are equal, and yet to remember that they had distinct names for printing purposes. A `multiset` would be just the type to do this.

7.6.4.3. Compound Containers

In addition to the sequential and associative containers, there are a few templates that can be used to build containers from other containers. For example, there is not a single `stack` class. Instead, there is a `stack` template that can use either a `vector`, a `list`, or a `deque` to implement the stack. Similarly, there is a `queue` container that works on top of some other container.

It is not necessary for these compound containers to built on top of standard containers; user-defined container classes can also be used as the basis for a `stack` or a `queue`, provided only that the user-defined containers have the right properties. Those properties are documented as part of the library specification.

7.6.5. Iterators

We have already noted that the various sequential containers have several properties in common. This suggests that it is desirable to be able to write programs that take advantage only of those properties, without direct knowledge of the types of containers they are using. The C++ library encapsulates knowledge of such properties into iterators. Loosely speaking, an iterator is an object of a type (or, sometimes, the type itself) that supports a set of operations that allow it to be used to mark a place in a container. More specifically, it is an object that acts enough like a pointer to make it possible to pretend it is a pointer.

The library recognizes five kinds of iterators. The two simplest, and most common, are input iterators and output iterators. If `p` is an input iterator, then `*p`, `p++`, `++p`, and `p->member` must have their usual meanings. Moreover, if `p` and `q` are input iterators, `p==q` must be true if and only if `p` and `q` refer to the same place in the input sequence.

Output iterators are similar to input iterators except for the meaning of `*p`. If `p` is an output iterator, `*p` can be used only on the left side of an assignment. Moreover, each distinct value of `p` must have `*p` used on the left of an assignment exactly once.

An example of an algorithm that uses input and output iterators is `copy`:

```
template<class In, class Out>
Out copy(In begin, In end, Out result)
{
    while (begin != end)
          *result++ = *begin++;
    return result;
}
```

This algorithm relies only on the properties of input and output iterators. It is clear that it can be used to copy elements of (built-in) arrays:

```
int x[100], y[100];
// ...
copy(x, x+100, y);
```

Recall that because `x` and `y` are arrays, uttering their names yields the addresses of their initial elements. Therefore, `x+100` is the address of one past the last element of the array `x`. The `copy` algorithm uses these pointers to copy the elements of the array `x` into `y`.

What is nice about this `copy` algorithm, though, is that it works with the library containers also. Among the operations supported by the sequential containers are `begin` and `end`, which yield appropriate iterators that refer to the first and one past the last elements of the container, and `back_inserter`, which is a nonmember function that yields an output iterator that can be used to append new elements at the back of the container. Therefore, if we wanted to copy the elements of `x` into a `vector` called `v`, we might say

```
vector<int> v;
copy(x, x+100, back_inserter(v));
```

and to copy the elements of `v` back into `x`, we might say

```
copy(v.begin(), v.end(), x);
```

and hope that `x` had enough elements to contain it.

Another interesting source of iterators in the library is the templates `istream_iterator` and `ostream_iterator`. They take input and output files and yield iterators that read from or write to the files. As a simple example, we can print all the elements of `v` by executing

```
copy(v.begin(), v.end(), ostream_iterator<int>(cout, "\n"));
```

Here, the call to `ostream_iterator<int>` constructs an object that acts like an output iterator; each time we dereference, assign, and increment that object, it writes the value assigned onto `cout` followed by a newline (the second argument to `ostream_iterator`).

If an iterator is capable of acting as an input iterator and an output iterator at the same time, we call it a *forward iterator*. We can think of a forward iterator as an idealization of a singly-linked list, or of any sequence that permits reading and writing but not backspacing. An example of an algorithm that requires a forward iterator is `replace`:

```
template<class Iter, class X>
void replace(Iter begin, Iter end, const X& x, const X& y)
{
    while (begin != end) {
        if (*begin == x)
            *begin = y;
        ++begin;
    }
}
```

This algorithm examines the elements of a sequence described by its first two arguments, replacing any element that is equal to the third argument by the fourth argument. So, for example, if we have a list of strings, we can replace any null strings by the string `(null)`:

```
list<string> ls;
// ...
replace(ls.begin(), ls.end(), "", "(null)");
```

Note that this algorithm works on lists in exactly the same way that it works on arrays; the iterators are different types, but the compiler takes that into account during template instantiation.

An iterator that has all the forward-iterator properties and also supports `--` is called a *reverse iterator*. Reverse iterators capture the idea of a doubly linked list; the `reverse` function that we saw earlier is an example of a standard library algorithm that takes advantage of reverse-iterator properties.

Finally, an iterator that has all the reverse-iterator properties and also supports arithmetic and subscripting the same way pointers do is called a *random-access iterator*. Among the algorithms that requires a random-access iterator is binary search.

Although iterators are related to each other in a way that suggests inheritance, that inheritance is entirely conceptual and not part of the language. In particular, pointers to ordinary array elements have all the random-access iterator properties, yet although pointers are iterators, they cannot participate in inheritance. The notion of the five kinds of iterators is part of the intellectual framework that the library provides; this framework allows users to write new containers or new algorithms and have them work with the containers and algorithms that already exist.

7.6.6. Algorithms

Many of the algorithms in the library are seemingly simple; yet they can do quite a bit in combination. We have already seen a few; although there are more of them than we can cover in detail, we can still summarize them.

The simplest algorithms deal with sequences without modifying them. These include linear searches, counting algorithms, comparisons, and subsequence searches. Among the most common of these algorithms is `find`:

```
template <class In, class X>
In find(In begin, In end, const X& x)
{
     while (begin != end && *begin != x)
          ++begin;
     return begin;
}
```

This algorithm is typical in several ways. It takes a pair of iterators to delimit the beginning and end of the sequence to be searched, which makes it easy to search subsequences of a container. It returns an iterator that refers to the element sought. If it does not find an element, it returns the one-past-the-end iterator `end` rather than trying to construct a unique iterator value. Most of the algorithms share one or more of these properties.

Other algorithms modify, or potentially modify, the sequences they use. They include copying, reversing, swapping, and other transformations such as `replace`. Finally, there are algorithms that are less easy to characterize. They include sorting, merging, heap manipulation, partitioning, and shuffling and other permutation algorithms.

7.6.7. Adaptors

In addition to the iterators and algorithms, the library provides an assortment of adaptors, which can build containers and iterators out of other containers and iterators. For example, there is a `reverse_iterator` template that, given a bidirectional iterator, yields a new bidirectional iterator that accesses the same sequence as the original iterator but in the opposite direction. This template makes it unnecessary to have separate find first and find last operations; instead, one can find the last element in a sequence with a given property by find the first element in the sequence obtained by reversing the iterators. Other adaptors offer convenient ways of constructing function objects, which are object that act like functions.

All these details should not be allowed to obscure the most important aspects of the container library:

- The standard containers provide reasonably efficient implementations of the most useful data structures, with interfaces that use similar means when they offer similar facilities.
- Iterators provide standard ways of accessing idealized containers. Each of the standard containers provides appropriate iterator types that allow these containers to be accessed efficiently in those standard ways.
- Most of the algorithms are written in terms of the properties of the iterators, not the individual containers.

This strategy implies that if there are M containers and N algorithms, the total complexity of the library is M+N instead of M×N. In effect, the iterators provide an intellectual framework for designing and extending the library that may prove to be more important than the detailed design of the library itself.

7.7. Summary

C++ is neither the smallest nor the most elegant programming language around. Why, then, bother with C++ at all?

The main reason is that even if C++ is not the best possible language for every application, it is a single language that does a wide variety of things well—more than well enough to be useful. It is possible to imagine building a system with one language for the low-level parts, another for the object-oriented parts, and still another to determine the overall structure, but C++ is a single language that can handle an entire system.

This ability to solve a wide range of problems did not arise by accident. Rather, it was the result of listening to actual users. C++ had an active, geographically dispersed user community remarkably early in its evolution. Many parts of C++ are the way they are because several different people, when using early versions, found that those versions lacked support for particular problems that they needed to solve. In that sense, the growth of C++ has been more organic than is common for programming languages.

This article has viewed C++ as comprising five major parts:

- The low-level facilities, on which all else depends;
- Classes, which permit programs that use abstract data types;

- Templates, which permit programmers to ignore the types of the objects they use until they compile their programs;
- Virtual functions, which support object-oriented programming and allow programs to defer knowledge of the types of objects until they use them while the program is running; and
- The library, which codifies common ways of using the language and offers an intellectual framework for extensions.

It would be a mistake to think that each of these parts of the language is suited only to particular kinds of problems. Rather, they offer the possibility of programming in a wide variety of styles, which, in turn, makes it possible to choose a style that is appropriate to the application.

7.8. Recommended Reading

The definitive work on C++ is, of course, Bjarne Stroustrup's *The C++ programming language* (3rd edition, Addison-Wesley, 1997). It covers the entire language, and library, in enough detail that a more detailed reference will often be unnecessary.

If a more detailed reference does turn out to be necessary, the ISO Standard (expected in 1998) is the place to look. Although not always easy to understand, the Standard is the definition of C++.

People who want a more leisurely tutorial introduction to C++ may wish to try Stanley Lippman's and Josée Lajoie *C++ Primer* (Addison-Wesley, 1998). Lippman has also written a book called *Inside the C++ object model* (Addison-Wesley, 1996), which is intended for programmers who want to understand in detail how to implement the language at the machine level.

For a deeper understanding of why the language is the way it is, consider Stroustrup's *Design and evolution of* C++ (Addison-Wesley, 1994). To learn more about how to solve problems in C++, read *Ruminations on* C++ by Andrew Koenig and Barbara E. Moo (Addison-Wesley, 1997). Marshall Cline offers a completely different way of understanding C++, by answering a wide variety of common questions in his *C++ FAQs* book (Addison-Wesley, 1995).

Finally, programmers who are building systems in C++ will want to understand the strategies described in *Design patterns* by Gamma, Helm, Johnson, and Vlissides (Addison-Wesley, 1995), and related programming techniques in Jim Coplien's *Advanced C++ styles and idioms* (Addison-Wesley, 1992).

7.9. References

Aho, A. V., B. W. Kernighan, and P. J. Weinberger. 1988. *The Awk programming language*. Reading, MA: Addison-Wesley.

Koenig, A., and B. E. Moo. 1997. 1997. *Ruminations on* C++. Reading, MA: Addison-Wesley.

7.10. Acknowledgments

Thanks to Jeffrey Oldham and Bjarne Stroustrup for reviewing drafts of this article.

CHAPTER 8

C++ Traps and Pitfalls

by Andrew Koenig

8.1. Why Programmers Get in Trouble

This chapter describes ways in which C++ programmers are likely to go wrong. It assumes a knowledge of C++, and therefore of C, but it concentrates on problems that C++ programmers encounter and C programmers do not.

How do programmers get in trouble? Typically, a programmer writes a program, expecting it to behave in a particular way, only to find that it does something else. Except for compiler bugs, which are relatively rare, such program misbehavior ultimately comes from programmer misunderstanding. The program did what the programmer asked, but what the programmer asked is not what the programmer wanted.

As an analogy, imagine a hiking trail with natural hazards. If those hazards occur in obvious places, hikers avoid them. If not, the hazards may injure people. We might be able to remove some of the hazards, but removing others might change the whole character of the trail. If we cannot remove a hazard, we can still make the trail less dangerous by warning people about where the hazards are. The deliberately vague phrase "traps and pitfalls" suggests such a trail.

On the surface, the mere existence of this chapter might be surprising. If it is possible to predict how people are likely to misunderstand C++, why was C++ not designed to match people's expectations in the first place and thereby avoid misunderstandings? A deeper look, however, reveals that all programming tools inevitably have pitfalls.

One reason that pitfalls are inevitable is that different people have different expectations. For example, consider the viewpoints implied by the questions, "If the compiler knows that I'm doing something wrong, why doesn't it do the right thing automatically?" and "Why can't the compiler do exactly what I say so that I know what is going on?" Any effort to fix the pitfalls that one of these questioners encounters is likely to cause trouble for the other one. Such differences of opinion are particularly prominent in large, diverse user communities.

Another reason for pitfalls is that people's expectations change as they gain experience. Catering to people's expectations changing as they learn is like putting training wheels on bicycles. At some point in most of our childhoods, we learn how to keep a bicycle upright, and we can put away the training wheels. Just as it does not always make sense to sell bicycles with training wheels already installed, it does not always make sense to design a programming language to cater to beginners in preference to experts.

A third reason that pitfalls are inevitable is that every useful language has users, and every user community has inertia. Users are accustomed to solving particular problems in a particular way. When new facilities enter the language, there is pressure to fit them into the same conceptual model as the facilities that already exist and to retain those existing facilities to let programmers continue to work in familiar ways. Once a part of a language is established, it is difficult to go back and change it later.

As an example of linguistic inertia, consider how hard it is to talk in English about a person without revealing that person's gender. This difficulty is not unique to English, but neither is it universal. In French, for example, the gender of possessive pronouns is the gender of what is possessed, rather than the gender of the person possessing it. Few English speakers believe that it is an advantage for them to be forced to ascribe genders to unknown people, and it is sometimes clearly a substantial disadvantage to have to do so. It would be easy enough to solve this problem with the English language completely by agreeing on a few new pronouns that carry no gender implications, so why does English still have the problem? Inertia.

A fourth reason that pitfalls are inevitable is that a programming language is usually a compromise among several conflicting goals. For example, one purpose of C++ is to express programs that run efficiently with a minimum of special-purpose operating-system support. This purpose argues for a small interface between the language and the operating system. The desire for portability and operating-system independence is another argument for keeping the interface between C++ and the operating system small. Yet some entirely plausible applications of C++ undoubtedly need to rely on specific features of a specific operating system, such as threads or shared memory, and those applications would be easier to write if the language included direct support for those features—even at the cost of allowing the language to work only with operating systems that support those features. It is hard to imagine how to cater to such conflicting goals without creating problems somewhere.

Fortunately, people are usually good at learning how to avoid hazards, especially if there is someone around to show them where the hazards are. Hikers learn how to avoid injury, authors learn how to write gender-independent English prose, and programmers learn which approaches are likely to get them into trouble and which ones are likely to avoid it.

8.1.1. Two Sources of Pitfalls

There are typically two main reasons why programmers expect programs to behave differently from the way they actually behave.

One reason is a mistaken assumption. A programmer looks at part of a program and makes an obvious guess about how it works—but the guess is wrong. For example, a programmer coming to C++ from Fortran might assume that the last element of an *n*-element array has index *n*. That assumption is wrong because C++ arrays start from zero. The last element of an *n*-element array therefore has index *n*-1.

The other reason for incorrect expectations is that some parts of a system are just plain complicated, and a programmer who has not learned those parts of the system thoroughly will make mistakes. For example, most programmers realize that floating-point numbers are not completely accurate, but they do not understand all the implications of working with approximate numbers. This incomplete understanding is often harmless, but it can result in programs that fail in subtle ways—in any language.

As a result, the problems that this chapter describes are typically either simple or complicated with few problems between the extremes.

8.1.2. The Relationship Between C++ and C

With one exception, this chapter discusses only pitfalls that are in C++ and not also in C. The reasons is that in 1988, I wrote a book called

C Traps and Pitfalls (Koenig, 1989) that summarized what I had learned until then about C pitfalls. Its coverage includes

- Purely syntactic pitfalls, such as writing `=` (assignment) instead of `==` (comparison).
- Why C counts from zero instead of from one, along with a description of how to use C's counting style to avoid fencepost errors.
- Declaration syntax, a common source of misunderstandings in C, especially including functions whose arguments or return values are functions.
- The subtle relationship between pointers and arrays, including multidimensional arrays.
- What happens when two parts of a program, compiled separately, say conflicting things about the type of a global object.
- The preprocessor, because of which the programs we write are not the programs we run.
- How C implementations differ from one another, even in matters as simple as arithmetic.

Although most C pitfalls appear in C++ as well, they are less important in C++ than they are in C. The reason is that C++ makes it easier to define classes that represent high-level abstractions; these abstractions often make it possible to avoid the C pitfalls entirely. For example, the standard C++ library provides a flexible vector class that avoids many of the pitfalls associated with C arrays, and inline functions in C++ make the C preprocessor, with its attendant pitfalls, much less important.

The one C pitfall that this chapter discusses is the notion of `const` as part of a type. At the time that *C Traps and Pitfalls* was published, the C standardization effort, already under way, had incorporated the idea of `const` into C from C++. However, it would be some time before the idea made it into C compilers and thence into widespread practice. There was therefore not enough user experience to know where the pitfalls were. The complexities of using `const` in C++ declarations therefore appear in this chapter, even though most of those complexities are present in C as well.

8.1.3. Synopsis

The point of this chapter is to give a programmer who already understands how to use C, and how to avoid its pitfalls, a feel for what kinds of hazards are particularly important to learn to avoid in C++. Although such hazards are intrinsically hard to classify, the chapter divides them into three broad categories. The boundary between the second and third category is slightly fuzzy.

The first area is syntax, which I discuss in section 8.2. Which syntactic aspects cause trouble in a language are largely a matter of taste and prior experience. C++ syntax is closely related to C syntax, so C programmers will find many parts of it familiar. Nevertheless, some parts of C++ syntax seem to cause trouble fairly regularly and are definitely worth mentioning.

Section 8.3 covers static semantics, particularly in the area of types. C++ is a compromise between the desire for the safety and efficiency of compile-time type checking and the desire for the flexibility and expressive power of dynamically varying types. Such compromises are bound to cause problems once in a while, and again some of those problems are worth pointing out.

Finally, in section 8.4, we discuss ways in which programs can go astray during execution, despite the programmer's and compiler's efforts to avoid trouble.

This chapter is not intended to be exhaustive. Instead, it presents a few important examples in each area, in an effort to give an understanding of what the problems are, why they exist, and how to learn to avoid them.

8.2. Syntactic Pitfalls

C++ inherits much of its syntax from C. It also inherits C's desire to keep the number of keywords, and other syntactic constructs, relatively small. As a result, C++ programs tend to be syntactically terse, and the language often gives several different meanings to a symbol, depending on the context.

For example, colons are part of labels both in C and in C++. In C++, however, colons are also used to indicate inheritance and to delimit constructor initializers. Moreover, C++ widens the syntactic contexts for labels to include class declarations.

The rest of this section gives examples of C++ syntax that beginners find particularly troublesome.

8.2.1 Lexical Pitfalls

The first problem that many C++ programmers encounter stems from the *maximal munch* strategy of lexical analysis: As the compiler reads characters to form a token, it takes the longest string of characters that could possibly form a token. When multiple tokens are written with no space separating them, the compiler might sometimes take several tokens to be one.

The most common example of this phenomenon is probably in the context of nested templates. For example, the C++ library includes a template class called `vector`. For any type `T` with appropriate properties, the library template gives a definition for `vector<T>`. The `vector` template meets its own requirements, which makes it possible to define vectors of vectors. Such two-level vectors are useful for stimulating two-dimensional matrices, which the library does not directly support.

One would think it possible to define a vector of vectors by writing, for example,

```
vector<vector<int>> matrix;            // wrong
```

Unfortunately, this obvious usage fails. Moreover, some implementations give obscure diagnostic messages that make the problem far from obvious. In this example, the problem is that the compiler takes two immediately adjacent `>` characters to be a shift-right operator, rather than two closing angle brackets. To ensure that the compiler treats the two brackets as brackets, one must say

```
vector<vector<int> > matrix;           // right
```

or, more symmetrically

```
vector< vector<int> > matrix;          // also right
```

The confusion between `>>` and `> >` is common enough that almost every C++ programmer will encounter it. There are other, similar lexical confusions that are so obscure that a programmer can go for an entire career without seeing them:

```
if (x<::sqrt(y))                       // wrong
     cout << "x is too small" << endl;
```

This example runs afoul of the fact that `<:` is an alternative way of spelling `[` in C++, to cater to systems that do not support the `[` character. Again, the solution is to use a space to separate the offending symbols:

```
if (x< ::sqrt(y))                      // right
     cout << "x is too small" << endl;
```

and again, adding another space makes the result more symmetric and possibly more attractive:

```
if (x < ::sqrt(y))                     // also right
     cout << "x is too small" << endl;
```

In both cases, the lesson is the same: Whenever you put two symbols next to each other, without intervening space, there is the possibility that they will combine to form a third symbol. When that happens, the result may be a diagnostic message that appears to have nothing to do with the original mistake. If you know that such mistakes can happen, they are usually easy to find.

8.2.2. Declarations and Specifiers

C++ inherits its declaration syntax from C, and along with that syntax, it inherits the notion of a *declarator*. A declaration normally consists of a type, followed by one or more declarators. Each declarator includes the name of an object and describes the relationship between that object and the given type.

For example, if we write

```
int x;
```

the type is `int` and the declarator is `x`. This declaration says that the object `x` has type `int`. Similarly, if we write

```
int *p;
```

the declarator is `*p`, and the declaration says, in effect, that `*p` has type `int`. By implication, `p` has type "pointer to `int`."

C++ programmers tend to write such declarations as

```
int* p;
```

to make it clearer that `p` has type `int*`. However, this style does not affect the fact that `*p` (or `* p`) is the declarator, not `p`.

Suppose that a C programmer wants to declare both `x` and `p` in a single declaration. The normal way to do that in C is to write

```
int *p, x;                          // *p and x have type int
```

which suggests that `*p` and `x` both have type `int`. However, if we rewrite this declaration in typical C++ style as

```
int* p, x;                          // * p and x have type int
```

the fact that p and x have different types becomes much less obvious. Indeed, even the C usage is marginal in this example; it might have been better to write

```
int (*p), x;
```

or

```
int* p;
int x;
```

either of which would make the programmer's intentions plain.

8.2.3. Where Does the const Go?

The const modifier is used to describe the type of an object whose value is promised not to change. Understanding how const works is easy in straightforward contexts, but there are potential surprises even in the C subset of C++. When C++ extends the notions of C to include constant member functions and pointers to members, one must keep a firm grasp to avoid becoming unstuck.

8.2.3.1. const in Type Specifiers

Introducing const into declarations can make it less obvious where the declarator begins. Let's start with some simple examples:

```
const extern int x;
const int extern x;
int const extern x;
int extern const x;
extern int const x;
extern const int x;
```

All six of these declarations mean the same thing: The object named x is a constant integer that is defined somewhere else (extern). In these examples, the order of the keywords const, extern, and int is immaterial.

Although we can scramble the first three words of this declaration, we can't move x:

```
int extern x const;
```

is illegal.

We know that x is part of the declarator because it is the first word in the declaration that cannot be part of the name of a type. Thus, for example,

```
extern const int a, b, c;
```

has three declarators, namely a, b, and c.

To figure out where the declarators start in a declaration is usually easy: Start at the beginning and skip over as many consecutive type names and keywords as you can. The first thing you reach that is neither a type name nor a keyword is the beginning of the first declarator.

The part of the declaration before the declarators doesn't have a universally common name but is sometimes called the *specifiers*. The specifiers may appear in any order without changing the meaning of a declaration.

8.2.3.2. Constant Pointers and Pointers to Constants

Now let's see how `const` and `*` interact. First, here's a common case:

```
const int* cp;
```

By looking for the first non-type, we see that the specifiers are `const` and `int` and the declarator is `*cp`. That means that we should treat `const int` as a unit, as if `const` modifies `int`. Viewed that way, it should be easy to see that `cp` is a pointer to a constant integer object. Moreover, changing the declaration to

```
int const* cp;
```

does not affect its meaning because the specifiers may be reordered freely.

If we want to say that the pointer itself is constant, we must move the `const` into the declarator:

```
int *const pc = &i;
```

and indeed this declaration requires an initializer because we won't be able to give `pc` a value later. Again applying the rule, we see that the `*` marks the beginning of the declarator, which means that the `const` is now part of the declarator and not part of the specifiers. Here is an example to emphasize this distinction:

```
int i, *const pc = &i;
```

This declaration has two declarators, namely `i` and `*const pc`.

Note that our rule implies that if a declaration has a `*` in it, that `*` is never part of the specifiers. The `*` always says that *something* is a pointer; to say that the pointer is a constant pointer, we always follow the `*` by `const`. In other words, to declare a constant pointer directly, look for a place to say `*const`.

Locating such a place can be confusing because it is possible to use `typedef` to define pointer types that conceal the `*`:

```
typedef int* IP;
```

In this declaration, the specifiers are `typedef` and `int` and the declarator is `*IP`. Once we have it, we can say

```
const IP p = &i;
```

which declares a pointer without using a `*`. What is the type of `p`?

Applying our rule again, we find that the specifiers are `const IP` (because `IP` is a type name) and the declarator is `p`. Therefore, it appears that the `const` modifies `IP` and `p` is therefore a constant pointer. Indeed, that is exactly what happens: It is as if we had written

```
int* const p = &i;
```

Indeed, it might be clearer if we had written

```
IP const p = &i;
```

To confirm your understanding of where the declarator begins, note that in

```
int* const p = &i;
```

the declarator is `* const p`, but in

```
IP const p = &i;
```

the declarator is just `p`.

From the foregoing examples, we learn that in the following example, the types of `cp` and `pc` are different:

```
const IP pc = &i;                    // constant pointer to int
const int* cp = &i;                  // pointer to constant int
```

because `pc` is a constant pointer and `cp` points to a constant. It is very important that you understand this distinction; if you don't, you might want to read this section again until you do.

8.2.3.3. Adding Member Functions and Pointers to Members

All the properties of `const` that we have considered so far are part of the syntax that C adopted from C++. In addition, C++ has the notions of member functions and pointers to members. Fortunately, the way C++ handles these notions fits well with how C does it, so once you've mastered the complexities of C declarations, the C++ rules aren't much harder. Accordingly, the following discussion does not describe a single, obvious source of misconceptions. Rather, the interactions between `const`, type declarations, and pointers to members are rich enough, and can occur in enough contexts, that the rules may not be easy to grasp at first. The main thing to remember while reading the discussion that follows is that these rules exist and can be looked up as needed.

Recall that classes may have constant member functions, which promise not to change the value of their objects:

```
class Thing {
public:
      int get() const;
      void put (int);
};
```

Here we've said that class `Thing` has two member functions called `get` and `put`. If `t` is a `Thing`, then calling `t.put(42)` might change the value of `t`, but calling `t.get()` does not.

Notice that when we declare a constant member function, the `const` goes at the end of the declarator. That now gives us three possible places for `const` to go, so that

```
class X {
public:
      const int* const f() const;
};
```

declares a class with a member function called `f` that returns a pointer to a constant integer (the first `const`) that cannot itself be modified (the second `const`). Moreover, the function promises not to modify its object (the third `const`).

Recall that we can declare pointers to class members:

```
void (Thing::*pp)(int) = &Thing::put;
```

declares `pp` as a variable that can potentially contain a pointer to any member function of class `Thing` that accepts an `int` argument and returns `void`. Of course, there happens to be only one such function in this case, namely `Thing::put`.

Suppose we want to declare a member pointer that could point to `Thing::get`. It might seem obvious that we could do it this way:

```
int (Thing::*gp)() = &Thing::get;    // error
```

but when we try it, we find that it doesn't work. The reason is that we're allowed to call `get` only on behalf of a `const` object:

```
const Thing ct;
int i = ct.get();
```

but if we try to do the same with our member pointer, the compiler stops us:

```
const Thing ct;
int i = (ct.*gp)();                    // error
```

Although `get` promises not to change its object, that promise is not carried along into `gp`. After all, `gp` could potentially point to some other member of `Thing` that might change its object, in which case evaluating `(ct.*gp)()` changes `ct` even though `ct` is not allowed to change. We therefore need some way of declaring a pointer that is like `gp` except that it must be restricted to pointing only at constant member functions.

The way to do that follows the form of the member function declaration itself:

```
int (Thing::*cgp)() const = &Thing::get;
```

Now we can say, for example

```
const Thing ct;
int i = (ct.*cgp)();
```

with no problems.

8.2.3.4. Constant Pointers to Members and Pointers to Constant Members

What if we want to declare a pointer such as `cgp` with the restriction that the pointer itself may not change? With ordinary pointers, we look for a place to say `* const`, so with member pointers, we similarly look for a place to say `::* const`. Knowing that, it is easy to see how to say it:

```
int (Thing:: *const cgpc)() const = &Thing::get;
```

Again, there is no difficulty saying

```
const Thing ct;
int i = (ct.*cgpc)();
```

8.2.3.5. `const` Summary

The first step in understanding a declaration is finding the boundary between the specifiers and the first declarator. The specifiers are keywords and type names; the declarators are everything afterwards. Because a `*` is neither a keyword nor a type name, an explicit `*` is always part of a declarator.

Changing the order of the specifiers doesn't change their meaning.

Saying `* const` (which, because of the `*`, is always part of a declarator) denotes an immutable pointer.

Saying `::* const` always denotes an immutable member pointer.

That leaves the possibility of saying `const` at the end of a declarator, which always says something about a constant member function.

Finally, one rule supersedes all the others: If you don't understand what you're saying, *don't say it*. Study it until you understand it, rewrite it in a simpler form, or break it into pieces you understand.

8.2.4. Constructor Initializers

Constructor initializers are one of the C++ facilities that beginners most often misunderstand. The unique initializer syntax is just common enough that virtually all C++ programmers must learn to use them, but just rare enough to be hard to understand at first.

The idea behind constructor initializers is simple enough. We can build a class on top of components of other types by using objects of those types either as members or as base classes. When we say how to initialize an object of our class, we must then say how to initialize those components.

We say how to initialize an object of our class by writing a constructor for that class. It is therefore tempting to write assignment statements in such a constructor to initialize the components:

```
class Person {
public:
      Person() { name = ""; address = ""; }
      Person (string n, string a) { name = n; address = a; }
      // ...

private:
      string name, address;
};
```

Although this example is not strictly wrong, it is dubious. The reason is that by the time control has reached the `{` of any of the constructors, `name` and `address` have already been initialized using the default constructor for the `string` class. If `string` is the class from the standard library, the default value is a null string. Then, once `name` and `address` have been initialized, the constructor gives them brand new values, obliterating the initial values that were already put in place.

It is much better to give the initial values directly:

```
class Person {
public:
      Person(): name (""), address("") { }
      Person (string n, string a): name(n), address(a) { }
      // ...
```

```
private:
      string name, address;
};
```

or, if the constructors were defined separately, as

```
class Person {
public:
      Person();
      Person(string, string);
      // ...

private:
      string name, address;
};
Person::Person(): name(""), address("") { }
Person::Person(string n, a): name(n), address(a) { }
```

In either case, we are now saying that `name` and `address` start off immediately with their given values.

We can even do slightly better: Instead of initializing `name` and `address` explicitly to null string literals, we can leave them uninitialized:

```
class Person {
public:
      Person () { }
      Person(string n, string a): name(n), address(a) { }
      // ...
private:
      string name, address;
};
```

By doing so, we allow `name` and `address` to be initialized automatically to their natural default values and avoid the extra overhead of explicitly converting `""` to a `string` in order to initialize `name` and `address`.

8.2.5. Summary of Syntactic Pitfalls

By far, the most common syntactic problems in C++ programs have to do with declarations. Part of the difficulty comes from the need for C++ to express a much wider range of declarations than is possible in C, while still retaining a syntax that is compatible with C. Another part comes about because of the C++ distinction between assignment and initialization, which C programmers can generally ignore. In C++, as in C, there is not much difference between writing

```
int n = 0
```

and

```
int n;
n = 0;
```

The distinction shows up in both C and C++ in declarations such as

```
const int n;                         // error--no initial value
```

but C programmers wouldn't write such a declaration anyway because there would be no way to give a value to n after declaring it.

The distinction becomes important when we switch from integers to types whose constructors do real work, such as

```
string s = "Hello, world";
```

versus

```
string s;
s = "Hello, world";
```

The distinction becomes even more important in the presence of user-defined types that have no default constructors and that therefore require every object of such a type to be initialized explicitly.

To avoid these pitfalls, then, one must avoid assuming that because part of the C++ declaration syntax works just like C, the rest of the syntax also works the same way.

8.3. Semantic Pitfalls

8.3.1. How Much Does const Promise?

Consider a function declared as

```
extern void f(const char*);
```

If we call f with the address of a char object c, as in

```
char c = ' ';
f(&c);
```

we are assured that c still has the value that it did before the call. Right?

The answer turns out to be "yes and no" for complicated reasons. To understand the reasons, we will first look at when it is legitimate to convert a pointer to const into an ordinary pointer. After that, we will be able to understand why such conversions might make it possible for a function such as f to break its promise not to change c. Finally, we will discuss how common such broken promises are likely to be in practice.

8.3.1.1. Casting Away const

The well-known C library function strchr opens a hole in the type system. The function takes two arguments: a pointer to the initial character of a null-terminated string and a character to seek in the string. If strchr finds the character, it returns a pointer to the first instance of the character; otherwise it returns 0.

The hole becomes easier to notice when we ask what should logically be the argument and return types of strchr. Consider the argument type first. It is clearly useful to be able to find a character in an array that we have promised not to modify. That implies that the first argument to strchr should be a pointer to const. Otherwise, we would not be allowed to declare a table that we promise not to change by saying something like

```
const char table[] = { /* ... */ };
```

and then to search it by calling strchr(table, c).

On the other hand, a similar line of reasoning argues that the *result* of strchr should *not* be a pointer to const. Otherwise, we cannot use strchr to locate a character in a modifiable character array that we want to modify.

In C, then, the strchr function ought logically to be declared like this:

```
char *strchr(const char *, char);
```

and indeed, this is how the C library defines it. But this definition implies that we can give strchr a pointer to const and get back a pointer to the same data structure that has no restrictions against modifying the data to which it points.

C++ closes this loophole by overloading strchr:

```
char* strchr(char*, char);
const char* strchr(const char*, char);
```

Now, if you call strchr with a char* argument, the result is also char*, and if you call strchr with a const char* argument, the result won't let you modify the underlying memory either. The loophole has been closed.

After understanding the strchr type loophole, we can turn our attention from the definition of strchr to its implementation. We have two versions to implement—one with const and the other without it—so it is natural to try to implement one in terms of the other. Suppose we implement the char* version first:

```
char* strchr(char* p, char x)
{
      while (*p != x) {
            if (*p == '\0')
                  return 0;
            ++p
      }
      return p;
}
```

If we now set out to implement the `const char*` version, we discover that indeed the two versions are identical except for the argument and result types. We might expect, therefore, that it should be trivial to implement one of them in terms of the other. Moreover, inline functions should let us do that with no overhead at execution time.

To implement one version of `strchr` in terms of the other, however, we must decide what will be the type of `p` in the version that we implement fully. Suppose, for example, that we try to implement the `const` version of `strchr` in terms of the one we already have:

```
// not quite right
const char* strchr(const char* p, char x)
{
      return ::strchr((char*) p, x);
}
```

It should be clear that the use of `(char*) p` in the argument to `::strchr` is dangerous indeed, at least from the viewpoint of the language. After all, it is possible that `p` might point to memory that is write protected in hardware. From a pedantic viewpoint, the conversion of `p` to `char*` is illegal.

The foregoing discussion implies that if we want to implement one version of `strchr` in terms of the other, we should do it this way:

```
const char* strchr(const char* p, char x)
{
      while (*p != x) {
            if (*p == '\0')
                  return 0;
            ++p;
      }
      return p;
}
char* strchr(char* p, char x)
{
      return (char*) ::strchr((const char*)p, x);
}
```

Here, the cast of the argument of `::strchr` is safe because converting from `char*` to `const char*` is safe. We need to cast only to ensure that the call to `::strchr` will select the appropriate overloaded version of `strchr` and not yield a recursion loop. On the other hand, we do need a cast to convert the result back to `char*`. Fortunately, this cast is also safe—because we execute it only when `p` is pointing to memory that we have permission to modify.

We can sum up the foregoing discussion by writing two rules:

- Converting a plain pointer into a pointer to `const` is always safe.
- Converting a pointer to `const` into a plain pointer is legal only when the pointer points to memory that was not `const` to begin with.

8.3.1.2. Sneaky Functions

Let us now consider a function that lies about what it is going to do to its argument:

```
void clobber(const int* p)
{
      int* q = (int*) p;
      *q = 0;
}
```

This function takes a pointer to memory that we have promised not to modify. It then goes ahead and uses that pointer to modify the memory. Can it do that?

In general, of course, the answer is no. For example, the effect of the following is undefined:

```
const int x = 42;
clobber(&x);
```

Here, `&x` points to memory that might be write-protected, so the moment `clobber` executes the cast `(int*)p`, the effect of anything after that is undefined. But consider the following:

```
int y = 42;
clobber(&y);
```

Here, everything is legal! The value of `&y` is a pointer to modifiable memory. Calling `clobber` converts that pointer into a `const int*`, and inside `clobber`, that pointer is converted back to an `int*`. Our second rule says that this conversion is safe. In other words, this use of `clobber` is legitimately defined to set `y` to `0`. The language does not prevent the function from violating its promise not to change `y`.

8.3.1.3. Theory and Practice

In theory, then, attaching a `const` to a pointer argument doesn't guarantee much. In practice, however, it is hard to write a function such as `clobber` that does anything useful.

The reason lies in the first example of using `clobber`:

```
const int x = 42;
clobber(&x);
```

Here, there is no question that the use of `clobber` violates the language rules, whether the compiler checks it or not. That means that the author of `clobber` has no legitimate reason to write it that way. In effect, when `clobber` violates its promise, that makes the *user* of `clobber` responsible for verifying that the program is never called with a `const` object as its argument. The author of `clobber` gains nothing significant, and the user loses.

8.3.1.4. `const` Promises Summary

A function that takes a pointer to `const` as an argument makes a promise to its users that it will not use that pointer to modify the memory that the pointer addresses. C++ offers the possibility of writing functions that accept such constant pointers and then modify the memory anyway.

On the surface, it might seem that such an ability is useless. However, it is a by-product of the desire to be able to have a single type that is able to store a pointer to memory that might, or might not, be modifiable. We did just that, for example, when we collapsed the two versions of `strchr` into one. To write such a function, however, one must be able to convert both `const` and non-`const` pointers to a single type, provided only that one remembers, by other means, the original type of a pointer. This ability gives rise to the rule that any pointer can be converted to a pointer to `const` and back to its original type with impunity.

On the surface, therefore, it might appear that it is meaningless for a function ever to promise that it will not change the memory at which one of its arguments points. In practice, however, a function that breaks such a promise runs afoul of the language definition if it is ever called with a pointer to genuinely constant memory. Such behavior can therefore rightfully be considered cheating. The way to avoid the temptation to cheat that way is to examine every cast that takes away a `const` from a pointer type and prove that the pointer must always point to memory that the program has permission to modify.

8.3.2. Functions That Return References

A reference is a way of attaching a name to an object. For example, after

```
int x = 42;
int& y = x;
```

the names `x` and `y` refer to the same object; the second declaration attaches `y` to the object denoted by `x`.

Often, the reason for giving an object a name is that it doesn't have one:

```
int& elem = a[i];
```

attaches the name `elem` to element `i` of array `a`. One might do this, for example, if one were about to use `a[i]` several times. Using a reference saves program text and might save computation time as well.

Although references usually have names directly associated with them, there is one common exception: Functions may return references. Here, for example, is a convoluted way of setting `x` to `0`:

```
int x;

int& f() { return x; }

main()
{
      f() = 0;                   // x = 0
}
```

Here the function `f` returns a reference to the global variable `x`; assigning a value to `f()` is therefore equivalent to assigning the value to `x`.

There are three common reasons for functions to return references.

One is for assignment operators:

```
class Thing {
public:
      // ...
      Thing& operator=(const Thing&);
      // ...
};
Thing& operator=(const Thing& t)
{
      // ...
      return *this;
}
```

The usual practice is for such operators to return `*this` as a reference. This practice makes it possible to chain assignments:

```
Thing t1, t2, t3;
// ...
t1 = t2 = t3;
```

Of course, such chaining is also possible if `operator=` returns a `Thing` instead of a `Thing&`:

```
class Thing {
public:
      // ...
      Thing operator=(const Thing&);
      // ...
};
Thing operator=)const Thing& t)
{
      // ...
      return *this;
}
```

but doing this is not a good idea: Without fairly clever compiler optimization, such an assignment operator always forms a copy of the object being assigned, even though that copy is usually thrown away.

The second common use for functions that return references is to allow member function calls to be chained easily. Consider, for example, a class `Text` whose objects represent strings of text. Such objects might have an associated font, size, and so on; the class might look something like this:

```
class Text {
public:
      Text(const String&);
      Text& setsize(int);
      Text& setfont(const  String&);
      // ...
};
```

If the `setsize` and `setfont` members each return `*this` as a reference, we can then write things such as

```
Text t("The quick brown fox");
t.setsize(12).setfont("Goudy");
```

Otherwise, it is necessary to write

```
t.setsize(12);
t.setfont("Goudy");
```

Of course, the gain is relatively minor in this particular example. It is easier to see the advantage when writing statements such as

```
cout << "x = " << x << ", y = " << y << endl;
```

This example works only because `ostream::operator<<` returns `*this` as a reference. Each call to `operator<<` therefore passes its left argument as its result; that result becomes the left argument of the next call to `operator<<`.

The third common use for such functions is accessing elements of a container. For example, consider a class intended to act like a built-in array:

```
template<classT> class Array {
public:
      Array(int);
      // ...
      T& operator[] (int);
      // ...
};
```

Such a class supports usages such as

```
Array<int> x(20);
// ...
x[i] = 0;
```

There are three things to remember when writing functions that return references.

First, never return a reference to a local variable. The local variable disappears as soon as the function returns and the reference leads nowhere. Be sure that if you do return a reference, it refers to an object that will still be around after the function returns.

There is nothing wrong with returning a formal parameter as a reference, provided that the formal parameter is itself a reference:

```
// Don't do this
int& f(int x) { return x; }

// ...but this is fine
int& g(int& x) { return x; }
```

The trouble with `f` is that the formal parameter `x` is essentially a local variable; it vanishes as soon as `f` returns. This is not a problem in `g` because here the parameter `x` is just an alternative name for something that existed before `g` was called and will presumably still exist after `g` has returned.

The second thing to remember is that whenever a function returns a reference, it is possible for the user of that function to convert the reference to a pointer, simply by taking the address of the object that the function returns. This may be hazardous for the same reason all pointer operations are:

```
main()
{
        int* p;
        {
                Array<int> x[20];
                p = &x[10];
        }
        *p = 42;        // Oops!
}
```

Here, the `Array<int>` object `x` goes away while the pointer `p` still contains the address of one of its elements. This is, of course, the same hazard one must avoid when using built-in arrays.

The third pitfall is a subtle corollary to the second. Some containers may be implemented using self-adjusting data structures: data structures that move their contents around implicitly in response to user requests. A simple example of such a data structure is an array that grows automatically in response to attempts to refer to nonexistent elements.

Such containers must never yield references to their elements. Otherwise, they get into trouble if the compiler evaluates expressions that use them in the wrong order:

```
z[i] = z[j];
```

Suppose that `z` is of a type that automatically relocates its elements when necessary. Then it is possible for things to happen in this order:

1. Evaluate `z[j]`, yielding a reference.
2. Evaluate `z[i]`, yielding a reference—but also causing the container to grow.
3. Assign to `z[i]` the object referred to by `z[j]`.

The trouble comes when growing the container moves the object referred to by `z[j]`: That reference is now invalid. If you use references to access elements of a container, be careful about your choice of data structures.

Of course, a well-designed data structure that offers an indexing operation is careful about when that operation might conceivably relocate its components. In particular, the standard library data structures do take pains not to move their components around when doing so might crash straightforward user programs. The more care that experienced library authors take to do the right thing, however, the more important it becomes for programmers who are just starting to write libraries to be aware that there is a right thing to do.

8.3.3. Multidimensional Arrays and `new` Expressions

The types built into C++ do not include multidimensional arrays. You allocate such arrays in C++ by allocating arrays of arrays. Programmers who want to allocate multidimensional arrays usually care the most about arrays with exactly two dimensions; higher dimensions are rarer. Nevertheless, if you can allocate a two-dimensional array, you can probably allocate a three- or four-dimensional one; the following discussion generalizes easily to any number of dimensions.

There is no particular problem in allocating arrays of arrays, as long as their sizes are known during compilation. The following discussion therefore concentrates on how to allocate arrays in dynamic memory.

8.3.3.1. Arrays or Isolated Objects?

The syntax for allocating multidimensional dynamic arrays is harder to understand than it might be because C++ tries to make two common usages particularly easy. One is allocating isolated objects. For example, if `tp` is a `Thing*`, then

```
tp = new Thing;
```

makes `tp` point at a newly allocated `Thing` object. The other is allocating one-dimensional arrays of objects, so that

```
tp = new Thing[5];
```

makes `tp` point at the initial element of an array of five objects of type `Thing`.

These two ways of allocating memory are so common that it makes sense to make them both as convenient as possible. That convenience comes at a cost: Although these two uses of `new` return the same type, they are really allocating two different types. We can make this clearer by giving a name to the type "array of `5` objects of type `Thing`":

```
typedef Thing Thingarray[5];
```

Now we might well expect

```
tp = new Thingarray;
```

to work the same way as

```
tp = new Thing[5];
```

and indeed it does—but it is exactly here that the problem lies.

Look again at the first example:

```
tp = new Thing;
```

Here we are allocating an object of type `Thing` and putting the resulting pointer into a `Thing*`. So when we say

```
tp = new Thingarray;
```

we might feel entitled to say that `tp` should be of type `Thingarray*`, not type `Thing*`. Why does this discrepancy occur? How do we resolve it?

The discrepancy comes from the fact that the size of an array is part of its type and from the desire to know the types of objects during compilation. We might be able to say that the type of the expression `new Thing[5]` is "pointer to array of 5 `Thing` objects," but if we did so, what would be the type of `new Thing[n]`? Because the value of `n` is not known during compilation, the type of `new Thing[n]` cannot include the value of `n`, which means that it cannot be an array type directly. If the type of a `new` expression were an array type for a constant size, and not otherwise, that would be even harder to understand the way the language is actually defined.

We can resolve the discrepancy by remembering two simple rules:

- Allocating an array always yields a pointer to its initial element.
- Allocating a single object always yields a pointer to the object.

8.3.3.2. Arrays of Arrays

We can apply these rules to understand what happens in

```
p = new Thing[10][5];
```

What should be the type of `p`? We note first that in C++, as in C, there are no true multidimensional arrays; instead we use arrays of arrays. Thus, for example, if we say

```
Thing t[10][5];
```

then `t` is a 10-element array, each element of which is a 5-element array of `Thing`s. That implies that `new Thing [10][5]` is a request to allocate an array of arrays. If we apply our rules, we see that evaluating `new Thing [10][5]` should yield a pointer to the first element of the array. Which array? The array of arrays. That array has 10 elements—each element of it is an array of 5 elements—so `p` should be a pointer to an array of 5 elements of type `Thing`. As it happens, we've already defined a name for that type, so

```
Thingarray* p = new Thing[10][5];
```

works fine. If we want to write it out longhand, we can do it this way:

```
Thing (*p)[5] = new Thing[10][5];
```

Readers who do not understand all the fine points of declaration syntax should think of `p` as something with the property that `*p` is an array of 5 elements of type `Thing`. In other words, `p` is a pointer to an array—in this case, the array that is the initial element of an array of 10 arrays.

Notice that the value `10` appears in only one place. In particular, it is not part of the type of `p`. This is what makes it possible to say, for instance,

```
p = new Thing[n][5];
```

without having to know the value of `n` during compilation. In that sense, the "type" `Thing[n][5]` isn't quite a type at all, but rather something that looks almost like a type.

Indeed, the variable dimension must always be the *first* one to appear after `new` because the "type" of `Thing[10][n]`, for example, must contain the value of `n` and that would never do if `n` were unknown until execution time.

8.3.3.3. Two Variable Dimensions

The foregoing discussion implies that although we have a way to allocate an array with *one* variable dimension, we do not have a way to allocate one with *two*. Suppose, for example, we want an `m` by `n` array of `Things`; how do we allocate such a beast?

One way is simply to allocate an `m*n`-element array and adopt the convention that the element at row `i` and column `j` is at position `i*m+j`. This technique essentially imitates the arithmetic that a compiler does anyway for two-dimensional arrays. It's a bit of a pain, but an appropriate class definition can make it easier. That approach is left to the reader as an exercise.

The other approach is more flexible: Instead of trying to allocate an array of arrays, allocate an array of pointers, each one of which points to the initial element of an array. For an `m` by `n` array, we want `m` pointers, each of which points at the initial element of an `n`-element array:

```
Thing** pp = new Thing* [m];
int i;
for (i = 0; i < m; i++)
      pp[i] = new Thing[n];
```

We can then pretend that `pp` is a two-dimensional array, and refer to `pp[i][j]`. Moreover, if we want, we can even make the "rows" of the matrix different sizes; nothing requires them all to be exactly `n` elements each.

8.3.3.4. Deleting Arrays

When we're done with memory, we should use `delete` to return it to the system. If we allocate a single object, we use plain `delete` to free it:

```
Thing* tp;                 // as before

tp = new Thing;
delete tp;
```

When we allocate an array, we must use `delete[]` when it comes time to free it:

```
tp = new Thing[100];
delete[] tp;
```

C++ imposes this rule for several reasons, the most important of which is that single objects are often small and allocated in great profusion. It is therefore potentially expensive for the runtime system to keep track of the size of each object; the overhead to do so might require as much memory as the objects themselves. Some programmers can afford that much overhead, but not all.

Arrays, especially when dynamically allocated, are usually large compared to the amount of memory needed to store their sizes. Therefore C++ adopts a compromise position: The programmer must remember whether what is allocated is an array, but not how big the array is.

Thus, for example, to free the memory allocated for `pp`, we might write

```
for (int i = 0; i < m; i++)
      delete[] pp[i];
delete[] pp;
```

Note that the requirement for `[]` depends on whether what is allocated is an array, *not* on whether it was allocated using `[]` syntax. That dependency is necessary to ensure that

```
tp = new Thing[5];
```

and

```
tp = new Thingarray;
```

impose the same requirements on `tp`. After all, `Thingarray` and `Thing[5]` are exactly the same type, so they should behave identically when allocated.

8.3.3.5. Arrays Summary

What trips people up the most about allocating arrays is failing to realize that `new` behaves differently depending on whether what is allocated is an array. The things to remember are

- Allocating an array yields a pointer to its initial element. Use `delete[]` to free the array when you're done with it.
- Allocating a single object yields a pointer to the object. Use `delete` (without `[]`) to free the object when you're done with it.
- There are no multidimensional arrays as such. Use either an array of arrays or an array of pointers.

Where possible, of course, wrap all this kind of stuff in a class so that you—and whoever might have to maintain your code—don't have to worry about the details more than once. Such classes have the additional advantage of making it possible to deal with memory management once, in the class definition, and not worry about it again.

8.3.4. Implicit Base Class Conversions

One of the fundamental properties of inheritance in C++ is that a pointer to a derived class object may be converted to a pointer to any base class of that object. Thus, for example, if we have declarations such as

```
class Vehicle { /* ... */ };
class LandVehicle: public Vehicle { /* ... */ };
class Automobile: public LandVehicle { /* ... */ };
```

then an `Automobile*` can be converted into a `LandVehicle*` or a `Vehicle*`. This conversion makes sense: Because every `Automobile` is a kind of `LandVehicle`, we can treat a pointer to an `Automobile` as if it were a pointer to the `LandVehicle` that it is a kind of.

Every use of virtual functions relies on this property of conversions. To see this, realize that virtual functions are interesting only when the particular function actually called at runtime is different from the one that, during compilation, might appear to be called. Thus, for example, if we have

```
class Vehicle {
public:
      virtual int weight () const;
      // ...
};
class LandVehicle: public Vehicle {
public:
      virtual int weight() const;
      // ...
};
class Automobile: public LandVehicle {
public:
      virtual int weight() const;
      // ...
};
```

then the fact that `weight` is virtual is relevant only when we use a pointer (or reference) to a base class that actually points (or refers) to an object of a derived class:

```
Automobile a;
Vehicle* vp = &a;
int n = vp->weight();          // automobile::weight
```

Here, even though `vp` is declared to point to a `Vehicle`, the fact that it actually points to an `Automobile` means that the call to `vp->weight` calls `Automobile::weight` and not `Vehicle::weight` as casual observation might suggest. Only in such circumstances do we care that weight is virtual; if `vp->weight` refers to `Vehicle::weight`, the `weight` member might as well not be virtual. It would make no difference either way.

All this is well known. Less well known is the implication this behavior has for copying between derived class and base class objects. To begin, note that unless the class author goes to some trouble to prevent it, it is possible to copy class objects:

```
Automobile a1;
Automobile a2 = a1;
```

Here, `a2` is created as a copy of `a1`, whatever that means. If the author of class `Automobile` doesn't say what it means, the compiler defines it recursively in terms of copying the components of an object of class `Automobile`. Only if the class author explicitly bars copying are such things prohibited.

This means that under ordinary circumstances, class `Vehicle`, say, has a copy constructor that behaves as if declared as

```
class Vehicle {
        // ...
        Vehicle(const Vehicle&);
        // ...
};
```

Earlier we saw that a reference to a class derived from `Vehicle` may be converted into a reference to a `Vehicle`. That implies that

```
Vehicle v = a1;
```

is completely legal even though `v` is a `Vehicle` and `a1` an `Automobile`; `a1` has a reference to `Vehicle` bound to it, which is then used to form `v`. In effect, `v` is a copy of the `Vehicle` part of `a1`.

When expressed this way, the behavior seems straightforward. After all, what else could it mean to ask that `v` be a copy of `a1`? However, straightforward behavior can be surprising if you forget that it is happening. Consider, for example, a function to test if a `Vehicle` is heavy:

```
int heavy(Vehicle v)
{
        return v.weight() > 12000;
}
```

For this example, we are arbitrarily saying that any `Vehicle` should be considered heavy if its weight exceeds 12,000 of whatever units we use to express weight.

Because of the conversion behavior we've seen so far, `heavy` accepts an argument of class `Vehicle` or any class derived from it. This accepting behavior is convenient. What might be less convenient is that the `heavy` function does not necessarily behave as intended.

For example, it is tempting to assume that `a1 > 12000` always yields the same result as `heavy(a1)`. That's why we wrote `heavy`, after all. Yet as it stands, that equivalence is not guaranteed. Think about why before reading on.

The reason is that the parameter `v` in function `heavy` is just a `Vehicle` and not a `Vehicle&`. It's an object, not a pointer or reference to an object. In the call `heavy(a1)`, the parameter `v` is created as a copy of the `Vehicle` part of the argument `a1`, which means that `v.weight()` calls `Vehicle::weight`. What else could it call? By the time we reach the point of calling `v.weight()`, there is nothing to distinguish `v` from any other `Vehicle` object. It is certainly not an `Automobile`.

On the other hand, `a1.weight()` will, of course, call `Automobile::weight`. In other words, the effect of calling `heavy(a1)` is to copy `a1` into a `Vehicle` object and then use `Vehicle::weight` to determine its weight.

Converting `a1` to a `Vehicle` and then calling the `weight()` member of the converted object might give the same answer as calling `Automobile::weight` directly, of course, or it might not. In general, though, there is no reason to suspect that the answer would be the same—else why bother defining `Automobile::weight` at all?

If you want `a1.heavy()` to mean the same thing as `a1.weight() > 12000`, here's how to do it:

```
int heavy(const Vehicle& v)
{
      return v.weight() > 12000;
}
```

Because `v` is now a reference to a `Vehicle` instead of a separate `Vehicle` object, no copies are made. That means that `v.weight()` is a virtual call, so calling `heavy(a1)` results in calling `Automobile::weight`, as intended.

8.3.4.1. Base Class Summary

Some classes are defined to make it easy to use their objects as values. That is, it is easy to copy objects of those classes, and there is no particular distinction between one object and another, aside from its address. Other classes are intended to have their objects used as objects. Copying an object of such a class may be difficult, or even meaningless, and the identity of each individual object becomes important.

The distinction between objects and values becomes particularly important in programs that pass objects as function arguments: Does the function take an object or a value? Giving an object to a function that expects a value is particularly troublesome.

This trouble can be compounded when the class of the object says nothing about how to copy objects of that class. In such cases, the compiler assumes that the objects are used as values and defines copying in terms of copying what it thinks are the relevant components of the objects. The compiler's guesswork is often right when the class is intended to be used as a value. In other cases, the class author must think about how the class objects are used and define (or prohibit) copying appropriately.

8.3.5. Containers and Comparisons

The distinction between objects and values can be particularly important in the context of container classes. The standard library containers are defined to contain values, rather than objects. That is, the containers store copies of the objects that are given to them, rather than the objects themselves. This distinction can be important when defining classes whose objects are intended to be placed in containers.

In addition, some container classes place additional requirements on their components. For example, the standard library `set` class requires that its components be of a type for which `<` is an order relation. Defining these operations appropriately is not always as easy as it looks.

8.3.5.1. Stating Requirements on Containers

Unlike some other languages that support generics, C++ has no way of saying, as part of a template definition, what properties the types must have that are used to instantiate the template. As an example, consider the standard library template `set`. If `T` is a type, then among the requirements that the `set` template places on type `T` is that objects of type `T` must be *comparable*. That is, if `t1` and `t2` are objects of type `T`, then `t1<t2` must be defined to be an appropriate order relation.

Why doesn't the C++ language have some way of saying explicitly that `T` must have `<` defined? Why leave it up to the documentation? There are at least three reasons:

- There are so many possible ways of defining `<` that it is hard to see how one might write such a requirement as part of the program.

- It is even harder to see how one might write the additional requirement that `<` represent an order relation only with respect to the elements that are actually compared during execution.
- Even if `<` does represent an order relation, that fact might still not be enough to force class `set` to behave properly.

We will consider each of these reasons in turn.

8.3.5.2. Requiring Particular Functions

Suppose we want to state a requirement that `t1<t2` be defined, where `t1` and `t2` are of type `T`. At first, it might seem sufficient to require that `T::operator<(T)` be defined. Unfortunately, that requirement is not nearly good enough. Also not good enough is the approach of requiring `T` to be derived from some other class, perhaps called `comparable`, that has an appropriate `operator<` defined.

For starters, we would like to cater to the possibility of defining `T::operator<(const T&)` instead; such a definition is probably more likely in practice than `T::operator<(T)`. Other possibilities include `operator<(T, T)` and `operator<(const T&, const T&)`. These possibilities may well be more realistic than either of the member functions because it is generally a good idea to avoid using member functions for operators that, like `<`, tend to treat their operands symmetrically for conversion purposes.

Another possibility is that `T` might be a built-in type, in which case `<` is a built-in operator and does not have a function that represents it at all. Moreover, there is no way to derive a built-in type from any particular base class.

Yet another possibility is that comparison between objects of type `T` might be defined in terms of any of the whole collection of functions of the form `operator<(const S1&, const S2&)`, where `S1` and `S2` are either `T` or public base classes of `T`.

If those were not enough, there is also the possibility that `<` might not be defined on objects of type `T` at all, but that there is a user-defined conversion that takes `T` into some other type (or types) for which `<` *is* defined.

Even if an appropriate function is defined, there might be more than one such function. That would render expressions such as `t1<t2` ambiguous, even though type `T`, when considered in isolation, might have every relevant function defined.

On the other hand, if the body of a template function uses the expression `t1<t2` and that template function is instantiated, the program does not compile unless `t1<t2` is uniquely defined. Therefore, the mere presence of `t1<t2` in a function body is a sufficient requirement all by itself.

8.3.5.3. Doing the Right Thing

Even if we had an explicit way of stating the requirement that our type `T` have `t1<t2` defined, that is not enough. It is also necessary for `<` actually to behave like a comparison. Typically, classes such as `set` maintain their elements in some kind of data structure that relies on ordering to implement fast searching. If `<` does not behave appropriately, the whole data structure collapses.

The problem of requiring appropriate behavior for operators becomes more acute when those requirements include names for which there is no universally accepted meaning. For example, most programmers assume that a class that defines `<` does so as an order relation of some kind, but what about `+`? Addition is not the only operation that classes use `+` to express. If a container requires its elements to have `+` defined, having a way to state that requirement in the language doesn't strengthen the specification much at all, unless there is also a way to talk about what `+` does.

Curiously, requiring that `<` represent an order relation is often too strong in practice; instead, it is important to require only that `<` represent an order relation *over the elements that are stored in each particular container*. It is desirable to loosen the requirement on `<` because some types have *singular values*, often used to represent error conditions, that do not obey the normal rules for comparison. These types are still appropriate to use with ordered containers, as long as one takes pains to keep the singular values out of the containers.

One example of such a type is IEEE floating point, which is probably the most popular floating-point format these days. It includes the notion of NaN (not a number) values, which have the curious property that any comparison involving a NaN value yields `false`. Thus, if `x` is NaN, `x<x` is `false`, as one would expect, but so are `x<=x`, `x==x`, and `x!=x`. Needless to say, any order-based algorithm that tries to use NaN values without taking their peculiarities into account is going to become confused.

If we agree to shun NaN values, `<` behaves completely reasonably on IEEE floating-point numbers. Therefore, if we have a `set` of IEEE values, it works fine as long as we avoid putting any NaN values into it.

The appropriate requirement to place on < is therefore impossible to check during compilation at all. The best we can do is to say that for set<T> to work correctly, < must behave properly on the values that are placed, or sought, in a set<T> object.

8.3.5.4. Object and Value Comparison

Are these all the comparison pitfalls we need to avoid? That is, suppose we have a < defined that always represents an order relation. Is that good enough to give us the behavior we want from our containers? Of course, the answer is no—or I wouldn't have asked the question. Having a correctly defined < gives us what we asked for, but what we ask for is not always what we want.

One example of the difference between what we ask for and what we might want comes when we consider the definition of string literals such as "abc". Recall that in C++, a string literal actually represents the address of the initial character of a null-terminated array; its type is "pointer to char." That definition implies that comparing two string literals is equivalent to comparing two pointers; the pointers are equal if they point to the same memory location and unequal otherwise.

In both C and C++, it is up to the implementation whether or not two identical string literals are stored in the same location. Although it is guaranteed that

```
"cat" == "dog"
```

is false, the value of

```
"cat" == "cat"
```

is up to the implementation.

The implication of this definition of comparison is that sets of character pointers may well behave counterintuitively if those pointers represent (the initial characters of) string literals. For example, if we write

```
set<char*> s;

s.insert("cat");
s.insert("cat");
```

it is up to the implementation whether s now contains one element or two. If s contains two elements, those elements are pointers to distinct memory locations, each of which is the initial c of a distinct instance of "cat".

The way to avoid this pitfall is to be careful when using sets of pointers, just as one should be careful when using pointers in other contexts. If, for example, we were to say

```
set<string> s;

s.insert("cat");
s.insert("cat");
```

then `s` is assured of containing only a single element because each insertion implicitly converts `"cat"` to a string, and the values of the strings then compare equal. In other words, `s` would have only a single element because

```
string("cat") == string("cat")
```

is assured of being `true` even if

```
"cat" == "cat"
```

is `false`. The point is that comparison of `string` values is defined in terms of comparing the characters that constitute the strings, not in terms of the addresses of those characters.

8.3.5.5. Containers and Comparisons Discussion

When connecting two pieces of software together, it is important to think about the interface between them and tempting to believe that there is some way to specify that interface that will ensure appropriate behavior.

The world is rarely as neat as that in practice. There may be more than one way of obtaining appropriate behavior, to the point that it is difficult to specify the behavior beyond saying "it has to work if you use it in the following way." The behavior may be inappropriate in some cases, but by avoiding those cases, it may still be possible to make the combined software work as intended. Finally, your intentions may not be as obvious as they may appear at first. Even a value as simple as a built-in string literal may behave in a surprising way when used with the built-in comparison operators.

These real-world complexities are among the reasons we talk about software engineering instead of software mathematics.

8.3.6. Pointer Comparisons and Order Relations

Our next example comes from a finely tuned portability compromise that C++ inherited from C. In this particular case, the compromise is right for C most of the time but has the potential to cause trouble for C++.

Accordingly, the C++ standard library circumvents the problem. As a result, most C++ programmers do not even need to know that the problem exists—but library designers, especially designers of container classes, may need to know about it.

To help us understand the problem, let's begin by asking what is wrong with this example:

```
int* p[100];
// ...
sort(p, p+100);
```

On the surface, nothing is wrong. We have declared an array of pointers, called `p`, and called a function named `sort`, which presumably sorts the elements of the array.

Unfortunately, this example conceals a nasty pitfall, which is rendered all the nastier by the fact that it works without trouble on many machines. The problem is that what is being sorted is an array of pointers, and to sort the elements of the array, we must be able to compare them. Moreover, ordered comparison between pointers is defined only when the pointers both point to elements of the same array (or one past the end of the array, as in the case of `p+100` in this example). For example, if we have two arrays

```
int x[10], y[10];
```

the mere evaluation of the expression `x<y` (which is equivalent to `&x[0]<&y[0]`) is undefined. It is not just that the implementation has a choice about whether to return `true` or `false` as the result of such a comparison; rather, the implementation is permitted to do *anything* it likes, including deleting all your files and sending hate mail in your name to all your friends.

Yet there is nothing wrong with expressions such as `&x[0]<&x[3]` (which is required to yield `true`) or even `x==y` (which is required to yield `false`). The point is that you are allowed to use `==` or `!=` to compare arbitrary pointers—and, if the pointers have well-defined values, those pointers compare equal if and only if they point to the same object (or are both zero)—but the moment you use any of the other four relational operators (`<`, `>`, `<=`, or `>=`), the pointers must point to elements of the same array or all bets are off.

This restriction actually has its origin in C, but the C++ standard library offers a way around the restriction that does not work readily in C. We will first explore the reason for the restriction, then detail its effects, and finally explain the solution.

8.3.6.1. Segmented Architectures

One of the engineering decisions to be made when designing a computer architecture is how to store memory addresses as part of machine instructions. The difficulty stems from the fact that many instructions do not need to be able to address completely arbitrary memory locations. Instead, they use local variables (whose addresses are usually a small offset from a stack register) or variables that are already in registers. This difficulty is compounded by machines whose memory addresses exceed the machine's natural word size. Such machines often need to store memory addresses in two registers, rather than one, and manipulate those registers as needed to form full addresses.

The most common such machine architecture today is found on so-called 16-bit personal computers. The idea is that the machine's internal registers are 16 bits long, but the available memory addresses exceed 2^{16}. In general, then, it may be necessary to store pointers as two words, one of which contains high-order bits of the address and the other of which contains low-order bits.

The following discussion is somewhat simplified from the actual situation on these machines but is a good description of the general problem. Suppose that every pointer `p` is represented by two values `p0` and `p1`, where `p0` contains some number of low-order bits of `p` and `p1` contains the remaining, high-order bits. Assume the same relationship between `q`, `q0`, and `q1`. Then it is fairly easy to say what it means to claim that `p=q`: We say that `p=q` if an only if `p0=q0` and `p1=q1`.

Moreover, the test for `p=q` is likely to be quite fast as long as we test for `p0=q0` first because most of the time `p0` and `q0` differ and we do not even have to inspect `p1` or `q1`. For instance, in a loop like

```
while (p != q) {
        // ...
        ++p;
}
```

most of the time, the test `p!=q` is satisfied after comparing `p0` and `q0`.

Now consider what it means to test whether `p<q`. It does not help to compare `p0` and `q0` because the result of that comparison gives no useful information if the high-order bits in `p1` and `q1` differ.

To see this, consider the analogy of two-digit decimal numbers. You cannot learn that 37<54 by comparing 7 and 4; you must look at the high-order digits first.

The first order of business, then, must be to compare `p1` and `q1`. If `p1<q1`, then we know that `p<q` and similarly if `p1>q1`. But if `p1=q1`, we must then compare `p0` and `q0` before we have the final answer. In other words, `p<q` if and only if `p1<q1` or (`p1=q1` and `p0<q0`).

Now consider a loop such as

```
while (p < q) {
        // ...
        ++p;
}
```

If we are going to count on `p` and `q` eventually becoming equal, it is likely that their high-order bits will be equal in many of the comparisons in the loop. That implies that most of the pointer comparisons will have to do two machine-level comparisons (`p1<q1` and then `p0<q0`) instead of the one comparison (`p0=q0`) that was necessary most of the time when checking for `p!=q`. It appears, therefore, that loops on machines of this kind are much slower if they use `<` than if they use `!=`.

The definition of C circumvented this problem in a clever way. Consider the `p<q` comparison. If `p` and `q` point to elements of different arrays, it is up to the implementation which array comes first in memory. Therefore, goes the reasoning, there is never a legitimate use for comparisons such as `p<q` unless `p` and `q` point to elements of the same array. For that reason, C defines such comparisons *only* if `p` and `q` point to elements of the same array. That way, if a compiler knows that `p1=q1` whenever and `p` and `q` point to elements of the same array (and it is possible for a compiler to arrange that in many cases), it is not necessary to compare `p1` and `q1` at all; the compiler can translate `p<q` directly into `p0<q0`.

Because C imposes this restriction, it was necessary for C++ to do so as well. To do otherwise would place C++ at a performance disadvantage compared to C when executing programs that use pointers in common ways.

The detailed reasoning here may be hard to follow without reading it several times. The important thing to remember is that, for efficiency reasons, C and C++ define `p==q` and `p!=q` for arbitrary pointers, but they define `p<q` only if `p` and `q` point to elements of the same array.

8.3.6.2. Order-Based Containers

Now let's look at library containers. The standard C++ library offers a number of containers, and related algorithms, that assume the ability to do order-based comparisons on the elements in the containers. One such container is `set<T>`, which has the property that an object of type `set<T>` contains objects of type `T`, and that every element of any particular `set<T>` object is unequal to every other element of that object.

Now consider objects of type `set<int*>`. It is certainly desirable to be able to have a set of integer pointers. It should not be hard to imagine a lot of uses for such sets. Yet without special pleading in the library, such a set works only if it contains only pointers to elements of the same array. The reason should not be hard to find: If a `set<int*>` object contains pointers to elements of two different arrays, the library evokes undefined behavior the moment it tries to compare two such pointers.

The problem is even worse than it appears at first because `set<int*>` objects work just fine on any machine that happens to implement pointer comparisons so that they work correctly on all pointers. The number of such machines is large and growing rapidly. How is it possible to define a container class that will work correctly across all machines?

Some people may claim there is no problem: Instead of comparing `p<q`, just compare `(int)p<(int)q`. That isn't really a solution, though, because there is no guarantee that it is possible to convert a pointer to an `int` (or even to a `long`), or, if it is, that the result of that conversion has sensible properties with respect to comparison.

Other people might claim that this example points out a fundamental limitation of order-based containers, and this problem would be entirely avoided if we had hash-based containers instead. But hash-based containers are useless unless the elements have a hash function defined, which means that container elements of user-defined type must have a user-defined hash function as well. In effect, this "solution" works by dumping the problem on the user's shoulders. How does a user go about defining a portable hash function on pointers if conversion from pointer to integer is not always defined under every implementation?

8.3.6.3. A Likely Solution

The key to the solution is to realize that, although different machine architectures might offer different ways of comparing pointers, every machine must make it possible *somehow*. After all, it is already guaranteed that two pointers are equal if and only if they point to the same object (or are both zero), which already rules out assigning the same address (whatever an address is on the machine) to two different objects. All we need, then, is a way to name the "correct" comparison between pointers, along with a requirement that the library make that kind of comparison available with the same name for all implementations.

The C++ standard library does exactly that and makes the comparisons available through function object templates. To compare two integer pointers, we use a function object of type `less<int*>` so that even if `p<q` is not guaranteed to work correctly for arbitrary `p` and `q`, `less<int*>()(p,q)` provides an appropriate guarantee. Here, the first pair of parentheses constructs an object of type `less<int*>`, and the second pair "calls" that object with arguments `p` and `q`. Of course, the "call" is actually an invocation of `operator()` on the object, but from the user's viewpoint, it looks like a call.

The "guarantee" that `less<int*>()` offers is that whenever `p<q` is guaranteed to be well defined, `less<int*>()(p,q)` has the same value. Moreover, `less<int*>()(p,q)` is a total order relation over all possible values of `p` and `q`.

With those definitions and guarantee, it should be obvious that the right way to define `set<T>` is to use `less<T>` as the normal comparison operation for the container, rather than just to use the `<` operation. Then all that is necessary is for `less<T>` to use `<` when `less<T>` is not overridden by a specialized definition for particular types (such as pointer types).

For example, an implementation in which `<` works for all pointers might define a template along the following lines:

```
template<class T> class less:
   public binary_function<T, T, bool> {
public:
      bool operator()(T x, T y) {
             return x < y;
      }
};
```

In this example, the `binary_function` base class is there to make our `less` class conform to library conventions that are irrelevant to this chapter. What is important is the definition of `operator()`, which simply defines class `less` so that "calling" an object of type `less<T>` with two arguments of type `T` compares the arguments.

Now, suppose we are on an implementation where `<` does not work with pointers to objects in different arrays, but on which it is possible to simulate such comparisons by casting the pointers to `long`. On such an implementation, the library must define a partial specialization of the `less` template, along the following lines:

```
template<classT> class less<T*>:
   public binary_function<T*, T*, bool> {
public:
      bool operator()(T* x, T* y) {
            return (long) x < (long)y;
      }
};
```

This specialization defines the `less` template for all pointer types. The net effect of the specialization is to say that `less<T>(x,y)` means `(long)x<(long)y` whenever `T` is a pointer type and `x<y` otherwise.

It is important to realize that these implementation-dependent definitions are part of the library for each individual machine, rather than something that users generally have to consider on their own initiative. Ultimately, the user will apply a library function, such as `sort`, to an array, and it will work correctly whether that array contains pointers, integers, or objects of some other type.

8.3.7. Semantic Pitfalls Summary

C++ classes give programmers a way to define new types, along with fine-grained control over the behavior of those types. Along with that control comes a corresponding responsibility. If one class expects a particular behavior of another, combining those two classes successfully depends on the behavior of the latter class matching the expectations of the former.

One place where mismatches are particularly likely is when class objects are copied. There are two common styles for using objects—as pure objects and as values—and although each style has its own uses, the two do not mix terribly well. Moreover, as a convenience to the class author, the compiler sometimes makes assumptions about operations that the author has not defined. Whether these assumptions are right or wrong depends on the context, which means that programmers must be aware of that context.

Another source of mismatches is in defining comparison. Not everything that looks like a comparison operation is actually an appropriate order relation. Moreover, for reasons of hardware efficiency and C compatibility, pointer comparisons are defined in a way that does not always meet naive expectations.

8.4. Execution Pitfalls

C++ compilers check for many potential problems during compilation, but no compiler can detect all such problems in advance. Moreover, some problems that could be detected in principle are often deliberately left undetected in practice.

For example, most C++ compilers do not defend against programs that overrun array boundaries. To do so would impose an overhead that many programmers would find unacceptable. Moreover, a C++ programmer who does not want to incur the risk of unchecked indexing operations can write a class that does the checking explicitly, whether the compiler offers such a feature or not.

More generally, the ability to wrap potentially hazardous operations in a class definition, and then debug those operations only once, means that well-written C++ programs avoid many execution pitfalls as a side effect of their design. Accordingly, the pitfalls described in this section tend to occur at a low level of abstraction.

They are important, however, for two reasons.

First, library authors must ultimately use low-level abstractions as a way of implementing the higher-level abstractions that they offer to their users. It is easy to avoid bounds errors by using an appropriate class—but someone must write that class, and that someone must also understand how to avoid bounds errors.

Second, C++ is designed to grant access to low-level facilities because such facilities can be essential for writing efficient applications. Of course, it is usually wise to isolate the low-level parts of a program and give them special care, but it is often impossible to avoid them entirely.

8.4.1. Cheating on Array Bounds

There is one kind of array bounds violation that is both common and deliberate in C programs, even though C does not officially sanction such programs. The practical effect of such violations is much greater in C++ programs than in C programs, however, which means that this pitfall deserves special attention from C programmers who are beginning to use C++.

8.4.1.1. A C Problem Solved

Suppose we want to design a C data structure that represents a variable-length array of characters. The object is to have a single data structure that holds both the length of the array and the characters that constitute the array. Here is one way to do it:

```
struct string1 {
      int length;
      char *data;
};
```

Here, the `length` member says how many characters the structure represents and the `data` member is a pointer to the initial character of the array; that array is presumably dynamically allocated.

Copying such a data structure is a bit of a nuisance. Suppose we have a pointer to a `string1` object:

```
struct string1 *p;
```

and we want to create a new `string1` object that is a copy of the original. Then we must do something like this:

```
struct string1 *q = malloc(sizeof(struct string1));
q->length = p->length;
q->data = malloc(p->length);
strncpy(q->data, p->data, p->length);
```

Copying a `string1` object requires an extra call to `malloc`. Similarly, freeing one of these objects requires an extra call to `free` to deallocate the memory to which the `data` member points.

8.4.1.2. Another Apparent C Solution

Part of being a good programmer is creative laziness. Why do by hand what a computer can do instead? It is therefore no surprise that C programmers look for an easier way of doing things. Here is one common way:

```
struct string2 {
      int length;
      char data[1];                    /* [sic] */
};
```

Of course, the character array is not just a single character long. Instead, when allocating a `string2`, we leave extra memory at the end. Anyone using the `data` member runs off the end of the officially defined array, but because the extra memory was allocated, that formal violation is harmless—at least in C.

Accordingly, if `p2` points to a `string2`, we might copy it this way:

```
struct string2 *q2 =
      malloc(sizeof(struct string2) + p2->length - 1);
q2->length = p2->length;
strncpy(q2->data, p2->data, p2->length);
```

This technique makes it slightly easier to copy a `string2` than a `string1`. It makes it significantly easier to free it, too:

```
free(q2);
```

8.4.1.3. Technicalities

This technique has the disadvantage of relying on a property of C that the language definition does not guarantee.

Consider this example:

```
struct string1 *p1;
struct string2 *p2;

if (p1->length > 3)
      p1->data[3] = '?';
if (p2->length > 3)
      p2->data[3] = '?'
```

We assign a new value to the `data[3]` element of each of our strings only if the length is big enough to accommodate it. Nothing is wrong there, but look at the assignment to `p2->data[3]`. Here, `p2->data` is an array with only one element. How can it be legal to assign to element number `3`?

On the other hand, the way we are allocating memory for our `string2` objects guarantees that there will actually be usable memory at the place where `p2->data[3]` would have to be if it existed at all. So what is the harm in using it?

I put that question to the C standards committee, pointing out that the answer would determine whether a debugging C implementation would be allowed to reject an assignment to `p2->data[3]` on the basis of bounds checking. I found out later that my question provoked the longest debate on any such issue that had ever occurred in the C committee. The eventual answer was that the use of `p2->data[3]` was indeed illegal, whether memory was effectively accessible or not. Of course, implementations would not be required to check for such errors. Because I agreed with the conclusion, I did not inquire about the details. Despite its popularity, the `string2` technique is not valid C; programmers who want to write maximally portable code should avoid it even though it is likely to work on most compilers.

8.4.1.4. The Rigorous Nature of C++

So far, we have been talking only about C. It turns out that in C++, there is a much stronger reason to avoid the `string2` technique: It will fail horribly in many C++ implementations if the class later acquires a virtual function.

Most C++ programmers know that if a class has a virtual function, the usual implementation technique is for the compiler to store an extra pointer in each object of that class. That pointer contains the address of a table that describes the type of the object and points to all that class's virtual functions.

What is less widely known is that this extra pointer is often stored at the *end* of the object, not the beginning. Part of the reason for this strategy is that it makes it easier to interchange data between C and C++ programs if the C part of a structure is at the beginning; it then requires no extra step to convert the value of a pointer when passing it between C and C++ programs.

For instance, if we had a structure such as

```
struct string3 {
      virtual void foo();
      int length;
      char data[1];
};
```

it would be entirely possible that the compiler might decide to store the virtual table pointer immediately after the data member, as if the structure had been declared this way:

```
struct string3a {
      int length;
      char data[1];
      virtual_table *vptr;
};
```

It is clear that trying to use data[n], where n is greater than 1, would eventually lead to disaster.

8.4.1.5. Array Bounds Summary

Formally speaking, array bounds are intended to be taken seriously in both C and C++. C programmers often fail to do so, particularly in ways similar to those shown here. Such transgressions usually go unpunished in practice—but only in C, not in C++. In particular, the presence of virtual functions effectively guarantees that this kind of memory cheating does not work in C++.

The way to do this kind of thing in C++ is to use a library, if an appropriate one is available. If it isn't, then resist the temptation to cheat. Instead, put the memory allocation and deallocation into a constructor and destructor, get it right once, and then forget about it. The resulting class is easier to use than its C counterpart, even if the C version cheats.

8.4.2. Input/Output and Order of Evaluation

Suppose we have a variable named x and we want to use the standard C++ library to print its value with an appropriate label. Then we can say something like

```
cout << "x = " << x << endl;
```

and be confident that the three values that we are printing will appear in the order we requested: First the string `x =`, then the value of `x`, and finally a newline.

Suppose next that `p` is a pointer to an element of an array and we want to print the value of that element and the next element of that array. Similarly to before, we can say

```
cout << *p << ", " << *(p+1) << endl;
```

or, equivalently,

```
cout << p[0] << ", " << p[1] << endl;
```

It is therefore tempting to assume that we can also say

```
cout << *p++ << ", " << *p << endl;
```

but, perhaps surprisingly, that doesn't work.

One way to understand this surprise is as a consequence of two rules:

- The implementation is permitted to evaluate the arguments to a function or operator in any order.
- The implementation must necessarily evaluate all the arguments to a function before calling the function itself.

These two rules seem straightforward enough: The first one should be well known to all C and C++ programmers and the second applies to any call-by-value language. Let's see how they might apply to the previous expressions.

Note first that when we write an expression such as

```
cout << "x = " << x << endl;
```

the `<<` operator is left associative. In other words, that expression is equivalent to

```
((cout << "x = ") << x) << endl;
```

We can view this expression as applying the `<<` operator to two operands, the second of which is `endl` and the first of which is complicated. That application, in turn, has one of two possible meanings, depending on whether the particular `operator<<` being used is a member of the class of `cout` or not. Specifically, the expression above is equivalent either to

```
operator<<(((cout << "x = ") << x), endl);
```

or to

```
((cout << "x = ") << x).operator<<(endl);
```

Either way, our two rules apply. The first rule says that the implementation is allowed to evaluate our complicated expression and `endl` in either order. The second rule says that the complicated expression must be completely evaluated before executing `operator<<`. That implies that the string `x =` and the value of `x` must be written before writing `endl`, which is what we want.

A similar analysis of the complicated expression shows that `x =` must be written before the value of `x`.

Now let's look at the expression that doesn't work:

```
cout << *p++ << ", " << *p << endl;
```

As before, the uses of `<<` group to the left, so that this statement means

```
((((cout << *p++) << ", ") << *p) << endl);
```

Consider the subexpression

```
(((cout << *p++) << ", ") << *p)
```

Similarly to before, we can view this as a call to `operator<<` whose right operand is `*p` and whose left operand is complicated, so that it means either

```
operator<<(((cout << *p++) << ", "), *p);
```

or

```
((cout << *p++) << ", ").operator<<(*p);
```

depending on whether or not the `operator<<` being used is a member of the class of `cout`. As before, both operands must be evaluated before calling `operator<<`. However, in this case, one operand uses the value of `p` and the other operand (uses and) modifies it. Because the operands are permitted to be evaluated in either order, it is up to the implementation whether `*p` uses the value of `p` before or after it has been modified. In other words, even though the `<<` operation in the subexpression

```
cout << *p++
```

must be evaluated before the `<<` operation that prints `*p`, that says nothing about the relative order in which `*p++` and `*p` are evaluated. The implementation is permitted to evaluate them in either order and have their results until it is time to print them.

The lesson from the foregoing discussion may be familiar: Expressions with side effects can be dangerous. Although they can be useful, they always require thought. In particular, even though parts of an expression might be guaranteed to be evaluated in particular order, that guarantee is not universal.

8.4.3. Dangling Pointers

It's virtually impossible to learn C++ without learning about the hazards of dangling pointers. For example, in

```
int* p = new int;
delete p;
*p = 42;              // <*>?!%#@
```

the assignment to `*p` is an error because `p` no longer points anywhere meaningful. Indeed, the implementation is permitted to change the value of `p` itself to make it easier to detect the error.

8.4.3.1. Pointers to Dynamic Memory

Pointers often point to dynamically allocated memory, and it is hard to say how to avoid dangling pointers in such circumstances except by a very general rule: Don't delete an object while there's still a pointer to it somewhere. Most of the time, figuring out whether a use of `delete` meets this rule is either very easy or very difficult; in either case, the application of this rule is beyond the scope of this chapter.

However, one thing is well worth noting: Many uses of dynamic memory are intended as *containers*, which are flexible data structures that grow as needed to contain the objects placed in them. The way to make such things safe is to wrap them in appropriate container classes, think hard enough about those classes to ensure they're safe, and then use them.

Thus, for instance, instead of saying

```
int* p = new int[n];
// ...
delete[] p;
```

think about whether what you really want might be a flexible array. If it is, use an appropriate class from the standard library:

```
vector<int> p(n);
```

8.4.3.2. Pointers to Local Variables

There are a lot of cases where pointers address things that were *not* allocated by `new`. Even if we did not use `new`, we can still get into trouble:

```
main()
{
        int* p;
        {
                int x;
                p = &x;
```

```
        }
        *p = 42;              // #!?@#%^
}
```

The problem here is the same as previously: We are assigning to `*p` after `p` no longer points anywhere useful.

Note that this example includes an inner block in which `x` is created and destroyed. Indeed, it is fairly difficult to create a dangling pointer without using `delete` or an inner block. The reason is that local variables are usually destroyed in reverse order of creation. To destroy an object while still retaining a pointer to it, it is therefore necessary to create the pointer before creating the object. Because the object does not exist when creating the pointer, we must give the pointer some other value and then change the value to refer to the object. The inner block is necessary to make is possible to use the pointer after the object has been destroyed.

In effect, our general rule has a corollary when dealing with local variables: When giving a value to a local pointer variable, make sure it's the address of something that existed when the pointer was created. That ensures that the pointer is destroyed first.

Most of the time it is obvious when an assignment might violate this rule. For example, it is always safe to copy an old pointer into a new one:

```
Thing* p;
// ...
        {
                Thing* q = p;
                // ...
        }
```

because the new pointer is destroyed before the old one. Copying a new pointer into a old one is potentially dangerous, but the hazard exists only when the new pointer addresses an object created after the old pointer:

```
Thing* p;
// ...
        {
                Thing* q;
                // ...
                p = q;                  // potentially dangerous
        }
```

Here, the assignment `p=q` is dangerous if `q` refers to an object created more recently than `p` itself. Of course, if `q` refers to an object more recent than `q`, it is dangerous even without assigning `q` to `p`.

8.4.3.3. Pointers and Functions

Most of the time, these hazards are obvious upon inspection. One case, however, deserves special attention: returning a pointer from a function. This is a special case because the act of returning from a function destroys the function's local variables while preserving the return value. If that return value points to a local variable, there's trouble:

```
int* fun()
{
        int x = 42;
        return &x;   // error
}
```

Of course, if a function accepts a pointer as an argument, it's safe to return that pointer as a result.

8.4.4. References and Aliasing

Here is an implementation of the standard library `find` function:

```
template<class It, class X>
It find(It begin, It end, const X& x)
{
        while (begin != end && *begin != x)
              ++begin;
        return begin;
}
```

The types `It` and `X` are both template parameters. In principle, they can be arbitrary types. Yet the arguments of type `It` are passed by value and the argument of type `X` is passed by reference. Why?

One might be tempted at first to say that objects of type `X` are likely to be larger than objects of type `It`. After all, in many common uses of this function, type `It` is just a pointer, where type `X` might be a floating-point number, string, or other "large" type. It is therefore no more efficient to copy an object of type `It` than a pointer to it, but it might be more efficient to avoid copying an object of type `X`.

These arguments are valid, as far as they go, but they do not capture the whole truth. There are other reasons to use references or not to use them.

8.4.4.1. Aliasing and Reasons for Using References

We begin with the obvious observation that calling a function ordinarily copies the arguments into the parameters—unless the parameter type is a reference. That implies that a parameter whose type is not a reference must be capable of being copied.

There is no corresponding requirement on the type of a parameter that is a reference. That means that type X in the `find` function does not need to be copyable. It is perfectly acceptable for the third argument to `find` to be of a type that prohibits copying outright, as long as the type supports the `!=` operation. Of course, for that to work, the `!=` operation itself must be defined to take a reference parameter, rather than copy its argument.

Now what about the first parameter? It can't be a reference to a constant because the function modifies it. Of course, we can change the function to copy it explicitly:

```
template<class It, class X>
It find (const It& begin, It end, const X& x)
{
      It b = begin;
      while (b != end && *b != x)
            ++b;
      return begin;
}
```

but what is the point of using a reference to avoid copying something that we immediately copy anyway? We could also make the first parameter a plain reference, but only at the cost of having the function destroy the value of the corresponding argument.

What about the second parameter? Here there is no obvious reason that it could not be made a reference. One practical reason it is not a reference is for consistency with the first parameter. Another is that this is one of those cases in which copying the argument is likely to be *more* efficient than not copying it because it avoids the extra memory reference associated with following a pointer each time `begin` and `end` are compared.

8.4.4.2. Aliases

In a slightly different context, there is yet another reason to avoid references. Consider this function, which multiplies every element of an array by a given constant:

```
void scale(double* p, int n, const double& x)
{
      for (int i = 0; i < n; ++i)
            p[i] *=x;
}
```

Unless you were reading unusually carefully, you probably did not notice the misstatement in the description of the function. To see it, consider this example:

```
double d[3] = { 2.0, 4.0, 6.0 };
scale(d, 3, d[1]);
```

The value of `d[1]` is `4.0`, so after calling `scale`, the elements of `d` should be `8.0`, `16.0`, and `24.0`, right? Wrong. Because the third parameter to scale is a reference, it is fetched each time through the loop. After the second iteration, `d[1]` has been set to `16.0`, so `x` is now bound to an object with value `16.0`. This, in turn, causes `d[2]` to be set to `96.0`, not `24.0`.

This phenomenon is called *aliasing*. It comes about when a pointer or reference is bound to a component of a data structure that is potentially modified while the pointer or reference is active. In this particular example, the aliasing comes from the possibility that `x` might be bound to an element of the array that has `p` pointing to an element of it. Although `x` is a reference to `const`, that is no bar to the value being changed through a different access path, such as by assignment to `p[i]`.

Of course, the way to avoid this problem is to ensure that `x` is a copy of its argument, rather than a reference to it:

```
void scale(double* p, int n, double x)
{
        for (int i = 0; i < n; ++i)
                p[i] *= x;
}
```

8.4.4.3. Referencing and Aliasing Summary

Aside from the obvious efficiency considerations, the reasons to use or not to use references as function parameters include

- A parameter of reference type is not copied, which means it can potentially be of a type that does not support copying at all.
- There is little to be gained from avoiding copying a value that is going to be changed—unless one is sure that the original value is expendable.
- If a parameter is to be used many times, it may be more efficient to copy it than to follow a reference each time it is used.
- References can cause aliasing.

Efficiency is often important, of course, but it is not the only thing that influences design. Every use of a pointer or reference implies that the object pointed or referred to can potentially be fetched more than once; at times, that might not be easy to predict in advance. This might or might not be a problem. As ever, the way to avoid difficulties is to be aware of them.

8.5. Conclusion

C++ is based on C, so it has many of the same pitfalls. C++ offers facilities that C does not offer, so C++ has additional pitfalls that C does not have. Nevertheless, many experienced C++ programmers find that the total effort needed to write reliable C++ programs—avoiding both the C and C++ pitfalls—is less than it is to write corresponding programs in C. How can such things be?

The most important reason is that C++ supports abstractions better than C does. For example, a C program that does any significant string processing must take memory allocation into account almost every time it touches a string. A well-written C++ version of the same program defines a class that captures the desired properties of strings (or uses an appropriate library class that already exists) and then worries about memory allocation only once, in that class. In other words, although most of the C pitfalls still exist in C++, they are much less important because programmers can avoid them most of the time by using the C++ abstraction facilities.

Of course, those abstraction facilities introduce their own pitfalls. Those pitfalls, however, are often of a different nature from their C counterparts. Instead of a sharply defined hazard to avoid, the typical C++ pitfall is often a body of knowledge to understand. Understand it poorly, and the pitfall is always there. Understand it well, and the pitfall goes away.

The most obvious example of this kind of pitfall is the difference between assignment and initialization. Experience shows that beginning C++ programmers have more trouble with the distinction than with any other part of the language. Yet once a beginner understands the distinction completely, it ceases to be a problem.

Similar pitfalls exist in C as well. However, they tend to come from using libraries, rather than from the language itself. Libraries in any language offer higher-level abstractions than the language itself offers, which means that problems that arise when using libraries in any language are likely to come from understanding those abstractions incompletely.

Where C++ is unusual is in the range of abstractions that it offers. Accordingly, the corresponding pitfalls also cover a wide range. This chapter therefore included both high- and low-level pitfalls but did not attempt to be exhaustive. Instead, it gave a sample of problems that C++ programmers encounter in practice, and, perhaps, even gave a feel for where to look for other potential problems—and for their solutions.

8.6. Acknowledgments
This chapter is a revision of articles collected from an ongoing series in *C++ Report* magazine, published by SIGS Publications. Thanks to Barbara Moo and Bjarne Stroustrup for their many helpful comments on earlier drafts of this chapter.

8.7. Reference
Koenig, A. 1989. *C traps and pitfalls*. Reading, MA: Addison-Wesley.

Part IV
Eiffel

CHAPTER 9

Eiffel

by Bertrand Meyer

9.1. Eiffel Overview

Eiffel is a method and language for the efficient description and development of quality systems.

Eiffel is more than a programming language. It covers not just programming in the restricted sense of implementation but the whole spectrum of software development:

- Analysis, modeling, and specification, where Eiffel can be used as a purely descriptive tool to analyze and document the structure and properties of complex systems (even nonsoftware systems).
- Design and architecture, where Eiffel can be used to build solid, flexible system structures.
- Implementation, where Eiffel provides practical software solutions with an efficiency comparable to solutions based on such traditional approaches as C and Fortran.
- Maintenance, where Eiffel helps because of the architectural flexibility of the resulting systems.
- Documentation, where Eiffel permits automatic generation of documentation, textual and graphical, from the software itself, as a partial substitute for separately developed and maintained software documentation.

Although the language is the most visible part, Eiffel is best viewed as a *method*, which guides system analysts and developers through the process of software construction. The Eiffel method is focused on both productivity (the ability to produce systems on time and within budget) and quality, with particular emphasis on the following quality factors:

- *Reliability*—Producing bug-free systems, which perform as expected.
- *Reusability*—Making it possible to develop systems from prepackaged, high-quality components and to transform software elements into such reusable components for future reuse.
- *Extendibility*—Developing software that is truly *soft*—easy to adapt to the inevitable and frequent changes of requirements and other constraints.
- *Portability*—Freeing developers from machine and operating system peculiarities and enabling them to produce software that runs on many different platforms.
- *Maintainability*—Yielding software that is clear, readable, well structured, and easy to continue enhancing and adapting.

9.2. General Properties

Here is an overview of the facilities supported by Eiffel:

- *Completely object-oriented (OO) approach*—Eiffel is a full-fledged application of object technology, not a hybrid of OO and traditional concepts.
- *External interfaces*—Eiffel is a software composition tool and is easily interfaced with software written in lower-level languages such as C, C++, and Java.
- *Full lifecycle support*—Eiffel is applicable throughout the development process, including analysis, design, implementation, and maintenance.
- *Classes as the basic structuring tool*—A class is the description of a set of runtime objects, specified through the applicable operations and abstract properties. An Eiffel system is made entirely of classes, serving as the only module mechanism.
- *Fully consistent type system*—Every type is based on a class, including basic types such as integer, boolean, real, character, string, and array.

- *Design by contract*—Every system component can be accompanied by a precise specification of its abstract properties, governing its internal operation and its interaction with other components.
- *Assertions*—The method and notation support writing the logical properties of object states to express the terms of the contracts. These properties, known as assertions, can be monitored at runtime for testing and quality assurance. They also serve as a documentation mechanism. Assertions include preconditions, postconditions, class invariants, and loop invariants and are also used in check instructions.
- *Exception handling*—Abnormal conditions, such as unexpected operating system signals or more generally contract violations, can be caught and corrected.
- *Information hiding*—Each class author decides, for each feature, whether it is available to all client classes, to specific clients only, or for internal purposes only.
- *Self-documentation*—The notation is designed to enable environment tools to produce abstract views of classes and systems, textual or graphical, and is suitable for reusers, maintainers, and client authors.
- *Inheritance*—One can define a class as extension or specialization of others.
- *Redefinition*—An inherited feature (operation) can be given a different implementation or signature.
- *Explicit redefinition*—Any feature redefinition must be explicitly stated.
- *Subcontracting*—Redefinition rules require new assertions to be compatible with inherited ones.
- *Deferred features and classes*—It is possible for a feature, and the enclosing class, to be specified—including with assertions—but not implemented. Deferred classes are also known as abstract classes.
- *Polymorphism*—An entity (variable, argument, and so on) can become attached to objects of many different types.
- *Dynamic binding*—Calling a feature on an object always triggers the version of the feature specifically adapted to that object, even in the presence of polymorphism and redefinition.

- *Static typing*—A compiler can check statically that all type combinations are valid so that no runtime situation occurs in which an attempt is made to apply a nonexistent feature to an object.
- *Assignment attempt (type narrowing)*—It is possible to check at runtime whether the type of an object conforms to a certain expectation—for example, if the object comes from a database or a network.
- *Multiple inheritance*—A class can inherit from any number of others.
- *Feature renaming*—To remove name clashes under multiple inheritance, or to give better names locally, a class can give a new name to an inherited feature.
- *Repeated inheritance: sharing and replication*—If, as a result of multiple inheritance, a class inherits from another through two or more paths, the class author can specify, for each repeatedly inherited feature, that it yields either one feature (sharing) or two (replication).
- *No ambiguity under repeated inheritance*—Conflicting redefinitions under repeated inheritance are resolved through a selection mechanism.
- *Unconstrained genericity*—A class can be parameterized, or generic, to describe containers of objects of an arbitrary type.
- *Constrained genericity*—A generic class can be declared with a generic constraint to indicate that the corresponding types must satisfy some properties, such as the presence of a particular operation.
- *Garbage collection*—The dynamic model is designed so that memory reclamation, in a supporting environment, can be automatic rather than programmer-controlled.
- *No-leak modular structure*—All software is built out of classes, with only two interclass relations, client and inheritance.
- *Once routines*— A feature can be declared as once so that it is executed only for its first call, subsequently returning always the same result (if required). This serves as a convenient initialization mechanism and for shared objects.
- *Standardized library*—The kernel library, providing essential abstractions, is standardized across implementations.

- *Other libraries*—Eiffel development is largely based on high-quality libraries covering many common needs of software development, from general algorithms and data structures to networking and databases.

It is also useful, as in any design, to list some of what is *not* present in Eiffel. The approach is indeed based on a small number of coherent concepts so that it remains easy to master. Eiffel typically takes a few hours to a few days to learn, and users seldom need to return to the reference manual once they have understood the basic concepts. In fact, the description given in this chapter is, save for a few details, essentially complete. Part of this simplicity results from the explicit decision to exclude a number of possible facilities:

- *No global variables*, which would break the modularity of systems and hamper extendibility, reusability, and reliability.
- *No union types* (or record type with variants), which force the explicit enumeration of all variants; in contrast, inheritance is an open mechanism that permits the addition of variants at any time without changing existing code.
- *No in-class overloading* which, by assigning the same name to different features within a single context, can cause confusion, errors, and conflicts with object-oriented mechanisms such as dynamic binding. (Dynamic binding itself is a powerful form of interclass overloading without any of these dangers.)
- *No goto instructions* or similar control structures (break, exit, or multiple-exit loops), which break the simplicity of the control flow and make it harder or impossible to reason about the software (in particular through loop invariants and variants).
- *No exceptions to the type rules.* To be credible, one type system must not allow unchecked casts converting from one type to another. (Safe cast-like operations are available through assignment attempt.)
- *No side-effect expression operators* confusing computation and modification.
- *No low-level pointers and no pointer arithmetic*, a well-known source of bugs. (There is, however, a type POINTER with no available operations except assignment, comparison, copying, and argument passing, used solely for interfacing Eiffel with C and other languages.)

9.3. The Software Process in Eiffel

Eiffel, as noted, supports the entire lifecycle. The underlying view of the system development lifecycle is radically different not only from the traditional Waterfall model (implying a sequence of discrete steps, such as analysis, global design, detailed design, and implementation, separated by major changes of method and notation) but also from its more recent variants such as the spiral model or rapid prototyping, which remains predicated on a synchronous, full-product process and retains the gaps between successive steps.

Clearly, not everyone using Eiffel will follow to the letter the principles outlined in this chapter; in fact, some competent and successful Eiffel developers may disagree with some of them and prefer a somewhat different process model. In the author's mind, however, these principles fit best with the language and the rest of the method, even if practical developments may fall short of applying their ideal form.

9.3.1. Clusters and the Cluster Model

Unlike earlier approaches, the Eiffel model assumes that the system is divided into a number of subsystems or *clusters*. It keeps from the Waterfall a sequential approach to the development of each cluster (without the gaps) but promotes *concurrent engineering* for the overall process, as suggested by Figure 9.1.

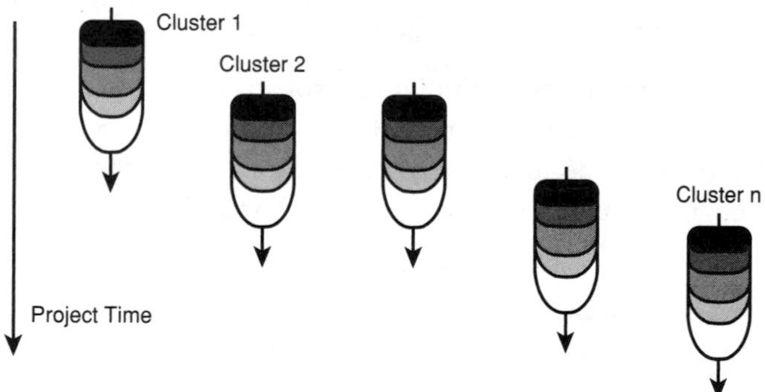

FIGURE 9.1. *The cluster model: sequential and concurrent engineering.*

The Eiffel techniques developed in this chapter, in particular information hiding and design by contract, make the concurrent engineering process possible by letting the clusters rely on other clusters through clearly defined interfaces, strictly limiting the amount of knowledge that must be acquired about a cluster to use it, and permitting separate testing. When the inevitable surprises of a project happen, the project leader can take advantage of the model's flexibility, advancing or delaying various clusters and steps through dynamic reallocation of resources.

Each of the individual cluster lifecycles is based on a continuous progression of activities, from the more abstract to the more implementation-oriented, as shown in Figure 9.2.

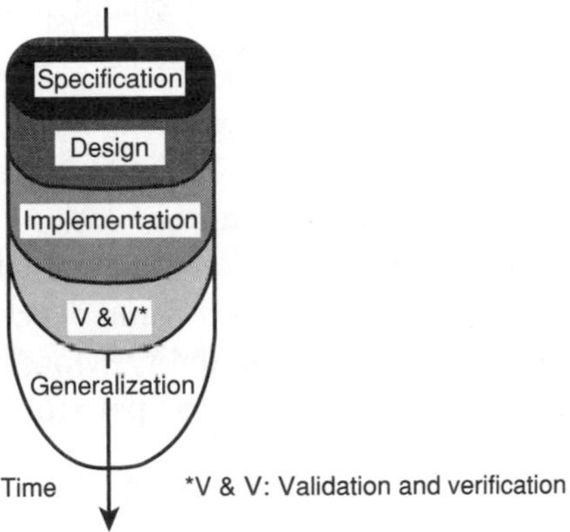

FIGURE 9.2. *The individual cluster lifecycle.*

Figure 9.2 should be understood as describing a process of accretion (as with a stalactite), where each steps *enriches* the results of the previous one. Unlike traditional views, which emphasize the multiplicity of software products—analysis document, global and detailed design documents, program, and maintenance reports—the principle here is to treat the software as a *single product* that is repeatedly refined, extended, and improved. The Eiffel language supports this view by providing high-level notations that can be used throughout the lifecycle, from the most general and software-independent activities of system modeling to the most exacting details of implementation tuned for optimal runtime performance.

These properties make Eiffel span the scope of both object-oriented methods (whereas most such methods do not yield an executable result) and programming languages (whereas most such languages are not suitable for design and analysis).

9.3.2. Seamlessness and Reversibility

The preceding ideas define the seamless approach embodied by Eiffel. With seamlessness goes reversibility: the ability to go back, even late in the process, to earlier stages. Because the developers work on a single product, they can take advantages of bouts of late wisdom—such as a great idea for adding a new function, discovered only at implementation time—and integrate them in the product. Traditional approaches tend to discourage reversibility because it is difficult to guarantee that the analysis and design will be updated with the late changes. With the single-product principle, this is much easier to achieve.

Seamlessness and reversibility enhance extendibility by providing a direct mapping from the structure of the solution to the structure of the problem description, making it much easier to take care of customers' change requests quickly and efficiently. They promote reliability by avoiding possible misunderstandings between customers' and developers' views. They are obviously a major boost to maintainability. More generally, they yield a smooth, consistent software process that is particularly favorable to both quality and productivity.

9.3.3. Generalization and Reuse

The latest part of the cluster lifecycles, generalization, is unheard of in traditional models. It is meant to prepare the results of a cluster for reuse across projects by looking for elements of general applicability and transform them for inclusion in libraries.

Of course, not all companies using the method will be ready to include this phase in their lifecycles. But those who do will see the reusability of their software greatly improved.

9.3.4. Constant Availability

Complementing the preceding principles is the idea that, in the cluster lifecycle, the development team (under the responsibility of the project leader) should at all times maintain a *current working demo* that, although covering only a part of the final system, works well and can be demonstrated or—after a certain stage—shipped as an early release. It is not a prototype in the sense of a mockup meant to be thrown away, but an initial iteration toward the final product; the successive iterations progress continuously until they become that final product.

9.3.5. Compilation Technology

The preceding goals benefit from the ability to check frequently that the current iteration is correct and robust. Eiffel compiler writers have developed considerable effort to supporting efficient compilation mechanisms, such as Interactive Software Engineering's (ISE's) Melting Ice Technology, which ensures immediate recompilation after a change. The recompilation time is a function of the size of the changes, never of the system's overall size. Even for a system of several thousand classes and several hundred thousand lines, the time until restarting after a change to a few classes is a few seconds on a typical modern computer.

Such a "quick melt" (recompilation) immediately catches (along with any syntax errors) the type errors—often the symptoms of conceptual errors that, if left undetected, could cause grave damage later in the process or even during operation. Once the type errors are corrected, the developers should start testing the new functionalities, relying on the power of assertions—explained in section 9.8—to kill the bugs while they are still larvae. Such extensive unit and system testing, constantly interleaved with development, plays an important part in making sure that the current demo is trustworthy and eventually yields a correct and robust product.

9.3.6. Quality and Functionality

Throughout the process, the method suggests maintaining a constant quality level: Apply all the style rules, put in all the assertions, handle erroneous cases (rather than the all too common practice of thinking that one will make the product robust later), and enforce the proper architecture. This applies to all the quality factors except possibly reusability (because one might not know ahead of time how best to generalize a component, and trying to make everything fully general may conflict with solving the specific problem at hand quickly). All that varies is functionality: As the project progresses and clusters come into place, more and more of the final product's intended coverage becomes available. The only question—for example, to answer the more practical one "Can we ship something yet?"—is "Do we cover enough?" and never "Is it good enough?" (as in "Will it not crash?").

Of course, not everyone using Eiffel can, any more than in another approach, guarantee that the ideal just presented will always hold, but it is the theoretical scheme to which the method tends. It explains Eiffel's emphasis on getting everything right: the grandiose and the mundane, the structure and the details. Regarding the details, the Eiffel books cited in the bibliography include many rules, some petty at first sight, about such low-level aspects as the choice of names for classes and features (including their grammatical categories), the indentation of software texts, the style for comments (including the presence or absence of a final period), and the use of spaces. Applying these rules does not, of course, guarantee quality, but they are part of a quality-oriented process, along with the more ambitious principles of design. In addition, they are particularly important for the construction of quality libraries, one of the central goals of Eiffel.

Whenever they are compatible with the space constraints, the present chapter applies these rules in its Eiffel examples.

9.4. Hello, World

When discovering any approach to software construction, however ambitious its goals, it is reassuring to see first a small example of the big picture—a complete program to print the famous "Hello, World" string. Here is how to perform this fascinating task in the Eiffel notation.

You write a class *HELLO* with a single procedure, say *make*, also serving as creation procedure. Here is a minimal version of the class:

```
class HELLO creation make feature
      make is
            do io.put_string ("Hello, World%N") end
end
```

In practice, however, the recommended Eiffel style rules suggest a better documented version:

```
indexing
     description: "Root class for one-class system printing a simple message"
class HELLO creation
      make
feature
      make is
               -- Print a simple message.
            do
              io.put_string ("Hello, World")
              io.new_line
            end
end -- class HELLO
```

The two versions perform identically; the following comments cover the more complete second one.

Note the typesetting conventions: Language keywords such as **class** appear in boldface monotype; identifiers such as the class name HELLO appear in italic monotype in this text, although the standard is italics; and comments appear in monotype, except for occurrences of identifiers in them.

The **indexing** clause does not affect execution semantics but serves to associate documentation with the class so that browsers and other indexing and retrieval tools can help users in search of reusable components satisfying certain properties. Here there is a single indexing entry, `description`.

The name of the class is `HELLO`. Any class may contain `features`; `HELLO` has just one, called `make`. The **creation** clause indicates that `make` is a creation procedure, that is, an operation to be executed at class instantiation time. The class could have any number of creation procedures.

The definition of that creation procedure, `make`, appears in the **feature** clause. Again, there can be any number of such clauses (to separate features into logical categories), and each one of them can contain any number of feature declarations. Here the code has only one.

The line starting with `--` is a comment; more precisely, it is a header comment, which style rules invite software developers to write for every such feature, just after the **is**. (As will be seen in section 9.8.5, environment tools know about this convention and use it to include the header comment in the automatically generated class documentation.)

The body of the feature is introduced by the **do** keyword and terminated by **end**. It consists of two output instructions. They both use `io`, a generally available reference to an object that provides access to standard input and output mechanisms. The notation `io.f`, for some feature `f` of the corresponding library class (`STD_FILES`), means "apply `f` to `io`." Here I use two such features:

- `put_string` outputs a string, passed as an argument, here `"Hello, World"`.
- `new_line` terminates the line.

Rather than use a call to `new_line`, the first version simply integrates a newline character, denoted as `%N`, at the end of the string. Either technique is acceptable.

To execute the software and print `Hello, World`, you need to construct a small *system* (the term preferred to *program* in Eiffel to emphasize the idea of building software by assembly of reusable components) and designate class `HELLO` as the system's root class, with `make` specified as the system's root procedure. Eiffel environments provide simple ways to construct an Ace file that specifies the root class, the root creation procedure, and other compilation options. In ISE Eiffel, for example, an interactive tool lets you enter the names of these two elements and builds the Ace file for you with all compilation options initialized to the most common defaults. You then click the Melt (quick compile) button to compile the system; after a few seconds, you are ready to click the Run button, which causes execution of the system. This outputs `Hello World` on the appropriate medium: a console on Windows or OS/2 or the starting window on UNIX or VMS.

9.5. The Static Picture: System Organization

We now look at the overall organization of Eiffel software.

9.5.1. Systems

An Eiffel system is a collection of classes, one of which is designated as the root class. One of the features of the root class, which must be one of its creation procedures, is designated as the root procedure.

To execute such a system is to create an instance of the root class (an object created according to the class description) and to execute the root procedure. In anything more significant than "Hello World" systems, this creates new objects and applies features to them, in turn triggering further creations and feature calls.

For the system to make sense, it must contain all the classes on which the root depends directly or indirectly. A class `B` depends on a class `A` if it is either a client of `A`, that is, it uses objects of type `A`, or an heir of `A`, that is, it extends or specializes `A`. (These two relations, *client* and *inheritance*, are described in more detail later in the chapter.)

The rest of section 9.5 describes the nuts and bolts of an Eiffel system and of its execution.

9.5.2. Classes

The notion of class is central to the Eiffel approach. A class is the description of a type of runtime data structures (`objects`), characterized by common operations (`features`) and properties. Examples of classes include

- In a banking system, a class `ACCOUNT` may have features such as `deposit`, adding a certain amount to an account, `all_deposits`, yielding the list of deposits since the account's opening, and `balance`, yielding the current balance, with properties stating that `deposit` must add an element to the `all_deposits` list and update `balance` by adding the sum deposited and that the current value of `balance` must be consistent with the lists of deposits and withdrawals.

- A class COMMAND in an interactive system of any kind may have features such as `execute` and `undo`, as well as a feature `undoable`, which indicates whether a command can be undone, with the property that `undo` is only applicable if `undoable` yields the value `true`.
- A class LINKED_LIST may have features such as `put`, which adds an element to a list, and `count` yielding the number of elements in the list with properties stating that `put` increases `count` by one and that `count` is always non-negative.

We may characterize the first of these examples as an analysis class, directly modeling objects from the application domain; the second one as a design class, describing a high-level solution; and the third as an implementation class, reused whenever possible from a library such as EiffelBase. In Eiffel, however, there is no strict distinction between these categories; it is part of the approach's seamlessness that the same notion of class, and the associated concepts, may be used at all levels of the software development process.

9.5.3. Class Relations

Two relations can exist between classes:

- You can define a class C as a client of a class A to enable the features of C to rely on objects of type A.
- You may define a class B as an heir of a class A to provide B with all the features and properties of A, letting B add its own features and properties and modify some of the inherited features if appropriate.

If C is a client of A, A is a supplier of C. If B is an heir of A, A is a parent of B. A descendant of A is either A itself or, recursively, a descendant of an heir of A; in more informal terms, a descendant is a direct or indirect heir, or the class itself. To exclude A itself, we talk of proper descendant. In the reverse direction, the terms are ancestor and proper ancestor.

The client relation can be cyclic; an example involving a cycle would be classes PERSON and HOUSE, modeling the corresponding informal everyday object types and expressing the properties that every person has a home and every home has an architect. The inheritance (heir) relation may not include any cycle.

In modeling terms, client roughly represents the relation "has," and heir roughly represents "is." For example, we may use Eiffel classes to model a certain system and express that every child *has* a birth date (client relation) and *is* a person (inheritance).

Distinctive of Eiffel is the rule that classes can only be connected through these two relations. This excludes the behind-the-scenes dependencies often found in other approaches, such as the use of global variables, which jeopardize the modularity of a system. Only through a strict policy of limited and explicit interclass relations can we achieve the goals of reusability and extendibility.

9.5.4. The Global Inheritance Structure

If you write an Eiffel class, it does not come into a vacuum but fits in a preordained structure, shown in Figure 9.3 and involving a few library classes: GENERAL, ANY, and NONE.

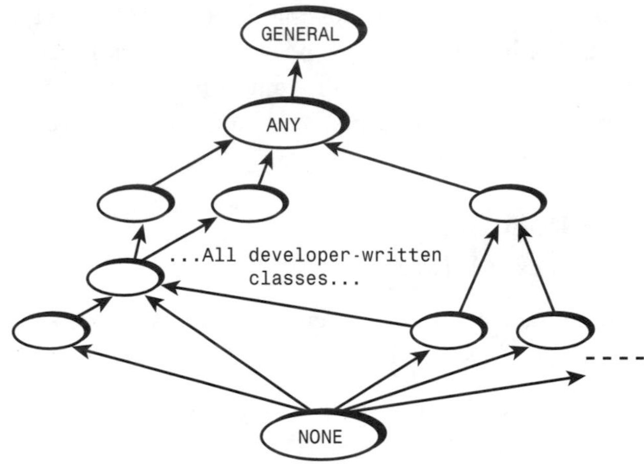

FIGURE 9.3. *The global inheritance structure.*

Any class that does not explicitly inherit from another is considered to inherit from ANY, which itself inherits from GENERAL. This makes GENERAL an ancestor of all developer-written classes (with an exception explained later). GENERAL introduces a number of general-purpose features useful everywhere; examples include copying, cloning, and equality testing operations (section 9.6.10), and default input/output mechanisms.

ANY, as delivered, is empty except for the clause stating that it inherits from GENERAL. Individual companies, groups, or projects can add features to it to provide general mechanisms available to all classes developed in a certain environment. This also gives the ability (not frequently useful) to produce classes that are not descendants of GENERAL: Just redefine ANY so that it ceases to be an heir of GENERAL.

NONE is a fictitious class, which is considered to be an heir of any class that has no explicit heir. Because inheritance has no cycles, NONE cannot have proper descendants. This makes it useful, as you will see, to specify non-exported features and to denote the type of void values.

9.5.5. Clusters

Classes are the only form of module in Eiffel. As is explained in more detail later, they also provide the basis for the only form of type. This module-type identification is at the heart of object technology and yields the fundamental simplicity of the Eiffel method.

Efforts to introduce a higher-level notion of module above classes are misguided because they introduce a whole new set of issues (namespace, name visibility, information hiding, separate compilation, and module inclusion) to which the solutions would clash with the class-level techniques. This would also hamper reusability (by making it harder to reuse a class by itself) and extendibility.

There is a need, however, for an *organizational* concept: cluster. A cluster is a group of related classes. The cluster is a property of the method, enabling managers to organize the development into teams, but it does not require a specific Eiffel language construct. As we have already seen (section 9.3.1), it also plays a central role in the lifecycle model.

9.5.6. External Software

The subsequent sections show how to write Eiffel classes with their features. In an Eiffel system, however, not everything has to be written in Eiffel: Some features may be **external**, coming from external languages such as C, C++, Java, Fortran, or others. For example, a feature declaration may appear (in lieu of the forms seen later in this chapter) as

```
file_status ( filedesc: INTEGER): INTEGER is
        -- Status indicator for filedesc
    external
        "C" alias "_fstat"
    end
```

to indicate that it is actually an encapsulation of a C function whose original name is _fstatv. (The **alias** clause is optional, but here it is needed because the C name, starting with an underscore, is not valid as an Eiffel identifier.)

Similar syntax exists in several Eiffel compilers to interface with C++ classes. ISE Eiffel includes a tool called Legacy++, which automatically produces, from a C++ class, an Eiffel class that encapsulates its facilities, making them available to the rest of the Eiffel software as bona fide Eiffel features.

These mechanisms illustrate one of the roles of Eiffel: a system architecture and software composition tool, used at the highest level to produce systems with robust, flexible structures ready for extendibility, reusability. and maintainability. In these structures, not everything must be written in the Eiffel language: Existing software elements and library components can play their part too, with the structuring capabilities of Eiffel (classes, information hiding, inheritance, clusters, and other techniques in this chapter) serving as the overall wrapping mechanism.

9.6. The Dynamic Structure: Execution Model

A system with a certain static structure describes a set of possible executions. The runtime model governs the structure of the data (*objects*) created during such executions.

The properties of the runtime model are not just of interest to implementers; they also involve concepts directly relevant to the needs of system modelers and analysts at the most abstract levels.

9.6.1. Objects, Fields, Values, and References

A class is defined as the static description of a type of runtime data structure. The data structure described by a class is called an *instance* of the class, which in turn is called the *generating class* (or just *generator*). An instance of ACCOUNT is a data structure representing a bank account; an instance of LINKED_LIST is a data structure representing a linked list.

An *object*, as created during the execution of a system, is an instance of some class of the system.

Classes and objects belong to different worlds. A class is an element of the software text; an object is a data structure created during execution. Although it is possible to define a class whose instances represent classes (as class E_CLASS in the ISE libraries, used to access properties of classes at runtime), this does not eliminate the distinction between a static, compile-time notion, class, and a dynamic, runtime notion, object.

An object is either an atomic object (integer, real, boolean, or double) or a composite object made of a number of *fields*, represented by adjacent rectangles on the conventional runtime diagrams (see Figure 9.4).

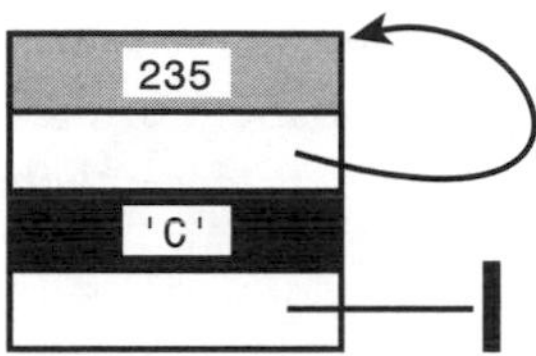

FIGURE 9.4. *A composite object with four fields, including self-reference and void reference.*

Each field is a *value*. A value can be either an object or an object reference:

- When a field is an object, it is in most cases an atomic object, as on the figure where the first field from the top is an integer and the third a character. A field can also be a composite object, in which case it is called a *subobject*.
- A *reference* is either void or uniquely identifies an object, to which it is said to be *attached*. In Figure 9.4, the second field from the top is a reference—attached in this case, as represented by the arrow, to the enclosing object itself. The bottom field is a void reference.

9.6.2. Features

A feature, as noted, is an operation available on instances of a class. A feature can be either an attribute or a routine. This classification, which can be followed by starting from the right on Figure 9.5, is based on implementation considerations.

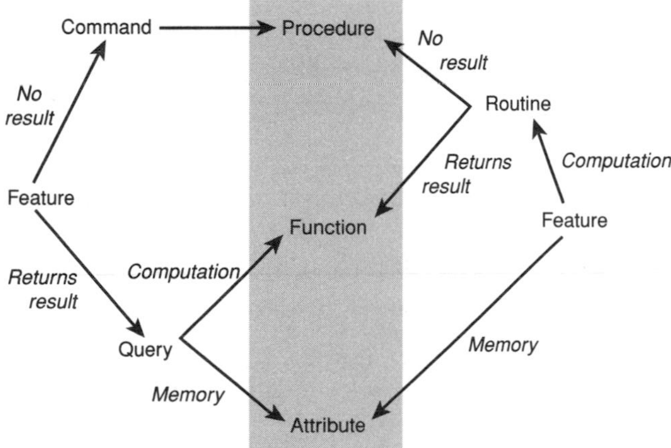

FIGURE 9.5. *Feature categories (two complementary classifications).*

- An attribute is a feature implemented through memory: It describes a field that is found in all instances of the class. For example, class `ACCOUNT` may have an attribute `balance`; then all instances of the class have a corresponding field containing each account's current balance.
- A routine describes a computation applicable to all instances of the class. `ACCOUNT` may have a routine `withdraw`.

Routines are further classified into functions, which return results, and procedures, which do not. Routine `withdraw` is a procedure; an example of a function may be `highest_deposit`, which returns the highest deposit made so far to the account.

From the viewpoint of classes relying on a certain class (its *clients*), the more relevant classification is the one coming from the left on Figure 9.5:

- *Commands* have no result and can modify an object. They can only be procedures.
- *Queries* have a result: They return information about an object. They can be implemented as either attributes (by reserving space for the corresponding information in each instance of the class, a memory-based solution) or functions (a computation-based solution). An attribute is only possible for a query without argument, such as `balance`; a query with arguments, such as `balance_on (d)`, returning the balance at date `d`, can only be a function.

From the outside, there is no difference between a query implemented as an attribute and one implemented as a function: To obtain the balance of an account `a`, you always write `a.balance`.

In the implementation suggested previously, `a` is an attribute so that the notation denotes an access to the corresponding object field. It is also possible to implement `a` as a function, whose algorithm explores the lists of deposits and withdrawals and computes their accumulated value. To the clients of the class, and in the official class documentation as produced by the environment tools, the difference is not visible.

This principle of uniform access supports Eiffel's goals of extendibility, reusability, and maintainability: You can change the implementation without affecting clients, and you can reuse a class without having to know the details of its features' implementations.

9.6.3. A Simple Class

The following simple class text illustrates the preceding concepts:

```
indexing
    description: "Simple bank accounts"
class
    ACCOUNT
feature -- Access
    balance: INTEGER
            -- Current balance
    deposit_count: INTEGER is
            -- Number of deposits made since opening
        do
            if all_deposits /= Void then
                Result := all_deposits.count
            end
        end
feature -- Element change
    deposit (sum: INTEGER) is
            -- Add sum to account.
        do
            if all_deposits= Void then
                !! all_deposits
            end
            all_deposits.extend (sum)
            balance := balance + sum
        end
feature {NONE} -- Implementation
    all_deposits: DEPOSIT_LIST
            -- List of deposits since account's opening.
invariant
    consistent_balance: (all_deposits /= Void)
        implies (balance = all_deposits.total)
    zero_if_no_deposits: (all_deposits = Void)
        implies (balance = 0)
end -- class ACCOUNT
```

(The `{NONE}` qualifier and the **invariant** clause, used here to make the example closer to a real class, are explained shortly. `DEPOSIT_LIST` refers to another class, which can be written separately using library classes.)

The category to which each feature belongs is easy to deduce from its syntactic appearance. Here only `deposit` and `deposit_count`, which include a **do**... clause, are routines; `balance` and `all_deposits`, which are simply declared with a type, are attributes. Note that even for attributes it is recommended to have a header comment.

Routine `deposit_count` is declared as returning a result (of type `INTEGER`), so it is a function. Routine `deposit` has no such result and hence is a procedure.

9.6.4. Creating and Initializing Objects

Classes, as noted, are a static notion. Objects appear at runtime; they are created explicitly.

The instruction that creates an object of type ACCOUNT and attaches it to x is written

```
!! x
```

assuming that x has been declared of type ACCOUNT. Such an instruction must be in a routine of some class—the only place where instructions can appear—and its effect at runtime is threefold: Create a new object of type ACCOUNT, initialize its fields to default values, and attach the value of x to it. Here the object has two fields corresponding to the two attributes of the generating class: an integer for balance, which is initialized to 0, and a reference for all_deposits, which is initialized to a void reference (see Figure 9.6).

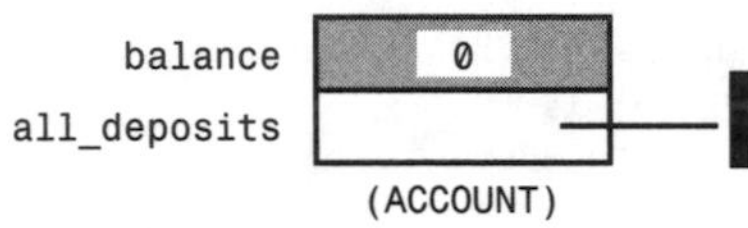

FIGURE 9.6. *An instance of ACCOUNT with fields initialized to defaults.*

The default initialization values are specified for all possible types (see Figure 9.7).

Type	Default value
INTEGER.REAL.DOUBLE	Zero
BOOLEAN	False
CHARACTER	Null
Reference types (such as ACCOUNT and DEPOSIT_LIST)	Void reference
Composite expanded types	Same rules, applied recursively to all fields

FIGURE 9.7. *Types and corresponding default initialization values.*

It is possible to override the initialization values by providing—as in the earlier example of class HELLO—one or more creation procedures. For example, we might change ACCOUNT to make sure that every account is created with an initial deposit:

```
indexing
    description: "Simple bank accounts, initialized with a first
                  deposit"
class
    ACCOUNT1
creation
    make
```

```
feature   -- Initialization
        make (sum: INTEGER) is
            -- Initialize account with sum.
        do
            deposit (sum)
        end
... The rest of the class as for ACCOUNT ...
end   -- class ACCOUNT1
```

The newly added **creation** clause lists one or more (here just one) procedures of the class. In this case, the original form `!! x` is not valid any more for creating an instance of ACCOUNT1; a creation instruction must be of a form such as

```
!! x.make (2000)
```

known as a creation call. Such a creation call has the same effect as the original form (creation, initialization, and attachment to `x`) followed by the effect of calling the selected creation procedure, which here calls `deposit` with the given argument.

Note that in this example all that `make` does is to call `deposit`. An alternative to introducing a new procedure `make` would have been simply to introduce a creation clause of the form **creation** `deposit`, elevating `deposit` to the status of creation procedure. Then a creation call would be of the form `!! x.deposit (2000)`.

9.6.5. Entities

The example assumes `x` declared of type ACCOUNT (or ACCOUNT1). Such an `x` is an example of an entity, a notion generalizing the well-known concept of a variable. An entity is a name that appears in a class text to represent possible runtime values (a value being, as defined earlier, an object or a reference). An entity is one of the following:

- An attribute of the enclosing class, such as `balance` and `all_deposits`.
- A formal argument of a routine, such as `sum` for `deposit` and `make`.
- A local entity declared for the needs of a routine.
- The special entity `Result` in a function.

The third case, local entities, arises when a routine needs some auxiliary values for its computation. Here is an example of the syntax:

```
deposit (sum: INTEGER) is
        -- Add sum to account.
    local
        new: AMOUNT
```

```
    do
        !! new.make (sum)
        all_deposits.extend (new)
        balance := balance + sum
    end
```

This example is a variant of `deposit` for which we assume that the elements of a `DEPOSIT_LIST` such as `all_deposits` are no longer just integers, but objects, instances of a new class, `AMOUNT`. Such an object contains an integer value and possibly other information as well. For the purpose of procedure `deposit`, we create an instance of `AMOUNT` and insert it, using procedure `extend`, into the list `all_deposits`. The object is identified through the local entity `new`, which is only needed within each execution of the routine (as opposed to an attribute, which yields an object field that remains in existence for as long as the object).

The last case of entity, `Result`, serves to denote, within the body of a function, the final result to be returned by that function. This was illustrated by the function `deposits_count`, which reads

```
deposit_count: INTEGER is
     -- Number of deposits made since opening (provisional version)
    if all_deposits /= Void then
        Result := all_deposits.count
    end
```

The value returned by any call is the value of the expression `all_deposits.count` (to be explained in detail shortly) for that call, unless `all_deposits` has value `Void`, denoting a void reference (`/=` is not equal).

The default initialization rules seen earlier for attributes (Figure 9.7) also serve to initialize all local entities and `Result` on entry to a routine. In the last example, if `all_deposits` is void (as in the case on initialization with the class as given so far), `Result` keeps its default value of 0, which is returned as the result of the function.

9.6.6. Calls

Apart from object creation, the basic computational mechanism, in the object-oriented style of computation represented by Eiffel, is the feature call. In its basic form, it appears as

```
target.feature (argument1, ...)
```

where *`target`* is an entity (it can more generally be an expression), *`feature`* is a feature name, and there may be zero or more *`argument`* expressions. In the absence of any *`argument`*, the part in parentheses should be removed.

We have already seen such calls. If *feature* denotes a procedure, the call is an instruction, as in

```
all_deposits.extend (new)
```

If *feature* denotes a query (function or attribute), the call is an expression, as in the right-hand side of

```
Result := all_deposits.count
```

The principle of uniform access (section 9.6.2) implies that this form is the same for an attribute and for a function without arguments. (The feature used in this example, count from class DEPOSIT_LIST, could indeed be implemented in either of these two ways: We can keep a count field in each list, updating it for each insertion and removal, or we can compute count, whenever requested, by traversing the list to count the number of elements.)

In the case of a routine with arguments—procedure or function—the routine is declared, in its class, as

```
feature ( formal1: TYPE1; ...) is
    do ... end
```

meaning that, at the time of each call, the value of each formal is set to the corresponding actual (formal1 to argument1 and so on). In the routine body, it is not permitted to change the value of a formal argument, although it is possible to change the value of an attached object through a procedure call such as formal1.some_procedure (...).

9.6.7. Infix and Prefix Notation

Basic types such as INTEGER are, as noted, part of Eiffel's uniform type system, so they are declared as classes (part of the kernel library). INTEGER, for example, is characterized by the features describing integer operations: plus, minus, times, division, less than, and so on.

With the dot notation seen so far, this would imply that simple arithmetic operations would have to be written with a syntax such as i.plus (j) instead of the usual i + j. This is awkward. Infix and prefix features solve the problem, reconciling the object-oriented view of computation with common notational practices of mathematics. The addition function is declared in class INTEGER as

```
infix "+" (other: INTEGER): INTEGER is
    do ... end
```

Such a feature has all the properties and prerogatives of a normal identifier feature, except for the form of the calls, which is infix, as in `i + j`, rather than dot notation. An infix feature must be a function and take exactly one argument. Similarly, a function can be declared as **prefix** "--", with no argument, permitting calls of the form `--3` rather than `(3).negated`.

Predefined library classes covering basic types such as `INTEGER`, `CHARACTER`, `BOOLEAN`, `REAL`, and `DOUBLE` are known to the Eiffel compiler so that a call of the form `i + j`, although conceptually equivalent to a routine call, can be processed just as efficiently as the corresponding arithmetic expression in an ordinary programming language. This brings the best of both worlds: conceptual simplicity, enabling Eiffel developers, when they want to, to think of integers and the like as objects and efficiency as good as in lower-level approaches.

Infix and prefix features can be used in any class, not just predefined classes for basic types. For example, a graphics class could use the name **infix** "|--|" for a function computing the distance between two points, to be used in expressions such as `point1 |--| point2`.

9.6.8. Type Declaration

Every entity in Eiffel is declared as a certain type, using the syntax already encountered in the preceding examples:

```
entity_name: TYPE_NAME
```

This applies to attributes, formal arguments of routines, and local entities. The result type is also declared for a function, as in the earlier example

```
deposit_count: INTEGER is ...
```

Here the type also serves as the type implicitly declared for `Result` in the function's body.

What is a type? With the elements seen so far, every type is a class. `INTEGER`, used in the declaration of `deposits_count`, is, as we have seen, a library class, and the declaration `all_deposits: DEPOSIT_LIST` assumes the existence of a class `DEPOSIT_LIST`.

Three mechanisms introduced later in this chapter—expanded types (section 9.6.9), genericity (section 9.7) and anchored declarations (section 9.9.16)—generalize the notion of type slightly. But they do not change the fundamental property that *every type is based on a class*, called the type's *base class*. In the examples seen so far, each type is a class, serving as its own base class. An instance of a class `C` is also called an object of type `C`.

9.6.9. Type Categories

It was noted previously that a value is either an object or a reference. This corresponds to two kinds of type: reference types and expanded types.

If a class is declared as just

```
class CLASS_NAME ...
```

it defines a reference type. The entities declared of that type denote references. In the declaration

```
x: ACCOUNT
```

the possible runtime values for x are references, which are either void or attached to instances of class ACCOUNT.

Instead of **class**, however, you can use the double keyword **expanded class**, as in the library class definition

```
indexing
     description: "Integer values"
expanded class
     INTEGER
feature  -- Basic operations
     infix "+" (other: INTEGER): INTEGER is
          do ... end
... Other feature declarations ...
end  -- class INTEGER
```

In this case, the value of an entity declared as n: INTEGER is not a reference to an object, but the object itself—in this case, an atomic object, an integer value.

It is also possible, for some non-expanded class C, to declare an entity as

```
x: expanded C
```

so that the values for x are objects of type C, rather than references to such objects. This is our first example of a type—**expanded** C—that is not directly a class, although it is based on a class, C. The base type of such a type is C.

Note that the value of an entity of expanded type can never be void; only a reference can. Extending the earlier terminology, an expanded entity is always *attached to* an object, atomic (as in the case of n: INTEGER) or composite (as in x: **expanded** ACCOUNT).

Expanded declarations make it possible to construct composite objects with subobjects, as in the following abbreviated class declaration (indexing clause and routines omitted):

```
class CAR feature
    engine: expanded ENGINE
    originating_plant: PLANT
end  -- class CAR
```

Figure 9.8 shows the structure of a typical instance of CAR:

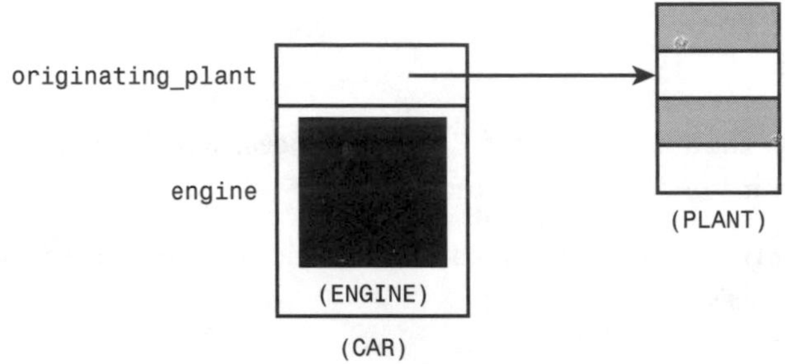

FIGURE 9.8. *A composite object with reference and subobject.*

This example also illustrates that the distinction between expanded and reference types is important not just for system implementation purposes but for high-level system modeling as well. To understand the conceptual distinction, note that many cars share the same `originating_plant`, but an `engine` belongs to just one car. References represent the modeling relation "knows about"; subobjects, as permitted by expanded types, represent the relation "has part," also known as aggregation. The key difference is that sharing is possible in the former case but not in the latter.

9.6.10. Basic Operations

The basic operations described in this section are available on entities and expressions.

Assignment uses the symbol `:=`. The assignment instruction

```
x := y
```

updates the value of `x` to be the same as that of `y`. This means that

- For entities of reference types, the value of `x` is a void reference if the value of `y` is void; otherwise, `x` is attached to the same object `OBJ2` as `y` (see Figure 9.9).

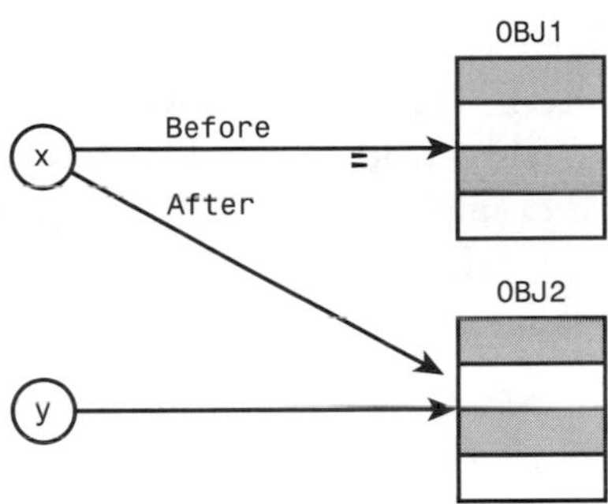

FIGURE 9.9. *The effect of reference reattachment* `x := y`.

- For entities of expanded types, the values are objects; the object attached to `x` is overwritten with the contents of the object attached to `y`. In the case of atomic objects, as in `n := 3` with the declaration `n: INTEGER`, this has the expected effect of assigning to `n` the integer value `3`; in the case of composite objects, this overwrites the fields for `x`, one by one, with the corresponding `y` fields.

To copy an object, use `x.copy (y)`, which assumes that both `x` and `y` are non-void and copies the contents of `y`'s attached object onto those of `x`'s. Note that for expanded entities, the effect is the same as that of the assignment `x :=y`.

A variant of the *copy* operation is `clone`. The expression `clone (y)` produces a newly created object, initialized with a copy of the object attached to `y`, or a void value if `y` itself is void. For a reference type (the only interesting case) the returned result for non-void `y` is a reference to the new object. In other words, `clone` can be viewed as a function that performs

```
!! Result
Result.copy (y)
```

In the assignment `x := clone (y)`, assuming that both entities of reference types and `y` are not void, attaches `x` to a new object identical to `y`'s attached object, as opposed to the assignment `x :=y`, which attaches `x` to the same object as `y`.

To determine whether two values are equal, use the expression `x = y`. (The expression `x /= y` yields `true` if they are *not* equal.) For references, the equality comparison yields true if the values are either both void or both attached to the same object; this is the case on Figure 9.9 in the state *after* the assignment, but not before.

As with assignment, there is also a variant that works on objects rather than references: `x.is_equal (y)` returns `true` when `x` and `y` are both non-void and attached to field-by-field identical objects. This can be true even when `x = y` is not—for example, on Figure 9.9, *before* the assignment, if the two objects shown are field-by-field equal.

A more general variant of `is_equal` is used under the form `equal (x, y)`. This is always defined, even if `x` is void, returning `true` whenever `is_equal` would but also if `x` and `y` are both void. (In contrast, `x.is_equal (y)` is not defined for void *x* and would, if evaluated, yield an exception as explained in section 9.8.6.)

The predefined feature `Void` denotes a void reference. You can make `x` void through the assignment `x := Void` and test whether it is void through **`if`** `x = Void` **`then`** .... The type of `Void` is `NONE`, the least interesting class (section 9.5.4).

The features introduced in this section—`copy`, `clone`, `is_equal`, `equal`, and `Void`—are not language constructs but features defined in the highest-level class `GENERAL` (section 9.5.4) and hence available to all classes. `Void` is of type `NONE`. Using the redefinition mechanisms mentioned in the discussion of inheritance, a class can redefine `copy` and `is_equal` to describe specific notions of copy and equality. (The assertions ensure that the two remain compatible: After `x.copy (y)`, the property `x.is_equal (y)` must always be true.) Redefining `copy` automatically causes `clone` to follow, and redefining `is_equal` automatically causes `equal` to follow. `Void` too should not be redefined. To avoid any mistake, these features are declared as "frozen"—not redefinable. To guarantee the original, non-redefined semantics, you can use the frozen variants `standard_copy`, `standard_clone`, `standard_equal`, and so on.

9.6.11. Deep Operations and Persistence

Feature `clone` only duplicates one object. If some of the fields of that object are references to other objects, the references themselves are copied, not those other objects.

It is useful, in some cases, to duplicate not just one object but an entire object structure. The expression `deep_clone (y)` achieves this goal: Assuming non-void `y`, it produces a duplicate not just of the object attached to `y` but of the entire object structure starting at that object. The mechanism of course respects all the possible details of that structure, such as cyclic reference chains. As earlier features, `deep_clone` comes from class `GENERAL`.

A related mechanism provides a powerful *persistence* facility. A call of the form

```
x.store (Some_file_or_network_connection)
```

(using the conventions of ISE Eiffel) stores a copy of the entire object structure starting at `x`, under a suitable representation. Like `deep_clone`, procedure `store` follows all references to the end and maintains the properties of the structure. The function `retrieved` can then be used—in the same system, or another—to recreate the structure from the stored version.

As the name suggests, `Some_file_or_network_connection` can be an external medium of various possible kinds, not just a file but possibly a database or network. ISE's EiffelNet client/server library indeed uses the `store`-`retrieved` mechanism to exchange object structures over a network, between compatible or different machine architectures—for example, a Windows client and a UNIX server.

9.6.12. Memory Management

Reference reattachments `x := y` of the form illustrated by Figure 9.9 can cause objects to become unreachable. This is the case for the object identified as `OBJ2` on that figure (the object to which `x` was attached before the assignment) if no other reference was attached to it.

In all but toy systems, it is essential to reclaim the memory that has been allocated for such objects; otherwise, memory usage could grow forever, as a result of creation instructions `!! x ...` and calls to `clone` and the like, leading to thrashing and eventually to catastrophic termination.

Unlike some other approaches, the Eiffel method suggests that the task of detecting and reclaiming such unused object space should be handled by an automatic mechanism (part of the Eiffel runtime environment), not manually by developers (through calls to procedures such as Pascal's `dispose` and C/C++'s `free`). The arguments for this view are

- *Convenience*—Handling memory reclamation manually can add enormous complication to the software, especially when—as is often the case in object-oriented development—the system manipulates complex runtime data structures with many links and cycles.
- *Reliability*—Memory management errors, such as the incorrect reclamation of an object that is still referenced by a distant part of the structure, are a notorious source of particularly dangerous and hard-to-correct bugs.

Eiffel environments have developed sophisticated *garbage collectors* that efficiently handle the automatic reclamation process, while causing no visible degradation of a system's performance and response time.

Reliance on automatic garbage collection is a key part of the Eiffel method's contribution to both ease of development and software reliability.

9.6.13. Information Hiding and the Call Rule

The basic form of computation, it has been noted, is a call of the form `target.feature (...)`. This is only meaningful if `feature` denotes a feature of the generating class of the object to which `target` (assumed to be non-void) is attached. The precise rule is the following:

Feature call rule

A call of the form `target.feature (...)` appearing in a class `C` is only valid if `feature` is a feature of the base class of `target`'s type and is available to `C`.

The first condition simply expresses that if `target` has been declared as `target: A`, then `feature` must be the name of one of the features of `A`. The second condition reflects Eiffel's application of the principles of information hiding. A **feature** clause, introducing one or more feature declarations, may not just appear as

```
feature   -- Comment identifying the feature category
     ... Feature declaration ...
     ... Feature declaration ...
     ...
```

but also include a list of classes in braces, **feature** `{A, B, ...}`, as illustrated for `ACCOUNT`:

```
feature {NONE}   -- Implementation
     all_deposits: DEPOSIT_LIST
           -- List of deposits since account's opening.
```

This form indicates that the features appearing in that clause are only available—in the sense of available for calls, as used in the feature call rule—to the classes listed. In the sample feature, `all_deposits` is only available to `NONE`. Because of the global inheritance structure (section 9.5.4), this means it is in fact available to no useful client at all and is equivalent in practice to **feature** `{ }` with an empty class list, but the form listing `NONE` explicitly is more visible and hence preferred.

With this specification, a class text including the declaration `acc: ACCOUNT` and a call of the form

```
acc.all_deposits
```

violates the feature call rule and is rejected by the Eiffel compiler.

Besides fully exported features (introduced by **`feature`** ... without further qualification) and fully secret ones (**`feature`** `{}` or **`feature`** `{NONE}`), it is possible to export features selectively to some specified classes, using the specification **`feature`** `{A, B, ...}` for arbitrary classes `A`, `B`, and so on. By enabling a group of related classes to provide each other with privileged access, this selective export mechanism is one of the techniques that avoids the heavier solution of using meta-modules above the class level (section 9.5.5).

Exporting features selectively to a set of classes `A`, `B`, and so on also makes them available to the descendants of these classes. A feature clause beginning with just **`feature`** is equivalent to one starting with **`feature`** `{ANY}`.

These rules enable successive feature clauses to specify exports to different clients. In addition, the recommended style, illustrated in the examples of this chapter, suggests writing separate feature clauses—regardless of their use for specifying export privileges—to group features into separate categories. Typical categories, appearing in the order given, are Initialization (for creation procedures), Access (for general queries), Status report, Status setting, Element change, and Implementation (for selectively exported or secret features).

The feature call rule is the first of the rules that make Eiffel a *statically typed* approach, where the applicability of operations to objects is verified at compile time rather than during execution. Static typing is one of the principal components of Eiffel's support for reliability in software development.

9.6.14. Execution Scenario

The preceding elements make it possible to understand the overall scheme of an Eiffel system's execution.

At any time during the execution of a system, one object is the *current object* of the execution, and one of the routines of the system, the *current routine*, is executed with the current object as its target. (You will see later in this chapter how the current object and current routine are determined.) The text of a class, in particular its routines, make constant implicit references to the current object. For example, in the instruction

```
balance := balance + sum
```

appearing in the body of procedure deposit of class ACCOUNT, the name of the attribute balance, in both occurrences, denotes the balance field of the current object, assumed to be an instance of ACCOUNT. In the same way, the procedure body that we have used for the creation procedure make in the ACCOUNT1 variant

```
make (sum: INTEGER) is
        -- Initialize account with sum.
do
      deposit (sum)
end
```

contains a call to the procedure deposit. Contrary to earlier calls written in dot notation as *target.feature* (...), the call to deposit has no explicit target; this means its target is the current object, an instance of ACCOUNT1. Such a call is said to be *unqualified*; those using dot notations are *qualified* calls.

Although most uses of the current object are implicit, a class may need to name it explicitly. The predefined expression Current is available for that purpose. A typical use, in a routine merge (other: ACCOUNT) of class ACCOUNT, would be a test of the form

```
if other = Current then
      report_error ("Error: trying to merge an account with itself !")
else
      ... Normal processing (merging two different accounts) ...
end
```

With these notions, it is not hard to define precisely the overall scenario of a system execution by defining what object and routine will be the current object and the current routine at each instant:

- Starting a system execution, as we have seen, consists in creating an instance of the root class, the root object, and executing a designated creation procedure, the root procedure, with the root object as its target. The root object is the initial current object, and the root procedure is the initial current procedure.
- From then on, only two events can change the current object and current procedure: a qualified routine call and the termination of a routine.

- In a call of the form *target.routine* (...), *target* denotes a certain object TC. (If *target* is an attribute, TC is the object attached to the corresponding field of the current object, which must be non-void for the call to proceed.) Then TC becomes the new current object. The generating class of TC must, according to the feature call rule, contain a routine of name routine, which becomes the new current routine.
- When a routine execution terminates, the target object and routine of the most recent non-terminated call (which just before the terminated call were the current object and the current routine) assume again the role of current object and current routine. This does not apply, of course, to the termination of the original root procedure call; in this case, the entire execution terminates and there is nothing more to say about it.

9.6.15. Abstraction

The description of assignments stated that in x := y, the target x must be an entity. More precisely, it must be a *writable* entity; this excludes formal routine arguments. As noted, a routine r (arg: SOME_TYPE) cannot assign to arg (reattaching it to a different object), although it can change the attached objects through calls of the form *arg.procedure* (...).

The restriction to an entity precludes in particular assignments of the form *obj.some_attribute* := *some_value* because the left-hand side, *obj.some_attribute*, is an expression (a feature call), not an entity, and you can no more assign to *obj.some_attribute* than to, say, a + b—another expression that is also, formally, a feature call.

To obtain the intended effect of the invalid assignment, you can use a procedure call of the form *obj.set_attribute* (*some_value*), where the base class of obj's type has defined the procedure

```
set_attribute (v: VALUE_TYPE) is
        -- Set value of attribute to v.
    do
        attribute := v
    end
```

This rule is essential to enforcing the method. Permitting direct assignments to an object's fields would violate all the tenets of information hiding by circumventing the interface carefully crafted by the author of the supplier class. It is the responsibility of each class author to define the exact privileges that the class gives to each of its clients, in particular field modification rights. A field can be totally hidden (when the corresponding attribute is exported to NONE); it can be exported in read-only mode (when the attribute is exported, but no procedure modifies it); it can be exported in free-write mode (as with `set_attribute` if the class exports this procedure); it can also be exported in restricted-write mode, as with procedure `deposit` of class ACCOUNT, which allows addition of a certain amount to the balance field, but not direct setting of the balance. In such a case, the exported procedures may, thanks to the assertion mechanism reviewed later (section 9.8), place some further restrictions on the permitted modifications—for example, by requiring the withdrawn amount to be positive.

The more general view is that each class describes a well-understood abstraction, for which the class designer decides exactly what operations are permitted. The class documentation (the *short form* described in section 9.8.5) makes this view clear to client authors; no violation of that interface is permitted, as it would make a mockery of the principles of object technology. This approach also paves the way for future generalization (9.3.3) of the most promising components and their inclusion into reusable libraries.

9.7. Genericity

Some of the classes that we need, particularly (but not solely) in libraries, are container classes, describing data structures made of a number of objects of the same type, or compatible types. Examples of containers include arrays, stacks, and lists. The class `DEPOSIT_LIST` posited in earlier examples describes containers.

It is not hard, with the mechanisms seen so far, to write a class such as `DEPOSIT_LIST`, which includes such features as `count` (query returning the number of elements) and `put` (command to insert a new element).

Most of the operations, however, are the same for lists of objects other than deposits. To avoid undue replication of efforts and promote reuse, we need a way to describe generic container classes, which can be applied to describe containers of elements of many different types.

The notation

```
class C[G] ... The rest as for any other class declaration ...
```

introduces such a generic class. A name such as `G` appearing in brackets after the class name is known as a *formal generic parameter*; it represents an arbitrary type.

Within the class text, feature declarations can freely use G even though it is not known what type G stands for. Class LIST of ISE's EiffelBase libraries, for example, includes features

```
first: G
      -- Value of first list element

extend (val: G) is
      -- Add a new element of value val at end of list
     ...
```

The operations available on an entity such as first and x, whose type is a formal generic parameter, are the operations available on all types: use as source y of an assignment x := y, use as target x of such an assignment (although not for val, which as a formal routine argument is not writable), use in equality comparisons x = y or x /= y, and application of universal features from ANY such as clone, equal, and copy.

To use a generic class such as list, a client provides a type name as an actual generic parameter; for example, instead of using DEPOSIT_LIST, the class ACCOUNT could include the declaration

```
all_deposits: LIST [DEPOSIT]
```

using LIST as a generic class and DEPOSIT as the actual generic parameter. Then all features declared in LIST as working on entities of type G work, when called on the target all_deposits, on entities of type DEPOSIT. With the target

```
all_accounts: LIST [ACCOUNT]
```

these features would work on entities of type ACCOUNT.

A note on terminology: To avoid confusion, Eiffel literature uses the word *argument* for routine arguments, reserving *parameter* for the generic parameters of classes.

Genericity reconciles extendibility and reusability with the static type checking demanded by reliability. A typical error, such as confusing an account and a deposit, is detected immediately at compile time because the call all_accounts.extend (dep) is invalid for dep declared of type DEPOSIT. (What is valid is something like all_accounts.extend (acc) for acc of type ACCOUNT.) In other approaches, the same effect might require costly runtime checks (as in Java or Smalltalk) with the risk of runtime errors.

Further flexibility is provided by providing a *constrained* form of genericity that allows assuming other operations, on a formal generic parameter, than just those of *ANY*. This will be seen in the discussion of inheritance.

An example of generic class from the kernel library is `ARRAY [G]`, which describes direct-access arrays. Features include

- `put` to replace an element's value, as in `my_array.put (val, 25)`, which replaces by `val` the value of the array entry at index 25.
- `item` to access an entry, as in `my_array.item (25)` yielding the entry at index 25. A synonym is **`infix`** `"@"` so that the same result can be obtained more tersely as `my_array @ 25`.
- `lower`, `upper`, and `count`: queries yielding the bounds and the number of entries.
- The creation procedure `make`, as in `!! my_array.make (1, 50)`, which creates an array with the given index bounds. It is also possible to resize an array through `resize`, keeping of course the old elements. In general, the Eiffel method shuns built-in limits and favors automatically resizable structures.

The comment made about `INTEGER` and other basic classes applies to `ARRAY` too: Eiffel compilers know about this class and can process expressions of the form `my_array.put (val, 25)` and `my_array @ 25` in essentially the same way as a C or Fortran array access (`my_array [25]` in C). It is consistent and practical to let developers treat `ARRAY` as a class and arrays as objects; many library classes in EiffelBase, for example, inherit from `ARRAY`. Once again, the idea is to get the best of both worlds: the convenience and uniformity of the object-oriented way of thinking and the efficiency of traditional approaches. A similar technique applies to another kernel library class, one that is not generic: `STRING`, describing character strings with a rich set of string manipulation features.

The introduction of genericity brings up a small difference between classes and types. A generic class `C` is not directly a type because you cannot declare an entity as type `C` (you must use some actual generic parameter `T`—itself a type). Rather, `C` is a type pattern. To obtain an actual type `C [T]`, you must provide an actual generic parameter `T`. This is known as a *generic derivation.* (`T` itself is, recursively, a type—either a non-generic class or again a generically derived type `D [U]` for some `D` and `U`, as in `LIST [ARRAY [INTEGER]]`.)

It remains true, however, that every type is based on a class. The base class of a generically derived type `C [T]` is `C`.

9.8. Design by Contract, Assertions, and Exceptions

Eiffel directly implements the ideas of design by contract, which enhance software reliability and provide a sound basis for software specification, documentation, and testing, as well as exception handling and the proper use of inheritance.

9.8.1. Design by Contract Basics

A system—a software system in particular, but the ideas are more general—is made of a number of cooperating components. Design by contract states that their cooperation should be based on precise specifications—*contracts*—describing each party's expectations and guarantees.

An Eiffel contract is similar to a real-life contract between two people or two companies, which it is convenient to express in the form of tables listing the expectations and guarantees. Here for example is how we could sketch the contract between a homeowner and the telephone company:

`provide_service`	**Obligations**	**Benefits**
Client	*(Satisfy precondition:)* Pay bill	*(From postcondition:)* Get telephone service
Supplier	*(Satisfy postcondition:)* Provide telephone service	*(From precondition:)* No need to provide anything if bill not paid

Note how the obligation for each of the parties maps onto a benefit for the other. This is a general pattern.

The client's obligation, which protects the supplier, is called a *precondition.* It states what the client must satisfy before requesting a certain service. The client's benefit, which describes what the supplier must do (assuming the precondition was satisfied), is called a *postcondition.*

In addition to preconditions and postconditions, there are also invariants applying to a class as a whole. More precisely, a class invariant must be ensured by every creation procedure (or by the default initialization if there is no creation procedure) and maintained by every exported routine of the class.

9.8.2. Expressing Assertions

Eiffel provides syntax for expressing preconditions (`require`), postconditions (`ensure`), and class invariants (`invariant`), as well as other assertion constructs studied later (section 9.10.3): loop invariants and variants, check instructions.

Here is a partial update of class `ACCOUNT` with more assertions:

```
indexing
    description: "Simple bank accounts"
class
    ACCOUNT
feature  -- Access
    balance: INTEGER
            -- Current balance
    deposit_count: INTEGER is
            -- Number of deposits made since opening
        do
            ... As before ...
        end
feature  -- Element change
    deposit (sum: INTEGER) is
            -- Add sum to account.
        require
            non_negative: sum >= 0
        do
            ... As before ...
        ensure
            one_more_deposit: deposit_count = old deposit_count + 1
            updated: balance = old balance + sum
        end
feature {NONE}  -- Implementation
    all_deposits: DEPOSIT_LIST
            -- List of deposits since account's opening.
invariant
    consistent_balance: (all_deposits /= Void)
        implies (balance = all_deposits.total)
    zero_if_no_deposits: (all_deposits = Void)
        implies (balance = 0)
end  -- class ACCOUNT
```

Each assertion is made of one or more subclauses, each of them a boolean expression (with the additional possibility of the **`old`** construct). If there is more than one subclause, as in the postcondition of `deposit` and in the invariant, they are treated as if they were connected by an **`and`**. Each clause may be preceded by a label, such as `consistent_balance` in the invariant, and a colon; the label is optional and does not affect the assertion's semantics, except for error reporting as explained in the next section, but including it systematically is part of the recommended style as applied by this chapter. The boolean expression `a` **`implies`** `b` is `true` if `a` is `false` and otherwise if both `a` and `b` are `true`.

Because assertions benefit from the full power of boolean expressions, they may include function calls. This makes it possible to express sophisticated consistency conditions, such as "*the graph contains no cycle*," which is not otherwise expressible through simple expressions, or even through first-order predicate calculus, but which are easy to implement as Eiffel functions returning boolean results.

The precondition of a routine expresses conditions that the routine is imposing on its clients. Here a call to `deposit` is correct if and only if the value of the argument is non-negative. The routine does not guarantee anything for a call that does not satisfy the precondition. It is in fact part of the Eiffel method that a routine body should *never* test for the precondition because it is the client's responsibility to ensure it. (An apparent paradox of design by contract, which is reflected in the bottom-right entries of the preceding and following contract tables, and should not be a paradox any more at the end of this discussion, is that one can get *more* reliable software by having *fewer* explicit checks in the software text.)

The postcondition of a routine expresses what the routine does guarantee to its clients for calls satisfying the precondition. The notation **old** `expression`, valid in postconditions (**ensure** clauses) only, denotes the value that *expression* had on entry to the routine.

The precondition and postcondition state the terms of the contract between the routine and its clients, similar to the earlier example of a human contract:

`deposit`	**Obligations**	**Benefits**
Client	*(Satisfy precondition:)* Use a non-negative argument.	*(From postcondition:)* Get deposits list and balance updated.
Supplier	*(Satisfy postcondition:)* Update deposits list and balance.	*(From precondition:)* No need to handle negative arguments.

The class `invariant`, as noted, applies to all features. It must be satisfied on exit by any creation procedures and is implicitly added to both the precondition and postcondition of every exported routine. In this respect, it is both good news and bad news for the routine implementer: good news because it guarantees that the object is initially in a stable state, averting the need in the preceding example to check that the total of `all_deposits` is compatible with the `balance`, and bad news because, in addition to its official contract as expressed by its specific postcondition, every routine must take care of restoring the invariant on exit.

A requirement on meaningful contracts is that they should be in good faith: satisfiable by an honest partner. This implies a consistency rule: If a routine is exported to a client (either generally or selectively), any feature appearing in its precondition must also be available to that client. Otherwise—for example, if the precondition included `require n > 0`, where `n` is a secret attribute—the supplier would be making demands that a good-faith client cannot possibly check for.

It should be noted in this respect that ensuring a precondition does not necessarily mean testing for it explicitly. Assuming `n` is indeed exported, a client can make a correct call as

```
if x.n > 0 then x.r end
```

possibly with an `else` part, but this is not the only possible form: If `n` is known to be positive, perhaps because some preceding call set it to the sum of two squares, then there is no need for protection by an `if` or equivalent. In such a case, a `check` instruction as introduced later (section 9.10.3) is recommended if the reason for omitting the test is non-trivial.

9.8.3. Using Assertions for Built-in Reliability

The first use of assertions is purely methodological. By applying a discipline of expressing, as precisely as possible, the logical assumptions behind software elements, one can write software whose reliability is built-in: software that is developed hand-in-hand with the rationale for its correctness.

This simple observation—usually not clear to people until they have practiced design by contract thoroughly on a large-scale project—brings as much change to software practices and quality as the rest of object technology.

9.8.4. Runtime Assertion Monitoring

Assertions in Eiffel are not just wishful thinking. They can be monitored at runtime under the control of compilation options.

It should be clear from the preceding discussion that assertions are not a mechanism to test for special conditions—for example, erroneous user input. For that purpose, the usual control structures (`if deposit_sum >= 0 then ...`) are available, complemented in applicable cases by the exception-handling mechanism reviewed next. An assertion is instead a *correctness condition* governing the relationship between two software modules (not a software module and a human or a software module and an external device). If `sum` is negative on entry to `deposit`, violating the precondition, the culprit is some other software element, whose author was not careful enough to observe the terms of the deal. Bluntly:

Assertion violation rule

A runtime assertion violation is the manifestation of a bug.

To be more precise:

- A precondition violation signals a bug in the client, which did not observe its part of the deal.
- A postcondition (or invariant) violation signals a bug in the supplier—the routine—which did not do its job.

That violations indicate bugs explains why it is possible to enable or disable assertion monitoring through mere compilation options: for a correct system—one without bugs—assertions always hold, so the compilation option makes no difference to the semantics of the system.

Of course, for an incorrect system, the best way to find out where the bug is—or just that there is a bug—is often to check the assertions. As a result, Eiffel environments typically provide compilation options at several levels (here as supported in ISE Eiffel, which makes them settable separately for each class, with defaults at the system and cluster levels):

- **`no`**—assertions have no runtime effect.
- **`require`**—check preconditions only, on routine entry.
- **`ensure`**—preconditions on entry, postconditions on exit.
- **`invariant`**—as **`ensure`**, plus class invariant on both entry and exit for qualified calls.
- **`all`**—as **`invariant`**, plus **`check`** instructions, loop invariants, and loop variants (section 9.10.3).

An assertion violation, if detected at runtime under one of these options other than the first, causes an exception (section 9.8.6). Unless the software has an explicit "retry" plan as explained later, the violation causes production of an exception trace and termination (or, in development environment such as EiffelBench, a return to the browsing and debugging facilities of the environment at the point of failure). If present, the label of the violated subclause is displayed, serving to identify the cause precisely.

The default is **`require`**. This is particularly interesting in connection with the Eiffel method's insistence on using libraries: With libraries such as EiffelBase that are richly equipped with preconditions expressing terms of use, an error in the client software often leads, for example through an incorrect argument, to violating one of these preconditions. A somewhat paradoxical consequence is that even an application developer who does not apply the method too well (out of carelessness, haste, indifference, or ignorance) still benefits from the presence of assertions in someone else's library code.

During development and testing, assertion monitoring should be turned on at the highest possible level. Combined with static typing and the immediate feedback of compilation techniques such as the Melting Ice Technology, this permits the development process mentioned in section 9.3.6, where errors are exterminated at birth. No one who has not practiced the method in a real project can imagine how many mistakes are found in this way; surprisingly often, a violation turns out to affect an assertion that was just included for goodness's sake, the developer being convinced that it could not "possibly" fail to be satisfied.

By providing a precise reference (the description of what the software is supposed to do) against which to assess the reality (what the software actually does), design by contract profoundly transforms the activities of debugging, testing, and quality assurance.

When releasing the final version of a system, it is usually appropriate to turn off assertion monitoring, at least down to the **`require`** level. The exact policy depends on the circumstances; it is a tradeoff between efficiency considerations, the potential cost of mistakes, and how much the developers and quality assurance team trust the product. When developing the software, however, one should always assume that monitoring will be turned off in the end (to avoid loosening one's guard).

9.8.5. The Short Form of a Class

Another application of assertions regards documentation. Environment mechanisms—such as clicking the short button of a class tool in ISE's EiffelBench—produce, from a class text, an abstracted version, the short form, which only includes the information relevant for client authors. Here is the short form of class ACCOUNT in its latest version:

```
indexing
    description: "Simple bank accounts"
class interface
    ACCOUNT
```

```
feature  -- Access
    balance: INTEGER
            -- Current balance
    deposit_count: INTEGER
            -- Number of deposits made since opening
feature  -- Element change
    deposit (sum: INTEGER)
        -- Add sum to account.
        require
            non_negative: sum >= 0
        ensure
            one_more_deposit: deposit_count = old deposit_count + 1
            updated: balance = old balance + sum
invariant
    consistent_balance: balance = all_deposits.total
end  -- class interface ACCOUNT
```

The words **`class interface`** are used instead of just **`class`** to avoid any confusion with actual Eiffel text because this is documentation, not executable software. (It is in fact possible to generate a compilable variant of the short form in the form of a deferred class, a notion defined in section 9.9.5.)

Compared to the full text, the short form keeps all the elements that are part of the abstract interface relevant to client authors:

- Names and signatures (argument and result type information) for the exported features.
- Header comments of these features, which carry informal descriptions of their purpose (hence the importance, mentioned in section 9.4, of always including such comments and writing them carefully).
- Preconditions and postconditions of these routines (at least the subclauses involving only exported features, which may exclude certain postcondition subclauses).
- Class invariant (at least the subclauses involving only exported features, which may exclude certain postcondition subclauses).

The following elements are removed, however: any information about non-exported features; all the routine bodies (**`do`** clauses, or the **`external`** and **`once`** variants in sections 9.5.6 and 9.10.1); assertion subclauses involving non-exported features; and some keywords not useful in the documentation, such as **`is`** for a routine.

In accordance with the uniform access principle (section 9.6.2), the short form does not distinguish between attributes and argument-less queries. In the preceding example, `balance` could be one or the other, as it makes no difference to clients, except possibly for performance.

The short form is the fundamental tool for using supplier classes in the Eiffel method. It protects client authors from the need to read the source code of software on which they rely. This is a crucial requirement in large-scale industrial developments.

The result is also particularly interesting because it satisfies the property that should always be required of good software documentation:

- It is truly abstract, free from the implementation details of what it describes but concentrating on its functionality.
- Instead of being produced separately—an unrealistic requirement, hard to impose on developers initially and becoming impossible in practice if we expect the documentation to remain up to date as the software evolves—the documentation is extracted from the software itself. It is not a separate product but a different view of the same product. This prolongs the single product principle that lies at the basis of Eiffel's seamless development (section 9.3.1).

Other views are possible. For example, the EiffelCase tool of ISE's environment and a cluster-level tool integrated in Visual Eiffel propose graphical "bubble-and-arrow" diagram representations of system structures, showing classes and their relations—client and inheritance—according to the conventions of BON (the *business object notation*) with, in the first case, the possibility to edit these diagrams and generate updated Eiffel text in accordance with the principles of seamlessness and reversibility.

The short form—or its variant, the flat-short form, which takes account of inheritance (section 9.9.12)—is the standard form of library documentation, used extensively, for example, in the book *Reusable Software* (Meyer, 1994). Assertions play a central role in such documentation by expressing the terms of the contract. As demonstrated *a contrario* by the widely publicized $500-million crash of the Ariane-5 rocket launcher in June 1996 due to the incorrect reuse of a software module from the Ariane-4 project, reuse without a contract documentation is the path to disaster. Non-reuse would, in fact, be preferable.

9.8.6. Exception Handling

Another application of design by contract governs the handling of unexpected cases. The vagueness of many discussions of this topic follows from the lack of a precise definition of terms such as exception. With design by contract, we are in a position to be specific:

- Any routine has a contract to achieve.
- Its body defines a strategy to achieve it—a sequence (or other control structure) involving instructions. Some of these operations are themselves routines with their own contracts, but even an atomic operation, such as the computation of an arithmetic operation, has an implicit contract, stating that the result is representable.
- Any one of these operations may fail, that is, be unable to meet its contract; for example, an arithmetic operation may produce an overflow (non-representable result).
- Failure of one of these operations is an exception for the routine.
- As a result, the routine may fail too—causing an exception in its own caller.

Note how the two basic concepts, failure and exception, are defined precisely. Although failure is the more basic concept—because it is defined for atomic, non-routine operations—the definitions are mutually recursive because an exception may cause a failure of the recipient routine, and a routine's failure causes an exception in its own caller.

Why only the observation that an exception "may" cause a failure? The reason is that a routine may have planned for the exception and defined a rescue policy. This is done through a clause with the corresponding keyword, as in

```
read_next_character (f: FILE) is
          -- Make next character available in last_character;
          -- if impossible, set failed to True.
     require
          readable: file.readable
     local
          impossible: BOOLEAN
     do
          if impossible then
               failed := True
          else
               last_character := low_level_read_function (f)
          end
     rescue
          impossible := True
          retry
     end
```

This example includes the only two constructs needed for exception handling: **rescue** and **retry**. The **retry** instruction is only permitted in a rescue clause; its effect is to start again the execution of the routine, without repeating the initialization of local entities (such as `impossible` in the example, which was initialized to `False` on first entry). Features `failed` and `last_character` are assumed to be attributes of the enclosing class.

This example is typical of the use of exceptions: as a last resort, for situations that should not occur. The routine has a precondition, `file.readable`, which ascertains that the file exists and is accessible for reading characters. Clients should check that everything is fine before calling the routine. Although this check is almost always a guarantee of success, a rare combination of circumstances could cause a change of file status (because a user or some other system is manipulating the file) between the check for `readable` and the call to `low_level_read_function`. If we assume this latter function fails if the file is not readable, we must catch the exception.

A variant is

```
local
    attempts: INTEGER
do
    if attempts < Max_attempts then
        last_character := low_level_read_function (f)
    else
        failed := True
    end
rescue
    attempts := attempts + 1
    retry
end
```

which tries again up to `Max_attempts` times before giving up.

The preceding routine, in either variant, never fails: It always fulfills its contract, which states that it should either read a character or set `failed` to record its inability to do so. In contrast, consider the variant

```
local
    attempts: INTEGER
do
    last_character := low_level_read_function (f)
end
rescue
    attempts := attempts + 1
    if attempts < Max_attempts then
        retry
    end
end
```

with no more role for `failed`. In this case, after `Max_attempts` unsuccessful attempts, the routine executes its **`rescue`** clause to the end, with no **`retry`** (the **`if`** having no **`else`** clause). This is how a routine fails. As noted, it passes on the exception to its caller.

Such a rescue clause should, before returning, restore the invariant of the class so that the caller and possible subsequent **retry** attempts from higher up find the objects in a consistent state. As a result, the rule for an absent **rescue** clause (the case, of course, for the vast majority of routines in most systems) is that it is equivalent to

```
rescue
    default_rescue
```

where procedure `default_rescue` comes from `GENERAL`, where it is defined to do nothing; in a system built for robustness, classes subject to non-explicitly rescued exceptions should redefine `default_rescue` (perhaps using a creation procedure, which is bound by the same formal requirement) so that it always restores the invariant.

Behind Eiffel's exception-handling scheme lies the principle—at first an apparent platitude, but violated by many existing mechanisms—that a routine should either succeed or fail. This is all a result of the contract notion: Succeeding means being able to fulfill the contract (possibly after one or more **retry**); failure is the other case, which must always trigger an exception in the caller. Without this principle, it is possible for a routine to miss its contract and yet to return to its caller in a seemingly normal state. That is the worst possible way to handle an exception.

Concretely, exceptions result from the following events:

- A routine failure (**rescue** clause executed to the end with no **retry**), as just seen.
- Assertion violation, if they are monitored.
- Attempt to call a feature on a void reference: `x.f (...)`, the fundamental computational mechanism, can only work if `x` is attached to an object and causes an exception otherwise.
- Developer exception, as seen next.
- Operating system signal: no memory available for a requested creation or clone (even after garbage collection has rummaged everything to find some space), arithmetic overflow (but no C/C++-like "wrong pointer address," which cannot occur thanks to the statically typed nature of Eiffel).

It may in some cases be useful, when handling exceptions in **rescue** clauses, to ascertain the exact nature of the exception that got the execution there. For this, it suffices to inherit from the kernel library class

EXCEPTIONS, which provides queries such as exception, giving the code for the last exception, and symbolic names (constant attributes, see section 9.10.2) for all such codes, such as No_more_memory and so on. Then by testing exception against various possibilities, one can have specific exception handling. The method strongly suggests, however, that exception-handling code should remain simple; a complicated algorithm in a **rescue** clause is probably a sign of abuse.

Class EXCEPTIONS also provide various facilities for fine-tuning the exception facilities, such as a procedure raise that explicitly triggers a "developer exception" with a code than can then be detected and processed.

Exception handling makes it possible to produce Eiffel software that is not just correct but robust, by planning for cases that should *not* normally arise, but might out of Murphy's law, and ensuring they do not affect the software's basic safety and simplicity.

9.8.7. Other Applications of Design by Contract

The design by contract ideas pervade the Eiffel method. In addition to the applications just mentioned, they have two particularly important consequences:

- They make it possible to use Eiffel for analysis and design. At a high level of abstraction, it is necessary to be precise too. With the exception of BON, object-oriented analysis and design methods tend to favor abstraction over precision. Thanks to assertions, it is possible to express precise properties of a system ("At what speed should the alarm start sounding?") without making any commitment to implementation. The discussion of deferred classes (section 9.9.6) shows how to write a purely descriptive, non-software model in Eiffel, using assertions to describe the essential properties of a system without any computer or software aspect.
- Assertions also serve to control the power of inheritance-related mechanisms—redeclaration, polymorphism, and dynamic binding—and channel them to correct uses by assigning the proper semantic limits. This is reviewed in section 9.9.9.

9.9. The Inheritance Mechanism

Inheritance is a powerful and attractive technique. A look at either the practice or literature shows, however, that it is not always well applied. Eiffel has made a particular effort to tame inheritance for the benefit of modelers and software developers. Many of the techniques are original with Eiffel. Paul Dubois has written (comp.lang.python Usenet newsgroup, 23 March 1997): "There are two things that [Eiffel] got right that nobody else got right anywhere else: support for design by contract and multiple inheritance." Everyone should understand these correct answers if only to understand how to work around the limitations in other languages.

9.9.1. Basic Inheritance Structure

To make a class inherit from another, simply use an **inherit** clause:

```
indexing ... class D creation ... inherit
     A
     B
     ...
feature
     ...
```

This makes D an heir of A, B, and any other class listed. Eiffel supports multiple inheritance: A class can have as many parents as it needs. Later sections (see in particular 9.9.8 and 9.9.13) explain how to handle the possible conflicts created by parent features.

By default, D simply includes all the original features of A, B, and so on, to which it may add its own through its **feature** clauses if any. The inheritance mechanism is more flexible, allowing D to adapt the inherited features in many ways. Each parent name—A, B, and so on in the example—can be followed by a feature adaptation clause, with subclauses, all optional, introduced by keywords **rename, export, undefine, redefine**, and **select**, enabling the author A to make the best use of the inheritance mechanism by tuning the inherited features to the precise needs of D. This makes inheritance a principal tool in the Eiffel process, mentioned earlier, of carefully crafting each individual class for the benefit of its clients. The various feature adaptation subclauses are reviewed in the following sections.

9.9.2. Redefinition

The first form of feature adaptation is the ability to change the implementation of an inherited feature. Assume a class SAVINGS_ACCOUNT that specializes the notion of account. It is probably appropriate to define it as an heir to class ACCOUNT, to benefit from all the features of ACCOUNT still applicable to savings accounts, and express the conceptual relationship that every savings account "is" an account (apart from its own specific properties). However, we may need to produce a different effect for procedure deposit so that besides recording the deposit and updating the balance, it also updates the interest, for instance.

This example is typical of the form of reuse promoted by inheritance and crucial to effective reusability in software: the case of *reuse with adaptation*. Traditional forms of reuse are all-or-nothing: Either you take a component exactly as it is, or you build your own. Inheritance gets us out of this "reuse or redo" dilemma by allowing us to reuse *and* redo. The mechanism is feature redefinition:

```
indexing
    description: "Savings accounts"
class
    SAVINGS_ACCOUNT
inherit
    ACCOUNT
        redefine deposit end
feature  -- Element change
    deposit (sum: INTEGER) is
              -- Add sum to account.
        do
             ... New implementation (see below) ...
        end
    ... Other features ...
end  -- class SAVINGS_ACCOUNT
```

Without the **redefine** subclause, the declaration of deposit would be invalid, yielding two features of the same name, the inherited one and the new one. The subclause makes this valid by specifying that the new declaration overrides the old one.

In a redefinition, the original version—such as the ACCOUNT implementation of deposit in this example—is called the *precursor* of the new version. It is common for a redefinition to rely on the precursor's algorithm and add some other actions; the reserved word Precursor helps achieve this goal simply. Permitted only in a routine redefinition, it denotes the parent routine being redefined. Here the body of the new deposit could be of the form

```
Precursor (sum)      -- Apply algorithm of ACCOUNT's version of deposit
... Instructions to update the interest ...
```

Besides changing the implementation of a routine, a redefinition can turn an argument-less function into an attribute; for example, a proper descendant of ACCOUNT could redefine deposits_count, originally a function, as an attribute. The principle of uniform access (section 9.6.2) guarantees that the redefinition makes no change for clients, which continues to use the feature under the form *acc.deposits_count*.

9.9.3. Polymorphism

The inheritance mechanism is relevant to both roles of classes: module and type. Its application as a mechanism to reuse, adapt, and extend features from one class to another, as just seen, covers the module role. But inheritance is also a subtyping mechanism. To say that `D` is an heir of `A`, or more generally, a descendant of `A`, is to express that instances of `D` can be viewed as instances of `A`.

The mechanism that supports this idea is polymorphic assignment. In an assignment `x := y`, the types of `y` do not, thanks to inheritance, have to be identical; the rule is that the type of `y` must simply conform to another. A class `D` conforms to a class `A` if and only if it is a descendant (which of course includes the case in which `A` and `D` are the same class); if these classes are generic, conformance of `D [U]` to `C [T]` requires in addition that type `U` conform to type `T` (through the recursive application of the same rules).

With the inheritance relations suggested earlier, the declarations

```
acc: ACCOUNT; sav: SAVINGS_ACCOUNT
```

make it valid to write the assignment

```
acc := sav
```

which assigns to `acc` a reference attached (if not void) to a direct instance of type `SAVINGS_ACCOUNT`, not `ACCOUNT`.

Such an assignment, where the source and target types are different, is said to be polymorphic. An entity such as `acc`, which as a result of such assignments may become attached at runtime to objects of types other than the one declared for it, is itself called a polymorphic entity.

For polymorphism to respect the reliability requirements of Eiffel, it must be controlled by the type system and enable static type checking. We certainly do not want an entity of type `ACCOUNT` to become attached to an object of type `DEPOSIT`. The second typing rule:

Type conformance rule

An assignment `x := y`, or the use of `y` as actual argument corresponding to the formal argument `x` in a routine call, is only valid if the type of `y` conforms to the type of `x`.

The second case is that of a call such as `target.routine (..., y, ...)` where the corresponding routine declaration is of the form `routine (..., x: SOME_TYPE, ...)`. The rules governing the setting of `x` to the value of `y` at the beginning of the call are exactly the same as those of an assignment `x := y`: not just the type rule, as expressed by type conformance (the type of `y` must conform to `SOME_TYPE`), but also the actual runtime effect which, as for assignments, is either a reference attachment or, for expanded types, a copy.

Note that the ability to accept the assignment `x := Void` for `x` of any reference type (section 9.6.10) is a consequence of the type conformance rule because `Void` is of type `NONE`, which by construction (section 9.5.4) conforms to all types.

Polymorphism also yields a more precise definition of "instance." A direct instance of a type `A` is an object created from the exact pattern defined by the declaration of `A`'s base class, with one field for each of the class attributes; you obtain it through a creation instruction of the form `!! x...`, for `x` of type `A`, or by cloning an existing direct instance. An instance of `A` is a direct instance of any type conforming to `A`: `A` itself, but also many types based on descendant classes. An instance of `SAVINGS_ACCOUNT` is also an instance, although not a direct instance, of `ACCOUNT`.

A consequence of polymorphism is the ability to define polymorphic data structures. With a declaration such as

```
accounts: LIST [ACCOUNT]
```

the procedure call `accounts.extend (acc)`, because it uses a procedure *extend* which in this case expects an argument of any type conforming to `ACCOUNT`, is valid not only if `acc` is of type `ACCOUNT` but also if it is of a descendant type such as `SAVINGS_ACCOUNT`. Successive calls of this kind make it possible to construct a data structure that, at runtime, might contain objects of several types, all conforming to `ACCOUNT` (see Figure 9.10).

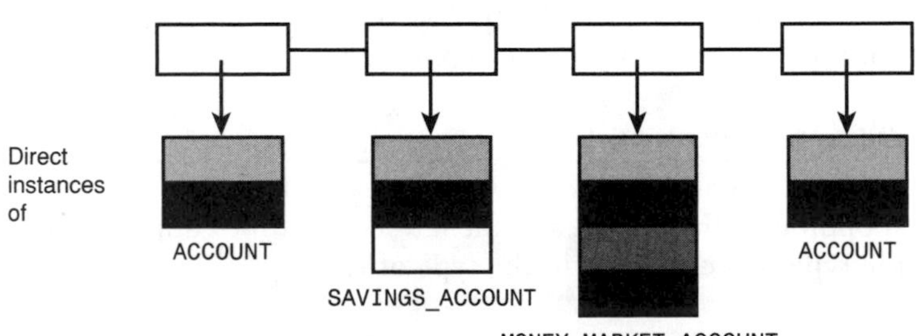

FIGURE 9.10. *Polymorphic data structure.*

Such polymorphic data structures combine the flexibility and safety of genericity and inheritance. They can be more or less general depending on the type, here ACCOUNT, chosen as actual generic parameter; static typing is again precious, prohibiting for example a mistaken insertion of the form `accounts.extend (dep)` where `dep` is of type DEPOSIT, which does not conform to ACCOUNT.

It remains possible to produce unrestrictedly polymorphic data structures, such as a `general_list: LIST [ANY]`, which makes the call `general_list.extend (x)` valid for any `x`. The price to pay is that the operations applicable to an element retrieved from such a list are only the most general ones (assignment, clone, equality comparison, and the like)—although assignment attempt, studied later, makes it possible to apply more specific operations after checking that a retrieved object is the appropriate type.

9.9.4. Dynamic Binding

The complement of polymorphism and dynamic binding is the answer to the question "What version of a feature is applied in a call whose target is polymorphic?" For example, if `acc` is of type ACCOUNT, the attached objects may now, thanks to polymorphism, be direct instances not just of ACCOUNT but also SAVINGS_ACCOUNT or other descendants. Some of these descendants, indeed SAVINGS_ACCOUNT among them, redefine features such as `deposit`. What then is the effect of a call of the form `acc.deposit (some_value)`?

Dynamic binding is the clearly correct answer: The call executes the version of `deposit` from the generating class of the object attached to `acc` at runtime. If `acc` is attached to a direct instance of ACCOUNT, execution uses the original ACCOUNT version; if `acc` is attached to a direct instance of SAVINGS_ACCOUNT, the call executes the version redefined in that class.

This is a clear correctness requirement. A policy of *static binding* (as available, for example, by default in C++ or Borland's Delphi) would take the declaration of `acc` as an ACCOUNT literally. But that declaration is only meant to ensure generality, to enable the use of a single name `acc` in many different cases: What counts at execution time is the object that `acc` represents. Applying the ACCOUNT version to a SAVINGS_ACCOUNT object would be wrong, possibly leading in particular to objects that violate the invariant of their own generating class (because there is no reason a routine of ACCOUNT will preserve the specific invariant of a proper descendant such as SAVINGS_ACCOUNT, which it does not even know about).

Note that in some cases the choice between static and dynamic binding does not matter: This is the case, for example, if a call's target is not polymorphic or if the feature of the call is redefined nowhere in the system. In such cases, the use of static binding permits slightly faster calls (because the feature is known at compile time). This application of static binding should, however, be treated as a compiler optimization. Good Eiffel compilers detect such cases and process them accordingly—unlike approaches that make developers responsible for specifying what should be static and what dynamic (a tedious and error-prone task, especially delicate because a minute change in the software can make a static call, far away in another module of a large system, suddenly become dynamic). Eiffel developers are protected from such concerns; they can rely on the semantics of dynamic binding in all cases, with the knowledge that an optimizing compiler applies static binding when safe and desirable.

Even in cases that require dynamic binding, the design of Eiffel, in particular the typing rules, enables compilers to make the penalty over the static-binding calls of traditional approaches very small and, most importantly, constant bounded: It does not grow with the depth or complexity of the inheritance structure. The discovery in 1985 of a technique for constant-time dynamic binding calls, even in the presence of multiple and repeated inheritance, was the event that gave the green light to the development of Eiffel.

Dynamic binding is particularly interesting for polymorphic data structures. If we iterate over the list of accounts of various kinds, `accounts: LIST [ACCOUNT]`, illustrated in Figure 9.10, and at each step let `acc` represent the current list element, we can repeatedly apply `acc.deposit (...)` to have the appropriate variant of the `deposit` operation triggered for each element.

The benefit of such techniques appears clearly if we compare them with the traditional way to address such needs: using multibranch discriminating instructions of the form `if "Account is a savings account" then ...elseif "It is a money market account" then ...` and so on, or the corresponding `case ... of ...or inspect` instructions. Apart from their heaviness and complexity, such solutions cause many components of a software system to rely on the knowledge of the exact set of variants available for a certain notion, such as bank account. Then, any addition, change, or removal of variants can cause a ripple of changes throughout the architecture. This is one of the major obstacles to extendibility and reusability in traditional approaches. In contrast, using the combination of inheritance, redefinition, polymorphism, and dynamic binding makes it possible to have a point of single choice—a unique location in the system that knows the exhaustive list of variants. Every client then manipulates entities of the most general type, ACCOUNT, through dynamically bound calls of the form acc.*some_account_feature* (...).

These observations make dynamic binding appear for what it is: not an implementation mechanism, but an architectural technique that plays a key role (along with information hiding, which it extends, and design by contract, to which it is linked through the assertion redefinition rules seen later) in providing the modular system architectures of Eiffel, the basis for the method's approach to reusability and extendibility. These properties apply as early as analysis and modeling, and continue to be useful throughout the subsequent steps.

9.9.5. Deferred Features and Classes

In the preceding examples of dynamic binding, all classes were assumed to be fully implemented, and dynamically bound features had a version in every relevant class, including the most general ones such as ACCOUNT.

It is also useful to define classes that leave the implementation of some of their features entirely to proper descendants. Such an abstract class is known as *deferred*; so are its unimplemented features. The reverse of deferred is *effective*, meaning fully implemented.

LIST is a typical example of deferred class. As it describes the general notion of list, it should not favor any particular implementation; that is, the task of its effective descendants, such as LINKED_LIST (linked implementation), TWO_WAY_LIST (linked both ways), and ARRAYED_LIST (implementation by an array), all effective, and all indeed to be found in ISE's EiffelBase libraries.

At the level of the deferred class LIST, some features such as extend (add an item at the end of the list) have no implementation and hence are declared as deferred. Here is the corresponding form, illustrating the syntax for both deferred classes and their deferred features:

```
indexing
    description: "Sequential finite lists,
        without a commitment to a representation"
deferred class
    LIST [G]
feature  -- Access
    count: INTEGER is
            -- Number of items in list
        do
            ... See below; this feature can be effective ...
        end
```

```
feature  -- Element change
    extend (x: G) is
            -- Add x at end of list.
        require
            space_available: not full
        deferred
        ensure
            one_more: count = old count + 1
        end
... Other feature declarations and invariant ...
end  -- class LIST
```

A deferred feature (considered to be a routine, although it can yield an attribute in a proper descendant) has the single keyword **deferred** in lieu of the **do** *Instructions* clause of an effective routine. A deferred class—defined as a class that has at least one deferred feature—must be introduced by **deferred class** instead of just **class**.

As the example of `extend` shows, a deferred feature, although it has no implementation, can be equipped with assertions. They are binding on implementations in descendants, in a way to be explained later.

Deferred classes do not have to be fully deferred. They can contain some effective features along with their deferred ones. Here, for example, we may express `count` as a function:

```
count: INTEGER is
        -- Number of items in list
    do
        from start until after loop
            Result := Result + 1; forth
        end
end
```

This implementation relies on the loop construct described later (**from** introduces the loop initialization) and on deferred features of the class that allow traversal of a list based on moving a fictitious cursor: `start` to bring the cursor to the first element if any, `after` to find out whether all relevant elements have been seen, and `forth` (with precondition **not** after) to advance the cursor to the next element. For example, `forth` appears as

```
forth is
        -- Advance cursor by one position
    require
        not_after: not after
    deferred
    ensure
        moved_right: index = old index + 1
    end
```

where index—another deferred feature of the class—is the integer position of the cursor.

Although the preceding version of feature count is time-consuming—it implies a whole traversal just for the purpose of determining the number of elements—it has the advantage of being applicable to all variants, without any commitment to a choice of implementation, as would follow, for example, if we decided to treat count as an attribute. Proper descendants can always redefine count for more efficiency.

Function count illustrates one of the most important contributions of the method to reusability: the ability to define behavior classes that capture common behaviors (such as count) while leaving the details of the behaviors (such as start, after, and forth) open to many variants. As noted earlier, traditional approaches to reusability provide closed reusable components. A component such as LIST, although equipped with directly usable behaviors such as count, is open to many variations, to be provided by proper descendants.

A class B inheriting from a deferred class A may provide implementations—effective declarations—for the features inherited in deferred form. In this case, there is no need for the equivalent of a **redefine** subclause; the effective versions simply replace the inherited versions. The class is said to *effect* the corresponding features. If after this process, there remain any deferred features, B is still considered deferred, even if it introduces no deferred features of its own, and must be declared as **deferred class**.

In the example, classes such as LINKED_LIST and ARRAYED_LIST effect all the deferred features they inherit from LIST—extend, start, and so on—and hence be effective.

Note that—except in some applications restricted to pure system modeling—deferred classes and features only make sense thanks to polymorphism and dynamic binding. Because extend has no implementation in class LIST, a call of the form *my_list.extend* (...) with *my_list* of type LIST [T] for some T can only be executed if *my_list* is attached to a direct instance of an effective proper descendant of LIST, such as LINKED_LIST; then it uses the corresponding version of extend. Static binding would not even be meaningful here.

Even an effective feature of LIST such as count may depend on deferred features (start and so on) so that a call of the form *my_list.count* can only be executed in the context of an effective descendant.

All this indicates that a deferred class must have no direct instance (it has instances, the direct instances of its effective descendants). If it had any, we could call deferred features on them, leading to execution-time impossibility. The rule that achieves this goal is simple: If the base type of `x` is a deferred class, no creation instruction of target `x`, of the form `!! x ...`, is permitted.

9.9.6. Applications of Deferred Classes

Deferred classes cover abstract notions with many possible variants. They are widely used in Eiffel where they cover various needs:

- Capturing high-level classes, with common behaviors.
- Defining the higher levels of a general taxonomy, especially in the inheritance structure of a library.
- Defining the components of an architecture during system design, without commitment to a final implementation.
- Describing domain-specific concepts in analysis and modeling.

As the reader will have noted, these applications make deferred classes a central tool of the Eiffel method's support for seamlessness and reversibility. The last one in particular uses deferred classes and features to model objects from an application domain, without any commitment to implementation, design, or even software (and computers). Deferred classes are the ideal tool here: They express the properties of the domain's abstractions, without any temptation of implementation bias, yet with the precision afforded by type declarations, inheritance structures (to record classifications of the domain concepts), and assertions to express the abstract properties of the objects being described.

Unlike approaches using a separate object-oriented analysis and design method and notation (Booch, OMT, UML, and so on), this technique integrates seamlessly with the subsequent phases (assuming the decision is indeed taken to develop a software system): It suffices to develop the deferred classes progressively by introducing effective elements, either by modifying the classes themselves or by introducing design- and implementation-oriented descendants. In the resulting system, the classes that played an important role for analysis, and are the most meaningful for customers, remain important; as we have seen (section 9.3.2) this *direct mapping* property is a great help for extendibility.

The following sketch (from the book *Object-Oriented Software Construction* [Meyer, 1997]) illustrates these ideas on the example of scheduling the programs of a TV station. This is pure modeling of an application domain; no computers or software are involved yet. The class describes the notion of program segment.

Note the use of assertions to define semantic properties of the class, its instances, and its features. Although often presented as high-level, most object-oriented analysis methods (with the exception of Waldèn's and Nerson's BON) have no support for the expression of such properties, limiting themselves instead to the description of broad structural relationships:

```
indexing
    description:"Individual fragments of a broadcasting schedule"
deferred class
    SEGMENT
feature  -- Access
    schedule: SCHEDULE is deferred end
              -- Schedule to which segment belongs
    index: INTEGER is deferred end
              -- Position of segment in its schedule
    starting_time, ending_time: INTEGER is deferred end
              -- Beginning and end of scheduled air time
    next: SEGMENT is deferred end
              -- Segment to be played next, if any
    sponsor: COMPANY is deferred end
              -- Segment's principal sponsor
    rating: INTEGER is deferred end
              -- Segment's rating (for children's viewing etc.)
    Minimum_duration: INTEGER is 30
              -- Minimum length of segments, in seconds
    Maximum_interval: INTEGER is 2
              -- Maximum time between two successive segments, in sec-
onds
feature  -- Element change
    set_sponsor (s: SPONSOR) is
        require
            not_void: s /= Void
        deferred
        ensure
            sponsor_set: sponsor = s
        end
    ... change_next, set_rating omitted ...
invariant
    in_list:(1 <= index) and (index <= schedule.segments.count)
    in_schedule: schedule.segments.item (index)= Current
    next_in_list:(next /= Void) implies
        (schedule.segments.item (index + 1)= next)
    no_next_iff_last:(next = Void)=(index = schedule.segments.count)
    non_negative_rating: rating >= 0
    positive times:(starting_time > 0) and (ending_time > 0)
    sufficient_duration: ending_time--starting_time>=Minimum_duration
    decent_interval:(next.starting_time)--ending_time<=Maximum_interval
end
```

9.9.7. Structural Property Classes

An interesting category of deferred classes includes classes whose purpose is to describe a structural property, which may be useful to the description of many other classes. Typical examples are covered by classes of the kernel library:

- NUMERIC describes objects on which the arithmetic operations +, --, *, and / are available, with the properties of a ring (associativity, distributivity, zero elements, and so on). Kernel library classes such as INTEGER and REAL—but not, for example, STRING—are descendants of NUMERIC. An application that defines a class MATRIX may also make it a descendant of NUMERIC.

- COMPARABLE describes objects on which the comparison operations <, <=, >, and >= are available, with the properties of a total preorder (transitivity and irreflexivity). Kernel library classes such as CHARACTER, STRING and INTEGER—but not our MATRIX example—are descendants of NUMERIC.

For such classes, it is again essential to permit the inclusion of effective features in a deferred class and to include assertions. For example, class COMPARABLE declares **infix** "<" as deferred and expresses the other features effectively in terms of it. The type **like** Current is explained in section 9.9.16; it may be considered equivalent, in the following class text, to the type COMPARABLE:

```
indexing
    description:"Objects that can be compared
        according to a total preorder relation"
deferred class
    COMPARABLE
feature  -- Comparison
    infix "<" (other: like Current): BOOLEAN is
            -- Is current object less than other?
        require
            other_exists: other /= Void
        deferred
        ensure
            asymmetric: Result implies not (other < Current)
        end
    infix "<=" (other: like Current): BOOLEAN is
            -- Is current object less than or equal to other?
        require
            other_exists: other /= Void
        do
            Result := (Current < other) or is_equal (other)
        ensure
            definition: Result = (Current < other) or is_equal (other)
        end
```

```
... Other features: infix ">", min, max, ...
invariant
    irreflexive: not (Current < Current)
end -- class COMPARABLE
```

Note how <= is defined in terms of < and >= in terms of <=.

9.9.8. Multiple Inheritance and Feature Renaming

It is often necessary to define a new class in terms of several existing ones:

- The kernel library classes INTEGER and REAL must inherit from both NUMERIC and COMPARABLE.
- A class TENNIS_PLAYER, in a system for keeping track of player ranking, inherits from COMPARABLE, as well as from other domain-specific classes.
- A class COMPANY_PLANE may inherit from both PLANE and ASSET.
- Class ARRAYED_LIST, describing an implementation of lists through arrays, may inherit from both LIST and ARRAY.

In all such cases, multiple inheritance provides the answer.

Multiple inheritance can cause *name clashes*: Two parents can include a feature with the same name. This would conflict with the ban on name overloading within a class—the rule that no two features of a class may have the same name. Eiffel provides a simple way to remove the name clash at the point of inheritance through the **rename** subclause, as in

```
indexing
    description:"Sequential finite lists implemented as arrays"
class
    ARRAYED_LIST [G]
inherit
    LIST [G]

    ARRAY [G]
        rename
            count as capacity, item as array_item
        end
feature
    ...
end -- class ARRAYED_LIST
```

Here both LIST and ARRAY have features called count and item. To make the new class valid, we give new names to the features inherited from ARRAY, which are known within ARRAYED_LIST as capacity and array_item. Of course, we could have renamed the LIST versions instead or renamed along both inheritance branches.

Every feature of a class has a *final name*. For a feature introduced in the class itself (immediate feature), it is the name appearing in the declaration; for an inherited feature that is not renamed, it is the feature's name in the parent; for a renamed feature, it is the name resulting from the renaming. This definition yields a precise statement of the rule against in-class overloading:

Final name rule

Two different features of a class may not have the same final name.

It is interesting to compare renaming and redefinition. The important distinction is between features and feature names. Renaming keeps a feature but changes its name. Redefinition keeps the name but changes the feature. In some cases, it is, of course, appropriate to do both.

Renaming is interesting even in the absence of name clashes. A class may inherit from a parent a feature that it finds useful for its purposes, but whose name, appropriate for the context of the parent, is not consistent with the context of the heir. This is the case with ARRAY's feature `count` in the last example. The feature that defines the number of items in an array—the total number of available entries—becomes, for an arrayed list, the *maximum* number of list items. The truly interesting indication of the number of items is the count of how many items have been inserted in the list, as given by feature `count` from LIST. Even if we did not have a name clash because of the two inherited `count` features we should rename ARRAY's `count` as `capacity` to maintain the consistency of the local feature terminology.

The **`rename`** subclause appears before all the other feature adaptation subclauses—**`redefine`** already seen and the remaining ones **`export`**, **`undefine`**, and **`select`**—because an inherited feature that has been renamed sheds its earlier identity once and for all. Within the class, and to its own clients and descendants, it is known solely through the new name. The original name has simply disappeared from the namespace. This is essential to the view of classes presented earlier: self-contained, consistent abstractions prepared carefully for the greatest enjoyment of clients and descendants.

9.9.9. Inheritance and Contracts

A proper understanding of inheritance requires looking at the mechanism in the framework of design by contract, where it appears as a form of *subcontracting*.

The first rule is that invariants accumulate down an inheritance structure:

Invariant accumulation rule

The invariants of all the parents of a class apply to the class itself.

The invariant of a class is automatically considered to include—in the sense of logical and—the invariants of all its parents. This is a consequence of the view of inheritance as an "is" relation: If we may consider every instance of B as an instance of A, then every consistency constraint on instances of A must also apply to instances of B.

Next, we consider routine preconditions and postconditions. The rule here follows from an examination of what contracts mean in the presence of polymorphism and dynamic binding.

Consider a parent A and a proper descendant B (a direct heir on Figure 9.11), which redefines a routine r inherited from A.

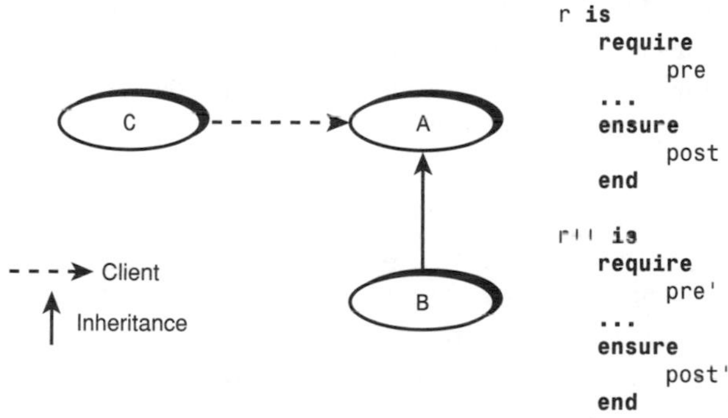
C
A
B
Client
Inheritance
r is
require
pre
...
ensure
post
end
r'' is
require
pre'
...
ensure
post'
end

FIGURE 9.11. *Client, parent, and heir.*

As a result of dynamic binding, a call a1.r from a client C may be serviced not by A's version of r but by B's version if a1, although declared of type A, becomes at runtime attached to an instance of B. This shows the combination of inheritance, redefinition, polymorphism, and dynamic binding as providing a form of subcontracting; A subcontracts certain calls to B.

The problem is to keep subcontractors honest. Assuming preconditions and postconditions as shown on Figure 9.11, a call in C of the form

```
if a1.pre then a1.r end
```

or just `a1.q; a1.r`, where the postcondition of `q` implies the precondition `pre` of `r`, satisfies the terms of the contract and hence is entitled to be handled correctly—to terminate in a state satisfying `a1.post`. If we let the subcontractor `B` redefine the assertions to arbitrary `pre'` and `post'`, this is not necessarily the case: `pre'` could be stronger than `pre`, enabling `B` not to process correctly certain calls that are correct from `A`'s perspective, and `post'` could be weaker than `post`, enabling `B` to do less of a job than advertised for `r` in the short form of `A`, the only official reference for authors of client classes such as `C`. (An assertion `p` is stronger than or equal to an assertion `q` if `p` implies `q` in the sense of boolean implication.)

The rule, then, is that for the redefinition to be correct, the new precondition `pre'` must be weaker than or equal to the original `pre`, and the new postcondition `post'` must be stronger than or equal to the original `post'`.

Because it is impossible to check simply that an assertion is weaker or stronger than another, the language rule relies on new variants of the assertion constructs: **`require else`** and **`ensure then`**, relying on the mathematical property that, for any assertions `p` and `q`, `p` implies `(p or q)`, and `(p and q)` implies `p`. For a precondition, using **`require else`** with a new assertion performs an **`or`**, which can only weaken the original; for a postcondition, **`ensure then`** performs an **`and`**, which can only strengthen the original. Hence, the rule:

Assertion redeclaration rule

In the redeclared version of a routine, it is not permitted to use a **`require`** or **`ensure`** clause. Instead, you may

- Use a clause introduced by **`require else`**, to be or-ed with the original precondition.
- Use a clause introduced by **`ensure then`**, to be and-ed with the original postcondition.

In the absence of such a clause, the original assertion is retained.

The last case—retaining the original—is frequent, but by no means universal.

The assertion redeclaration rule applies to *redeclarations*. This terms covers not just redefinition but also effecting (the implementation, by a class, of a feature that it inherits deferred). The rules—not just for assertions but also, as reviewed below, for typing—are indeed the same in both cases. Without the assertion redeclaration rule, assertions on deferred features, such as those on `extend`, `count`, and `forth` in section 9.9.5, would be almost useless—wishful thinking; the rule makes them binding on all effectings in descendants.

From the assertion redeclaration rule follows an interesting technique: abstract preconditions. What needs to be weakened for a precondition (or strengthened for a postcondition) is not the assertion's concrete semantics but its abstract specification as seen by the client. A descendant can change the *implementation* of that specification as it pleases, even to the effect of strengthening the concrete precondition, as long as the abstract form is kept or weakened. The precondition of procedure `extend` in the deferred class `LIST` provided an example. We wrote the routine (section 9.9.5) as

```
extend (x: G) is
        -- Add x at end of list.
    require
        space_available: not full
    deferred
    ensure
        one_more: count = old count + 1
    end
```

The precondition expresses that it is only possible to add an item to a list if the representation is not full. We may well consider—in line with the Eiffel principle that whenever possible structures should be of unbounded capacity—that `LIST` should by default make `full` always return `false`:

```
full: BOOLEAN is
        -- Is representation full?
        -- (Default: no)
    do
        Result := False
    end
```

Now a class `BOUNDED_LIST` that implements bounded-size lists (inheriting, like the earlier `ARRAYED_LIST`, from both `LIST` and `ARRAY`) may redefine `full`:

```
full: BOOLEAN is
        -- Is representation full?
        -- (Answer: if and only if number of items is capacity)
    do
        Result := (count = capacity)
    end
```

Procedure `extend` remains applicable as before; any client that used it properly with `LIST` can rely polymorphically on the `FIXED_LIST` implementation. The abstract precondition of `extend` has not changed, even though the concrete implementation of that precondition has in fact been strengthened.

Note that a class such as `BOUNDED_LIST`, the likes of which indeed appear in EiffelBase, is not a violation of the Eiffel advice to stay away from fixed-size structures. The corresponding structures are bounded, but the bounds are changeable. Although `extend` requires **`not`** `full`, another feature, called `force` by convention, is available to work in all cases, resizing (and possibly reallocating) the structure if necessary. Even arrays in Eiffel are not fixed-size and have a procedure *force* with no precondition, accepting any index position.

The assertion redeclaration rule, together with the invariant accumulation rule, provides the right methodological perspective for understanding inheritance and the associated mechanisms. Defining a class as inheriting from another is a strong commitment; it means inheriting not only the features but also the logical constraints. Redeclaring a routine is a committing decision: It means that you are providing a new implementation (or, for an effecting, a first implementation) of a previously defined semantics, as expressed by the original contract. Usually you have a wide margin for choosing your implementation because the contract only defines a range of possible behaviors (rather than just one behavior), but you *must* remain within that range. Otherwise, you would be perverting the goals of redeclaration, using this mechanism as a sort of late-stage hacking to override bugs in ancestor classes.

9.9.10. Joining and Uneffecting

It is not an error to inherit two deferred features from different parents under the same name, provided they have the same signature (number and types of arguments and result). In that case, a *feature join* takes place: The features are merged into just one—with their preconditions and postconditions, if any, respectively or-ed and and-ed.

More generally, it is permitted to have any number of deferred features and *one* effective feature that share the same name: The effective version applies to all the others.

All this is not a violation of the final name rule (section 9.9.8) because the name clashes prohibited by the rule involve two *different* features having the same final name; here the result is just *one* feature, resulting from the join of all the inherited versions.

Sometimes we may want to join *effective* features inherited from different parents, assuming again the features have compatible signatures. One way is to redefine them all into a new version; then they again become one feature, with no name clash in the sense of the final name rule. In other cases, we may simply want one of the inherited implementations to take over the others. The solution is to revert to the preceding case by uneffecting the other features; uneffecting an inherited effective feature makes it deferred (this is the reverse of effecting, which turns an inherited deferred feature into an effective one). The syntax uses the **`undefine`** subclause:

```
class D inherit
    A
        rename
            g as f          -- g was effective in A
        undefine
            f
        end
    B
        undefine f end      -- f was effective in B
    C
         -- C also has an effective f, which will serve as implementa-
tion
         -- for the result of the join.
feature
    ...
```

Again what counts, to determine if there is an invalid name clash, is the final name of the features. In this example, two of the joined features were originally called f; the one from A was called g, but in D, it is renamed as f, so without the undefinition it would cause an invalid name clash.

Feature joining is the most common application of uneffecting. In some non-joining cases, however, it may be useful to forget the original implementation of a feature and let it start a new life devoid of any burden from the past.

9.9.11. Changing the Export Status

Another feature adaptation subclause makes it possible to change the export status of an inherited feature. By default—covering the behavior desired in the vast majority of practical cases—an inherited feature keeps its original export status (exported, secret, or selectively exported). In some cases, however, this is not appropriate:

- A feature may have played a purely implementation-oriented role in the parent but become interesting to clients of the heir. Its status changes from secret to exported.
- In implementation inheritance (for example, ARRAYED_LIST inheriting from ARRAY), an exported feature of the parent may not be suitable for direct use by clients of the heir. The change of status in this case is the reverse of the previous one.

You can achieve either of these goals by writing

```
class D inherit
    A
        export {X, Y, ...} feature1, feature2, ... end
    ...
```

This gives a new export status to the features listed (under their final names because, as noted, **export**, like all other subclauses, comes after **rename** if present): They become exported to the classes listed. In most cases, this list of classes (X, Y, and so on) consists of just ANY, to re-export a previously secret feature, or NONE, to hide a previously exported feature. It is also possible, in lieu of the feature list, to use the keyword **all** to apply the new status to all features inherited from the listed parent. Then there can be more than one class-feature list, as in

```
class ARRAYED_LIST [G] inherit
     ARRAY [G]
          rename
               count as capacity, item as array_item, put as array_put
          export
               {NONE} all
               {ANY} capacity
          end
     ...
```

where any explicit listing of a feature, such as capacity, takes precedence over the export status specified for **all**. Here most features of ARRAY are secret in ARRAYED_LIST because the clients should not be permitted to manipulate array entries directly. They manipulate them indirectly through list features such as extend and item, whose implementation relies on array_item and array_put, but ARRAY's feature count remains useful, under the name capacity, to the clients of ARRAYED_LIST.

9.9.12. Flat and Flat-Short Forms

Thanks to inheritance, it is possible to write a concise class text that achieves a lot, relying on all the features inherited from direct and indirect ancestors.

This is part of the power of the object-oriented form of reuse, but can create a comprehension and documentation problem when the inheritance structures become deep: How does one understand such a class, either as client author or as maintainer? For clients, the short form, which only considers the class text, does not tell the full story about available features, and for maintainers, much of the information must be sought in proper ancestors.

These observations suggest a need for mechanisms that produce, from a class text, a version that is equivalent feature-wise and assertion-wise but has no inheritance dependency at all. This is called the *flat form* of the class. It is a class text that has no inheritance clause and includes all the features of the class, immediate (declared in the class itself) as well as inherited. For the inherited features, the flat form must, of course, take account of all the feature adaptation mechanisms: renaming (each feature must appear under its final name), redefinition, effecting, uneffecting, and export status change. For redeclared features, **require else** clauses are or-ed with the precursors' preconditions, and **ensure then** clauses are and-ed with precursors' postconditions. For invariants, all the ancestors' clauses are concatenated. As a result, the flat form yields a view of the class, its features, and its assertions that conforms exactly to the view offered to clients and (except for polymorphic uses) heirs.

An Eiffel environment should provide tools to produce the flat form of a class. (In the ISE environment, users click the Flat button in the class tool to get it.)

The short form (see section 9.8.5) of the flat form of a class, known as its *flat-short form*, is the complete interface specification, documenting all exported features and assertions—immediate or inherited—and hiding implementation aspects. It is the appropriate documentation for a class.

9.9.13. Repeated Inheritance and Selection

An inheritance mechanism, following from multiple inheritance, remains to be seen. Through multiple inheritance, a class can be a proper descendant of another through more than one path. This is called repeated inheritance and can be indirect, as in Figure 9.12, or even direct, when a class D lists a class A twice in its **inherit** clause.

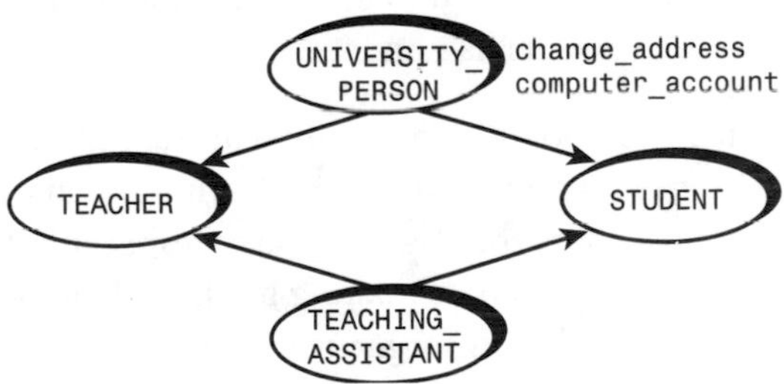

FIGURE 9.12. *Indirect repeated inheritance.*

This particular example is in fact often used by introductory presentations of multiple inheritance, which is a grave pedagogical mistake: Simple multiple inheritance examples (such as INTEGER inheriting from NUMERIC and COMPARABLE, COMPANY_PLANE from ASSET and PLANE, and so on) should involve the combination of *separate abstractions*. Repeated inheritance is an advanced technique; although precious, it does not arise in elementary uses and requires a little more care.

In fact, there is only one non-trivial issue in repeated inheritance: What does a feature of the repeated ancestor, such as `change_address` and `computer_account`, mean for the repeated descendant, here `TEACHING_ASSISTANT`? (The sample features chosen involve a routine and an attribute; the basic rules are the same.)

There are two possibilities: sharing (the repeatedly inherited feature yields just one feature in the repeated descendant) and duplication (it yields two). Examination of various cases shows quickly that a fixed policy, or one that would apply to all the features of a class, would be inappropriate. A feature such as `change_address` calls for sharing: As a teaching assistant, you may be both teacher and student, but you are just one person and have just one official domicile. If there are different computers and accounts for students doing course work and for faculty, you probably have two accounts, one as a student and one as a teacher.

The Eiffel rule enables, once again, the software developer to craft the resulting class to tune it to the exact requirements. Not surprisingly, it is based on names. In accordance with the final name rule (no in-class overloading):

Repeated inheritance rule

- A feature inherited multiply under one name is shared: It is considered to be just one feature in the repeated descendant.
- A feature inherited multiply under different names is replicated, yielding as many variants as names.

To tune the repeated descendant, feature by feature, for sharing and replication, it suffices to use renaming. If you do nothing, you obtain sharing, which is indeed in most cases the desired policy (especially for those cases of unintended repeated inheritance: making `D` inherit from `A` even though it also inherits from `B`, which you forgot is already a descendant of `A`). If you use renaming somewhere along the way, so that the final names are different, you obtain two separate features. Note that it does not matter where the renaming occurs; all that counts is whether in the common descendant, `TEACHING_ASSISTANT` in Figure 9.12, the names are the same or different. You can use renaming at that last stage to cause replication, but if the features have been renamed higher, you can also use last-minute renaming to avoid replication, by bringing them back to a single name.

The repeated inheritance rule gives the desired flexibility to disambiguate the meaning of repeatedly inherited features. There remains a problem in case of redeclaration and polymorphism. Assume that somewhere along the inheritance paths, one or both of two replicated versions of a feature f, such as computer_account in the example, has been redeclared. We need to define the effect of a call a.f (a.computer_account in the example) if a is of the repeated ancestor type, here UNIVERSITY_PERSON, and has become attached as a result of polymorphism to an instance of the repeated descendant, here TEACHING_ASSISTANT. If one or more of the intermediate ancestors has redefined its version of the feature, the dynamically bound call has two or more versions to choose from.

The ambiguity is resolved here through a **select** clause, as in

```
class TEACHING_ASSISTANT inherit
    TEACHER
        rename
            computer_account as faculty_account
        select
            faculty_account
        end
    STUDENT
        rename
            computer_account as student_account
        end
...
```

The assumption here is that no other renaming has occurred—TEACHING_ASSISTANT takes care of the renaming to ensure replication—but that one of the two parents has redefined computer_account, for example TEACHER to express the special privileges of faculty accounts. In such a case, the rule is that one (and exactly one) of the two parent clauses in TEACHING_ASSISTANT must select the corresponding version. Note that no problem arises for an entity declared as

```
ta: TEACHING_ASSISTANT
```

because the valid calls are of the form ta.faculty_account and ta.student_account, neither of them ambiguous (the call ta.computer_account would be invalid because after the renamings, class TEACHING_ASSISTANT has no feature of that name). The **select** only applies to a call

```
up.computer_account
```

with up of type UNIVERSITY_PERSON, dynamically attached to an instance of TEACHING_ASSISTANT; then the **select** resolves the ambiguity by causing the call to use the version from TEACHER. For example, if we traverse a data structure of the form computer_users: LIST [UNIVERSITY_PERSON] to print some information about the computer account of each element in the list, the account used for a teaching assistant is the faculty account, not the student account. (Note that we can, if desired, redefine faculty_account in class TEACHING_ASSISTANT, using student_account, if necessary, to take into consideration the existence of another account. In all cases, we need a precise disambiguation of what `computer_account` means for a `TEACHING_ASSISTANT` object known only through a `UNIVERSITY_PERSON` entity.)

The **`select`** is only needed in case of replication. If the repeated inheritance rule would imply sharing, as with `change_address`, and one or both of the shared versions has been redeclared, the final name rule makes the class invalid because it now has two different features with the same name. (This is only a problem if both versions are effective; if one or both are deferred, there is no conflict but a mere case of feature joining as explained in section 9.9.10.) The two possible solutions follow from the previous discussions:

- If you do want sharing, one of the two versions must take precedence over the other. It suffices to undefine the other, and everything gets back to order. Alternatively, you can redefine both into a new version, which takes precedence over both.
- If you want to keep both versions, switch from sharing to replication. Rename one or both of the features so that they have different names; then you must select one of them.

9.9.14. Constrained Genericity

Eiffel's inheritance mechanism has an important application to extending the flexibility of the *genericity* mechanism. In a class `SOME_CONTAINER [G]`, as noted (section 9.7), the only operations available on entities of type `G`, the formal generic parameter, are those applicable to entities of all types. A generic class may, however, need to assume more about the generic parameter, as with a class `SORTABLE_ARRAY [G... ]`, which has a procedure `sort` that needs, at some stage, to perform tests of the form

```
if item (i) < item ( j) then ...
```

where `item (i)` and `item ( j)` are of type `G`. This requires the availability of a feature **`infix`** `"<"` in all types that may serve as actual generic parameters corresponding to `G`. Using the type `SORTABLE_ARRAY [INTEGER]` should be permitted because `INTEGER` has such a feature—but not `SORTABLE_ARRAY [MATRIX]` if there is no total order relation on `MATRIX`.

To cover such cases, declare the class as

```
class SORTABLE_ARRAY [G  --> COMPARABLE] ... The rest as before ...
```

making it constrained generic. The symbol `-->` recalls the arrow of inheritance diagrams; what follows it is a type, known as the generic constraint. Such a declaration means that

- Within the class, all features of the generic constraint—here all features of `COMPARABLE`: **infix** `"<"`, **infix** `"<="` and so on—may be applied to entities of type `G`.
- A generic derivation is only valid if the chosen actual generic parameter conforms to the constraint. Here we can use `SORTABLE_ARRAY [INTEGER]` because `INTEGER` is a descendant of `COMPARABLE` but not `SORTABLE_ARRAY [INTEGER]` if `MATRIX` is not a descendant of `COMPARABLE`.

A class can have a mix of constrained and unconstrained generic parameters, as in the EiffelBase class `HASH_TABLE [G, H --> HASHABLE]`, whose first parameter represents the types of objects stored in a hash table, the second representing the types of the keys used to store them, which must be `HASHABLE`. As these examples suggest, structural property classes such as `COMPARABLE`, `NUMERIC`, and `HASHABLE` are the most common choice for generic constraints.

Unconstrained genericity, as in `C [G]`, is defined as equivalent to `C [G --> ANY]`.

9.9.15. Assignment Attempt

The type conformance rule (section 9.9.3) ensures type safety by requiring all assignments to be from a more specific source to a more general target.

In some cases, the type of the target object cannot be known for sure. This happens, for example, when the target comes from the outside—a file, a database, or a network. The persistence storage mechanism studied in section 9.6.11 includes, along with the procedure `store` seen there, the reverse operation, a function `retrieved`, which yields an object structure retrieved from a file or network, to which it was sent using `store`. But `retrieved` as declared in the corresponding class `STORABLE` of EiffelBase can only return the most general type, `ANY`; the exact type can only be ascertained at execution time because the corresponding objects are not under the control of the retrieving system and might even have been corrupted by some external agent.

In such cases, we cannot trust the declared type, but must check it against the type of an actual runtime object. Eiffel introduces for this purpose the assignment attempt operation, written

```
x ?= y
```

with the following effect (only applicable if x is a writable entity of reference type):

- If y is attached, at the time of the instruction's execution to an object whose type conforms to the type of x, perform a normal reference assignment.
- Otherwise (if y is void, or attached to a non-conforming object), make x void.

Using this mechanism, a typical object structure retrieval is of the form

```
x ?= retrieved
if x = Void then
    "We did not get what we expected"
else
    "Proceed with normal computation, which will typically involve
    calls of the form x.some_ feature"
end
```

As another application, assume we have a LIST [ACCOUNT], and class SAVINGS_ACCOUNT, a descendant of ACCOUNT, has a feature interest_rate that was not in ACCOUNT. We want to find the maximum interest rate for savings accounts in the list. Assignment attempt easily solves the problem:

```
local
    s: SAVINGS_ACCOUNT
do
    from account_list.start until account_list.after loop
            s ?= acc_list.item -- item from LIST yields
                the element at cursor position
        if s /= Void and then s.interest_rate > Result then
                -- Using and then (rather than and) ensures that
                -- s.interest_rate not evaluated if s = Void is true.
            Result := s.interest_rate
        end
        account_list.forth
    end
end
```

Note that if there is no savings account at all in the list, the assignment attempt always yields void so that the result of the enclosing function is 0, the default initialization.

Assignment attempt is useful in the cases cited—access to external objects beyond the software's own control and access to specific properties in a polymorphic data structure. The form of the instruction precisely serves these purposes; not being a general type comparison (but only a verification of a specific expected type), it does not carry the risk of encouraging developers to revert to multibranch instruction structures, for which Eiffel provides the far preferable alternative of polymorphic, dynamically bound feature calls.

9.9.16. Covariance and Anchored Declarations

The final property of Eiffel inheritance involves the rules for adapting not only the implementation of inherited features (through redeclaration of either kind, redeclaration and redefinition, as seen so far) and their contracts (through the assertion redeclaration rule), but also their types. More general than type is the notion of a feature's signature, defined by the number of its arguments, their types, the indication of whether it has a result (that is, is a function or attribute rather than a procedure) and, if so, the type of the result.

In many cases, the signature of a redeclared feature remains the same as the original's. But in some cases, we may want to adapt it to the new class—for example, if we assume that class ACCOUNT has features

```
owner: HOLDER
set_owner (h: HOLDER) is
        -- Make h the account owner.
    require
        not_void: h /= Void
    do
        owner := h
    end
```

Assume that we introduce an heir BUSINESS_ACCOUNT of ACCOUNT to represent special business accounts, corresponding to class BUSINESS inheriting from HOLDER (see Figure 9.13).

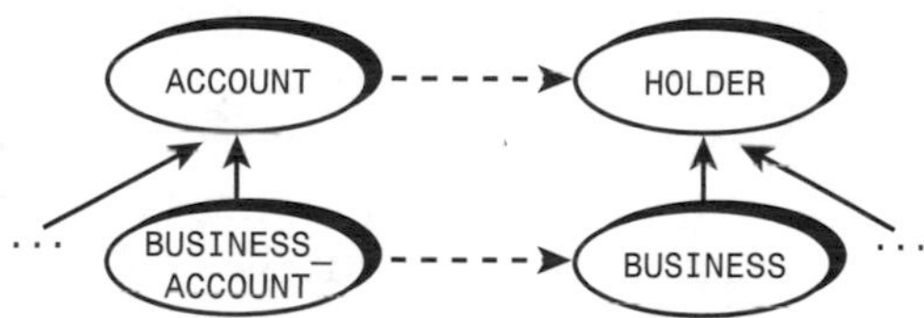

FIGURE 9.13. *Parallel hierarchies.*

Clearly, owner must be redefined in class BUSINESS_ACCOUNT to yield a result of type BUSINESS; the same signature redefinition must be applied to the argument of set_owner. This case is fully typical of the general scheme of signature redefinition: In a descendant, you may need to redefine both query results and routine arguments to types conforming to the originals. This is reflected by a language rule:

Covariance rule

In a feature redeclaration, both the result type if the feature is a query (attribute or function) and the type of any argument if it is a routine (procedure or function) must conform to the original type as declared in the precursor version.

The term *covariance* reflects the property that all types—those of arguments and those of results—vary together in the same direction as the inheritance structure.

If a feature such as set_owner has to be redefined for more than its signature—to update its implementation or assertions—explicit signature redefinition is acceptable. For example, set_owner could do more for business owners than it does for ordinary owners. Then the redefinition is of the form

```
set_owner (b: BUSINESS) is
        -- Make b the account owner.
    ... New routine body ...
    end
```

In many cases, the body is the same as in the precursor. Then explicit redefinition is unbearably tedious, implying constant text duplication. The mechanism of anchored redeclaration solves this problem. The original declaration of set_owner in ACCOUNT should be of the form

```
set_owner (h: like Current) is
        -- Make h the account owner.
        -- The rest as before:
    require
        not_void: h /= Void
    do
        owner := h
    end
```

A **like** anchor type, known as an anchored type, may appear in any context in which anchor has a well-defined type T: anchor can be an attribute or function of the enclosing class or an argument of the enclosing routine. Then, in the class in which it appears, type **like** anchor means the same as T; for example, in set_owner, the declaration of h has the same effect as if h had been declared of type HOLDER, the type of the anchor owner in class ACCOUNT. The difference comes in proper descendants: If a type redefinition changes the type of the anchor, any entity declared **like** the anchor is considered to have been redefined too. This is a form of implicit type redeclaration.

In the example, class BUSINESS_ACCOUNT need only redefine the type of owner (to BUSINESS). Then there is no need to redefine set_owner—unless we want to change its implementation or assertions.

It is possible to use Current as anchor; the declaration **like** Current denotes a type based on the current class (with the same generic parameters, if any). This is in fact a common case; we saw in section 9.9.7 that it applies in class COMPARABLE to features such as

```
infix "<" (other: like Current): BOOLEAN is ...
```

because we only want to compare two comparable elements of compatible types—but not, for example, integer and strings, even if both types conform to COMPARABLE. (A "balancing rule" makes it possible, however, to mix the various arithmetic types, consistently with mathematical traditions, in arithmetic expressions such as 3 + 45.82 or boolean expressions such as 3 < 45.82.)

Similarly, procedure copy is declared in class GENERAL as

```
copy (other: like Current) is ...
```

with both the argument anchored to the current object. Function clone, for its part, has signature clone (other: ANY): **like** other, showing a result anchored to the argument so that the type of clone (x) for any x is the same as the type of x.

A final, more application-oriented example of anchoring to Current is the feature merge posited in an earlier example (section 9.6.14) with the signature merge (other: ACCOUNT). By using instead merge (other: **like** Current), we can ensure that in any descendant class—BUSINESS_ACCOUNT, SAVINGS_ACCOUNT, MINOR_ACCOUNT, and so on—an account is only mergeable with another of a compatible type.

Covariance complicates somewhat the static type checking mechanism; mechanisms of system validity and catcalls address the problem, which is discussed in detail in the book *Object-Oriented Software Construction* (Meyer, 1997).

9.10. Other Important Mechanisms

We now examine a few supplementary mechanisms that complement the preceding picture: shared objects, constants, instructions, and lexical conventions.

9.10.1. once Routines and Shared Objects

The Eiffel's method obsession with extendibility, reusability, and maintainability yields, as has been seen, highly modular and decentralized architectures, where intermodule coupling is limited to the strictly necessary, interfaces are clearly delimited, and all the temptations to introduce obscure dependencies, in particular global variables, have been removed. There is a need, however, to let various components of a system have access to common objects without requiring their routines to pass these objects around as arguments (which is only slightly better than global variables). For example, various classes may need to perform output to a common console window, represented by a shared object.

Eiffel addresses this need through an original mechanism that also takes care of another important issue, poorly addressed by many design and programming approaches: initialization. The basic idea is very simple: If instead of **do**, the implementation of an effective routine is introduced by the keyword **once**, it is only executed the first time the routine is called during a system execution (or, in a multithreaded environment, the first time in each thread), regardless of what the caller is. Subsequent calls from the same caller or others have no effect; if the routine is a function, it always returns the result computed by the first call—object if an expanded type, reference otherwise.

In the case of procedures, this provides a convenient initialization mechanism. A delicate problem in the absence of a **once** mechanism is how to provide the users of a library with a set of routines that they can call in any order, but that all need, to function properly, the guarantee that some context had been properly set up. Asking the library clients to precede the first call with a call to an initialization procedure `setup` is not only user-unfriendly but silly: In a well-engineered system, we want to check setup in every of the routines and report an error if necessary. But then if we were able to detect improper setup, we might as well shut up and set up (by calling `setup`) ourselves instead. This is not easy, however, because the object on which we call `setup` must itself be properly initialized, so we are only pushing the problem further. Making `setup` a **once** procedure solves it: We can simply include a call

```
setup
```

at the beginning of each affected routine; the first one performs the needed initializations; subsequent calls have, as desired, no effect.

`once` functions give us shared objects. A common scheme is

```
console: WINDOW is
        -- Shared console window
    once
        !! Result.make (...)
    end
```

The first call creates the appropriate window and returns a reference to it. Subsequent calls, from anywhere in the system, return that same reference. The simplest way to make this function available to a set of classes is to include it in a class `SHARED_STRUCTURES`, which the classes needing a set of related shared objects simply inherit.

For the classes using it, `console`, although a function, looks very much as if it were an attribute—only one referring to a shared object.

The "Hello, World" system at the beginning of this chapter (section 9.4) uses an output instruction of the form `io.put_string ("Some string")`. This is another example of the general scheme illustrated by `console`. Feature `io`, declared in `GENERAL` and hence usable by all classes, is a `once` function that returns an object of type `STANDARD_FILES` (another kernel library class) providing access to basic input and output mechanisms. Procedure `put_string` is one of them. Because basic input and output must all work on the same files, `io` should clearly be a `once` function, shared by all classes that need these mechanisms.

9.10.2. Constant Attributes

The attributes studied earlier were variable: Each represents a field present in each instance of the class and changeable by its routines.

It is also possible to declare constant attributes, as in

```
Solar_system_planet_count: INTEGER is 9
```

These have the same value for every instance and hence do not need to occupy any space in objects at execution time. (In other approaches, similar needs would be addressed by constants, as in Pascal or Ada, or macros, as in C.)

What comes after the **is** is a manifest constant: a self-denoting value of the appropriate type. Manifest constants are available for integers, reals (also used for doubles), booleans (`True` and `False`), and characters (in single quotes, as `'A'`, with special characters expressed using a percent sign as in `'%N'` for newline, `'%B'` for backspace, and `'%U'` for null).

For integer constants, it is also possible to avoid specifying the values. A declaration of the form

```
a, b, c, ... n: INTEGER is unique
```

introduces `a, b, c, ... n` as constant integer attributes, whose values are assigned by the Eiffel compiler rather than explicitly by the developer. The values are different for all **unique** attributes in a system; they are all positive, and, in a single declaration such as the preceding, guaranteed to be consecutive (so that an invariant property of the form `code >= a and code <= n` can be used to express that `code` should be one of the values). This mechanism replaces the enumerated types found in Pascal and subsequent languages without suffering from the same problems. (Enumerated types have an ill-defined place in the type system, and it is not clear what operations are permitted.) Unique values can be used in conjunction with the **inspect** multibranch instruction studied in the next section. They are only appropriate for codes that can take on a fixed number of well-defined values—not as a way to program operations with many variants, a need better addressed by the object-oriented technique studied earlier and relying on inheritance, polymorphism, redeclaration, and dynamic binding.

Manifest constants are also available for strings, using double quotes, as in

```
User_friendly_error_message: INTEGER is "Go get a life!"
```

with special characters again using the `%` codes. It is also possible to declare manifest arrays using double angle brackets:

```
<<1, 2, 3, 5, 7, 11, 13, 17, 19>>
```

This example is an expression of type `ARRAY [INTEGER]`. Manifest arrays and strings are not atomic but denote instances of the kernel library classes `STRING` and `ARRAY`, as can be produced by `once` functions.

9.10.3. Instructions

Eiffel has a remarkably small set of instructions. The basic computational instructions have been seen: creation, assignment, assignment attempt, procedure call, and **`retry`**. They are complemented by control structures: conditional, multibranch, and loop, as well as **`debug`** and **`check`**.

A conditional instruction has the form **`if...then...elseif...else...end`**. The **`elseif`**... part (of which there may be more than one) and the **`else`**... part are optional. After the **`if`** comes a boolean expression; after **`then`**, **`elseif`** and **`else`** come zero or more instructions.

A multibranch instruction has the form

```
inspect
     exp
when v1 then
     inst1
when v2 then
     inst2
...
else
     inst0
end
```

where the **`else`** $inst_0$ part is optional, `exp` is a character or integer expression, v_1, v_2, ... are constant values of the corresponding type, all different, and $inst_0$, $inst_1$, $inst_2$, ... are sequences of zero or more instructions. In the integer case, it is often convenient to use **`unique`** value for the v_i.

The effect of such a multibranch instruction, if the value of `exp` is one of the v_i, is to execute the corresponding $inst_i$. If none of the v_i matches, the instruction executes $inst_0$, unless there is no **`else`** part, in which case it triggers an exception. (This is the desired behavior because the absence of an **`else`** part indicates explicitly that the author guarantees that one of the values matches; to ensure that the instruction does nothing in this case, rather than cause an exception, use an **`else`** part with an empty $inst_0$. In contrast, the instruction **`if`** `c` **`then`** `inst` **`end`** with no **`else`** clause does nothing in the absence of an **`else`** part because in this case, there is no implied claim that `c` must hold.)

The loop construct has the form

```
from
    initialization
until
    exit
invariant
    inv
variant
    var
loop
    body
end
```

The **`invariant`** `inv` and **`variant`** `var` parts are optional; the others are required. `initialization` and `body` are sequences of zero or more instructions; `exit` and `inv` are boolean expressions (more precisely, `inv` is an assertion); `var` is an integer expression.

The effect is to execute `initialization`, then, zero or more times until `exit` is satisfied, to execute `body`. (If after `initialization` the value of `exit` is already `true`, `body` is not executed at all.) Note that the syntax of loops always includes an initialization, as most loops require some preparation. If not, just leave `initialization` empty while including the **`from`** because it is a required component.

The assertion `inv`, if present, expresses a **`loop invariant`** (not to be confused with class invariants). For the loop to be correct, `initialization` must ensure `inv`, and then every iteration of `body` executed when `exit` is false must preserve the invariant, so the effect of the loop is to yield a state in which both `inv` and `exit` are true. The loop must terminate after a finite number of iterations, of course; this can be guaranteed by using a **`loop variant`** *`var`*. It must be an integer expression whose value is non-negative after execution of `initialization` and decreased by at least one, while remaining non-negative, by any execution of `body` when `exit` is `false`; because a non-negative integer cannot be decreased forever, this ensures termination. The full-assertion-monitoring mode checks these properties of the invariant and variant after initialization and after each loop iteration, triggering an exception if the invariant does not hold or the variant is negative or does not decrease.

An occasionally useful instruction is `debug (Debug_key, ...) instructions end` where `instructions` is a sequence of zero or more instructions and the part in parentheses is optional, containing if present one or more strings (debug keys). Compilation options of the environment (specifying explicit debug keys or just yes or no to govern the effect of debug instructions with no keys) make it possible to treat this instruction as executing the `instructions` or doing nothing at all. The obvious use is for instructions that should be part of the system but executed only in some circumstances; for example, to provide extra debugging information.

The final instruction is connected with design by contract. The instruction `check Assertions end`, where `Assertions` is a sequence of zero or more assertions, has no effect unless assertion monitoring is turned on at the check level or higher. In that case, it evaluates all the assertions listed, having no further effect if they are all satisfied; if any one of them does not hold, however, the instruction triggers an exception.

This instruction serves to state properties that are expected to be satisfied at some stages of the computation—other than the specific stages, such as routine entry and exit, already covered by the other assertion mechanisms such as preconditions, postconditions, and invariants. A recommended use of **check** involves calling a routine with a precondition, where the call, for good reason, does not explicitly test for the precondition. Consider a routine of the form

```
r (ref: SOME_REFERENCE_TYPE) is
    require
        not_void: r /= Void
    do
        r.some_feature
        ...
    end
```

Because of the call to `some_feature`, the routine does not work unless its precondition is satisfied. A call `a.r (x)` can appear as `if x /= Void then a.r (x) end`, but this is not the only possible scheme; for example, if the preceding instruction is `!! x`, then we know `x` is not void and do not need to protect the call at all. In some cases, however, the argument showing that `x` is not void might be less obvious; for example, `x` could have been obtained, in a non-adjacent part of the algorithm, as `clone (y)` for some `y` that we know is not void. It is good practice in this case to write the call as

```
        check
            x_not_void: x /= Void end
              -- Because x was obtained as a clone of y,
                 and y is not void because [etc.]
        end
    a.r (x)
```

Note the recommended convention: extra indentation of the **check** part to separate it from the algorithm proper, and inclusion of a comment listing the rationale behind the developer's decision not to check explicitly for the precondition.

In production mode with assertion monitoring turned off, this instruction has no effect. But it is precious for a maintainer of the software who is trying to figure out what it does and in the process to reconstruct the original developer's reasoning. (The maintainer might of course be the same person as the developer, six months later.) If the rationale is wrong somewhere, turning on assertion checking immediately uncovers the bug.

9.10.4. Lexical Conventions

Eiffel software texts are free-format: Distribution into lines is not semantically significant, and any number of successive space and line-return characters is equivalent to just one space. The style rules suggest indenting software texts as illustrated by the examples in this chapter.

About 65 names—all unabbreviated single English words, except for **elseif**, which is made of two words—are reserved, meaning that they cannot be used to declare new entities.

Most of them are keywords, serving only as syntactic markers, and conventionally written in boldface in texts such as the present one: **class**, **feature**, **inherit**, and so on. Other reserved words, such as `Current`, directly carry a semantic denotation.

Except in manifest character constants (appearing in single quotes, such as `'A'`) and character strings (appearing in double quotes, such as `"lower and UPPER"`), letter case is not significant, to avoid errors due to subtle differences in writing an identifier. The style rules are again quite strict: They suggest writing class names in uppercase, as `ACCOUNT`, non-constant feature names and keywords in lowercase, as `balance` and **class**, and constant features and predefined entities and expressions with an initial lowercase, as `Avogadro` and `Current`.

Successive declarations or instructions may be separated by semicolons. Eiffel's syntax has been so designed, however, that (except in rare cases) the semicolon is optional. Omitting semicolons for elements appearing on separate lines lightens text and is the recommended practice. For clarity, however, successive elements appearing on a single line should always be separated by semicolons. These are the rules applied in this chapter.

9.11. Concurrency and Further Developments

Recent work has resulted in advanced mechanisms being made available to the Eiffel community in the area of concurrency, Internet development, multithreading, and CORBA.

9.11.1. SCOOP

Many proposals have been made to make Eiffel support concurrent programming; an extensive bibliography may be found at `http://www.eiffel.com`. The most developed of these proposals in the process of being submitted to the NICE Eiffel consortium at the time of this writing is known as SCOOP—simple concurrent object-oriented programming—and is the result of work performed between 1991 and 1996.

The key word in SCOOP is the first: simple. SCOOP represents a minimal extension to Eiffel—one keyword, `separate`—and takes full advantage of the existing sequential Eiffel mechanisms, remaining fully compatible with the spirit of the method that it prolongs to its natural concurrent counterparts. In spite of its simplicity, it is extremely general, covering all known forms of concurrency, from multiple processes to Internet programming, multithreading, and distributed computation (all implemented or being implemented in ISE's environment at the time of writing). The following summary is drawn from the chapter on concurrency in *Object-Oriented Software Construction* (Meyer, 1997).

We use the fundamental scheme of OO computation: feature call, `x.f (a)`, executed on behalf of some object `O1` and calling `f` on the object `O2` attached to `x`, with the argument `a`. Instead of a single processor that handles operations on all objects, we may now rely on different processors for `O1` and `O2`—so that the computation on `O1` can move ahead without waiting for the call to terminate because another processor handles it.

Because the effect of a call now depends on whether the objects are handled by the same processor or different ones, the software text must tell us unambiguously what the intent is for any `x`. Hence the need for the single new keyword—rather than just `x: SOME_TYPE`, we declare `x: separate`

`SOME_TYPE` to indicate that `x` is handled by a different processor so that calls of target `x` can proceed in parallel with the rest of the computation. With such a declaration, any creation instruction `!! x.make (...)` spawns a new processor—a new thread of control—to handle future calls on `x`.

Nowhere in the software text should we have to specify *which* processor to use. All we state, through the **`separate`** declaration, is that two objects are handled by different processors because this radically affects the system's semantics. Actual processor assignment can wait until runtime. Nor do we settle too early on the exact nature of processors: A processor can be implemented by a piece of hardware (a computer), but just as well by a task (process) of the operating system, or, on a multithreaded OS, just a thread of such a task. Viewed by the software, "processor" is an abstract concept; you can execute the same concurrent application on widely different architectures (time-sharing on one computer, distributed network with many computers, or threads within one UNIX or Windows task) without any change to its source text. All you change is a *concurrency configuration file* that specifies the last-minute mapping of abstract processors to physical resources.

We need to specify synchronization constraints. The conventions are straightforward:

- No special mechanism is required for a client to resynchronize with its supplier after a separate call `x.f (a)` has gone off in parallel. The client waits when and if it needs to: when it requests information on the object through a query call, as in `value := x.some_query`. This automatic mechanism is called *wait by necessity*.
- To obtain exclusive access to a separate object `O2`, it suffices to use the attached entity `a` as an argument to the corresponding call, as in `r (a)`.
- A routine precondition involving a separate argument such as `a` causes the client to wait until the precondition holds.
- To guarantee that we can control our software and predict the result (in particular, rest assured that class invariants are maintained), we must allow the processor in charge of an object to execute at most one routine at any given time.
- We may, however, need to *interrupt* the execution of a routine to let a new, high-priority client take over. This causes an exception so that the spurned client can take the appropriate corrective measures—most likely retrying after a while.

This covers most of the mechanism, which enables us to build the most advanced concurrent and distributed applications through the full extent of Eiffel techniques reviewed in this chapter, from multiple inheritance and behavior classes to static typing, dynamic binding, and design by contract.

9.11.2. Other Developments

As part of the growth of Eiffel usage in large projects and its openness to the rest of the software world, a number of important developments, some already in the form of products, and still others in progress, have recently occurred:

- Development of multithreading libraries (which may be used without the SCOOP extensions of the preceding section for users using sequential Eiffel or in conjunction with SCOOP).
- CORBA interfaces, as a result of a cooperation between ISE and ICL Ltd. and of a multivendor effort leading to a proposed official Eiffel binding for IDL, the Interface Definition Language of CORBA.
- Interfaces to Microsoft's OLE 2 and ActiveX.
- Interfaces to relational and object-oriented databases.
- Libraries or reusable components in many different areas (such as ISE's EiffelMath for scientific and financial applications).
- Java and Java bytecode generation, Java interfaces.
- Interfaces to many other industry-standard products.

9.12. Eiffel History

I designed Eiffel on September 23, 1985. It was initially intended as an internal tool for the newly created ISE. The first internal implementation was ready in mid-1986.

The main influences on the design of Eiffel have been

- The object-oriented concepts introduced by Simula 67, which I was able to practice starting at the end of 1973.
- Work on formal specification, in particular Abrial's original version of the Z specification language, with which I had been associated (and which I documented in a 1978 book).

- Work on abstract data types by Liskov, Zilles, Guttag, and me.
- The Algol 60/Algol W/Pascal/Ada line of programming languages.
- Work on program proving and axiomatic semantics (Floyd, Hoare, and Dijkstra).
- Modern concepts of software engineering, in particular the work on software quality.

A presentation at the first OOPSLA conference (Object-Oriented Programming, Systems, Languages, and Applications, Portland, September 1986) revealed that many of the concepts and their implementation were ahead of the rest of the industry as well as of academic research and led to the transformation of the compiler into a commercial product, which started to be sold to companies and universities worldwide in December 1986. Version 2 was introduced in 1988.

The book *Object-Oriented Software Construction* (Meyer, 1988, 1997) enjoyed a large success and introduced Eiffel to a broader community.

In 1990, ISE decided to relinquish control of the Eiffel language and kernel library to an independent organization, NICE (the Nonprofit International Consortium for Eiffel), which was incorporated in the same year. This enabled the development of compilers and tools from other sources and the birth of an Eiffel industry.

At the same time, a general cleanup of the language was undertaken, which led to a number of simplifications and a few extensions. These changes did not, however, affect the essential concepts and techniques of the language and method; Eiffel has been remarkably stable and remains close today to the original 1985 design. The language reference, *Eiffel: The Language* (Meyer, 1992), the result of this revision, was published in 1991 and revised the following year. Under the control of NICE, a few further adaptations are planned, meant to make the practice of Eiffel usage more pleasurable without causing any upward-compatibility problems or introducing any major conceptual change.

ISE's own original technology reached its peak with Version 2.3, released in 1990. From 1990 to 1993, the technology was reengineered in Eiffel (the first versions, for obvious reasons of necessity, had been written in C), using Version 2.3 for the initial bootstrap. This led to ISE Eiffel 3, a complete graphical development environment first released in 1993, and to its successor ISE Eiffel 4 (1997), incorporating multithreading and concurrency.

Another notable event was the publication in 1995 of *Seamless Object-Oriented Software Construction* (Waldén & Nerson, 1995), which introduced the business object notation, prolonging Eiffel on the analysis and design side in a form that is attractive to managers, analysts, and system architects.

Today Eiffel is used to develop some of the largest, most ambitious successful software projects in the world. Areas of application include banking, financial systems, accounting, telecommunications, health care, CAD-CAM, simulation, real-time, scientific computing, and scientific visualization. Some of the most visible projects (such as CALFP Bank's Rainbow system, initially a derivative trading system but having grown to oversee most of the bank's operation) have been extensively documented in the press and are also featured at `http://www.eiffel.com`.

Eiffel is also popular as a teaching tool in universities and even high schools. A large number of universities are in fact using Eiffel as the first programming language taught to students. Others use it at various levels in the curriculum, aided by attractive packages from the Eiffel product providers.

The name *Eiffel* is a homage to Gustave Eiffel, the man who built the eponymous tower in Paris as well as many other durable constructions such as the metallic armature of the Statue of Liberty in New York and the Budapest railway station. The Eiffel Tower, started in 1887 for the 1889 World's Fair, was completed on time and within budget; it has survived political hostility and attempts at destruction, found many new uses (such as radio and television), and proved to be robust and efficient. Built out of a small number of robust, elegant design patterns, combined and varied repeatedly to yield a powerful result, it is the best symbol of what Eiffel can achieve for the software world.

9.13. More Information on Eiffel

9.13.1. Documentation

A large body of literature exists on Eiffel. Here is a selection of the most relevant titles.

Dubois, P. 1996. *Object technology for scientific computing—Object-oriented numerical software in Eiffel and C*. Upper Saddle River, NJ: Prentice Hall. Describes the application of the Eiffel method and language to numerical computation and the design of the EiffelMath library.

Gore, J. 1996. *Object structures: Building object-oriented software components*. Reading, MA: Addison-Wesley. Covers data structures using Eiffel with an emphasis on abstraction, reusability, and the proper use of inheritance.

Jézéquel, J.-M. 1996. *Object-oriented software engineering with Eiffel*. Reading, MA: Addison-Wesley. Emphasizes the application of the Eiffel method and modern software engineering principles to the development of large, mission-critical systems.

Meyer, B. 1988. *Object-oriented software construction* (1st ed.). Englewood Cliffs, NJ: Prentice Hall. This is not a book about Eiffel per se, but about object technology in general, using the Eiffel approach and relying on the Eiffel notation. (See second edition.)

Meyer, B. 1992. *Eiffel: The language*. Englewood Cliffs, NJ: Prentice Hall. This serves as both a detailed language description and the language reference.

Meyer, B. 1994. *Reusable software: The base object-oriented component libraries*. Englewood Cliffs, NJ: Prentice Hall. A discussion of library design principles as supported by Eiffel and their application to the EiffelBase libraries.

Meyer, B. 1997. *Object-oriented software construction* (2nd ed.). Englewood Cliffs, NJ: Prentice Hall. This is not a book about Eiffel per se, but about object technology in general, using the Eiffel approach and relying on the Eiffel notation. Considerably expanded in both breadth and depth from the first edition.

Meyer, B., and J.-M. Nerson (Eds.). 1994. *Object-oriented applications*. Englewood Cliffs, NJ: Prentice Hall. This is a collection of chapters written by various project leaders from industrial companies (CAD-CAM, telecommunications, and AI) and describing Eiffel projects in detail: system goals, techniques used, issues encountered, architectural decisions, and practical status.

Rist, R., and R. Terwilliger. 1995. *Object-oriented programming in Eiffel*. Englewood Cliffs, NJ: Prentice Hall. A textbook that serves as an introduction to programming with an emphasis on software design principles.

Switzer, R. 1993. *Eiffel: An introduction*. Englewood Cliffs, NJ: Prentice Hall. A short and clear presentation of Eiffel, suitable for anyone having had prior experience in another language. Written by one of the authors of the Eiffel/S system.

Thomas, P., and R. Weedon. 1995. *Object-oriented programming in Eiffel.* Reading, MA: Addison-Wesley. A textbook that serves as an introduction to programming with emphasis on data abstraction and design by contract.

Waldén, K., and J.-M. Nerson. 1995. *Seamless object-oriented software architecture—Analysis and design of reliable systems.* Upper Saddle River, NJ: Prentice Hall. A lucid description of issues and principles of object-oriented analysis and design, using ideas close to those of Eiffel. Introduces the BON method (business object notation).

Wiener, R. 1995. *Software development using Eiffel—There can be life other than C++.* Englewood Cliffs, NJ: Prentice Hall. A presentation particularly aimed at readers already familiar with another OO language such as C++.

Wiener, R. 1996. *An object-oriented introduction to computer science using Eiffel.* Englewood Cliffs, NJ: Prentice Hall.

Wiener, R. 1997. *Data structures using Eiffel.* Englewood Cliffs, NJ: Prentice Hall.

9.13.2. Information Sources

ISE's home page at `http://www.eiffel.com` is an extensive repository of information about Eiffel with numerous introductory presentations on the technology and its application, and online technology papers on concurrency, multithreading, external interfaces, Eiffel projects, and so on.

GUERL, (for Geoff [Eldridge]'s Universal Eiffel Resource Locator) `http://www.el;.com`, provides considerable amounts of Eiffel information and links to other Eiffel pages.

9.13.3. Compiler Sources

The following companies provide Eiffel compilers. They are listed here in chronological order of appearance of their initial products.

ISE Eiffelsoft, a division of Interactive Software Engineering Inc., offers the ISE Eiffel 4 environment running on a large number of platforms (Windows, UNIX, Linux, VMS, etc.) including numerous tools and libraries and resells Object Tools's visual Eiffel (see next). ISE Eiffelsoft, 270 Storke Road Suite 7, Santa Barbara, CA 93117, phone 805-685-1006, fax 805-685-6869, `info@eiffel.com`, `http://www.eiffel.com`. A time-limited free version can be downloaded from the Web site.

Object Tools is the originator of both the Eiffel/S and Visual Eiffel compilers, as well as a reseller of other compilers. Object Tools GmbH, zu den Bettern 4, 35619 Braunfels, Germany, phone +49 6472 2096, fax +49/6472-911-031, `info@object-tools.com`, `http://www.object-tools.com`.

Tower Technology offers the Tower Eiffel compiler and environment, available on a number of platforms, and the Eiffel Booch components. Tower Technology Corporation, 1501 West Koenig Lane, Austin, TX 78756, phone 512-452-9455, fax 512-452-1721, `tower@twr.com`, `http://www.twr.com`.

Halstenbach GmbH provides the ISS-Base tools based on Eiffel. Halstenbach ACT, Briedenbrucher Strasse 2, D-51674 Wiehl-Bomig, Germany, phone +49-2261- 9902-0, fax +49-2261-9902-99, `info@hact.de`, `http://www.hact.de`.

The **Centre de Recherche en Informatique de Nancy** (**CRIN**) is the source of the SmallEiffel compiler, also known as GNU Eiffel and distributed under the terms of the GNU General Public License. It is available from `http://www.loria.fr/projects/SmallEiffel`.

PART V
Ada 95

CHAPTER 10

Ada 95 in Context

by Michael B. Feldman

10.1. Introduction

Ada is alive and well and might well be found in your trains, planes, and automobiles, not to mention satellites, steel mills, and—if you live in Switzerland—your bank.

This chapter introduces you to the Ada programming language. The chapter is organized as follows:

- Section 10.2, "Preliminaries": Ada history, the Ada 95 project, and Ada compiler validation
- Section 10.3, "Ada in Today's World": Defense and non-defense projects, Ada in education, Ada compiler availability
- Section 10.4, "Programming in Ada": A tour of the language via annotated complete, compilable, tested examples
- Section 10.5, "Bibliography": A list of useful sources for further information

The current Ada standard is Ada 95; the language of the original Ada standard is now referred to as Ada 83. Throughout this chapter, when I refer to Ada I mean Ada 95, except in the historical section. Where necessary to full understanding, I distinguish between Ada 83 and Ada 95, but I keep this distinction to a minimum.

Frequently, I refer to the wealth of materials available on the World Wide Web. With the exception of published books, nearly every conceivable Ada document is available on the Web, as are freely downloadable compilers. These resources are collected at five main Web sites, whose uniform resource locators (URLs, or addresses) are given in section 10.5. The sites are

- Ada Programming Language Resources for Educators and Students, sponsored by the Education Working Group of the ACM Special Interest Group on Ada (SIGAda), which I maintain and refer to here as the "Educator site"
- Ada Information Clearinghouse (Ada IC), operated by IIT Research Institute under contract to the Ada Joint Program Office (AJPO) in the U.S. Government and referred to as the "Ada IC site"
- Public Ada Library (PAL), a very large collection of Ada documents, programs, compilers, and so on, maintained by Richard Conn on the Washington University (St. Louis) Internet archive server and referred to as "the PAL"
- Home of the Brave Ada Programmers, maintained in Switzerland by Magnus Kempe and referred to as "HBAP"
- ACM Special Interest Group on Ada, referred to as "SIGAda"

In referring to specific files and other resources on the Web, I have refrained from giving detailed URLs, as these have an annoying tendency to change. All the sites are organized for quick search and retrieval and contain many references to resources on the other sites, so I deem it better just to mention the overall site name and leave it the reader to pay an electronic visit.

10.2. Preliminaries

This section briefly reviews the history of Ada 83 and Ada 95 and discusses the important process of validation of Ada implementations.

10.2.1. A Brief Historical Sketch of Ada 83

This chapter is not intended as a historical document, but one can best assess a technical contribution if one acquires some understanding of the history and context of that contribution. This section therefore provides a historical sketch of Ada.

10.2.1.1. The Early History of Ada 83

The history of Ada 83 has been written exhaustively—and entertainingly—in a paper in the Second History of Programming Languages Conference (HOPL-II) by William Whitaker (Whitaker, 1996). Whitaker led the original High Order Language Working Group (HOLWG) effort at the U.S. Department of Defense (DoD). This group wrote the requirements for, and oversaw the competition for the design of, the language that became Ada. Whitaker's article also makes fascinating reading for its insights into the workings of a large organization. For this early history, excerpts from Whitaker's account serve much more effectively than could my attempt to reword it.

To begin, I quote from Whitaker's (1996) commentary on the reasons for desiring a common DoD language:

> The proposal for language commonality across DoD was extremely radical at the time and initially met almost universal opposition. In fact, it was regarded as unrealistic to expect to use a high order language for embedded systems. It may be surprising that a consensus did not mandate a common high order language for embedded systems much earlier. There are, however, a number of managerial and technical constraints that acted against this. For many DoD systems, severe timing and memory considerations were dominant, governed by real-time interaction with the exterior environment.
>
> Because of these constraints, and restrictions in developmental cost and time scale, many systems opted for assembly language programming. This decision was influenced by past experience with poor quality compilers and the fact that an assembler routinely comes with the machine, while the compiler and its tools usually must be developed after the project has begun. The advantages of high order languages, however, were compelling, and more systems turned to them. Because of limitations of available high order languages, the programs generated often included very large portions done in assembly code and linked to an HOL structure, negating many of the HOL advantages.
>
> Further, many systems found it convenient to produce their own high order language or some incompatible dialect of an existing one. Since there was no general facility for control of existing languages, each systems office did the configuration control on its language and compilers and continued this for their particular dialect through the entire maintenance phase of the system. This had the effect of reducing the contractual flexibility of the Government and restricting competition in maintenance and further development.
>
> This lack of commonality negated many advantages of high order languages including transportability, sharing of tools, the development of very powerful tools of high efficiency and, in fact, not only raised the total cost of existing tools, but in some cases essentially priced them out of the market. Development projects were very poorly supported and forced to live with technology far below what should be the state-of-the-art.

> The target for a major language project was to be DoD "software in the large." This is often given a limited interpretation, namely that DoD programs are individually large, which is certainly true and drives many of the technical requirements on the language. But the fact that the DoD has hundreds of such large programs provides an opportunity for economies of scale that are potentially much greater than the sum of individual projects. The problem is not just that of producing a subsystem of 200,000 lines of code, but of the servicing of a "system" that is all the code produced by the DoD for (by 1990) $30 billion per year ("programming in the very large"). This path drives other requirements and properties, like machine independence which forces the validation requirement and the rejection of subsets. But these advantages can be realized only if the technology is applied with consistency over the whole of the DoD, and an even larger community if possible. So a strong position from the DoD was vital to the plan.

Once the working group was formed, it agreed on these goals for a common DoD language:

- The language should facilitate the reduction of software costs. The costs must be reckoned on the total burden of the lifecycle including maintenance, not just the cost of production or program writing.
- Transportability allows the reusing of major portions of software and tools from previous projects and the flexibility for a system to change hardware while keeping the same software.
- The maintenance of very long-lived software in an ever-changing threat situation requires responsiveness and timely flexibility.
- Reliability is an extremely severe requirement in many Defense systems and is often reflected in the high cost of extensive testing and verification procedures.
- The readability of programs produced for such long-term systems use is clearly more important than coding speed or writability.
- The general acceptability of high-order languages is often determined by the efficiency and quality of the compiled code. Although rapidly falling costs of hardware may make this difficult to substantiate in the abstract, each project manager will compare the efficiency of the object code produced against an absolute standard of the best possible machine language programming. Very little degradation is acceptable.

The abstract of the Whitaker (1996) article summarizes the early stages of the actual project very nicely. I have interpolated a few bits of text, in brackets:

> The Department of Defense (DoD) High Order Language Commonality program began in 1975 with the goal of establishing a single high order computer programming language appropriate for DoD real-time embedded computer systems. A High Order Language Working Group (HOLWG) was chartered to formulate the DoD requirements for high order languages, to evaluate existing languages against those requirements, and to implement the minimal set of languages required for DoD use.
>
> Other parts of the effort included administrative initiatives toward the eventual goal—specifically, DoD Directive 5000.29 which provided that new defense systems should be programmed in a DoD "approved" and centrally controlled high order language and DoD Instruction 5000.31 which gave the interim defining list of approved languages. [These included Fortran, COBOL, TACPOL, CMS-2, SPL/1, Jovial J3 and Jovial J73.]
>
> The HOLWG language requirements were widely distributed for comment throughout the military and civil communities worldwide. Each successive version of the requirements, from STRAWMAN [1975] through [WOODENMAN, TINMAN, and IRONMAN, to] STEELMAN [HOLWG, 1978], produced a more refined definition of the proposed language. During the requirement development process, it was determined that the set of requirements generated was both necessary and sufficient for all major DoD applications (and the analogous large commercial applications). Formal evaluations were performed on dozens of existing languages.
>
> It was concluded that no existing language could be adopted as a single common high order language for the DoD, but that a single language meeting essentially all the requirements was both feasible and desirable. Four contractors were funded [in August 1977] to produce competitive prototypes. A first-phase evaluation [starting in February 1978] reduced the designs to two, which were carried to completion. In turn, [in May 1979] a single language design [submitted by the Frenchman Jean Ichbiah and his team at CII-Honeywell Bull] was subsequently chosen. [The *Reference Manual* and Rationale for this design were published as a two-part set of *SIGPLAN Notices,* June 1979.]
>
> Follow-on steps included the test and evaluation of the language, control of the language and validation of compilers. The production of compilers and a program development and tool environment

> were to be accomplished separately by the individual service components. The general requirements and expectations for the environment and the control of the language were addressed in another iterative series of documents. A language validation capability (the test code suite) and associated facilities were established to assure compliance to the language definition of compilers using the name "Ada." The name Ada was initially protected by a DoD-owned trademark [which was relinquished, along with the copyright on the *Reference Manual*, in 1987].

Several refinements of the language design took place between 1979 and 1983. Here is Whitaker's (1996) summary of those years:

> Upon the completion of the development project in late 1980...the loose organization of the HOLWG was superseded by a DoD Ada Joint Program Office (AJPO), chartered 12 December 1980....This office managed the standardization processes with ANSI and ISO. One consequence of the transition was that this new organization was exclusively involved in the control and support of Ada, not in the overall DoD software problem. While initially proposed and budgeted to generate tools and applications libraries, the AJPO abandoned that role and concerned itself mainly with the control and with DoD policies.
>
> The chief task was to continue to polish the language definition in connection with an ANSI canvass process leading to ANSI, and eventually ISO, standardization. A major challenge was to maintain close international involvement in the development and assure that national and international standards did not differ (a real possibility in the standards world of that time, but much less likely today). Through the usual Ada open process, the definition was refined to MIL-STD 1815A, and this was endorsed by ANSI in February 1983 [U.S. Dept. of Defense 1983], with updated Rationale [Ichbiah *et al.* 1987]. Ada was endorsed as ISO Standard 8652 in 1987. [The ISO standard was a one-page document incorporating the ANSI standard by reference; there were no technical changes at all.]

One final quotation from Whitaker (1996), about the language evaluation process, is revealing:

> Other languages were considered for formal evaluation, but were not included because preliminary examination led one to believe that they would not meet the requirements so were not viable candidates for the purposes of the DoD. One such language was C. At that time DARPA was working with Western Electric/Bell Labs on UNIX, contractually supporting some DARPA contractors and

other Government facilities using UNIX. It was the evaluation policy to have the owners provide assessments of their own languages, in addition to the contracted evaluations, so HOLWG took advantage of this connection between DARPA and Bell Labs to request their cooperation. When Bell Labs were invited to evaluate C against the DoD requirements, they said that there was no chance of C meeting the requirements of readability, safety, etc., for which we were striving, and that it should not even be on the list of evaluated languages. We recognized the truth in their observation and honored their request.

Some have claimed that Ada was "designed by a committee." This claim is simply not true. The HOLWG represented the intended *users* of the new language. This group oversaw the design competition, but each of the four full language designs was firmly in the hands of a small team in industry. The team that won the competition consisted of Jean Ichbiah and six other members who attest to Ichbiah's strong leadership. It is true that the process was an open one, which was unprecedented in language development, and that many in the community reviewed the design and advised on its refinement, but Ada was designed by its designers.

10.2.1.2. The Name

The name *Ada* honors Countess Augusta Ada Lovelace (1815–1852), a mathematician and the only legitimate daughter of poet Lord Byron. While in her twenties, she worked with Charles Babbage on his Difference Engine and thus is considered the world's first computer programmer. The name was suggested in 1978 by Jack Cooper, a member of the HOLWG, at a meeting of the group in Paris. Whitaker, who was not in Paris at the time, is unable to confirm that the meeting took place in a Paris café. On the other hand, his article does contain verbatim copies of a wonderful series of letters in which DoD requested—and received—permission from Ada's rightful heir, Lord Lytton, to name the language for her.

Ada's life has been chronicled in a number of biographies, including Dorothy Stein's 1985 work (Stein, 1985). Many Ada language enthusiasts are known to be quite emphatic in their reminders that the Ada language honors a real—and interesting—person and therefore is *not* to be spelled ADA, which refers to (depending on context) the American Dental Association and the Americans with Disabilities Act. The military version of the Ada 83 standard carries reference number MIL-STD 1815A. This number was not chosen idly; the inside joke is that the real Ada was born in 1815.

10.2.2. From Ada 83 to Ada 95

Under ANSI practice, a standard is revisited five years after its adoption, and a process is begun to determine whether the standard should be retained as is, modified, or withdrawn. Accordingly, in 1988 the Ada standard was opened formally for a second look. (Naturally, during the five years, many informal comments had been collected.) In the words of the Ada IC flier *Introducing Ada 95:*

> A Board of Distinguished Reviewers representing six different countries and comprising 28 world-renowned leaders in academia and industry provided oversight and evaluation of the immense input from the international community of users. Over 750 recommendations were received by individuals who were invited to submit Revision Requests.... Conferences, workshops, small-group meetings and one-on-one consultations were held with various segments of the Ada community, and advice was received from some of the world's finest software engineers and Government technology leaders.
>
> ...The revision is an update of the 1987 International Organization for Standardization (ISO) release and the equivalent 1983 American National Standards Institute (ANSI) Ada standard. Drafts of the revised standard were formally considered by the ISO between September 1993 and October 1994; ballots were cast over a period of 15 months by the 22 member countries, and officially tallied on November 1, 1994.
>
> ISO delegates accepted the revision unanimously and the revised standard reference manual was published 15 February 1995. The ISO approval made Ada 95 the first internationally standardized, fully object oriented programming (OOP) language. Ada 95 also received ANSI approval [in April 1995], following a period of public review and comment....
>
> The design of the language revisions, as well as creation of a new reference manual, was completed by Intermetrics, Inc., of Cambridge, MA.

The Intermetrics team leader was S. Tucker Taft, and the Ada 95 language design shows his imprint as vividly as Ada 83 shows that of Jean Ichbiah. As was the case with Ada 83, the Ada 95 process was an especially open one, with input solicited from any and all in the community, but Ada 95, like its predecessor, was designed by its designers, not by a "committee."

Six or seven years may seem a long time to revise a language standard, but in fact, most other language standardization processes have taken longer, sometimes much longer. Designing a language is complex and highly specialized, and convincing a large number of organizations to approve the design and vote favorably on a national or international standard is time-consuming and requires much skill in the art of human persuasion. This is borne out by the lengthy process of developing a standard for C++ and also the current (fall 1997) controversies raging among those who would produce a standard for Java.

10.2.2.1. Language Features

Ada 95 is a smooth and upward-compatible extension of Ada 83. Revisions to Ada 83 were requested, and designed, in several key areas. I quote again from the Ada IC summary. These features are explored in some depth in section 10.4:

> The capabilities of Ada 83 were enhanced for Ada 95 through the definition of a small number of new "building blocks" in three basic areas: object oriented programming, programming in the large, and real-time and parallel programming. In each case, the revision team used existing features as the basis for enhanced capabilities: The derived and universal types were the basis for object-oriented programming features; the existing notion of library units formed the basis for hierarchical namespace and program partitioning; and the concepts of private types, functions, procedures, and entries provided the basis for protected record construct, supporting fast mutual exclusion, and asynchronous task communication.

10.2.2.2. The Annexes

One important aspect of the Ada 95 design is that the standard is now divided into a core language—which provides all the syntactic structures—and a set of Annexes. The Annexes provide predefined types and packages (modules) as well as specifying certain implementation recommendations and requirements; no new syntax is introduced in the Annexes.

Annex A describes the rich set of standard libraries, which support text, binary, and stream input/output, command-line parameters, math functions, random number generators, character mapping and translation, dynamic strings, and other assorted capabilities. Implementations are required to provide a complete Annex A. Annex B describes Ada's standard interfaces to C, COBOL, and Fortran, including mechanisms for importing foreign-language routines to Ada programs and exporting Ada routines to other languages. Also specified are types corresponding to those of the other languages and storage-allocation conventions to match those of the other languages. (Fortran-style array storage is a good example.)

Annexes C through H are referred to as "special needs" annexes; implementations are not required to provide support for these but must follow the standard if they do. These annexes are

- Annex C, Systems Programming (access to machine instructions, interrupts, and so on)
- Annex D, Real-Time Systems (policies for real-time optimization of multiple tasks)
- Annex E, Distributed Systems (programs spread over multiple nodes)
- Annex F, Information Systems (exact arithmetic for decimal types, edit-directed output)
- Annex G, Numerics (complex-number types and operations, floating-point accuracy requirements)
- Annex H, Safety and Security

These annexes are described further in section 10.4.

10.2.2.3. The Role of the GNU Ada 95 (GNAT) Compiler

A critically important aspect of the growing acceptance of Ada 95 is the availability of a freely available compiler, known as GNAT. This Ada 95 implementation is integrated into the GNU (*GNU's not UNIX*) family of languages and uses the same back-end code generator. It supports the full Ada 95 language, including all annexes. The compiler can be downloaded from the PAL and all its mirror sites, and—as is the case with all software released under the GNU General Public License—full source code is available along with the binaries.

The GNAT project was originally located at New York University and funded by AJPO from 1993 to 1995. Starting in mid-1995, development and commercial support continued at Ada Core Technologies (ACT), a company founded by principals of the NYU GNAT project.

GNAT has made Ada 95 accessible to a large number of users around the world. Further, because full source code for the compiler and runtime system can be freely downloaded, Ada is once again becoming an interesting subject of academic and other research.

10.2.3. Validation, or "Just Which Language Does This Compiler Compile?"

One critically important aspect of the Ada project is *validation* of implementations (compilers and associated linkers and runtime support libraries). DoD desired to have, above all, a *common* language, supported by a strong standard that described the language. In that vision, hardware could be procured competitively, without concern about whether the compilers from hardware vendors A and B compiled the same source language. Similarly, once the hardware platform was determined, compilers for that platform could be procured competitively based on price and performance because all compilers would support the same language. Validation demonstrates the conformance of a compiler to the standard.

Compiler validation is necessarily a *testing* process because there is no other effective way to demonstrate standard conformance. DoD therefore commissioned the development of a set of test programs called the Ada Compiler Validation Capability (ACVC). This test suite was made readily available to interested parties, originally on magnetic tape; with the growing use of the Internet, the ACVC was distributed by FTP.

Over the roughly ten years of Ada 83, the ACVC was, of course, updated a number of times, to take account of practical experience with the compilers, add new tests as compiler bugs were discovered, and so on. The final operative Ada 83 test suite was ACVC 1.11, containing more than 2000 distinct test segments. Various forms of the applicable regulations determined the frequency with which a validated compiler was required to be retested with a newer test suite.

With the advent of Ada 95, the validation process was changed somewhat to accommodate Ada 95's structure as a core language with specialized-needs annexes; vendors can now choose to submit any or all annexes for separate validation.

Because the reader is probably unfamiliar with the compiler validation process, it is useful to go into it in a bit of detail, to put the process in perspective. The following section, describing Ada 95 validation, is adapted directly from the Ada IC flyer *The Ada Compiler Validation Process.*

10.2.3.1. The Validation Process

The administrative structure of validation is, at this writing, in transition as part of the implementation of the revised Ada policy described in section 10.3.1.1. This section therefore describes the process historically. It is safe to assume that the technical process will continue in a similar fashion, but the names of the administrative player organizations will probably change.

Historically, the validation process was carried out by the Ada certification body. This body consisted of the Ada Joint Program Office (AJPO) and the Ada Validation Facilities (AVFs).

The AJPO issued validation certificates for AVF-tested Ada implementations, registered Ada implementations that were derived by an AVF, maintained the Ada Compiler Validation Capability (ACVC), reviewed all Validation Summary Reports (VSRs), reviewed and adjudicated all disputes regarding the Ada test instrument, and maintained current operating agreements with the AVFs. The AJPO had the responsibility for establishing and maintaining a certification system for the ISO.

To obtain a validation certificate, the following six steps were completed by the customer and the Ada certification body:

1. A formal validation agreement between the customer and an AVF was required in order to obtain validation services.
2. Pre-validation, consisting of customer testing, submission of results to the AVF, and resolution of any test issues (e.g., a missing or incomplete result to a test) preceded the actual validation.
3. Validation testing was performed by an AVF at a site mutually agreed upon by the customer and the AVF (usually the customer's site).
4. A Declaration of Conformance was then completed and signed by the customer no later than the time of validation testing.
5. A Validation Summary Report (VSR) was prepared by the AVF to document the validation.
6. A Validation Certificate (VC) was then issued to the customer by the authority of the AJPO for a successfully tested Ada implementation.

With Ada 95 compilers, compliance is measured only within the limits of the collection of test programs contained in the ACVC for the core language and specialized needs annexes. An Ada implementation passes a given ACVC version if 1) it processes each test of the customized test suite in accordance with criteria for individual tests and 2) the test result profile matches the passing requirements for the specific ACVC version.

Matrices displaying the test result profiles for Core Ada 95 Test Categories and Special Needs Annexes are shown in the VSR. The information contained in the matrix is reformatted and provided in the Validated Compilers List (VCL) to allow easy access for buyers and users.

10.2.3.2. A Sample Test Profile

To give the reader some flavor of the tests, I show an example of the test profile that is published in the VCL.

The first matrix displays the number of tests that were Passed, Not Applicable (NA), Not Supported (NS), and Withdrawn for each of seven test categories: Ada 9X Basic, Real-Time, OOP, Type Extensions in Child Units, Child Library Units, Predefined Language Environment, and Mixed Features. Here is a list of the test categories and a short description for each:

- *Ada 9X Basic:* This is the subset of tests from ACVC 1.11 after removal of tests not applicable to Ada 95. These tests focus on support expected from Ada for features of Ada 83 that have been updated to be compatible with revised rules.

Note: The following subsets of tests validate features that are new to Ada 95. Each test has been allocated into exactly one of several test subsets, based upon a general categorization of Ada features used in the test. These tests are designed to reflect the features that programmers are likely to use to solve a programming problem.

- *Real-Time:* This subset is composed of tests for the new Ada 95 features from Section 9, Tasks and Synchronization. These features include protected objects, modifications to task types, select statements, and delay alternatives.
- *OOP:* This subset of tests focuses on some necessary facilities for achieving object-oriented programming in Ada 95. Features validated include tagged types, class attributes, and abstract types and subprograms. Other Ada 95 facilities commonly used in object-oriented programs are included in subsequent subsets.
- *Type Extensions in Child Units:* These tests focus on the interaction of the two new Ada features of type extensions of tagged types and child library units. This includes the related semantics of visibility, accessibility, and calls on primitive operations of tagged types.
- *Child Library Units:* These tests focus on the support for the new Ada capability to provide a hierarchical organization of the compilation units of an Ada program with the associated capabilities of granting access to the contents of private declarations and of hiding selected units within subsystems.

- *Predefined Language Environment:* This subset of tests includes some Ada 83 facilities and some new features defined in Annex A. Annex A provides specifications for root library units for Ada, Interface, and System, character and string handling, and input/output.
- *Mixed Features:* This relatively large subset of tests focuses on the interaction of Ada features that are a mixture of familiar Ada 83 and new Ada 95 features.

Tables 10.1 and 10.2, quoted from the VCL with minor reformatting, show the actual ACVC 2.01 test profile run in March 1997, for the GNU Ada 95 (GNAT) compiler under Solaris.

TABLE 10.1. *Test Profile for Ada 95 Test Categories*

Test Categories	*Passed*	*NA*	*NS*	*Withdrawn*	*Totals*
Ada 9X Basic	2817	33	0	11	2861
Real Time	51	0	0	0	51
OOP	54	0	0	0	54
Type Extensions in Child Units	32	0	0	2	34
Child Library Units	37	0	0	0	37
Predefined Language Environment	26	0	0	1	27
Mixed Features	180	0	0	8	188
Totals	**3197**	**33**	**0**	**22**	**3252**

TABLE 10.2. *Test Profile for Specialized Needs Annexes*

Annex	*Passed*	*NA*	*NS*	*Withdrawn*	*Totals*
C Syst Prog	4	0	0	3	7
D Real Time Syst	26	4	0	1	31
E Dist Syst	8	0	0	0	8
F Info Systems	3	0	0	3	6
G Numerics	5	0	0	0	5
H Safety/Security	0	0	0	0	0
Totals	**46**	**4**	**0**	**7**	**57**

10.2.3.3. What Does It All Mean?

Ada compiler validation, for all its openness, has been widely misunderstood in the community at large. It is important to understand what validation does *not* demonstrate.

First, validation does not, and cannot, demonstrate that a compiler is free of bugs. All we can say is that a validated compiler has passed a large set of standard, publicly distributed, conformance tests. However, to use a maxim attributed to Edsger Dijkstra, "Testing can show only the *presence* of bugs; it cannot show the *absence* of bugs." On the other hand, compiler developers would like their products to be as bug-free as possible, so they continue to develop tests. Compiler vendors have their own (highly proprietary) test libraries, in addition to the ACVC; these libraries (we assume) not only implement the vendor's internal test design, but also incorporate regression suites based on the experiences of that vendor's actual users. As with all programs of nontrivial size, as compilers mature, they exhibit fewer and fewer bugs over time.

Second, validation does not assess the *performance* (time and space resources) of a compiler. For this purpose, various benchmark suites have been developed, but running these is not a part of the validation process.

We cannot expect validation magically to suspend all the laws of large-program development. Validation cannot guarantee perfection. However, it can, and, in the Ada case, it does, contribute much to our confidence in a compiler's adherence to the language standard. An Ada compiler compiles *Ada,* accepting and properly translating our valid programs and rejecting our invalid ones, according to the *Reference Manual*, to the extent that it is humanly possible to test it. In a software industry in which languages have tended to be poorly defined "moving targets," with weak or nonexistent standards and no public validation process, this is real progress.

10.3. Ada in Today's World

This section discusses the general state of Ada in use in defense and non-defense projects, Ada in education, and the general availability of Ada 95 compilers.

10.3.1. Ada in Use

As we know, Ada was originally commissioned by the Department of Defense. On the other hand, it was never DoD "property" and has, from its inception in the early 1980s, been chosen for projects well outside the defense sector. Some of its earliest applications were in purely commercial management systems: a payroll system at a truck manufacturer and a job scheduling system at a printing company. The purpose of this section is to bring you up to date on the general state of Ada usage in the world.

10.3.1.1. Ada in U.S. Defense Applications: The Ada Policy

Defense projects are, by their very nature, not discussed in much detail in the open literature. On the other hand, enough information has come to light to lead to a conclusion that Ada has been reasonably successful in the weapons-building community.

In 1996, DoD commissioned the National Research Council to convene a task force to recommend the future course of the DoD Ada policy. The final report of this study group (National Research Council, 1996) contains a chart showing 50 million lines of active Ada code (MLOC) in DoD weapons systems, with 33 MLOC of C, 5 MLOC C++, 20 MLOC Fortran, 19 MLOC CMS-2, and 14 MLOC Jovial. Considering the long life cycles of DoD systems, this is a good record for Ada. It is interesting to note that the first validated Ada 95 compiler, validated in mid-1995, was hosted on a Sun Sparc and targeted to a proprietary board used in the revised Patriot missile system.

Published reports have discussed a number of successful military management information systems written in Ada, including a recent one in Ada 95 with SQL integration. The AdaSAGE system, developed by Idaho National Engineering Laboratory and consisting of a relational database manager, interface builder, and other support for secure PC-based information systems, won a "best product" award at a non-Ada object-technology conference and is said to have many customers within DoD.

The NRC report recommended that DoD maintain its Ada requirement for "warfighting software" but eliminate the requirement for other applications, and DoD management (Paige, 1997) subsequently decided to eliminate the requirement altogether, opting to embed language choice into a Software Engineering Plan Review process for each project. It will be interesting to observe the degree to which Ada continues to be chosen for U.S. military applications in the absence of a firm requirement to choose it.

It is useful to comment on the Ada "mandate." The term "mandate" has acquired a negative connotation in current U.S. political life, but its use to describe DoD's Ada policy is inappropriate. In its negative sense, mandate has meant the Federal Government compelling action from state or local governments, the business sector, or the general public, without providing a suitable level of Federal funding for these actions. On-the-job safety regulations, air and water quality standards, and requirements placed on educational institutions are sometimes assailed in the daily press as "unfunded mandates."

Whatever one's opinion on Federal regulation in general, one must agree that the Ada requirement is simply not a mandate in this sense. DoD has never required *anyone* to use Ada except vendors developing software under DoD contract for DoD use. Whether DoD should impose such a requirement—or whether such a requirement could be consistently enforced—has been, of course, a hotly debated issue; the fact remains that the Ada requirement was a contractual requirement, nothing more.

10.3.1.2. Non-Defense Applications

I have been tracking non-defense Ada projects for a number of years and participate in a joint SIGAda-Ada IC effort to prepare and publish application briefs for projects whose sponsors are willing to see some publicity. Several dozen of these "success stories" are online and accessible from the Ada IC and SIGAda Educator Web sites.

It is often difficult to get authoritative information for attribution. Many companies are, understandably, uncomfortable seeing details of their projects—including languages and tools used—described in print. These details are often considered trade secrets and sometimes are deemed to be unwanted invitations to "head hunters" to approach key employees. On the other hand, the published stories, combined with inside tips from software developers, yield enough information for a useful summary of the state of Ada in the non-defense world.

I can say with confidence that software written in Ada can be found in

- On-board software in most new commercial aircraft, including the Boeing 777 with several million lines of Ada, other recent Boeing and Airbus models, the latest Russian Ilyushin and Tupolev airliners, Canadair and Embraer regional aircraft, and so on

- Many countries' latest air traffic control systems, including nations in North America, Europe, Asia, Africa, and Australia
- A number of commercial communications satellites, including Intelsat VII, NSTAR, PanAmSat, ChinaSat, and others
- New railway signaling and control, including the French TGV, Channel Tunnel, and Paris suburban systems, as well as urban metro lines in Paris, London, Hong Kong, Cairo, Calcutta, Caracas, and elsewhere
- The secondary shutdown system in a Czech nuclear power plant
- A U.S. commercially marketed power-plant emission monitoring system
- A significant proportion of the U.S. military and civilian Global Positioning System (GPS) receivers, including some of the mass-produced GPS receivers used in U.S. rental cars
- A major U.S. computer-controlled steel rolling mill, an early adopter of Ada now moving to a second-generation Ada 95 control system
- Major banking and financial systems, including the Swiss Postbank electronics funds transfer system
- Several major commercially marketed medical-analytical systems

It goes without saying that these projects were under no U.S. DoD requirement to use Ada. Further, although many of the projects are government-sponsored (by air traffic control agencies, national railway administrations, and so on), the governments involved generally did not impose the use of Ada. It follows that Ada was chosen as the implementation language by the companies doing the implementing. Why did they choose to go with Ada?

In some cases—avionics, for example—it can be conjectured that a company's experience with Ada in the defense sector led them to choose it for similar commercial projects. There are other reasons as well. In the various published articles and success story briefs, a recurring theme is that Ada was chosen because of its technical characteristics. Among other attributes, strong typing and language-supported multitasking are often mentioned; also, the confidence engendered by compiler validation seems to be an important reason for choosing Ada. In Ada 95 projects, the ease with which new Ada code can interface with existing subsystems such as SQL, CORBA, and the like is starting to be an important factor.

10.3.2. Education and Ada

This section briefly discusses the Ada 95 textbook literature and surveys the use of Ada in college and university education.

10.3.2.1. Ada 95 Textbooks

At this writing, 17 published books, at different levels but with Ada 95 as their focus, have appeared since 1995. Anyone wishing to learn the language has an excellent range of books from which to choose.

The Ada 95 *Reference Manual* (Taft & Duff, 1997) and *Rationale* (Barnes, 1997), both available on the Web, but until recently only with difficulty in paper form, have now been formally published as books.

Five texts (Culwin, 1997; English, 1997; Feldman & Koffman, 1996; Lopes, 1997; Skansholm, 1997) introduce Ada to first-year students and other readers with no programming experience. Two works (Beidler, 1997; Feldman, 1997c) focus on data structures and algorithms, and one (Smith, 1996) deals specifically with object-oriented programming. Two texts (Burns & Wellings, 1995, 1997) discuss concurrency and real-time systems. An interesting work in French (Rosen, 1995) discusses software engineering methods with Ada 95.

Finally, four works (Barnes, 1995; Cohen, 1996; Naiditch, 1995; Wheeler, 1997) introduce Ada 95 to experienced programmers, and one book (Johnston, 1997) introduces the language specifically to readers experienced with C or C++.

10.3.2.2. Ada as a Foundation Programming Language

Since 1991, I have tracked the colleges and universities that have adopted Ada as a "foundation language," that is, in one of the first few computing courses taken by students majoring in the field.

Computing curricula are far from standardized, and there is much variation from institution to institution depending upon local needs and politics. The courses I have tracked are

- The introductory-level course taught to majors in the first year (some refer to this as "CS1")
- The second course, which follows the "CS1" course, which is, in general, devoted mostly to algorithms and data structures (some refer to this as "CS2")

In some institutions, one or both of these courses are "pre-major," so the third course is the first one taught specifically to majors. This is often a more advanced data structures course or something similar.

Given the local variations, it is difficult to write a one-size-fits-all definition of the courses I follow, but I choose to keep track of precisely these courses because they are taken by majors in either first or second year and thus early enough to serve as a foundation upon which to build a large portion of the software curriculum. The following chart shows the trend since 1991:

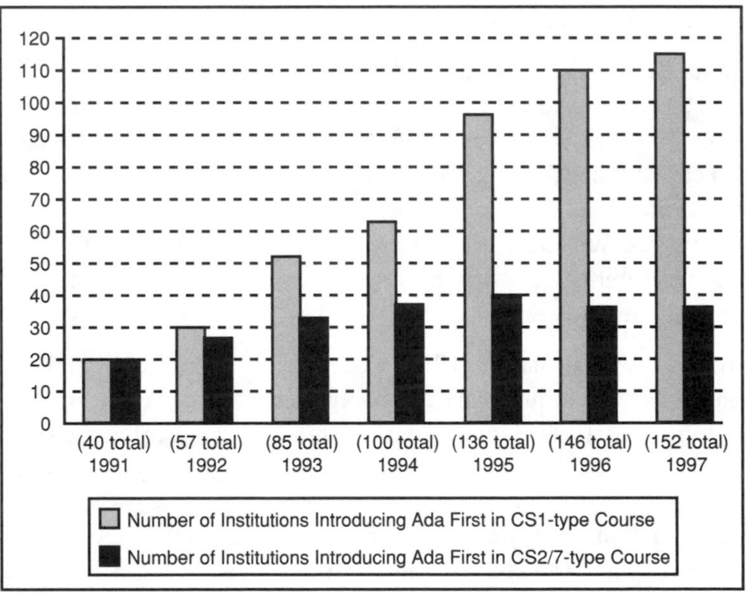

10.3.2.3. The Ada IC CREASE Database

The Ada Information Clearinghouse maintains a WWW database called CREASE (Catalog of Resources for Education in Ada and Software Engineering) that keeps track of Ada-related courses in both academic institutions and training companies. They send occasional canvasses, follow up to ensure that their data is current, and make an electronic questionnaire available at the site. At this writing, 445 organizations are present in the database, describing 799 different courses.

10.3.3. Ada 95 Compiler Availability

Ada 95 compilers are readily available for all the popular computing host and target platforms and many specialized targets as well.

For example, at this writing freely downloadable ports of GNU Ada 95 (GNAT), with full source code, exist for

- Sun Solaris (Sun SPARC and 80x86/Pentium)
- Sun OS (Sun SPARC)
- IBM OS/2 (Warp), Windows 95 or NT, DOS, Linux (Elf object format); all for 80x86/Pentium
- IRIX (SGI)
- Digital UNIX (OSF), OpenVMS (DEC Alpha)
- AIX (PowerPC/RS6000)
- HP-UX (HP PA)
- MachTen host, MachTen and MacOS targets (Power Mac)
- Sinix (Siemens Nixdorf)

These can be downloaded from various FTP servers and are included on the Walnut Creek Ada CD-ROM.

A fully functional Aonix ObjectAda development system for Windows 95 and NT is included on a CD-ROM with at least two textbooks (Feldman, 1996; Johnston, 1997).

Other suppliers offer proprietary compilers for popular host platforms, supporting targets for these platforms as well as for various bare boards, real-time operating systems, digital signal processors, and so on. Two suppliers—Aonix and Intermetrics—support a Java Virtual Machine target, and a GNAT version targeting the JVM is under active development. At this writing, the official Validated Compiler List (available on the Ada IC Web site) shows over 80 validated implementations from 10 different suppliers.

10.4. Programming

I introduce programming in Ada using a series of complete examples, which serve better than rules and fragments to illustrate the use of the language. Each of these programs has been compiled and tested. In each case, I have numbered the lines so that I can refer to them in the discussion; the line numbers are not part of the programs themselves and are not entered into a source file.

The first several examples introduce the basic structure of an Ada program; the rest introduce more interesting concepts of program construction using modules, object-oriented programming, and concurrent programming. Each program introduces several new concepts.

10.4.1. Examples of Basic Structure and Syntax

Two of the most fundamental Ada concepts are the *type* and the *package.*

10.4.1.1. Types and Objects

A type consists of two sets: a set of values and a set of operations appropriate for those values. Each variable and constant in Ada has a type; variables and constants are thus holders for values. The Ada standard defines a number of standard types either in the language—for example, `Integer`, `Float`, `Boolean`, `Duration` (elapsed time), `Character`, and `String`—or in standard library packages—for example, `Time` and `Complex`. Further, the programmer can define application-specific types of various kinds (for example, enumerations, records, arrays, and tasks). Conversion among types can be done with explicit type-conversion operations; implicit type conversion does not occur in Ada.

The Ada standard requires that the compiler ensure that operations are appropriate for the values to which they are applied. Appropriateness is checked statically at compilation time, wherever possible; otherwise, runtime checks are compiled into the executable program. If a runtime check fails (for example, the program attempts to store a computed negative value in a variable declared as nonnegative), a standard exception is raised (in this case, `Constraint_Error`). A raised exception can be handled by the program if code has been provided to do so; otherwise, the program terminates.

Because in Ada, each variable or constant has a state—its value—and a well-defined behavior—the set of operations defined for its type, it is entirely appropriate to refer to variables and constants as *objects,* and I shall do so in this development.

10.4.1.2. Packages and Files

A package encapsulates a collection of resources: type declarations, functions, procedures, variables, and constants. A package generally consists of two compilation units, which developers generally choose to place in distinct source files. The package *specification* or *interface* unit gives a list of those resources intended to be directly visible to clients; the *body* or *implementation* unit contains the code bodies of the procedures and functions, as well as any internal resources used by the packages but not exported to the client.

A package interface is roughly analogous to a "header file" as used in other languages but differs in that it is required and its contents are strictly structured. The package interface can be seen as a required "contract" between a package's developer and its user.

In other languages—the C family in particular—source programs are organized into physical files. These files have semantic meaning in the language—they create scope and visibility—so the precise contents of each file are of critical importance. In Ada, this semantic content is embodied in the *compilation unit.*

Package interfaces, package implementations, and main procedures are all compilation units; whether the units making up a program are distributed into individual files or collected together in a single file, or something in between, is irrelevant to the program semantics, and is, in fact, never discussed in the standard. Some compilers have a preferred file structure, but this can be overridden. Thus the organization of a program into physical files is a matter of one's organizational style and does not affect the program's meaning.

The Ada standard libraries are implemented as packages; application programs are constructed from these and application-specific or generally reusable but non-standard packages. In this major section, the package examples all come from the standard libraries; in the next one, I introduce some packages of my own.

10.4.1.3. The Usual "Hello World" Program

The first example is `Hello`.

```
 1 with Ada.Text_IO;
 2 procedure Hello is
 3
 4   -- A first very small, obligatory program
 5
 6 begin -- Hello
 7
 8   Ada.Text_IO.Put_Line
 9     (Item => "This is the obligatory Hello program!");
10
11 end Hello;
```

An Ada program usually consists of a main procedure, whose statements make reference to resources that are either locally declared or imported from packages. Each package is mentioned in a `with` clause—officially called a *context clause*—at the top of the program; in line 1 of `Hello`, the standard Ada input/output library `Ada.Text_IO` is indicated.

Lines 8 and 9 use the procedure `Put_Line` to display the quoted string on the standard output file and move to a new line. I have used the full form of the call: The package name `Ada.Text_IO` precedes the call and the name of the formal parameter `Item` is associated with its actual value, using the symbol `=>`. This may seem a bit verbose; I show some terser forms later.

The words `with`, `procedure`, `is`, `begin`, and `end` are five of Ada's *reserved words*. These are used for various syntactic purposes and cannot be used in other contexts, such as variable names. By the end of this section, you will have seen most of the reserved words.

`Put_Line`, on the other hand, is the name of a standard procedure. Procedure names are not reserved; you could write another package that provided a procedure `Put_Line` and call this procedure in a program, as long as the compiler had enough information to resolve the potential ambiguity in the name.

The layout of a program in terms of lines is not specified by the language, nor is the case of reserved words and identifiers. A program is treated syntactically as a sequence of characters; indentation and use of blank lines and other whitespace is purely a matter of programmer style. The style I use here—lowercase reserved words, mixed-case identifiers, and whitespace—is generally consistent with the *Reference Manual* and most textbooks and with generally accepted practice.

The only exception regarding lines is that a *comment*—inserted for the human reader and ignored by the compiler—begins with `--` and ends at the end of the same line. This line-oriented comment style—used in Fortran and assembler and adopted by C++—was chosen in preference to the bracketed style of Pascal and C to make it obvious that a block of code has been "commented out." Lines 4 and 6 show comments used in two ways: an entire line and following some Ada code.

This section's examples do not include space-taking program comments but concentrate on numbered lines and prose explanations.

A note on context clauses: A context clause is only superficially similar to the `#include` of C and other languages. It serves two purposes:

- At compilation time, the clause provides context for the compilation: The compiler reads each package interface (in source or intermediate form, depending on the compiler) and checks the correctness of each reference made to resources in that package.

- At binding and linking time, the clause is used to bind the compiled form of the main with the compiled form of the packages; the binder and linker must ensure that the compiled form of each package is up to date.

There is no exact equivalent in Ada to the `#include`, which simply copies the contents of another file. One could in theory use a preprocessor to get the equivalent, but it is almost never necessary to do so because context clauses provide similar functionality with more integrity-checking.

A final point on the standard libraries: The many Ada 95 standard libraries are easy to recognize. Their names all begin with `Ada`. They are in fact *child packages* of the root package `Ada`. More on child packages later.

10.4.1.4. A Less Verbose Coding Style

`Hello_Terse` shows two ways of reducing the "verbosity" of a program. As you shall see, one programmer's verbosity may well be another's clarity.

```
1 with Ada.Text_IO;
2 use  Ada.Text_IO;
3 procedure Hello_Terse is
4 -- A terse version of the Hello program
5 begin
6   Put_Line ("This is the obligatory Hello program!");
7 end Hello_Terse;
```

First, I add a `use` clause (line 2), which makes all the resources of the given package directly visible. That is, you can name a resource (as in line 6) without preceding the reference with the package name. This may seem like an obvious advantage, but for longer programs using a number of packages, omitting package names tends to obscure the meaning of the statements and to lead to reader confusion. I return to this issue later in the chapter.

Second, I omit the formal parameter name. This, too, may seem like an obvious advantage, but for procedures with a number of parameters, using the named association allows you to supply actual parameters in any order and may also lead to clearer, less error-prone procedure calls.

10.4.1.5. The Calendar Package

The next several examples examine the standard library package, `Ada.Calendar`, and use it while introducing several Ada data and control structures.

Here is an extract from the package interface of `Ada.Calendar`, which provides date and time services in a standard fashion. The resources listed in the interface are exported to client programs.

```
 1 package Ada.Calendar is
 2   type Time is private;
 3
 4   subtype Year_Number  is Integer range 1901..2099;
 5   subtype Month_Number is Integer range 1..12;
 6   subtype Day_Number   is Integer range 1..31;
 7   subtype Day_Duration is Duration range 0.0..86_400.0;
 8
 9   function Clock return Time;
10
11   function Year    (Date : Time) return Year_Number;
12   function Month   (Date : Time) return Month_Number;
13   function Day     (Date : Time) return Day_Number;
14   function Seconds(Date : Time) return Day_Duration;
15    ...
16 end Ada.Calendar;
```

`Time` is declared (line 2) as a *private type,* which signals that its structure—its set of values—is not directly available to me. I use time values only via package operations.

Lines 4–7 define four *subtypes*. A subtype declaration creates a subset of the values of the original type; subtypes are commonly used, as here, to restrict the appropriate ranges of certain variables. The three `Integer` subtypes here have obvious meanings in the calendar; the three functions in lines 11–13 extract the corresponding components from a `Time` value. The `Duration` subtype `Day_Duration` provides the elapsed time values in a 24-hour period; the function `Seconds` returns the time elapsed since midnight of the given day.

10.4.1.6. Displaying the Current Date

The next example, `Show_Date`, displays the current date in the form 05 AUG 1997.

```
with Ada.Text_IO;
with Ada.Calendar;
procedure Show_Date is

  Now  : Ada.Calendar.Time;

  type Months is
    (Jan, Feb, Mar, Apr, May, Jun,
     Jul, Aug, Sep, Oct, Nov, Dec);

begin

```

```
13    Now := Ada.Calendar.Clock;
14
15    Ada.Text_IO.Put_Line("Today is"
16      & Integer'Image(Ada.Calendar.Day(Now)) & ' '
17      & Months'Image
18          (Months'Val( Ada.Calendar.Month(Now) - 1))
19      & Integer'Image(Ada.Calendar.Year (Now)));
20
21 end Show_Date;
```

The context clause in line 2 mentions `Ada.Calendar`; line 7 declares a time variable `Now`, which, in line 13, is set to the current time by a call to `Ada.Calendar.Clock`. Line 13 is an *assignment statement;* the symbol `:=` means *assignment;* the statement

```
Now := Ada.Calendar.Clock;
```

assigns to the variable `Now` the value returned by the `Clock` call.

To display the date, I must extract the month, day, and year from the time value. I extract the day in line 16 with the function call `Ada.Calendar.Day(Now)` and extract the month and year in lines 18 and 19 with similar calls.

I choose to display the date (lines 15–19) by constructing a string from substrings concatenated together using the `&` operator. The expression (line 16)

```
Integer'Image(Ada.Calendar.Day(Now))
```

extracts the day as an integer value and then produces its *image* (`Integer'Image`) as a numeric string. The form `Integer'Image` is known as an *attribute;* each type in Ada has a set of retrievable attributes.

To display the month as a 3-letter abbreviation instead of a number 1 .. 12, I introduce an *enumeration type* in lines 5–7. An enumeration type is declared by listing—enumerating—its values. This creates an ordered set of values, with no value appearing more than once. The values are, syntactically, either characters or (as in this case) identifiers.

Two especially useful attributes of enumeration types are `'Pos` and `'Val`. `Months'Pos(Jan)` returns a nonnegative integer representing the *position* of `Jan` in the type, or `0`. `Months'Val(0)` goes the other way, returning `Jan`; `Months'Pos(May)` returns `4`; `Months'Val(8)` returns `Sep`. Because `Ada.Calendar.Month` returns an integer in the range 1 .. 12, the expression

```
Months'Val(Ada.Calendar.Month(Now) - 1)
```

returns just the right enumeration value, and so

```
Months'Image(Months'Val(Ada.Calendar.Month(Now) - 1))
```

produces the desired output substring.

10.4.1.7. Displaying the Date and Time

The program `Show_Date_and_Time` extends the previous example to display both the time and the date.

```
with Ada.Text_IO, Ada.Integer_Text_IO;
with Ada.Calendar;
procedure Show_Date_and_Time is

  type Months is
    (Jan, Feb, Mar, Apr, May, Jun,
     Jul, Aug, Sep, Oct, Nov, Dec);

  Now           : Ada.Calendar.Time := Ada.Calendar.Clock;
  SecsPast_0h00: Natural
                    := Natural(Ada.Calendar.Seconds(Now));
  MinsPast_0h00: Natural := SecsPast_0h00 / 60;
  Secs          : Natural := SecsPast_0h00 rem 60;
  Mins          : Natural := MinsPast_0h00 rem 60;
  Hrs           : Natural := MinsPast_0h00 / 60;

begin

  Ada.Text_IO.Put("The date and time is"
    & Integer'Image(Ada.Calendar.Day(Now)) & ' '
    & Months'Image
         (Months'Val(Ada.Calendar.Month(Now) - 1))
    & Integer'Image(Ada.Calendar.Year (Now)) & ' ');

  if Hrs  < 10 then
    Ada.Text_IO.Put (Item => '0');
  end if;
  Ada.Integer_Text_IO.Put (Item => Hrs, Width => 1);
  Ada.Text_IO.Put (Item => ':');

  if Mins < 10 then
    Ada.Text_IO.Put (Item => '0');
  end if;
  Ada.Integer_Text_IO.Put (Item => Mins, Width => 1);
  Ada.Text_IO.Put (Item => ':');

  if Secs < 10 then
    Ada.Text_IO.Put (Item => '0');
  end if;
  Ada.Integer_Text_IO.Put (Item => Secs, Width => 1);

  Ada.Text_IO.New_Line;

end Show_Date_and_Time;
```

Using the `'Image` attribute to display a number is convenient, but it gives us little control over the format of the output value. Therefore, the context clause in line 1 mentions another standard package, `Ada.Integer_Text_IO`, which provides extended facilities for reading and writing integer values.

In line 9 I declare `Now` as before and then add five more variables. These are all given as type `Natural`, a subtype of `Integer`, declared in the standard as

```
subtype Natural is Integer range 0..Integer'Last;
```

where `Integer'Last` returns the largest positive integer supported by the type.

This is a good time to mention that the Ada standard does not specify the range of `Integer` but requires that the range –2**15+1 .. +2**15–1 (16 bits) be included. In current practice on popular computers, it is usually safe to assume that `Integer` is represented using 32 bits. For absolute certainty, Ada allows you to declare your own numeric types and specify the required width in bits; this is an example of the way Ada provides simple default structures but allows the programmer much flexibility in overriding the defaults where necessary.

Returning to the example, each of the six declarations includes an *initial expression,* which is evaluated at runtime when the declaration is *elaborated.* Note that each of these expressions is dynamic, depending on the current clock value. The expression

```
Natural(Ada.Calendar.Seconds(Now))
```

returns the `Seconds` component converted from `Day_Duration` to `Natural`. `Duration` is actually a fixed-point type, not an integer one, so fractions of seconds can be represented. Converting to `Natural` truncates the value, discarding the fractional part; I am interested only in whole seconds here.

The expressions

```
SecsPast_0h00 / 60
SecsPast_0h00 rem 60
```

are integer expressions, computing the quotient and the remainder respectively. In Ada, the interpretation of arithmetic operators, including division, depends on the types of their operands. `SecsPast_0h00` (seconds since midnight) and `60` are both integer values, so the division is a truncating one.

There is no C-style promotion or implicit conversion in Ada; for example, mixed integer/real expressions are rejected by the compiler. One can use explicit type conversions to adjust the types in expressions that would otherwise be mixed. The requirement for explicit type conversion ensures that the result of an arithmetic expression is obvious to the human reader.

In the example, because the values of all the variables are computed at the time their declarations are elaborated, the statement-sequence part of the program need only display the result. Lines 19–23 display the date just as before; the rest of the program displays the time in 24-hour hh:mm:ss form. The `if` statements in lines 25–27, 31–33, and 37–39 are used to display leading zeroes where necessary, for example, 09:15:08. if statements are *fully bracketed*; that is, the `if` must have a closing `end if`. An `if` can include a single `else` or one or more `elsif` clauses. Two other `if` variations are

```
if ... then
  ...
else
  ...
end if;
```

```
if ... then
  ...
elsif ... then
  ...
elsif ... then
  ...
else
  ...
end if;
```

Lines 28, 34, and 40 are calls to `Ada.Integer_Text_IO.Put`. `Width=>1` is a formatting parameter that requests *at least* one position for the output value. A value of one or more digits is displayed properly; the effect of this width parameter is to left-adjust the value.

`Width` is a parameter that is defined with a default value so that a call to `Put` can omit `Width`. The default width is one larger than the width of `Integer'Last`, typically `11`.

Note in passing that the integer `Put` has yet another parameter, `Base`, which defaults to `10` and indicates the desired number base (bases in the range 2..16 are allowed). The call

```
Ada.Integer_Text_IO(Item => 19, Base => 8);
```

displays the octal value `8#23#` (base first, then value delimited by `#` signs); substituting `Base=>2` displays `2#10011#`. Using this syntax, it is possible to format *input* values in non-decimal bases. Again you see that Ada provides simple defaults with much capability to override these.

10.4.1.8. The Brevity/Clarity Tradeoff

Ada has been criticized for its apparent "verbosity." Ada's proponents respond that Ada was designed for the development and maintenance of programs of nontrivial size with long life cycles. Such programs are written once but read and modified many times over their lives, so the language definitely favors the reader over the writer, and Ada programmers tend to become conditioned to write less for their own eyes than for others'. This courtesy to the reader of a program is not considered to be a disadvantage!

On the other hand, it is possible to write Ada more tersely. Single-character variable names are legal and the language does not compel the use of whitespace. Also, as I observed earlier, you can add use clauses and employ positional parameters instead of named ones. Consider `Show_Use_Clause`, which is a terse version of `Show_Date_and_Time`. If it were a program of a few thousand lines instead of 44 lines, making reference to 5 or 10 different packages, the reader would probably miss the explicit package and formal parameter names.

```
with Ada.Text_IO, Ada.Integer_Text_IO;
use  Ada.Text_IO, Ada.Integer_Text_IO;
with Ada.Calendar;
use  Ada.Calendar;
procedure Show_Use_Clause is

  type Months is
    (Jan, Feb, Mar, Apr, May, Jun,
     Jul, Aug, Sep, Oct, Nov, Dec);

  Now            : Time := Clock;
  SecsPast_0h00: Natural := Natural(Seconds(Now));
  MinsPast_0h00: Natural := SecsPast_0h00/60;
  Secs           : Natural := SecsPast_0h00 rem 60;
  Mins           : Natural := MinsPast_0h00 rem 60;
  Hrs            : Natural := MinsPast_0h00 / 60;

begin

  Put("The date and time is"
    & Integer'Image(Day(Now)) & ' '
    & Months'Image (Months'Val(Month(Now) - 1))
    & Integer'Image(Year(Now)) & ' ');

```

```
  if Hrs  < 10 then
    Put ('0');
  end if;
  Put (Hrs, 1);
  Put (':');

  if Mins < 10 then
    Put ('0');
  end if;
  Put (Mins, 1);
  Put (':');

  if Secs < 10 then
    Put ('0');
  end if;
  Put (Secs, 1);

  New_Line;

end Show_Use_Clause;
```

Note that in this program, there are calls to three different `Put` procedures: one for single characters, one for strings, and one for integers. This is an example of *overloading,* or giving the same name to several different subprograms. Overloading is quite common in Ada; the compiler readily distinguishes the three procedures by examining the profile (order, number, and type) of the parameters.

If, by some chance, two different procedures with the same name *and* the same parameter profile were made directly visible by `use` clauses (this could happen if the procedures were in different packages), the compiler would discover the ambiguity and give an error message. The programmer could easily correct the ambiguity by prefixing the package names.

I have designed the examples here to explicate the language and some of its standard libraries; therefore, I generally use a verbose style for maximum clarity. Occasionally, I add use clauses and omit parameter names where there is no loss of clarity. Programming style issues should really be managed by each project team.

10.4.1.9. Loops, Arrays, and Files—the Advantage of Subtypes

The next example produces a simple letter-frequency histogram, a horizontal bar graph that shows the number of times each alphabet letter occurs in an input file. For example, given the input

```
This is a test of an Ada 95
simple histogram program.
```

the program displays

```
a | *****
d | *
e | **
f | *
g | **
h | **
i | ****
l | *
m | ***
n | *
o | ***
p | **
r | ***
s | *****
t | ***
A | *
T | *
```

Input is taken from the standard input file, which for most operating systems defaults to the terminal keyboard. Input can be "redirected" from an external disk file if the operating system permits this; redirection is an operating system feature and lies outside the Ada standard.

```
with Ada.Text_IO;
procedure Histogram is

  subtype UpperCase is Character range 'A'..'Z';
  subtype LowerCase is Character range 'a'..'z';

  Uppers : array(UpperCase) of Natural := (others => 0);
  Lowers : array(LowerCase) of Natural := (others => 0);

  NextCh   : Character;
  PlotChar : constant Character := '*';

begin

  while not Ada.Text_IO.End_Of_File loop
    while not Ada.Text_IO.End_Of_Line loop

      Ada.Text_IO.Get(NextCh);

      case NextCh is
        when UpperCase =>
          Uppers(NextCh) := Uppers(NextCh) + 1;
        when LowerCase =>
          Lowers(NextCh) := Lowers(NextCh) + 1;
        when others =>
          null;
      end case;

    end loop;
    Ada.Text_IO.Skip_Line;
```

```
31     end loop;
32
33     for C in LowerCase loop
34
35       if Lowers(C) /= 0 then
36         Ada.Text_IO.Put(Item => C & " ¦ ");
37         for Count in 1..Lowers(C) loop
38           Ada.Text_IO.Put(PlotChar);
39         end loop;
40         Ada.Text_IO.New_Line;
41       end if;
42
43     end loop;
44
45     for C in UpperCase loop
46
47       if Uppers(C) /= 0 then
48         Ada.Text_IO.Put(Item => C & " ¦ ");
49         for Count in 1..Uppers(C) loop
50           Ada.Text_IO.Put(PlotChar);
51         end loop;
52         Ada.Text_IO.New_Line;
53       end if;
54
55     end loop;
56
57   end Histogram;
```

Lines 4 and 5 introduce subtypes for the uppercase and lowercase letters, respectively; lines 7 and 8 introduce two *arrays* to hold the letter frequency counts. An array is an *indexed,* or *subscripted,* collection of elements; the index set is given in parentheses. All elements of a given array have the same type, but this type can be arbitrary, chosen for the application needs. Because all the elements have the same type, we say that an array type is *homogeneous.* In this case, I need nonnegative counters for the letters, so the array elements are of type `Natural`. The initial expression (`others => 0`) initializes all elements of both arrays to `0`.

Line 11 introduces the constant `PlotChar`, as the asterisk I use to plot the histogram. A constant *must* have an initial expression; once the constant is set, it cannot be changed during its lifetime (in this case, the duration of the program execution). A `constant` value is set at the time its declaration is elaborated; it need not be static but can be computed at that time.

Lines 15 and 16 are the opening lines of the two nested `while` loops that drive the program. `End_Of_Line` and `End_Of_File` are Boolean-returning standard functions. Line 18 is a `Get` that reads a single character from the standard input file; it is because `Get` skips over line terminators that I need to test explicitly for `End_Of_Line` in line 16. Lines 29–31 bracket the loops.

Once a character is read, the `case` statement in lines 20–27 classifies it and acts accordingly, incrementing the appropriate counter. Note the case form: The first two `when` clauses refer to subtype ranges `UpperCase` and `LowerCase` and the `when others` covers all other possible values of the character variable. An Ada case statement is safe: *All* values of the case expression must be covered, using an `others` clause if necessary.

Once the input file has been completely read, I draw the bar graph. Line 33 starts a `for` (counting) loop, which is bracketed by the `end loop` in line 43. The meaning of the `for` is evident: It covers, in succession, each value in the subtype range of `LowerCase`.

I choose to plot bars only for those characters that actually appear in the input. The expression `Lowers(C) /= 0` (line 35) returns `true` if the number of occurrences of C was non-zero; `/=` is Ada's "unequal" symbol. In line 37, I show a loop expression whose bounds are given explicitly instead of by naming a subtype.

The loop in lines 45–55 just repeats the logic of the earlier loop, plotting bars for the uppercase characters.

The control structures in this example show the value of using subtype ranges. Once a subtype is carefully defined with a range determined by the application, it can be used repeatedly throughout the program. This ensures that appropriate ranges are used in loops and, especially, in loops that run through arrays. Programming without subtype ranges—either in Ada or in languages such as those in the C family that do not support subtypes—often results in runtime errors due to overrunning subscripts; such errors do not occur with carefully designed subtypes.

10.4.1.10. Type Composition: Arrays and Records

The next example is a miniature information systems application. A company sells five kind of gadgets, indicated by the colors `Red`, `Blue`, `Green`, `Yellow`, and `Black`. In a given time period, a transaction file is created in which a transaction indicates a kind of gadget and a positive (sale) or negative (return) monetary quantity. The program `Gadget_Report` summarizes the sales, giving, for each of the five gadget types, the number of transactions and the total monetary value. For example, an input transaction file containing

```
green 56.00
blue 25.00
green 2078.00
black -2065.00
```

results in this report:

```
Gadget Type  Transactions  Value
-------------------------------
RED                 0         0.00
BLUE                1        25.00
GREEN               2      2134.00
YELLOW              0         0.00
BLACK               1     -2065.00
```

```
with Ada.Text_IO;
with Ada.Integer_Text_IO;
with Ada.Float_Text_IO;
procedure Gadget_Report is

  subtype Money is
    Float range -1_000_000_000.00..1_000_000_000.00;

  type Gadgets is (Red, Blue, Green, Yellow, Black);
  package Gadget_IO is
    new Ada.Text_IO.Enumeration_IO (Enum => Gadgets);

  type SummaryEntry is record
    HowMany: Natural := 0;
    Net    : Money := 0.00;
  end record;

  type Summary is array(Gadgets) of SummaryEntry;

  TodaysSummary : Summary;
  InputData: Ada.Text_IO.File_Type;
  WhichKind: Gadgets;
  Amount: Money;

begin

  Ada.Text_IO.Open(File => InputData,
    Mode => Ada.Text_IO.In_File, Name => "today.dat");

  while not
    Ada.Text_IO.End_of_File(File => InputData) loop

    Gadget_IO.Get(File => InputData, Item => WhichKind);
    Ada.Float_Text_IO.Get
      (File => InputData, Item => Amount);
    Ada.Text_IO.Skip_line(File => InputData);

    TodaysSummary(WhichKind).HowMany :=
      TodaysSummary(WhichKind).HowMany + 1;
    TodaysSummary(WhichKind).Net :=
      TodaysSummary(WhichKind).Net + Amount;

  end loop;

  Ada.Text_IO.Close (File => InputData);

```

```
47     Ada.Text_IO.Put_Line
48       (Item => "Gadget Type  Transactions  Value");
49     Ada.Text_IO.Put_Line
50       (Item => "-----------------------------");
51
52     for WhichKind in Gadgets loop
53       Gadget_IO.Put(Item => WhichKind, Width => 7);
54       Ada.Integer_Text_IO.Put(
55         Item => TodaysSummary(WhichKind).HowMany,
56         Width => 12);
57       Ada.Float_Text_IO.Put(
58         Item => TodaysSummary(WhichKind).Net,
59         Fore => 10, Aft => 2, Exp => 0);
60       Ada.Text_IO.New_Line;
61     end loop;
62
63   end Gadget_Report;
```

I represent the monetary type as a subtype of the predefined type `Float`. Line 3 mentions `Ada.Float_Text_IO`, which allows me to read and write these quantities; lines 6–7 show the subtype declaration. The underscore characters group the digits by threes; they are just used to improve readability.

I declare `Gadgets` as an enumeration type (line 9). Lines 10–11 constitute a *generic instance* of the standard generic package `Ada.Text_IO.Enumeration_IO`. A generic package is a *template* for a package; in this case, `Enumeration_IO` is generic because I must supply the name of an enumeration type on whose values input and output is being done. The instance `Gadget_IO` is capable of reading and writing *exactly* the five gadget values.

This generic specialization is especially advantageous in reading input values because the input routine (`Gadget_IO.Get`) *validates* that an input token in fact belongs to the set of desired values. If the token does not belong to the desired set, the standard exception `Ada.Text_IO.Data_Error` is raised at the point of the `Get` call; the exception can be handled by program code, as you shall see in the next example.

In the reporting program, each transaction is read from the input file and the appropriate summaries—number of transactions and net income per gadget kind—are updated. The transaction can then be discarded. To define a summary entry, lines 13–16 declare a *record type*. A record type—in this case, `SummaryEntry`—has fields or *components*—in this case, `HowMany` and `Net`; a record type is heterogeneous because in general, each component has its own type. This type declaration creates no objects; it just gives a rule for creating objects from object declarations.

To hold the gadget summaries, line 18 declares an array type `Summary`. The components of the array are of type `SummaryEntry`, which illustrates *type composition*: a programmer-defined array type each of whose elements is a programmer-defined record type. Types can be composed at will in this fashion.

Now, lines 20–23 declare four objects (variables): an array object `TodaysSummary`, a file object `InputData`, and two variables to hold the current transaction.

Instead of reading from standard input, this program reads from an external file whose name as seen by the operating system is `today.dat`. This external file is associated with the file object `InputData` by the `Open` call in lines 27–28. The `File` and `Name` parameters are obvious; `Mode` refers to one of the standard sequential file modes `In_File`, `Out_File`, and `Append_File` (an output mode in which writing begins at the end of an existing file). (Ada's standard library for direct access files also has an `InOut_File` mode to open a direct file for both reading and writing).

The main loop of this program (lines 30–43) is straightforward: It reads a transaction from the file and updates the summaries. The expression

```
TodaysSummary(WhichKind).HowMany
```

selects the `HowMany` field of the `WhichKind` element of the array object `TodaysSummary`.

Finally, lines 45–61 close the input file and then loop through the summary array to display the results. The formatting parameters `Fore` and `Aft` (line 59) for `Ada.Float_Text_IO.Put` indicate the desired number of displayed places before and after the decimal point. A non-zero `Exp` calls for the number to be displayed in "E-notation" and gives the number of places in the exponent. Thus `Fore =>1, Aft=>2, Exp=>2` displays `-2065.00` as `–2.07E+3`. This is fine for an engineering application but not for data processing.

10.4.1.11. Exception Handling, Command Parameters, and Information Systems Features

The last "inner syntax" example, `Show_Exception`, is a modification of `Gadget_Report` that illustrates exception handling, the decimal-types and edit-directed-output features of the Ada 95 Information Systems Annex (Annex F), and the standard package `Ada.Command_Line`. For the input file `today.dat` as used previously, issuing the operating system command

```
show_exception today.dat
```

produces the output

```
show_exception: Input file is today.dat
Gadget Type  Transactions  Value
--------------------------------
RED                   0          $0.00
BLUE                  1         $25.00
GREEN                 2      $2,134.00
YELLOW                0          $0.00
BLACK                 1      $2,065.00CR
```

The command `show_exception` produces the output

```
show_exception: No input file provided.
```

A transaction containing bad data is ignored (in a real application, it would be written to an error report); for the file `bad.dat` containing a misspelled gadget type (`gren`),

```
green 56.00
blue 25.00
gren 20.00
black -20.00
```

the command `show_exception bad.dat` results in

```
show_exception: Input file is bad.dat
Ignoring Bad Transaction
Gadget Type  Transactions  Value
--------------------------------
RED                   0          $0.00
BLUE                  1         $25.00
GREEN                 1         $56.00
YELLOW                0          $0.00
BLACK                 1         $20.00CR
```

```
with Ada.Text_IO, Ada.Text_IO.Editing;
with Ada.Integer_Text_IO;
with Ada.Command_Line;
use Ada.Text_IO, Ada.Integer_Text_IO;
procedure Show_Exception is

  type Money is delta 0.01 digits 12;
  package Money_In is
    new Ada.Text_IO.Decimal_IO(Num => Money);
  package Money_Out is new
    Ada.Text_IO.Editing.Decimal_Output (Num => Money);

  type Gadgets is (Red, Blue, Green, Yellow, Black);
  package Gadget_IO is
    new Ada.Text_IO.Enumeration_IO (Enum => Gadgets);

  type Transaction is record
    Kind: Gadgets;
    Amount: Money := 0.00;
```

```
   end record;

   type Database is
     array(Integer range <>) of Transaction;

   type SummaryEntry is record
     HowMany: Natural := 0;
     Net    : Money := 0.00;
   end record;

   type Summary  is array(Gadgets) of SummaryEntry;

   TodaysActivity: Database(1..100);
   TodaysSummary : Summary;

   InputData: Ada.Text_IO.File_Type;

   TransactionCount: Natural := 0;
   WhichKind: Gadgets;

begin

   Put(Item => Ada.Command_Line.Command_Name);

   if Ada.Command_Line.Argument_Count = 0 then
     Put_Line (Item => ": No input file provided.");
     return;
   else
     Put_Line(Item => ": Input file is "
       & Ada.Command_Line.Argument(Number => 1));
   end if;

   Open(File => InputData,
        Mode => Ada.Text_IO.In_File,
        Name => Ada.Command_Line.Argument(Number => 1));

   while not End_of_File(File => InputData) loop
     TransactionCount := TransactionCount + 1;

     begin
       Gadget_IO.Get(File => InputData,
         Item => TodaysActivity(TransactionCount).Kind);
       Money_In.Get (File => InputData,
         Item=>TodaysActivity(TransactionCount).Amount);
       Skip_line(File => InputData);
     exception
       when Constraint_Error =>
         Put_Line(Item =>
           "Out of range amount; ignoring transaction");
         Skip_Line(File => InputData);
         TransactionCount := TransactionCount - 1;
       when Ada.Text_IO.Data_Error =>
         Put_Line(Item =>
           "Bad gadget or amount; ignoring transaction");
         Skip_Line(File => InputData);
         TransactionCount := TransactionCount - 1;
     end;
```

```
77    end loop;
78
79    Ada.Text_IO.Close (File => InputData);
80
81    for Count in 1..TransactionCount loop
82      WhichKind := TodaysActivity(Count).Kind;
83      TodaysSummary(WhichKind).HowMany :=
84        TodaysSummary(WhichKind).HowMany + 1;
85      TodaysSummary(WhichKind).Net :=
86        TodaysSummary(WhichKind).Net
87      + TodaysActivity(Count).Amount;
88    end loop;
89
90    Ada.Text_IO.Put_Line
91      (Item => "Gadget Type  Transactions  Value");
92    Ada.Text_IO.Put_Line
93      (Item => "-------------------------------");
94
95    for WhichKind in Gadgets loop
96      Gadget_IO.Put(Item => WhichKind, Width => 7);
97      Put(Item => TodaysSummary(WhichKind).HowMany,
98        Width => 12);
99      Money_Out.Put(Item => TodaysSummary(WhichKind).Net,
100       Pic => Ada.Text_IO.Editing.To_Picture
101         ("$$_$$$_$$9.99CR"));
102     Ada.Text_IO.New_Line;
103   end loop;
104
105 exception
106
107   when Ada.Text_IO.Name_Error =>
108     Put_Line (Item => "File Not Found, Goodbye.");
109
110 end Show_Exception;
```

The context clause in line 1 mentions `Ada.Text_IO.Editing`. This Annex F package provides for COBOL or PL/I-style edit-directed output, which is widely used in business reports. The context clause in line 3 mentions `Ada.Command_Line`, which provides a platform-independent equivalent of C's `argc/argv` capability. Using this package, a program can read its own command-line name as well as any other command-line parameters the user has supplied.

In the original `Gadget_Report`, the monetary type was a subtype of `Float`. This is not the best way to represent money because `Float` is just an approximation of the real numbers and there is always a danger of accumulated rounding errors. For monetary quantities, it is better to use a decimal type that stores quantities exactly within a given accuracy. Accordingly, I write (line 7)

```
type Money is delta 0.01 digits 12;
```

which specifies a new numeric type with 12 decimal digits of representation, accurate to the nearest 0.01. This gives us, according to the standard, a range of $\pm 10^{10} - 0.01$ or ±999,999,999.99. Lines 8–11 create instances of the two generic packages `Ada.Text_IO.Decimal_IO` (which I use for input) and `Ada.Text_IO.Editing` (which I use for edit-directed output).

In `Gadget_Report`, I discarded each transaction after reading it. Here I choose to retain all the transactions in an array, so that, for example, I could extend the program to support queries. Accordingly, I declare (lines 17–20) a transaction record type, and (lines 22–23) an array type I shall call `Database`. This is an example of an *unconstrained array type;* the range expression

```
Integer range <>
```

indicates that the bounds of each object will be *some* integer subrange, but that I choose *not* to specify the array bounds in the type declaration, preferring instead to pin down the bounds in the object declarations. This would allow me to declare a number of array objects, each with different bounds. In this example, I declare just one array object, namely (line 32)

```
TodaysActivity: Database(1..100);
```

which allocates one array with bounds 1..100.

Moving now to the program statements, I retrieve and display the program name (as actually seen in the file system) using (line 42) `Ada.Command_Line.Command_Name` and then (lines 44–50) ascertain that the user has supplied an input file, using `Ada.Command_Line.Argument_Count` (similar to `argc`). If a file is supplied, I open it, using `Ada.Command_Line.Argument` (similar to `argv`) to retrieve its name.

Suppose the filename is incorrect so that `Open` cannot find the proper file and thus fails. `Ada.Text_IO` raises an exception, generally `Ada.Text_IO.Name_Error`. At this point, control passes to the *exception handler* for `Name_Error` if the programmer has coded one; otherwise, control passes to the runtime system and the program terminates.

Syntactically, exception handlers in Ada are associated with “frames,” that is, with `begin-end` blocks. The structure of a `begin-end` block is

```
begin

   --sequence of statements

[exception
   --one or more exception handlers]

end
```

where the brackets indicate that the exception handler part is optional. `exception` is a reserved word.

The example contains two exception-handler sections. The one governing the file-open operation begins at line 105. In this simple program, if the file open fails, there is no point in continuing execution, so I associate the handler with the main `begin-end` pair. If the file open fails, control immediately passes here. There is only one handler here, for `Name_Error`. The handler code displays a message and then control passes out of the frame. In this case, because the frame is the main frame, the program terminates.

If the file can be opened successfully, the main `while` loop (lines 56–77) reads transactions from the file, storing them this time in the array `TodaysActivity`. For example,

```
Gadget_IO.Get(File => InputData,
              Item => TodaysActivity(TransactionCount).Kind);
```

reads a gadget kind from the file, storing it in the `Kind` field of the transaction record at `TodaysActivity(TransactionCount)`.

Now suppose that in a given transaction, the first token does not represent a valid gadget, or the monetary amount is ill-formed or out of range. This condition results in either `Ada.Text_IO.Date_Error` or `Constraint_Error` being raised. The invalid transaction should not be recorded, but the program should continue to process other transactions. I need to handle the exception locally and therefore provide a `begin/end` frame (lines 59–76) with its own exception-handler part (lines 65–75).

If either of the `Get` calls raises an exception, the statement containing the call is abandoned, control immediately passes to this handler section, and the relevant handler (the appropriate `when` clause) is selected. The appropriate actions are taken and then control passes out of this frame, namely, just below the end at line 76. Now control—still in the `while` loop—passes back to the top of this loop to read the next transaction.

Language-provided exception-handling models are of two varieties: *resumption* or *termination*. In a resumption model, control passes from a handler directly back to the failed statement. Ada uses the *termination* model. The designers observed that it is often fruitless and unreliable to *automatically* resume a failed statement; in any case, the programmer can provide for resumption using loops and local exception handlers, much as I have done here.

As another example of this, an Ada idiom commonly used for interactive input is

```
loop
  begin
    Get(...);
    exit;
  exception
    when ...
    when ...
  end;
end loop;
```

Here the exception handler protects just the one `Get`. If the call succeeds, the `exit` statement passes control to just below the `end loop`. If the `Get` fails on an exception, the handlers recover, perhaps writing a message to the interactive user, after which control passes below the `end`, back around the loop for another attempt.

Completing the example, lines 81–88 loop through the transaction database and create the summary array and then lines 90–103 display the results. The statement

```
Money_Out.Put(Item => TodaysSummary(WhichKind).Net,
              Pic => Ada.Text_IO.Editing.To_Picture
                ("$$_$$$_$$9.99CR"));
```

displays the monetary quantity in edited form, using a parameter `Pic` of type `Ada.Text_IO.Editing.Picture` to provide the desired format. These picture strings are similar to those in COBOL and in spreadsheet programs. In this case, I have indicated a floating dollar sign, commas to separate groups of digits, and `CR` to indicate a negative monetary value. Thus –2065.00 displays as `$2,065.00CR`.

As in other systems used to program financial reports, Ada picture strings have many rules and much flexibility. Edited formats need not even be programmed statically. Because a picture is, syntactically, just a string, it need not be supplied as a literal but can be constructed on-the-fly depending on other conditions and passed to `Put` at the last moment.

This is the last example of the brief Ada programs designed to illustrate types and objects, the "inner syntax" of the language, and a number of the standard library packages. The next section shows how programs are constructed from packages.

10.4.2. Packages: The Ada Encapsulation Mechanism

This section illustrates the use of packages with some of my own. Before doing so, it is useful to examine a standard library package, namely the full interface of `Ada.Calendar`, taken verbatim from the *Reference Manual* because it is an especially good example of careful design of appropriate operations. Also, many Ada packages—standard and application specific—follow the general structure of `Ada.Calendar`.

```
package Ada.Calendar is

  type Time is private;

  subtype Year_Number  is Integer range 1901 ..  2099;
  subtype Month_Number is Integer range 1 ..  12;
  subtype Day_Number   is Integer range 1 .. 31;
  subtype Day_Duration is Duration range 0.0 .. 86_400.0;

  function Clock return Time;

  function Year   (Date: Time) return Year_Number;
  function Month  (Date: Time) return Month_Number;
  function Day    (Date: Time) return Day_Number;
  function Seconds(Date: Time) return Day_Duration;

  procedure Split (Date    : in Time;
                   Year    : out Year_Number;
                   Month   : out Month_Number;
                   Day     : out Day_Number;
                   Seconds: out Day_Duration);

  function Time_Of(Year    : Year_Number;
                   Month   : Month_Number;
                   Day     : Day_Number;
                   Seconds: Day_Duration := 0.0)
    return Time;

  function "+" (Left: Time; Right: Duration) return Time;
  function "+" (Left: Duration; Right: Time) return Time;
  function "-" (Left: Time; Right: Duration) return Time;
  function "-" (Left: Time; Right: Time) return Duration;

  function "<" (Left, Right: Time) return Boolean;
  function "<="(Left, Right: Time) return Boolean;
  function ">" (Left, Right: Time) return Boolean;
  function ">="(Left, Right: Time) return Boolean;

  Time_Error: exception;

private
     ... -- not specified by the language
end Ada.Calendar;
```

You have seen lines 1–15 earlier and I do not belabor them. Lines 17–20 define a procedure that accepts a `Time` value and returns, in four `out` parameters, the four components that the functions in lines 12–15 return separately. The four functions and this procedure are, in object-oriented design, generally called *selector* operations because they return selected information from an object—in this case a `Time` object—without modifying the original object.

Lines 23–27 provide a *constructor* function that goes the other way: Given the four component values, `Time_Of` produces a time. The `Seconds` parameter (line 26) is provided with a default value of `0.0`. If a calling program does not supply an actual parameter for this formal parameter, the default is used. If `T` is a `Time` variable, then

```
T := Ada.Calendar.Time_Of(7, 29, 1997);
```

returns a value corresponding to midnight at the start of July 29, 1997. On the other hand,

```
T := Ada.Calendar.Time_Of(6, 31, 1997);
```

is invalid because June has 30 days, and

```
T := Ada.Calendar.Time_Of(2, 29, 1997);
```

is invalid because 1997 is not a leap year. In both of these cases, `Ada.Calendar.Time_Error` (as defined in line 39) is raised at the point of each call; it is up to the calling program to handle the exception. I return shortly to package-defined exceptions.

Lines 29–32 define *infix operators* for `Time` values. Note that there is no operator to add two times; it is physically meaningless to add 2 o'clock to 3 o'clock. On the other hand, adding a `Duration` and a `Time` is meaningful—`Duration` represents *elapsed* time, and 2 o'clock plus 15 minutes gives 2:15. Note that I need one operator for the `Time` value on the left and another for the `Duration` value on the left.

Finally, you see (lines 34–37) comparison operators for `Time` values. `Time` is ordered, so comparing two times is meaningful.

This quick look at `Ada.Calendar` has introduced constructor and selector operations and Ada's style for defining new infix operators. I consider these issues in more detail later in this chapter in introducing some of my own packages.

10.4.2.1. A Root Package

First we introduce our structure and naming convention. By analogy with the standard library structure in which all standard packages are descendants ("children" or "grandchildren") of a root package `Ada`, in this chapter all the packages are descendants of a root package `HB`:

```
package HB is
-- Root package for Handbook examples
end HB;
```

This package interface provides no resources; it exists purely to serve as the root. Because this interface is empty, there is no need to provide an implementation.

Ada does not require you to use a root package. I choose to do so in conformity with a growing trend in the Ada literature, in which the provider of a given collection of packages uses a root package to provide a distinctive top-level name for all packages in the collection. In this way, the user of different collections can tell the origin of a given package; further, the likelihood of duplicated package names is minimized.

10.4.2.2. A Package for Rational-Number Arithmetic

The first package example is `HB.Rationals`, which provides a type and a set of programmer-defined operations on rational numbers (fractions). The Ada standard provides for integer, fixed-point, and floating-point scalar arithmetic, and Annex G, the standard numerics annex, provides for complex numbers and arithmetic. On the other hand, Ada provides no predefined support for rationals, which have many applications.

A rational value has two components: the numerator and the denominator. Here is the package interface for `HB.Rationals`.

```
package HB.Rationals is

  type Rational is private;

  ZeroDenominator: exception;

  function "/" (X, Y: Integer) return Rational;
  -- constructor:
  -- Pre :   X and Y are defined
  -- Post:   returns a rational number
  --    If Y > 0, returns X/Y
  --    If Y < 0, returns (-X)/(-Y)
  -- Raises: ZeroDenominator if Y = 0

  function Numer (R : Rational) return Integer;
```

```
16    function Denom (R : Rational) return Positive;
17    -- selectors:
18    -- Pre: R is defined
19    -- Post: return numerator and denominator respectively
20
21    function "=" (R1, R2 : Rational) return Boolean;
22    function "<" (R1, R2 : Rational) return Boolean;
23    function "<="(R1, R2 : Rational) return Boolean;
24    function ">" (R1, R2 : Rational) return Boolean;
25    function ">="(R1, R2 : Rational) return Boolean;
26    -- comparators:
27    -- Pre : R1 and R2 are defined
28    -- Post: return the obvious Boolean results
29
30    function "+"(R: Rational)   return Rational;
31    function "-"(R: Rational)   return Rational;
32    function "ABS"(R: Rational) return Rational;
33    function "+"(R1, R2 : Rational) return Rational;
34    function "-"(R1, R2 : Rational) return Rational;
35    function "*"(R1, R2 : Rational) return Rational;
36    function "/"(R1, R2 : Rational) return Rational;
37    -- Pre : R, R1 and R2 are defined
38    -- Post: return the obvious arithmetic results
39
40 private
41
42    type Rational is record
43      Numerator  : Integer  := 0;
44      Denominator: Positive := 1;
45    end record;
46
47 end HB.Rationals;
```

Line 3 gives a *partial view* of a type `Rational`: The type is declared as `private`; its structure is not provided here. I make the type `private` for encapsulation purposes: The structural details of a private type are not visible to client programs, and the only operations predefined on private types are assignment and equality/inequality tests.

Using a private type gives me the flexibility to choose—and later change—the internal structure without requiring any changes to client programs. Further, I can provide a complete set of operations on the type with no worry that a client will be able to use any additional operations. This gives me control over the abstraction provided by the package.

Ada also provides for `limited private` types, which have no predefined operations at all, not even assignment and equality test. That is, the programmer of a package providing a `limited private` type is assured that a client program can do *nothing* with objects of the type except those operations explicitly provided in the package. This is useful in situations where, for example, it is necessary or desirable to prohibit clients from copying one object to another. The type `Ada.Text_IO.File_Type` is a predefined limited `private` type.

The *full view* of the `private` type `Rational` is given in the `private` part of the interface (lines 40–46). You see that a rational is represented as a record, that its numerator can be an arbitrary integer but that its denominator is positive, and that each rational quantity is initialized. Human readers of the package interface can obviously see this full view, but client programs cannot. A client program therefore cannot refer directly to the numerator and denominator fields but must use package-provided operations to do so.

Line 5 defines a package-specific exception `ZeroDenominator`; you shall see later how this is raised if a client tries to assign `0` to the denominator of a rational.

The declaration (line 7)

```
function "/" (X, Y: Integer) return Rational;
```

declares an operator `"/"`, which clients can use to construct a rational. This operator allows you to write, in client programs, statements such as

```
R: Rational := 1/3;
```

Defining, in this fashion, additional meanings for the existing operator symbols is called *operator overloading*. Ada allows you to overload any of the existing operator symbols and prohibits you from defining any new operator symbols.

In this interface, I have documented the various groups of operations with comments indicating preconditions and postconditions. These lie outside Ada but are increasingly commonly used in Ada and other languages to give concise and consistent descriptions of sets of operations. The precondition (line 9)

```
-- Pre :   X and Y are defined
```

indicates that the behavior of this operation can be assured *only* if the client program refrains from passing it uninitialized variables. In Ada, variables are not initialized by default and there is no requirement that the programmer provide initialization expressions in declarations. Moreover, there is, in general, no assured compile-time or runtime check that variables are initialized. The precondition is therefore very important in Ada: As in most programming languages, initialization is a programmer responsibility.

The postcondition

```
-- Post:   returns a rational number
--    If Y > 0, returns X/Y
--    If Y < 0, returns (-X)/(-Y)
-- Raises: ZeroDenominator if Y = 0
```

describes the behavior of the `"/"` operator in succinct terms. Lines 15–38 declare a full set of operations on rational quantities; their intent is obvious from their declarations and postconditions.

Line 21

```
function "=" (R1, R2 : Rational) return Boolean;
```

merits a bit of discussion. The equality-test operation is predefined in Ada for most types, including private ones. Here I *override* the predefined equality test because it may give incorrect results. Predefined equality compares its two operands bitwise; any disagreement yields a `False` result. Algebraically, 1/3 = 2/6 = 24/72, and so on. Ada's predefined equality would return `False` if applied to 1/3 and 2/6. I need my own equality test, so I provide it in the package interface and deliver it in the package body I examine shortly.

I defined all the operators as *functions* because, in fact, mathematically an operator *is* just a function with certain restrictions on its arguments. Indeed, the standard defines the operators on the predefined types using just this function syntax.

10.4.2.3. A Child Package for Rational Input and Output

To provide clients with an easy way to input and display rationals, I provide a child package `HB.Rationals.IO`, in which `Get` and `Put` operations are provided for the standard and named input and output files. There is no requirement that this package be a child of `Rationals`; I simply chose to make it so.

```
with Ada.Text_IO;
use Ada.Text_IO;
package HB.Rationals.IO IS

  procedure Get (Item : out Rational);
  procedure Get
     (File: in File_Type; Item : out Rational);

  procedure Put (Item : in Rational);
  procedure Put
     (File: in File_Type; Item : in Rational);

end HB.Rationals.IO;
```

In this package interface, note how the various procedure parameters are specified. In writing Ada procedures, you choose a *mode* for each parameter. That is, you declare each parameter as `in`, `out`, or `in out`; in the absence of a mode specifier, `in` is specified by default.

Ada separates the intended use of parameters from the mechanism by which they are passed. An `in` parameter is treated as a constant, or read-only value, within the body of the procedure. Because no code within the procedure can attempt to modify an in parameter—this is, of course, checked by the compiler—it is of no concern whether the parameter is passed by copy or by reference.

In fact, the Ada standard requires that scalar parameters be passed by value; an `in out` scalar is copied from actual to formal at the start of a procedure execution, and the possibly new value is copied back from formal to actual at procedure completion. On the other hand, composite (record and array) parameters can be legally passed either by copy or by reference; most compilers pass them by reference.

Parameters or functions must be `in`; programmers generally omit the explicit `in` from function parameter declarations, and I have omitted it in the packages here.

10.4.2.4. Using the Rationals Package

Before I investigate the implementations of the rational-number packages, examine a typical interactive client program. A session with this program might be

```
A = 1/3
B = -2/4
Enter rational number C > 2/5
Enter rational number D > 3/4

E = A + B is -2/12
A + E * B is 60/144
B's numerator is -2
```

Results such as `-2/12` and `60/144` make it obvious that nothing in this package is reducing rationals to lowest terms. A good rationals package should do so; I have chosen to omit it in the interest of brevity. It would not be difficult to add to the `"/"` operator.

```
with Ada.Text_IO, Ada.Integer_Text_IO;
with HB.Rationals, HB.Rationals.IO;
use HB.Rationals;
```

```
 4 procedure Show_Package is
 5
 6   A, B, C, D, E: Rational;
 7
 8 begin
 9
10   A := 1/3;
11   B := 2/(-4);
12   Ada.Text_IO.Put(Item => "A = ");
13   HB.Rationals.IO.Put(Item => A);
14   Ada.Text_IO.New_Line;
15   Ada.Text_IO.Put(Item => "B = ");
16   HB.Rationals.IO.Put(Item => B);
17   Ada.Text_IO.New_Line;
18
19   Ada.Text_IO.Put(Item => "Enter rational number C > ");
20   HB.Rationals.IO.Get(Item => C);
21   Ada.Text_IO.Put(Item => "Enter rational number D > ");
22   HB.Rationals.IO.Get(Item => D);
23   Ada.Text_IO.New_Line;
24
25   E := A + B;
26   Ada.Text_IO.Put(Item => "E = A + B is ");
27   HB.Rationals.IO.Put(Item => E);
28   Ada.Text_IO.New_Line;
29
30   Ada.Text_IO.Put(Item => "A + E * B is ");
31   HB.Rationals.IO.Put(Item => A + E * B);
32   Ada.Text_IO.New_Line;
33
34   Ada.Text_IO.Put(Item => "B's numerator is ");
35   Ada.Integer_Text_IO.Put
36     (Item => Numer(B), Width => 1);
37   Ada.Text_IO.New_Line;
38
39 exception
40   when ZeroDenominator =>
41     Ada.Text_IO.Put_Line(Item =>
42       "Zero not allowed in denominator; bye-bye.");
43 end Show_Package;
```

Lines 1–3 provide the expected context clauses and a `use` for `Rationals`. The `use` allows me to use the rational operators in infix form; without a `use`, I would have to say, for example, in line 10,

```
A := Rationals."/"(1,3);
```

which is unpleasant. The rest of the program illustrates some simple rational arithmetic; note line 25, for example, which looks like an ordinary arithmetic assignment, but in fact, all the operations are rational ones.

In analyzing `E := A + B`, the compiler can determine that the `+` is intended to be that for rationals because its two operands (`A` and `B`) are of type `Rational`, as is the return type (`E`). Similarly in line 31, the expression `A + E * B` is a rational one because all three operands are, as is the desired `Item` sent to `HB.Rationals.IO.Put`. Determining which of several like-named operators is intended is called *overload resolution;* the compiler can resolve the overloads if and only if it has enough information to do so.

If `X` is `Integer` and `Y` is `Rational`, the expression `X + Y` results in a compilation error. This is simply because there is no `+` defined for this combination of operands; I could add one to the package if I chose to do so; its line in the interface would be

```
function "+"(X: Integer; R: Rational) return Rational;
```

Indeed, nothing prevents me from writing a package providing other mixed operations, such as

```
function "+"(X: Integer; F: Float) return Float;
```

This observation reveals that although mixed operations are not *predefined* in Ada, you could add these to the language via a suitable (large) collection of overloaded operators. Doing so would not be desirable, however: The compiler would have no trouble resolving all the overloads in a program that used these mixed expressions, but the human reader would quickly get confused. Operator overloading is convenient when used in moderation.

10.4.2.5. Implementing the `Rationals` and `Rationals.IO` Packages

Now examine the implementation of the `Rationals` package. In Ada, the implementation is called a `package body`, as line 1 shows.

```
 1 package body HB.Rationals is
 2
 3   function "/" (X, Y : Integer) return Rational is
 4   begin
 5     if Y = 0 then
 6       raise ZeroDenominator;
 7     elsif X = 0 then
 8       return (Numerator => 0, Denominator => 1);
 9     elsif Y > 0 then
10       return (Numerator => X, Denominator => Y);
11     else
12       return (Numerator => -X, Denominator => -Y);
13     end if;
14   end "/";
15
16   function Numer (R : Rational) return Integer is
```

```
begin
  return R.Numerator;
end Numer;

function Denom (R : Rational) return Positive is
begin
  return R.Denominator;
end Denom;

function "=" (R1, R2 : Rational) return Boolean is
begin
  return Numer(R1)*Denom(R2) = Numer(R2)*Denom(R1);
end "=";

function "<" (R1, R2 : Rational) return Boolean is
begin
  return Numer(R1)*Denom(R2) < Numer(R2)*Denom(R1);
end "<";

function ">" (R1, R2 : Rational) return Boolean is
begin
  return Numer(R1)*Denom(R2) > Numer(R2)*Denom(R1);
end ">";

function "<=" (R1, R2 : Rational) return Boolean is
begin
  return Numer(R1)*Denom(R2) <= Numer(R2)*Denom(R1);
end "<=";

function ">=" (R1, R2 : Rational) return Boolean is
begin
  return Numer(R1)*Denom(R2) >= Numer(R2)*Denom(R1);
end ">=";

function "+"(R : Rational) return Rational is
begin
  return R;
end "+";

function "-"(R : Rational) return Rational is
begin
  return (-Numer(R)) / Denom(R);
end "-";

function "abs"(R : Rational) return Rational is
begin
  return (abs Numer(R)) / Denom(R);
end "abs";

function "+"(R1, R2 : Rational) return Rational is
begin
  return (Numerator =>
               Numer(R1)*Denom(R2) + Numer(R2)*Denom(R1),
            Denominator => Denom(R1)*Denom(R2));
end "+";

function "-"(R1, R2 : Rational) return Rational is
```

```
74    begin
75      return (Numerator =>
76                 Numer(R1)*Denom(R2) - Numer(R2)*Denom(R1),
77               Denominator => Denom(R1)*Denom(R2));
78    end "-";
79
80    function "*"(R1, R2 : Rational) return Rational is
81    begin
82      return (Numerator => Numer(R1)*Numer(R2),
83               Denominator => Denom(R1)*Denom(R2));
84    end "*";
85
86    function "/"(R1, R2 : Rational) return Rational is
87    begin
88      return (Denominator => Numer(R1)*Numer(R2),
89               Numerator => Denom(R1)*Denom(R2));
90    end "/";
91
92  end HB.Rationals;
```

Lines 3–14 implement the `"/"` operator. This is simply a matter of checking the various cases. In the first case (line 6), an attempt to store `0` in the denominator, we

```
raise ZeroDenominator;
```

Because there is no exception handler in this function, the exception is *propagated* to the point where the client called the function. If the client provides a nearby handler, control is passed to it; otherwise, control passes to the next higher level in the call chain and so forth until either the exception is handled somewhere in the application or it passes beyond the main program to the runtime system.

It is quite common in Ada to declare exceptions in package interfaces and then raise them in package implementations. This sort of exception responds to a client program's violation of the abstraction provided by the package—in this case, the mathematical prohibition against 0 in the denominator of a rational number. The package cannot be expected to "clean up" a violation such as this: The client caused the problem and the client is responsible for solving it. Ada's exception-propagation rules encourage programmers to design such that responsibility for anomalies and violations is passed to, and handled by, just the right layer of the overall program.

The other cases in `"/"` are straightforward. Note (line 10) the `return` statement

```
return (Numerator => X, Denominator => Y);
```

in which the parenthesized expression is an *aggregate* expression, returning a record to the calling program, with its fields set as indicated.

This statement illustrates that in Ada there is no restriction on the return type of a function; specifically, a function may return a record or even an array, as the abstraction requires. This is a significant advantage over languages that require pointers to data structures to be explicitly passed to, and returned from, functions. Because in Ada composite types are generally passed by reference, pointers are indeed involved, but the compiler, not the programmer, is responsible for them.

Lines 16–24 implement `Numer` and `Denom`; lines 26–29 implement the equality test. The statement

```
return Numer(R1)*Denom(R2) = Numer(R2)*Denom(R1);
```

returns `True` or `False`, depending on whether the two cross-products are equal. Recalling that 2/6 = 3/9, algebraically, confirms the correctness of the boolean cross-product expression.

Note that it is neither necessary nor legal to overload `"/="`; overloading `"="` automatically overloads `"/="`.

Lines 31–49 give the bodies of the other four comparison operators; lines 51–64 implement the three monadic (unary) arithmetic operators, and lines 66–90 implement the dynadic (binary) arithmetic operators. These bodies are all straightforward.

I complete the rationals system by showing the implementation of `HB.Rationals.IO`; these four procedure bodies are straightforward. Note only that the `Get` for standard input is implemented by a simple call (line 19) to the other `Get` for a named file, using `Ada.Text_IO.Standard_Input` as the filename.

```
 1 with Ada.Text_IO, Ada.Integer_Text_IO;
 2 use  Ada.Text_IO, Ada.Integer_Text_IO;
 3 package body HB.Rationals.IO is
 4
 5   procedure Get
 6     (File: in File_Type; Item : out Rational) is
 7     N: Integer;
 8     D: Integer;
 9     Dummy: Character;  -- dummy character to hold the "/"
10   begin
11     Get(File => File, Item => N);
12     Get  (File => File, Item => Dummy);
13     Get(File => File, Item => D);
14     Item := N/D;
```

```
   end Get;

   procedure Get (Item : out Rational) is
   begin
     Get(File => Standard_Input, Item => Item);
   end Get;

   procedure Put
     (File: in File_Type; Item : in Rational) is
   begin
     Put(File => File, Item => Numer(Item), Width => 1);
     Put(File => File, Item => '/');
     Put(File => File, Item => Denom(Item), Width => 1);
   end Put;

   procedure Put (Item : in Rational) is
   begin
     Put(File => Standard_Output, Item => Item);
   end Put;

end HB.Rationals.IO;
```

10.4.2.6. Unconstrained Array Types and Vectors

The next example gives a basic package for manipulating mathematical vectors.

```
package HB.Vectors is

   type Vector is array(Integer range <>) of Float;

   Bounds_Error : exception;

   function "*" (K : Float; Right : Vector) return Vector;
   -- Pre:  K and Right are defined
   -- Post: scales the vector by the scalar
   --    Result(i) := K * Right(i)

   function "*" (Left, Right : Vector) return Float;
   -- Pre:    Left and Right are defined
   -- Post:   returns the inner product of Left and Right
   -- Raises: Bounds_Error if Left and Right
   --          have different numbers of elements

   function "+" (Left, Right : Vector) return Vector;
   -- Pre:    Left and Right are defined
   -- Post:   returns the sum of Left and Right
   --          Result(i) := Left(i) + Right(i)
   --          Result has Left's bounds
   -- Raises: Bounds_Error if Left and Right
   --          have different numbers of elements

end HB.Vectors;
```

In line 3, a vector is defined as an array of `Float` values. Recall from the earlier gadgets example that the expression `Integer range <>` indicates an unconstrained array type. This means that each vector's bounds are an `Integer` subrange and that these bounds are set not in the type declaration but in the object declaration. For example,

```
V: Vector (1..100);
W: Vector (25..40);
Z: Vector (-5..10);
```

are all legal object declarations. Each object is now said to be *constrained*; its bounds (and the space allocated for it) are set for its lifetime.

Under Ada's rules, two such constrained objects are assignment-compatible if they have the same *length*, that is, the same number of elements; thus the bounds do not have to be equal. Because `W` and `Z` have the same length (16 elements),

```
W := Z;
Z := W;
```

are both valid assignments. Moreover, you can work with *slices,* that is, subarrays. For example,

```
V (5..10) := W (32..37);
```

is valid because both lengths are 6. The slice bounds don't have to be static; they can be computed as the program executes, so slicing turns out to give considerable expressiveness in array-handling algorithms.

Ada's predefined `String` type is, in fact, an unconstrained array type:

```
type String is array (Positive range <>) of Character;
```

so slicing operations operate as substring operations. The standard library packages `Ada.Strings`, `Ada.Strings.Bounded`, and `Ada.Strings.Unbounded` provide full sets of operations on bounded and unbounded strings of varying length, built on top of the basic support for strings as unconstrained arrays. For brevity's sake, I do not go into more detail on the string operations.

In `HB.Vectors`, I provide an exception `Bounds_Error` and several overloaded operators. The sum (`+`) of two equal-length vectors is a vector of that same length, in which each element is the sum of the corresponding elements in the operand vectors. The inner product (`"*"`) of two equal-length vectors with `Float` elements is a `Float` value, the accumulated sum of all the pairwise products of the operand vectors (a pairwise product is the product of the first elements of the two vectors, or of the second elements, and so on).

As the postconditions show, this exception is raised if the client violates the vector abstraction, that is, attempts to add or multiply vectors of different lengths. If we have

```
V: Vector (1..10);
W: Vector (11..20);
X: Vector (6..11);
Z: Vector (26..35);
```

then

```
W := V + Z;
```

is valid but

```
W := X + Z;
```

is not and the exception is raised.

This, and the vector arithmetic operations, are shown in the package implementation.

```
package body HB.Vectors is

  function "*"
    (K : Float; Right : Vector) return Vector is
    Result: Vector(Right'Range);
  begin
    for I in Right'Range loop
      Result(I) := K * Right(I);
    end loop;
    return Result;
  end "*";

  function "+" (Left, Right : Vector) return Vector is
    Result : Vector(Left'Range);
  begin
    if Left'Length /= Right'Length then
      raise Bounds_Error;
    else
      for I in Left'range loop
        Result(I) :=
          Left(I) + Right(I - Left'First + Right'First);
      end loop;
      return Result;
    end if;
  end "+";

```

```
27   function "*" (Left, Right : Vector) return Float is
28     Sum : Float := 0.0;
29   begin
30     if Left'Length /= Right'Length then
31       raise Bounds_Error;
32     else
33       for I in Left'Range loop
34         Sum := Sum +
35           Left(I) * Right(I - Left'First + Right'First);
36       end loop;
37       return Sum;
38     end if;
39   end "*";
40
41 end HB.Vectors;
```

The implementation makes heavy use of unconstrained array attributes, as seen in the first function, which scales the vector by multiplying each of its elements by the same `Float` value. Line 5

```
Result: Vector(Right'Range);
```

creates a temporary result vector `Result` whose bounds are given by `Right'Range`. Equivalently you could say

```
Result: Vector(Right'First..Right'Last);
```

`Right'First` is the value of the first *index* or *subscript* of `Right`, not the first *element* value. This line, then, "sizes" the result vector to be the same as the input vector. Similarly, the loop in lines 7–9 is also bounded by `Right'Range` and thus multiplies each vector element by the `Float` value `K`.

The operator `+` (lines 13–25) first sizes a result vector (line 14), choosing `Left`'s bounds as the ones to use. Because the operation makes mathematical sense only if the two vectors have the same length, I check this in lines 16–17, raising the exception if the lengths disagree.

If the vectors are conformable (the lengths agree), I compute the sum by looping through both vectors. Because the *bounds* will not, in general, be the same, I loop using `Left`'s bounds and adjust the index into `Right` accordingly, selecting

```
Left(I) + Right(I - Left'First + Right'First)
```

The inner product (`"*"`, lines 27–39) is similar to the sum, but this time I multiply the elements pairwise, accumulating them in a scalar `Result`.

As this package has shown, unconstrained arrays and their attributes provide a concise way to operate on arrays whose bounds are unknown at compilation time. This gives you great expressive power to write general-purpose mathematical algorithms that can operate on vectors and matrices of any size, without knowing their specific bounds.

10.4.2.7. Generic Packages and Matrices

`HB.Vectors` shows the power of unconstrained array types, but only in a single dimension. Also, the vector element type is specified as `Float`, which makes the package insufficiently general. In the next example, I extend `HB.Vectors` in two ways: I illustrate multidimensional unconstrained array types and I show a generic or template package for vector and matrix operations that allows instantiation for an arbitrary element type. Here is the interface for `HB.Matrices_Generic`.

```
generic

   type   ElementType is private;
   Zero:  ElementType;
   Unity: ElementType;

   with function
      "+"(Left, Right: ElementType) return ElementType;
   with function
      "*"(Left, Right: ElementType) return ElementType;

package HB.Matrices_Generic is

   type Vector is array(Integer range <>) of ElementType;
   type Matrix is
      array (Integer range <>, Integer range <>)
      of ElementType;

   Bounds_Error: exception;

   function "*"
      (K: ElementType; Right: Vector) return Vector;
   function "*" (Left, Right: Vector) return ElementType;
   function "+" (Left, Right: Vector) return Vector;

   function "*"
      (K: ElementType; Right: Matrix) return Matrix;
   function Transpose (Left: Matrix) return Matrix;
   function "+" (Left, Right: Matrix) return Matrix;
   function "*" (Left, Right: Matrix) return Matrix;

   function "*"
      (Left: Vector; Right: Matrix) return Vector;
   function "*"
      (Left: Matrix; Right: Vector) return Vector;

end HB.Matrices_Generic;
```

Lines 1–11 give the generic part of a package template. Syntactically, this generic part precedes an otherwise ordinary-looking package interface. Lines 3–10 give the *generic formal parameters*. Just as the caller of an ordinary procedure or function must supply actual parameters to match that subprogram's formal parameters, so a client of a generic template must supply actual parameters for each of the generic formals.

Line 3 declares a generic formal *type* parameter. Syntactically, this looks similar to an ordinary type declaration, but it is not; it declares a type *parameter.* Ada provides for different categories of generic formal parameters, such as integer types, float types, enumeration types, constrained and unconstrained array types, and so on. Each parameter category has its own bit of syntax for describing the category.

In this case, the parameter is a `private` type parameter. This does not mean that the actual *must* be `private`, but rather that the actual may be *any* type, including a private one. This excludes from consideration only `limited` and `tagged` types (which I have not introduced yet) and thus allows great flexibility in the kinds of types that can serve as matrix elements. I could instantiate with predefined scalar types such as `Integer`, or `Float`, or `Boolean` (there are many applications for boolean matrices) or even programmer-defined private composite types such as `Rational`.

To understand the remaining formal parameters, first recall from `HB.Vectors` that the inner product operation first initializes a `Sum` variable to `0.0` and then, as it loops through the vectors, carries out `Float` addition and multiplication on the vector elements and `Sum`. In the generic package, the element type is no longer `Float`, but an arbitrary type to be supplied by the client. This means that 0.0 no longer is a correct zero value. In fact, each possible element type has its own zero: 0 (`Integer`), 0/1 (`Rational`), `False` (`Boolean`), and so on. In return for the ability to instantiate a matrix package for any type, the client gains the responsibility to tell us (line 4) what the zero is for that type. Similarly, I ask the client to supply a unity value (line 5) for the type.

Furthermore, because any programmer-defined type can be used as an element, it is not self-evident that addition and multiplication are defined for this type. I therefore list formal parameters for these operations (lines 7–10) and the client must supply the corresponding actuals. To instantiate for `Float`, you would write

```
package Float_Matrices is new HB.Matrices_Generic
  (ElementType => Float,
   Zero        => 0.0,
   Unity       => 1.0,
   "+" => "+",
   "*" => "*");
```

and to instantiate for `Boolean` (say, for a graph-theory application that represents graphs as `Boolean` matrices), you would write

```
package Boolean_Matrices is new HB.Matrices_Generic
  (ElementType => Boolean,
   Zero        => False,
   Unity       => True,
   "+" => "or",
   "*" => "and");
```

Returning to the package interface, lines 14–17 declare two types, `Vector` and `Matrix`. The second declaration shows a matrix as a two-dimensional unconstrained array. This lets me declare objects such as

```
M: Matrix(1..3, 25..100);
```

which I view as having three rows and 76 columns.

The `Matrix` type raises two related issues. First, a two-dimensional (2D) array is *not* a 1D array of 1D arrays (as it would be in Pascal or C, for example); it is a different type entirely. Second, the Ada standard does *not* specify a storage structure for multidimensional arrays; an implementer could choose row-major, or column-major, or another scheme entirely (such as a tree structure). This is an advantage because the storage structure can be tailored to the underlying computer's memory structure. Generally, a programmer need not be concerned about the storage structure.

On the other hand, in a program using the Ada 95 interface to Fortran (as described in Annex B of the standard), for example, to call preexisting Fortran subprograms, I could attach to a matrix type a compiler directive—`pragma` in Ada—of the form

```
pragma Convention(Fortran, Matrix);
```

indicating that all objects of the Ada type `Matrix` must be stored to match the column-major convention used by the related Fortran compiler.

Lines 19–24 are essentially repeated from `HB.Vectors`. Lines 26–27 declare a scaling operation for matrices; line 28 declares a matrix transposition operation in which rows are interchanged with columns, line 29 gives a matrix sum (similar to the vector sum), and line 30 provides the matrix product. In this last operation, given matrices `Left`, `Right`, and `Result`, for a given row `R` and column `C` of `Result`, `Result(R,C)` is the vector inner product of row `R` of `Left` and column `C` of `Right`. The conformability condition is that `Left` must have as many columns as `Right` has rows; `Result` has the number of rows of `Left` and the number of columns of `Right`.

Finally, lines 32–35 provide "mixed" vector/matrix operations. In the first `"*"`, `Left` is a row vector; multiplying it by the matrix `Right` produces another vector. This is similar to a matrix product operation in which `Left` has only one row. Similarly, the second `"*"` operation provides for multiplying a matrix `Left` by a vector `Right`.

A comment on package design: That I choose to export *two* types from this package shows clearly that the Ada package is an encapsulation mechanism that gives us flexibility to export one or more types—or, indeed, not to export any types at all, as in `HB.Rationals.IO`. This is a clearly different style from "class"-oriented languages in which the type and the encapsulation mechanisms are the same. Naturally, there is debate about the superiority of one style over another; however, neither side can prove its case because these are just different syntactic mechanisms—matters of preference, really—for reaching similar program-design goals.

10.4.2.8. Using the Generic Matrix Package

Before examining the implementation of `HB.Matrices_Generic`, see how it might be used. `Show_Matrices` is a sample client in which the matrix element type is `Rational`.

```
with Ada.Text_IO; use Ada.Text_IO;
with HB.Rationals; use HB.Rationals;
with HB.Rationals.IO; use HB.Rationals.IO;
with HB.Matrices_Generic;
procedure Show_Matrices is

  package Rational_Matrices is new HB.Matrices_Generic
    (ElementType => Rational,
     Zero        => 0/1,
     Unity       => 1/1,
     "+" => HB.Rationals."+",
     "*" => HB.Rationals."*");
  use Rational_Matrices;

  procedure Put(Item: in Vector) is
```

```
16    begin
17      for Element in Item'Range loop
18        Put(Item(Element));
19        Put("  ");
20      end loop;
21      New_Line(Spacing => 2);
22    end Put;
23
24    procedure Put(Item: in Matrix) is
25    begin
26      for Row in Item'Range(1) loop
27        for Col in Item'Range(2) loop
28          Put(Item(Row, Col));
29          Put("  ");
30        end loop;
31        New_Line;
32      end loop;
33      New_Line;
34    end Put;
35
36    V: Vector(1..3) := (1/3, 2/3, 0/1);
37    M: Matrix(1..3, 1..4) := ((0/1, 1/3, 1/2, 1/4),
38                              (1/1, 1/2, 1/2, 0/1),
39                              (1/4, 2/3, 1/4, 1/5));
40
41  begin
42
43    Put_Line("V ="); Put(V);
44    Put_Line("M ="); Put(M);
45    Put_Line("1/2 * M ="); Put(1/2 * M);
46    Put_Line("V * M ="); Put(V * M);
47
48    begin
49      Put_Line("M * V ="); Put(M * V);
50      Put_Line("Exception should have been raised");
51    exception
52      when Bounds_Error =>
53        Put_Line("Exception properly raised");
54    end;
55
56  end Show_Matrices;
```

This program is in "terse" style with `use` clauses supplied and named parameters used only where extra clarity is needed. Lines 7–12 create an instance `Rational_Matrices` of the generic template. In line 11, the association

```
"+" => HB.Rationals."+"
```

is written verbosely, just for clarity's sake. Indeed, the instantiation could have been written (tersely but more opaquely) as

```
package Rational_Matrices is
  new HB.Matrices_Generic (Rational, 0/1, 1/1, "+", "*");
```

The instance is now a `use`-able package, so I can supply a `use` clause (line 13). This instance gives me the types `Rational_Matrices.Vector` and `Rational_Matrices.Matrix`; the `use` lets me refer to these just as `Vector` and `Matrix`.

Lines 15–22 is a procedure to display the elements of a vector. There is nothing new here except (line 21) the use of the `Spacing` parameter to `New_Line`, which has the obvious meaning of "move the cursor to the next line and then move it again."

Lines 24–34 show a procedure to display a matrix, row-by-row. Note in line 26 the attribute `Item'Range(1)`, which means "the range of `Item`'s first dimension," and in line 27, the attribute `Item'Range(2)`, which means "the range of `Item`'s second dimension." Here again you see the power of attributes to work with arrays whose bounds are unknown at compilation time.

Lines 36–39 declare a vector and matrix, both initialized with aggregates of rational quantities. The 2D aggregate initializes `M` row-by-row. Lines 43–46 display the vector and the matrix, followed by the matrix scaled by 1/2 and then by the product of the vector and the matrix.

Lines 48–54 are used to illustrate a frame style that is commonly used in writing a program designed to test a package. The product `M*V` is mathematically impossible because `M` has 4 columns, but there, column vector `V` has only 3 columns. `Bounds_Error` is raised to signal this abstraction violation, if and only if the product operation is correctly implemented in the package.

The actual output of this program should be

```
V =
1/3  2/3  0/1

M =
0/1  1/3  1/2  1/4
1/1  1/2  1/2  0/1
1/4  2/3  1/4  1/5

1/2 * M =
0/2  1/6  1/4  1/8
1/2  1/4  1/4  0/2
1/8  2/6  1/8  1/10

V * M =
24/36  72/162  72/144  15/180

M * V =
Exception properly raised
```

10.4.2.9. Implementing the Generic Matrix Package

From the exploration of `HB.Vectors` and `Show_Matrices`, the package implementation is easy to understand.

```
package body HB.Matrices_Generic is

  function "*"
    (K : ElementType; Right : Vector) return Vector is
    Result: Vector(Right'Range);
  begin
    for I in Right'Range loop
      Result(I) := K * Right(I);
    end loop;
    return Result;
  end "*";

  function "+" (Left, Right : Vector) return Vector is
    Result : Vector(Left'Range);
  begin
    if Left'Length /= Right'Length then
      raise Bounds_Error;
    else
      for I in Left'Range loop
        Result(I) :=
          Left(I) + Right(I - Left'First + Right'First);
      end loop;
      return Result;
    end if;
  end "+";

  function "*"
    (Left, Right : Vector) return ElementType is
    Sum : ElementType := Zero;
  begin
    if Left'Length /= Right'Length then
      raise Bounds_Error;
    else
      for I in Left'Range loop
        Sum := Sum +
          Left(I) * Right(I - Left'First + Right'First);
      end loop;
      return Sum;
    end if;
  end "*";

  function "*"
    (K : ElementType; Right : Matrix) return Matrix is
    Result: Matrix(Right'Range(1), Right'Range(2));
  begin
    for I in Right'Range(1) loop
      for J in Right'Range(2) loop
        Result(I,J) := K * Right(I,J);
      end loop;
    end loop;
    return Result;
  end "*";

```

```
function Transpose (Left: Matrix) return Matrix is
  Result: Matrix(Left'Range(2), Left'Range(1));
begin
  for I in Result'Range(1) loop
    for J in Result'Range(2) loop
      Result(I,J) := Left(J,I);
    end loop;
  end loop;
  return Result;
end Transpose;

function "+" (Left, Right : Matrix) return Matrix is
  Result : Matrix(Left'Range(1), Left'Range(2));
begin
  if Left'Length(1) /= Right'Length(1) or
     Left'Length(2) /= Right'Length(2) then
    raise Bounds_Error;
  else
    for I in Left'Range(1) loop
      for J in Left'Range(2) loop
        Result(I, J) := Left(I, J) +
          Right(I - Left'First(1) + Right'First(1),
                J - Left'First(2) + Right'First(2));
      end loop;
    end loop;
    return Result;
  end if;
end "+";

function "*" (Left, Right : Matrix) return Matrix is
  Result: Matrix(Left'Range(1), Right'Range(2)) :=
    (others => (others => Zero));
begin
  if Left'Length(2) /= Right'Length(1) then
    raise Bounds_Error;
  else
    for RowL in Left'Range(1) loop
      for ColR in Right'Range(2) loop
        for ColL in Left'Range(2) loop
          Result(RowL, ColR) := Result(RowL, ColR) +
            Left(RowL, ColL) *
            Right((ColL-Left'First(2))+Right'First(1),
                  ColR);
        end loop;
      end loop;
    end loop;
  end if;
  return Result;
end "*";

function "*"
  (Left: Vector; Right: Matrix) return Vector is
  Result: Vector(Right'Range(2)) := (others => Zero);
begin
  if Left'Length /= Right'Length(1) then
    raise Bounds_Error;
```

```
110       else
111         for C in Right'Range(2) loop
112           for R in Right'Range(1) loop
113             Result(C) := Result(C) + Right(R, C) *
114               Left(Left'First + (R-Right'First(1)));
115           end loop;
116         end loop;
117       end if;
118       return Result;
119     end "*";
120
121     function "*"
122       (Left: Matrix; Right: Vector) return Vector is
123       Result: Vector(Left'Range(1)) := (others => Zero);
124     begin
125       if Left'Length(2) /= Right'Length then
126         raise Bounds_Error;
127       else
128         for R in Left'Range(1) loop
129           for C in Left'Range(2) loop
130             Result(R) := Result(R) + Left(R, C) *
131               Right(Right'First + (C-Left'First(2)));
132           end loop;
133         end loop;
134       end if;
135       return Result;
136     end "*";
137
138   end HB.Matrices_Generic;
```

I do not belabor the algorithms embodied in the various operations; these are well-known and straightforward algorithms from matrix algebra. From the Ada perspective, I point out the declaration (lines 84–85)

```
Result: Matrix(Left'Range(1), Right'Range(2)) :=
        (others => (others => Zero));
```

which "sizes" a result matrix in terms of the `Left` and `Right` matrix operands and further initializes all elements of this matrix to `0`, the parameter representing the zero of the element type. This aggregate initialization is very concise and can be implemented efficiently because the programmer leaves it up to the compiler just *how* all the elements are initialized at execution time.

Finally, lines 87–88 give the conformability condition for matrix multiplication: `Left` must have as many columns as `Right` has rows.

10.4.3. Type Extension, Inheritance, and Polymorphism

Even in its original 1983-standard form, Ada contained most of the important ingredients for object-oriented software development.

First, packages, together with private types, provide a strong *encapsulation* mechanism that gives the programmer tight control over the visibility, state, and behavior of objects.

Further, two kinds of *polymorphism* are provided: The generic package facility gives the ability to parameterize packages with respect to types and operations, and overloading allows you to use the same name for a number of different operations with different parameter profiles.

Finally, *inheritance* is provided through *type derivation.* In Ada 83 you can write, for example,

```
package Credit_Cards is
   type Credit_Card is private;
   procedure P1 (X: in Credit_Card; ...);
   procedure P2 (X: in out Credit_Card; ...);
   ...
private
   type Credit_Card is...
end Credit_Cards;
```

and then derive new types such as

```
type Personal_Card is new Credit_Card;
type Business_Card is new Credit_Card;
```

These three types form a type hierarchy. `Personal_Card` and `Business_Card` inherit the structural details of `Credit_Card` and also the operations `P1` and `P2`. The three types are not compatible with each other but can be explicitly converted so that if you have

```
C: Credit_Card;
P: Personal_Card;
B: Business_Card;
```

then

```
C := B;
P := B;
B := C;
```

are all disallowed, but

```
C := Credit_Card(B);
P := Personal_Card(B);
B := Business_Card(P);
```

are all valid. Furthermore,

```
P1(C);
P1(P);
P1(B);
```

are all valid and the compiler can determine which one to dispatch for each object.

The common characteristic in generics, overloading, and Ada 83 type derivation is that given an object and a set of similarly-named operations, the operation to be executed can be determined essentially at compilation time.

Why, then, did the Ada 83 designers not go the rest of the distance and provide for the kind of inheritance and runtime polymorphism programmers have come to expect for object-oriented programming (OOP)? There is considerable folklore about the discussions at the time, but not much available written record on this issue. It is a matter of fact, though, that Ichbiah and his team were well aware of, and considered carefully, the costs and benefits of these features. The *Ada 83 Rationale* says just this on the subject (in the introduction to Chapter 9):

> Facilities for modularization have appeared in many languages. Some of them—such as Simula, Clu, and Alphard—provide dynamic facilities which may entail large run-time overhead. The facility provided in Ada is more static—in the spirit of previous solutions offered in Lis, Euclid, Mesa, and Modula. At the same time it retains the best aspects of solutions in earlier languages such as Fortran and Jovial.

I conclude that given the slow speed and memory constraints of the computers of that period, the main concern was about runtime costs. The Ada 83 designers—who did most of their work in the late 1970s—provided the "hooks" for full OOP but left it to the second generation of designers—who produced Ada 95 beginning in 1988, when far more powerful hardware was common and other OO languages had become popular—to implement it fully.

The Ada 95 designers recognized the strength of the existing Ada 83 type declaration and derivation facilities and so determined that extending the type facility—not, for example, attempting to build C++-style classes by providing a "package type"—was the proper way to provide for inheritance. Indeed, in this way a large increase in expressive power for OOP is achieved with remarkably little additional syntax.

10.4.3.1. Classical Polymorphic Types: Variant Records

Consider a typical Ada application in the software controlling the instrument cluster in an automobile. There are several kinds of instruments; all have some common features but each is also different from the others. A classical solution—in Ada 83 and earlier languages—is to represent the instrument type as a *variant record,* sometimes called a *discriminated record* or, more formally, *discriminated union.* In Ada, given some basic types

```
subtype Speeds is Integer range 0 .. 85; -- mph
subtype Percent is Integer range 0 .. 100;
type InstrumentKinds is (Speedometer, Gauge, Graphic_Gauge);
```

the variant record type might look like

```
type Instrument (Kind: InstrumentKinds) is record
  Name: String(1 .. 14):= "              ";
  case Kind is
    when Speedometer =>
      SpeedValue: Speeds;
    when Gauge =>
      GaugeValue: Percent;
    when Graphic_Gauge =>
      Reading: Percent;
      Size : Integer:= 20;
      Fill : Character:= '*';
      Empty: Character:= '.';
  end case;
end record;
```

The phrase `(Kind: InstrumentKinds)` defines a special record component called the *discriminant;* in other languages, such a field is called a *tag.* The discriminant serves to parameterize the type; a typical variable declaration might be

```
S: Instrument(Kind => Speedometer);
```

which *constrains* `S` to that variant. If I wanted to allow an instrument variable to contain different instruments at different times—to be *unconstrained* or *mutable*—I could provide a default discriminant value in the type declaration, say,

```
type Instrument (Kind: InstrumentKinds := Gauge) is record...
```

in which case I could declare

```
I: Instrument;
```

whose value is *initially* a gauge but could change over time.

In Ada, a variant type declaration *must* include a discriminant component; "free union" types without discriminants such as those in C or Pascal do not exist. Further, Ada rules—whose details I do not belabor here—ensure that in a mutable variant object, the value of the discriminant is always consistent with the actual values in the variant part.

The variant parts are specified with a `case` construct, and operations on variant objects typically use `case` statements to manipulate the variant parts. Variant records represent yet another kind of static polymorphism in that mutable objects can effectively change their type over time and operations can be written that select among the various type possibilities.

The inconvenience in using a variant record type is that if, in the future of the program, a new variant must be added, it must be added to the original type declaration. Worse, each operation that manipulates objects of the type must be explicitly modified with a new case choice to account for the new variant. In many applications, this additional maintenance is quite acceptable; further, the static solution is appealing to developers of real-time systems in which *predictability* of execution time and space overhead is of paramount concern.

For full OOP, programmers are interested precisely in being able to extend a variant type ad infinitum without imposing any changes to existing code. In other words, we are interested in inheritance and dynamic polymorphism. In Ada 95, this is provided by a syntactically simple extension of the type system.

10.4.3.2. Type Extension: Ada 95 Tagged Types

Support in Ada 95 for full inheritance and polymorphism is done using *type extension,* building on the existing type, type derivation, and package capabilities of Ada 83. I introduce this in the context of the automobile instrument cluster mentioned in the last section. By the end of this discussion, I display a dashboard such as

```
Speed          : 45 Miles per Hour
Fuel           : 60 %
Water          : <****************....>
Oil            : <******..............>
Time           : 12:15:00
Chronometer    : <<79976>>
```

using the following type hierarchy:

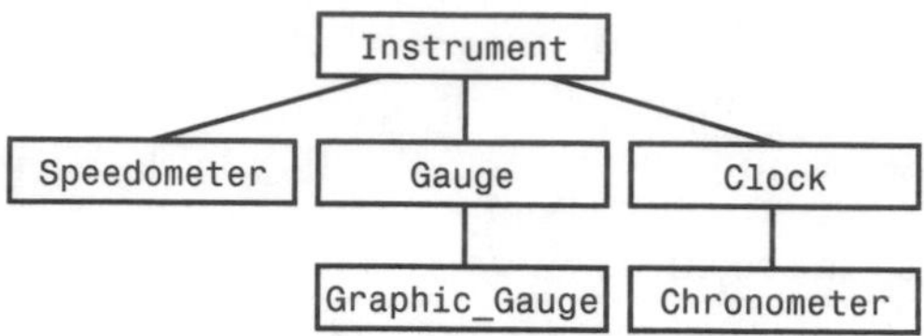

Recall that in the variant-record solution, adding a new variant required adding a new case choice to every operation on objects of the variant type. Using type extension, I can add new variants without touching existing code. `HB.Instruments` is the interface of a package exporting a root type `Instrument`.

```
package HB.Instruments is

  type Instrument is abstract tagged record
    Name: String(1 .. 14):= (others => ' ');
  end record;

  procedure Set_Name(I: in out Instrument; S: String);
  procedure Display_Value(I: Instrument);

end HB.Instruments;
```

The reserved word `tagged` is the key to type extension. Adding it to a record type declaration causes the declaration to function as the root of a type hierarchy. I can derive new types from it, as in the earlier `Credit_Card` example, but now I can also add components to the derived type.

Primitive operations of the parent type—essentially those procedures and functions declared in the same package interface, just after the parent type—are inherited by the child type but can be *overridden* by similar operations with the same name but with formal parameters of the parent type replaced by those of the child type. In this example, `Set_Name` and `Display_Value` are primitive operations of the type `Instrument`.

The reserved word `abstract` mentioned in the type declaration indicates that this type serves simply as a root for derivations; that is, I cannot declare any objects of the type. For an abstract type, it is possible to declare abstract operations; an abstract operation has no function or procedure body and is used simply to serve as a root operation for inheritance. An ordinary primitive operation *can* be overridden; an abstract primitive operation *must* be overridden.

Now the child package `HB.Instruments.Basic` provides a set of three instrument kinds, all derived from `Instrument`.

```
1 package HB.Instruments.Basic is
2
3   subtype Speeds is Integer range 0 .. 85; -- mph
4
5   type Speedometer is new Instrument with record
6     Value: Speeds;
7   end record;
8
9   procedure Set_Value(S: in out Speedometer; V: Speeds);
10  procedure Display_Value(S: Speedometer);
11
12  subtype Percent is Integer range 0 .. 100;
13
14  type Gauge is new Instrument with record
15    Value: Percent;
16  end record;
17
18  procedure Display_Value(G: Gauge);
19
20  type Graphic_Gauge is new Gauge with record
21    Size : Integer:= 20;
22    Fill : Character:= '*';
23    Empty: Character:= '.';
24  end record;
25
26  procedure Display_Value(G: Graphic_Gauge);
27
28 end HB.Instruments.Basic;
```

Lines 5–7 declare a new type `Speedometer`, derived from `Instrument`. Each `Speedometer` object has the name component of `Instrument`, but also an additional component `Value`, specific to the new type. `Speedometer` is not `abstract`; I can declare objects of this type, which of course was just the intent.

The new type has a total of three operations, each in a different category:

- `Set_Name`, which it inherits unchanged from its parent. That is, I have implicitly declared a new operation

  ```
  procedure Set_Name(I: in out Instrument; S: in String);
  ```

- `Set_Value`, a new operation specific to `Speedometer`
- `Display_Value`, a `Speedometer`-specific operation that overrides the corresponding `Instrument` one

Similarly, the type `Gauge`, another extension of `Instrument`, is declared (lines 12–18) with one overriding operation and one inherited one. Now `Graphic_Gauge` is declared (lines 20–24) as an extension of `Gauge`. I now have a three-level hierarchy of types, namely `Instrument`, `Gauge`, and `Graphic_Gauge`.

`HB.Instruments.Clocks` introduces two more instrument types.

```
package HB.Instruments.Clocks is

  subtype Sixty is Integer range 0 .. 60;
  subtype Twenty_Four is Integer range 0 .. 24;

  type Clock is new Instrument with record
    Seconds : Sixty := 0;
    Minutes : Sixty := 0;
    Hours : Twenty_Four := 0;
  end record;

  procedure Display_Value (C : Clock);
  procedure Init (C : in out Clock;
                  H : Twenty_Four := 0;
                  M, S : Sixty := 0);

  procedure Increment(C: in out Clock; Inc: Integer :=1);

  type Chronometer is new Clock with null record;

  procedure Display_Value (C : Chronometer);

end HB.Instruments.Clocks;
```

`Clock` extends `Instrument`. Its operations are `Set_Name` (inherited from `Instrument`), `Display_Value` (overrides the one inherited from `Instrument`), `Init` (new primitive), and `Increment` (new primitive).

Now `Chronometer` extends `Clock`. The construct `with null record` satisfies a rule that a type derived from a tagged type *must* have an extension, even if no new components are added.

Chronometer has the following operations:

- `Set_Name`, inherited from `Clock` but declared higher, with `Instrument`
- `Display_Value`, overriding the one inherited from `Clock`
- `Init` and `Increment`, inherited from `Clock`

That an extensible type has three kinds of primitive operations—inherited from somewhere above it, overriding inherited ones, and new ones—is not unique to Ada, but inherent in the nature of OOP with inheritance, sometimes called "classification-first design."

For large "industrial-strength" type hierarchies, where each object can have many applicable operations, this can lead to real confusion for programmers and for the readers of their programs. For both groups, an important question is "Given an object of type `T`, exactly which operations are applicable to it?" Keeping a mental list of these operations is difficult: Some operations—new and overriding—are declared in the same place with the type, but inherited operations could have been declared *anywhere* above this type in the hierarchy. In comparison, using classical packages—sometimes called "composition-first design"—results in *all* operations of a given type being declared with the type.

The software industry has recognized that here, as almost everywhere in computing, there is no "free lunch" in OOP: There is an important tradeoff between the flexibility of classification-first design and the ease of understanding and maintainability in composition-first design. Systems of nontrivial size will probably use both paradigms. Ada supports both paradigms equally well, so the language need not drive the design.

One might ask why Ada requires the use of `tagged` to indicate an extensible type, that is, why all types—or, at least, all record types—are not potentially extensible. The answer is that extensible types require additional overhead: space for an internal tag, time to distinguish at runtime which of several (potentially many) derived types a given value has, and so forth. Requiring `tagged` supports a key Ada principle: "You don't have to pay for features you don't use."

If a type is *not* tagged, there will *not* be the associated overhead. The compiler will not generate such overhead; the human developer is assured that there will be none. This is very important to developers of real-time systems, to whom knowledge of sources of potential runtime overhead is critical. Finally, compiling an Ada 83 program with an Ada 95 compiler produces no new overhead; an Ada 83 program cannot have tagged types because these do not exist in Ada 83!

10.4.3.4. Using the Instruments Hierarchy: Polymorphic Dispatch

Before examining the implementations of the instruments packages, see how they might be used. Specifically, the next few listings show how to build a linked list of instruments, which will constitute a dashboard. First I give a package interface `HB.Instruments.Aux` (for "auxiliary").

```
with HB.Instruments.Basic, HB.Instruments.Clocks;
use  HB.Instruments.Basic, HB.Instruments.Clocks;
package HB.Instruments.Aux is

```

```
 5    type InstrumentPointer is access all Instrument'Class;
 6
 7    Speed : aliased Speedometer;
 8    Fuel : aliased Gauge;
 9    Oil, Water : aliased Graphic_Gauge;
10    Time : aliased Clock;
11    Chrono : aliased Chronometer;
12
13    SpeedPointer: InstrumentPointer := Speed'Access;
14    FuelPointer:  InstrumentPointer := Fuel'Access;
15    OilPointer:   InstrumentPointer := Oil'Access;
16    WaterPointer: InstrumentPointer := Water'Access;
17    TimePointer:  InstrumentPointer := Time'Access;
18    ChronoPointer:InstrumentPointer := Chrono'Access;
19
20    procedure Display (P: InstrumentPointer);
21
22 end HB.Instruments.Aux;
```

This package declares a general access type `InstrumentPointer` that can designate (point to) instrument objects. The reserved word `all` (in this context) indicates that an object of type `InstrumentPointer` can designate either a statically declared instrument or one whose space is heap-allocated; if `all` were omitted, only heap-allocated objects could be designated.

The designated type `Instrument'Class` consists of the entire type hierarchy of which `Instrument` is the root. An `InstrumentPointer` object can thus be made to point to an object of type `Speedometer`, `Gauge`, `Graphic_Gauge`, `Clock`, or `Chronometer`, or of any additional types that may be derived from any of these in the future. (Recall that `Instrument` itself is `abstract`, so no `Instrument` objects can exist.)

Lines 7–11 declare some objects in the class `Instrument'Class`. The reserved word `aliased` indicates that these statically declared objects may be designated by access objects; omitting aliased would disallow such designation. Lines 13–18 declare some access objects. Each is initialized with a "pointer" to its associated instrument, using the `'Access` attribute.

The procedure `Display` takes an access value as its parameter; its implementation is shown here.

```
package body HB.Instruments.Aux is

  procedure Display (P: InstrumentPointer) is
  begin
    Display_Value (P.all);
  end Display;

end HB.Instruments.Aux;
```

In line 5, the expression `P.all` *dereferences* `P`—that is, finds the object designated by `P`. The type of `P.all` can be anything in `Instrument'Class` and can change each time `Display` is called. Moreover, each type in this class has its own `Display_Value`. Every time line 5 is executed, the actual type of `P.all`, *at that instant,* determines which of many `Display_Value` operations is called. This is an example of *dynamic* or *runtime polymorphism.* The Ada term for this is *dispatching;* line 5 is a *dispatching operation.*

10.4.3.5. Building a Dashboard

I build a dashboard as a linked list of instruments. This linked list is *heterogeneous*; it is a "container" consisting of nodes, each of whose contained object can be a different instrument. Indeed, sometime in the future I could define more instruments, and the list structure must be flexible enough to contain them as well.

I shall use an instance of a generic list package `HB.Lists_Generic`, which supports creating lists like this one:

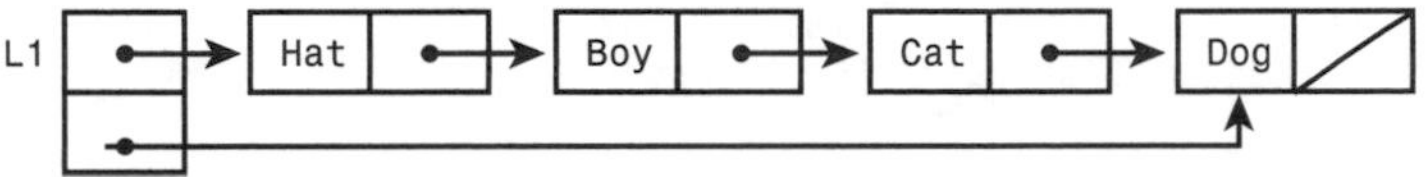

This is an interesting package that illustrates several important concepts.

```
with HB.Lists_Generic;
with HB.Instruments.Aux;
package HB.Dashboards is new HB.Lists_Generic
  (ElementType => HB.Instruments.Aux.InstrumentPointer,
   DisplayElement => HB.Instruments.Aux.Display);
```

`HB.Dashboards` is an instance of `HB.Lists_Generic`. The generic requires a client to supply two parameters. The first, `ElementType`, must specify the type of contained objects; the second, a procedure parameter `DisplayElement`, must specify how to display an element of type `ElementType`.

The instantiated package provides a type `List` and several operations. Of these, I use `AddToEnd`—which, given a list and a contained value, adds a new node containing that value to the tail of the list—and `Display`—which walks through a list node-by-node, displaying all the contained objects.

I now have all the pieces with which to build and display a dashboard; the main program, `Show_Dashboard`, accomplishes the task.

```
with HB.Instruments.Basic; use HB.Instruments.Basic;
with HB.Instruments.Clocks; use HB.Instruments.Clocks;
with HB.Instruments.Aux; use HB.Instruments.Aux;
```

```
 4 with HB.Dashboards; use HB.Dashboards;
 5 procedure Show_Dashboard is
 6
 7    Dashboard : List;
 8
 9 begin
10
11    Set_Name (Speed, "Speed");
12    Set_Name (Fuel, "Fuel");
13    Set_Name (Water, "Water");
14    Set_Name (Oil, "Oil");
15    Set_Name (Time, "Time");
16    Set_Name (Chrono, "Chronometer");
17
18    Speed.Value := 45; --  mph
19    Fuel.Value := 60; --  %
20    Water.Value := 80; -- %
21    Oil.Value := 30; --  %
22    Init (Time, 12, 15, 00);
23    Init (Chrono, 22, 12, 56);
24
25    AddToEnd (Dashboard, SpeedPointer);
26    AddToEnd (Dashboard, FuelPointer);
27    AddToEnd (Dashboard, WaterPointer);
28    AddToEnd (Dashboard, OilPointer);
29    AddToEnd (Dashboard, TimePointer);
30    AddToEnd (Dashboard, ChronoPointer);
31
32    Display (Dashboard);
33
34 end Show_Dashboard;
```

The context clauses do not include the root package `HB.Instruments` because this program makes no direct reference to anything there.

Line 7 declares a list variable; the type `List` is provided by `HB.Dashboards`. The variables `Speed`, `Fuel`, and so on, and their associated pointers `SpeedPointer`, `FuelPointer`, and so on, were declared in `HB.Instruments.Aux`. Lines 11–16 set the various display names; lines 18–23 set various values. Lines 25–30 build the dashboard by adding each of the pointer objects to the list. Finally, line 32 displays the entire dashboard as promised at the start of this discussion. The output, once again, is

```
Speed          : 45 Miles per Hour
Fuel           : 60 %
Water          : <****************....>
Oil            : <******..............>
Time           : 12:15:00
Chronometer    : <<79976>>
```

10.4.3.6. Comments on Pointers in Ada

In building the heterogeneous list, why must the nodes contain pointers to the instrument objects and not the objects themselves? That is, why must I instantiate with `InstrumentPointer` and not something more like `Instrument'Class`? The answer relates to storage allocation. A list node must have a component indicating its contained object; space must be allocated for this object, but how much? I do not know, and cannot know, the space required for each type in `Instrument'Class` because `Instrument` is an extensible type that allows types derived from it to grow indefinitely. On the other hand, pointers are the same size regardless of the size of their designated objects. Ada could have been designed so that these pointers were created implicitly, by the runtime system, but the designers chose to require explicit pointers, to accommodate real-time system designers who prefer not to have pointers generated "behind their backs."

Why are Ada pointers called *access objects*? In other languages, *pointer* has been directly associated with *address*, and also the term acquired a negative reputation because pointers are so easily abused. In Ada, an access value has no direct relationship to an address. Access values and addresses may or may not have the same internal form; this is intentionally left up to the implementer. Further, no arithmetic operations are predefined on access values. This minimizes the likelihood that pointers will point to inappropriate memory locations.

Another important characteristic of Ada pointers is that each pointer object is guaranteed by the standard to have the initial value `Null`, a special value that denotes an "empty" pointer. An execution-time attempt to dereference a `Null` pointer results in `Constraint_Error` being raised. Automatic initialization of pointers ensures that uninitialized pointers containing "garbage" cannot be used to access unpredictable blocks of storage. This makes programs that use pointers inherently safer and also significantly easier to write and debug.

Finally, Ada rules require that any object accessed by `'Access` have a lifetime at least as long as that of the corresponding general access type. This rule prevents a possible dangling pointer. For example, consider this short main program.

```
with HB.Instruments; use HB.Instruments;
with HB.Instruments.Basic; use HB.Instruments.Basic;
procedure Main is
  type Pointer is access all Speedometer;
  Pointer1: Pointer;
```

```
 6 begin
 7   declare
 8     Pointer2: Pointer;
 9     S: aliased Speedometer;
10   begin
11     Pointer2 := S'Access;
12     Pointer1 := Pointer2;
13   end;
14   Pointer1.all.Value := 50;
15 end Main;
```

In the exception-handling example, you observed that you can create frames—`begin`/`end` blocks—within a program unit. In line 7, `declare` opens an inner frame that allows me to declare local entities whose lifetimes begin when their declarations are elaborated and end when control passes through the end of the frame. Local objects are typically stack-allocated, so their space is reclaimed at the end of the frame.

This example has a big problem: `Pointer2` and `S` are allocated and reclaimed in the inner frame, but `Pointer1` is not. This means that in line 14, `Pointer1` is "dangling" and the statement will try to write a value into space that has already been reclaimed. Dangling pointers are usually not this obvious and can be horribly difficult to debug. Luckily, Ada programs such as this are invalid. The compiler rejects programs that use the `'Access` attribute at a level deeper than the one in which the corresponding general access type is declared; this simple rule guarantees that no pointer of this kind can outlive its designated value.

10.4.3.7. Implementation of the Instruments Hierarchy

I return now to the implementations of the various instrument packages.

```
with Ada.Text_IO; use Ada.Text_IO;
package body HB.Instruments is

  procedure Set_Name(I: in out Instrument; S: String) is
  begin
    I.Name (1..S'Length) := S;
  end Set_Name;

  procedure Display_Value(I: Instrument) is
  begin
    New_Line;
    Put(I.Name);
    Put(": ");
  end Display_Value;

end HB.Instruments;
```

The body of `HB.Instruments` is straightforward and contains nothing new. Note that `Display_Value` just displays the string name of the instrument. Next, consider the body of `HB.Instruments.Basic`.

```
 1 with Ada.Text_IO; use Ada.Text_IO;
 2 with Ada.Integer_Text_IO; use Ada.Integer_Text_IO;
 3 package body HB.Instruments.Basic is
 4
 5   procedure Display_Value(S: Speedometer) is
 6   begin
 7     Display_Value(Instrument (S));
 8     Put(S.Value, 1);
 9     Put(" Miles per Hour");
10   end Display_Value;
11
12   procedure Set_Value
13    (S: in out Speedometer; V: Speeds) is
14   begin
15     S.Value := V;
16   end Set_Value;
17
18   procedure Display_Value(G: Gauge) is
19   begin
20     Display_Value(Instrument (G));
21     Put(G.Value, 1);
22     Put(" %");
23   end Display_Value;
24
25   procedure Display_Value(G: Graphic_Gauge) is
26     Lg: constant Integer := G.Size * G.Value / 100;
27     S1: constant String(1 .. Lg) := (others => G.Fill);
28     S2: constant String(Lg + 1 .. G.Size)
29       := (others => G.Empty);
30   begin
31     Display_Value(Instrument (G));
32     Put('<');
33     Put(S1);
34     Put(S2);
35     Put('>');
36   end Display_Value;
37
38 end HB.Instruments.Basic;
```

The code here is entirely familiar except for one new detail. In line 7,

```
Display_Value(Instrument (S));
```

calls the `Display_Value` defined for `Instrument`. To make this happen, its actual parameter is converted to an Instrument value. What happens to the extension component that turned `Instrument` into `Speedometer`? It is effectively stripped off in this *up-conversion* process. In programming languages supporting OOP, up-conversions are common and down-conversions are disallowed. In the package, lines 20 and 31 do similar up-conversions to `Instrument`.

Given the preceding discussion, `HB.Instruments.Clocks` contains much detail but no new concepts at all; it is included just for completeness.

```
with Ada.Text_IO; use Ada.Text_IO;
with Ada.Integer_Text_IO; use Ada.Integer_Text_IO;
package body HB.Instruments.Clocks is

  procedure Display_Value(C: Clock) is
  begin
    Display_Value(Instrument (C));
    if C.Hours < 10 then
      Put('0');
    end if;
    Put(C.Hours,1);
    Put(":");
    if C.Minutes < 10 then
      Put('0');
    end if;
    Put(C.Minutes,1);
    Put(":");
    if C.Seconds < 10 then
      Put('0');
    end if;
    Put(C.Seconds,1);
  end Display_Value;

  procedure Increment
    (C: in out Clock; Inc: Integer:=1) is
    nInc: Integer;
  begin
    C.Seconds :=(C.Seconds + Inc) mod 60;
    nInc :=(C.Seconds + Inc) / 60;
    C.Minutes :=(C.Minutes + nInc) mod 60;
    nInc :=(C.Minutes + nInc) / 60;
    C.Hours :=(C.Hours + nInc) mod 24;
  end Increment;

  procedure Init(C: in out Clock;
                 H: Twenty_Four := 0;
                 M, S: Sixty := 0) is
  begin
    C.Seconds := S;
    C.Minutes := M;
    C.Hours := H;
  end Init;

  procedure Display_Value(C: Chronometer) is
  V: Integer;
  begin
    Display_Value(Instrument (C));
    V := C.Seconds + C.Minutes * 60 + C.Hours * 3600;
    Put("<<");
    Put(V, 1);
    Put(">>");
  end Display_Value;

end HB.Instruments.Clocks;
```

10.4.3.8. Dynamic Data Structures

The dashboard example made use of a generic linked list package, `HB.Lists_Generic`, detailed discussion of which was deferred until this point. Here is the interface of `Lists_Generic`.

```
with Ada.Finalization;
generic
  type ElementType is private;
  with procedure DisplayElement (Item: in ElementType);
package HB.Lists_Generic is

  type List is private;

  procedure MakeEmpty (L : in out List);
  procedure AddToEnd
    (L: in out List; Element: in ElementType);
  function "="(L1, L2: List) return Boolean;
  procedure Display (L: in List);

private

  type ListNode;
  type ListPtr is access ListNode;
  type ListNode is record
    Element: ElementType;
    Next: ListPtr;
  end record;

  type List is new Ada.Finalization.Controlled
  with record
    Head: ListPtr;
    Tail: ListPtr;
  end record;

  procedure Initialize (L : in out List);
  procedure Finalize (L: in out List);
  procedure Adjust (L : in out List);

end HB.Lists_Generic;
```

Like most modern linked-structure systems, this package depends on the language support for dynamic storage allocation. Ada provides for such allocation; the term *storage pool* is used to refer to the "heap" from which blocks of memory are dynamically drawn. Ada also provides for deallocation of individual blocks; a deallocated block is returned to the storage pool.

The Ada standard allows, but does not require, *automatic* deallocation, sometimes called "garbage collection." In simple terms, garbage collection is not required because developers of real-time systems feel strongly that this would lead to unpredictable runtime overhead and therefore prefer that programmers control their own storage reclamation. As you shall see shortly, Ada does provide useful mechanisms to make it easier for programmers to do this reliably.

I return shortly to the meaning of the context clause in line 1. Meanwhile, lines 3 and 4 give, as usual, the generic formal parameters, actuals for which an instantiating client is required to supply. The first parameter is `ElementType`, which describes the kind of object to be contained in each node. Recall from the earlier matrices discussion that in this context, `private` indicates that any type, including a `private` one, but not including a `limited` or `tagged` one, can be supplied to "match" `ElementType` (the dashboard example used `HB.Instruments.Aux.InstrumentPointer`). The second parameter is `DisplayElement`, which describes how to display an object of type `ElementType` (the dashboard case used `HB.Instruments.Aux.Display`).

Now the public part of the interface provides a private type `List` and four operations, just enough to be illustrative. Additional operations would be straightforward linked-list manipulations; I choose here to omit them for brevity's sake.

`MakeEmpty` removes all the nodes in a list and returns them explicitly to the storage pool. In the absence of garbage collection, one cannot simply disconnect a linked list from its header; all the lists's nodes would remain allocated but inaccessible.

`AddToEnd` is straightforward; given an element, this operation just adds a node containing the element to the tail of the list. Display is equally straightforward; it iterates through the list, calling `DisplayElement` at each node.

Before discussing `"="`, I examine the data structures in the `private` section of the interface. First, lines 19–22 describe the node type as a record with an element and a forward link to the next node. This link is of type `NextPtr`. Because Ada requires types to be declared before they are used, line 18

```
type ListPtr is access ListNode;
```

declares the pointer type. Now `ListNode` seems to be used before it is declared. I therefore declare it as an incomplete ("forward") declaration in line 17. This three-part declaration is the conventional Ada idiom for declaring linked structures.

Now lines 24–28 declare the list structure itself as a header block, a pair of pointers designating the first and last nodes, respectively, of the list (I explain shortly why it is an extension of a tagged type `Ada.Finalization.Controlled`).

The overloaded operator (`"="`) is interesting. Given lists `L1` and `L2`, this is a "deep" equality test that returns `True` if and only if the *contents* of the lists are equal, that is, if the element in each node of `L1` is equal to the element in the corresponding node of `L2`. Recall from the `Rationals` discussion that equality-test (and inequality test) are *predefined* for `private` types, so this `"="` overrides the predefined one.

All I can expect of predefined equality is that it will compare these header blocks. If the two header blocks are equal, they are pointing to the same list. If they are unequal, predefined equality will return `False`, of course, but the two lists might still be equal in the "deep" sense I require. I need my own `"="` operator to provide this deep testing.

10.4.3.9. Controlled Types and Finalization

I hinted previously that Ada provides a mechanism that facilitates writing an application-specific garbage-collection scheme. Three activities must be supported:

- Initialization of an object just after its elaboration
- Finalization of the object just before its destruction
- User-defined assignment

This support is embodied in the standard library package `Ada.Finalization`.

```
package Ada.Finalization is

  type Controlled is abstract tagged private;
  procedure Initialize(Object : in out Controlled);
  procedure Adjust    (Object : in out Controlled);
  procedure Finalize  (Object : in out Controlled);

  type Limited_Controlled is
    abstract tagged limited private;
  procedure Initialize
    (Object : in out Limited_Controlled);
  procedure Finalize
    (Object : in out Limited_Controlled);
private
  ... -- not specified by the language
end Ada.Finalization;
```

The type `Ada.Finalization.Controlled` is

- `abstract`—it is a root type; clients cannot declare objects.
- `tagged`—it is extensible; its operations are inherited by types derived from it.
- `private`—its internal structure cannot be directly accessed by a client.

The operations `Initialize`, `Adjust`, and `Finalize` can be overridden for a derived type. They are not abstract operations, however, so they need not be overridden. In this case, the root operations are essentially "no-ops" that have no discernible effect.

How do these operations work? Suppose you have

```
type MyType is new Ada.Finalization.Controlled
  with some_extension

declare
  Object: MyType;
begin
  Object := some_expression;
  ...
end;
```

When control passes into the `declare` block, the declaration of `Object` is elaborated. Because `MyType` is derived from `Controlled`, its (inherited or overriding) `Initialize` operation is now automatically called.

Now control passes to the assignment statement. Three actions occur:

1. `Finalize(Object)` is automatically called to "clean up" `Object` before copying a new value into it.
2. The expression is evaluated and the result copied into `Object`, as usual in an assignment.
3. `Adjust(Object)` is automatically called.

Finally, when control passes out of the block, `Object` goes out of scope and is destroyed (typically, popped off the system stack). Before this happens, `Finalize(Object)` is automatically called.

Suppose `MyType` represents a linked list. Deriving it from `Controlled` allows me to develop my own garbage collection in terms of overriding operations.

- `Finalize` walks through the linked list, returning nodes one-by-one to the storage pool. This means that whenever a list variable goes out of scope, the entire list is reclaimed.
- `Adjust` provides a "deep copy." Given `L1` and `L2`, the assignment `L1:=L2` first deallocates all the nodes of `L1` (because `Finalize(L1)` is called automatically). The assignment itself does a "shallow copy" operation, that is, it just copies the header block of `L2` to `L1`, but the overriding `Adjust` procedure copies its elements into newly allocated and linked nodes.

`Ada.Finalization` provides a clean and easy-to-understand equivalent of the constructor and destructor operations of other languages and moreover provides user-defined assignment in a fashion that is well-integrated with the other operations.

It is now easy to understand the rest of the interface of `HB.Lists_Generic`. The type `List` is derived from `Ada.Finalization.Controlled`. I declare three overriding operations; putting them in the `private` part ensures that a client cannot call them directly.

10.4.3.10. Implementing the Linked List Package

Now I examine the body of `HB.Lists_Generic`, which, given the preceding discussion, is mostly straightforward.

```
with Ada.Unchecked_Deallocation;
package body HB.Lists_Generic is

  procedure Display(L: in List) is
    Current: ListPtr := L.Head;
  begin
    while Current /= Null loop
      DisplayElement(Current.Element);
      Current := Current.Next;
    end loop;
  end Display;

  procedure AddToEnd
    (L: in out List; Element: in ElementType) is
  begin
    if L.Tail = Null then
      L.Tail := new ListNode'(Element, Null);
      L.Head := L.Tail;
    else
      L.Tail.Next := new ListNode'(Element, Null);
      L.Tail := L.Tail.Next;
    end if;
  end AddToEnd;

```

```
  function "="(L1, L2: List) return Boolean is
    Current1: ListPtr := L1.Head;
    Current2: ListPtr := L2.Head;
  begin
    while Current1 /= Null and Current2 /= Null loop
      if Current1.Element /= Current2.Element then
        return False;
      end if;
      Current1 := Current1.Next;
      Current2 := Current2.Next;
    end loop;
    return (Current1 = Null and Current2 = Null);
  end "=";

  procedure Adjust (L: in out List) is
    TempList: List;
    Current: ListPtr;
  begin
    Current := L.Head;
    while Current /= Null loop
      AddToEnd (TempList, Current.Element);
      Current := Current.Next;
    end loop;
    L.Head := TempList.Head;
    L.Tail := TempList.Tail;
    TempList.Head := Null;
    TempList.Tail := Null;
  end Adjust;

  procedure Dispose is
    new Ada.Unchecked_Deallocation
      (Object => ListNode, Name => ListPtr);

  procedure Finalize (L: in out List) is
    Current: ListPtr := L.Head;
    Leading: ListPtr;
  begin
    while Current /= Null loop
      Leading := Current.Next;
      Dispose(Current);
      Current := Leading;
    end loop;
    L.Head := Null;
    L.Tail := Null;
  end Finalize;

  procedure MakeEmpty (L: in out List) is
  begin
    Finalize(L);
  end MakeEmpty;

  procedure Initialize (L: in out List) is
  begin
    Finalize (L);
  end Initialize;

end HB.Lists_Generic;
```

Refer again to the linked list:

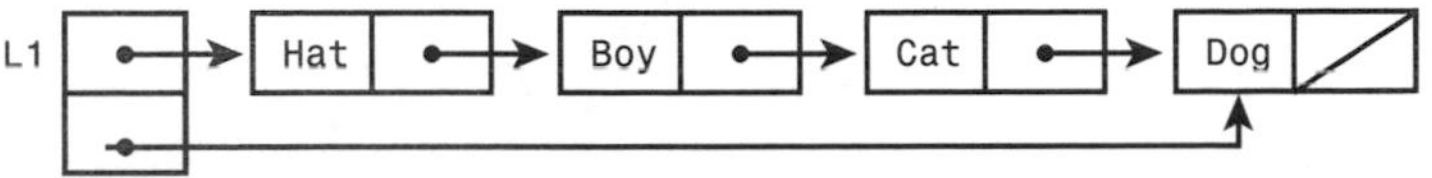

The context clause in line 1 mentions `Ada.Unchecked_Deallocation`. I explain this shortly. Now given a list like the preceding one, it is easy to see that the procedure in lines 4–11 declares a temporary pointer `Current`, initialized to the first node in the list. The `while` loop, in traditional linked-list programming style, walks down the list, calling `DisplayElement` to display each element in turn.

In `AddToEnd` (lines 13–23), I allocate a new node, store the element in it, and connect it to the list. If the list is initially empty, the new node is the first and only one, and

```
L.Tail := new ListNode'(Element, Null);
```

stores in `L.Tail` a pointer to a new (heap-allocated) node with `Element` and `Null` in the corresponding fields. (Strictly speaking, the `Null` could have been omitted because that field is already `Null`; I include it for emphasis.) If the list already contains some nodes, then I connect the new node to the end of the list and change the `Tail` pointer accordingly (lines 20–21).

The overloaded (`"="`) operator (lines 25–37) simply moves two temporary pointers down the two lists in parallel, returning `False` to the calling program if, at a given point in both lists, their elements disagree. The loop iterates until the end of one or both lists is reached. The two lists are equal (line 36) if and only both ends are reached at the same time.

Lines 39–52 give the implementation of the overriding `Adjust` procedure. Because `Adjust` has only one parameter, `L`, I make `Adjust` work as a deep copy operation by copying `L` into a temporary list, `TempList`, using `AddToEnd` in a straightforward `while` loop, and then I copy the head and tail pointers of `TempList` back into `L`. In this manner I return in `L` a list that is distinct from the one received in `L`. Now suppose a client program executes

```
L1 := L2;
```

Because `List` is a controlled type, `L1` is first finalized. Then the header block (head and tail pointers) of `L2` are copied into `L1`. At this point, the `Adjust` is called. The client now has, in `L1`, a complete but distinct copy of `L2`, as desired.

Lines 54–56 instantiate the generic procedure `Ada.Unchecked_Deallocation` to produce a procedure `Dispose`. If `P` and `Q` are of type `ListPtr`, then executing

```
Q := P;
Dispose(P);
```

causes these standard actions:

1. `P` is `Null` after the `Dispose` call.
2. If `P` was already `Null`, the `Dispose` call has no effect.
3. The storage designated by `P` is deallocated. Actually reclaiming the storage is recommended but not required by the standard; practical implementations will, of course, reclaim the storage.

Because `P` is now `Null`, an attempt to dereference `P` raises `Constraint_Error` (as discussed earlier). On the other hand, setting `P` to `Null` does not—cannot—magically set `Q` to `Null`, so `Q` is now a dangling pointer, and the behavior of an attempt to dereference it is *erroneous*. The Ada standard defines erroneous execution as one whose effect is not predictable. In this case, the standard cannot require that dangling pointers be detected at execution time; in general, the overhead to do so would be unacceptable. It is for this reason that the generic procedure is called `Unchecked_Deallocation`; it cannot be expected to check for dangling pointers.

In `HB.Lists_Generic`, the `Dispose` instance is called in the overriding `Finalize` (lines 58–69), in which two temporary pointers, `Current` and `Leading`, are used to walk down the list, calling `Dispose` on each node in turn.

Finally, the exported operation `MakeEmpty`, and the overriding operation `Initialize`, are both implemented (lines 71–79) as simple calls to `Finalize`.

The final set of examples illustrates some of Ada's concurrent programming constructs.

10.4.4. Concurrent Programming

Before examining a concurrent programming example, it is useful to consider the background against which concurrent programming was introduced in Ada 83.

There is still no universally accepted terminology to describe this subdiscipline; various authors disagree on the proper use of *concurrency, parallelism, multitasking*, and other related terms. This is not the place in which to enter at length into this debate. Here I choose to understand the term *concurrent program* as a program in which several things can happen—or at least appear to happen—simultaneously. This usage allows me to focus on program structures without undue concern for either the underlying operating system, or hardware configuration, or intended application.

10.4.4.1. Why Concurrency?

Section 9 of the STEELMAN Report (HOLWG, 1978) is titled *Parallel Processing*. It is interesting to read several paragraphs of that section:

> 9A. Parallel Processing. It shall be possible to define parallel processes. Processes (that is, activation instances of such a definition) may be initiated at any point within the scope of the definition. Each process (activation) must have a name. It shall not be possible to exit the scope of a process name unless the process is terminated (or uninitiated).
>
> 9B. Parallel Process Implementation. The parallel processing facility shall be designed to minimize execution time and space. Processes shall have consistent semantics whether implemented on multicomputers, multiprocessors, or with interleaved execution on a single processor.
>
> 9H. Passing Data. It shall be possible to pass data between processes that do not share variables. It shall be possible to delay such data transfers until both the sending and receiving processes have requested the transfer.

Recall that STEELMAN (HOLWG, 1978) was a requirements document, setting out the desired capabilities of a new programming language. It is clear from the preceding paragraphs that this language was intended to support concurrent processing with constructs that did not depend on either a particular operating system or, indeed, a particular hardware configuration. STEELMAN is, in fact, using the term "parallel" in the sense in which I defined "concurrent" previously. To the STEELMAN authors, it was of critical importance to be able to develop sophisticated concurrent programs, with long life-cycles, that could be recompiled with minimal change for new generations of competitively procured hardware, running new underlying operating systems.

Language-level concurrency was (and to some, still is) a controversial requirement; many argued (and some still do) that concurrency is best handled via straightforward calls to operating-system processes or threads. Opinions aside, it is a fact that Ada's concurrency constructs derive directly from the STEELMAN (HOLWG, 1978) requirements. The Ada designers studied all the research on concurrent programming and developed a practical model as an extended version of the constructs proposed in such lab models as Dijkstra's guarded commands (Dijkstra, 1975) and Hoare's monitors (Hoare, 1974) and Communicating Sequential Processes (CSP; Hoare, 1978).

10.4.4.2. A Concurrent Application

Consider a program containing three independent subtasks, `A`, `B`, and `C`, which are required to execute (or, on a uniprocessor machine, appear to execute) simultaneously. Each subtask executes a given number of cycles; during each cycle, each program rests (idles or "sleeps") a random number of seconds. View the terminal screen as divided vertically into three equal-width "windows"; as each subtask reaches a "nap" period, it displays its state in its own "window."

Because different subtasks are sleeping for different time periods, each subtask must control its own "window" and be able to write into it without interference from the other subtasks. The output from a typical execution might be

```
A nap 7 secs          B nap 9 secs          C nap 5 secs
A nap 10 secs         B nap 1 secs          C nap 3 secs
A nap 1 secs          B nap 1 secs          C nap 1 secs
A nap 6 secs          B nap 10 secs         C nap 7 secs
A nap 1 secs          B nap 3 secs
                      B nap 10 secs
                      B nap 1 secs
```

This program is skeletal without much real functionality; its purpose is to illustrate the Ada concurrency model concisely. The model is very rich, providing a number of constructs I cannot touch on in the space available here.

I construct the program using two packages and a main procedure; I present the package interfaces and main procedure first and then examine the package bodies.

10.4.4.3. A Tasking-Safe Random Number Generator

The "naps" taken by the three subtasks are to be of random duration. The package `HB.Random_Task` provides a random number facility that is "concurrency-safe," that is, it ensures that the random number generator cannot be simultaneously called by more than one subtask. This prevents the seed of the generator from being corrupted by a second call arriving in the midst of a computation. The interface of this package is shown here.

```
1 package HB.Random_Task is
2
3   subtype RandomRange is Natural range 1..10;
4
5   task Randomizer is
6     entry GiveNumber (Result: out RandomRange);
7   end Randomizer;
8
9 end HB.Random_Task;
```

Lines 3–5 give the interface to a task `Randomizer`. The task is Ada's construct for a concurrent subtask. A task cannot be a compilation unit; it must be declared within a package or main unit. A task has an interface and an implementation (body); the task can provide services by means of *entries,* which are called by other tasks. An entry declaration is syntactically similar to a procedure declaration; an entry call is syntactically similar to a procedure call, but its behavior is different. Specifically, the Ada standard ensures that multiple calls to a given task's entries are executed one at a time. Given a variable, in some other task,

```
R: HB.Random_Task.RandomRange;
```

the entry call, in that other task,

```
HB.Random_Task.Randomizer.GiveNumber(Result=>R);
```

deposits in `R` a random number in the range 1..10. Moreover, this call is guaranteed to complete before another is allowed to begin. You will see how this is done when I examine the body of `HB.Random_Task`.

10.4.4.5. A Tasking-Safe Screen Manager

Each of the subtasks must be able to write to its own "window" on the screen. The second package is `HB.Screen`. This package provides a "tasking-safe" manager for the terminal screen, which I assume has ANSI or VT100 screen-control characteristics.

```
package HB.Screen is

  ScreenHeight : constant Integer := 24;
  ScreenWidth : constant Integer := 80;

  subtype Height is Integer range 1..ScreenHeight;
  subtype Width  is Integer range 1..ScreenWidth;

  type Position is record
```

```
    Row   : Height := 1;
    Column: Width := 1;
  end record;

  task Manager is
    entry Beep;
    entry ClearScreen;
    entry Write (Item: in String; Where: in Position);
  end Manager;

end HB.Screen;
```

The package exports a task `Manager` with entries providing `Beep`, `ClearScreen`, and `Write` services. Why is this task necessary?

To write a given string at a given row/column position requires two operations: positioning the cursor at the correct position and writing the string there. Using ANSI standard screen-control commands, positioning the cursor to row 15, column 35 requires me to send, to the terminal, the string

```
ESC [ 15 ; 35 f
```

where `ESC` is the "escape" character and the blanks are included for clarity here but are not sent. This is a total of eight characters; moreover, this control string must be immediately followed by the string to be displayed.

It is fundamental to concurrent programming that wherever multiple processes (threads, tasks) are running and writing to a shared resource (in this case, the standard output file), it is possible that one of the processes will be interrupted (preempted, swapped out) and one of its sibling processes will gain control. If this interruption happens to occur in the midst of a "transaction" to the screen, that is, the command followed by the string, the process gaining control might start another screen transaction. Because the terminal itself has no idea that this has occurred, it interprets the incoming character stream as best it can; this is likely to result in a chaotic mess on the screen because half-completed commands can be randomly intermixed with displayed strings. For example, here is the output from an execution of a similar program without this protection:

```
1;21fA nap 7 secs41fB nap 7 secsC nap 4 secs
                                C nap 4 secs[2;1f21fA nap 4 secsB nap 7
A nap 1 secs    B nap 8 secs    C nap 1 secs
A nap 4 secs    B nap 9 secs    C nap 6 secs
A nap 8 secs    B nap 7 secs
                B nap 5 secs
                B nap 2 secs
```

I cannot allow this chaos to occur, so I must provide *mutual exclusion* that allows at most one task at a time to send a screen transaction and ensures that this transaction is completed before another one is begun.

Implementing the screen services as entries of a task provides the desired mutual exclusion; I return to the details after examining the main program.

A "real" program normally uses a window manager of some sort for this window-like display style. Window managers are, of course, generally provided by platform-dependent application programming interfaces (APIs); it is interesting to note that APIs are not necessarily concurrency-safe, and an API-using concurrent program—in Ada or another language—may well have to provide its own safety mechanisms. I recently developed some multitasking Ada programs using the Apple Macintosh Toolbox API (Feldman, 1997b); the window manager and event handler design required me to develop Ada-level safety mechanisms similar to the one here.

10.4.4.6. The Main Multitask Program

Here is the main program `Show_Tasks`.

```
with Ada.Text_IO;
with HB.Random_Task;
with HB.Screen;
procedure Show_Tasks is

  task type SimpleTask (Message: Character;
                        HowMany: HB.Screen.Height;
                        Column:  HB.Screen.Width) is
    entry StartRunning;
  end SimpleTask;

  task body SimpleTask is
    Nap: HB.Random_Task.RandomRange;
  begin
    accept StartRunning;
    for Count in 1..HowMany loop
      HB.Random_Task.Randomizer.GiveNumber(Result=>Nap);
      HB.Screen.Manager.Write(
        Where => (Row => Count, Column => Column),
        Item => Message & " nap"
                         & Natural'Image(Nap) & " secs");
      delay Duration(Nap);
    end loop;
  end SimpleTask;

  Task_A: SimpleTask
    (Message => 'A', HowMany => 5, Column => 1);
  Task_B: SimpleTask
    (Message => 'B', HowMany => 7, Column => 21);
  Task_C: SimpleTask
    (Message => 'C', HowMany => 4, Column => 41);

begin -- Show_Tasks

  HB.Screen.Manager.ClearScreen;
  Task_B.StartRunning;
```

```
37    Task_A.StartRunning;
38    Task_C.StartRunning;
39
40 end Show_Tasks;
```

In this main unit, I declare the three subtasks. I could as easily have enclosed these in a package but chose to illustrate tasks declared in a main program. Lines 6–10 declare a task type `SimpleTask`. This implies that I can declare task objects; in fact, I do so in this program in lines 26–31. Ada tasks are, in fact, a form of active concurrent objects.

Each task declared in a program is *activated* (starts running) just after control reaches the `begin` of the block in which it is declared; the order of activation is not defined by the language. Each task declared in a package is activated when that package is elaborated, that is, just before control passes to the main procedure. Here, as each task of type `SimpleTask` is activated, the actual parameters (strictly speaking, discriminant values) for `Message`, `HowMany`, and `Column` are passed to it. `Message` indicates the constant message to be displayed in each cycle, `HowMany` indicates the number of cycles this task is to run, and `Column` indicates the screen column in which to display its message.

Because an Ada task is activated implicitly based on the enclosing program's block structure, it is sometimes necessary to inhibit the task from doing any work until this "start button" is "pressed" by an entry call. To illustrate how this is done, `SimpleTask` also provides one entry, `StartRunning`.

Lines 12–24 show the body of the task type. When task objects are declared, each one has (in effect) a copy of this code. Each object may be mapped to an OS-level thread, but the precise mapping depends, of course, on the nature of the underlying OS support. The point is that the application programmer generally has no need to worry about this; the Ada implementation takes care of it just as it takes care of all the other platform dependencies such as memory structures, floating-point arithmetic, and so on.

I choose one task object arbitrarily and follow the execution expressed in the task body. Line 15 says

```
accept StartRunning;
```

Upon reaching an `accept`, a task waits at the accept until the corresponding entry is called by another task. The task is put into a suspended or blocked state, which allows other tasks sharing the same CPU to run. The corresponding entry calls are issued here in lines 36–38. If the start button is never pressed, the task waits forever. I show in the package bodies how to guard against this eventuality.

Lines 16–23 are a simple `for` loop that runs for the desired number of cycles, according to the task's `HowMany` parameter. The task calls for a random number (line 17) and then formats and displays a line via the screen manager (lines 18–21). Finally, line 22,

```
delay Duration(Nap);
```

causes the task to sleep (suspend, block) for the desired number of seconds. The type conversion `Duration(Nap)` is required because the delay period must be of type `Duration`. Note that the nap length—delay period—is recomputed in each cycle, based on the random number. I have used a relative `delay` here, that is, the `delay` is relative to the current time. Ada also provides an absolute `delay until`, whose argument is a `Time` value.

It is important to understand that the Ada standard provides that a task becomes ready at the expiration of a delay period. This means that the task is not blocked and starts running again when it gains control of a CPU. The standard cannot guarantee that a CPU is available at precisely the right instant; this obviously depends on contention with other tasks in the program, or, in a multiprogramming environment, on contention with unrelated programs.

This is a simple example of the general concurrent-programming problem of ensuring that a cyclic process meets its deadline. In real-time system design, this is an important subdiscipline. It is certainly helpful to have clear and platform-independent concurrency constructs in the coding language, but these do not—cannot—substitute for careful analysis and design.

10.4.4.7. Implementing the Random Number Generator

Examine the body of `HB.Random_Task`.

```
with Ada.Numerics.Discrete_Random;
package body HB.Random_Task is

  task body Randomizer is
    package RandomTen is
      new Ada.Numerics.Discrete_Random
        (Result_Subtype => RandomRange);
    G: RandomTen.Generator;
  begin
    RandomTen.Reset(Gen => G);
    loop
      select
        accept GiveNumber (Result: out RandomRange) do
          Result := RandomTen.Random(Gen => G);
        end GiveNumber;
```

```
16        or
17          terminate;
18        end select;
19      end loop;
20    end Randomizer;
21
22 end HB.Random_Task;
```

The context clause mentions `Ada.Numerics.Discrete_Random`. This standard generic library package can be instantiated for any integer or enumeration type or subtype; one could use it, for example, to produce random coin flips of the enumeration type (`Heads, Tails`). Here I instantiate it (lines 6–7) for the `RandomRange` of 1..10.

Using the random number generator requires declaring a generator variable, as I declare `G` in line 8. The type `Generator` is `limited private`; as such, it has no operations except those provided by the package. A generator variable retains the current seed of the number generator, so I can run multiple random number sequences—each with its own generator variable—using the same instance of the package.

The standard provides three ways to initialize a pseudo-random sequence:

- If I do nothing at all, the sequence is initialized with an unknown value that is the same for each initialization. This gives a repeatable pseudo-random sequence.
- If I call `Reset` as in line 10, the sequence is initialized with a value that depends on the current time of day. The pseudo-random sequence is then effectively random because I cannot predict this value, which will obviously be different in successive `Reset` calls.
- If I call `Reset` with two parameters, a generator variable and an integer value, I can make the sequence repeatable by using the same integer value in successive `Reset` calls.

If I had written lines 11–19 as

```
loop
  accept GiveNumber (Result: out RandomRange) do
    Result := RandomTen.Random(Gen => G);
  end GiveNumber;
end loop;
```

the task would loop repeatedly, waiting at the accept in each cycle, until another task called `GiveNumber`. The `accept/do/end` frame is called a *rendezvous;* while this task is executing the rendezvous code, the calling task is blocked and waiting for the result. Once the rendezvous is completed, both tasks become ready and each can run again when it gains control of a CPU.

The Ada runtime system provides a FIFO (first in, first out) queue for each entry of each task. If several other tasks call the entry (quasi) simultaneously—for example, another call arrives while the first caller's rendezvous is being executed—the calls are queued in this entry queue. *One* call is accepted per cycle, so the queued caller is handled in the next cycle.

The simple loop above has no way to terminate, so if, at a given point, no further calls arrive, the task "hangs," waiting at the `accept` for a call that will never come. The `select` statement that enclose the `accept` (lines 12–18) provides two `select` alternatives. The behavior of this strange-looking construct is that calls are accepted as long as they continue to arrive. However, if no calls are pending on the entry, and the other tasks in the program are ready to terminate, then this task terminates as well.

The `terminate` alternative provides a kind of graceful implicit termination of a task. A task also terminates if control passes to the end of its body, so I could use program logic to force this task out of its main loop. For example, I could write a finite one:

```
while the time is earlier than 5 PM loop
   ...
end loop;
```

and the task would terminate just after 5 p.m. The disadvantage here is that I would strand any pending calls. Other strategies are also possible; the programmer has substantial flexibility here.

10.4.4.8. Implementing the Screen Manager

Finally, I present the body of `HB.Screen`.

```
with Ada.Text_IO, Ada.Integer_Text_IO;
use  Ada.Text_IO, Ada.Integer_Text_IO;
package body HB.Screen is

  task body Manager is
  begin
    loop
      select
        accept Beep do
          Put (Item => ASCII.BEL);
          Ada.Text_IO.Flush;
        end Beep;
      or
        accept ClearScreen do
          Put (Item => ASCII.ESC & "[2J");
          Ada.Text_IO.Flush;
        end ClearScreen;
      or
        accept Write
          (Item: in String; Where: in Position) do
          Put (Item => ASCII.ESC & '[');
```

```
          Put (Item => Where.Row, Width => 1);
          Put (Item => ';');
          Put (Item => Where.Column, Width => 1);
          Put (Item => 'f');
          Put(Item => Item);
          Ada.Text_IO.Flush;
        end Write;
      or
        terminate;
      end select;
    end loop;

  end Manager;
end HB.Screen;
```

The task body for `Manager` is similar to that of the random number generator. It is intended to operate as a background task, similar to a device driver, and therefore is allowed to activate. It has a main loop, inside of which is a select statement. This statement is an example of nondeterministic selection and is based on the concurrent programming research of the 1970s, especially CSP and its later implementation in Occam.

In each cycle of the main loop, control reaches the `select`. If no calls are pending on any of the three entries, the task then waits at the `select` for one of these entries to be called and responds to the one that arrives first, entering a rendezvous with the calling task. The `Put` statements in the rendezvous blocks are generally obvious; `Ada.Text_IO.Flush` is used to send the OS output buffer contents directly to the terminal. As before, the calling task blocks during the rendezvous, and furthermore `Manager` can take no other action until the rendezvous completes. This ensures that the screen transaction can be fully sent to the terminal before another begins and prevents the messed-up screen I described earlier.

Once the rendezvous completes, the `select` is satisfied and `Manager` loops back for another cycle. Suppose now that several calls have arrived from different tasks so that at least two of the entry queues have callers pending. In this case, `Manager` makes an arbitrary selection of one of the queues and then enters a rendezvous with the caller at the head of that queue. This arbitrariness—the algorithm for it is not defined by the Ada standard—makes the selection nondeterministic.

Generally, this nondeterminism is desirable; where it is not, the programmer can use Boolean conditions—so-called guard clauses—on the various `accept` alternatives to gain more control. For example, a priority selection can be imposed by guarding one of the queues so that it is not selected unless another queue is empty. This *guarded command* idea was also developed in the laboratory concurrent languages of the 1970s.

The `select` statement here also has a `terminate` alternative, which acts as it did in the random-number example. If no calls are pending on any of the entry queues, and if the other tasks are ready to terminate, `Manager` terminates as well.

It is also possible to set a timer as one of the alternatives, to trigger an action if no other call has occurred within the time-out period. There are other possibilities as well; the select is a "feature-rich" construct.

Ada 95 provides another, complementary, concurrency construct called the *protected type*. Protected objects have behavior similar to tasks in that mutual exclusion is automatically provided for their operations. However, protected objects are less general than tasks. They were designed not as general-purpose concurrency structures, but rather to support the special case of providing very efficient mutual exclusion on relatively simple objects, for high-performance real-time situations. In these special cases, protected operations can be implemented much more efficiently than general rendezvous-based communication. Space does not permit me to go into more detail on these special structures.

10.4.4.9. Comments on Concurrent Programming

It is a fact that even today, there is no effective, working standard, across operating systems, for processes or threads. Even within the UNIX family, syntactic and semantic differences persist between threads libraries. Given this state of affairs, it is far more efficient and reliable for a small group of compiler experts, working with a well-designed platform-independent model, to tailor a compiler and runtime system to a particular hardware/OS platform than for a large community of application programmers to deal explicitly with OS-specific concurrency constructs in every program.

Ada 83 compilers and runtimes were targeted to dozens of different platforms, from small embedded processors to supercomputers, workstation networks, and personal computers. Ada 95 compilers and runtimes support nearly as many targets already. It is not difficult to write a single concurrent program—with no "conditional compilation" for different platforms—that compiles and executes properly on all available platforms.

Indeed, I developed an interesting implementation of the concurrent-programming classic Dining Philosophers (Feldman, 1992) that compiled and ran—without changing a character of source code—on 26 different compiler/OS combinations, using compilers from 12 different vendors. An Ada 95 version of this program is included in the GNAT examples library; it compiles and runs without change using ObjectAda on Windows and also on the 12 GNAT-supported platforms. The GNAT runtime systems on these platforms support Ada-level concurrency using whatever underlying OS thread support is available or a threads emulator if nothing suitable exists at the OS level.

Concurrent programming is an abstraction method, not just an implementation method for real-time systems. It is often said that the world is concurrent, so modeling the world is best done with concurrent programming. Often, performance of concurrent programs is adequate using straightforward, platform-independent constructs. Programs with real-time performance constraints might require some platform-dependent performance tuning, perhaps with the help of facilities provided by the Ada Real-Time Annex; here the maxim applies that "it is much easier to make a correct program fast than to make a fast program correct."

As is the case with all newly designed language structures, in immature Ada 83 compilers, the performance of Ada tasking left much to be desired and caused many developers to abandon tasking for more familiar OS-level operations. Over time, however, compilers and runtime systems have reached maturity and performance of Ada-level concurrency compares favorably with platform-specific calls. As the word spreads on this, developers are taking a second look and beginning to realize just how forward-looking the concurrency model was and how effective it can be.

If STEELMAN (HOLWG, 1978) had failed to require concurrency, and the resulting language had therefore failed to support it, the notion of a common language, in which programs could be written with a high degree of platform independence, would have been significantly undermined. The language would have left developers to write *precisely* the interesting and complex code—the concurrent code—in highly platform-dependent terms. With the current emphasis on multitasking in personal-computer operating systems, and the difficulty many programmers have in coding programs for it, Ada's higher-level constructs have much to offer.

10.5. Bibliography

This selected bibliography is divided in two sections: Ada Web sites and Ada books, articles, and other publications of interest. A textbook bibliography containing brief reviews, and other reference lists, are available on the Web; where texts have their own associated Web sites, links to these are provided in the various online bibliographies.

10.5.1. World Wide Web Resources on Ada

There are five main sites on the World Wide Web intended for use by those interested in Ada. All these sites mirror, or link to, most of the files on the others, but each site is somewhat different from the others in its emphasis and organizational structure.

ACM Special Interest Group on Ada (SIGAda). The major professional organization for those interested in Ada. This is a membership organization, with very attractive rates for students. `http://info.acm.org/sigada`

Ada Information Clearinghouse. The "official" U.S. Government-sponsored Ada site. A good place to look for Ada manuals and other documents. Most of this site is copied to the PAL, but this one is less crowded. `http://sw-eng.falls-church.va.us`

Ada Programming Language Resources for Educators and Students. I maintain this SIGAda-sponsored site that collects the sets of links most useful to educators and students in an easy-to-use fashion. `http://www.acm.org/sigada/education`

Home of the Brave Ada Programmers. A World Wide Web page for anyone interested in Ada. Contains links to the other Internet sites. `http://www.adahome.com`

Public Ada Library (PAL). A comprehensive collection of freely available Ada documents, compilers, tutorials, and source code libraries. Nearly everything Ada-related on the Internet is mirrored to this site. `http://wuarchive.wustl.edu/languages/ada`

10.5.2. Books, Selected Articles, and Other Publications of Interest on Ada 95

Barnes, J. G. P. 1995. *Programming in Ada 95.* Reading, MA: Addison-Wesley. The latest in a series of popular Ada texts by this author. Barnes covers the whole language well and readably, with a fine sense of humor.

Barnes, J. (Ed.). 1997. *Ada 95 Rationale.* Berlin: Springer-Verlag. *Ada 95 Rationale* is the companion to the *Reference Manual* (language standard); it introduces Ada 95 and its attractive new features and explains the rationale behind them. It should be studied in parallel with the *Ada 95 Reference Manual.* Various electronic forms are also available; a searchable HTML version is on the Web.

Beidler, J. 1997. *Data structures and algorithms: An object-oriented approach using Ada 95.* Berlin: Springer-Verlag. An interesting approach to this subject; its special strength is the development in parallel of two libraries of software components, one generics-based, the other inheritance-based.

Burns, A., and A. Wellings. 1995. *Concurrency in Ada.* Cambridge, England: Cambridge University Press. A readable and complete text on concurrent programming and real-time systems in Ada 95.

Burns, A., and A. Wellings. 1997. *Real-time systems and programming languages*. Reading, MA: Addison-Wesley. An excellent text on the issues in designing real-time systems. Ada 95 is emphasized, but other languages such as Occam and various C dialects are also considered.

Cohen, N. 1996. *Ada as a second language,* 2nd ed. New York: McGraw-Hill. An encyclopedic work, over 1100 pages long. Its strength is in its thorough, exhaustive coverage of the language and its realistic examples.

Culwin, F. 1997. *Ada: A developmental approach,* 2nd ed. Englewood Cliffs, NJ: Prentice Hall. A text for students without previous programming experience. The author emphasizes design issues as well as programming.

Dijkstra, E. W. 1975. Guarded commands, nondeterminacy, and formal derivation of programs. *Communications of the ACM 18*(8):453–457. Introduces much of the theory used in the Ada select statement.

English, J. 1997. *Ada 95: The Craft of object-oriented programming.* Englewood Cliffs, NJ: Prentice Hall. This book introduces Ada as a first language, using an example-driven approach that gradually develops small programs into large case studies.

Feldman, M. B. 1992. Portable dining philosophers: a movable feast of concurrency and software engineering. *Proc. 23rd ACM-SIGCSE Technical symposium on computer science education.* Also on the Web at my site.

Feldman, M. B. 1997a. *Ada as a foundation programming language.* This is a frequently updated document reporting the use of Ada in first-year programming courses. Available on the Web.

Feldman, M. B. 1997b. An Ada 95 sort race construction set. *Proc. AdaEurope '97.* Also available on the Web at my site.

Feldman, M. B. 1997c. *Software construction and data structures with Ada 95.* Reading, MA: Addison-Wesley. An undergraduate text focusing on algorithms and data structures with a definite software-engineering flavor and a heavy emphasis on developing generic and polymorphic software components.

Feldman, M. B., and E. B. Koffman. 1996. *Ada 95: Problem solving and program design.* Reading, MA: Addison-Wesley. A text that introduces Ada 95 to readers with no previous programming experience in any language. The text is shipped with an Aonix ObjectAda CD-ROM containing an Ada 95 development system for Windows 95/NT.

Guttag, J. V., E. Horowitz, and D. R. Musser. 1978. Abstract data types and software validation. *Communications of the ACM 21*(12):1048–1064. One of the early papers on abstract data types.

Hoare, C. A. R. 1974. Monitors: An operating system structuring concept. *Communications of the ACM 17*(10):549–557. Introduces much of the theory behind Ada's protected types.

Hoare, C. A. R. 1978. Communicating sequential processes. *Communications of the ACM 21*(8):666–677. Introduces much of the theory behind rendezvous.

HOLWG. 1978. *STEELMAN*. This is the famous requirements document for a new defense programming language, which led to Ada 83. The previous versions of this document were named, in sequence, STRAWMAN, WOODENMAN, TINMAN, and IRONMAN. This document was never accessibly published but is now available on the Web.

Ichbiah, J., et al. 1979a. Preliminary Ada reference manual. *SIGPLAN Notices 14*(6A).

Ichbiah, J., et al. 1979b. Rationale for the design of the Ada programming language. *SIGPLAN Notices 14*(6B).

Ichbiah, J., et al. 1987. *Rationale for the design of the Ada programming language*. Honeywell. Available on the Web at Ada IC.

Johnston, S. 1997. *Ada 95 for C and C++ programmers*. Reading, MA: Addison Wesley. The correspondences between C/C++ idioms and Ada 95 ones are described; both the core language and the annexes are presented. Shipped with the Aonix ObjectAda CD-ROM.

Liskov, B. H., and S. N. Zilles. 1977. Abstraction mechanisms in CLU. *Communications of the ACM 20*(8):564–576. Specification versus implementation.

Lopes, A. V. 1997. *Introcão à Programmacão com Ada 95*, (in Portuguese). Canos RS, Brazil: Editoria ULBRA

Naiditch, D. J. 1995. *Rendezvous with Ada 95*. John Wiley and Sons. (ISBN 0-471-01276-9) A very readable, often humorous, survey of Ada 95.

National Research Council. 1996. *Ada and Beyond: Software Policies for the Department of Defense*. Available from NRC; also on the Web at the Ada IC site.

Paige, E. 1997. *Memorandum of April 29, 1997 on the Use of the Ada Programming Language*. This is the Ada policy announcement by Emmett Paige, Jr., then U.S. Assistant Secretary of Defense for Command, Control, Communications and Intelligence, "to eliminate the mandatory requirement for use of the Ada programming language in favor of an engineering approach to selection of the language to be used."

Rosen, J.-P. 1995. *Méthodes de génie logiciel avec Ada 95* (*Software Engineering Methods with Ada 95*; in French). Paris: InterEditions. Introduces Ada 95 in the context of several important software engineering methodologies.

Skansholm, J. 1997. *Ada from the beginning* (3rd ed.) Reading, MA: Addison-Wesley. This book was one of the first to use Ada with CS1-style pedagogy. There are excellent sections on the idiosyncrasies of interactive I/O (a problem in all languages) and a sufficient number of fully worked examples to satisfy students.

Smith, M. A. 1996. *Object-oriented software in Ada 95*. International Thomson Computer Press. For those interested in pursuing object-oriented programming with Ada 95, this book can serve as an excellent follow-up to the present work.

Stein, D. 1985. *Ada: A life and a legacy.* Cambridge, MA: MIT Press. A biography of the real Ada, after whom the language is named.

Stroustrup, B. 1982. Classes: an abstract data type facility for the C language. *SIGPLAN Notices 17*(1):354–356. An early article on what became C++.

Taft, T. and R. A. Duff (Eds.). 1997. *Ada 95 reference manual.* Berlin: Springer-Verlag. *Ada 95 reference manual* completely documents the Ada 95 standard and thus is an indispensable working companion for anybody using Ada 95 professionally or learning the language systematically. Various electronic forms are also available; a searchable HTML version is on the Web.

Wheeler, D. A. 1997. *Ada 95: The Lovelace tutorial.* Berlin: Springer-Verlag. This book, based on a successful World Wide Web tutorial, introduces the basic elements of Ada 95 to those who already know another programming language.

U.S. Dept. of Defense. 1983. ANSI/MIL-STD-1815A-1983. *Reference manual for the Ada programming language*. This is the definition of the language now called Ada 83. Available on the Web at Ada IC.

Whitaker, W. 1996. Ada—The project: The DoD High Order Language Working Group. *History of programming languages—II*. Reading, MA: Addison-Wesley. This definitive paper, written for the 1993 Second History of Programming Languages Conference (HOPL-II), is also on the Web.

Part VI
Modula-3

11

The Modula-3 Programming Language[1]

by Farshad Nayeri

> *The language designer should be familiar with many alternative features designed by others and should have excellent judgment in choosing the best and rejecting any that are mutually inconsistent....One thing he should not do is to include untried ideas of his own. His task is consolidation, not innovation.*
>
> —*C. A. R. Hoare*

11.1. Preface

If you were to choose *one* programming language for developing and maintaining all your programs, what would it be? Modula-3 is designed to be the answer to this question, as it is a practical programming language for systems development at-large. Based on programming language demographics at the time of press, however, you are likely to have chosen C, C++, Java, Smalltalk, or Ada95. Therefore, some justification is required.

[1]The Modula-3 language specification was designed and written by Luca Cardelli, Jim Donahue, Mick Jordan, Bill Kalsow, and Greg Nelson. Farshad Nayeri edited the language reference for inclusion in this book.

First and foremost, Modula-3 designers emphasized safety unlike the approach taken by the designers of the C programming language. Designed in the late 1980s, Modula-3 is a pioneer in the adoption of the trio of modern systems programming features—garbage collection, exceptions, and threads—which were later popularized by Java. The language design does not stop there; it provides interfaces and modules, a squeaky-clean type-system, and a simple but scalable object system. The well-integrated set of features has resulted in a language that makes code maintenance much more straightforward.

In contrast to the approaches taken by C++ and Ada designers, however, Modula-3 designers refused to give up on simplicity in order to achieve. To combat "featuritis," the designers limited the language definition to 50 pages. (Indeed, the language definition for Modula-3 is the only one that fits into a chapter of this handbook.) This language definition economy has paid off in the long run: It is much easier to build tools for Modula-3, and to maintain the compiler and the runtime. It also made it easier for early developers to build a complete reference implementation of the compiler and the runtime that has stood the test of time.

Last but not least, Modula-3 does not forgo practical systems programming features in order to achieve its foremost goals. This is a an essential differentiating feature of Modula-3 when compared with Smalltalk or Java. Like traditional systems programming language, Modula-3 permits bit arithmetic, untraced pointer references, and unsafe casts. However, to eliminate contamination of safe code, the language only allows unsafe operations in clearly marked *unsafe* modules. In addition, the language design provides a bridge for smooth integration of safe and unsafe code under the same language.

Despite syntactic differences, many of the Modula-3 design ideals were embodied in Java's design, about five years later. Modula-3 has done well on its own, too, especially given the relatively small amount of resources spent on its promotion. Modula-3 has so far met the challenges for developing and maintaining large, high-performance systems quite well, for example, in building life-critical 911 emergency call systems, highly available network object systems, Internet commerce and distribution management systems, high-performance graphics systems, extensible operating systems, and even a commercial-grade Java virtual machine.[2]

---

[2]You can find out more about these by visiting `http://www.m3.org`.

This chapter of the *Handbook of Programming Languages* includes the *entire* language definition for Modula-3.

11.2. Introduction

He that will not apply new remedies must expect new evils: For time is the greatest innovator, and if time or course alters things to the worse, and wisdom and counsel shall not alter them to the better, what shall be the end?

—Francis Bacon

11.2.1. History

On November 6, 1986, Maurice Wilkes wrote to Niklaus Wirth proposing that the Modula-2+ language be revised and standardized as a successor to Modula-2. Wirth gave this project his blessing, and the Modula-3 committee was born.

At the first meeting, the committee unanimously agreed to be true to the spirit of Modula-2 by selecting simple, safe, proven features rather than experimenting with our own untried ideas. We found that unanimity was harder to achieve when we got to the details.

Modula-3 supports interfaces, objects, generics, lightweight threads of control, the isolation of unsafe code, garbage collection, exceptions, and subtyping. Some of the more problematic features of Modula-2 have been removed, such as variant records and the built-in unsigned numeric data type. Modula-3 is substantially simpler than other languages with comparable power.

Modula-3 is closely based on Modula-2+, which was designed at the Digital Equipment Corporation Systems Research Center and used to build the Topaz system. The Modula-3 design was a joint project by Digital and Olivetti. The language definition was published in August 1988 and immediately followed by implementation efforts at both companies. In January 1989, the committee revised the language to reflect the experiences of these implementation teams. A few minor corrections to the language definition were made since then.

11.2.2. Perspective

Most systems programming today is done in the BCPL family of languages, which includes B, Bliss, and C. The beauty of these languages is the modest cost with which they were able to take a great leap forward from assembly language. To fully appreciate them, you must consider the engineering constraints of machines in the 1960s. What language designed in the 1980s has a compiler that fits into 4,000 18-bit words, like Ken Thompson's B compiler for the PDP-7? The most successful of these languages was C, which by the early 1970s had almost completely displaced assembly language in the UNIX system.

The BCPL-like languages are easy to implement efficiently for the same reason they are attractive to skeptical assembly language programmers: They present a programming model that is close to the target machine. Pointers are identified with arrays, and address arithmetic is ubiquitous. Unfortunately, this low-level programming model is inherently dangerous. Many errors are as disastrous as they would be in machine language. The type system is scanty and reveals enough quirks of the target machine that even experienced and disciplined programmers sometimes write unportable code simply by accident. The most modern language in this family, C++, has enriched C by adding objects, but it has also given up C's best virtue—simplicity—without relieving C's worst drawback—its low-level programming model.

At the other extreme are languages such as Lisp, ML, Smalltalk, and CLU, whose programming models originate from mathematics. Lisp is the hybrid of the lambda calculus and the theory of a pairing function; ML stems from polymorphic type theory; Smalltalk from a theory of objects and inheritance; CLU from a theory of abstract data types. These languages have beautiful programming models, but they tend to be difficult to implement efficiently because the uniform treatment of values in the programming model invites a runtime system in which values are uniformly represented by pointers. If the implementer doesn't take steps to avoid it, as simple a statement as `n := n + 1` could require an allocation, a method lookup, or both. Good implementations avoid most of the cost, and languages in this family have been used successfully for systems programming. But their general disposition toward heap allocation rather than stack allocation remains, and they have not become popular with systems programmers. The runtime systems required to make these languages efficient often isolate them in closed environments that cannot accommodate programs written in other languages. If you are a fan of these languages, you may find Modula-3 overly pragmatic, but read on anyway, and give us a chance to show that pragmatic constraints do not exclude attractive solutions.

Between the extremes of BCPL and Lisp is the Algol family of languages, whose modern representatives include Pascal, Ada, Modula-2, and Modula-3. These languages have programming models that reflect the engineering constraints of random-access machines but conceal the details of any particular machine. They give up the beauty and mathematical symmetry of the Lisp family to make efficient implementations possible without special tricks; they also have strong type systems that avoid most of the dangerous and machine-dependent features of the BCPL family.

In the 1960s, the trend in the Algol family was toward features for control flow and data structuring. In the 1970s, the trend was toward information-hiding features such as interfaces, opaque types, and generics. More recently, the trend in the Algol family has been to adopt a careful selection of techniques from the Lisp and BCPL families. This trend is demonstrated by Modula-3, Oberon, and Cedar, to name three languages that have floated portable implementations in the past few years.

Modula-3, Oberon, and Cedar all provide garbage collection, previously viewed as a luxury available only in the closed runtime systems of the Lisp family. The world is starting to understand that garbage collection is the only way to achieve an adequate level of safety, and that modern garbage collectors can work in open runtime environments.

At the same time, these three languages allow a small set of unsafe, machine-dependent operations of the sort usually associated with the BCPL family. In Modula-3, unsafe operations are allowed only in modules explicitly labeled unsafe. The combination of garbage collection with the explicit isolation of unsafe features produces a language suitable for programming entire systems from the highest-level applications down to the lowest-level device drivers.

11.2.3. Features

The following sections give an overview of the most important features of Modula-3.

11.2.3.1. Interfaces

One of Modula-2's most successful features is the provision for explicit interfaces between modules. Interfaces are retained with essentially no changes in Modula-3. An interface to a module is a collection of declarations that reveal the public parts of a module; things in the module that are not declared in the interface are private. A module imports the interfaces it depends on and exports the interface (or, in Modula-3, the interfaces) that it implements.

Interfaces make separate compilation type-safe, but it does them an injustice to look at them in such a limited way. Interfaces make it possible to think about large systems without holding the whole system in your head at once.

Programmers who have never used Modula-style interfaces tend to underestimate them, observing, for example, that anything that can be done with interfaces can also be done with C-style include files. This misses the point: Many things can be done with include files that cannot be done with interfaces. For example, the meaning of an include file can be changed by defining macros in the environment into which it is included. Include files tempt programmers into shortcuts across abstraction boundaries. To keep large programs well structured, you either need superhuman willpower or proper language support for interfaces.

11.2.3.2. Objects

The better we understand our programs, the bigger the building blocks we use to structure them. After the instruction came the statement, after the statement came the procedure, after the procedure came the interface. The next step seems to be the abstract type.

At the theoretical level, an abstract type is a type defined by the specifications of its operations instead of by the representation of its data. As realized in modern programming languages, a value of an abstract type is represented by an object whose operations are implemented by a suite of procedure values called the object's methods. A new object type can be defined as a subtype of an existing type, in which case the new type has all the methods of the old type and possibly new ones as well (inheritance). The new type can provide new implementations for the old methods (overriding).

Objects were invented in the mid-1960s by the farsighted designers of Simula. Objects in Modula-3 are very much like objects in Simula: They are always references, they have both data fields and methods, and they have single inheritance but not multiple inheritance.

Small examples are often used to get across the basic idea: truck as a subtype of vehicle or rectangle as a subtype of polygon. Modula-3 aims at larger systems that illustrate how object types provide structure for large programs. In Modula-3, the main design effort is concentrated into specifying the properties of a single abstract type—a stream of characters or a window on the screen. Then dozens of interfaces and modules are coded that provide useful subtypes of the central abstraction. The abstract type provides the blueprint for a whole family of interfaces and modules. If the central abstraction is well-designed, then useful subtypes can be produced easily, and the original design cost will be repaid with interest.

The combination of object types with Modula-2 opaque types produces something new: the partially opaque type, where some of an object's fields are visible in a scope and others are hidden. Because the committee had no experience with partially opaque types, the first version of Modula-3 restricted them severely, but after a year of experience, it was clear that they were a good thing, and the language was revised to remove the restrictions.

It is possible to use object-oriented techniques even in languages that were not designed to support them by explicitly allocating the data records and method suites. This approach works reasonably smoothly when there are no subtypes; however, it is through subtyping that object-oriented techniques offer the most leverage. The approach works badly when subtyping is needed: Either you allocate the data records for the different parts of the object individually (which is expensive and notationally cumbersome) or you must rely on unchecked type transfers, which is unsafe. Whichever approach is taken, the subtype relations are all in the programmer's head: Only with an object-oriented language is it possible to get object-oriented static type-checking.

11.2.3.3. Generics

A generic module is a template in which some of the imported interfaces are regarded as formal parameters to be bound to actual interfaces when the generic is instantiated. For example, a generic hash table module could be instantiated to produce tables of integers, tables of text strings, or tables of any desired type. The different generic instances are compiled independently: The source program is reused, but the compiled code will generally be different for different instances.

To keep Modula-3 generics simple, they are confined to the module level: Generic procedures and types do not exist in isolation, and generic parameters must be entire interfaces.

In the same spirit of simplicity, there is no separate type-checking associated with generics. Implementations are expected to expand the generic and type-check the result. The alternative would be to invent a polymorphic type system flexible enough to express the constraints on the parameter interfaces that are necessary for the generic body to compile. This has been achieved for ML and CLU, but it has not yet been achieved satisfactorily in the Algol family of languages, where the type systems are less uniform. (The rules associated with Ada generics are too complicated for our taste.)

11.2.3.4. Threads

Dividing a computation into concurrent processes (or threads of control) is a fundamental method of separating concerns. For example, suppose you are programming a terminal emulator with a blinking cursor: The most satisfactory way to separate the cursor blinking code from the rest of the program is to make it a separate thread. Suppose you are augmenting a program with a new module that communicates over a buffered channel. Without threads, the rest of the program will be blocked whenever the new module blocks on its buffer, and conversely, the new module will be unable to service the buffer whenever any other part of the program blocks. If this is unacceptable (as it almost always is), there is no way to add the new module without finding and modifying every statement of the program that might block. These modifications destroy the structure of the program by introducing undesirable dependencies between what would otherwise be independent modules.

The provisions for threads in Modula-2 are weak, amounting essentially to co-routines. Hoare's monitors are a sounder basis for concurrent programming. Monitors were used in Mesa, where they worked well, except that the requirement that a monitored data structure be an entire module was irksome. For example, it is often useful for a monitored data structure to be an object instead of a module. Mesa relaxed this requirement, made a slight change in the details of the semantics of Hoare's Signal primitive, and introduced the Broadcast primitive as a convenience. The Mesa primitives were simplified in the Modula-2+ design, and the result was successful enough to be incorporated with no substantial changes in Modula-3.

A threads package is a tool with a very sharp edge. A common programming error is to access a shared variable without obtaining the necessary lock. This introduces a race condition that can lie dormant throughout testing and strike after the program is shipped. Theoretical work on process algebra has raised hopes that the rendezvous model of concurrency may be safer than the shared memory model, but the experience with Ada, which adopted the rendezvous, lends at best equivocal support for this hope; Ada still allows shared variables, and apparently they are widely used.

11.2.3.5. Safety

A language feature is unsafe if its misuse can corrupt the runtime system so that further execution of the program is not faithful to the language semantics. An example of an unsafe feature is array assignment without bounds checking: If the index is out of bounds, then an arbitrary location can be clobbered and the address space can become fatally corrupted. An error in a safe program can cause the computation to abort with a runtime error message or to give the wrong answer, but it can't cause the computation to crash in a rubble of bits.

Safe programs can share the same address space, each safe from corruption by errors in the others. Getting similar protection for unsafe programs requires placing them in separate address spaces. As large address spaces become available, and programmers use them to produce tightly coupled applications, safety becomes more and more important.

Unfortunately, it is generally impossible to program the lowest levels of a system with complete safety. Neither the compiler nor the runtime system can check the validity of a bus address for an I/O controller, nor can they limit the ensuing havoc if it is invalid. This presents the language designer with a dilemma. If he holds out for safety, then low level code will have to be programmed in another language. But if he adopts unsafe features, then his safety guarantee becomes void everywhere.

The languages of the BCPL family are full of unsafe features; the languages of the Lisp family generally have none (or none that are documented). In this area, Modula-3 follows the lead of Cedar by adopting a small number of unsafe features that are allowed only in modules explicitly labeled unsafe. In a safe module, the compiler prevents any errors that could corrupt the runtime system; in an unsafe module, it is the programmer's responsibility to avoid them.

11.2.3.6. Garbage Collection

A classic unsafe runtime error is to free a data structure that is still reachable by active references (or dangling pointers). The error plants a time bomb that explodes later, when the storage is reused. If on the other hand the programmer fails to free records that have become unreachable, the result will be a storage leak and the computation space will grow without bound. Problems due to dangling pointers and storage leaks tend to persist long after other errors have been found and removed. The only sure way to avoid these problems is the automatic freeing of unreachable storage, or garbage collection.

Modula-3 therefore provides traced references, which are like Modula-2 pointers except that the storage they point to is kept in the traced heap where it will be freed automatically when all references to it are gone.

Another great benefit of garbage collection is that it simplifies interfaces. Without garbage collection, an interface must specify whether the client or the implementation has the responsibility for freeing each allocated reference and the conditions under which it is safe to do so. This can swamp the interface in complexity. For example, Modula-3 supports text strings by a simple required interface Text, rather than with a built-in type. Without garbage collection, this approach would not be nearly as attractive.

New refinements in garbage collection have appeared continually for more than 20 years, but it is still difficult to implement efficiently. For many programs, the programming time saved by simplifying interfaces and eliminating storage leaks and dangling pointers makes garbage collection a bargain, but the lowest levels of a system may not be able to afford it. For example, in SRC's Topaz system, the part of the operating system that manages files and heavy-weight processes relies on garbage collection, but the inner "nub" that implements virtual memory and thread context switching does not. Essentially, all Topaz application programs rely on garbage collection.

For programs that cannot afford garbage collection, Modula-3 provides a set of reference types that are not traced by the garbage collector. In most other respects, traced and untraced references behave identically.

11.2.3.7. Exceptions

An exception is a control construct that exits many scopes at once. Raising an exception exits active scopes repeatedly until a handler is found for the exception and transfers control to the handler. If there is no handler, the computation terminates in some system-dependent way—for example, by entering the debugger.

There are many arguments for and against exceptions, most of which revolve around inconclusive issues of style and taste. One argument in their favor that has the weight of experience behind it is that exceptions are a good way to handle any runtime error that is usually, but not necessarily, fatal. If exceptions are not available, each procedure that might encounter a runtime error must return an additional code to the caller to identify whether an error has occurred. This can be clumsy and has the practical drawback that even careful programmers may inadvertently omit the test for the error return code. The frequency with which returned error codes are ignored has become something of a standing joke in the UNIX/C world. Raising an exception is more robust because it stops the program unless there is an explicit handler for it.

11.2.3.8. Type System

Like all languages in the Algol family, Modula-3 is strongly typed. The basic idea of strong typing is to partition the value space into types, restrict variables to hold values of a single type, and restrict operations to apply to operands of fixed types. In actuality, strong typing is rarely so simple. For example, each of the following complications is present in at least one language of the Algol family: A variable of type `[0..9]` may be safely assigned to an `INTEGER`, but not vice versa (subtyping). Operations such as absolute value may apply both to `REAL`s and to `INTEGER`s instead of to a single type (overloading). The types of literals (for example, `NIL`) can be ambiguous. The type of an expression may be determined by how it is used (target-typing). Type mismatches may cause automatic conversions instead of errors (as when a fractional `REAL` is rounded upon assignment to an integer).

We adopted several principles to make Modula-3's type system as uniform as possible. First, there are no ambiguous types or target-typing: The type of every expression is determined by its subexpressions, not by its use. Second, there are no automatic conversions. In some cases, the representation of a value changes when it is assigned (for example, when assigning to a packed field of a record type), but the abstract value itself is transferred without change. Third, the rules for type compatibility are defined in terms of a single subtype relation. The subtype relation is required for treating objects with inheritance, but it is also useful for defining the type compatibility rules for conventional types.

11.2.3.9. Simplicity

In the early days of the Ada project, a general in the Ada Program Office opined that "obviously the Department of Defense is not interested in an artificially simplified language such as Pascal." Modula-3 represents the opposite point of view. We used every artifice that we could find or invent to make the language simple.

C. A. R. Hoare has suggested that as a rule of thumb, a language is too complicated if it can't be described precisely and readably in 50 pages. The Modula-3 committee elevated this to a design principle: We gave ourselves a "complexity budget" of 50 pages and chose the most useful features that we could accommodate within this budget. In the end, we were over budget by six lines plus the syntax equations. This policy is a bit arbitrary, but there are so many good ideas in programming language design that some kind of arbitrary budget seems necessary to keep a language from getting too complicated.

In retrospect, the features that made the cut were directed toward two main goals. Interfaces, objects, generics, and threads provide fundamental patterns of abstraction that help to structure large programs. The isolation of unsafe code, garbage collection, and exceptions help make programs safer and more robust. Of the techniques that we used to keep the language internally consistent, the most important was the definition of a clean type system based on a subtype relation. There is no special novelty in any one of these features individually, but there is simplicity and power in their combination.

11.3. Definitions

A Modula-3 program specifies a computation that acts on a sequence of digital components called *locations*. A *variable* is a set of locations that represents a mathematical value according to a convention determined by the variable's type. If a value can be represented by some variable of type T, then we say that the value is a member of T and T contains the value.

An *identifier* is a symbol declared as a name for a variable, type, procedure, and so on. The region of the program over which a declaration applies is called the *scope* of the declaration. Scopes can be nested. The meaning of an identifier is determined by the smallest enclosing scope in which the identifier is declared.

An *expression* specifies a computation that produces a value or variable. Expressions that produce variables are called *designators*. A designator can denote either a variable or the value of that variable, depending on the context. Some designators are read-only, which means that they cannot be used in contexts that might change the value of the variable. A designator that is not read-only is called *writable*. Expressions whose values can be determined statically are called *constant expressions*; they are never designators.

A *static error* is an error that the implementation must detect before program execution. Violations of the language definition are static errors unless they are explicitly classified as runtime errors.

A *checked runtime error* is an error that the implementation must detect and report at runtime. The method for reporting such errors is implementation dependent. (If the implementation maps them into exceptions, then a program could handle these exceptions and continue.)

An *unchecked runtime error* is an error that is not guaranteed to be detected and can cause the subsequent behavior of the computation to be arbitrary. Unchecked runtime errors can occur only in unsafe modules.

11.4. Types

I am the voice of today, the herald of tomorrow.... I am the leaden army that conquers the world—I am TYPE.

—Frederic William Goudy

Modula-3 uses structural equivalence, instead of the name equivalence of Modula-2. Two types are the same if their definitions become the same when expanded—that is, when all constant expressions are replaced by their values and all type names are replaced by their definitions. In the case of recursive types, the expansion is the infinite limit of the partial expansions. A type expression is generally allowed wherever a type is required.

A type is empty if it contains no values. For example, `[1..0]` is an empty type. Empty types can be used to build non-empty types (for example, `SET OF [1..0]`, which is not empty because it contains the empty set). It is a static error to declare a variable of an empty type.

Every expression has a statically determined type, which contains every value that the expression can produce. The type of a designator is the type of the variable it produces.

Assignability and type compatibility are defined in terms of a single syntactically specified subtype relation with the property that if `T` is a subtype of `U`, then every member of `T` is a member of `U`. The subtype relation is reflexive and transitive.

Every expression has a unique type, but a value can be a member of many types. For example, the value `6` is a member of both `[0..9]` and `INTEGER`. It would be ambiguous to talk about the type of a value. Thus the phrase type of `x` means type of the expression `x`, whereas `x` is a member of `T` means the value of `x` is a member of `T`.

However, there is one sense in which a value can be said to have a type: Every object or traced reference value includes a code for a type, called the *allocated type* of the reference value. The allocated type is tested by `TYPECASE`. The type constructors and subtyping rules are discussed later in the chapter.

11.4.1. Ordinal Types

There are three kinds of ordinal types: enumerations, subranges, and `INTEGER`. An enumeration type is declared like this:

```
TYPE T = {id1, id2, ..., idn}
```

where the `ids` are distinct identifiers. The type `T` is an ordered set of *n* values; the expression $T.id_i$ denotes the *i*th value of the type in increasing order. The empty enumeration `{}` is allowed.

Integers and enumeration elements are collectively called *ordinal values*. The base type of an ordinal value `v` is `INTEGER` if `v` is an integer; otherwise, it is the unique enumeration type that contains `v`.

A subrange type is declared like this:

```
TYPE T = [Lo..Hi]
```

where `Lo` and `Hi` are two ordinal values with the same base type, called the base type of the subrange. The values of `T` are all the values from `Lo` to `Hi` inclusive. `Lo` and `Hi` must be constant expressions. If `Lo` exceeds `Hi`, the subrange is empty.

The operators `ORD` and `VAL` convert between enumerations and integers. The `VAL` convert, `LAST`, and `NUMBER` applied to an ordinal type return the first element, last element, and number of elements.

Here are the predeclared ordinal types:

`INTEGER`	All integers represented by the implementation
`CARDINAL`	Behaves just like the subrange `[0..LAST(INTEGER)]`
`BOOLEAN`	The enumeration `{FALSE, TRUE}`
`CHAR`	An enumeration containing at least 256 elements

The first 256 elements of type CHAR represent characters in the ISO-Latin-1 code, which is an extension of ASCII. The language does not specify the names of the elements of the CHAR enumeration. The syntax for character literals is specified in the section on literals. FALSE and TRUE are predeclared synonyms for BOOLEAN.FALSE and BOOLEAN.TRUE.

Each distinct enumeration type introduces a new collection of values, but a subrange type reuses the values from the underlying type:

```
TYPE
     T1 = {A, B, C};
     T2 = {A, B, C};
     U1 = [T1.A..T1.C];
     U2 = [T1.A..T2.C]; (* error *)
     V =  {A, B}
```

T1 and T2 are the same type because they have the same *expanded definition*. In particular, T1.C equals T2.C and therefore U1 and U2 are also the same type. But the types T1 and U1 are distinct, although they contain the same values, because the expanded definition of T1 is an enumeration whereas the expanded definition of U1 is a subrange. The type V is a third type whose values V.A and V.B are not related to the values T1.A and T1.B.

11.4.2. Floating-Point Types

There are three floating-point types, which in order of increasing range and precision are REAL, LONGREAL, and EXTENDED. The properties of these types are specified by required interfaces.

11.4.3. Arrays

An *array* is an indexed collection of component variables, called the elements of the array. The indexes are the values of an ordinal type, called the *index type* of the array. The elements all have the same size and the same type, called the *element type* of the array.

There are two kinds of array types, *fixed* and *open*. The length of a fixed array is determined at compile time. The length of an open array type is determined at runtime, when it is allocated or bound. The length cannot be changed thereafter.

The shape of a multidimensional array is the sequence of its lengths in each dimension. More precisely, the shape of an array is its length followed by the shape of any of its elements; the shape of a non-array is the empty sequence.

Arrays are assignable if they have the same element type and shape. If either the source or target of the assignment is an open array, a runtime shape check is required.

A fixed array type declaration has the form:

```
TYPE T = ARRAY Index OF Element
```

where `Index` is an ordinal type and `Element` is any type other than an open array type. The values of type `T` are arrays whose element type is `Element` and whose length is the number of elements of the type `Index`.

If `a` has type `T`, then `a[i]` designates the element of `a` whose position corresponds to the position of `i` in `Index`. For example, consider the declarations:

```
VAR a := ARRAY [1..3] OF REAL {1.0, 2.0, 3.0};
VAR b: ARRAY [-1..1] OF REAL := a;
```

Now `a = b` is `TRUE`; yet `a[1] = 1.0` while `b[1] = 3.0`. The interpretation of indexes is determined by an array's type, not its value; the assignment `b := a` changes `b`'s value, not its type. (This example uses variable initialization and array constructors.)

An expression of the form

```
ARRAY Index1, ..., Indexn OF Element
```

is shorthand for

```
ARRAY Index1 OF ... OF ARRAY Indexn OF Element
```

This shorthand is eliminated from the expanded type definition used to define structural equivalence. An expression of the form $a[i_1, \ldots, i_n]$ is shorthand for $a[i_1]\ldots[i_n]$.

An open array type declaration has the form

```
TYPE T = ARRAY OF Element
```

where `Element` is any type. The values of `T` are arrays whose element type is `Element` and whose length is arbitrary. The index type of an open array is the integer subrange `[0..n-1]`, where `n` is the length of the array.

An open array type can be used only as the type of a formal parameter, the referent of a reference type, the element type of another open array type, or as the type in an array constructor.

Examples of array types:

```
TYPE
  Transform = ARRAY [1..3], [1..3] OF REAL;
  Vector = ARRAY OF REAL;
  SkipTable = ARRAY CHAR OF INTEGER
```

11.4.4. Records

A *record* is a sequence of named variables, called the *fields* of the record. Different fields can have different types. The name and type of each field are statically determined by the record's type. The expression `r.f` designates the field named `f` in the record `r`.

A record type declaration has the form

```
TYPE T = RECORD FieldList END
```

where `FieldList` is a list of field declarations, each of which has the form

```
fieldName: Type := default
```

where `fieldName` is an identifier, `Type` is any non-empty type other than an open array type, and `default` is a constant expression. The field names must be distinct. A record is a member of `T` if it has fields with the given names and types, in the given order, and no other fields. Empty records are allowed.

The constant `default` is a default value used when a record is constructed or allocated. Either `:= default` or `: Type` can be omitted, but not both. If `Type` is omitted, it is taken to be the type of default. If both are present, the value of `default` must be a member of `Type`.

When a series of fields shares the same type and default, any `fieldName` can be a list of identifiers separated by commas. Such a list is shorthand for a list in which the type and default are repeated for each identifier. That is

f_1, ..., f_m: Type := default

is shorthand for

f_1: Type := default; ...; f_m: Type := default

This shorthand is eliminated from the expanded definition of the type. The default values are included.

Examples of record types:

```
TYPE
  Time = RECORD seconds: INTEGER; milliseconds: [0..999]  END;
  Alignment = {Left, Center, Right};
  TextWindowStyle = RECORD
    align              := Alignment.Center;
    font               := Font.Default;
    foreground         := Color.Black;
    background         := Color.White;
    margin, border     := 2
END
```

11.4.5. Packed Types

A declaration of a packed type has the form

```
TYPE T = BITS n FOR Base
```

where `Base` is a type and `n` is an integer-valued constant expression. The values of type `T` are the same as the values of type `Base`, but variables of type `T` that occur in records, objects, or arrays will occupy exactly `n` bits and be packed adjacent to the preceding field or element. For example, a variable of type

```
ARRAY [0..255] OF BITS 1 FOR BOOLEAN
```

is an array of 256 booleans, each of which occupies one bit of storage.

The values allowed for `n` are implementation dependent. An illegal value for `n` is a static error. The legality of a packed type can depend on its context; for example, an implementation could prohibit packed integers from spanning word boundaries.

11.4.6. Sets

A *set* is a collection of values taken from some ordinal type. A set type declaration has the form

```
TYPE T = SET OF Base
```

where `Base` is an ordinal type. The values of `T` are all sets whose elements have type `Base`. For example, a variable whose type is `SET OF [0..1]` can assume the following values:

```
{}  {0}  {1}  {0,1}
```

Implementations are expected to use the same representation for a `SET OF T` as for an `ARRAY T OF BITS 1 FOR BOOLEAN`. Hence, programmers should expect `SET OF [0..1023]` to be practical, but not `SET OF INTEGER`.

11.4.7. References

A *reference* value is either `NIL` or the address of a variable, called the referent.

A reference type is either *traced* or *untraced*. When all traced references to a piece of allocated storage are gone, the implementation reclaims the storage. Two reference types are of the same *reference class* if they are both traced or both untraced. A general type is traced if it is a traced reference type, a record type any of whose field types is traced, an array type whose element type is traced, or a packed type whose underlying unpacked type is traced.

A declaration for a traced reference type has the form:

```
TYPE T = REF Type
```

where `Type` is any type. The values of `T` are traced references to variables of type `Type`, which is called the *referent type* of `T`.

A declaration for an untraced reference type has the form

```
TYPE T = UNTRACED REF Type
```

where `Type` is any untraced type. (This restriction is lifted in unsafe modules.) The values of `T` are the untraced references to variables of type `Type`.

In both the traced and untraced cases, the keyword `REF` can optionally be preceded by `BRANDED b` where `b` is a text constant called the *brand*. Brands distinguish types that would otherwise be the same; they have no other semantic effect. All brands in a program must be distinct. If `BRANDED` is present and `b` is absent, the implementation automatically supplies a unique value for `b`. Explicit brands are useful for persistent data storage.

The following reference types are predeclared:

`REFANY`	Contains all traced references
`ADDRESS`	Contains all untraced references
`NULL`	Contains only `NIL`

The `TYPECASE` statement can be used to test the referent type of a `REFANY` or object, but there is no such test for an `ADDRESS`. Examples of reference types:

```
TYPE
  TextLine = REF ARRAY OF CHAR;
  ControllerHandle = UNTRACED REF RECORD
    status: BITS 8 FOR [0..255];
    filler: BITS 12 FOR [0..0];
    pc: BITS 12 FOR [0..4095]
  END;
  T = BRANDED "ANSI-M3-040776" REF INTEGER;
  Apple = BRANDED REF INTEGER;
  Orange = BRANDED REF INTEGER;
```

11.4.8. Procedures

A procedure is either NIL or a triple consisting of

- The body, which is a statement
- The signature, which specifies the procedure's formal arguments, result type, and raises set (the set of exceptions that the procedure can raise)
- The environment, which is the scope with respect to which variable names in the body will be interpreted

A procedure that returns a result is called a *function* procedure; a procedure that does not return a result is called a *proper* procedure. A *top-level* procedure is a procedure declared in the outermost scope of a module. Any other procedure is a local procedure. A local procedure can be passed as a parameter but not assigned because in a stack implementation, a local procedure becomes invalid when the frame for the procedure containing it is popped.

A *procedure constant* is an identifier declared as a procedure (as opposed to a procedure variable, which is a variable declared with a procedure type).

A procedure type declaration has the form

```
TYPE T = PROCEDURE sig
```

where sig is a signature specification, which has the form

```
(formal1; ...; formaln): R RAISES S
```

- Each $formal_i$ is a formal parameter declaration, as described later in this chapter.
- R is the result type, which can be any type but an open array type. The : R can be omitted, making the signature that of a proper procedure.
- S is the raises set, which is either an explicit set of exceptions with the syntax {E_1, ..., E_n} or the symbol ANY representing the set of all exceptions. If RAISES S is omitted, RAISES {} is assumed.

A formal parameter declaration has the form

```
Mode Name: Type := Default
```

- `Mode` is a parameter mode, which can be `VALUE`, `VAR`, or `READONLY`. If `Mode` is omitted, it defaults to `VALUE`.
- `Name` is an identifier that names the parameter. The parameter names must be distinct.
- `Type` is the type of the parameter.
- `Default` is a constant expression, the default value for the parameter. If `Mode` is `VAR`, `:= Default` must be omitted; otherwise, either `:= Default` or `: Type` can be omitted, but not both. If `Type` is omitted, it is taken to be the type of `Default`. If both are present, the value of `Default` must be a member of `Type`.

When a series of parameters share the same mode, type, and default, `Name` can be a list of identifiers separated by commas. Such a list is shorthand for a list in which the mode and type are repeated for each identifier:

```
Mode v1, ..., vn: Type := Default
```

is shorthand for

```
Mode v1: Type := Default; ...; Mode vn: Type := Default
```

This shorthand is eliminated from the expanded definition of the type. The default values are included.

A procedure value `P` is a member of the type `T` if it is `NIL` or its signature is covered by the signature of `T`, where $\texttt{signature}_1$ covers $\texttt{signature}_2$ if

- They have the same number of parameters, and corresponding parameters have the same type and mode.
- They have the same result type, or neither has a result type.
- The raises set of $\texttt{signature}_1$ contains the raises set of $\texttt{signature}_2$.

The parameter names and defaults affect the type of a procedure, but not its value. For example, consider the declarations:

```
PROCEDURE P(txt: TEXT := "P") =
BEGIN
  Wr.PutText(Stdio.stdout, txt)
END P;
VAR q: PROCEDURE(txt: TEXT := "Q") := P;
```

Now `P = q` is `TRUE`, yet `P()` prints `P` and `q()` prints `Q`. The interpretation of defaulted parameters is determined by a procedure's type, not its value; the assignment `q := P` changes `q`'s value, not its type.

The following are examples of procedure types:

```
TYPE
  Integrand = PROCEDURE (x: REAL): REAL;
  Integrator = PROCEDURE(f: Integrand; lo, hi: REAL): REAL;
  TokenIterator = PROCEDURE(VAR t: Token) RAISES {TokenError};
  RenderProc = PROCEDURE(
    scene: REFANY;
    READONLY t: Transform := Identity)
```

In a procedure type, `RAISES` binds to the closest preceding `PROCEDURE`. That is, the parentheses are required in

```
TYPE T = PROCEDURE (): (PROCEDURE ()) RAISES {}
```

11.4.9. Objects

An *object* is either `NIL` or a reference to a data record paired with a method suite, which is a record of procedures that will accept the object as a first argument.

An object type determines the types of a prefix of the fields of the data record, as if `OBJECT` were `REF RECORD`. But in the case of an object type, the data record can contain additional fields introduced by subtypes of the object type. Similarly, the object type determines a prefix of the method suite, but the suite can contain additional methods introduced by subtypes.

If `o` is an object, then `o.f` designates the data field named `f` in `o`'s data record. If `m` is one of `o`'s methods, an invocation of the form `o.m( ... )` denotes an execution of `o`'s `m` method. An object's methods can be invoked but not read or written.

If `T` is an object type and `m` is the name of one of `T`'s methods, then `T.m` denotes `T`'s `m` method. This notation makes it convenient for a subtype method to invoke the corresponding method of one of its supertypes.

A field or method in a subtype masks any field or method with the same name in the supertype. To access such a masked field, use `NARROW` to view the subtype variable as a member of the supertype, as illustrated later in this chapter.

Object assignment is reference assignment. Objects cannot be dereferenced because the static type of an object variable does not determine the type of its data record. To copy the data record of one object into another, the fields must be assigned individually.

There are two predeclared object types:

```
ROOT            {The traced object type with no fields or methods}
UNTRACED ROOT   {The untraced object type with no fields or methods}
```

The declaration of an object type has the form

```
TYPE T = ST OBJECT Fields METHODS Methods OVERRIDES Overrides END
```

where ST is an optional supertype, Fields is a list of field declarations, exactly as in a record type, Methods is a list of *method declarations*, and Overrides is a list of *method overrides*. The fields of T consist of the fields of ST followed by the fields declared in Fields. The methods of T consist of the methods of ST modified by Overrides and followed by the methods declared in Methods. T has the same reference class as ST.

The names introduced in Fields and Methods must be distinct from one another and from the names overridden in Overrides. If ST is omitted, it defaults to ROOT. If ST is untraced, then the fields must not include traced types. (This restriction is lifted in unsafe modules.) If ST is declared as an opaque type, the declaration of T is legal only in scopes where ST's concrete type is known to be an object type.

The keyword OBJECT can optionally be preceded by BRANDED or by BRANDED b, where b is a text constant. The meaning is the same as in non-object reference types.

A method declaration has the form

```
m sig := proc
```

where m is an identifier, sig is a procedure signature, and proc is a top-level procedure constant. It specifies that T's m method has signature sig and value proc. If := proc is omitted, := NIL is assumed. If proc is non-nil, its first parameter must have mode VALUE and type some supertype of T, and dropping its first parameter must result in a signature that is covered by sig.

A method override has the form

```
m := proc
```

where m is the name of a method of the supertype ST and proc is a top-level procedure constant. It specifies that the m method for T is proc, rather than ST.m. If proc is non-nil, its first parameter must have mode VALUE and type some supertype of T, and dropping its first parameter must result in a signature that is covered by the signature of ST's m method.

Consider the following declarations:

```
TYPE
  A = OBJECT a: INTEGER; METHODS p() END;
  AB = A OBJECT b: INTEGER END;
  PROCEDURE Pa(self: A) = ... ;
  PROCEDURE Pab(self: AB) = ... ;
```

The procedures Pa and Pab are candidate values for the p methods of objects of types A and AB:

```
TYPE T1 = AB OBJECT OVERRIDES p := Pab END
```

declares a type with an AB data record and a p method that expects an AB.T1 is a valid subtype of AB. Similarly,

```
TYPE T2 = A OBJECT OVERRIDES p := Pa END
```

declares a type with an A data record and a method that expects an A. T2 is a valid subtype of A. A more interesting example is

```
TYPE T3 = AB OBJECT OVERRIDES p := Pa END
```

which declares a type with an AB data record and a p method that expects an A. Because every AB is an A, the method is not too choosy for the objects in which it will be placed. T3 is a valid subtype of AB. In contrast,

```
TYPE T4 = A OBJECT OVERRIDES p := Pab END
```

attempts to declare a type with an A data record and a method that expects an AB; because not every A is an AB, the method is too choosy for the objects in which it would be placed. The declaration of T4 is a static error.

The following example illustrates the difference between declaring a new method and overriding an existing method. After the declarations

```
TYPE
  A = OBJECT METHODS m() := P END;
  B = A OBJECT OVERRIDES m := Q END;
  C = A OBJECT METHODS m() := Q END;
VAR
  a := NEW(A); b := NEW(B); c := NEW(C);
```

we have that

a.m() activates P(a)

b.m() activates Q(b)

c.m() activates Q(c)

So far there is no difference between overriding and extending. But c's method suite has two methods, whereas b's has only one, as can be revealed if b and c are viewed as members of type A:

NARROW(b, A).m() activates Q(b)

NARROW(c, A).m() activates P(c)

Here, NARROW is used to view a variable of a subtype as a value of its supertype. It is more often used for the opposite purpose when it requires a runtime check.

The last example uses object subtyping to define reusable queues. First the interface:

```
TYPE
     Queue = RECORD head, tail: Queue Elem END;
     QueueElem = OBJECT link: QueueElem END;
  PROCEDURE Insert (VAR q: Queue; x: QueueElem);
  PROCEDURE Delete (VAR q: Queue): QueueElem;
  PROCEDURE Clear (VAR q: Queue);
```

Then a sample client:

```
TYPE
  IntQueueElem = QueueElem OBJECT val: INTEGER END;
VAR
  q: Queue;
  x: IntQueueElem;
   ...
  Clear(q);
  x := NEW(IntQueueElem, val := 6);
  Insert(q, x);
  ...
  x := Delete(q)
```

Passing x to Insert is safe because every IntQueueElem is a QueueElem. Assigning the result of Delete to x cannot be guaranteed valid at compile time because other subtypes of QueueElem can be inserted into q, but the assignment will produce a checked runtime error if the source value is not a member of the target type. Thus IntQueueElem bears the same relation to QueueElem as [0..9] bears to INTEGER.

11.4.10. Subtyping Rules

We write T <: U to indicate that T is a subtype of U and U is a supertype of T.

If T <: U, then every value of type T is also a value of type U. The converse does not hold: For example, a record or array type with packed fields contains the same values as the corresponding type with unpacked fields, but there is no subtype relation between them. This section presents the rules that define the subtyping relation.

For ordinal types `T` and `U`, we have `T <: U` if they have the same basetype and every member of `T` is a member of `U`. That is, subtyping on ordinal types reflects the subset relation on the value sets.

For array types,

```
(ARRAY OF)^m ARRAY J_1 OF ... ARRAY J_n OF ARRAY K_1 OF ... ARRAY K_p OF T
     <:
       (ARRAY OF)^m (ARRAY OF)^n ARRAY I_1 OF ... ARRAY I_p OF T

  if NUMBER(I_i) = NUMBER(K_i) for i = 1, ..., p.
```

That is, an array type `A` is a subtype of an array type `B` if they have the same ultimate element type and the same number of dimensions, and for each dimension, either both are open (as in the first *m* dimensions), or `A` is fixed and `B` is open (as in the next *n* dimensions), or they are both fixed and have the same size (as in the last *p* dimensions).

For reference types,

```
NULL <: REF T <: REFANY
NULL <: UNTRACED REF T <: ADDRESS
```

That is, `REFANY` and `ADDRESS` contain all traced and untraced references, respectively, and `NIL` is a member of every reference type. These rules also apply to branded types.

For procedure types,

```
NULL <: PROCEDURE(A): R RAISES S for any A, R, and S.
```

That is, `NIL` is a member of every procedure type.

```
PROCEDURE(A): Q RAISES E <: PROCEDURE(B): R RAISES F
if signature (B): R RAISES F covers signature (A): Q RAISES E.
```

That is, for procedure types, `T <: U` if they are the same except for parameter names, defaults, and the raises set, and the raises set for `T` is contained in the raises set for `U`.

For object types,

```
ROOT <: REFANY
UNTRACED ROOT <: ADDRESS
NULL <: T OBJECT ... END <: T
```

That is, every object is a reference, `NIL` is a member of every object type, and every subtype is included in its supertype. The third rule also applies to branded types.

For packed types,

```
BITS n FOR T <: T
```

and

```
T <: BITS n FOR T
```

That is, `BITS FOR T` has the same values as `T`.

Finally, for all types,

```
T <: T for all T
T <: U and U <: V implies T <: V for all T, U, V.
```

That is, `<:` is reflexive and transitive.

Note that `T <: U` and `U <: T` does not imply that `T` and `U` are the same because the subtype relation is unaffected by parameter names, default values, and packing.

For example, consider the following:

```
TYPE
  T = [0..255];
  U = BITS 8 FOR [0..255];
  AT = ARRAY OF T;
  AU = ARRAY OF U;
```

The types `T` and `U` are subtypes of one another but are not the same. The types `AT` and `AU` are unrelated by the subtype relation.

11.4.11. Predeclared Opaque Types

The language predeclares the two types:

```
TEXT    <: REFANY
MUTEX    <: ROOT
```

which represent text strings and mutual exclusion semaphores, respectively. These are opaque types. Their properties are specified in the required interfaces `Text` and `Thread`.

11.5. Statements

Look into any carpenter's tool-bag and see how many different hammers, chisels, planes, and screwdrivers he keeps there—not for ostentation or luxury, but for different sorts of jobs.

—Robert Graves and Alan Hodge

Executing a statement produces a computation that can halt (normal outcome), raise an exception, cause a checked runtime error, or loop forever. If the outcome is an exception, it can optionally be paired with an argument.

We define the semantics of `EXIT` and `RETURN` with exceptions called the *exit-exception* and the *return-exception*. The exit-exception takes no argument; the return-exception takes an argument of arbitrary type. Programs cannot name these exceptions explicitly.

Implementations should speed up normal outcomes at the expense of exceptions (except for the return-exception and exit-exception). Expending a thousand instructions per exception raised to save one instruction per procedure call would be reasonable.

If an expression is evaluated as part of the execution of a statement, and the evaluation raises an exception, then the exception becomes the outcome of the statement.

The empty statement is a no-op. In this chapter, empty statements are written `(*skip*)`.

11.5.1. Assignment

To specify the type-checking of assignment statements, we need to define *assignable*, which is a relation between types and types, between expressions and variables, and between expressions and types.

A type `T` is assignable to a type `U` if

- `T <: U`.
- `U <: T` and `T` is an array or a reference type other than `ADDRESS`. (This restriction is lifted in unsafe modules.)
- `T` and `U` are ordinal types with at least one member in common.

An expression `e` is assignable to a variable `v` if

- The type of `e` is assignable to the type of `v`.
- The value of `e` is a member of the type of `v` and is not a local procedure, and if it is an array, then it has the same shape as `v`.

The first point can be checked statically; the others generally require runtime checks. Because there is no way to determine statically whether the value of a procedure parameter is local or global, assigning a local procedure is a runtime rather than a static error.

An expression e is assignable to a type T if e is assignable to some variable of type T. (If T is not an open array type, this is the same as saying that e is assignable to any variable of type T.)

An assignment statement has the form

```
v := e
```

where v is a writable designator and e is an expression assignable to the variable designated by v. The statement sets v to the value of e. The order of evaluation of v and e is undefined, but e will be evaluated before v is updated. In particular, if v and e are overlapping subarrays, the assignment is performed in such a way that no element is used as a target before it is used as a source.

Examples of assignments:

```
VAR
  x: REFANY;
  a: REF INTEGER;
  b: REF BOOLEAN;
  a := b; (* static error *)
  x := a; (* no possible error *)
  a := x (* possible checked runtime error *)
```

The same comments would apply if x had an ordinal type with non-overlapping subranges a and b or if x had an object type and a and b had incompatible subtypes. The type ADDRESS is treated differently from other reference types because a runtime check cannot be performed on the assignment of raw addresses:

```
VAR
  x: ADDRESS;
  a: UNTRACED REF INTEGER;
  b: UNTRACED REF BOOLEAN;
  a := b; (* static error *)
  x := a; (* no possible error *)
  a := x (* static error in safe modules *)
```

11.5.2. Procedure Calls

A procedure call has the form

```
P(Bindings)
```

where P is a procedure-valued expression and Bindings is a list of keyword or positional bindings. A keyword binding has the form name := actual, where actual is an expression and name is an identifier. A positional binding has the form actual, where actual is an expression. When keyword and positional bindings are mixed in a call, the positional bindings must precede the keyword bindings. If the list of bindings is empty, the parentheses are still required.

The list of bindings is rewritten to fit the signature of `P`'s type as follows: First, each positional binding `actual` is converted and added to the list of keyword bindings by supplying the name of the `i`th formal parameter, where `actual` is the `i`th binding in `Bindings`. Second, for each parameter that has a default and is not bound after the first step, the binding `name := default` is added to the list of bindings, where `name` is the name of the parameter and `default` is its default value. The rewritten list of bindings must bind only formal parameters and must bind each formal parameter exactly once. For example, suppose that the type of `P` is

```
PROCEDURE(ch: CHAR; n: INTEGER := 0)
```

Then the following calls are all equivalent:

```
P('a', 0)
P('a')
P(ch := 'a')
P(n := 0, ch := 'a')
P('a', n := 0)
```

The call `P()` is illegal because it doesn't bind `ch`. The call `P(n := 0, 'a')` is illegal because it has a keyword parameter before a positional parameter.

For a `READONLY` or `VALUE` parameter, the actual can be any expression assignable to the type of the formal (except that the prohibition against assigning local procedures is relaxed). For a `VAR` parameter, the actual must be a writable designator whose type is the same as that of the formal, or, in case of a `VAR` array parameter, assignable to that of the formal (see section 11.7.3).

A `VAR` formal is bound to the variable designated by the corresponding actual; that is, it is aliased. A `VALUE` formal is bound to a variable with an unused location and initialized to the value of the corresponding actual. A `READONLY` formal is treated as a `VAR` formal if the actual is a designator and the type of the actual is the same as the type of the formal (or an array type that is assignable to the type of the formal); otherwise, it is treated as a `VALUE` formal.

Implementations are allowed to forbid `VAR` or `READONLY` parameters of packed types.

To execute the call, the procedure `P` and its arguments are evaluated, the formal parameters are bound, and the body of the procedure is executed. The order of evaluation of `P` and its actual arguments is undefined. It is a checked runtime error to call an undefined or `NIL` procedure.

It is a checked runtime error for a procedure to raise an exception not included in its raises set (if an implementation maps this runtime error into an exception, the exception is implicitly included in all RAISES clauses) or for a function procedure to fail to return a result.

A procedure call is a statement only if the procedure is proper. To call a function procedure and discard its result, use EVAL.

A procedure call can also have the form

```
o.m(Bindings)
```

where o is an object and m names one of o's methods. This is equivalent to

```
(o's m method) (o, Bindings)
```

11.5.3. EVAL

An EVAL statement has the form

```
EVAL e
```

where e is an expression. The effect is to evaluate e and ignore the result, as in:

```
EVAL Thread.Fork(p)
```

11.5.4. Block Statements

A block statement has the form

```
Decls BEGIN S END
```

where Decls is a sequence of declarations and S is a statement. The block introduces the constants, types, variables, and procedures declared in Decls and then executes S. The scope of the declared names is the block.

11.5.5. Sequential Composition

A statement of the form

S_1; S_2

executes S_1 and then if the outcome is normal, executes S_2. If the outcome of S_1 is an exception, S_2 is ignored.

Some programmers use the semicolon as a statement terminator, some as a statement separator. Similarly, some use the vertical bar in case statements as a case initiator, some as a separator. Modula-3 allows both styles. This chapter uses both operators as separators.

11.5.6. RAISE

A RAISE statement without an argument has the form

```
RAISE e
```

where e is an exception that takes no argument. The outcome of the statement is the exception e. A RAISE statement with an argument has the form

```
RAISE e(x)
```

where e is an exception that takes an argument and x is an expression assignable to e's argument type. The outcome is the exception e paired with the argument x.

11.5.7. TRY-EXCEPT

A TRY-EXCEPT statement has the form

```
TRY
    Body
EXCEPT
    id1 (v1) => Handler1
| ...
| idn (vn) => Handlern
ELSE Handler0
END
```

where Body and each Handler are statements, each id names an exception, and each v_i is an identifier. The ELSE $Handler_0$ and each (v_i) are optional. It is a static error for an exception to be named more than once in the list of ids.

The statement executes Body. If the outcome is normal, the except clause is ignored. If Body raises any listed exception id_i, then $Handler_i$ is executed. If Body raises any other exception and ELSE $Handler_0$ is present, then it is executed. In either case, the outcome of the TRY statement is the outcome of the selected handler. If Body raises an unlisted exception and ELSE $Handler_0$ is absent, then the outcome of the TRY statement is the exception raised by Body.

Each (v_i) declares a variable whose type is the argument type of the exception id_i and whose scope is $Handler_i$. When an exception id_i paired with an argument x is handled, v_i is initialized to x before $Handler_i$ is executed. It is a static error to include (v_i) if exception id_i does not take an argument.

If (v_i) is absent, then id_i can be a list of exceptions separated by commas, as shorthand for a list in which the rest of the handler is repeated for each exception:

```
id1, ..., idn => Handler
```

is shorthand for

```
id1 => Handler | ... | idn => Handler
```

It is a checked runtime error to raise an exception outside the dynamic scope of a handler for that exception. A TRY EXCEPT ELSE counts as a handler for all exceptions.

11.5.8. TRY-FINALLY

A statement of the form

```
TRY S1 FINALLY S2 END
```

executes statement S_1 and then statement S_2. If the outcome of S_1 is normal, the TRY statement is equivalent to S_1; S_2. If the outcome of S_1 is an exception and the outcome of S_2 is normal, the exception from S_1 is reraised after S_2 is executed. If both outcomes are exceptions, the outcome of the TRY is the exception from S_2.

11.5.9. LOOP

A statement of the form

```
LOOP S END
```

repeatedly executes S until it raises the exit-exception. Informally, it is like

```
TRY S; S; S; ... EXCEPT exit-exception => (*skip*) END
```

11.5.10. EXIT

The statement

```
EXIT
```

raises the exit-exception. An EXIT statement must be textually enclosed by a LOOP, WHILE, REPEAT, or FOR statement.

We define EXIT and RETURN in terms of exceptions in order to specify their interaction with the exception-handling statements. As a pathological example, consider the following code, which is an elaborate infinite loop:

```
LOOP
  TRY
  TRY EXIT FINALLY RAISE E END
  EXCEPT
    E => (*skip*)
  END
END
```

11.5.11. RETURN

A RETURN statement for a proper procedure has the form

```
RETURN
```

The statement raises the return-exception without an argument. It is allowed only in the body of a proper procedure.

A RETURN statement for a function procedure has the form

```
RETURN Expr
```

where Expr is an expression assignable to the result type of the procedure. The statement raises the return-exception with the argument Expr. It is allowed only in the body of a function procedure.

Failure to return a value from a function procedure is a checked runtime error.

The effect of raising the return exception is to terminate the current procedure activation. To be precise, a call on a proper procedure with body B is equivalent (after binding the arguments) to

```
TRY B EXCEPT return-exception => (*skip*) END
```

A call on a function procedure with body B is equivalent to

```
TRY
  B; (error: no returned value)
EXCEPT
  return-exception (v) => (the result becomes v)
END
```

11.5.12. IF

An IF statement has the form

```
IF B1 THEN S1
ELSIF B2 THEN S2
...
ELSIF Bn THEN Sn
ELSE S0
END
```

where the Bs are boolean expressions and the Ss are statements. The ELSE S_0 and each ELSIF B_i THEN S_i are optional.

The statement evaluates the Bs in order until some B_i evaluates to TRUE and then executes S_i. If none of the expressions evaluates to TRUE and ELSE S_0 is present, S_0 is executed. If none of the expressions evaluates to TRUE and ELSE S_0 is absent, the statement is a no-op (except for any side effects of the Bs).

11.5.13. WHILE

If B is an expression of type BOOLEAN and S is a statement:

```
WHILE B DO S END
```

is shorthand for

```
LOOP IF B THEN S ELSE EXIT END END
```

11.5.14. REPEAT

If B is an expression of type BOOLEAN and S is a statement:

```
REPEAT S UNTIL B
```

is shorthand for

```
LOOP S; IF B THEN EXIT END END
```

11.5.15. WITH

A WITH statement has the form

```
WITH id = e DO S END
```

where id is an identifier, e an expression, and S a statement. The statement declares id with scope S as an alias for the variable e or as a readonly name for the value e. The expression e is evaluated once at entry to the WITH statement.

The statement is like the procedure call P(e), where P is declared as

```
PROCEDURE P(mode id: type of e) = BEGIN S END P;
```

If e is a writable designator, mode is VAR; otherwise, mode is READONLY. The only difference between the WITH statement and the call P(e) is that free variables, RETURNs, and EXITs that occur in the WITH statement are interpreted in the context of the WITH statement, not in the context of P (see Section 11.7.3).

A single WITH can contain multiple bindings, which are evaluated sequentially. That is, WITH id_1 = e_1, id_2 = e_2, ... is equivalent to WITH id_1 = e_1 DO WITH id_2 = e_2 DO ....

11.5.16. FOR

A FOR statement has the form

```
FOR id := first TO last BY step DO S END
```

where `id` is an identifier, `first` and `last` are ordinal expressions with the same base type, `step` is an integer-valued expression, and `S` is a statement. `BY step` is optional; if omitted, `step` defaults to `1`.

The identifier `id` denotes a readonly variable whose scope is `S` and whose type is the common basetype of `first` and `last`.

If `id` is an integer, the statement steps `id` through the values `first`, `first+step`, `first+2*step`, and so on, stopping when the value of `id` passes `last`. `S` executes once for each value; if the sequence of values is empty, `S` never executes. The expressions `first`, `last`, and `step` are evaluated once before the loop is entered. If `step` is negative, the `loop` iterates downward.

The case in which `id` is an element of an enumeration is similar. In either case, the semantics are defined precisely by the following rewriting, in which `T` is the type of `id` and in which `i`, `done`, and `delta` stand for variables that do not occur in the `FOR` statement:

```
VAR
  i := ORD(first); done := ORD(last); delta := step;
BEGIN
  IF delta >= 0 THEN
    WHILE i <= done DO
      WITH id = VAL(i, T) DO S END; INC(i, delta)
    END
  ELSE
    WHILE i >= done DO
      WITH id = VAL(i, T) DO S END; INC(i, delta)
    END
  END
END
```

If the upper bound of the loop is `LAST(INTEGER)`, it should be rewritten as a `WHILE` loop to avoid overflow.

11.5.17. CASE

A `CASE` statement has the form

```
CASE Expr OF
  L1  => S1
| ...
| Ln => Sn
ELSE S0
END
```

where `Expr` is an expression whose type is an ordinal type and each `L` is a list of constant expressions or ranges of constant expressions denoted by $e_1..e_2$, which represent the values from e_1 to e_2 inclusive. If e_1 exceeds e_2, the range is empty. It is a static error if the sets represented by any two `L`s overlap or if the value of any of the constant expressions is not a member of the type of `Expr`. The `ELSE` S_0 is optional.

The statement evaluates Expr. If the resulting value is in any L_i, then S_i is executed. If the value is in no L_i and ELSE S_0 is present, then it is executed. If the value is in no L_i and ELSE S_0 is absent, a checked runtime error occurs.

11.5.18. TYPECASE

A TYPECASE statement has the form

```
TYPECASE Expr OF
  T1 (v1) => S1
| ...
| Tn (vn) => Sn
ELSE S0
END
```

where Expr is an expression whose type is a reference type, S_0,...,S_n are statements, the Ts are reference types, and the vs are identifiers. It is a static error if Expr has type ADDRESS or if any T is not a subtype of the type of Expr. The ELSE S_0 and each (v) are optional.

The statement evaluates Expr. If the resulting reference value is a member of any listed type T_i, then S_i is executed, for the minimum such i. (Thus a NULL case is useful only if it comes first.) If the value is a member of no listed type and ELSE S_0 is present, then it is executed. If the value is a member of no listed type and ELSE S_0 is absent, a checked runtime error occurs.

Each (v_i) declares a variable whose type is T_i and whose scope is S_i. If v_i is present, it is initialized to the value of Expr before S_i is executed.

If (v_i) is absent, then T_i can be a list of type expressions separated by commas, as shorthand for a list in which the rest of the branch is repeated for each type expression:

```
T1, ..., Tn => S
```

is shorthand for

```
T1 => S | ... | Tn => S
```

Here is an example:

```
PROCEDURE ToText(r: REFANY): TEXT =
  (* Assume r = NIL or r^ is a BOOLEAN or INTEGER. *)
BEGIN
  TYPECASE r OF
    NULL => RETURN "NIL"
  | REF BOOLEAN (rb) => RETURN Fmt.Bool(rb^)
  | REF INTEGER (ri) => RETURN Fmt.Int(ri^)
  END
END ToText;
```

11.5.19. LOCK

A LOCK statement has the form

```
LOCK mu DO S END
```

where S is a statement and mu is an expression. It is equivalent to

```
WITH m = mu DO
  Thread.Acquire(m);
  TRY S FINALLY Thread.Release(m) END
END
```

where m stands for a variable that does not occur in S.

11.5.20. INC and DEC

INC and DEC statements have the form

```
INC(v, n)
DEC(v, n)
```

where v designates a variable of an ordinal type and n is an optional integer-valued argument. If omitted, n defaults to 1. The statements increment and decrement v by n, respectively. The statements are equivalent to

```
WITH x = v DO x := VAL(ORD(x) + n, T) END
WITH x = v DO x := VAL(ORD(x) - n, T) END
```

where T is the type of v and x stands for a variable that does not appear in n. As a consequence, the statements check for range errors. In unsafe modules, INC and DEC are extended to ADDRESS.

11.6. Declarations

> *There are two basic methods of declaring high or low before the showdown in all High-Low Poker games. They are (1) simultaneous declarations and (2) consecutive declarations....It is a sad but true fact that the consecutive method spoils the game.*
>
> *—John Scarne's Guide to Modern Poker*

A declaration introduces a name for a constant, a type, a variable, an exception, or a procedure. The scope of the name is the block containing the declaration. A block has the form

```
Decls BEGIN S END
```

where Decls is a sequence of declarations and S is a statement, the executable part of the block. A block can appear as a statement or as the body of a module or procedure. The declarations of a block can introduce a name at most once, although a name can be redeclared in nested blocks, and a procedure declared in an interface can be redeclared in a module exporting the interface. The order of declarations in a block does not matter except to determine the order of initialization of variables.

11.6.1. Types

If T is an identifier and U a type (or type expression because a type expression is allowed wherever a type is required), then

```
TYPE T = U
```

declares T to be the type U.

11.6.2. Constants

If id is an identifier, T a type, and C a constant expression, then

```
CONST id: T = C
```

declares id as a constant with the type T and the value of C. The : T can be omitted, in which case the type of id is the type of C. If T is present, it must contain C.

11.6.3. Variables

If id is an identifier, T a non-empty type other than an open array type, and E an expression, then

```
VAR id: T := E
```

declares id as a variable of type T whose initial value is the value of E. Either := E or : T can be omitted, but not both. If T is omitted, it is taken to be the type of E. If E is omitted, the initial value is an arbitrary value of type T. If both are present, E must be assignable to T.

The initial value is a shorthand that is equivalent to inserting the assignment id := E at the beginning of the executable part of the block. If several variables have initial values, their assignments are inserted in the order they are declared:

```
VAR i: [0..5] := j; j: [0..5] := i; BEGIN S END
```

initializes i and j to the same arbitrary value in [0..5]; it is equivalent to

```
VAR i: [0..5]; j: [0..5]; BEGIN i := j; j := i; S END
```

If a sequence of identifiers share the same type and initial value, id can be a list of identifiers separated by commas. Such a list is shorthand for a list in which the type and initial value are repeated for each identifier:

```
VAR v1, ..., vn: T := E
```

is shorthand for

```
VAR v1: T := E; ...; VAR vn: T := E
```

This means that E is evaluated n times.

11.6.4. Procedures

There are two forms of procedure declaration:

```
PROCEDURE id sig = B id
PROCEDURE id sig
```

where id is an identifier, sig is a procedure signature, and B is a block. In both cases, the type of id is the procedure type determined by sig. The first form is allowed only in modules; the second form is allowed only in interfaces.

The first form declares id as a procedure constant whose signature is sig, whose body is B, and whose environment is the scope containing the declaration. The parameter names are treated as if they were declared at the outer level of B; the parameter types and default values are evaluated in the scope containing the procedure declaration. The procedure name id must be repeated after the END that terminates the body.

The second form declares id to be a procedure constant whose signature is sig. The procedure body is specified in a module exporting the interface by a declaration of the first form.

11.6.5. Exceptions

If id is an identifier and T a type other than an open array type, then

```
EXCEPTION id(T)
```

declares id as an exception with argument type T. If (T) is omitted, the exception takes no argument. An exception declaration is allowed only in an interface or in the outermost scope of a module. All declared exceptions are distinct.

11.6.6. Opaque Types

An *opaque type* is a name that denotes an unknown subtype of some given reference type. For example, an opaque subtype of REFANY is an unknown traced reference type; an opaque subtype of UNTRACED ROOT is an unknown untraced object type. The actual type denoted by an opaque type name is called its concrete type.

Different scopes can reveal different information about an opaque type. For example, what is known in one scope only to be a subtype of REFANY could be known in another scope to be a subtype of ROOT.

An opaque type declaration has the form

```
TYPE T <: U
```

where T is an identifier and U an expression denoting a reference type. It introduces the name T as an opaque type and reveals that U is a supertype of T. The concrete type of T must be revealed elsewhere in the program.

11.6.7. Revelations

A *revelation* introduces information about an opaque type into a scope. Unlike other declarations, revelations introduce no new names.

There are two kinds of revelations, *partial* and *complete*. A program can contain any number of partial revelations for an opaque type; it must contain exactly one complete revelation.

A partial revelation has the form

```
REVEAL T <: V
```

where V is a type expression (possibly just a name) and T is an identifier (possibly qualified) declared as an opaque type. It reveals that V is a supertype of T.

In any scope, the revealed supertypes of an opaque type must be ordered linearly by the subtype relation. That is, if it is revealed that T <: U1 and T <: U2, it must also be revealed either that U1 <: U2 or that U2 <: U1.

A complete revelation has the form

```
REVEAL T = V
```

where V is a type expression (not just a name) whose outermost type constructor is a branded reference or object type and T is an identifier (possibly qualified) that has been declared as an opaque type. The revelation specifies that V is the concrete type for T. It is a static error if any type revealed in any scope as a supertype of T is not a supertype of V. Generally, this error is detected at link time.

Distinct opaque types have distinct concrete types because V includes a brand and all brands in a program are distinct.

A revelation is allowed only in an interface or in the outermost scope of a module. A revelation in an interface can be imported into any scope where it is required, as illustrated by the stack example.

For example, consider the following:

```
INTERFACE I; TYPE T <: ROOT; PROCEDURE P(x:T): T; END I.
INTERFACE IClass; IMPORT I; REVEAL I.T <: MUTEX; END IClass.
INTERFACE IRep; IMPORT I;
  REVEAL I.T = MUTEX BRANDED OBJECT count: INTEGER END;
END IRep.
```

An importer of `I` sees `I.T` as an opaque subtype of `ROOT` and is limited to allocating objects of type `I.T`, passing them to `I.P`, or declaring subtypes of `I.T`. An importer of `IClass` sees that every `I.T` is a `MUTEX` and can therefore lock objects of type `I.T`. Finally, an importer of `IRep` sees the concrete type and can access the `count` field.

11.6.8. Recursive Declarations

A constant, type, or procedure declaration `N = E`, a variable declaration `N: E`, an exception declaration `N(E)`, or a revelation `N = E` is recursive if `N` occurs in any partial expansion of `E`. A variable declaration `N := I` where the type is omitted is recursive if `N` occurs in any partial expansion of the type `E` of `I`. Such declarations are allowed if every occurrence of `N` in any partial expansion of `E` is within some occurrence of the type constructor `REF` or `PROCEDURE`, within a field or method type of the type constructor `OBJECT`, or within a procedure body.

Examples of legal recursive declarations:

```
TYPE
  List = REF RECORD x: REAL; link: List END;
  T = PROCEDURE(n: INTEGER; p: T);
  XList = X OBJECT link: XList END;
CONST N = BYTESIZE(REF ARRAY [0..N] OF REAL);
PROCEDURE P(b: BOOLEAN) = BEGIN IF b THEN P(NOT b) END END P;
EXCEPTION E(PROCEDURE () RAISES {E});
VAR v: REF ARRAY [0..BYTESIZE(v)] OF INTEGER;
```

Examples of illegal recursive declarations:

```
TYPE
  T = RECORD x: T END;
  U = OBJECT METHODS m() := U.m END;
CONST N = N+1;
REVEAL I.T = I.T BRANDED OBJECT END;
VAR v := P(); PROCEDURE P(): ARRAY [0..LAST(v)] OF T;
```

Examples of legal non-recursive declarations:

```
VAR n := BITSIZE(n);
REVEAL T <: T;
```

11.7. Modules and Interfaces

Art, it seems to me, should simplify. That, indeed, is very nearly the whole of the higher artistic process; finding what conventions of form and what detail one can do without and yet preserve the spirit of the whole.

—*Willa Cather*

A *module* is like a block, except for the visibility of names. An entity is visible in a block if it is declared in the block or in some enclosing block; an entity is visible in a module if it is declared in the module or in an interface that is imported or exported by the module.

An *interface* is a group of declarations. Declarations in interfaces are the same as in blocks, except that any variable initializations must be constant, and procedure declarations must specify only the signature, not the body.

A module `X` exports an interface `I` to supply bodies for one or more of the procedures declared in the interface. A module or interface `X` imports an interface `I` to make the entities declared in `I` visible in `X`.

A program is a collection of modules and interfaces that contains every interface imported or exported by any of its modules or interfaces and in which no procedure, module, or interface is multiply defined. The effect of executing a program is to execute the bodies of each of its modules. The order of execution of the modules is constrained by the initialization rule.

The module whose body is executed last is called the *main module*. Implementations are expected to provide a way to specify the main module, in case the initialization rule does not determine it uniquely. The recommended rule is that the main module be the one that exports the interface `Main`, whose contents are implementation dependent.

Program execution terminates when the body of the main module terminates, even if concurrent threads of control are still executing.

The names of the modules and interfaces of a program are called *global* names. The method for looking up global names—for example, by file system search paths—is implementation dependent.

11.7.1. Import Statements

There are two forms of import statements. All imports of both forms are interpreted simultaneously: Their order doesn't matter.

The first form is

```
IMPORT I AS J
```

which imports the interface whose global name is `I` and gives it the local name `J`. The entities and revelations declared in `I` become accessible in the importing module or interface, but the entities and revelations imported into `I` do not. To refer to the entity declared with name `N` in the interface `I`, the importer must use the qualified identifier `J.N`.

The statement `IMPORT I` is short for `IMPORT I AS I`.

The second form is

```
FROM I IMPORT N
```

which introduces `N` as the local name for the entity declared as `N` in the interface `I`. A local binding for `I` takes precedence over a global binding. For example,

```
IMPORT I AS J, J AS I; FROM I IMPORT N
```

simultaneously introduces local names `J`, `I`, and `N` for the entities whose global names are `I`, `J`, and `J.N`, respectively.

It is illegal to use the same local name twice:

```
IMPORT J AS I, K AS I;
```

would be a static error if `J` and `K` were the same.

11.7.2. Interfaces

An interface has the form

```
INTERFACE id;  Imports;  Decls END id.
```

where `id` is an identifier that names the interface, `Imports` is a sequence of import statements, and `Decls` is a sequence of declarations that contains no procedure bodies or non-constant variable initializations. The names declared in `Decls` and the visible imported names must be distinct. It is a static error for two or more interfaces to form an import cycle.

11.7.3. Modules

A module has the form:

```
MODULE id EXPORTS Interfaces;  Imports; Block id.
```

where `id` is an identifier that names the module, `Interfaces` is a list of distinct names of interfaces exported by the module, `Imports` is a list of import statements, and `Block` is a block, the body of the module. The name `id` must be repeated after the `END` that terminates the body. `EXPORTS Interfaces` can be omitted, in which case `Interfaces` defaults to `id`.

If module M exports interface I, then all declared names in I are visible without qualification in M. Any procedure declared in I can be redeclared in M, with a body. The signature in M must be covered by the signature in I. To determine the interpretation of keyword bindings in calls to the procedure, the signature in M is used within M; the signature in I is used everywhere else.

Except for the redeclaration of exported procedures, the names declared at the top level of Block, the visible imported names, and the names declared in the exported interfaces must be distinct.

For example, the following is illegal because two names in exported interfaces coincide:

```
INTERFACE I;   INTERFACE J;     MODULE M EXPORTS I, J;
  PROCEDURE X(); PROCEDURE X(); PROCEDURE X() = ...;
```

The following is also illegal because the visible imported name X coincides with the top-level name X:

```
INTERFACE I;  MODULE M EXPORTS I;  FROM I IMPORT X;
  PROCEDURE X(); PROCEDURE X() = ...;
```

But the following is legal, although peculiar:

```
INTERFACE I;  MODULE M EXPORTS I;  IMPORT I;
  PROCEDURE X(...); PROCEDURE X(...) = ...;
```

because the only visible imported name is I, and the coincidence between X as a top-level name and X as a name in an exported interface is allowed, assuming the interface signature covers the module signature. Within M, the interface declaration determines the signature of I.X and the module declaration determines the signature of X.

11.7.4. A Sample Module and Interface

Here is the canonical example of a public stack with hidden representation:

```
INTERFACE Stack;
  TYPE T <: REFANY;
  PROCEDURE Create(): T;
  PROCEDURE Push(VAR s: T; x: REAL);
  PROCEDURE Pop(VAR s: T): REAL;
END Stack.

MODULE Stack;
  REVEAL T = BRANDED OBJECT item: REAL; link: T END;
  PROCEDURE Create(): T = BEGIN RETURN NIL END Create;
  PROCEDURE Push(VAR s: T; x: REAL) =
    BEGIN
      s := NEW(T, item := x, link := s)
    END Push;
```

```
    PROCEDURE Pop(VAR s: T): REAL =
      VAR res: REAL;
      BEGIN
        res := s.item; s := s.link; RETURN res
      END Pop;
  BEGIN
  END Stack.
```

If the representation of stacks is required in more than one module, it should be moved to a private interface so that it can be imported wherever it is required:

```
INTERFACE Stack (* ... as before ... *) END Stack.
INTERFACE StackRep; IMPORT Stack;
  REVEAL Stack.T = BRANDED OBJECT item: REAL; link: Stack.T END
END StackRep.

MODULE Stack; IMPORT StackRep;
  (* Push, Pop, and Create as before *)
BEGIN
END Stack.
```

11.7.5. Generics

In a generic interface or module, some of the imported interface names are treated as formal parameters to be bound to actual interfaces when the generic is instantiated.

A generic interface has the form

```
GENERIC INTERFACE G(F_1, ..., F_n);  Body END G.
```

where `G` is an identifier that names the generic interface, $F_1, \ldots, F_n$ is a list of identifiers, called the formal imports of `G`, and `Body` is a sequence of imports followed by a sequence of declarations, exactly as in a nongeneric interface.

An instance of `G` has the form

```
INTERFACE I = G(A_1, ..., A_n) END I.
```

where `I` is the name of the instance and $A_1, \ldots, A_n$ is a list of actual interfaces to which the formal imports of `G` are bound. The instance `I` is equivalent to an ordinary interface defined as follows:

```
INTERFACE I;  IMPORT A_1 AS F_1, ..., A_n AS F_n;  Body END I.
```

A generic module has the form

```
GENERIC MODULE G(F_1, ..., F_n);  Body G.
```

where `G` is an identifier that names the generic module, $F_1, \ldots, F_n$ is a list of identifiers, called the formal imports of `G`, and `Body` is a sequence of imports followed by a block, exactly as in a nongeneric module.

An instance of G has the form

```
MODULE I EXPORTS E = G(A_1, ..., A_n) END I.
```

where I is the name of the instance, E is a list of interfaces exported by I, and $A_1, \ldots, A_n$ is a list of actual interfaces to which the formal imports of G are bound. EXPORTS E can be omitted, in which case it defaults to EXPORTS I. The instance I is equivalent to an ordinary module defined as follows:

```
MODULE I EXPORTS E;  IMPORT A1 AS F1, ..., An AS Fn; Body I.
```

Notice that the generic module itself has no exports; they are supplied only when it is instantiated.

For example, here is a generic stack package:

```
GENERIC INTERFACE Stack(Elem);
  (* where Elem.T is not an open array type. *)
  TYPE T <: REFANY;
  PROCEDURE Create(): T;
  PROCEDURE Push(VAR s: T; x: Elem.T);
  PROCEDURE Pop(VAR s: T): Elem.T;
END Stack.

GENERIC MODULE Stack(Elem);
  REVEAL
    T = BRANDED OBJECT n: INTEGER; a: REF ARRAY OF Elem.T END;
  PROCEDURE Create(): T =
    BEGIN RETURN NEW(T, n := 0, a := NIL) END Create;
  PROCEDURE Push(VAR s: T; x: Elem.T) =
    BEGIN
      IF s.a = NIL THEN
        s.a := NEW(REF ARRAY OF Elem.T, 5)
      ELSIF s.n > LAST(s.a^) THEN
        WITH temp = NEW(REF ARRAY OF Elem.T,
                2 * NUMBER(s.a^)) DO
          FOR i := 0 TO LAST(s.a^) DO temp[i] := s.a[i] END;
          s.a := temp
        END
      END;
      s.a[s.n] := x;
      INC(s.n)
    END Push;
  PROCEDURE Pop(VAR s: T): Elem.T =
    BEGIN DEC(s.n); RETURN s.a[s.n] END Pop;
BEGIN END Stack.
```

To instantiate these generics to produce stacks of integers, you would use this:

```
INTERFACE Integer; TYPE T = INTEGER; END Integer.
INTERFACE IntStack = Stack(Integer) END IntStack.
MODULE IntStack = Stack(Integer) END IntStack.
```

Implementations are not expected to share code between different instances of a generic module because this will not be possible in general.

Implementations are not required to type-check uninstantiated generics, but they must type-check their instances. For example, if you made the following mistake:

```
INTERFACE String; TYPE T = ARRAY OF CHAR; END String.
INTERFACE StringStack = Stack(String) END StringStack.
MODULE StringStack = Stack(String) END StringStack.
```

everything would go well until the last line, when the compiler would attempt to compile a version of `Stack` in which the element type was an open array. It would then complain that the `NEW` call in `Push` does not have enough parameters.

11.7.6. Initialization

The order of execution of the modules in a program is constrained by the following rule:

If module `M` depends on module `N` and `N` does not depend on `M`, then `N`'s body will be executed before `M`'s body, where

- A module `M` depends on a module `N` if `M` uses an interface that `N` exports or if `M` depends on a module that depends on `N`.
- A module `M` uses an interface `I` if `M` imports or exports `I` or if `M` uses an interface that (directly or indirectly) imports `I`.

Except for this constraint, the order of execution is implementation dependent.

11.7.7. Safety

The keyword `UNSAFE` can precede the declaration of any interface or module to indicate that it is *unsafe*—that is, uses the unsafe features of the language. An interface or module not explicitly labeled `UNSAFE` is called *safe*.

An interface is *intrinsically safe* if there is no way to produce an unchecked runtime error by using the interface in a safe module. If all modules that export a safe interface are safe, the compiler guarantees the intrinsic safety of the interface. If any of the modules that export a safe interface are unsafe, it is the programmer, rather than the compiler, who makes the guarantee.

It is a static error for a safe interface to import an unsafe one or for a safe module to import or export an unsafe interface.

11.8. Expressions

The rules of logical syntax must follow of themselves, if we only know how every single sign signifies.
—*Ludwig Wittgenstein*

An expression prescribes a computation that produces a value or variable. Syntactically, an expression is either an operand or an operation applied to arguments, which are themselves expressions. Operands are identifiers, literals, or types. An expression is evaluated by recursively evaluating its arguments and performing the operation. The order of argument evaluation is undefined for all operations except AND and OR.

11.8.1. Conventions for Describing Operations

To describe the argument and result types of operations, we use a notation such as procedure signatures. Because most operations are too general to be described by a true procedure signature, we extend the notation in several ways.

The argument to an operation can be required to have a type in a particular class, such as an ordinal type, set type, and so on. In this case, the formal specifies a type class instead of a type:

```
ORD (x: Ordinal): INTEGER
```

The formal type Any specifies an argument of any type.

A single operation name can be overloaded, which means that it denotes more than one operation. In this case, we write a separate signature for each of the operations:

```
ABS    (x: INTEGER) : INTEGER
       (x: Float) : Float
```

The particular operation will be selected so that each actual argument type is a subtype of the corresponding formal type or a member of the corresponding formal type class.

The argument to an operation can be an expression denoting a type. In this case, we write Type as the argument type:

```
BYTESIZE (T: Type): CARDINAL
```

The result type of an operation can depend on its argument values (although the result type can always be determined statically). In this case, the expression for the result type contains the appropriate arguments:

```
FIRST (T: FixedArrayType): IndexType(T)
```

`IndexType(T)` denotes the index type of the array type `T` and `IndexType(a)` denotes the index type of the array `a`. The definitions of `ElemType(T)` and `ElemType(a)` are similar.

11.8.2. Operation Syntax

The operators that have special syntax are classified and listed here in order of decreasing binding power:

Operator	*Description*
`x.a`	Infix dot
`f(x) a[i] T{x}`	Applicative `(`, `[`, `{`
`p^`	Postfix `^`
`+ -`	Prefix arithmetics
`* / DIV MOD`	Infix arithmetics
`+ - &`	Infix arithmetics
`= # < <= >= > IN`	Infix relations
`NOT`	Prefix `NOT`
`AND`	Infix `AND`
`OR`	Infix `OR`

All infix operators are left associative. Parentheses can be used to override the precedence rules. Here are some examples of expressions together with their fully parenthesized forms:

Expression	*Parenthesized Form*	*Reason*
`M.F(x)`	`(M.F)(x)`	Dot before application
`Q(x)^`	`(Q(x))^`	Application before `^`
`- p^`	`- (p^)`	`^` before prefix `-`
`- a * b`	`(- a) * b`	Prefix `-` before `*`
`a * b - c`	`(a * b) - c`	`*` before infix `-`

`x IN s - t`	`x IN (s - t)`	Infix - before IN
`NOT x IN s`	`NOT (x IN s)`	IN before NOT
`NOT p AND q`	`(NOT p) AND q`	NOT before AND
`A OR B AND C`	`A OR (B AND C)`	AND before OR

Operators without special syntax are *procedural*. An application of a procedural operator has the form `op(args)`, where `op` is the operation and `args` is the list of argument expressions. For example, `MAX` and `MIN` are procedural operators.

11.8.3. Designators

An identifier is a *writable* designator if it is declared as a variable, is a VAR or VALUE parameter, is a local of a TYPECASE or TRY EXCEPT statement, or is a WITH local that is bound to a writable designator. An identifier is a read-only designator if it is a READONLY parameter, a local of a FOR statement, or a WITH local bound to a non-designator or read-only designator.

The only operations that produce designators are dereferencing, subscripting, selection, and SUBARRAY. This section defines these operations and specifies the conditions under which they produce designators. In unsafe modules, LOOPHOLE can also produce a designator:

- `r^`—Denotes the referent of `r`; this operation is called *dereferencing*. The expression `r^` is always a writable designator. It is a static error if the type of `r` is REFANY, ADDRESS, NULL, an object type, or an opaque type and a checked runtime error if `r` is NIL. The type of `r^` is the referent type of `r`.
- `a[i]`—Denotes the `(i + 1 - FIRST(a))`th element of the array `a`. The expression `a[i]` is a designator if `a` is and is writable if `a` is. The expression `i` must be assignable to the index type of `a`. The type of `a[i]` is the element type of `a`.

  An expression of the form `a[`i_1`, ..., `i_n`]` is shorthand for `a[`i_1`]...[`i_n`]`. If `a` is a reference to an array, then `a[i]` is shorthand for `a^[i]`.
- `r.f, o.f, I.x, T.m, E.id`—If `r` denotes a record, `r.f` denotes its `f` field. In this case, `r.f` is a designator if `r` is and is writable if `r` is. The type of `r.f` is the declared type of the field.

  If `r` is a reference to a record, then `r.f` is shorthand for `r^.f`.

If o denotes an object and f names a data field specified in the type of o, then o.f denotes that data field of o. In this case, o.f is a writable designator whose type is the declared type of the field.

If I denotes an imported interface, then I.x denotes the entity named x in the interface I. In this case, I.x is a designator if x is declared as a variable; such a designator is always writable.

If T is an object type and m is the name of one of T's methods, then T.m denotes the m method of type T. In this case, T.m is not a designator. Its type is the procedure type whose first argument has mode VALUE and type T and whose remaining arguments are determined by the method declaration for m in T. The name of the first argument is unspecified; thus in calls to T.m, this argument must be given positionally, not by keyword. T.m is a procedure constant.

If E is an enumerated type, then E.id denotes its value named id. In this case, E.id is not a designator. The type of E.id is E.

- SUBARRAY(a: Array; from, for: CARDINAL): ARRAY OF ElemType(a)—SUBARRAY produces a subarray of a. It does not copy the array; it is a designator if a is and is writable if a is. If a is a multidimensional array, SUBARRAY applies only to the top-level array.

  The operation returns the subarray that skips the first from elements of a and contains the next for elements. Note that if from is zero, the subarray is a prefix of a, whether the type of a is zero based. It is a checked runtime error if from+for exceeds NUMBER(a).

  Implementations may restrict or prohibit the SUBARRAY operation for arrays with packed element types.

11.8.4. Numeric Literals

Numeric literals denote constant non-negative integers or reals. The types of these literals are INTEGER, REAL, LONGREAL, and EXTENDED.

A literal INTEGER has the form base_digits, where base is one of 2, 3, ..., 16, and digits is a non-empty sequence of the decimal digits 0 through 9 plus the hexadecimal digits A through F. The base_ can be omitted, in which case base defaults to 10. The digits are interpreted in the given base. Each digit must be less than base. For example, 16_FF and 255 are equivalent integer literals.

If no explicit base is present, the value of the literal must be at most LAST(INTEGER). If an explicit base is present, the value of the literal must be less than 2^Word.Size, and its interpretation uses the convention of the Word interface. For example, on a 16-bit two's complement machine, 16_FFFF and -1 represent the same value.

A literal REAL has the form decimal E exponent, where decimal is a non-empty sequence of decimal digits followed by a decimal point followed by a non-empty sequence of decimal digits, and exponent is a non-empty sequence of decimal digits optionally beginning with a + or -. The literal denotes decimal times 10^exponent. If E exponent is omitted, exponent defaults to 0.

LONGREAL and EXTENDED literals are like REAL, but instead of E, they use D and X, respectively.

Case is not significant in digits, prefixes, or scale factors. Embedded spaces are not allowed.

For example, 1.0 and 0.5 are valid, 1. and .5 are not; 6.624E-27 is a REAL, and 3.1415926535d0 a LONGREAL.

11.8.5. Text and Character Literals

A character literal is a pair of single quotes enclosing either a single ISO-Latin-1 printing character (excluding single quote) or an escape sequence. The type of a character literal is CHAR.

A text literal is a pair of double quotes enclosing a sequence of ISO-Latin-1 printing characters (excluding double quote) and escape sequences. The type of a text literal is TEXT.

Here are the legal escape sequences and the characters they denote:

\n	Newline (linefeed)
\f	Form feed
\t	Tab
\\	Backslash
\r	Carriage return
\"	Double quote
\'	Single quote
\nnn	Char with code 8_nnn

A \ followed by exactly three octal digits specifies the character whose code is that octal value. A \ that is not a part of one of these escape sequences is a static error.

For example, `'a'` and `'\''` are valid character literals, `'''` is not; `""` and `"Don't\n"` are valid text literals; `"""` is not.

11.8.6. NIL

The literal `"NIL"` denotes the value `NIL`. Its type is `NULL`.

11.8.7. Function Application

A procedure call is an expression if the procedure returns a result. The type of the expression is the result type of the procedure.

11.8.8. Set, Array, and Record Constructors

A set constructor has the form

```
S{e1, ..., en}
```

where `S` is a set type and the `e`s are expressions or ranges of the form `lo..hi`. The constructor denotes a value of type `S` containing the listed values and the values in the listed ranges. The `e`s, `lo`s, and `hi`s must be assignable to the element type of `S`.

An array constructor has the form

```
A{e1, ..., en}
```

where `A` is an array type and the `e`s are expressions. The constructor denotes a value of type `A` containing the listed elements in the listed order. The `e`s must be assignable to the element type of `A`. This means that if `A` is a multidimensional array, the `e`s must themselves be array-valued expressions.

If `A` is a fixed array type and `n` is at least 1, then `e`*n* can be followed by

```
, ..
```

to indicate that the value of `e`*n* will be replicated as many times as necessary to fill out the array. It is a static error to provide too many or too few elements for a fixed array type.

A record constructor has the form

```
R{Bindings}
```

where `R` is a record type and `Bindings` is a list of keyword or positional bindings, exactly as in a procedure call. The list of bindings is rewritten to fit the list of fields and defaults of `R`, exactly as for a procedure call; the record field names play the role of the procedure formal parameters. The expression denotes a value of type `R` whose field values are specified by the rewritten binding.

The rewritten binding must bind only field names and must bind each field name exactly once. Each expression in the binding must be assignable to the type of the corresponding record field.

11.8.9. NEW

An allocation operation has the form

```
NEW(T, ...)
```

where T is a reference type other than REFANY, ADDRESS, or NULL. The operation returns the address of a newly-allocated variable of T's referent type; or if T is an object type, a newly allocated data record paired with a method suite. The reference returned by NEW is distinct from all existing references. The allocated type of the new reference is T.

It is a static error if T's referent type is empty. If T is declared as an opaque type, NEW(T) is legal only in scopes where T's concrete type is known completely or is known to be an object type.

The initial state of the referent generally represents an arbitrary value of its type. If T is an object type or a reference to a record or open array, then NEW takes additional arguments to control the initial state of the new variable.

If T is a reference to an array with k open dimensions, the NEW operation has the form

NEW(T, n_1, ..., n_k)

where the ns are integer-valued expressions that specify the lengths of the new array in its first k dimensions. The values in the array will be arbitrary values of their type.

If T is an object type or a reference to a record, the NEW operation has the form

```
NEW(T, Bindings)
```

where Bindings is a list of keyword bindings used to initialize the new fields. Positional bindings are not allowed.

Each binding f := v initializes the field f to the value v. Fields for which no binding is supplied will be initialized to their defaults if they have defaults; otherwise, they will be initialized to arbitrary values of their types. The order of the field bindings makes no difference.

If T is an object type, then Bindings can also include method overrides of the form m := P, where m is a method of T and P is a top-level procedure constant. This is syntactic sugar for the allocation of a subtype of T that includes the given overrides, in the given order. For example, NEW(T, m := P) is syntactic sugar for NEW(T OBJECT OVERRIDES m := P END).

11.8.10. Arithmetic Operations

The basic arithmetic operations are built into the language; additional operations are provided by the required floating-point interfaces.

To test or set the implementation's behavior for overflow, underflow, rounding, and division by zero, see the required interface FloatMode. Modula-3 arithmetic was designed to support the IEEE floating-point standard but not to require it.

To perform unsigned word arithmetic operations, programs should use the routines in the required interface Word.

Implementations must not rearrange the computation of expressions in a way that could affect the result. For example, (x+y)+z generally cannot be computed as x+(y+z) because addition is not associative either for bounded integers or for floating-point values:

Operator + definition

```
prefix    +(x: INTEGER)      : INTEGER
          +(x: Float)        : Float
infix     +(x,y: INTEGER)    : INTEGER
          (x,y: Float)       : Float
          (x,y: Set)         : Set
```

As a prefix operator, +x returns x. As an infix operator on numeric arguments, + denotes addition. On sets, + denotes set union. That is, e IN (x + y) if and only if (e IN x) OR (e IN y). The types of x and y must be the same, and the result is the same type as both. In unsafe modules, + is extended to ADDRESS.

Operator - is defined as

```
prefix   -(x: INTEGER)     : INTEGER
         (x: Float)        : Float
infix    -(x,y: INTEGER)   : INTEGER
         (x,y: Float)      : Float
         (x,y: Set)        : Set
```

As a prefix operator, -x is the negative of x. As an infix operator on numeric arguments, - denotes subtraction. On sets, - denotes set difference. That is, e IN (x - y) if and only if (e IN x) AND NOT (e IN y). The types of x and y must be the same, and the result is the same type as both. In unsafe modules, - is extended to ADDRESS.

Operator * is defined as

```
infix   *(x,y: INTEGER)    : INTEGER
        (x,y: Float)       : Float
        (x,y: Set)         : Set
```

On numeric arguments, * denotes multiplication. On sets, * denotes intersection. That is, `e IN (x * y)` if and only if `(e IN x) AND (e IN y)`. The types of x and y must be the same, and the result is the same type as both.

Operator / is defined as

```
infix   /(x,y: Float)      : Float
        (x,y: Set)         : Set
```

On reals, / denotes division. On sets, / denotes symmetric difference. That is, `e IN (x / y)` if and only if `(e IN x) # (e IN y)`. The types of x and y must be the same, and the result is the same type as both.

DIV and MOD operators are defined as

```
infix   DIV  (x,y: INTEGER)  : INTEGER
infix   MOD  (x,y: INTEGER)  : INTEGER
        MOD  (x, y: Float)   : Float
```

The value `x DIV y` is the floor of the quotient of x and y—that is, the maximum integer not exceeding the real number z such that `z * y = x`. For integers x and y, the value of `x MOD y` is defined to be `x - y * (x DIV y)`.

This means that for positive y, the value of `x MOD y` lies in the interval `[0 .. y-1]`, regardless of the sign of x. For negative y, the value of `x MOD y` lies in the interval `[y+1 .. 0]`, regardless of the sign of x.

If x and y are floats, the value of `x MOD y` is `x - y * FLOOR(x / y)`. This may be computed as a Modula-3 expression or by a method that avoids overflow if x is much greater than y. The types of x and y must be the same, and the result is the same type as both.

ABS operator is defined as

```
ABS   (x: INTEGER)    : INTEGER
      (x: Float)      : Float
```

`ABS(x)` is the absolute value of x. If x is a float, the type of `ABS(x)` is the same as the type of x.

FLOAT operator is defined as

```
FLOAT   (x: INTEGER; T: Type := REAL)   : T
        (x: Float; T: Type := REAL)     : T
```

`FLOAT(x, T)` is a floating-point value of type `T` that is equal to or very near `x`. The type `T` must be a floating-point type; it defaults to `REAL`. The exact semantics depend on the thread's current rounding mode, as defined in the required interface `FloatMode` (see section 11.10.6).

`FLOOR` and `CEILING` operators are defined as

```
FLOOR    (x: Float)  : INTEGER
CEILING  (x: Float)  : INTEGER
```

`FLOOR(x)` is the greatest integer not exceeding `x`. `CEILING(x)` is the least integer not less than `x`.

`ROUND` and `TRUNC` operators are defined as

```
ROUND   (r: Float)  : INTEGER
TRUNC   (r: Float)  : INTEGER
```

`ROUND(r)` is the nearest integer to `r`; ties are broken according to the constant `RoundDefault` in the required interface `FloatMode`. `TRUNC(r)` rounds `r` toward zero; it equals `FLOOR(r)` for positive `r` and `CEILING(r)` for negative `r`.

`MAX` and `MIN` operators are defined as

```
MAX, MIN  (x,y: Ordinal)  : Ordinal
          (x,y: Float)    : Float
```

`MAX` returns the greater of the two values `x` and `y`; `MIN` returns the lesser. If `x` and `y` are ordinals, they must have the same base type, which is the type of the result. If `x` and `y` are floats, they must have the same type, and the result is the same type as both.

11.8.11. Relations

Operators `=` and `#` are defined as

```
infix   =, #  (x, y: Any)  : BOOLEAN
```

The operator `=` returns `TRUE` if `x` and `y` are equal. The operator `#` returns `TRUE` if `x` and `y` are not equal. It is a static error if the type of `x` is not assignable to the type of `y` or vice versa.

Ordinals are equal if they have the same value. Floats are equal if the underlying implementation defines them to be; for example, on an IEEE implementation, `+0` equals `-0` and `NaN` (not a number) does not equal itself. References are equal if they address the same location. Procedures are equal if they agree as closures—that is, if they refer to the same procedure body and environment. Sets are equal if they have the same elements. Arrays are equal if they have the same length and corresponding elements are equal. Records are equal if they have the same fields and corresponding fields are equal.

Operators `<=` and `>=` are defined as

```
infix  <=, >=  (x,y: Ordinal)    : BOOLEAN
               (x,y: Float)      : BOOLEAN
               (x,y: ADDRESS)    : BOOLEAN
               (x,y: Set)        : BOOLEAN
```

In the first three cases, `<=` returns `TRUE` if `x` is at most as large as `y`. In the last case, `<=` returns `TRUE` if every element of `x` is an element of `y`. In all cases, it is a static error if the type of `x` is not assignable to the type of `y` or vice versa. The expression `x >= y` is equivalent to `y <= x`.

Operators `<` and `>` are defined as

```
infix  >, <  (x,y: Ordinal)  : BOOLEAN
             (x,y: Float)    : BOOLEAN
             (x,y: ADDRESS)  : BOOLEAN
             (x,y: Set)      : BOOLEAN
```

In all cases, `x < y` means `(x <= y) AND (x # y)`, and `x > y` means `y < x`. It is a static error if the type of `x` is not assignable to the type of `y` or vice versa.

Note that with IEEE floating-point, `x <= y` is not the same as *not* `x > y`.

Operator `IN` is defined as

```
infix  IN   (e: Ordinal; s: Set)    : BOOLEAN
```

`IN` returns true if `e` is an element of set `s`. It is a static error if the type of `e` is not assignable to the element type of `s`. If the value of `e` is not a member of the element type, no error occurs, but `IN` returns `FALSE`.

11.8.12. Boolean Operations

The following are some examples of Boolean operators:

```
prefix   NOT   (p: BOOLEAN)     : BOOLEAN
infix    AND   (p,q: BOOLEAN)   : BOOLEAN
infix    OR    (p,q: BOOLEAN)   : BOOLEAN
```

`NOT p` is the complement of `p`.

`p AND q` is `TRUE` if both `p` and `q` are `TRUE`. If `p` is `FALSE`, `q` is not evaluated.

`p OR q` is `TRUE` if at least one of `p` and `q` is `TRUE`. If `p` is `TRUE`, `q` is not evaluated.

11.8.13. Type Operations

ISTYPE is defined as

```
ISTYPE  (x: Reference; T: RefType)  : BOOLEAN
```

ISTYPE(x, T) is TRUE if and only if x is a member of T. T must be an object type or traced reference type, and x must be assignable to T:

NARROW is defined as

```
NARROW  (x: Reference; T: RefType)  : T
```

NARROW(x, T) returns x after checking that x is a member of T. If the check fails, a runtime error occurs. T must be an object type or traced reference type, and x must be assignable to T.

TYPECODE is defined as

```
TYPECODE   (T: RefType)          : CARDINAL
           (r: REFANY)           : CARDINAL
           (r: UNTRACED ROOT)    : CARDINAL
```

Every object type or traced reference type (including NULL) has an associated integer code. Different types have different codes. The code for a type is constant for any single execution of a program but may differ for different executions. TYPECODE(T) returns the code for the type T and TYPECODE(r) returns the code for the allocated type of r. It is a static error if T is REFANY or is not an object type or traced reference type.

ORD and VAL operators are defined as

```
ORD   (element: Ordinal)             : INTEGER
VAL   (i: INTEGER; T: OrdinalType)   : T
```

ORD converts an element of an enumeration to the integer that represents its position in the enumeration order. The first value in any enumeration is represented by zero. If the type of element is a subrange of an enumeration T, the result is the position of the element within T, not within the subrange.

VAL is the inverse of ORD; it converts from a numeric position i into the element that occupies that position in an enumeration. If T is a subrange, VAL returns the element with the position i in the original enumeration type, not the subrange. It is a checked runtime error for the value of i to be out of range for T.

If n is an integer, ORD(n) = VAL(n, INTEGER) = n.

NUMBER operator is defined as

```
NUMBER    (T: OrdinalType)     : CARDINAL
          (A: FixedArrayType)  : CARDINAL
          (a: Array)           : CARDINAL
```

For an ordinal type T, NUMBER(T) returns the number of elements in T. For a fixed array type A, NUMBER(A) is defined by NUMBER(IndexType(A)). Similarly, for an array a, NUMBER(a) is defined by NUMBER(IndexType(a)). In this case, the expression a will be evaluated only if it denotes an open array.

FIRST and LAST are defined as

```
FIRST (T: OrdinalType)      : BaseType(T)
      (T: FloatType)        : T
      (A: FixedArrayType)   : BaseType(IndexType(A))
      (a: Array)            : BaseType(IndexType(a))
LAST  (T: OrdinalType)      : BaseType(T)
      (T: FloatType)        : T
      (A: FixedArrayType)   : BaseType(IndexType(A))
      (a: Array)            : BaseType(IndexType(a))
```

For a non-empty ordinal type T, FIRST returns the smallest value of T and LAST returns the largest value. If T is the empty enumeration, FIRST(T) and LAST(T) are static errors. If T is any other empty ordinal type, the values returned are implementation dependent, but they satisfy FIRST(T) > LAST(T).

For a floating-point type T, FIRST(T) and LAST(T) are the smallest and largest values of the type, respectively. On IEEE implementations, these are minus and plus infinity.

For a fixed array type A, FIRST(A) is defined by FIRST(IndexType(A)) and LAST(A) by LAST(IndexType(A)). Similarly, for an array a, FIRST(a) and LAST(a) are defined by FIRST(IndexType(a)) and LAST(IndexType(a)). The expression a will be evaluated only if it is an open array. Note that if a is an open array, FIRST(a) and LAST(a) have type INTEGER.

The following operations return size information for variables or types:

```
BITSIZE    (x: Any)     : CARDINAL
           (T: Type)    : CARDINAL
BYTESIZE   (x: Any)     : CARDINAL
           (T: Type)    : CARDINAL
ADRSIZE    (x: Any)     : CARDINAL
           (T: Type)    : CARDINAL
```

BITSIZE returns the number of bits, BYTESIZE the number of 8-bit bytes, and ADRSIZE the number of addressable locations. In all cases, x must be a designator and T must not be an open array type. A designator x will be evaluated only if its type is an open array type.

11.8.14. Text Operations

The following is the concatenation of a and b, as defined by Text.Cat:

```
infix   & (a,b: TEXT) : TEXT
```

11.8.15. Constant Expressions

Constant expressions are a subset of the general class of expressions, restricted by the requirement that it be possible to evaluate the expression statically. All operations are legal in constant expressions except for ADR, LOOPHOLE, TYPECODE, NARROW, ISTYPE, SUBARRAY, NEW, and dereferencing (explicit or implicit). The only procedures that can be applied to constant expressions are the functions in the Word interface.

A variable can appear in a constant expression only as an argument to FIRST, LAST, NUMBER, BITSIZE, BYTESIZE, or ADRSIZE, and such a variable must not have an open array type. Literals and top-level procedure constants are legal in constant expressions.

11.9. Unsafe Operations

There are some cases that no law can be framed to cover.

—Aristotle

The features defined in this section can potentially cause unchecked runtime errors and are thus forbidden in safe interfaces and modules.

An unchecked type transfer operation has the form

```
LOOPHOLE(e, T)
```

where e is an expression whose type is not an open array type and T is a type. It denotes e's bit pattern interpreted as a variable or value of type T. It is a designator if e is and is writable if e is. An unchecked runtime error can occur if e's bit pattern is not a legal T or if e is a designator and some legal bit pattern for T is not legal for e.

If T is not an open array type, BITSIZE(e) must equal BITSIZE(T). If T is an open array type, its element type must not be an open array type, and e's bit pattern is interpreted as an array whose length is BITSIZE(e) divided by BITSIZE (the element type of T). The division must come out even.

The following operations are primarily used for address arithmetic:

```
ADR       (VAR x: Any)                 : ADDRESS
infix   + (x: ADDRESS, y:INTEGER)      : ADDRESS
infix     (x: ADDRESS, y:INTEGER)      : ADDRESS
infix     (x,y: ADDRESS)               : INTEGER
```

`ADR(x)` is the address of the variable `x`. The actual argument must be a designator but need not be writable. The operations `+` and `-` treat addresses as integers. The validity of the addresses produced by these operations is implementation dependent. For example, the address of a variable in a local procedure frame is probably valid only for the duration of the call. The address of the referent of a traced reference is probably valid only as long as traced references prevent it from being collected (and not even that long if the implementation uses a compacting collector).

In unsafe modules, the `INC` and `DEC` statements apply to addresses as well as ordinals:

```
INC  (VAR x: ADDRESS; n: INTEGER := 1)
DEC  (VAR x: ADDRESS; n: INTEGER := 1)
```

These are short for `x := x + n` and `x := x - n`, except that `x` is evaluated only once.

A `DISPOSE` statement has the form

```
DISPOSE (v)
```

where `v` is a writable designator whose type is not `REFANY`, `ADDRESS`, or `NULL`. If `v` is untraced, the statement frees the storage for `v`'s referent and sets `v` to `NIL`. Freeing storage to which active references remain is an unchecked runtime error. If `v` is traced, the statement is equivalent to `v := NIL`. If `v` is `NIL`, the statement is a no-op.

In unsafe interfaces and modules, the definition of assignable for types is extended: Two reference types `T` and `U` are assignable if `T <: U` or `U <: T`. The only effect of this change is to allow a value of type `ADDRESS` to be assigned to a variable of type `UNTRACED REF T`. It is an unchecked runtime error if the value does not address a variable of type `T`.

In unsafe interfaces and modules, the type constructor `UNTRACED REF T` is allowed for traced as well as untraced `T`, and the fields of untraced objects can be traced. If `u` is an untraced reference to a traced variable `t`, then the validity of the traced references in `t` is implementation dependent because the garbage collector probably will not trace them through `u`.

11.10. Required Interfaces

There are several fundamental interfaces that every Modula-3 implementation must provide:

- `Text` provides operations on text strings.
- `Thread` provides synchronization primitives for multiple threads of control.
- `Word` provides operations on unsigned words.
- `Real`, `LongReal`, and `ExtendedReal` define the properties of the three floating-point types—for example, their bases and ranges.
- `RealFloat`, `LongFloat`, and `ExtendedFloat` provide numerical operations related to the floating-point representation—for example, extracting the exponent of a number.
- `FloatMode` provides operations for testing (and possibly setting) the behavior of the implementation in response to numeric conditions—for example, overflow.

Implementations are free to extend the required interfaces, provided they do not invalidate clients of the unextended interfaces.

Most Modula-3 implementations provide many other interfaces. A few that are recommended to other implementers, but not required are

- `Fmt` and `Lex` provide for textual formatting and scanning of numbers and other data.
- `Pickle` provides type-safe persistent storage via binary files called pickles.
- `Table` provides generic hash tables.

The interfaces in this section are included verbatim as a Modula-3 program in a literate-programming style. Each call in the interface is followed by a description of the call.

See `http://www.research.digital.com/SRC/modula-3/html` or `http://www.m3.org/` for other standard interfaces.

11.10.1. The `Text` Interface

This section defines the Text interface that defines text operations.

```
INTERFACE Text;
TYPE
  T = TEXT;
```

A non-nil `TEXT` represents a zero-based sequence of characters. `NIL` does not represent any sequence of characters, it will not be returned from any procedure in the interface, and it is a checked runtime error to pass it to any procedure in the interface.

```
PROCEDURE Cat(t, u: T): T;
```

The concatenation of `t` and `u`.

```
PROCEDURE Equal(t, u: T): BOOLEAN;
```

`TRUE` if `t` and `u` have the same length and (case-sensitive) contents.

```
PROCEDURE GetChar(t: T; i: CARDINAL): CHAR;
```

Character `i` of `t`. A checked runtime error if `i >= Length(t)`.

```
PROCEDURE Length(t: T): CARDINAL;
```

The number of characters in `t`.

```
PROCEDURE Empty(t: T): BOOLEAN;
```

`TRUE` if `Length(t) = 0`.

```
PROCEDURE Sub(t: T; start, length: CARDINAL): T;
```

Return a subsequence of `t`: empty if `start >= Length(t)` or `length = 0`; otherwise, the subsequence ranging from `start` to the minimum of `start+length-1` and `Length(t)-1`.

```
PROCEDURE SetChars(VAR a: ARRAY OF CHAR; t: T);
```

For each `i` from `0` to `MIN(LAST(a), Length(t)-1)`, set `a[i]` to `GetChar(t, i)`.

```
PROCEDURE FromChar(ch: CHAR): T;
```

A text containing the single character `ch`.

```
PROCEDURE FromChars(READONLY a: ARRAY OF CHAR): T;
```

A text containing the characters of `a`.

```
PROCEDURE Hash(t: T): INTEGER;
```

Return a hash function of the contents of `t`.

```
END Text.
```

11.10.2. The Thread Interface

If a shared variable is written concurrently by two threads, or written by one and read concurrently by another, the effect is to set the variable to an implementation-dependent value of its type. For example, if one thread writes `a[0]` while another concurrently writes `a[1]`, one of the writes might be lost. Thus, portable programs must use the `Thread` interface to provide mutual exclusion for shared variables.

```
INTERFACE Thread;
TYPE
  T <: REFANY;
  Mutex = MUTEX;
  Condition <: ROOT;
  Closure = OBJECT METHODS apply(): REFANY END;
```

A `Thread.T` is a handle on a thread. A `Mutex` is locked by some thread or unlocked. A `Condition` is a set of waiting threads. A newly allocated `Mutex` is unlocked; a newly allocated `Condition` is empty. It is a checked runtime error to pass the `NIL` `Mutex`, `Condition` or `T` to any procedure in this interface.

```
PROCEDURE Fork(cl: Closure): T;
```

A handle on a newly created thread executing `cl.apply()`.

```
PROCEDURE Join(t: T): REFANY;
```

Wait until `t` has terminated and return its result. It is a checked error to call this more than once for any `t`.

```
PROCEDURE Wait(m: Mutex; c: Condition);
```

The calling thread must have `m` locked. Atomically unlocks `m` and waits on `c`. Then relocks `m` and returns.

```
PROCEDURE Acquire(m: Mutex);
```

Wait until `m` is unlocked and then lock it.

```
PROCEDURE Release(m: Mutex);
```

The calling thread must have `m` locked. Unlocks `m`.

```
PROCEDURE Broadcast(c: Condition);
```

All threads waiting on `c` become eligible to run.

```
PROCEDURE Signal(c: Condition);
```

One or more threads waiting on `c` become eligible to run.

```
PROCEDURE Self(): T;
```

Return the handle of the calling thread.

```
EXCEPTION Alerted;
```

Used to approximate asynchronous interrupts.

```
PROCEDURE Alert(t: T);
```

Mark `t` as an alerted thread.

```
PROCEDURE TestAlert(): BOOLEAN;
```

`TRUE` if the calling thread has been marked alerted.

```
PROCEDURE AlertWait(m: Mutex; c: Condition) RAISES {Alerted};
```

Like `Wait`, but if the thread is marked alerted at the time of call or sometime during the wait, lock `m` and raise `Alerted`.

```
PROCEDURE AlertJoin(t: T): REFANY RAISES {Alerted};
```

Like `Join`, but if the calling thread is marked alerted at the time of call or sometime during the wait, raise `Alerted`.

```
CONST
  AtomicSize = ...;
```

An implementation-dependent integer constant: the number of bits in a memory-coherent block. If two components of a record or array fall in different blocks, they can be accessed concurrently by different threads without locking.

```
END Thread.
```

11.10.3. The `Word` Interface

The `Word` interface describes operations for unsigned arithmetic.

```
INTERFACE Word;
TYPE T = INTEGER;
CONST Size = BITSIZE(T);
```

A `Word.T w` represents a sequence of `Word.Size` bits w_0, ..., $w_{(Word.Size-1)}$. It also represents the unsigned number `SUM` $(w_i * 2i)$. Finally, it also represents a signed `INTEGER` by some implementation-dependent encoding (for example, two's complement). The built-in operations of the language deal with the signed value; the operations in this interface deal with the unsigned value or with the bit sequence.

Here are the arithmetic operations on unsigned words:

```
PROCEDURE Plus (x,y: T): T;  (* (x + y) MOD 2^Word.Size *)
PROCEDURE Times (x,y: T): T;  (* (x * y) MOD 2^Word.Size *)
PROCEDURE Minus (x,y: T): T;  (* (x - y) MOD 2^Word.Size *)
PROCEDURE Divide(x,y: T): T;  (* x DIV y *)
PROCEDURE Mod(x,y: T): T;  (* x MOD y *)
PROCEDURE LT(x,y: T): BOOLEAN; (* x < y *)
PROCEDURE LE(x,y: T): BOOLEAN; (* x <= y *)
PROCEDURE GT(x,y: T): BOOLEAN; (* x > y *)
PROCEDURE GE(x,y: T): BOOLEAN; (* x >= y *)
```

Here are the logical operations on bit sequences:

```
PROCEDURE And(x,y: T): T;  (* Bitwise AND of x and y *)
PROCEDURE Or (x,y: T): T;  (* Bitwise OR of x and y *)
PROCEDURE Xor(x,y: T): T;  (* Bitwise XOR of x and y *)
PROCEDURE Not (x: T): T;  (* Bitwise complement of x *)
```

Here are additional operations on bit sequences:

```
PROCEDURE Shift(x: T; n: INTEGER): T;
```

For all `i` such that both `i` and `i - n` are in the range `[0..Word.Size - 1]`, bit `i` of the result equals bit `i - n` of `x`. The other bits of the result are `0`. Thus shifting by `n > 0` is like multiplying by 2^n.

Because Modula-3 has no exponentiation operator, `Word.Shift(1, n)` is the usual way of writing 2^n in a constant expression.

```
PROCEDURE Rotate(x: T; n: INTEGER): T;
```

Bit `i` of the result is bit `((i - n) MOD Word.Size)` of `x`.

```
PROCEDURE Extract(x: T; i, n: CARDINAL): T;
```

Take `n` bits from `x`, with bit `i` as the least significant bit, and return them as the least significant `n` bits of a word whose other bits are `0`. A checked runtime error if `n + i > Word.Size`.

```
PROCEDURE Insert(x: T; y: T; i, n: CARDINAL): T;
```

Result of replacing `n` bits of `x`, with bit `i` as the least significant bit, by the least significant `n` bits of `y`. The other bits of `x` are unchanged. A checked runtime error if `n + i > Word.Size`.

```
END Word.
```

11.10.4. The `Real`, `LongReal`, and `Extended` Interfaces

For definitions of the terms used in these interfaces, see the ANSI/IEEE Standard 754-1985 for floating-point arithmetic.

These interfaces define constant attributes of the three built-in floating-point types:

```
INTERFACE Real; TYPE T = REAL;
CONST
  Base: INTEGER = ...;
  Precision: INTEGER = ...;
  MaxFinite: T = ...;
  MinPos: T = ...;
  MinPosNormal: T = ...;
END Real.
INTERFACE LongReal; TYPE T = LONGREAL;
CONST
  Base: INTEGER = ...;
  Precision: INTEGER = ...;
  MaxFinite: T = ...;
  MinPos: T = ...;
  MinPosNormal: T = ...;
END LongReal.
INTERFACE Extended; TYPE T = EXTENDED;
CONST
  Base: INTEGER = ...;
  Precision: INTEGER = ...;
  MaxFinite: T = ...;
  MinPos: T = ...;
  MinPosNormal: T = ...;
END Extended.
```

The specification is the same for all three interfaces:

- `Base` is the radix of the floating-point representation for `T`.
- `Precision` is the number of digits of precision for `T`.
- `MaxFinite` is the maximum finite value in `T`. For non-IEEE implementations, this is the same as `LAST(T)`.
- `MinPos` is the minimum positive value in `T`.
- `MinPosNormal` is the minimum positive normal value in `T`; it differs from `MinPos` only for implementations (such as IEEE) with denormalized numbers.

11.10.5. The `RealFloat`, `LongFloat`, and `ExtendedFloat` Interfaces

For definitions of the terms used in these interfaces, see the ANSI/IEEE Standard 754-1985 for floating-point arithmetic.

These interfaces define operations that depend on the floating-point representation. They are all are instances of a generic interface `Float`:

```
INTERFACE RealFloat = Float(Real) END RealFloat.
INTERFACE LongFloat = Float(LongReal) END LongFloat.
INTERFACE ExtendedFloat = Float(Extended) END ExtendedFloat.
GENERIC INTERFACE Float(R); TYPE T = R.T;
```

This generic interface provides access to the floating-point operations required or recommended by the IEEE floating-point standard. Consult the standard for the precise specifications of the procedures, including when their arguments are NaNs, infinities, and signed zeros and including what exceptions they can raise. The comments here specify their effect when the arguments are ordinary numbers and no exception is raised. Implementations on non-IEEE machines that have values similar to NaNs and infinities should explain how those values behave in an implementation guide.

```
PROCEDURE Scalb(x: T; n: INTEGER): T;
```

Return `x * 2`^{n}.

```
PROCEDURE Logb(x: T): T;
```

Return the exponent of `x`. More precisely, return the unique *n* such that the ratio `ABS(x) / Base`^{n} is in the range`[1..Base-1]`, unless `x` is denormalized, in which case return the minimum exponent value for `T`.

```
PROCEDURE ILogb(x: T): INTEGER;
```

Like `Logb`, but returns an integer, never raises an exception, and always returns the *n* such that `ABS(x) / Base`^{n} is in the range `[1..Base-1]`, even for denormalized numbers.

```
PROCEDURE NextAfter(x, y: T): T;
```

Return the next representable neighbor of `x` in the direction towards `y`. If `x = y`, return `x`.

```
PROCEDURE CopySign(x, y: T): T;
```

Return `x` with the sign of `y`.

```
PROCEDURE Finite(x: T): BOOLEAN;
```

Return TRUE if x is strictly between minus infinity and plus infinity. This always returns TRUE on non-IEEE machines.

```
PROCEDURE IsNaN(x: T): BOOLEAN;
```

Return FALSE if x represents a numerical (possibly infinite) value, and TRUE if x does not represent a numerical value. For example, on IEEE implementations, returns TRUE if x is a NaN, FALSE otherwise.

```
PROCEDURE Sign(x: T): [0..1];
```

Return the sign bit of x. For non-IEEE implementations, this is the same as ORD(x >= 0); for IEEE implementations, Sign(-0) = 1 and Sign(+0) = 0.

```
PROCEDURE Differs(x, y: T): BOOLEAN;
```

Return (x < y OR y < x). Thus, for IEEE implementations, Differs(NaN,x) is always FALSE; for non-IEEE implementations, Differs(x,y) is the same as x # y.

```
PROCEDURE Unordered(x, y: T): BOOLEAN;
```

Return NOT (x <= y OR y <= x).

```
PROCEDURE Sqrt(x: T): T;
```

Return the square root of T. This must be correctly rounded if FloatMode.IEEE is TRUE.

```
TYPE IEEEClass =
  {SignalingNaN, QuietNaN, Infinity, Normal, Denormal, Zero};
PROCEDURE Class(x: T): IEEEClass;
```

Return the IEEE number class containing x.

```
END Float.
```

11.10.6. The FloatMode Interface

The FloatMode interface allows you to test the behavior of rounding and of numerical exceptions. On some implementations, it also allows you to change the behavior on a per-thread basis. For definitions of the terms used in this interface, see the ANSI/IEEE Standard 754-1985 for floating-point arithmetic.

```
INTERFACE FloatMode;
CONST IEEE: BOOLEAN = ...;
TRUE for fully-compliant IEEE implementations.
EXCEPTION Failure;
```

Raised by attempts to set modes that are not supported by the implementation.

```
TYPE RoundingMode = {NearestElseEven, TowardMinusInfinity,
  TowardPlusInfinity, TowardZero, NearestElseAwayFromZero,
  IBM370, Other};
```

Rounding modes. the first four are the IEEE modes.

```
CONST RoundDefault: RoundingMode = ...;
```

Implementation dependent: the default mode for rounding arithmetic operations, used by a newly forked thread. This also specifies the behavior of the `ROUND` operation in halfway cases.

```
PROCEDURE SetRounding(md: RoundingMode) RAISES {Failure};
```

Change the rounding mode for the calling thread to `md`, or raise the exception if this cannot be done. This affects the implicit rounding in floating-point operations; it does not affect the `ROUND` operation. Generally, this can be done only on IEEE implementations and only if `md` is an IEEE mode.

```
PROCEDURE GetRounding(): RoundingMode;
```

Return the rounding mode for the calling thread.

```
TYPE Flag =  {Invalid, Inexact, Overflow, Underflow,  DivByZero,
  IntOverflow, IntDivByZero};
```

Associated with each thread is a set of boolean status flags recording whether the condition represented by the flag has occurred in the thread since the flag was last reset. The meaning of the first five flags is defined precisely in the IEEE floating-point standard. Roughly, they mean

`Invalid`—Invalid argument to an operation.

`Inexact`—An operation produced an inexact result.

`Overflow`—A floating-point operation produced a result whose absolute value is too large to be represented.

`Underflow`—A floating-point operation produced a result whose absolute value is too small to be represented.

`DivByZero`—Floating-point division by zero.

The meaning of the last two flags is

`IntOverflow`—An integer operation produced a result whose absolute value is too large to be represented.

`IntDivByZero`—Integer `DIV` or `MOD` by zero.

```
CONST NoFlags = SET OF Flags {};
PROCEDURE GetFlags(): SET OF Flag;
```

Return the set of flags for the current thread.

```
PROCEDURE SetFlags(s: SET OF Flag): SET OF Flag RAISES{Failure};
```

Set the flags for the current thread to `s`, and return their previous values.

```
PROCEDURE ClearFlag(f: Flag);
```

Turn off the flag `f` for the current thread.

```
EXCEPTION
  Trap(Flag);
TYPE
  Behavior = {Trap, SetFlag, Ignore};
```

Calls in this interface may raise the `Trap` exception:

The behavior of an operation that causes one of the flag conditions is either

> `Ignore`—Return some result and do nothing.
>
> `SetFlag`—Return some result and set the condition flag. For IEEE implementations, the result of the operation is defined by the standard.
>
> `Trap`—Possibly set the condition flag; in any case, raise the `Trap` exception with the appropriate flag as the argument.

```
PROCEDURE SetBehavior(f: Flag; b: Behavior) RAISES {Failure};
```

Set the behavior of the current thread for the flag `f` to be `b`, or raise `Failure` if this cannot be done.

```
PROCEDURE GetBehavior(f: Flag): Behavior;
```

Return the behavior of the current thread for the flag `f`.

```
END FloatMode.
```

11.11. Syntax

> *Care should be taken, when using colons and semicolons in the same sentence, that the reader understands how far the force of each sign carries.*
>
> *—Robert Graves and Alan Hodge*

This section includes an overview of the language syntax.

11.11.1. Keywords

AND	DO	FROM	NOT	REPEAT	UNTIL
ANY	ELSE	GENERIC	OBJECT	RETURN	UNTRACED
ARRAY	ELSIF	IF	OF	REVEAL	VALUE
AS	END	IMPORT	OR	ROOT	VAR
BEGIN	EVAL	IN	OVERRIDES	SET	WHILE
BITS	EXCEPT	INTERFACE	PROCEDURE	THEN	WITH
BRANDED	EXCEPTION	LOCK	RAISE	TO	
BY	EXIT	LOOP	RAISES	TRY	
CASE	EXPORTS	METHODS	READONLY	TYPE	
CONST	FINALLY	MOD	RECORD	TYPECASE	
DIV	FOR	MODULE	REF	UNSAFE	

11.11.2. Reserved Identifiers

ABS	CARDINAL	FIRST	LONGREAL	NIL	SUBARRAY
ADDRESS	CEILING	FLOAT	LOOPHOLE	NULL	TEXT
ADR	CHAR	FLOOR	MAX	NUMBER	TRUE
ADRSIZE	DEC	INC	MIN	ORD	TRUNC
BITSIZE	DISPOSE	INTEGER	MUTEX	REAL	TYPECODE
BOOLEAN	EXTENDED	ISTYPE	NARROW	REFANY	VAL
BYTESIZE	FALSE	LAST	NEW	ROUND	

11.11.3. Operators

```
+    <     #    =    ;    ..   :
-    >     {    }    |    :=   <:
*    <=    (    )    ^    ,    =>
/    >=    [    ]    .    &
```

11.11.4. Comments

A comment is an arbitrary character sequence opened by `(*` and closed by `*)`. Comments can be nested and can extend over more than one line.

11.11.5. Pragmas

A pragma is an arbitrary character sequence opened by `<*` and closed by `*>`. Pragmas can be nested and can extend over more than one line. Pragmas are hints to the implementation; they do not affect the language semantics.

We recommend supporting the two pragmas `<*INLINE*>` and `<*EXTERNAL*>`. The pragma `<*INLINE*>` precedes a procedure declaration to indicate that the procedure should be expanded at the point of call. The pragma `<*EXTERNAL N:L*>` precedes an interface or a declaration in an interface to indicate that the entity it precedes is implemented by the language `L`, where it has the name `N`. If `:L` is omitted, then the implementation's default external language is assumed. If `N` is omitted, then the external name is determined from the Modula-3 name in some implementation-dependent way.

11.11.6. Conventions for Syntax

We use the following notation for defining syntax:

```
X Y     X followed by Y
X|Y     X or Y
[X]     X or empty
{X}     A possibly empty sequence of X's
X&Y     X or Y or X Y
```

"Followed by" has greater binding power than `|` or `&`; parentheses are used to override this precedence rule. Non-terminals begin with an upper-case letter. Terminals are either keywords or quoted operators. The symbols `Ident`, `Number`, `TextLiteral`, and `CharLiteral` are defined in the token grammar. Each production is terminated by a period. The syntax does not reflect the restrictions that revelations and exceptions can be declared only at the top level; nor does it include explicit productions for NEW, INC, and DEC, which parse like procedure calls.

11.11.7. Compilation Unit Productions

```
Compilation     = [UNSAFE] (Interface | Module) | GenInf | GenMod.
Interface       = INTERFACE Id ";" {Import} {Decl} END Id "."
                | INTERFACE Id "=" Id GenActls END Id ".".
Module          = MODULE Id [EXPORTS IdList] ";" {Import} Block Id "."
                | MODULE Id [EXPORTS IdList] "=" Id GenActls END Id ".".
GenInf          = GENERIC INTERFACE Id GenFmls ";"
                {Import} {Decl} END Id ".".
GenMod          = GENERIC MODULE Id GenFmls ";"
                {Import} Block Id ".".
Import          = AsImport | FromImport.
AsImport        = IMPORT ImportItem {"," ImportItem} ";".
FromImport      = FROM Id IMPORT IdList ";".
Block           = {Decl} BEGIN S END.
Decl            = CONST {ConstDecl ";"}
                | TYPE {TypeDecl ";"}
                | EXCEPTION {ExceptionDecl ";"}
                | VAR {VariableDecl ";"}
                | ProcedureHead ["=" Block Id] ";"
                | REVEAL {QualId ("=" | "<:") Type ";"}.
GenFmls         = "(" [IdList] ")".
GenActls        = "(" [IdList] ")".
ImportItem      = Id | Id AS Id.
ConstDecl       = Id [":" Type] "=" ConstExpr.
TypeDecl        = Id ("=" | "<:") Type.
ExceptionDecl   = Id ["(" Type ")"].
VariableDecl    = IdList (":" Type & ":=" Expr).
ProcedureHead   = PROCEDURE Id Signature.
Signature       = "(" Formals ")" [":" Type] [RAISES Raises].
Formals         = [ Formal {";" Formal} [";"] ].
Formal          = [Mode] IdList (":" Type & ":=" ConstExpr).
Mode            = VALUE | VAR | READONLY.
Raises          = "{" [ QualId {"," QualId} ] "}" | ANY.
```

11.11.9. Statement Productions

```
Stmt        = AssignSt | Block | CallSt | CaseSt | ExitSt | EvalSt | ForSt
            | IfSt | LockSt | LoopSt | RaiseSt | RepeatSt |  ReturnSt
            | TCaseSt | TryXptSt | TryFinSt | WhileSt |  WithSt.
S           = [ Stmt {";" Stmt} [";"] ].
AssignSt    = Expr ":=" Expr.
CallSt      = Expr "(" [Actual {"," Actual}] ")".
CaseSt      = CASE Expr OF [Case] {"|" Case} [ELSE S] END.
ExitSt      = EXIT.
EvalSt      = EVAL Expr.
ForSt       = FOR Id ":=" Expr TO Expr [BY Expr] DO S END.
IfSt        = IF Expr THEN S {ELSIF Expr THEN S} [ELSE S] END.
```

```
LockSt       = LOCK Expr DO S END.
LoopSt       = LOOP S END.
RaiseSt      = RAISE QualId ["(" Expr ")"].
RepeatSt     = REPEAT S UNTIL Expr.
ReturnSt     = RETURN [Expr].
TCaseSt      = TYPECASE Expr OF [TCase] {"|" TCase} [ELSE S] END.
TryXptSt     = TRY S EXCEPT [Handler] {"|" Handler} [ELSE S] END.
TryFinSt     = TRY S FINALLY S END.
WhileSt      = WHILE Expr DO S END.
WithSt       = WITH Binding {"," Binding} DO S END.
Case         = Labels {"," Labels} "=>" S.
Labels       = ConstExpr [".." ConstExpr].
Handler      = QualId {"," QualId} ["(" Id ")"] "=>" S.
TCase        = Type {"," Type} ["(" Id ")"] "=>" S.
Binding      = Id "=" Expr.
Actual       = Type | [Id ":="] Expr.
```

11.11.9. Type Productions

```
Type           = TypeName | ArrayType | PackedType | EnumType
               | ObjectType  | ProcedureType | RecordType
               | RefType |  SetType | SubrangeType  | "(" Type ")".
ArrayType      = ARRAY [Type {"," Type}] OF Type.
PackedType     = BITS ConstExpr FOR Type.
EnumType       = "{" [IdList] "}".
ObjectType     = [TypeName | ObjectType] [Brand] OBJECT Fields
                 [METHODS Methods] [OVERRIDES Overrides] END.
ProcedureType = PROCEDURE Signature.
RecordType     = RECORD Fields END.
RefType        = [UNTRACED] [Brand] REF Type.
SetType        = SET OF Type.
SubrangeType   = "[" ConstExpr ".." ConstExpr "]".
Brand          = BRANDED [ConstExpr].
Fields         = [ Field {";" Field} [";"] ].
Field          = IdList (":" Type & ":=" ConstExpr).
Methods        = [ Method {";" Method} [";"] ].
Method         = Id Signature [":=" ConstExpr].
Overrides      = [ Override {";" Override} [";"] ].
Override       = Id ":=" ConstExpr .
```

11.11.10. Expression Productions

```
ConstExpr = Expr.
Expr      = E1 {OR E1}.
   E1     = E2 {AND E2}.
   E2     = {NOT} E3.
   E3     = E4 {Relop E4}.
   E4     = E5 {Addop E5}.
   E5     = E6 {Mulop E6}.
   E6     = {"+" | "-"} E7.
   E7     = E8 {Selector}.
   E8     = Id     | Number | CharLiteral | TextLiteral  | Constructor
          |  "(" Expr ")".
```

```
Relop         =  "="  | "#" | "<" | "<=" | ">" | ">=" | IN.
Addop         =  "+"  | "-" | "&".
Mulop         =  "*"  | "/" | DIV | MOD.
Selector      =  "^"  | "." Id | "[" Expr {"," Expr} "]"
              |  "(" [ Actual {"," Actual} ] ")".
Constructor =  Type "{" [ SetCons | RecordCons | ArrayCons ] "}".
SetCons       =  SetElt {"," SetElt}.
SetElt        =  Expr [".." Expr].
RecordCons    =  RecordElt {"," RecordElt}.
RecordElt     =  [Id ":="] Expr.
ArrayCons     =  Expr {"," Expr} ["," ".."].
```

11.11.11. Miscellaneous Productions

```
IdList        =  Id {"," Id}.
QualId        =  Id ["." Id].
TypeName      =  QualId | ROOT | UNTRACED ROOT.
```

11.11.12. Token Productions

To read a token, first skip all blanks, tabs, newlines, carriage returns, vertical tabs, form feeds, comments, and pragmas. Then read the longest sequence of characters that forms an operator or an `Id` or `Literal`.

An `Id` is a case-significant sequence of letters, digits, and underscores that begins with a letter. An `Id` is a keyword if it appears in the list of keywords, a reserved identifier if it appears in the list of reserved identifiers, and an ordinary identifier otherwise.

In the following grammar, terminals are characters surrounded by double-quotes and the special terminal `DQUOTE` represents double-quote itself:

```
Id             = Letter {Letter | Digit | "_"}.
Literal        = Number | CharLiteral | TextLiteral.
CharLiteral    = "'" (PrintingChar | Escape | DQUOTE) "'".
TextLiteral    = DQUOTE {PrintingChar | Escape | "'"} DQUOTE.
Escape         = "\" "n" | "\" "t"  | "\" "r"  | "\" "f"  | "\" "\"
               |  "\" "'"  | "\" DQUOTE
               |  "\" OctalDigit OctalDigit OctalDigit.
Number         = Digit {Digit}
               |  Digit {Digit} "_" HexDigit {HexDigit}
               |  Digit {Digit} "." Digit {Digit} [Exp].
Exp            = ("E" | "e" | "D" | "d" | "X" | "x")
               ["+" | "-"] Digit {Digit}.
PrintingChar   = Letter | Digit | OtherChar.
HexDigit       = Digit | "A" | "B" | "C" | "D" | "E" | "F"
               |  "a" | "b" | "c" | "d" | "e" | "f".
Digit          = "0" | "1" | ... | "9".
OctalDigit     = "0" | "1" | ... | "7".
Letter         = "A" | "B" | ... | "Z" | "a" | "b" | ... | "z".
```

```
OtherChar     =  " " | "!" | "#" | "$" | "%" | "&" | "(" | ")"
              |  "*" | "+" | "," | "-" | "." | "/" | ":" | ";"
              |  "<" | "=" | ">" | "?" | "@" | "[" | "]" | "^"
              |  "_" | "`" | "{" | "|" | "}" | " "
              |  ExtendedChar
ExtendedChar  =  any char with ISO-Latin-1 code in
              [8_ 240.. 8_ 377].
```

11.12. Acknowledgments

The original definition of Modula-3 was given in SRC Research Report 31, August 1988. It was revised in Report 52, November 1989 and finally published in *Systems Programming with Modula-3*, November 1989. This edition of the language definition is derived from all of these reports.

Modula-3 was designed by Luca Cardelli, Jim Donahue, Mick Jordan, Bill Kalsow, and Greg Nelson, as a joint project by the Digital Equipment Corporation Systems Research Center and the Olivetti Research Center. Paul Rovner made many contributions as a founding member of the design committee. The language specification was written by Lucille Glassman and Greg Nelson under the watchful supervision of the whole committee.

Maurice Wilkes had the inspiration that sparked the project.

Our technical starting point was Modula-2+, which was designed by Paul Rovner, Roy Levin, John Wick, Andrew Birrell, Butler Lampson, and Garret Swart. We made good use of the ruthlessly complete description of Modula-2+ in Mary-Claire van Leunen's *Modula-2+ User's Manual*. The ideas in the + part of Modula-2+ were mostly derived from the Mesa and Cedar languages developed at Xerox PARC.

Niklaus Wirth designed Modula-2, the starting point of our starting point. He also reviewed the evolving design and made many valuable suggestions—not one of which was a suggested addition. Indeed, he inspired us with the courage to pull out a number of deep-rooted weeds.

SRC Modula-3 was implemented by Bill Kalsow and Eric Muller. Olivetti Modula-3 was implemented by Mick Jordan, Trevor Morris, David Chase, Steve Glassman, and Marion Sturtevant.

The language and this chapter were greatly improved by the helpful feedback from Bob Ayers, Andrew Black, Regis Crelier, Dan Craft, Hans Eberle, John Ellis, Stu Feldman, Michel Gangnet, Lucille Glassman,

David Goldberg, Stephen Harrison, Sam Harbison, Jim Horning, Solange Karsenty, Mike Kupfer, Butler Lampson, Mark Manasse, Tim Mann, Eliot Moss, Dick Orgass, Sharon Perl, Norman Ramsey, Lyle Ramshaw, Eric Roberts, Peter Robinson, Ed Satterthwaite, Jorge Stolfi, Garret Swart, Chuck Thacker, and Ken Zadeck.

We are grateful for the support of Digital Equipment Corporation in general and Bob Taylor and Sam Fuller in particular.

For more information about Modula-3 see `http://www.m3.org` and `http://www.research.digital.com/modula-3/html/`.

PART VII

Java

CHAPTER 12

What Is Java?[1]

by James Gosling, Bill Joy, and Guy Steele

Java was originally called Oak and designed for use in embedded consumer-electronic applications by James Gosling. After several years of experience with the language, and significant contributions by Ed Frank, Patrick Naughton, Jonathan Payne, and Chris Warth, it was retargeted to the Internet, renamed Java, and substantially revised to be the language specified here. The final form of the language was defined by James Gosling, Bill Joy, Guy Steele, Richard Tuck, Frank Yellin, and Arthur van Hoff, with help from Graham Hamilton, Tim Lindholm, and many other friends and colleagues.

Java is a general-purpose, concurrent, class-based, object-oriented programming language, specifically designed to have as few implementation dependencies as possible. Java allows application developers to write a program once and then be able to run it everywhere on the Internet.

We believe that Java is a mature language, ready for widespread use. Nevertheless, we expect some evolution of the language in the years to come. We intend to manage this evolution in a way that is completely compatible with existing applications. To do this, we intend to make relatively few new versions of the language and to distinguish each new version with a different filename extension. Java compilers and systems will be able to support the several versions simultaneously, with complete compatibility.

---

[1]This chapter is reprinted with permission from Gosling, J., B. Joy, and G. Steele. 1996. *The Java Language Specification*. Reading, MA: Addison-Wesley.

Much research and experimentation with Java is already underway. We encourage this work and will continue to cooperate with external groups to explore improvements to Java. For example, we have already received several interesting proposals for parameterized types. In technically difficult areas, near the state of the art, this kind of research collaboration is essential.

CHAPTER 13

Working with Java[1]

by Ken Arnold and James Gosling

See Europe! Ten Countries in Seventeen Days!

—Sign in a travel agent's window

This chapter is a whirlwind tour of the Java programming language that gets you started writing Java code quickly.[2] We cover the main points of the language quickly, without slowing you down with full-blown detail.

13.1. Getting Started

Java programs are built from *classes*. From a class definition, you can create any number of *objects* that are known as *instances* of that class. Think of a class as a factory with blueprints and instructions to build gadgets—objects are the gadgets that factory makes.

A class contains two kinds of *members*, called *fields* and *methods*. Fields are data belonging either to the class itself or to objects of the class; they make up the *state* of the object or class. Methods are collections of *statements* that operate on the fields to manipulate the state.

[1]This chapter is reprinted with the permission of Sun Microsystems from Arnold, K., and J. Gosling. 1996. *The Java Programming Language*. Reading, MA: Addison-Wesley.

[2]The Java programming language is written simply as "Java" throughout.

The first sample program in many languages prints "Hello, world." Here is the Java version:

```
class HelloWorld {
     Public static void main (String[] args) {
          System.out.println("Hello, world");
     }
}
```

Use your favorite text editor to type this program source into a file. Then run the Java compiler to compile the source of this program into Java *bytecodes*, the "machine language" for the Java virtual machine. Details of editing source and compiling vary from system to system and aren't described here—consult your system manuals for specific information. When you run the program, it displays:

```
Hello, world
```

Now you have a small Java program that does something, but what does it mean?

The program above declares a class called `HelloWorld` with a single method called `main`. Class members appear between curly braces `{` and `}` following the class name. `HelloWorld` has only one method, and no fields.

The `main` method's only *parameter* is an array of `String` objects that are the program's arguments from the command line with which it was invoked. Arrays and strings are covered later, as well as what `args` means for the `main` method.

The `main` method is declared `void` because it doesn't return a value. It is one of a few special method names in Java: The `main` method of a class, if declared as above, is executed when you run the class as an application. When run, `main` can create objects, evaluate expressions, invoke other methods, and do anything else needed to define an application's behavior.

In the example above, `main` contains a single statement that invokes a method on the `System` class's `out` object. Methods are invoked by supplying an object reference and a method name, separated by a dot (`.`). `HelloWorld` uses the `out` object's `println` method to print a newline-terminated string on the standard output stream.

Exercise 13.1

Enter, compile, and run `HelloWorld` on your system.

Exercise 13.2

Try changing parts of `HelloWorld` and see what errors you get.

13.2. Variables

The next example prints the *Fibonacci sequence*—an infinite sequence whose first few terms are

```
1
1
2
3
5
8
13
21
34
```

The Fibonacci sequence starts with the terms 1 and 1, and successive terms are the sum of the previous two terms. A Fibonacci printing program is simple, but it demonstrates how to declare variables, write a simple loop, and perform basic arithmetic. Here is the Fibonacci program:

```
class Fibonacci {
    /** Print out the Fibonacci sequence for values < 50 */
    public static void main (String[] args) {
        int lo = 1;
        int hi = 1;

        System.out.println(lo);
        while (hi < 50) {
            System.out.println(hi);
            hi = lo + hi;       // new hi
            lo = hi - lo;       /* new lo is (sum-old lo)
                                   i.e., the old hi */
        }
    }
}
```

This example declares a Fibonacci class that, like `HelloWorld`, has a `main` method. The first two lines of `main` declare two variables, `hi` and `lo`. Every variable must have a *type* that precedes its name. `hi` and `lo` are of type `int`, 32-bit signed integers with values in the range -2^{32} through $2^{32}-1$.

Java has built-in "primitive" data types to support integers, floating-point, Boolean, and character values. These primitive types hold data that Java understands directly, as opposed to object types defined by programmers. Java has no "default" types; the type of every variable must be defined explicitly. The primitive data types of Java are

`boolean`	Either `true` or `false`
`char`	16-bit Unicode 1.1 character
`byte`	8-bit integer (signed)
`short`	16-bit integer (signed)

`int`	32-bit integer (signed)
`long`	64-bit integer (signed)
`float`	32-bit floating point (IEEE 754-1985)
`double`	64-bit floating point (IEEE 754-1985)

In the Fibonacci program, we declared `hi` and `lo` with initial values of `1`. The starting values are set by initialization expressions, using the `=` operator, when the variables are declared. The `=` operator sets the variable named on the left-hand side to the value of the expression on the right-hand side. In this program, `hi` is the last term in the series and `lo` is the previous term.

Variables are *undefined* prior to initialization. Should you try to use variables before assigning a value, the Java compiler will refuse to compile your program until you fix the problem.

The `while` statement in the example provides one way of looping in Java. The expression inside the `while` is evaluated—if true, the body of the loop is executed and the expression tested again. The `while` is repeated until the expression becomes false. If it never becomes false, the program will run forever, unless something intervenes to break out of the loop, like a `break` statement, or an exception happening.

The expression that `while` tests is a Boolean expression that has the value `true` or `false`. The Boolean expression above tests whether the current high value of the sequence is less than 50. If the high value is less than 50, its value is printed and the next value calculated. If the high value equals or exceeds 50, control passes to the first line of code following the body of the `while` loop. That is the end of the main method in this example, so the program is finished.

Notice that the `println` method accepts an integer argument in the Fibonacci example above, whereas it accepted a string argument in the `HelloWorld` example. The `println` method is one of many methods that are *overloaded* such that they can accept arguments of different types.

Exercise 13.3

Add a title to the printed list.

Exercise 13.4

Write a program that generates a different sequence, such as a table of squares (multiplication is done using `*`, such as `i * i`).

13.3. Comments in Code

The English-like things scattered through the code are *comments*. Java has three styles of comments, all illustrated in the example.

Text following `//` up to the end of the line is ignored by the compiler, as is text between `/*` and the next `*/`.

Comments enable you to write descriptive text beside your code, to annotate it for future programmers who may read your code in the future. The "future programmer" may well be *you* months or years later. You save yourself effort by commenting your own code. Also, you often find bugs when you write comments: because explaining what the code is supposed to do forces you to think about it.

The third kind of comment appears at the very top, between `/**` and `*/`. A comment starting with two asterisks is a *documentation comment* ("doc comment" for short). Documentation comments are intended to describe declarations that follow them. The comment in the above example is for the `main` method. A tool called `javadoc` extracts documentation comments and generates HTML documentation.

13.4. Named Constants

Constants are values like `12`, `17.9`, and `"Strings Like This"`. Constants are how you specify values that are not computed and recomputed, but remain, well, constant for the life of a program.

Programmers prefer *named constants* for two reasons. One reason is that the name of the constant is a form of documentation. The name can (and should) describe what the particular value is used for.

Another reason is that you define a named constant in a single place in a program. When the constant needs to be changed or corrected, it can be changed in only one place, easing program maintenance. Named constants in Java are created by declaring a variable as `static` and `final`, and providing its initial value in the declaration:

```
class CircleStuff {
        static final double π = 3.1416;
}
```

The value of π can be changed in just one place when we discover that five significant digits of precision are not enough. We declared π as `double`—a double-precision 64-bit floating-point number. Now we could change π to a more precise value, like 3.14159265358979323846.

You can group related constants within a class. For example, a card game might use these constants:

```
class Suit {
      final static int CLUBS     = 1;
      final static int DIAMONDS  = 2;
      final static int HEARTS    = 3;
      final static int SPADES    = 4;
};
```

With this declaration, `Suit` in a program would be accessed as `Suit.HEARTS`, `Suit.SPADES`, and so on, thus grouping all the suit names within the single name `Suit`.

13.4.1. Unicode Characters

We take a minor diversion to note the π symbol as the name of a constant in the previous example. In most programming languages, identifiers are usually limited to the letters and digits available in the ASCII character set.

Java moves you toward the modern world of internationalized software: You write Java code in *Unicode*—an international character-set standard. Unicode characters are 16 bits and provide a character range large enough to write the major languages used in the world, which is why we can use π for the name of the value in the example above. π is a valid letter from the Greek section of Unicode, and therefore valid in Java source. Most existing Java code is written in ASCII, a 7-bit character standard, or ISO-Latin-1, an 8-bit character standard commonly called "Latin-1." But, they are translated into Unicode before processing so the Java character set is always Unicode.

Exercise 13.5

Change the `HelloWorld` application to use a named string constant as the string to print.

Exercise 13.6

Change the `Fibonacci` application to use a named constant in its loop instead of a literal constant.

13.5. Flow of Control

"Flow of control" is the term for deciding which statements in a program are executed. The `while` loop in the Fibonacci program above is one way. Other flow-of-control statements include `if/else`, `for`, `switch`, `do/while`, and *blocks*—multiple statements grouped within `{` and `}`. We change the

Fibonacci sequence program by numbering the elements of the sequence, and marking even numbers with an asterisk:

```
class ImprovedFibonacci {
     /** Print out the first few Fibonacci
       * numbers, marking evens with a '*' */
     static final int MAX_INDEX = 10;

     public static void main(String[] args) {
          int lo = 1;
          int hi = 1;
          String mark;

          System.out.println("1: " + lo);
          for (int I=2; I < MAX_INDEX; I++) {
               if (hi % 2 == 0_
                   mark = " *";
               else
                   mark = "";
               System.out.println(i + ": " + hi + mark);
               hi = lo + hi;           // new hi
               /* new lo is (sum - old lo) i.e., the old hi */
               lo = hi - lo;
          }
     }
}
```

Here is the new output:

```
1: 1
2: 1
3: 2 *
4: 3
5: 5
6: 8 *
7: 13
8: 21
9: 34 *
```

To number the elements of the sequence, we used a `for` loop instead of a `while` loop. A `for` loop is shorthand for a `while` loop, but with an initialization and increment phase added. The `for` loop above is equivalent to this `while` loop:

```
{
     int I = 2;
     while (I < MAX=INDEX) {
          // .. do the printing stuff
          I++;
     }
}
```

The `++` operator in the code fragment above may be unfamiliar if you're new to C-derived programming languages. The plus-plus operator increments by one the value of any variable it abuts—the contents of variable `i` in this case. The `++` operator is a *prefix* operator when it comes before its operand, and *postfix* when it comes after. Similarly, minus-minus decrements by one the value of any variable it abuts, and can also be prefix or postfix. The ++ and – operators come from the C programming language. In the context of the example above, a statement like

```
i++;
```

is equivalent to

```
i = i + 1;
```

Beyond simple assignment, Java supports other assignment operators that apply an arithmetic operation to the value on the left-hand side of the operator. For example, another way to write `i++` in the `for` loop above would be to write

```
i += 1;
```

which adds the value on the right-hand side of the `+=` operator (namely `1`) to the variable on the left-hand side (namely `i`). Many of the binary operators in Java (operators that take two operands) can be joined with the `=` in a similar way.

Inside the `for` loop we use an `if/else` to see if the current `hi` value is even. The `if` statement tests the expression between the parentheses. If the expression is `true`, the first statement or block in the body of the `if` is executed. If the expression is `false`, the statement or block following the `else` clause is executed. The `else` part is optional: If the `else` is not present, nothing is done when the expression is false. After figuring out which (if any) clause to execute, control passes to the code following the body of the `if` statement.

The example tests if `hi` is even, using the `%` or *remainder* operator. It produces the remainder after dividing the value on the left side by the value on the right. If the left-side value is even, the remainder is 0, and the following statement assigns a string containing the even-number indicator to `marker`. The `else` clause is executed for odd numbers, setting `marker` to an empty string.

The `println` invocation is more complex, using the `+` operator to concatenate strings representing `i`, a separator, a string representing `hi`, and the marker string. The `+` operator is a concatenation operator when used with strings, whereas it is an addition operator when used in arithmetic expressions.

Exercise 13.7

Change the loop so that `i` counts backward instead of forward.

13.6. Classes and Objects

Java, like any object-oriented programming language, provides a tool to solve programming problems using the notions of classes and objects. Objects in Java have a type; that type is the object's class. Each class type has two kinds of members, namely, fields and methods.

- Fields are data variables associated with a class and its objects. Fields store results of computations performed by the class's methods.
- Methods contain the executable code of a class. Methods are built from statements. The way in which methods are *invoked* and the statements contained within those methods are what ultimately directs program execution.

Here is the declaration of a simple class that might represent a point on a two-dimensional plane:

```
class Point {
     public double x, y;
}
```

This `Point` class has two fields representing the x and y coordinates of a point, and has (as yet) no methods. A class declaration like this one is, conceptually, a plan that defines what objects manufactured from that class look like, plus sets of instructions that define the behavior of those objects. The blueprint of an object adds its maximum value when you use the plans and instructions in the blueprint to manufacture goods (objects) from those plans.

Members of a class can have various levels of visibility. The `public` declaration of `x` and `y` in the `Point` class means that any code with access to a `Point` object can read or modify those values. Other levels of visibility limit member access to code in the class itself, or to other related classes.

13.6.1 Creating Objects

Objects are created using an expression containing the `new` keyword. Creating an object from a class definition is also known as *instantiation*; thus, objects are often called instances.

In Java, newly created objects are allocated within an area of system memory known as the *heap*. All objects in Java are accessed via *object references*—any variable that appears to hold an object actually contains a reference to that object. Object references are `null` when they do not reference any object.

Most of the time, you can be imprecise in the distinction between actual objects and references to objects. You can say "pass the object to the method" when you really mean "pass an object reference to the method." We are careful about this distinction only where it makes a difference. Most of the time, you can use "object" and "object reference" interchangeably.

Getting back to the `Point` class defined previously, suppose you are building a graphics application in which you need to track lots of points. You represent each point by its own concrete `Point` object. Here is how you might create and initialize `Point` objects:

```
Point  lowerLeft = new Point ();
Point  upperRight = new Point ();
Point  middlePoint = new Point ();

lowerLeft.x = 0.0;
lowerLeft.y = 0.0;

upperRight.x = 1280.0;
upperRight.y = 1024.0;

middlePoint.x = 640.0;
middlePoint.y = 512.0;
```

Each `Point` object is unique and has its own copy of the `x` and `y` fields. Changing `x` in the `lowerLeft`, for example, does not affect the value of `x` in `upperRight` object. The fields in objects are known as *instance variables*, because there is a unique copy of the field in each object (instance) of the class.

13.6.2. Static or Class Fields

Per-object fields are usually what you need. You usually want a field in one object to be distinct from the similarly named field in every other object instantiated from that class.

Sometimes, though, you want fields that are shared among all objects of that class. These shared variables are known as *class variables*—variables specific to the class as opposed to objects of the class.

Why would you want to use class variables? Consider the Sony Walkman factory. Each Walkman has a unique serial number. In object terms, each Walkman object has its own unique serial number field. However, the factory needs to keep a record of the next serial number to be assigned. You don't want to keep that number with every Walkman object—you'd keep only one copy of that number in the factory, or in object terms, as a class variable.

In Java, you obtain class-specific fields by declaring them `static`, and they are therefore sometimes called *static fields*. For example, a `Point` object to represent the origin might be common enough that you should provide it as a `static` field in the `Point` class:

```
public static Point origin = new Point ();
```

If this declaration appears inside the declaration of the `Point` class, there will be exactly one piece of data called `Point.origin` that always refers to an object at (0,0). This `static` field is there no matter how many `Point` objects are created, even if none is created. The values of `x` and `y` are zero because that is the default for numeric fields that are not explicitly initialized to a different value.

You saw one `static` object in your first program. The `System` class is a standard Java class that has a `static` field named `out` for printing output to the standard output stream.

When you see "field" in this chapter, it generally means a per-object field, although the term "non-static field" is sometimes used for clarity.

13.6.3. The Garbage Collector

After creating an object using `new`, how do you get rid of the object when you no longer want it? The answer is simple: You don't. Unused Java objects are automatically reclaimed by a *garbage collector*. The garbage collector runs in the background and tracks object references. When an object no longer has any reference, it can be removed from the storage allocation heap, although its actual removal may be delayed until a propitious time.

13.7. Methods and Parameters

Objects of the `Point` class as defined above are exposed to manipulation by any code that has a reference to a `Point` object, because its fields are declared `public`. The `Point` class is an example of the very simplest kind of class. Indeed, some classes are this simple, when they are designed to fit purely internal needs for a package, or when simple data containers are all you need.

The real benefits of object orientation, however, come from hiding the implementation of a class behind operations performed on its internal data. In Java, operations of a class are declared via its methods—instructions that operate on an object's data to obtain results. Methods access internal implementation details that are otherwise hidden from other objects. Hiding data behind methods so that it is inaccessible to other objects is the fundamental basis of data encapsulation.

Methods have zero or more parameters. A method can return a value, or it can be declared `void` to indicate that it does not return any value. A method's statements appear in a block of code between curly braces `{` and `}` that follow the method's name and the declaration of its *signature*. The signature is the name of the method and the number and types of the method's parameters. If we enhance the `Point` class with a simple `clear` method, it might look like this:

```
public void clear() {
      x=0;
      y=0;
}
```

The `clear` method has no parameters, hence the empty `(` and `)` after its name; in addition, `clear` is declared `void` because it does not return any value. Inside a method, fields and other methods of the class can be named directly—we can simply say `x` and `y` without an explicit object reference.

13.7.1. Invoking a Method

Objects in general do not operate directly on the data of other objects although, as you saw in the `Point` class, a class can make its fields publicly accessible. In general, though, well-designed classes hide their data so that it can be changed only by methods of that class. To invoke a method, you provide an object reference and the method name, separated by a dot (.). Parameters are passed to the method as a comma-separated list of values enclosed in parentheses. Methods that take no parameters still require the parentheses, with nothing between them. The object on which the method is invoked (the object receiving the method invocation) is often known as the *receiving object* of the *receiver*.

A method may return a single value as a result. To return more than one value from a method, create an object whose sole purpose is to hold return values in a single unit, and return that object.

Here is a method called `distance` that's part of the `Point` class shown in previous examples. The `distance` method accepts another `Point` object as a parameter, computes the Euclidean distance between itself and the other point, and returns a double-precision floating-point result:

```
public double distance(Point that) {
      double xdiff, ydiff;
      xdiff = x - that.x;
      ydiff = y - that.y;
      return Math.sqrt(xdiff ( xdiff + ydiff * ydiff);
}
```

Based on our lowerLeft and upperRight objects created in the section on instantiating objects previously, you could invoke distance like this:

```
double d = lowerLeft.distance(upperRight);
```

After this statement executes, the variable d contains the Euclidean distance between lowerLeft and upperRight.

13.7.2. The this Reference

Occasionally, the receiving object needs to know its own reference. For example, the receiving object might want to add itself to a list of objects somewhere. An implicit reference named this is available to methods, and this is a reference to the current (receiving) object. The following definition of clear is equivalent to the one just presented:

```
public void clear() {
      this.x = 0;
      this.y = -'
}
```

You usually use this as a parameter to other methods that need an object reference. The this reference also can be used to explicitly name the members of the current object. Here's another one of Point's methods, named move, that sets the x and y fields to specified values:

```
public void move(double x, double y) {
      this.x = x;
      this.y = y;
}
```

This move method uses this to clarify which x and y are being referred to. Naming the parameters of move "x" and "y" is reasonable, because you pass x and y coordinates to the method. But then those parameters have the same names as Point's fields, and therefore the parameter names are said to *hide* the field names. If we simply wrote x=x we would assign the value x parameter to itself, not to the x field as required. The expression this.x refers to the object's x field, not the x parameter of move.

13.7.3. Static or Class Methods

Just as you can have per-class static fields, you also can have per-class static methods, often known as class methods. Class methods are usually intended to do class-like operations specific to the class itself, and usually on static fields, not on specific instances of that class. Class methods are declared using the static keyword, and therefore are also known as static methods.

As with the term "field," when you see "method," it generally means a per-object method, although the term "non-static method" is sometimes used for clarity.

Why would you need static methods? Consider the Sony Walkman factory again. The record of the next serial number to be assigned is held in the factory, not in every Walkman. A method to operate on the factory's copy of the next available serial number must be a static method, not a method to operate on specific Walkman objects.

The implementation of `distance` in the previous example uses the static method `Math.sqrt` to calculate a square root. The `Math` class supports many methods useful for general mathematical manipulation. These methods are declared as static methods because they do not act on any particular object, but group a related set of functionality in the class itself.

A static method cannot directly access non-static members. When a static method is invoked, there's no specific object reference for the method to operate on. You could work around this by passing an explicit object reference as a parameter to the static method. In general, however, static methods do class kinds of operations and non-static methods do object kinds of things. Asking a static method to work on object fields is like asking the Walkman factory to change the serial number of a Walkman hanging on the belt of a jogger in Golden Gate Park.

13.8. Arrays

Simple variables that hold one value are useful, but are not sufficient for many applications. A program that plays a game of cards would want a number of `Card` objects it can manipulate as a whole. To meet this need, Java provides *arrays*.

An array is a collection of variables all of the same type. The components of an array are accessed by simple integer indices. In a card game, a `Deck` object might look like this:

```
class Deck {
      final int DECK_SIZE = 52;
      Card[] cards = new Card[DECK_SIZE};

      public void print () {
            for (int I = 0; I < cards.length; I++)
                  System.out.println(cards[i]);
      }
}
```

First, we declare a constant called `DECK_SIZE` to define the number of cards in a deck. We declare a `cards` field as an array of type `Card` by following the type name in the declaration with brackets `[` and `]`. We initialize `cards` to a new array with `DeckSize` `Card` variables, initialized to `null`. An array's length is fixed when it is created, and can never change.

The `print` method invocation shows how array components are accessed by enclosing the index of the desired element within brackets `[` and `]` following the array name.

You can probably tell from reading the code that array objects have a `length` field that says how many elements the array contains. The *bounds* of an array are integers between 0 and `length-1`. An `IndexOutOfBoundsException` is thrown if you use an index outside the bounds of the array.

The example also introduced a new variable declaration mechanism—declaring the control variable of a `for` statement in its initialization clause. Declaring variables in the initialization section of a `for` loop is a concise and convenient way to declare simple loop variables. This construct is allowed only in the initialization of `for` statements; you cannot declare variables in the test clause of an `if` or `while` statement.

The loop variable `i` is available only within the code of the `for` statement. A loop variable declared in this manner disappears when the loop terminates, which means you can reuse that variable name in subsequent `for` statements.

Exercise 13.8

Modify the `Fibonacci` application to store the sequence into an array and print the list of values at the end.

Exercise 13.9

Modify the `ImprovedFibonacci` application to store its sequence in an array. Do this by creating a new class to hold both the value and a `boolean` value that says whether the value is even and then having an array of object references to objects of that class.

13.9. String Objects

Java provides a `String` object type to deal specifically with sequences of character data, and provides language-level support for initializing them. The Java `String` class provides a variety of methods to operate on `String` objects.

You've already seen `String` literals in examples like the `HelloWorld` program. When you write a statement like

```
System.out.println("Hello, world");
```

the Java compiler actually creates a `String` object initialized to the value of the specified string literal, and passes that `String` object as the parameter to the `println` method.

Unlike arrays, you don't need to specify the length of a `String` object when you create it. You can create a new `String` object and initialize it all in one statement, as shown in this example:

```
class StringsDemo {
      static public void main(String args[]) {
            String  myName = "Petronius";

            myName = myName + " Arbiter";
            System.out.println("Name=" + myName);
      }
}
```

Here we create a `String` object reference called `myName` and initialize it with a `String` literal. Following initialization, we use the `String` concatenation `+` operator to make a new `String` object with a new value. Finally, we print the value of `myName` on the standard output stream. The output when you run the above program is

```
Name=Petronius Arbiter
```

In addition to the `+` sign as a concatenation operator, you can use the `+=` operator as a shorthand for placing the variable name on the right-hand side of the assignment. Here's an upgraded version of the above example:

```
class BetterStringsDemo {
      static public void main(String args[]) {
            String myName = "Petronius";
            String occupation = "Reorganization Specialist";
            myName = myName = " Arbiter";
            myName += " ";
            myName += "(" + occupation + ")";
            System.out.println("Name = " + myName);
      }
}
```

Now, when you run the program you get this output:

```
Name = Petronius Arbiter (Reorganization Specialist)
```

`String` objects have a `length` method that returns the number of characters in the `String`. Characters are indexed from 0 through `length() -1`.

String objects are *read-only*, or *immutable*: The contents of a String never change. When you see statements like:

```
str = "redwood";
// ... do something with str ..
str = "oak";
```

the second assignment gives a new value to the *object reference* str, not to the *contents* of the string. Every time you perform operations that seem to modify a String object, such as += as used above, you end up with a new String object that is also read-only, while the original String object's contents remain unchanged. The StringBuffer class provides for mutable strings.

The equals method is the simplest way to compare two String objects to see if they have the same contents:

```
if (oneStr.equals(twoStr))
    foundDuplicate(oneStr, twoStr);
```

Exercise 13.10

Modify the StringsDemo application to use different strings.

Exercise 13.11

Modify ImprovedFibonacci to store the String objects it creates into an array instead of invoking println with them directly.

13.10. Extending a Class

One of the major benefits of object orientation is the ability to *extend*, or *subclass*, the behavior of an existing class and continue to use code written for the original class.

When you extend a class to create a new class, the new extended class *inherits* all the fields and methods of the class that was extended. The original class on which the extension is based is known as the *superclass*.

If the subclass does not specifically *override* the behavior of the superclass, the subclass inherits all the behavior of its superclass, because, as we said, the extended class inherits the fields and methods of its superclass.

The Walkman example can itself be extended in this way. Later models incorporated two sets of jacks so two people could listen to the same tape. In the object-oriented world, the two-jack model extends, or is a subclass of, the basic model. The two-jack model inherits the characteristics and behavior of the basic model and adds new behavior of its own.

Customers told Sony they wanted to talk to each other while sharing a tape in the two-jack model. Sony enhanced the two-jack model to include two-way communications so people could chat while listening to music. The two-way communications model is a subclass of the two-jack model, inherits all of its behavior, and adds new behavior.

Sony created many other Walkman models. Later models extend the capabilities of the basic model—they subclass the basic model and inherit features and behavior from it.

Let's look at an example of extending a Java class. Here we extend our former `Point` class to represent a screen pixel. The new `Pixel` class requires a color in addition to x and y coordinates:

```
class Pixel extends Point {
      Color color;

      public void clear() {
            super.clear();
            color = null;
      }
}
```

`Pixel` extends both *data* and *behavior* of its `Point` superclass. `Pixel` extends the data by adding an additional field, namely `color`, to `Point`. `Pixel` also extends the behavior of `Point` by overriding `Point`'s `clear` method. Here is an illustration of the concept:

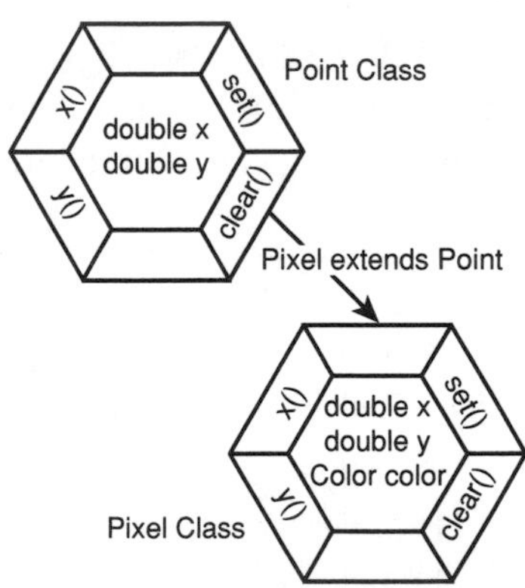

`Pixel` objects can be used by any code designed to work with `Point` objects. If a method expects a parameter of type `Point`, you can hand it a `Pixel` object and it just works. All the `Point` code can be used by anyone with a `Pixel` in hand. This feature is known as *polymorphism*: A single object like `Pixel` can have many (*poly-*) forms (*-morph*) and can be used as both a `Pixel` object and a `Point` object.

Pixel's behavior extends Point's behavior. Extended behavior could be entirely new (adding color in this example) or can be a restriction on old behavior that follows all the original requirements. An example of restricted behavior might be Pixel objects that live inside some kind of Screen object, restricting x and y to the dimensions of the screen. The original Point class made no restriction on coordinates, but a class with restricted range is still within the original unbounded range.

An extended class often overrides the behavior of its superclass (the class that was extended) by providing new implementations of one or more of the inherited methods. In the example above, we override clear to obtain proper behavior that Pixel requires—the clear that Pixel inherited from Point knows only about Point's fields, but obviously can't know about the new color field declared in the Pixel subclass.

Exercise 13.12

Write a set of classes that reflect the class structure of the Sony Walkman product family. Use methods to hide the data, making all the data private and the methods public. What methods would belong in the base Walkman class? Which methods would be added for which extended classes?

13.10.1. The Object Class

Classes that do not explicitly extend any other class implicitly extend the Object class. All object references are polymorphically of class Object, so Object is the generic class for references that can refer to objects of any class:

```
Object oref = new Pixel();
oref = "Some String";
```

In this example, oref is legally assigned references to Pixel and String objects, even though those classes have no relationship other than the direct or indirect implicit superclass of Object.

13.10.2. Invoking Methods from the Superclass

To make Pixel do the correct "clear" behavior, we provide a new implementation of clear that first invokes its superclass's clear using the super reference. The super reference is a lot like the this reference described previously, except that super references things from the superclass, whereas this references things from the current object.

The invocation super.clear() looks to the superclass to execute clear as it would for an object of the superclass type—namely, Point. After invoking super.clear(), we add new functionality, to set color to a reasonable empty value. We choose null—a reference to no object.

What would have happened had we not invoked `super.clear()`? `Pixel`'s `clear` method would set the color to its `null` value, but the `x` and `y` variables that `Pixel` inherited from `Point` would not be set to any "cleared" values. Not clearing all the values of a `Pixel` object, including its `Point` parts, is probably a bug.

When you invoke `super.`*`method`*`()`, the object runtime system looks back up the inheritance hierarchy to the first superclass that contains the required *`method`*`()`. If `Point` didn't have a `clear` method, for example, the object runtime would look at `Point`'s superclass for such a method, and invoke that, and so on.

For all other references you use, invoking a method uses the actual type of the object, not the type of the object reference. Here is an example:

```
Point point = new Pixel();

point.clear(); // uses Pixel's clear ()
```

In this example, `Pixel`'s version of `clear` is invoked, even though the variable that holds the `Pixel` is declared as a `Point` reference. But if we write `super.clear()` inside one of `Pixel`'s methods, `Point`'s clear method is invoked.

13.11. Interfaces

Sometimes you need only *define* methods an object must support, but not necessarily supply the *implementation* of those methods. As long as their behavior meets specific criteria, implementation details of the methods are irrelevant. For example, to ask whether a particular value is contained in a set of values, details of how those values are stored are irrelevant. You would want the methods to work equally well with a linked list of values, a hashtable of values, or any other data structure.

Java enables you to define an *interface*, which is a like a class, but with only declarations of its methods. The designer of the interface declares which methods are supported by classes that *implement* the interface, and what those methods should do. Here is a `Lookup` interface:

```
interface Lookup {
      /** Return the value associated with the name, or
       *  null if there is no such value */
      Object find(String name);
}
```

The `Lookup` interface defines one method, `find`, that takes a `String` and returns the value associated with that name, or `null` if there is no associated value. No implementation is given for the method—the class that implements the interface is responsible for the specific implementation. Code that uses references to `Lookup` objects (objects that implement the `Lookup` interface) can invoke the `find` method and get the expected results, no matter the actual type of the object:

```
void processValues(String[] names, Lookup table) {
      for (int I = 0; I < names.length; i++) {
            Object value = table.find(names[i]);
      if (value != null)
            processValue(names[i], value);
      }
}
```

A class can implement as many interfaces as it chooses. This example implements `Lookup` using a simple array (methods to set or remove values are left out for simplicity):

```
class SimpleLookup implements lookup {
      private String[] Names;
      private Object[] Values;

      public Object find(String name) {
            for (int I = 0; I < Names.length; I++) {
                  if (Names[i].equals(name))
                        return Values[i];
            }
            return null;   // not found
      }

      // ...
}
```

Interfaces can be extended, too, using the `extends` keyword. An interface can extend one or more other interfaces, adding new constants and new methods that must be implemented by any class that implements the extended interface.

A class's supertypes are the class it extends and the interfaces it implements, including all the supertypes of those classes and interfaces. So the type of an object is not only its class, but any of its supertypes, including interfaces. An object can be used polymorphically with both its superclass and any superinterfaces, including any of their supertypes.

Exercise 13.13

Write an extended interface of `Lookup` that has `add` and `remove` methods. Implement the extended interface in a new class.

13.12. Exceptions

What do you do when an error occurs in a program? In many languages, error conditions are signaled by unusual return values like `01`. Programmers often don't check for exceptional values because they may assume errors "can't happen." On the other hand, adding error-detection and recovery to what should be a straightforward flow of logic can obscure that logic to the point where the normal flow is incomprehensible. An ostensibly simple task such as reading a file into memory might require about seven lines of code. Error checking and reporting extend this to 40 or more lines. Making normal operation the needle in your code haystack is undesirable.

Java used *checked exceptions* to manage error handling. Exceptions force you to deal with errors. If a checked exception is not handled, this is noticed when the error happens, not later when problems have compounded because of the unchecked error.

A method that detects an unusual error condition *throws* an exception. Exceptions can be *caught* by code farther back on the calling stack—this prior code can handle the exception as needed and then continue executing. Uncaught exceptions are handled by a default handler in the Java implementation, which may report the exception and terminate the thread of execution.

An exception in Java is an object, with type, methods, and data. Representing exceptions as objects is useful, because an exception object can include data or methods or both to report on or recover from specific kinds of exceptions. Exception objects are generally derived from the `Exception` class, which provides a string field to describe the error. Java requires all exceptions to be extensions of a class named `Throwable`.

The general paradigm of exceptions in Java is the *try-catch-finally* sequence: You *try* something; if that something throws an exception, you *catch* the exception; and, *finally*, clean up from either the normal code path or the exception code path, whichever actually happened.

Below you see an `averageOf` method that returns the average of two elements in an array. If either index is outside the bounds of the array, it wants to throw an exception describing the error. First, we define a new exception type `IllegalAverageException` to describe such an error. Then we declare that the `averageOf` method throws that exception using a `throws` clause:

```
class IllegalAverageException extends Exception {
}

class MyUtilities {
     public double averageOf(double[] vals, int I, int j)
          throws IllegalAverageException
     {
          try {
               return (vals[i] + vals[j]) / 2;
          } catch(IndexOutOfBoundsException e) {
               throw new IllegalAverageException();
          }
     }
}
```

During the averaging calculation, if both `i` and `j` are within the array bounds, the calculation succeeds and the average value is returned. But if either index is out of bounds, an `IndexOutOfBoundsException` is thrown, and the matching `catch` clause is executed. The `catch` clause creates a new `IllegalAverageException` object and throws it, in effect translating the general array index exception into a specific exception that more precisely describes the real failure. Methods farther back on the execution stack have a chance to catch the new exception and react to it appropriately.

If execution of a method can result in checked exceptions, it must declare the types of these exceptions in a `throws` clause, as shown for `averageOf`. Other than exceptions of type `RuntimeException` and `Error`, or subclasses of these exception types, which can be thrown anywhere, a method can throw only those exceptions it declares, whether it throws those exceptions directly with `throw`, or indirectly by invoking a method that throws exceptions.

Declaring exceptions that a method throws means the compiler can ensure that the method throws only those exceptions it declared, and no others. This check prevents errors in cases where your method should handle another method's exceptions, but did not. In addition, the method that invokes your method is assured that your method will not result in unexpected exceptions. This is why the exceptions you must declare in a `throws` clause are called *checked exceptions*. Exceptions that are extensions of `RuntimeException` and `Error` need not be declared and are not checked; they are called *unchecked exceptions*.

Exercise 13.14

Add fields to `IllegalAverageException` to hold the array and indices so that whoever catches the exception will know details about the error.

13.13. Packages

Name conflicts are a major problem when developing reusable code. No matter how carefully you pick names for classes and methods, somebody else is likely to use that name for a different purpose. If you use simple, descriptive names, the problem gets worse—such names are more likely to be used by someone else who was also trying to use simple, descriptive names. Words like set, get, clear, and so on, are used a lot and are almost certain to clash with other people's uses.

The standard solution for name collision in many programming languages is to use a "package prefix" at the front of every class, type, global function, and so on. Prefix conventions create *naming contexts* to ensure that names in one package do not conflict with names in other packages. These prefixes are usually a few characters long and are usually an abbreviation of the package product name, such as `Xt` for "X Toolkit," or `WIN32` for the 32-bit Windows API.

When code uses only a few packages, the likelihood of prefix conflict is small. However, since prefixes are abbreviations, the probability of a name conflict increases with the number of packages used.

Java has adopted a more formal notion of packages that has a set of types and subpackages as members. Packages are named and can be imported. Package names are hierarchical, with components separated by dots. When you use part of a package, either you use its fully qualified name, or you import all or part of the package. Hierarchical package names enable longer package names. Hierarchical package names also give you control over name conflicts—if two packages contain classes with the same name, you can use a package-qualified form of the class name for one or both of them.

Here is an example of a method that uses fully qualified names to print the current day and time using Java's utility class `Date`:

```
class Date1 {
      public static void main(String[] args) {
            java.util.Date now = new java.util.Date();
            System.out.println(now);
      }
}
```

And here is a version that uses `import` to declare the type `Date`:

```
import java.util.Date;

class Date2 {
     public static void main(String[] args) {
          Date now = new Date();
          System.out.println(now);
     }
}
```

The name-collision problem is not completely solved by the Java package mechanism. Two projects can still give their packages the same name. This problem can be solved only by convention. The standard convention is to use the reversed Internet domain name of the organization to prefix the package name. For example, if the Acme Corporation had the Internet domain `acme.com`, it would use package names of the form `COM.acme.`*`package`*.

Having dots separate package components may occasionally cause confusion, because the dot is also used to invoke methods and access fields in object references. This may lead to confusion as to what can be imported. Java novices often try to import `System.out` so they don't have to type it in front of every `println`. This does not work because `System` is a class, in which `out` is a static field whose type supports the `println` method.

On the other hand, `java.util` is a package, so you can import `java.util.Date` (or `java.util.*` if you want everything from the package). If you are having problems importing something, setup and make sure that you are importing a type.

Java classes are always in a package. A package is named by providing a package declaration at the top of the source file:

```
package com.sun.games;

class Card
{
     // ...
}

// ...
```

If a name is not provided via a `package` declaration, the class is made part of an *unnamed package*. Although this is adequate for an application (or applet) that is not loaded with any other code, classes destined for a library should be written in named packages.

13.14. The Java Infrastructure

Java is designed to maximize portability. Many details about Java are specifically defined for all implementations. For example, an `int` is a 32-bit two's-complement signed integer. Many languages leave precise definitions to particular implementations, making only general guarantees such as minimum range, or provide a way to ask the system what the range is on the current platform.Java makes these definitions specific all the way down to the machine language into which Java code is translated. Java source code is compiled into Java bytecodes, designed to be run on a Java virtual machine. Bytecodes are a machine language for an abstract machine, but are interpreted by the virtual machine on each system that supports Java.[3]

The virtual machine assigns each application its own runtime, which both isolates applications from each other and provides a security model. Each runtime's security manager decides on the capabilities available to the application. The security manager could, for example, forbid the application from reading or writing the local disk, or allow network connections only to particular machines.

These features combined give Java code complete platform independence to provide a security model suitable for executing code downloaded across the network at varying levels of trust. Java source code compiled into Java bytecodes can be run on any machine with a Java virtual machine. The code can be executed with an appropriate level of protection to prevent careless or malicious class writers from harming the system. The level of trust can be adjusted depending on the source of the bytecodes—bytecodes on the local disk or protected network can be trusted more than bytecodes fetched from arbitrary machines elsewhere in the world.

---

[3]A system can, of course, implement the Java virtual machine in silicon—that is, using a special-purpose chip. This does not affect the portability of the bytecode; it is just another virtual machine implementation.

13.15. Other Topics Briefly Noted

Java has several other features which we mention briefly here:

- *Threads:* Java has built-in thread support for creating multithreaded applications. It uses per-object and per-class monitor-style locks to synchronize concurrent access to object and class data.
- *I/O:* Java provides a `java.io` package for many different kinds of input and output operations.
- *Type classes:* Java has classes to represent most of the primitive types (such as `integer`, `double`, and `boolean`) and a `Class` class to represent class types.
- *Utility classes and interfaces:* Java provides a `java.util` package that has many useful classes, such as `BitSet`, `Vector`, `Stack`, and `Date`.

CHAPTER 14

Programming in Java[1]

by David Flanagan

14.1. Getting Started with Java

When it was introduced in late 1995, Java took the Internet by storm. Java 1.1, released in early 1997, nearly doubles the speed of the Java interpreter and includes many important new features. With the addition of APIs to support database access, remote objects, an object component model, internationalization, printing, encryption, digital signatures, and many other technologies, Java is now poised to take the rest of the programming world by storm.

Despite all the hype surrounding Java and the new features of Java 1.1, it's important to remember that at its core, Java is just a programming language, like many others, and its APIs are just class libraries, like those of other languages. What is interesting about Java, and thus the source of much of the hype, is that it has a number of important features that make it ideally suited for programming in the heavily networked, heterogeneous world of the late 1990s. The rest of this section describes those interesting features of Java and demonstrates some simple Java code....

---

[1]This chapter is reprinted with permission from Flanagan, D. 1997. *Java in a Nutshell: A Desktop Quick Reference* (2nd ed., pp. 3–101). Sebastopol, CA: O'Reilly.

14.1.1. Why Is Java Interesting?

In one of their early papers about the language, Sun described Java as follows:

> Java: A simple, object-oriented, distributed, interpreted, robust, secure, architecture neutral, portable, high-performance, multithreaded, and dynamic language.

Sun acknowledges that this is quite a string of buzzwords, but the fact is that, for the most part, they aptly describe the language. In order to understand why Java is so interesting, let's take a look at the language features behind the buzzwords.

14.1.1.1. Object-Oriented

Java is an object-oriented programming language. As a programmer, this means that you focus on the data in your application and methods that manipulate that data, rather than thinking strictly in terms of procedures. If you're accustomed to procedure-based programming in C, you may find that you need to change how you design your programs when you use Java. Once you see how powerful this new paradigm is, however, you'll quickly adjust to it.

In an object-oriented system, a *class* is a collection of data and methods that operate on that data. Taken together, the data and methods describe the state and behavior of an *object*. Classes are arranged in a hierarchy, so that a subclass can inherit behavior from its superclass. A class hierarchy always has a root class; this is a class with very general behavior.

Java comes with an extensive set of classes, arranged in *packages*, that you can use in your programs. For example, Java provides classes that create graphical user interface components (the `java.awt` package), classes that handle input and output (the `java.io` package), and classes that support networking functionality (the `java.net` package). The `Object` class (in the `java.lang` package) serves as the root of the Java class hierarchy.

Unlike C++, Java was designed to be object-oriented from the ground up. Most things in Java are objects; the primitive numeric, character, and boolean types are the only exceptions. Strings are represented by objects in Java, as are other important language constructs like threads. A class is the basic unit of compilation and of execution in Java; all Java programs are classes.

While Java is designed to look like C++, you'll find that Java removes many of the complexities of that language. If you are a C++ programmer, you'll want to study the object-oriented constructs in Java carefully. Although the syntax is often similar to C++, the behavior is not nearly so analogous. For a complete description of the object-oriented features of Java, see "Classes and Objects in Java."

14.1.1.2. Interpreted

Java is an interpreted language: The Java compiler generates byte-codes for the Java Virtual Machine (JVM), rather than native machine code. To actually run a Java program, you use the Java interpreter to execute the compiled byte-codes. Because Java byte-codes are platform-independent, Java programs can run on any platform that the JVM (the interpreter and run-time system) has been ported to.

In an interpreted environment, the standard "link" phase of program development pretty much vanishes. If Java has a link phase at all, it is only the process of loading new classes into the environment, which is an incremental, lightweight process that occurs at runtime. This is in contrast with the slower and more cumbersome compile-link-run cycle of languages like C and C++.

14.1.1.3. Architecture Neutral and Portable

Because Java programs are compiled to an architecture neutral byte-code format, a Java application can run on any system, as long as that system implements the Java Virtual Machine. This is particularly important for applications distributed over the Internet or other heterogeneous networks. But the architecture neutral approach is useful beyond the scope of network-based applications. As an application developer in today's software market, you probably want to develop versions of your application that can run on PCs, Macs, and UNIX workstations. With multiple flavors of UNIX, Windows 95, and Windows NT on the PC, and the new PowerPC Macintosh, it is becoming increasingly difficult to produce software for all of the possible platforms. If you write your application in Java, however, it can run on all platforms.

The fact that Java is interpreted and defines a standard, architecture-neutral, byte-code format is one big part of being portable. But Java goes even further, by making sure that there are no "implementation-dependent" aspects of the language specification. For example, Java explicitly specifies the size of each of the primitive data types, as well as its arithmetic behavior. This differs from C, for example, in which an `int` type can be 16, 32, or 64 bits long depending on the platform.

While it is technically possible to write non-portable programs in Java, it is relatively easy to avoid the few platform-dependencies that are exposed by the Java API and write truly portable or "pure" Java programs. Sun's new "100% Pure Java" program helps developers ensure (and certify) that their code is portable. Programmers need only to make simple efforts to avoid non-portable pitfalls in order to live up to Sun's trademarked motto "Write Once, Run Anywhere."

14.1.1.4. Dynamic and Distributed

Java is a dynamic language. Any Java class can be loaded into a running Java interpreter at any time. These dynamically loaded classes can then be dynamically instantiated. Native code libraries can also be dynamically loaded. Classes in Java are represented by the `Class` class; you can dynamically obtain information about a class at runtime. This is especially true in Java 1.1, with the addition of the Reflection API....

Java is also called a distributed language. This means, simply, that it provides a lot of high-level support for networking. For example, the `URL` class and related classes in the `java.net` package make it almost as easy to read a remote file or resource as it is to read a local file. Similarly, in Java 1.1, the Remote Method Invocation (RMI) API allows a Java program to invoke methods of remote Java objects, as if they were local objects. (Java also provides traditional lower-level networking support, including datagrams and stream-based connections through sockets.)

The distributed nature of Java really shines when combined with its dynamic class loading capabilities. Together, these features make it possible for a Java interpreter to download and run code from across the Internet. (As we'll see below, Java implements strong security measures to be sure that this can be done safely.) This is what happens when a Web browser downloads and runs a Java applet, for example. Scenarios can be more complicated than this, however. Imagine a multimedia word processor written in Java. When this program is asked to display some type of data that it has never encountered before, it might dynamically download a class from the network that can parse the data, and then dynamically download another class (probably a Java "bean") that can display the data within a compound document. A program like this uses distributed resources on the network to dynamically grow and adapt to the needs of its user.

14.1.1.5. Simple

Java is a simple language. The Java designers were trying to create a language that a programmer could learn quickly, so the number of language constructs has been kept relatively small. Another design goal was to make the language look familiar to a majority of programmers, for ease of migration. If you are a C or C++ programmer, you'll find that Java uses many of the same language constructs as C and C++.

In order to keep the language both small and familiar, the Java designers removed a number of features available in C and C++. These features are mostly ones that led to poor programming practices or were rarely used. For example, Java does not support the `goto` statement; instead, it provides labeled `break` and `continue` statements and exception handling. Java does not use header files and it eliminates the C preprocessor. Because Java is object-oriented, C constructs like `struct` and `union` have been removed. Java also eliminates the operator overloading and multiple inheritance features of C++.

Perhaps the most important simplification, however, is that Java does not use pointers. Pointers are one of the most bug-prone aspects of C and C++ programming. Since Java does not have structures, and arrays and strings are objects, there's no need for pointers. Java automatically handles the referencing and dereferencing of objects for you. Java also implements automatic garbage collection, so you don't have to worry about memory management issues. All of this frees you from having to worry about dangling pointers, invalid pointer references, and memory leaks, so you can spend your time developing the functionality of your programs.

If it sounds like Java has gutted C and C++, leaving only a shell of a programming language, hold off on that judgment for a bit. As we'll see in the section "How Java Differs from C," Java is actually a full-featured and very elegant language.

14.1.1.6. Robust

Java has been designed for writing highly reliable or robust software. Java certainly doesn't eliminate the need for software quality assurance; it's still quite possible to write buggy software in Java. However, Java does eliminate certain types of programming errors, which makes it considerably easier to write reliable software.

Java is a strongly typed language, which allows for extensive compile-time checking for potential type-mismatch problems. Java is more strongly typed than C++, which inherits a number of compile-time laxities from C, especially in the area of function declarations. Java requires explicit method declarations; it does not support C-style implicit declarations. These stringent requirements ensure that the compiler can catch method invocation errors, which leads to more reliable programs.

One of the things that makes Java simple is its lack of pointers and pointer arithmetic. This feature also increases the robustness of Java programs by abolishing an entire class of pointer-related bugs. Similarly, all accesses to arrays and strings are checked at runtime to ensure that they are in bounds, eliminating the possibility of overwriting memory and corrupting data. Casts of objects from one type to another are also checked at runtime to ensure that they are legal. Finally, and very importantly, Java's automatic garbage collection relieves the developer of many of the mundane house-cleaning tasks normally associated with memory management, which helps avoid pernicious bugs related to memory allocation and deallocation.

Exception handling is another feature in Java that makes for more robust programs. An *exception* is a signal that some sort of exceptional condition, such as a "file not found" error, has occurred. Using the `try/catch/finally` statement, you can group all of your error handling code in one place, which greatly simplifies the task of error handling and recovery.

14.1.1.7. Secure

One of the most highly touted aspects of Java is that it's a secure language. This is especially important because of the distributed nature of Java. Without an assurance of security, you certainly wouldn't want to download code from a random site on the Internet and let it run on your computer. Yet this is exactly what people do with Java applets every day. Java was designed with security in mind, and provides several layers of security controls that protect against malicious code, and allow users to comfortably run untrusted programs such as applets.

At the lowest level, security goes hand-in-hand with robustness. As we've already seen, Java programs cannot forge pointers to memory, or overflow arrays, or read memory outside of the bounds of an array or string. These features are one of Java's main defenses against malicious code. By totally disallowing any direct access to memory, an entire huge, messy class of security attacks is ruled out.

The second line of defense against malicious code is the byte-code verification process that the Java interpreter performs on any untrusted code it loads. These verification steps ensure that the code is well-formed—that it doesn't overflow or underflow the stack or contain illegal byte-codes, for example. If the byte-code verification step was skipped, inadvertently corrupted or maliciously crafted byte-codes might be able to take advantage of implementation weaknesses in a Java interpreter.

Another layer of security protection is commonly referred to as the "sandbox model": Untrusted code is placed in a "sandbox," where it can play safely, without doing any damage to the "real world," or full Java environment. When an applet, or other untrusted code, is running in the sandbox, there are a number of restrictions on what it can do. The most obvious of these restrictions is that it has no access whatsoever to the local file system. There are a number of other restrictions in the sandbox as well. These restrictions are enforced by a `SecurityManager` class. The model works because all of the core Java classes that perform sensitive operations, such as filesystem access, first ask permission of the currently installed `SecurityManager`. If the call is being made, directly or indirectly, by untrusted code, the security manager throws an exception, and the operation is not permitted.

Finally, in Java 1.1, there is another possible solution to the problem of security. By attaching a digital signature to Java code, the origin of that code can be established in a cryptographically secure and unforgeable way. If you have specified that you trust a person or organization, then code that bears the digital signature of that trusted entity is trusted, even when loaded over the network, and may be run without the restrictions of the sandbox model.

Of course, security isn't a black-and-white thing. Just as a program can never be guaranteed to be 100% bug-free, no language or environment can be guaranteed 100% secure. With that said, however, Java does seem to offer a practical level of security for most applications. It anticipates and defends against most of the techniques that have historically been used to trick software into misbehaving, and it has been intensely scrutinized by security experts and hackers alike. Some security holes were found in early versions of Java, but these flaws were fixed almost as soon as they were found, and it seems reasonable to expect that any future holes will be fixed just as quickly.

14.1.1.8. High Performance

Java is an interpreted language, so it is never going to be as fast as a compiled language like C. Java 1.0 was said to be about 20 times slower than C. Java 1.1 is nearly twice as fast as Java 1.0, however, so it might be reasonable to say that compiled C code runs ten times as fast as interpreted Java byte-codes. But before you throw up your arms in disgust, be aware that this speed is more than adequate to run interactive, GUI, and network-based applications, where the application is often idle, waiting for the user to do something, or waiting for data from the network. Furthermore, the speed-critical sections of the Java runtime environment that do things like string concatenation and comparison are implemented with efficient native code.

As a further performance boost, many Java interpreters now include "just in time" compilers that can translate Java byte-codes into machine code for a particular CPU at runtime. The Java byte-code format was designed with these "just in time" compilers in mind, so the process of generating machine code is fairly efficient and it produces reasonably good code. In fact, Sun claims that the performance of byte-codes converted to machine code is nearly as good as native C or C++. If you are willing to sacrifice code portability to gain speed, you can also write portions of your program in C or C++ and use Java native methods to interface with this native code.

When you are considering performance, it's important to remember where Java falls in the spectrum of available programming languages. At one end of the spectrum, there are high-level, fully interpreted scripting languages such as Tcl and the UNIX shells. These languages are great for prototyping and they are highly portable, but they are also very slow. At the other end of the spectrum, you have low-level compiled languages like C and C++. These languages offer high performance, but they suffer in terms of reliability and portability. Java falls in the middle of the spectrum. The performance of Java's interpreted byte-codes is much better than the high-level scripting languages (even Perl), but it still offers the simplicity and portability of those languages.

14.1.1.9. Multithreaded

In a GUI-based network application such as a Web browser, it's easy to imagine multiple things going on at the same time. A user could be listening to an audio clip while she is scrolling a page and in the background the browser is downloading an image. Java is a multithreaded language; it provides support for multiple threads of execution (sometimes called lightweight processes) that can handle different tasks. An important benefit of multithreading is that it improves the interactive performance of graphical applications for the user.

If you have tried working with threads in C or C++, you know that it can be quite difficult. Java makes programming with threads much easier, by providing built-in language support for threads. The `java.lang` package provides a `Thread` class that supports methods to start and stop threads and set thread priorities, among other things. The Java language syntax also supports threads directly with the `synchronized` keyword. This keyword makes it extremely easy to mark sections of code or entire methods that should only be run by a single thread at a time.

While threads are "wizard-level" stuff in C and C++, their use is commonplace in Java. Because Java makes threads so easy to use, the Java class libraries require their use in a number of places. For example, any applet that performs animation does so with a thread. Similarly, Java does not support asynchronous, non-blocking I/O with notification through signals or interrupts—you must instead create a thread that blocks on every I/O channel you are interested in.

14.1.1.10. A Simple Example

By now, you should have a pretty good idea of why Java is such an interesting language. So we'll stop talking about abstract concepts and look at some concrete Java code. Before we look at an interesting applet, however, we are going to pay tribute to that ubiquitous favorite, "Hello World."

Hello World

Example 14.1 shows the simplest possible Java program: "Hello World."

EXAMPLE 14.1. *Hello World.*

```
public class HelloWorld {
    public static void main(String[] args) {
        System.out.println("Hello World!");
    }
}
```

This program, like every Java program, consists of a public class definition. The class contains a method named `main()`, which is the main entry point for all Java applications—that is, the point at which the interpreter starts executing the program. The body of `main()` consists of only a single line, which prints out the message:

```
Hello World!
```

This program must be saved in a file with the same name as the public class plus a `.java` extension. To compile it, you would use `javac`:[2]

```
% javac HelloWorld.java
```

This command produces the `HelloWorld.class` file in the current directory. To run the program, you use the Java interpreter, `java`:

```
% java HelloWorld
```

Note that when you invoke the interpreter, you do not supply the `.class` extension for the file you want to run.

[2]Assuming you're using Sun's Java Development Kit (JDK). If you're using a Java development environment from some other vendor, follow your vendor's instructions.

A Scribble Applet

Example 14.2 shows a less trivial Java program. This program is an applet, rather than a stand-alone Java application like the "Hello World" program above. Because this example is an applet, it has a different structure than a stand-alone application; notably, it does not have a `main()` method. Like all applets, this one runs inside an applet viewer or Web browser, and lets the user draw (or scribble) with the mouse, as illustrated in Figure 14.1.

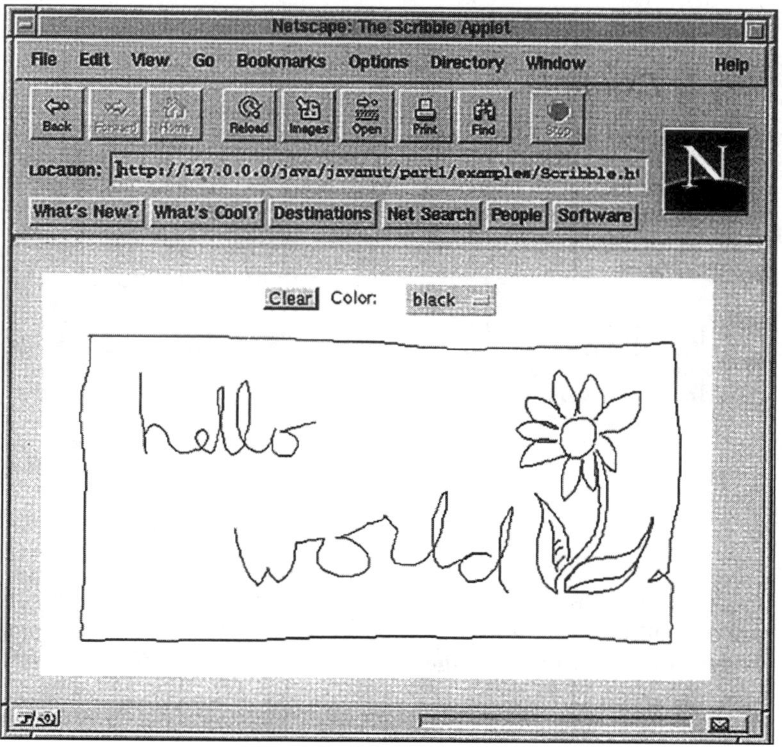

FIGURE 14.1. *A Java applet running in a Web browser.*

One of the major changes between Java 1.0 and Java 1.1 is in the way that Java programs are notified of "events," such as mouse motion. Example 14.2 uses the Java 1.0 event model rather than the preferred Java 1.1 event model. This is because the current generation of Web browsers (as this is written) still use Java 1.0. In order for this applet to be widely usable, it is coded with the old, "deprecated" event model.[3]

[3] If you are interested in updating this program to use Java 1.1, you must learn how to use the new 1.1 event model. In addition, you need to change the call to `bounds()` in the `action()` method to a call to `getBounds()`, if you want to avoid a compilation warning about using a deprecated method.

EXAMPLE 14.2. *A Java applet.*

```
import java.applet.*;
import java.awt.*;

public class Scribble extends Applet {
  private int last_x, last_y;
    // Store the last mouse position.
  private Color current_color = Color.black;
    // Store the current color.
  private Button clear_button;
    // The clear button.
  private Choice color_choices;
    // The color dropdown list.
    // This method is called to initialize the applet.
    // Applets don't have a main() method.
  public void init() {
    // Set the background color
    this.setBackground(Color.white);

    // Create a button and add it to the applet.
    // Set the button's colors
    clear_button = new Button("Clear");
    clear_button.setForeground(Color.black);
    clear_button.setBackground(Color.lightGray);
    this.add(clear_button);

    // Create a menu of colors and add it to the applet.
    // Also set the menu's colors and add a label.
    color_choices = new Choice();
    color_choices.addItem("black");
    color_choices.addItem("red");
    color_choices.addItem("yellow");
    color_choices.addItem("green");
    color_choices.setForeground(Color.black);
    color_choices.setBackground(Color.lightGray);
    this.add(new Label("Color: "));
    this.add(color_choices);
  }

    // This method is called when the user clicks
    // the mouse to start a scribble.
  public boolean mouseDown(Event e, int x, int y)
  {
    last_x = x; last_y = y;
    return true;
  }

  // This method is called when the user drags the mouse.
  public boolean mouseDrag(Event e, int x, int y)
  {
    Graphics g = this.getGraphics();
    g.setColor(current_color);
    g.drawLine(last_x, last_y, x, y);
    last_x = x;
    last_y = y;
    return true;
  }
    // This method is called when the user clicks
```

continues

```
      // the button or chooses a color
    public boolean action(Event event, Object arg) {
      // If the Clear button was clicked on, handle it.
      if (event.target =\^= clear_button) {
        Graphics g = this.getGraphics();
        Rectangle r = this.bounds();
        g.setColor(this.getBackground());
        g.fillRect(r.x, r.y, r.width, r.height);
        return true;
      }
      // Otherwise if a color was chosen, handle that
      else if (event.target =\^= color_choices) {
        if (arg.equals("black")) current_color = Color.black;
        else if (arg.equals("red")) current_color = Color.red;
        else if (arg.equals("yellow")) current_color = Color.yellow;
        else if (arg.equals("green")) current_color = Color.green;
        return true;
      }
      // Otherwise, let the superclass handle it.
      else return super.action(event, arg);
    }
  }
```

Don't expect to be able to understand the entire applet at this point. It is here to give you the flavor of the language. In the sections "How Java Differs from C" and "Classes and Objects in Java," we'll explain the language constructs you need to understand the example.

The first thing you should notice when browsing through the code is that it looks reassuringly like C and C++. The `if` and `return` statements are familiar. Assignment of values to variables uses the expected syntax. Procedures (called *methods* in Java) are recognizable as such.

The second thing to notice is the object-oriented nature of the code. As you can see at the top of the example, the program consists of the definition of a public class. The name of the class we are defining is `Scribble`; it is an extension, or subclass, of the `Applet` class. (The full name of the `Applet` class is `java.applet.Applet`. One of the `import` statements at the top of the example allows us to refer to `Applet` by this shorter name.)

Classes are said to "encapsulate" data and methods. As you can see, our `Scribble` class contains both variable and method declarations. The methods are actually defined inside of the class. The methods of a class are often invoked through an instance of the class. Thus you see lines like:

```
color_choices.addItem("black");
```

This line of code invokes the `addItem()` method of the object referred to by the `color_choices` variable. If you're a C programmer, but not a C++ programmer, this syntax may take a little getting used to. We'll see lots more of it later. Note that `this` is a keyword, not a variable name. It refers to the current object; in this example, it refers to the `Scribble` object.

The init() method of an applet is called by the Web browser or applet viewer when it is starting the applet up. In our example, this method creates a Clear button and a menu of color choices, and then adds these GUI components to the applet.

The mouseDown() and mouseDrag() methods are called when the user clicks and drags the mouse. These are the methods that are responsible for drawing lines as the user scribbles. The action() method is invoked when the user clicks on the Clear button or selects a color from the menu of colors. The body of the method determines which of these two events has occurred and handles the event appropriately. Recall that these methods are part of the Java 1.0 event model.

To compile this example, you'd save it in a file named Scribble.java and use javac:

```
% javac Scribble.java
```

This example is an applet, not a stand-alone program like our "Hello World" example. It does not have a main() method, and therefore cannot be run directly by the Java interpreter. Instead, we must reference it in an HTML file and run the applet in an applet viewer or Web browser. It is the applet viewer or Web browser that loads the applet class into its running Java interpreter and invokes the various methods of the applet at the appropriate times. To include the applet in a Web page, we'd use an HTML fragment like the following:

```
<APPLET code="Scribble.class" width=500 height=300>
</APPLET>
```

Example 14.3 shows a complete HTML file that we might use to display the applet....

EXAMPLE 14.3. *An HTML file that contains an applet.*

```
<HTML>
<HEAD>
<TITLE>The Scribble Applet</TITLE>
</HEAD>
<BODY>
Please scribble away in the applet below.
<P>
<APPLET code="Scribble.class" width=500 height=300>
Your browser does not support Java, or Java is not enabled. Sorry!
</APPLET>
</BODY>
</HTML>
```

Suppose we save this example HTML file as `Scribble.html`. Then to run this applet, you could use Sun's `appletviewer` command like this:

```
% appletviewer Scribble.html
```

You could also display the applet by viewing the `Scribble.html` file in your Web browser, if your browser supports Java applets. Figure 14.1 showed the `Scribble` applet running in Netscape Navigator.

14.2. How Java Differs from C

Java is a lot like C, which makes it relatively easy for C programmers to learn. But there are a number of important differences between C and Java, such as the lack of a preprocessor, the use of 16-bit Unicode characters, and the exception handling mechanism. This section explains those differences, so that programmers who already know C can start programming in Java right away!

This section also points out similarities and differences between Java and C++. C++ programmers should beware, though: While Java borrows a lot of terminology and even syntax from C++, the analogies between Java and C++ are not nearly as strong as those between Java and C. C++ programmers should be careful not to be lulled into a false sense of familiarity with Java just because the languages share a number of keywords.

One of the main areas in which Java differs from C, of course, is that Java is an object-oriented language and has mechanisms to define classes and create objects that are instances of those classes. Java's object-oriented features are a topic for a chapter of their own, and they'll be explained in detail in "Classes and Objects in Java."

14.2.1. Program Structure and Environment

A program in Java consists of one or more class definitions, each of which has been compiled into its own `.class` file of Java Virtual Machine object code. One of these classes must define a method `main()`, which is where the program starts running.[4]

To invoke a Java program, you run the Java interpreter, `java`, and specify the name of the class that contains the `main()` method. You should omit the `.class` extension when doing this. Note that a Java applet is not an application—it is a Java class that is loaded and run by an already running Java application such as a Web browser or applet viewer. The `main()` method that the Java interpreter invokes to start a Java program must have the following prototype:

```
public static void main(String args[])
```

[4]Method is an object-oriented term for a procedure or function. You'll see it used throughout this chapter.

The Java interpreter runs until the main() method returns, or until the interpreter reaches the end of main(). If no threads have been created by the program, the interpreter exits. Otherwise, the interpreter continues running until the last thread terminates.

14.2.1.1. Command-Line Arguments

The single argument to main() is an array of strings, conventionally named args or argv. The length of this array (which would be passed as the argc argument in C) is available as argv.length, as is the case with any Java array. The elements of the array are the arguments, if any, that appeared on the interpreter command line after the class name. Note that the first element of the array is not the name of the class, as a C programmer might expect it to be. Example 14.4. shows how you could write a UNIX-style echo command (a program that simply prints out its arguments) in Java.

EXAMPLE 14.4. *An echo program in Java.*

```
public class echo {
   public static void main(String argv[]) {
      for(int i=0; i < argv.length; i++)
          System.out.print(argv[i] + " ");
      System.out.print("\n");
      System.exit(0);
   }
}
```

14.2.1.2. Program Exit Value

Note that main() must be declared to return void. Thus, you cannot return a value from your Java program with a return statement in main(). If you need to return a value, call System.exit() with the desired integer value, as we've done in Example 14.4. Note that the handling and interpretation of this exit value are, of course, operating-system dependent. System.exit() causes the Java interpreter to exit immediately, whether or not other threads are running.

14.2.1.3. Environment

The Java API does not allow a Java program to read operating system environment variables because they are platform-dependent. However, Java defines a similar, platform-independent mechanism, known as the system properties list, for associating textual values with names.

A Java program can look up the value of a named property with the System.getProperty() method:

```
String homedir = System.getProperty("user.home");
String debug = System.getProperty("myapp.debug");
```

The Java interpreter automatically defines a number of standard system properties when it starts up. You can insert additional property definitions into the list by specifying the `-D` option to the interpreter:

```
% java -Dmyapp.debug=true myapp
```

See Chapter 14, "System Properties," for more information on system properties.

14.2.2. The Name Space: Packages, Classes, and Members

As a language that is designed to support dynamic loading of modules over the entire Internet, Java takes special care to avoid name space conflicts. Global variables are simply not part of the language. Neither are "global" functions or procedures, for that matter.

14.2.2.1. No Global Variables

In Java, every field and method is declared within a class and forms part of that class. Also, every class is part of a package (in Java 1.1, classes can also be declared within other classes). The fields and methods (and classes in 1.1) of a class are known as the *members* of a class. Every Java field or method may be referred to by its fully qualified name, which consists of the package name, the class name, and the member name (i.e., the field or the method name), all separated by periods. Package names are themselves usually composed of multiple period-separated components. Thus, the fully qualified name for a method might be:

```
david.games.tetris.SoundEffects.play()
```

14.2.2.2. Java Filenames and Directory Structure

A file of Java source code has the extension `.java`. It consists of an optional `package` statement followed by any number of `import` statements followed by one or more class or interface definitions. (The `package` and `import` statements will be introduced shortly.) If more than one class or interface is defined in a Java source file, only one of them may be declared `public` (i.e., made available outside of the package), and the source file must have the same name as that public class or interface, plus the `.java` extension.

Each class or interface definition in a `.java` file is compiled into a separate file. These files of compiled Java byte-codes are known as "class files," and must have the same name as the class or interface they define, with the extension `.class` appended. For example, the class `SoundEffects` would be stored in the file `SoundEffects.class`.

Class files are stored in a directory that has the same components as the package name. If the fully qualified name of a class is `david.games.tetris.SoundEffects`, for example, the full path of the class file must be `david/games/tetris/SoundEffects.class`.[5] This filename is interpreted relative to the Java "class path," described below.

14.2.2.3. Packages of the Java API

The Java 1.1 API consists of the classes and interfaces defined in the twenty-three packages listed in Table 14.1.

TABLE 14.1. *The packages of the Java API.*

Package Name	*Contents*
`java.applet`	Applet classes
`java.awt`	Graphics, window, and GUI classes
`java.awt.datatransfer`	Data transfer (e.g., cut-and-paste) classes
`java.awt.event`	Event processing classes and interfaces
`java.awt.image`	Image processing classes
`java.awt.peer`	GUI interfaces for platform independence
`java.beans`	JavaBeans component model API
`java.io`	Various types of input and output classes
`java.lang`	Core language classes
`java.lang.reflect`	Reflection API classes
`java.math`	Arbitrary precision arithmetic
`java.net`	Networking classes
`java.rmi`	Remote Method Invocation classes
`java.rmi.dgc`	RMI-related classes
`java.rmi.registry`	RMI-related classes
`java.rmi.server`	RMI-related classes
`java.security`	Security classes
`java.security.acl`	Security-related classes
`java.security.interfaces`	Security-related classes
`java.sql`	JDBC SQL API for database access
`java.text`	Internationalization classes
`java.util`	Various useful data types
`java.util.zip`	Compression and decompression classes

[5]We'll use UNIX-style directory specifications in this chapter. If you are a Windows programmer, simply change all the forward slashes in filenames to backward slashes. Similarly, in path specifications, change colons to semicolons.

14.2.2.4. The Java Class Path

The Java interpreter knows where its standard system classes are installed, and loads them from that location as needed. By default, it looks up user-defined classes in or relative to the current directory. You can set the `CLASSPATH` environment variable to tell the interpreter where to look for user-defined classes. The interpreter always appends the location of its system classes to the end of the path specified by this environment variable. The entries in a class path specification should be directories or ZIP files that contain the classes. The directories in a class path specification should be colon-separated on a UNIX system, and semicolon-separated on a Windows system. For example, on a UNIX system, you might use:

```
setenv CLASSPATH .:/home/david/classes:
    /usr/local/javatools/classes.zip
```

On a Windows system you could use:

```
set CLASSPATH .;C:\^\david\classes;D:\local\javatools\classes.zip
```

This tells Java to search in and beneath the specified directories for non-system classes. Note that the current directory (`.`) is included in these paths.

You can also specify a class path to the Java interpreter with the `-classpath` command-line argument . Setting this option overrides any path specified in the `CLASSPATH` environment variable. Note that the interpreter does not append the location of the system classes to the end of this path, so you must be sure to specify those system classes yourself. Finally, note that the Java compiler also recognizes and honors class paths specified with the `CLASSPATH` environment variable and the `-classpath` command-line argument.

14.2.2.5. Globally Unique Package Names

The Java designers have proposed an Internet-wide unique package naming scheme that is based on the Internet domain name of the organization at which the package is developed.

Figure 14.2 shows some fully qualified names, which include package, class, and field components.

Some organizations are following this naming scheme, and producing classes with names like `com.sybase.jdbc.SybDriver`. Another trend that is developing, however, is for companies to simply use their company name as the first component of their package names, and produce classes like `netscape.javascript.JSObject`.

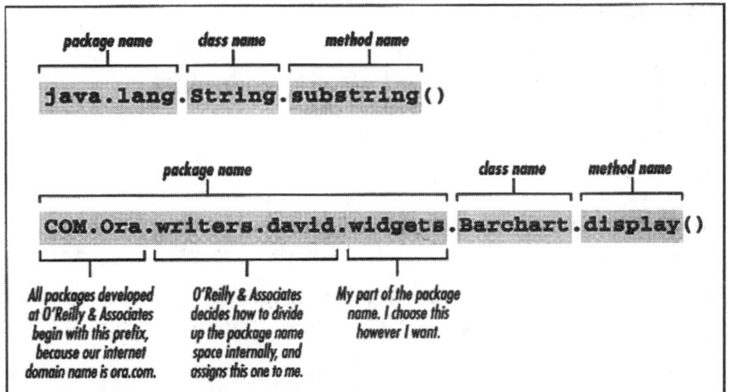

FIGURE 14.2. *Fully qualified names in Java.*

The top-level package names `java` and `sun` are reserved for use by Sun, of course. Developers should not define new classes within these packages.

14.2.2.6. The `package` Statement

The `package` statement must appear as the first statement (i.e., the first text other than comments and whitespace) in a file of Java source code, if it appears at all. It specifies which package the code in the file is part of. Java code that is part of a particular package has access to all classes (`public` and `non-public`) in the package, and to all non-`private` methods and fields in all those classes. When Java code is part of a named package, the compiled class file must be placed at the appropriate position in the `CLASSPATH` directory hierarchy before it can be accessed by the Java interpreter or other utilities.

If the `package` statement is omitted from a file, the code in that file is part of an unnamed default package. This is convenient for small test programs, or during development, because it means that the code can be interpreted from the current directory.

14.2.2.7. The `import` Statement

The `import` statement makes Java classes available to the current class under an abbreviated name. Public Java classes are always available by their fully qualified names, assuming that the appropriate class file can be found (and is readable) relative to the `CLASSPATH` environment variable. `import` doesn't actually make the class available or "read it in"; it simply saves you typing and makes your code more legible.

Any number of `import` statements may appear in a Java program. They must appear, however, after the optional `package` statement at the top of the file, and before the first class or interface definition in the file.

There are two forms of the `import` statement:

```
import package.class ;
import package.* ;
```

The first form allows the specified class in the specified package to be known by its class name alone. Thus, this `import` statement allows you to type `Hashtable` instead of `java.util.Hashtable`:

```
import java.util.Hashtable;
```

The second form of the `import` statement makes all classes in a package available by their class name. For example, the following `import` statement is implicit (you need not specify it yourself) in every Java program:

```
import java.lang.*;
```

It makes the core classes of the language available by their unqualified class names. If two packages imported with this form of the statement contain classes with the same name, it is an error to use either of those ambiguous classes without using its fully qualified name.

14.2.2.8. Access to Packages, Classes, and Class Members

Java has the following rules about access to packages, classes, and class members. (Class members are the variables, methods, and, in Java 1.1, nested classes defined within a class.) Note that the `public`, `private`, and `protected` keywords used in these rules will be explained in more detail later.

- A package is accessible if the appropriate files and directories are accessible (e.g., if local files have appropriate read permissions, or if they can be downloaded via the network).
- All classes and interfaces in a package are accessible to all other classes and interfaces in the same package. It is not possible to define classes in Java that are visible only within a single file of source code.
- A class declared `public` in one package is accessible within another package, assuming that the package itself is accessible. A non-`public` class is not accessible outside of its package.
- Members of a class are accessible from a different class within the same package, as long as they are not declared `private`. `private` members are accessible only within their own class.

- A member of a class `A` is accessible from a class `B` in different package if `A` is public and the member is public, or if `A` is `public`, the member is `protected`, and `B` is a subclass of `A`.
- All members of a class are always accessible from within that class.

14.2.2.9. Local Variables

The name space rules we've been describing apply to packages, classes, and the members within classes. Java also supports local variables, declared within method definitions. These local variables behave just like local variables in C—they do not have globally unique hierarchical names, nor do they have access modifiers like `public` and `private`. Local variables are quite different from class fields.

14.2.3. Comments

Java supports three types of comments:

- A standard C-style comment that begins with `/*` and continues until the next `*/`. As in most implementations of C, this style of comment cannot be nested.
- A C++-style comment that begins with `//` and continues until the end of the line.
- A special "doc comment" that begins with `/**` and continues until the next `*/`. These comments may not be nested. Doc comments are specially processed by the `javadoc` program to produce simple online documentation from the Java source code....

Since C-style comments do not nest, it is a good idea to use C++-style `//` comments for most of your short comments within method bodies. This allows you to use `/* */` comments to comment out large blocks of code when you need to do that during development. This is especially important because, as you will see, Java does not support a preprocessor that allows you to use `#if 0` to comment out a block.

14.2.4. No Preprocessor

Java does not include any kind of preprocessor like the C `cpp` preprocessor. It may seem hard to imagine programming without `#define`, `#include`, and `#ifdef`, but in fact, Java really does not require these constructs.

14.2.4.1. Defining Constants

Any variable declared `final` in Java is a constant—its value must be specified with an initializer when it is declared, and that value may never be changed. The Java equivalent of a C `#define`d constant is a `static final` variable declared within a class definition. If the compiler can compute the value of such a `static final` variable at compile time, it uses the computed value to precompute other compile-time constants that refer to the value. The variable `java.lang.Math.PI` is an example of such a constant. It is declared like this:

```
public final class Math {
     ...
     public static final double PI = 3.14159.....;
     ...
}
```

Note two things about this example. First, the C convention of using CAPITAL letters for constants is also a Java convention. Second, note the advantage Java constants have over C preprocessor constants: Java constants have globally unique hierarchical names, while constants defined with the C preprocessor always run the risk of a name collision. Also, Java constants are strongly typed and allow better type-checking by the compiler than C preprocessor constants.

14.2.4.2. Defining Macros

The C preprocessor allows you to define macros—a construct that looks like a function invocation but that is actually replaced directly with C code, saving the overhead of a function call. Java has no equivalent to this sort of macro, but compiler technology has advanced to a point where macros are rarely necessary any more. A good Java compiler should automatically be able to "inline" short Java methods where appropriate.

14.2.4.3. Including Files

Java does not have a `#include` directive, but it does not need one. Java defines a mapping of fully qualified class names (like `java.lang.Math`) to a directory and file structure (like `java/lang/Math.class`). This means that when the Java compiler needs to read in a specified class file, it knows exactly where to find it and does not need a special directive to tell it where to look.

Furthermore, Java does not make the distinction between *declaring* a variable or procedure and *defining* it that C does. This means that there is no need for C-style header files or function prototypes—a single Java object file serves as the interface definition and implementation for a class.

Java does have an `import` statement, which is superficially similar to the C preprocessor `#include` directive. What this statement does, however, is tell the compiler that the current file is using the specified classes, or classes from the specified package, and allows us to refer to those classes with abbreviated names. For example, since the compiler implicitly imports all the classes of the `java.lang` package, we can refer to the constant `java.lang.Math.PI` by the shorter name `Math.PI`.

14.2.4.4. Conditional Compilation

Java does not have any form of the C `#ifdef` or `#if` directives to perform conditional compilation. In theory, conditional compilation is not necessary in Java since it is a platform-independent language, and thus there are no platform dependencies that require the technique. In practice, however, conditional compilation is still often useful in Java—to provide slightly different user interfaces on different platforms, for example, or to support optional inclusion of debugging code in programs.

While Java does not define explicit constructs for conditional compilation, a good Java compiler (such as Sun's `javac`) performs conditional compilation implicitly—that is, it does not compile code if it can prove that the code will never be executed. Generally, this means that code within an `if` statement testing an expression that is always `false` is not included. Thus, placing code within an `if (false)` block is equivalent to surrounding it with `#if 0` and `#endif` in C.

Conditional compilation also works with constants, which, as we saw above, are `static final` variables. A class might define the constant like this:

```
private static final boolean DEBUG = false;
```

With such a constant defined, any code within an `if (DEBUG)` block is not actually compiled into the class file. To activate debugging for the class, it is only necessary to change the value of the constant to `true` and recompile the class.

14.2.5. Unicode and Character Escapes

Java characters, strings, and identifiers (e.g., variable, method, and class names) are composed of 16-bit Unicode characters. This makes Java programs relatively easy to internationalize for non-English-speaking users. It also makes the language easier to work with for non-English-speaking programmers—a Thai programmer could use the Thai alphabet for class and method names in her Java code.

If two-byte characters seem confusing or intimidating to you, fear not. The Unicode character set is compatible with ASCII and the first 256 characters (0x0000 to 0x00FF) are identical to the ISO8859-1 (Latin-1) characters 0x00 to 0xFF. Furthermore, the Java language design and the Java `String` API make the character representation entirely transparent to you. If you are using only Latin-1 characters, there is no way that you can even distinguish a Java 16-bit character from the 8-bit characters you are familiar with.

Most platforms cannot display all 38,885 currently defined Unicode characters, so Java programs may be written (and Java output may appear) with special Unicode escape sequences. Anywhere within a Java program (not only within character and string literals), a Unicode character may be represented with the Unicode escape sequence `\uxxxx`, where *xxxx* is a sequence of four hexadecimal digits.

Java also supports all of the standard C character escape sequences, such as `\n`, `\t`, and `\xxx` (where *xxx* is three octal digits). Note, however, that Java does not support line continuation with `\` at the end of a line. Long strings must either be specified on a single long line, or they must be created from shorter strings using the string concatenation (`+`) operator. (Note that the concatenation of two constant strings is done at compile time rather than at runtime, so using the `+` operator in this way is not inefficient.)

There are two important differences between Unicode escapes and C-style escape characters. First, as we've noted, Unicode escapes can appear anywhere within a Java program, while the other escape characters can appear only in character and string constants.

The second, and more subtle, difference is that Unicode `\u` escape sequences are processed before the other escape characters, and thus the two types of escape sequences can have very different semantics. A Unicode escape is simply an alternative way to represent a character that may not be displayable on certain (non-Unicode) systems. Some of the character escapes, however, represent special characters in a way that prevents the usual interpretation of those characters by the compiler. The following examples make this difference clear. Note that `\u0022` and `\u005c` are the Unicode escapes for the double-quote character and the backslash character.

```
// \" represents a " character, and prevents the normal
// interpretation of that character by the compiler.
// This is a string consisting of a double-quote character.
String quote = "\"";
```

```
// We can't represent the same string with a single Unicode escape.
// \u0022 has exactly the same meaning to the compiler as ".
// The string below turns into """: an empty string followed
// by an unterminated string, which yields a compilation error.
String quote = "\u0022";

// Here we represent both characters of an \" escape as
// Unicode escapes. This turns into "\"", and is the same
// string as in our first example.
String quote = "\u005c\u0022";
```

14.2.6. Primitive Data Types

Java adds `byte` and `boolean` primitive types to the standard set of C types. In addition, it strictly defines the size and signedness of its types. In C, an `int` may be 16, 32, or 64 bits, and a `char` may act signed or unsigned depending on the platform. Not so in Java. In C, an uninitialized local variable usually has garbage as its value. In Java, all variables have guaranteed default values, though the compiler may warn you in places where you rely, accidentally or not, on these default values. Table 14.2 lists Java's primitive data types. The subsections below provide details about these types.

TABLE 14.2. *Java primitive data types.*

Type	*Contains*	*Default*	*Size*	*Min Value*	*Max Value*
`boolean`	`true` or `false`	`false`	1 bit	N.A.	N.A.
`char`	Unicode character	`\u0000`	16 bits	`\u0000`	`\uFFFF`
`byte`	Signed integer	0	8 bits	–128	127
`short`	Signed integer	0	16 bits	–32768	32767
`int`	Signed integer	0	32 bits	–2147483648 2147483647	
`long`	Signed integer	0	64 bits	–9223372036854775808 9223372036854775807	
`float`	IEEE 754 floating-point	0.0	32 bits	±3.40282347E+38 ±1.40239846E–45	
`double`	IEEE 754 floating-point	0.0	64 bits	±1.79769313486231570E+308 ±4.94065645841246544E–324	

14.2.6.1. The `boolean` Type

`boolean` values are not integers, may not be treated as integers, and may never be cast to or from any other type. To perform C-style conversions between a `boolean` value `b` and an `int i`, use the following code:

```
b = (i != 0);     // integer-to-boolean: non-0 -> true; 0 -> false;
i = (b)?1:0;      // boolean-to-integer: true -> 1; false -> 0;
```

14.2.6.2. The `char` Type

`char` values represent characters. Character literals may appear in a Java program between single quotes. For example:

```
char c = 'A';
```

All of the standard C character escapes, as well as Unicode escapes, are also supported in character literals. For example:

```
char newline = '\n', apostrophe = '\'',
     delete = '\377', aleph='\u05D0';
```

Values of type `char` do not have a sign. If a `char` is cast to a `byte` or a `short`, a negative value may result.

The `char` type in Java holds a two-byte Unicode character. While this may seem intimidating to those not familiar with Unicode and the techniques of program internationalization, it is in fact totally transparent. Java does not provide a way to compute the size of a variable, nor does it allow any sort of pointer arithmetic. What this means is that if you are only using ASCII or Latin-1 characters, there is no way to distinguish a Java `char` from a C `char`.

14.2.6.3. Integral Types

The integral types in Java are `byte`, `short`, `char`, `int`, and `long`. Literals for these types are written just as they are in C. All integral types, other than `char`, are signed. There is no `unsigned` keyword as there is in C. It is not legal to write `long int` or `short int` as it is in C. A `long` constant may be distinguished from other integral constants by appending the character `l` or `L` to it.

Integer division by zero or modulo zero causes an `ArithmeticException` to be thrown.[6]

[6]Exceptions signal errors in Java. Exception handling is described later.

14.2.6.4. Floating-Point Types

The floating-point types in Java are `float` and `double`. Literals for these types are written just as they are in C. Literals may be specified to be of type `float` by appending an `f` or `F` to the value; they may be specified to be of type `double` by appending a `d` or `D`.

`float` and `double` types have special values that may be the result of certain floating-point operations: positive infinity, negative infinity, negative zero, and not-a-number. The `java.lang.Float` and `java.lang.Double` classes define some of these values as constants: `POSITIVE_INFINITY`, `NEGATIVE_INFINITY`, and `NaN`.

`NaN` is unordered—comparing it to any other number, including itself, yields `false`. Use `Float.isNaN()` or `Double.isNaN()` to test for `NaN`. Negative zero compares equal to regular zero (positive zero), but the two zeros may be distinguished by division: One divided by negative zero yields negative infinity; one divided by positive zero yields positive infinity.

Floating-point arithmetic never causes exceptions, even in the case of division by zero.

14.2.6.5. String Literals

Strings in Java are not a primitive type but are instances of the `String` class. However, because they are so commonly used, string literals may appear between quotes in Java programs, just as they do in C. When the compiler encounters such a string literal, it automatically creates the necessary `String` object.

14.2.7. Reference Data Types

The non-primitive data types in Java are objects and arrays. These non-primitive types are often called "reference types" because they are handled "by reference"—in other words, the address of the object or array is stored in a variable, passed to methods, and so on. By comparison, primitive types are handled "by value"—the actual primitive values are stored in variables and passed to methods.

In C, you can manipulate a value by reference by taking its address with the `&` operator, and you can "dereference" an address with the `*` and `->` operators. These operators do not exist in Java: Primitive types are always passed by value; arrays and objects are always passed by reference.

Because objects are passed by reference, two different variables may refer to the same object:

```
Button p, q;
p = new Button();              // p refers to a Button object
q = p;                         // q refers to the same Button.
p.setLabel("Ok");              // A change to the object through p...
String s = q.getLabel();       // ...is also visible through q.
                               // s now contains "Ok".
```

This is not true of primitive types, however:

```
int i = 3;                     // i contains the value 3.
int j = i;                     // j contains a copy of the value in i.
i = 2;                         // Changing i doesn't change j.
                               // Now, i =\^= 2 and j =\^= 3.
.\" djf: this is a new B-head
```

14.2.7.1. Terminology: Pass by Reference

The statement that Java manipulates objects "by reference" causes confusion for some programmers, because there are several different meanings of "by reference" in common use. Regardless of what we call it, it is important to understand what Java does. Java works with references to objects. A Java variable holds only a reference to an object, not the object itself. When an object is passed to a method, only a reference to the object is actually passed, not the entire object. It is in this sense that Java manipulates objects "by reference."

Some people use the term "pass by reference" to mean that a reference to a variable is passed to a method. Java does not do this. For example, it is not possible to write a working `swap()` function like the following in Java:

```
public void swap(Object a, Object b) {
  Object temp = a;
  a = b;
  b = temp;
}
```

The method parameters `a` and `b` contain references to objects, not addresses of variables. Thus, while this `swap()` function does compile and run, it has no effect except on its own local variables and arguments.

To solve this terminology problem, perhaps we should say that Java manipulates objects "by reference," but it passes object references to methods "by value."

14.2.7.2. Copying Objects

Because reference types are not passed by value, assigning one object to another in Java does not copy the value of the object. It merely assigns a reference to the object. Consider the following code:

```
Button a = new Button("Okay");
Button b = new Button("Cancel");
a = b;
```

After these lines are executed, the variable `a` contains a reference to the object that `b` refers to. The object that `a` used to refer to is lost.

To copy the data of one object into another object, use the `clone()` method:

```
Vector b = new Vector;
c = b.clone();
```

After these lines run, the variable `c` refers to an object that is a duplicate of the object referred to by `b`. Note that not all types support the `clone()` method. Only classes that implement the `Cloneable` interface may be cloned.

Arrays are also reference types, and assigning an array simply copies a reference to the array. To actually copy the values stored in an array, you must assign each of the values individually or use the `System.arraycopy()` method.

14.2.7.3. Checking Objects for Equality

Another implication of passing objects by reference is that the == operator tests whether two variables refer to the same object, not whether two objects contain the same values. To actually test whether two separate objects are the same, you must use a specially written method for that object type (just as you might use `strcmp()` to compare C strings for equality). In Java, a number of classes define an `equals()` method that you can use to perform this test.

14.2.7.4. Java Has No Pointers

The referencing and dereferencing of objects is handled for you automatically by Java. Java does not allow you to manipulate pointers or memory addresses of any kind:

- It does not allow you to cast object or array references into integers or vice-versa.
- It does not allow you to do pointer arithmetic.
- It does not allow you to compute the size in bytes of any primitive type or object.

There are two reasons for these restrictions:

- Pointers are a notorious source of bugs. Eliminating them simplifies the language and eliminates many potential bugs.

- Pointers and pointer arithmetic could be used to sidestep Java's run-time checks and security mechanisms. Removing pointers allows Java to provide the security guarantees that it does.

To a C programmer, the lack of pointers and pointer arithmetic may seem an odious restriction in Java. But once you get used to the Java object-oriented programming model, it no longer seems like a serious restriction at all. The lack of pointers does mean that you probably can't do things like write UNIX device drivers in Java (at least not without using native methods written in C). But big deal—most of us never have to do this kind of low-level programming anyway.

14.2.7.5. `null`

The default value for variables of all reference types is `null`. `null` is a reserved value that indicates "an absence of reference"—i.e., that a variable does not refer to any object or array.

In Java, `null` is a reserved keyword, unlike `NULL` in C, where it is just a constant defined to be 0. `null` is an exception to the strong typing rules of Java—it may be assigned to any variable of reference type (i.e., any variable that has a class, interface, or array as its type).

`null` can't be cast to any primitive type, including integral types and `boolean`. It shouldn't be considered equal to zero (although it may be implemented this way).

14.2.7.6. Reference Type Summary

The distinction between primitive types passed by value, and objects and arrays passed by reference is a crucial one in Java. Be sure you understand the following:

- All objects and arrays are handled by reference in Java. (Those object references are passed-by-value to methods, however.)
- The `=` and `==` operators assign and test references to objects. Use `clone()` and `equals()` to actually copy or test the objects themselves.
- The necessary referencing and dereferencing of objects and arrays is handled automatically by Java.
- A reference type can never be cast to a primitive type.
- A primitive type can never be cast to a reference type.
- There is no pointer arithmetic in Java.

- There is no `sizeof` operator in Java.
- `null` is a special value that means "no object" or indicates an absence of reference.

14.2.8. Objects

Now that you know objects are passed by reference, we should discuss how they are created, used, and destroyed. The following subsections provide a very brief overview of objects. The section "Classes and Objects in Java" explains classes and objects in much greater detail.

14.2.8.1. Creating Objects

Declaring a variable to hold an object does not create the object itself; the variable only holds the reference to the object. To actually create an object, you must use the `new` keyword. This is followed by the object's class (i.e., its type) and an optional argument list in parentheses. These arguments are passed to the constructor method for the class, which serves to initialize internal fields in the new object. For example:

```
java.awt.Button b = new java.awt.Button();
ComplexNumber c = new ComplexNumber(1.0, 1.414);
```

There are actually two other ways to create an object. First, you can create a `String` object simply by enclosing characters in double quotes:

```
String s = "This is a test";
```

Because strings are used so frequently, the Java compiler provides this technique as a shortcut. Another way to create objects is by calling the `newInstance()` method of a `Class` object. This technique is generally used only when dynamically loading classes, so we won't discuss it here. In Java 1.1, objects can also be created by "de-serializing" them—i.e., re-creating an object that had its state saved through "serialization."

The memory for newly created objects is dynamically allocated. Creating an object with `new` in Java is like calling `malloc()` in C to allocate memory for an instance of a `struct`. It is also, of course, a lot like using the `new` operator in C++. (Below, we'll see where this analogy to `malloc()` in C and `new` in C++ breaks down.)

14.2.8.2. Accessing Objects

As you've probably noticed in various example code fragments by now, the way you access the fields of an object is with a dot:

```
ComplexNumber c = new ComplexNumber();
c.x = 1.0;
c.y = -1.414;
```

This syntax is reminiscent of accessing the fields of a `struct` in C. Recall, though, that Java objects are always accessed by reference, and that Java performs any necessary dereferencing for you. Thus, the dot in Java is more like `->` in C. Java hides the fact that there is a reference here in an attempt to make your programming easier. The other difference between C and Java when accessing objects is that in Java you refer to an object's methods with the same syntax used for fields:

```
ComplexNumber c = new ComplexNumber(1.0, -1.414);
double magnitude = c.magnitude();
```

14.2.8.3. Garbage Collection

Objects in Java are created with the `new` keyword, but there is no corresponding `old` or `delete` keyword or `free()` method to get rid of them when they are no longer needed. If creating an object with `new` is like calling `malloc()` in C or using `new` in C++, then it would seem that Java is full of memory leaks, because we never call `free()` or use the `delete` operator.

In fact, this isn't the case. Java uses a technique called *garbage collection* to automatically detect objects that are no longer being used (an object is no longer in use when there are no more references to it) and to free them. This means that in our programs, we spend less time worrying about freeing memory and destroying objects—the garbage collector takes care of that.

If you are a C or C++ programmer, it may take some getting used to to just let allocated objects go without worrying about reclaiming their memory. Once you get used to it, however, you'll begin to appreciate what a nice feature this is. We'll discuss garbage collection in more detail later.

14.2.9. Arrays

Most of what we learned in the previous sections about reference types and objects applies equally well to arrays in Java:

- Arrays are manipulated by reference.
- They are dynamically created with `new`.
- They are automatically garbage collected when no longer referred to.

The following subsections explain these and other details.

14.2.9.1. Creating and Destroying Arrays

There are two ways to create arrays in Java. The first uses `new`, and specifies how large the array should be:

```
byte octet_buffer[] = new byte[1024];
Button buttons[] = new Button[10];
```

Since creating an array does not create the objects that are stored in the array, there is no constructor to call, and the argument list is omitted with this form of the `new` keyword. The elements of an array created in this way are initialized to the default value for their type. The elements of an array of `int` are initialized to `0`, for example, and the elements of an array of objects are initialized to `null`. This last point is important to remember: Creating an array of objects only allocates storage for object references, not objects themselves. The objects that will be referred to by the elements of the array must be created separately.

The second way to create an array is with an initializer, which looks just like it does in C:

```
int lookup_table[] = {1, 2, 4, 8, 16, 32, 64, 128};
```

This syntax dynamically creates an array and initializes its elements to the specified values. The elements specified in an array initializer may be arbitrary expressions. This is different than in C, where they must be constant expressions.

In Java 1.1, arrays may also be created and initialized "anonymously" by combining the `new` syntax with the initializer syntax. It looks like this:

```
Menu m = createMenu("File", new String[] { "Open...", "Save", "Quit" });
```

Arrays are automatically garbage collected, just like objects are.

14.2.9.2. Multidimensional Arrays

Java also supports multidimensional arrays. These are implemented as arrays-of-arrays, as they are in C. You specify a variable as a multidimensional array type simply by appending the appropriate number of `[]` pairs after it. You allocate a multidimensional array with `new` by specifying the appropriate number of elements (between square brackets) for each dimension. For example:

```
byte TwoDimArray[][] = new byte[256][16];
```

This statement does three things:

- Declares a variable named `TwoDimArray`. This variable has type `byte[][]` (array-of-array-of-`byte`).

- Dynamically allocates an array with 256 elements. The type of this newly allocated array is `byte[][]`, so it can be assigned to the variable we declared. Each element of this new array is of type `byte[]`—a single-dimensional array of `byte`.
- Dynamically allocates 256 arrays of bytes, each of which holds 16 bytes, and stores a reference to these 256 `byte[]` arrays into the 256 elements of the `byte[][]` array allocated in the second step. The 16 bytes in each of these 256 arrays are initialized to their default value of `0`.

When allocating a multidimensional array, you do not have to specify the number of elements that are contained in each dimension. For example:

```
int threeD[][][] = new int[10][][];
```

This expression allocates an array that contains 10 elements, each of type `int[][]`. It is a single-dimensional allocation, although when the array elements are properly initialized to meaningful values, the array will be multidimensional. The rule for this sort of array allocation is that the first *n* dimensions (where *n* is at least one) must have the number of elements specified, and these dimensions may be followed by *m* additional dimensions with no dimension size specified. The following is legal:

```
String lots_of_strings[][][][] = new String[5][3][][];
```

This is not:

```
double temperature_data[][][] = new double[100][][10];  // illegal
```

Multidimensional arrays can also be allocated and initialized with nested initializers. For example, you might declare the following multidimensional array of strings for use by the `getParameterInfo()` method of an applet:

```
String param_info[][] = {
     {"foreground", "Color",   "foreground color"},
     {"background", "Color",   "background color"},
     {"message",     "String", "the banner to display"}
};
```

Note that since Java implements multidimensional arrays as arrays-of-arrays, multidimensional arrays need not be "rectangular." For example, this is how you could create and initialize a "triangular array":

```
short triangle[][] = new short[10][];
// A single-dimensional array
```

```
for(int i = 0; i < triangle.length; i++) {
// For each element of that array
    triangle[i] = new short[i+1];
    // Allocate a new array
    for(int j=0; j < i+1; j++)
    // For each element of new array
        triangle[i][j] = (short) i + j;
        // Initialize it to a value
}
```

You can also declare and initialize non-rectangular arrays with nested initializers:

```
static int[][] twodim = {{1, 2}, {3, 4, 5}, {5, 6, 7, 8}};
```

To simulate multiple dimensions within a single-dimensional array, you'd use code just as you would in C:

```
final int rows = 600;
final int columns = 800;
byte pixels[] = new byte[rows*columns];

// access element [i,j] like this:
byte b = pixels[i + j*columns];
```

14.2.9.3. Accessing Array Elements

Array access in Java is just like array access in C—you access an element of an array by putting an integer-valued expression between square brackets after the name of the array:

```
int a[] = new int[100];
a[0] = 0;
for(int i = 1; i < a.length; i++) a[i] = i + a[i-1];
```

Notice how we computed the number of elements of the array in this example—by accessing the `length` field of the array. This is the only field that arrays support. Note that it is a constant (`final`) field—any attempt to store a value into the `length` field of an array will fail.

In all Java array references, the index is checked to make sure it is not too small (less than zero) or too big (greater than or equal to the array length). If the index is out of bounds, an `ArrayIndexOutOfBoundsException` is thrown.[7] This is another way that Java works to prevent bugs (and security problems).

[7]The discussion of exceptions and exception handling is still to come.

14.2.9.4. Are Arrays Objects?

It is useful to consider arrays to be a separate kind of reference type from objects. In some ways, though, arrays behave just like objects. As we saw, arrays use the object syntax `.length` to refer to their length. Arrays may also be assigned to variables of type `Object`, and the methods of the `Object` class may be invoked for arrays. (`Object` is the root class in Java, which means that all objects can be assigned to a variable of type `Object` and all objects can invoke the methods of `Object`.)

The evidence suggests that arrays are, in fact, objects. Java defines enough special syntax for arrays, however, that it is still most useful to consider them a different kind of reference type than objects.

14.2.9.5. Declaring Array Variables and Arguments

In C, you declare an array variable or array function argument by placing square brackets next to the variable name:

```
void reverse(char strbuf[], int buffer_size)  {
    char buffer[500];
        ...
}
```

In Java, you would have to declare `buffer` as an array variable, and then allocate the array itself with `new`, but otherwise you could use the same syntax, with the array brackets after the variable or argument name.

However, Java also allows you to put the array brackets after the type name instead. So you could rewrite this code fragment to look something like this:

```
void reverse(char[] strbuf, int buffer_size) {
    char[] buffer = new char[500];
        ...
}
```

In a lot of ways, this new array syntax is easier to read and easier to understand. (It doesn't work in C, by the way, because pointers make C's type declaration syntax a real mess.) The only problem with this new syntax is that if you get in the habit of using it, it will make it harder for you when you (hopefully only occasionally!) have to switch back and program in C.

Java even allows you to mix the declaration styles, which is something you may find occasionally useful (or frequently confusing!) for certain data structures or algorithms. For example:

```
// row and column are arrays of byte.
// matrix is an array of an array of bytes.
byte[] row, column, matrix[];
```

```
// This method takes an array of bytes and an
// array of arrays of bytes
public void dot_product(byte[] column, byte[] matrix[]) { ... }
```

A final point to note about array declarations is that (as we've seen throughout this section) the size of an array is not part of its type as it is in C. Thus, you can declare a variable to be of type `String[]`, for example, and assign any array of `String` objects to it, regardless of the length of the array:

```
String[] strings;            // this variable can refer to
                             // any String array
strings = new String[10];    // one that contains 10 Strings
strings = new String[20];    // or one that contains 20.
.XE "arrays"
```

14.2.10. Strings

Strings in Java are not null-terminated arrays of characters as they are in C. Instead, they are instances of the `java.lang.String` class. Java strings are unusual, in that the compiler treats them almost as if they were primitive types—for example, it automatically creates a `String` object when it encounters a double-quoted constant in the program. And, the language defines an operator that operates on `String` objects—the `+` operator for string concatenation.

An important feature of `String` objects is that they are immutable—i.e., there are no methods defined that allow you to change the contents of a `String`. If you need to modify the contents of a `String`, you have to create a `StringBuffer` object from the `String` object, modify the contents of the `StringBuffer`, and then create a new `String` from the contents of the `StringBuffer`.

Note that it is moot to ask whether Java strings are terminated with a `NULL` character (`\u0000`) or not. Java performs runtime bounds checking on all array and string accesses, so there is no way to examine the value of any internal terminator character that appears after the last character of the string.

Some of the more important String methods are `length()`, `charAt()`, `equals()`, `compareTo()`, `indexOf()`, `lastIndexOf()`, and `substring()`.

14.2.11. Operators

Java supports almost all of the standard C operators. These standard operators have the same precedence and associativity in Java as they do in C. They are listed in Table 14.3....

TABLE 14.3. *Java operators.*

Prec.	*Operator*	*Operand Types*	*Assoc.*	*Operation Performed*
1	++	Arithmetic	R	Pre-or-post increment (unary)
	--	Arithmetic	R	Pre-or-post decrement (unary)
	+, -	Arithmetic	R	Unary plus, unary minus
	-	Integral	R	Bitwise complement (unary)
	!	boolean	R	Logical complement (unary)
	(type)	Any	R	Case
2	*, /, %	Arithmetic	L	Multiplication, division, remainder
3	+, -	Arithmetic	L	Addition, subtraction
	+	String	L	String concatenation
4	<<	Integral	L	Left shift
	>>	Integral	L	Right shift with sign extension
	>>>	Integral	L	Right shift with zero extension
5	<, <=	Arithmetic	L	Less than, less than or equal
	>, >=	Arithmetic	L	Greater than, greater than or equal
	instanceof	Object, type	L	Type comparison
6	==	Primitive	L	Equal (have identical values)
	!=	Primitive	L	Note equal (have difference values)
	==	Object	L	Equal (refer to same object)
	!=	Object	L	Not equal (refer to difference objects)
7	&	Integral	L	Bitwise AND
	&	boolean	L	boolean AND
8	^	Integral	L	Bitwise XOR
	^	boolean	L	boolean XOR
9	|	Integral	L	Bitwise OR
	|	boolean	L	boolean OR

Prec.	*Operator*	*Operand Types*	*Assoc.*	*Operation Performed*
10	&&	boolean	L	boolean OR
11	||	boolean	L	Conditional AND
12	?:	boolean, any	R	Conditional (ternary) operator
13	=	Variable, any	R	Assignment
	*=, /=, %=, +=, -=, <<=, >>=, >>>=, &=, ^=, |=	variable, any	R	assignment with operators

Note the following Java operator differences from C. Java does not support the comma operator for combining two expressions into one (although the `for` statement simulates this operator in a useful way). Since Java does not allow you to manipulate pointers directly, it does not support the reference and dereference operators `*`, `->`, and `&`, nor the `sizeof` operator. Further, Java doesn't consider `[]` (array access) and `.` (field access) to be operators, as C does.

Java also adds some new operators:

`+` The `+` operator applied to `String` values concatenates them.[8] If only one operand of `+` is a `String`, the other one is converted to a string. The conversion is done automatically for primitive types, and by calling the `toString()` method of non-primitive types. This `String +` operator has the same precedence as the arithmetic `+` operator. The `+=` operator works as you would expect for `String` values.

`instanceof` The `instanceof` operator returns `true` if the object `o` on its left-hand side is an instance of the class `C` or implements the interface `I` specified on its right-hand side. It also returns `true` if `o` is an instance of a subclass of `C` or is an instance of a subclass of some class that implements `I`. `instanceof` returns `false` if `o` is not an instance of C or does not implement `I`. It also returns `false` if the value on its left is `null`. If `instanceof` returns `true`, it means that `o` is assignable to variables of type `C` or `I`. The `instanceof` operator has the same precedence as the `<`, `<=`, `>`, and `>=` operators.

[8]To C++ programmers, this looks like operator overloading. In fact, Java does not support operator overloading—the language designers decided (after much debate) that overloaded operators were a neat idea, but that code that relied on them became hard to read and understand.

`>>>` Because all integral types in Java are signed values, the Java `>>` operator is defined to do a right shift with sign extension. The `>>>` operator treats the value to be shifted as an unsigned number and shifts the bits right with zero extension. The `>>>=` operator works as you would expect.

`&` and `|` When `&` and `|` are applied to integral types in Java, they perform the expected bitwise AND and OR operations. Java makes a strong distinction between integral types and the `boolean` type, however. Thus, if these operators are applied to `boolean` types, they perform logical AND and logical OR operations. These logical AND and logical OR operators always evaluate both of their operands, even when the result of the operation is determined after evaluating only the left operand. This is useful when the operands are expressions with side effects (such as method calls) and you always want the side effects to occur. However, when you do not want the right operand evaluated if it is not necessary, you can use the `&&` and `||` operators, which perform "short-circuited" logical AND and logical OR operations just as in C. The `&=` and `|=` operators perform a bitwise or logical operation depending on the type of the operands, as you would expect.

14.2.12. Statements

Many of Java's control statements are similar or identical to C statements. This section lists and, where necessary, explains Java's statements. Note that the topic of exceptions and the `try/catch/finally` statement is substantial enough that it is covered later in a section of its own.

14.2.12.1. The `if/else`, `while`, and `do/while` Statements

The `if`, `else`, `do`, and `while` statements are exactly the same in Java as they are in C. The only substantial difference arises because the Java `boolean` type cannot be cast to other types. In Java, the values `0` and `null` are not the same as `false`, and non-zero and non-`null` values are not the same as `true`.

The conditional expression that is expected by the `if`, the `while`, and the `do/while` statements must be of `boolean` type in Java. Specifying an integer type or a reference type won't do. Thus, the following C code is not legal in Java:

```
int i = 10;
while(i--) {
    Object o = get_object();
    if (o) {
        do { ... } while(j);
    }
}
```

In Java, you must make the condition you are testing for clear by explicitly testing your value against `0` or `null`. Use code like the following:

```
int i = 10;
while(i-- > 0) {
    Object o = get_object();
    if (o != null) {
        do { ... } while(j != 0);
    }
}
```

14.2.12.2. The `switch` Statement

The `switch` statement is the same in Java as it is in C. You may use `byte`, `char`, `short`, `int`, or `long` types as the values of the `case` labels, and you may also specify a `default` label just as you do in C.

14.2.12.3. The `for` Loop

The `for` statement is perhaps the most useful looping construct available in Java. There are only two differences between the Java `for` loop and the C `for` loop. The first difference is that although Java does not support the C comma operator (which allows multiple expressions to be joined into a single expression), the Java `for` loop simulates it by allowing multiple comma-separated expressions to appear in the initialization and increment sections, but not the test section, of the loop. For example:

```
int i;
String s;
for(i=0, s = "testing";                  // Initialize variables.
    (i < 10) && (s.length() >= 1);       // Test for continuation.
    i++, s = s.substring(1))             // Increment variables.
{
    System.out.println(s);               // Loop body.
}
```

As you can see, this "difference" between the Java and C `for` loops is really a similarity.

The second difference is the addition of the C++ ability to declare local loop variables in the initialization section of the loop:

```
for(int i = 0; i < my_array.length; i++)
    System.out.println("a[" + i + "] = " + my_array[i]);
```

Variables declared in this way have the `for` loop as their scope. In other words, they are only valid within the body of the `for` loop and within the initialization, test, and increment expressions of the loop. Although variables declared in `for` loops have their own scope, the Java compiler won't let you declare a loop variable that has the same name as an already existing variable or parameter.

Note that because variable declaration syntax also uses the comma, the Java syntax allows you to either specify multiple comma-separated initialization expressions or to declare and initialize multiple comma-separated variables of the same type. You may not mix variable declarations with other, non-declaration expressions. For example, the following `for` loop declares and initializes two variables that are valid only within the `for` loop.

```
for(int i=0, j=10; i < j; i++, j—) System.out.println("k = " + i*j);
```

14.2.12.4. Labeled `break` and `continue` Statements

The `break` and `continue` statements, used alone, behave the same in Java as they do in C. However, in Java, they may optionally be followed by a label that specifies an enclosing loop (for `continue`) or any enclosing statement (for `break`). The labeled forms of these statements allow you to "break" and "continue" any specified statement or loop within a method definition, not only the nearest enclosing statements or loop.

The `break` statement, without a label, transfers control out of ("breaks out of" or terminates) the nearest enclosing `for`, `while`, `do`, or `switch` statement, exactly as in C. If the `break` keyword is followed by an identifier that is the label of an arbitrary enclosing statement, execution transfers out of that enclosing statement. After the `break` statement is executed, any required `finally` clauses are executed, and control resumes at the statement following the terminated statement. (The `finally` clause and the `try` statement it is associated with are exception handling constructs and are explained in the next section.) For example:

```
test: if (check(i)) {
    try {
        for(int j=0; j < 10; j++) {
            if (j > i) break;              // Terminate just this loop.
            if (a[i][j] =\^= null)
                break test;                // Do the finally clause and
        }                                  // terminate the if statement.
    }
    finally { cleanup(a, i, j); }
}
```

Without a label, the `continue` statement works exactly as in C: It stops the iteration in progress and causes execution to resume after the last statement in the `while`, `do`, or `for` loop, just before the loop iteration is to begin again. If the `continue` keyword is followed by an identifier that is the label of an enclosing loop, execution skips to the end of that loop instead. If there are any `finally` clauses between the `continue` statement and the end of the appropriate loop, these clauses are executed before control is transferred to the end of the loop.

The following code fragment illustrates how the `continue` statement works in its labeled and unlabeled forms.

```
big_loop: while(!done) {
    if (test(a,b) =\^= 0) continue;        // Control goes to point 2.
    try {
        for(int i=0; i < 10; i++) {
            if (a[i] =\^= null)
                continue;                  // Control goes to point 1.
            else if (b[i] =\^= null)
                continue big_loop;         // Control goes to point 2,
                                           // after executing the
                                           // finally block.
            doit(a[i],b[i]);
           // Point 1. Increment and start loop again with the test.
        }
    }
    finally { cleanup(a,b); }
    // Point 2. Start loop again with the (!done) test.
}
```

Note the non-intuitive feature of the labeled `continue` statement: The loop label must appear at the top of the loop, but `continue` causes execution to transfer to the very bottom of the loop.

14.2.12.5. No `goto` Statement

`goto` is a reserved word in Java, but the `goto` statement is not currently part of the language. Labeled `break` and `continue` statements replace some important and legitimate uses of `goto`, and the `try`/`catch`/`finally` statement replaces the others.

14.2.12.6. The `synchronized` Statement

Since Java is a multithreaded system, care must often be taken to prevent multiple threads from modifying objects simultaneously in a way that might leave the object's state corrupted. Sections of code that must not be executed simultaneously are known as "critical sections." Java provides the `synchronized` statement to protect these critical sections. The syntax is:

```
synchronized (expression) statement
```

`expression` is an expression that must resolve to an object or an array. The `statement` is the code of the critical section, which is usually a block of statements (within { and }). The `synchronized` statement attempts to acquire an exclusive lock for the object or array specified by `expression`. It does not execute the critical section of code until it can obtain this lock, and in this way, ensures that no other threads can be executing the section at the same time.

Note that you do not have to use the `synchronized` statement unless your program creates multiple threads that share data. If only one thread ever accesses a data structure, there is no need to protect it with `synchronized`. When you do have to use it, it might be in code like the following:

```
public static void SortIntArray(int[] a) {
    // Sort the array a. This is synchronized so that some other
    // thread can't change elements of the array while we're
    // sorting it.
    // At least not other threads that protect their changes to the
    // array with synchronized.
    synchronized (a) {
        // do the array sort here.
    }
}
```

The `synchronized` keyword is more often used as a method modifier in Java. When applied to a method, it indicates that the entire method is a critical section. For a `synchronized` class method (a static method), Java obtains an exclusive lock on the class before executing the method. For a `synchronized` instance method, Java obtains an exclusive lock on the class instance. (Class methods and instance methods are discussed in the next section.)

14.2.12.7. The `package` and `import` Statements

The `package` statement, as we saw earlier in the section, specifies the package that the classes in a file of Java source code are part of. If it appears, it must be the first statement of a Java file. The `import` statement, which we also saw earlier, allows us to refer to classes by abbreviated names. `import` statements must appear after the `package` statement, if any, and before any other statements in a Java file. For example:

```
package games.tetris;

import java.applet.*;
import java.awt.*;
```

14.2.13. Exceptions and Exception Handling

Exception handing is a significant new feature of Java.[9] There are a number of new terms associated with exception handling. First, an *exception* is a signal that indicates that some sort of exceptional condition (such as an error) has occurred. To *throw* an exception is to signal an exceptional condition. To *catch* an exception is to handle it—to take whatever actions are necessary to recover from it.

Exceptions propagate up through the lexical block structure of a Java method, and then up the method call stack. If an exception is not caught by the block of code that throws it, it propagates to the next higher enclosing block of code. If it is not caught there, it propagates up again. If it is not caught anywhere in the method, it propagates to the invoking method, where it again propagates through the block structure. If an exception is never caught, it propagates all the way to the `main()` method from which the program started, and causes the Java interpreter to print an error message and a stack trace and exit.

As we'll see in the subsections below, exceptions make error handling (and "exceptional condition" handling) more regular and logical by allowing you to group all your exception handling code into one place. Instead of worrying about all of the things that can go wrong with each line of your code, you can concentrate on the algorithm at hand and place all your error handling code (that is, your exception catching code) in a single place.

14.2.13.1. Exception Objects

An exception in Java is an object that is an instance of some subclass of `java.lang.Throwable`. `Throwable` has two standard subclasses: `java.lang.Error` and `java.lang.Exception`.[10] Exceptions that are subclasses of `Error` generally indicate linkage problems related to dynamic loading, or virtual machine problems such as running out of memory. They should almost always be considered unrecoverable, and should not be caught. While the distinction is not always clear, exceptions that are subclasses of `Exception` indicate conditions that may be caught and recovered from. They include such exceptions as `java.io.EOFException`, which signals the end of a file and `java.lang.ArrayAccessOutOfBounds`, which indicates that a program has tried to read past the end of an array.

[9]It is similar to, but not quite the same as, exception handling in C++.

[10]We'll use the term "exception" to refer to any subclass of `Throwable`, whether it is actually an `Exception` or an `Error`.

Since exceptions are objects, they can contain data and define methods. The `Throwable` object, at the top of the exception class hierarchy, includes a `String` message in its definition and this field is inherited by all exception classes. This field is used to store a human-readable error message that describes the exceptional condition. It is set when the exception object is created by passing an argument to the constructor method. The message can be read from the exception with the `Throwable.get.Message()` method. Most exceptions contain only this single message, but a few add other data. The `java.io.InterruptedIOException`, for example, adds the following field:

```
public int bytesTransferred;
```

This field specifies how much of the I/O was complete before the exceptional condition occurred.

14.2.13.2. Exception Handling

The `try/catch/finally` statement is Java's exception handling mechanism. `try` establishes a block of code that is to have its exceptions and abnormal exits (through `break`, `continue`, `return`, or exception propagation) handled. The `try` block is followed by zero or more `catch` clauses that catch and handle specified types of exceptions. The `catch` clauses are optionally followed by a `finally` block that contains "cleanup" code. The statements of a `finally` block are guaranteed to be executed, regardless of how the code in the `try` block exits. A detailed example of the `try/catch/finally` syntax is shown in Example 14.5.

EXAMPLE 14.5. *The* `try/catch/finally` *statement.*

```
try {
        // Normally this code runs from the top of the block to the
        // bottom without problems. But it sometimes may raise
        // exceptions or exit the block via a break, continue,
        // or return statement.
}
catch (SomeException e1) {
        // Handle an exception object e1 of type SomeException
        // or of a subclass of that type.
}
catch (AnotherException e2) {
        // Handle an exception object e2 of type AnotherException
        // or of a subclass of that type.
}
finally {
        // Always execute this code, after we leave the try clause,
        // regardless of whether we leave it:
        //    1) Normally, after reaching the bottom of the block.
        //    2) With an exception that is handled by a catch.
        //    3) With an exception that is not handled.
        //    4) Because of a break, continue, or return statement.
}
```

14.2.13.3. `try`

The `try` clause simply establishes a block of code that is to have its exceptions and abnormal exits (through `break`, `continue`, `return`, or exception propagation) handled. The `try` clause by itself doesn't do anything interesting; it is the `catch` and `finally` clauses that do the exception handling and clean-up operations.

14.2.13.4. `catch`

A `try` block may be followed by zero or more `catch` clauses that specify code to handle various types of exceptions. `catch` clauses have an unusual syntax: Each is declared with an argument, much like a method argument. This argument must be of type `Throwable` or a subclass. When an exception occurs, the first `catch` clause that has an argument of the appropriate type is invoked. The type of the argument must match the type of the exception object, or it must be a superclass of the exception. This `catch` argument is valid only within the `catch` block, and refers to the actual exception object that was thrown.

The code within a `catch` block should take whatever action is necessary to cope with the exceptional condition. If the exception was a `java.io.FileNotFound\%Exception` exception, for example, you might handle it by asking the user to check his or her spelling and try again. Note that it is not required to have a `catch` clause for every possible exception—in some cases the correct response is to allow the exception to propagate up and be caught by the invoking method. In other cases, such as a programming error signaled by `NullPointerException`, the correct response is to not catch the exception at all, but to allow it to propagate and to have the Java interpreter exit with a stack trace and an error message.

14.2.13.5. `finally`

The `finally` clause is generally used to clean up (close files, release resources, etc.) after the `try` clause. What is useful about the `finally` clause is that the code in a `finally` block is guaranteed to be executed, if any portion of the `try` block is executed, regardless of how the code in the `try` block completes. In the normal case, control reaches the end of the `try` block and then proceeds to the `finally` block, which performs any necessary cleanup.

If control leaves the `try` block because of a `return`, `continue`, or `break` statement, the contents of the `finally` block are executed before control transfers to its new destination.

If an exception occurs in the `try` block and there is a local `catch` block to handle the exception, control transfers first to the `catch` block, and then to the `finally` block. If there is not a local `catch` block to handle the exception, control transfers first to the `finally` block, and then propagates up to the nearest `catch` clause that can handle the exception.

Note that if a `finally` block itself transfers control with a `return`, `continue`, or `break` statement, or by raising an exception, the pending control transfer is abandoned, and this new transfer is processed.

Also note that `try` and `finally` can be used together without exceptions or any `catch` clauses. In this case, the `finally` block is simply cleanup code that is guaranteed to be executed regardless of any `break`, `continue`, or `return` statements within the `try` clause.

14.2.13.6. Declaring Exceptions

Java requires that any method that can cause a "normal exception" to occur must either catch the exception or specify the type of the exception with a `throws` clause in the method declaration.[11] Such a `throws` clause might look like these:

```
public void open_file() throws IOException {
     // Statements here that might generate
     // an uncaught java.io.IOException
}

public void myfunc(int arg) throws MyException1, MyException2 {
     ...
}
```

Note that the exception class specified in a `throws` clause may be a superclass of the exception type that is actually thrown. Thus if a method throws exceptions `a`, `b`, and `c`, all of which are subclasses of `d`, the `throws` clause may specify all of `a`, `b`, and `c`, or it may simply specify `d`.

We said above that the `throws` clause must be used to declare any "normal exceptions." This oxymoronic phrase refers to any subclass of `Throwable` that is not a subclass of `Error` or a subclass of `RuntimeException`. Java does not require these types of exceptions to be declared because practically any method can conceivably generate them, and it would quickly become tedious to properly declare them all. For example, every method running on a buggy Java interpreter can throw an `InternalError` exception (a subclass of `Error`) and it doesn't make sense to have to declare this in a `throws` clause for every method. Similarly, as far as the Java compiler is concerned, any method that accesses an array can generate an `ArrayIndexOutOfBoundsException` exception (a subclass of `RuntimeException`).

---

[11]C++ programmers note that Java uses `throws` where C++ uses `throw`.

The standard exceptions that you often have to declare are `java.io.IOException` and a number of its more specific subclasses. `java.lang.InterruptedException` and several other less commonly used exceptions must also be declared. How do you know when you have to declare a `throws` clause? One way is to pay close attention to the documentation for the methods you call—if any "normal exceptions" can be thrown, either catch them or declare them. Another way to know what exceptions you've got to declare is to declare none and wait for the compilation errors—the compiler will tell you what to put in your `throws` clause!

14.2.13.7. Defining and Generating Exceptions

You can signal your own exceptions with the `throw` statement. The `throw` keyword must be followed by an object that is `Throwable` or a subclass. Often, exception objects are allocated in the same statement that they are thrown in:

```
throw new MyException("my exceptional condition occurred.");
```

When an exception is thrown, normal program execution stops and the interpreter looks for a `catch` clause that can handle the exception. Execution propagates up through enclosing statements and through invoking functions until such a handler is found. Any `finally` blocks that are passed during this propagation are executed.

Using exceptions is a good way to signal and handle errors in your own code. By grouping all your error handling and recover code together within the `try/catch/finally` structure, you will end up with cleaner code that is easier to understand. Sometimes, when you are throwing an exception, you can use one of the exception classes already defined by Java API. Often, though, you will want to define and throw your own exception types.

Example 14.6 shows how you can define your own exception types, throw them, and handle them. It also helps clarify how exceptions propagate. It is a long example, but worth studying in some detail. You'll know you understand exception handling if you can answer the following: What happens when this program is invoked with no argument; with a string argument; and with integer arguments 0, 1, 2, and 99?

EXAMPLE 14.6. *Defining, throwing, and handling exceptions.*

```
// Here we define some exception types of our own.
// Exception classes generally have constructors but no data or
// other methods. All these do is call their superclass constructors.
class MyException extends Exception {
  public MyException() { super(); }
  public MyException(String s) { super(s); }
}
class MyOtherException extends Exception {
  public MyOtherException() { super(); }
  public MyOtherException(String s) { super(s); }
}
class MySubException extends MyException {
  public MySubException() { super(); }
  public MySubException(String s) { super(s); }
}

public class throwtest {
  // This is the main() method. Note that it uses two
  // catch clauses to handle two standard Java exceptions.
public static void main(String argv[]) {
    int i;

    // First, convert our argument to an integer.
    // Make sure we have an argument and that it is convertible.
    try {  i = Integer.parseInt(argv[0]);  }
    catch (ArrayIndexOutOfBoundsException e) { // argv is empty
      System.out.println("Must specify an argument");
      return;
    }
    catch (NumberFormatException e) { // argv[0] isn't an integer
      System.out.println("Must specify an integer argument.");
      return;
    }

    // Now, pass that integer to method a().
    a(i);
  }

  // This method invokes b(), which is declared to throw
  // one type of exception. We handle that one exception.
  public static void a(int i) {
    try {
      b(i);
    }
    catch (MyException e) {            // Point 1
      // Here we handle MyException and its subclass MySubException.
      if (e instanceof MySubException)
        System.out.print("MySubException: ");
      else
        System.out.print("MyException: ");
      System.out.println(e.getMessage());
      System.out.println("Handled at point 1");
    }
  }

  // This method invokes c(), and handles one of the two exception
  // types that that method can throw. The other exception type is
  // not handled, and is propagated up and declared in this method's
```

```
    // throws clause. This method also has a finally clause to finish
    // up the work of its try clause. Note that the finally clause is
    // executed after a local catch clause, but before a containing
    // catch clause or one in an invoking procedure.
    public static void b(int i) throws MyException {
      int result;
      try {
        System.out.print("i = " + i);
        result = c(i);
        System.out.print(" c(i) = " + result);
      }
      catch (MyOtherException e) {              // Point 2
        // Handle MyOtherException exceptions:
        System.out.println("MyOtherException: " + e.getMessage());
        System.out.println("Handled at point 2");
      }
      finally {
        // Terminate the output we printed above with a newline.
        System.out.print("\n");
      }
    }

    // This method computes a value or throws an exception.
    // The throws clause only lists two exceptions, because
    // one of the exceptions thrown is a subclass of another.
    public static int c(int i) throws MyException, MyOtherException {
      switch (i) {
      case 0:       // processing resumes at point 1 above
        throw new MyException("input too low");
      case 1:       // processing resumes at point 1 above
        throw new MySubException("input still too low");
      case 99:      // processing resumes at point 2 above
        throw new MyOtherException("input too high");
      default:
        return i*i;
      }
    }
  }
```

14.2.14. Miscellaneous Differences

A number of miscellaneous differences between Java and C are described in the sections that follow. Miscellaneous differences that were mentioned elsewhere, such as the lack of the `goto` statement and the `sizeof` operator, are not repeated here.

14.2.14.1. Local Variable Declarations

A feature that Java has borrowed from C++ is the ability to declare and initialize local variables anywhere in a method body or other block of code. Declarations and their initializers no longer have to be the first statements in any block—you can declare them where it is convenient and fits well with the structure of your code.

Don't let this freedom make you sloppy, however! For someone reading your program, it is nice to have variable declarations grouped together in one place. As a rule of thumb, put your declarations at the top of the block, unless you have some good organizational reason for putting them elsewhere.

14.2.14.2. Forward References

For compiler efficiency, C requires that variables and functions must be defined, or at least declared, before they can be used or called. That is, forward references are not allowed in C. Java does not make this restriction, and by lifting it, it also does away with the whole concept of a variable or function declaration that is separate from the definition.

Java allows very flexible forward references. A method may refer to a variable or another method of its class, regardless of where in the current class the variable or method is defined. Similarly, it may refer to any class, regardless of where in the current file (or outside of the file) that class is defined. The only place that forward references are not allowed is in variable initialization. A variable initializer (for local variables, class variables, or instance variables) may not refer to other variables that have not yet been declared and initialized.

14.2.14.3. Method Overloading

A technique that Java borrows from C++ is called *method overloading*. Overloaded methods are methods that have the same name, but have different signatures. In other words, they take different types of arguments, a different number of arguments, or the same type of arguments in different positions in the argument list. You cannot overload a method by changing only its return type. Two methods with the same name may have different return types, but only if the method arguments also differ. Similarly, two overloaded methods may throw different exceptions, but only if their arguments differ as well.

Method overloading is commonly used in Java to define a number of related functions with the same name, but different arguments. Overloaded methods usually perform the same basic operation, but allow the programmer to specify arguments in different ways depending on what is convenient in a given situation. Method overloading is discussed in more detail later.

14.2.14.4. The `void` Keyword

The `void` keyword is used in Java, as in C, to indicate that a function returns no value. (As we will see in the next section, constructor methods are an exception to this rule.)

Java differs from C (and is similar to C++) in that methods that take no arguments are declared with empty parentheses, not with the `void` keyword. Java does not have any `void *` type, nor does it use a `(void)` cast in order to ignore the result returned by a call to a non-`void` method.

14.2.14.5. Modifiers

Java defines a number of modifier keywords that may be applied to variable and/or method declarations to provide additional information or place restrictions on the variable or method:

`final`
: The `final` keyword is a modifier that may be applied to classes, methods, and variables. It has a similar, but not identical meaning in each case. A `final` class may never be subclassed. A `final` method may never be overridden. A `final` variable may never have its value set. In Java 1.1, this modifier may also be applied to local variables and method parameters. This modifier is discussed in more detail later.

`native`
: `native` is a modifier that may be applied to method declarations. It indicates that the method is implemented elsewhere in C, or in some other platform-dependent fashion. A `native` method should have a semicolon in place of its body.

`synchronized`
: We saw the `synchronized` keyword in a previous section where it was a statement that marked a critical section of code. The same keyword can also be used as a modifier for class or instance methods. It indicates that the method modifies the internal state of the class or the internal state of an instance of the class in a way that is not thread-safe. Before running a `synchronized` class method, Java obtains a lock on the class, to ensure that no other threads can be modifying the class concurrently. Before running a `synchronized` instance method, Java obtains a lock on the instance that invoked the method, ensuring that no other thread can be modifying the object at the same time.

`transient`
: The `transient` keyword is a modifier that may be applied to instance fields in a class. This modifier is legal but unused in Java 1.0. In Java 1.1, it indicates a field that is not part of an object's persistent state and thus needs not be serialized with the object.

`volatile` The `volatile` keyword is a modifier that may be applied to fields. It specifies that the field is used by synchronized threads and that the compiler should not attempt to perform optimizations with it. For example, it should read the variable's value from memory every time and not attempt to save a copy of it on the stack.

14.2.14.6. No Structures or Unions

Java does not support C `struct` or `union` types. Note, however that a `class` is essentially the same thing as a `struct`, but with more features. And you can simulate the important features of a `union` by subclassing.

14.2.14.7. No Enumerated Types

Java does not support the C `enum` keyword for defining types that consist of one of a specified number of named values. This is somewhat surprising for a strongly typed language like Java. Enumerated types can be partially simulated with the use of `static final` constant values.

14.2.14.8. No Method Types

C allows you to store the address of a function in a variable and to pass function addresses to other functions. You cannot do this in Java: Methods are not data, and cannot be manipulated by Java programs. Note, however, that objects are data, and that objects can define methods.[12] So, when you need to pass a method to another method, you declare a class that defines the desired method and pass an instance of that class. See, for example, the `FilenameFilter` interface in the `java.io` package.

14.2.14.9. No Bitfields

Java does not support the C ability to define variables that occupy particular bits within `struct` and `union` types. This feature of C is usually only used to interface directly to hardware devices, which is never necessary with Java's platform-independent programming model.

14.2.14.10. No `typedef`

Java does not support the C `typedef` keyword to define aliases for type names. Java has a much simpler type naming scheme than C does, however, and so there is no need for something like `typedef`.

---

[12]An interesting way to think about objects in Java is a kind of method that defines multiple entry points.

14.2.14.11. No Variable-Length Argument Lists

Java does not allow you to define methods that take a variable number of arguments, as C does. This is because Java is a strongly typed language and there is no way to do appropriate type checking for a method with variable arguments. Method overloading allows you to simulate C `varargs` functions for simple cases, but there is no general replacement for this C feature.

14.3. Classes and Objects in Java

Java is an object-oriented language. "Object-oriented" is a term that has become so commonly used as to have practically no concrete meaning. This section explains just what "object-oriented" means for Java. It covers:

- Classes and objects in Java
- Creating objects
- Garbage collection to free up unused objects
- The difference between class (or static) variables and instance variables, and the difference between class (or static) methods and instance methods
- Extending a class to create a subclass
- Overriding class methods and dynamic method lookup
- Abstract classes
- Interface types and their implementation by classes

If you are a C++ programmer, or have other object-oriented programming experience, many of the concepts in this list should be familiar to you. If you do not have object-oriented experience, don't fear: This section assumes no knowledge of object-oriented concepts.

We saw in the last section that close analogies can be drawn between Java and C. Unfortunately for C++ programmers, the same is not true for Java and C++. Java uses object-oriented programming concepts that are familiar to C++ programmers, and it even borrows from C++ syntax in a number of places, but the analogies between Java and C++ are not nearly as strong as those between Java and C.[13] C++ programmers may have an easier time with this section than C programmers will, but they should still read it carefully and try not to form preconceptions about Java based on their knowledge of C++.

---

[13]As we'll see, Java supports garbage collection and dynamic method lookup. This actually makes it a closer relative, beneath its layer of C-like syntax, to languages like Smalltalk than to C++.

14.3.1. Introduction to Classes and Objects

A class is a collection of data and methods that operate on that data.[14] The data and methods, taken together, usually serve to define the contents and capabilities of some kind of object.

For example, a circle can be described by the x, y position of its center and by its radius. There are a number of things we can do with circles: compute their circumference, compute their area, check whether points are inside them, and so on. Each circle is different (i.e., has a different center or radius), but as a class, circles have certain intrinsic properties that we can capture in a definition. Example 14.7 shows how we could partially define the class of circles in Java. Notice that the class definition contains data and methods (procedures) within the same pair of curly brackets.[15]

EXAMPLE 14.7. *The class of circles, partially captured in Java code.*

```
        public double x, y;     // The coordinates of the center
        public double r;        // The radius

        // Methods that return the circumference and area of the circle
        public double circumference() { return 2 * 3.14159 * r; }
        public double area() { return 3.14159 * r*r; }
    }
```

14.3.1.1. Objects Are Instances of a Class

Now that we've defined (at least partially) the class `Circle`, we want to do something with it. We can't do anything with the class of circles itself—we need a particular circle to work with. We need an *instance* of the class, a single circle object.

By defining the `Circle` class in Java, we have created a new data type. We can declare variables of that type:

```
Circle c;
```

But this variable `c` is simply a name that refers to a circle object; it is not an object itself. In Java, all objects must be created dynamically. This is almost always done with the `new` keyword:

```
Circle c;
c = new Circle();
```

Now we have created an instance of our `Circle` class—a circle object—and have assigned it to the variable `c`, which is of type `Circle`.

[14]A method is the object-oriented term for a procedure or a function. You'll see it used a lot in this chapter. Treat it as a synonym for "procedure."

[15]C++ programmers should note that methods go inside the class definition in Java, not outside with the `::` operator as they usually do in C++.

14.3.1.2. Accessing Object Data

Now that we've created an object, we can use its data fields. The syntax should be familiar to C programmers:

```
Circle c = new Circle();
c.x = 2.0;  // Initialize our circle to have
            // center (2, 2) and radius 1.0
c.y = 2.0;
c.r = 1.0;
```

14.3.1.3. Using Object Methods

This is where things get interesting! To access the methods of an object, we use the same syntax as accessing the data of an object:

```
Circle c = new Circle();
double a;
c.r = 2.5;
a = c.area();
```

Take a look at that last line. We did not say:

```
a = area(c);
```

We said:

```
a = c.area();
```

This is why it is called "object-oriented" programming; the object is the focus here, not the function call. This is probably the single most important feature of the object-oriented paradigm.

Note that we don't have to pass an argument to `c.area()`. The object we are operating on, `c`, is implicit in the syntax. Take a look at again: You'll notice the same thing in the definition of the `area()` method—it doesn't take an argument. It is implicit in the language that a method operates on an instance of the class within which it is defined. Thus our `area()` method can use the `r` field of the class freely—it is understood that it is referring to the radius of whatever `Circle` instance invokes the method.

14.3.1.4. How It Works

What's going on here? How can a method that takes no arguments know what data to operate on? In fact, the `area()` method does have an argument! `area()` is implemented with an implicit argument that is not shown in the method declaration. The implicit argument is named `this`, and refers to "this object"—the `Circle` object through which the method is invoked. `this` is often called the "`this` pointer."[16]

[16]"`this` pointer" is C++ terminology. Since Java does not support pointers, I prefer the term "`this` reference."

The implicit `this` argument is not shown in method signatures because it is usually not needed—whenever a Java method accesses the fields in its class, it is implied that it is accessing fields in the object referred to by the `this` argument. The same is true, as we'll see, when a method in a class invokes other methods in the class—it is implicit that the methods are being invoked for the `this` object.

We can use the `this` keyword explicitly when we want to make explicit that a method is accessing its own variables and/or methods. For example, we could rewrite the `area()` method like this:

```
public double area() { return 3.14159 * this.r * this.r; }
```

In a method this simple, it is not necessary to be explicit. In more complicated cases, however, you may find that it increases the clarity of your code to use an explicit `this` where it is not strictly required.

An instance where the `this` keyword *is* required is when a method argument or a local variable in a method has the same name as one of the fields of the class. In this case, you must use `this` to access the field. If you used the field name alone, you would end up accessing the argument or local variable with the same name. We'll see examples of this in the next section.

14.3.2. Object Creation

Take another look at how we've been creating our circle object:

```
Circle c = new Circle();
```

What are those parentheses doing there? They make it look like we're calling a function! In fact, that is exactly what we're doing. Every class in Java has at least one *constructor* method, which has the same name as the class. The purpose of a constructor is to perform any necessary initialization for the new object. Since we didn't define one for our `Circle` class, Java gave us a default constructor that takes no arguments and performs no special initialization.

The way it works is this: The `new` keyword creates a new dynamic instance of the class—i.e., it allocates the new object. The constructor method is then called, passing the new object implicitly (a `this` reference, as we saw above), and passing the arguments specified between parentheses explicitly.

14.3.2.1. Defining a Constructor

There is some obvious initialization we could do for our circle objects, so let's define a constructor. Example 14.8 shows a constructor that lets us specify the initial values for the center and radius of our new `Circle` object. The example also shows a use of the `this` keyword, as described in the previous section.

EXAMPLE 14.8. *A constructor for the* `Circle` *class.*

```
public class Circle {
    public double x, y, r;   // The center and the radius of the circle

    // The constructor method.
    public Circle(double x, double y, double r)
    {
        this.x = x;
        this.y = y;
        this.r = r;
    }
    public double circumference() { return 2 * 3.14159 * r; }
    public double area() { return 3.14159 * r*r; }
}
```

With the old, default constructor, we had to write code like this:

```
Circle c = new Circle();
c.x = 1.414;
c.y = -1.0;
c.r = .25;
```

With this new constructor, the initialization becomes part of the object creation step:

```
Circle c = new Circle(1.414, -1.0, .25);
```

There are two important notes about naming and declaring constructors:

- The constructor name is always the same as the class name.
- The return type is implicitly an instance of the class. No return type is specified in constructor declarations, nor is the `void` keyword used. The `this` object is implicitly returned; a constructor should not use a `return` statement to return a value.

14.3.2.2. Multiple Constructors

Sometimes you'll want to be able to initialize an object in a number of different ways, depending on what is most convenient in a particular circumstance. For example, we might want to be able to initialize the radius of a circle without initializing the center, or we might want to initialize a circle to have the same center and radius as another circle, or we might want to initialize all the fields to default values. Doing this is no problem: A class can have any number of constructor methods.

Example 14.9 shows how.

EXAMPLE 14.9. *Multiple circle constructors.*

```
public class Circle {
    public double x, y, r;

    public Circle(double x, double y, double r) {
        this.x = x; this.y = y; this.r = r;
    }
    public Circle(double r) { x = 0.0; y = 0.0; this.r = r; }
    public Circle(Circle c) { x = c.x; y = c.y; r = c.r; }
    public Circle() { x = 0.0; y = 0.0; r = 1.0; }

    public double circumference() { return 2 * 3.14159 * r; }
    public double area() { return 3.14159 * r*r; }
}
```

14.3.2.3. Method Overloading

The surprising thing in this example (not so surprising if you're a C++ programmer) is that all the constructor methods have the same name! So how can the compiler tell them apart? The way that you and I tell them apart is that the four methods take different arguments and are useful in different circumstances. The compiler tells them apart in the same way. In Java, a method is distinguished by its name, and by the number, type, and position of its arguments. This is not limited to constructor methods—any two methods are not the same unless they have the same name, and the same number of arguments of the same type passed at the same position in the argument list. When you call a method and there is more than one method with the same name, the compiler automatically picks the one that matches the data types of the arguments you are passing.

Defining methods with the same name and different argument types is called method overloading. It can be a convenient technique, as long as you only give methods the same name when they perform similar functions on slightly different forms of input data. Overloaded methods may have different return types, but only if they have different arguments. Don't confuse method overloading with *method overriding*, which we'll discuss later.

14.3.2.4. `this` Again

There is a specialized use of the `this` keyword that arises when a class has multiple constructors—it can be used from a constructor to invoke one of the other constructors of the same class. So we could rewrite the additional constructors from Example 14.9 in terms of the first one like this:

```
public Circle(double x, double y, double r) {
    this.x = x; this.y = y; this.r = r;
}
public Circle(double r) { this(0.0, 0.0, r); }
public Circle(Circle c) { this(c.x, c.y, c.r); }
public Circle() { this(0.0, 0.0, 1.0); }
```

Here, the `this()` call refers to whatever constructor of the class takes the specified type of arguments. This would be a more impressive example, of course, if the first constructor that we were invoking did a more significant amount of initialization, as it might, for example, if we were writing a more complicated class.

There is a very important restriction on this `this` syntax: It may only appear as the first statement in a constructor. It may, of course, be followed by any additional initialization that a particular version of the constructor needs to do. The reason for this restriction involves the automatic invocation of superclass constructor methods, which we'll explore later in this section.

14.3.3. Class Variables

In our `Circle` class definition, we declared three "instance" variables: `x`, `y`, and `r`. Each instance of the class—each circle—has its own copy of these three variables. These variables are like the fields of a `struct` in C—each instance of the `struct` has a copy of the fields. Sometimes, though, we want a variable of which there is only one copy—something like a global variable in C.

The problem is that Java doesn't allow global variables. (Actually, those in the know consider this a feature!) Every variable in Java must be declared inside a class. So Java uses the `static` keyword to indicate that a particular variable is a *class variable* rather than an *instance variable.* That is, that there is only one copy of the variable, associated with the class, rather than many copies of the variable associated with each instance of the class. The one copy of the variable exists regardless of the number of instances of the class that are created—it exists and can be used even if the class is never actually instantiated.

This kind of variable, declared with the `static` keyword, is often called a *static variable.* I prefer (and recommend) the name "class variable" because it is easily distinguished from its opposite, "instance variable." We'll use both terms in this chapter.

14.3.3.1. An Example

As an example (a somewhat contrived one), suppose that while developing the `Circle` class we wanted to do some testing on it and determine how much it gets used. One way to do this, would be to count the number of `Circle` objects that are instantiated. To do this, we obviously need a variable associated with the class, rather than with any particular instance. Example 14.10 shows how we can do it—we declare a `static` variable and increment it each time we create a `Circle`.

EXAMPLE 14.10. *Static variable example.*

```
public class Circle {
     static int num_circles = 0;
     // class variable: how many circles created
     public double x, y, r;
     // instance vars: the center and the radius

     public Circle(double x, double y, double r) {
          this.x = x; this.y = y; this.r = r;
          num_circles++;
     }
     public Circle(double r) { this(0.0, 0.0, r); }
     public Circle(Circle c) { this(c.x, c.y, c.r); }
     public Circle() { this(0.0, 0.0, 1.0); }

     public double circumference() { return 2 * 3.14159 * r; }
     public double area() { return 3.14159 * r*r; }
}
```

14.3.3.2. Accessing Class Variables

Now that we are keeping track of the number of `Circle` objects created, how can we access this information? Because static variables are associated with the class rather than with an instance, we access them through the class rather than through the instance. Thus, we might write:[17]

```
System.out.println("Number of circles
     created: " + Circle.num_circles);
```

Notice that in our definition of the constructor method in Example 14.10 we just used `num_circles` instead of `Circle.num_circles`. We're allowed to do this within the class definition of `Circle` itself. Anywhere else, though, we must use the class name as well.

[17]Recall that `System.out.println()` prints a line of text, and that the string concatenation operator, +, converts nonstring types to strings as necessary.

14.3.3.2. Global Variables?

Earlier we said that Java does not support global variables. In a sense, though, `Circle.num_circles` behaves just like one. What is different from a global variable in C is that there is no possibility of name conflicts. If we use some other class with a class variable named `num_circles`, there won't be a "collision" between these two "global" variables, because they must both be referred to by their class names. Since each class variable must be part of a class and must be referred to with its class name, each has a unique name. Furthermore, each class has a unique name because, as we saw in the section "How Java Differs from C," it is part of a package with a unique name.

14.3.3.3. Constants: Another Class Variable Example

Let's try a less forced example of why you might want to use a class variable with the `Circle` class. When computing the area and circumference of circles, we use the value π. Since we use the value frequently, we don't want to keep typing out 3.14159, so we'll define it as a class variable that has a convenient name:

```
public class Circle {
     public static final double PI = 3.14159265358979323846;
     public double x, y, r;
     // ... etc....
}
```

Besides the `static` keyword that we've already seen, we use the `final` keyword, which means that this variable can never have its value changed. This prevents you from doing something stupid like:

```
Circle.PI = 4;
```

which would tend to give you some pretty square-looking circles.

The Java compiler is smart about variables declared both `static` and `final`—it knows that they have constant values. When you write code like this:

```
double circumference = 2 * Circle.PI * radius;
```

the compiler precomputes the value `2 * Circle.PI`, instead of leaving it for the interpreter.

Java does not have a preprocessor with a C-style `#define` directive. `static final` variables are Java's substitute for C's `#define`d constants. Note that the C convention of capitalizing constants has been carried over into Java.

14.3.4. Class Methods

Let's define a new method in our `Circle` class. This one tests whether a specified point falls within the defined circle:

```
public class Circle {
    double x, y, r;

    // is point (a,b) inside this circle?
    public boolean isInside(double a, double b)
    {
        double dx = a - x;
        double dy = b - y;
        double distance = Math.sqrt(dx*dx + dy*dy);
        if (distance < r) return true;
        else return false;
    }
        .
        . // Constructor and other methods omitted
        .
}
```

What's this `Math.sqrt()` thing? It looks like a method call and, given its name and its context, we can guess that it is computing a square root. But the method calls we've discussed are done through an object. `Math` isn't the name of an object that we've declared, and there aren't any global objects in Java, so this must be a kind of method call that we haven't seen before.

14.3.4.1. `static` Methods

What's going on here is that `Math` is the name of a class. `sqrt()` is the name of a class method (or static method) defined in `Math`. It differs from the instance methods, such as `area()` in `Circle`, that we've seen so far.

Class methods are like class variables in a number of ways:

- Class methods are declared with the `static` keyword.
- Class methods are often referred to as "static methods."
- Class methods are invoked through the class rather than through an instance. (Although within the class they may be invoked by method name alone.)
- Class methods are the closest Java comes to "global" methods. Because they must be referred to by the class name, there is no danger of name conflicts.

14.3.4.2. No `this`

Class methods differ from instance methods in one important way: They are not passed as an implicit `this` reference. Thus, these `this`-less methods are not associated with any instance of the class and may not refer to any instance variables or invoke instance methods.

Since class methods are not passed a `this` reference, and are not invoked through an object, they are the closest thing that Java offers to the "normal" C procedures that you may be accustomed to, and may therefore seem familiar and comforting. If you're sick and tired of this object-oriented business, it is perfectly possible to write complete Java programs using only class methods, although this does defeat an important purpose of using the language!

But don't think that class methods are somehow cheating—there are perfectly good reasons to declare a method `static`. And indeed, there are classes like `Math` that declare all their methods (and variables) `static`. Since `Math` is a collection of functions that operate on floating-point numbers, which are a primitive type, there are no objects involved, and no need for instance methods. `System` is another class that defines only class metods—it provides a varied collection of system functions for which there is no appropriate object framework.

14.3.4.3. A Class Method for Circles

Example 14.11 shows two (overloaded) definitions of a method for our `Circle` class. One is an instance method and one is a class method.

EXAMPLE 14.11. *A class method and an instance method.*

```
public class Circle {
    public double x, y, r;

    // An instance method. Returns the bigger of two circles.
    public Circle bigger(Circle c) {
        if (c.r > r) return c; else return this;
    }
    // A class method. Returns the bigger of two circles
    public static Circle bigger(Circle a, Circle b) {
        if (a.r > b.r) return a; else return b;
    }
        .
        . // Other methods omitted here.
        .
}
```

You would invoke the instance method like this:

```
Circle a = new Circle(2.0);
Circle b = new Circle(3.0);
Circle c = a.bigger(b);           // or, b.bigger(a);
```

And you would invoke the class method like this:

```
Circle a = new Circle(2.0);
Circle b = new Circle(3.0);
Circle c = Circle.bigger(a,b);
```

Neither of these is the "correct" way to implement this method. One or the other will seem more natural, depending on circumstances.

14.3.4.4. A Mystery Explained

Now that we understand class variables, instance variables, class methods, and instance methods, we are in a position to explore that mysterious method call we saw in our very first Java "Hello World" example:

```
System.out.println("Hello world!");
```

One hypothesis is that `println()` is a class method in a class named `out`, which is in a package named `System`. Syntactically, this is perfectly reasonable (except perhaps that class names always seem to be capitalized by convention, and `out` isn't capitalized). But if you look at the API documentation, you'll find that `System` is not a package name; it is the name of a class (which is in the `java.lang` package, by the way). Can you figure it out?

Here's the story: `System` is a class. It has a class variable named `out`. `out` refers to an object of type `PrintStream`. The object `System.out` has an instance method named `println()`. Mystery solved!

14.3.4.5. Static Initializers

Both class and instance variables can have initializers attached to their declarations. For example:

```
static int num_circles = 0;
float r = 1.0;
```

Class variables are initialized when the class is first loaded. Instance variables are initialized when an object is created.

Sometimes we need more complex initialization than is possible with these simple variable initializers. For instance variables, there are constructor methods, which are run when a new instance of the class is created. Java also allows you to write an initialization method for class variables. Such a method is called a static initializer.

The syntax of static initializers gets kind of bizarre. Consider that a static initializer is invoked automatically by the system when the class is loaded. Thus, there are no meaningful arguments that can be passed to it (unlike the arguments we can pass to a constructor method when creating a new instance). There is also no value to return. So a static initializer has no arguments and no return value. Furthermore, it is not really necessary to give it a name, since the system calls the method automatically for us. What part of a method declaration is left? Just the `static` keyword and the curly brackets!

Example 14.12 shows a class declaration with a static initializer. Notice that the class contains a regular static variable initializer of the kind we've seen before, and also a static initializer—an arbitrary block of code between `{` and `}`.

EXAMPLE 14.12. *A static initializer.*

```
// We can draw the outline of a circle using trigonometric functions.
// Trigonometry is slow though, so we pre-compute a bunch of values.
public class Circle {
    // Here are our static lookup tables, and their own initializers.
    static private double sines[] = new double[1000];
    static private double cosines[] = new double[1000];

    // Here's a static initializer "method" that fills them in.
    // Notice the lack of any method declaration!
    static {
        double x, delta_x;
        int i;
        delta_x = (Circle.PI/2)/(1000-1);
        for(i = 0, x = 0.0; i < 1000; i++, x += delta_x) {
            sines[i] = Math.sin(x);
            cosines[i] = Math.cos(x);
        }
    }
        .
        . // The rest of the class omitted.
        .
}
```

The syntax gets even a little stranger than this. Java allows any number of static initializer blocks of code to appear within a class definition. What the compiler actually does is to internally produce a single class initialization routine that combines all the static variable initializers and all of the static initializer blocks of code, in the order that they appear in the class declaration. This single initialization procedure is run automatically, one time only, when the class is first loaded.

One common use of static initializers is for classes that implement `native` methods—i.e., methods written in C. The static initializer for such a class should call `System.load()` or `System.loadLibrary()` to read in the native library that implements these native methods.

14.3.4.6. Instance Initializers

In Java 1.1, a class definition may also include instance initializers. These look like static initializers, but without the `static` keyword. An instance initializer is like a constructor: It runs when an instance of the class is created.

14.3.5. Object Destruction

Now that we've seen how you can create and use objects, the next obvious question, a question that C and C++ programmers have been itching to have answered, is how do you destroy objects when they are no longer needed?

The answer is: You don't! Objects are not passed to any `free()` method, as allocated memory in C is. And there is no `delete` operator as there is in C++. Java takes care of object destruction for you, and lets you concentrate on other, more important things, like the algorithm you're working on.

14.3.5.1. Garbage Collection

The technique Java uses to get rid of objects once they are no longer needed is called garbage collection. It is a technique that has been around for years in languages such as Lisp. The Java interpreter knows what objects it has allocated. It can also figure out which variables refer to which objects, and which objects refer to which other objects. Thus, it can figure out when an allocated object is no longer referred to by any other object or variable. When it finds such an object, it knows that it can destroy it safely, and does so. The garbage collector can also detect and destroy "cycles" of objects that refer to each other, but are not referred to by any other objects.

The Java garbage collector runs as a low-priority thread, and does most of its work when nothing else is going on. Generally, it runs during idle time while waiting for user input in the form of keystrokes or mouse events. The only time the garbage collector must run while something high-priority is going on (i.e., the only time it will actually slow down the system) is when the interpreter has run out of memory. This doesn't happen often because there is that low-priority thread cleaning things up in the background.

This scheme may sound extremely slow and wasteful of memory. Actually though, good garbage collectors can be surprisingly efficient. No, garbage collection will never be as efficient as explicit, well-written memory allocation and deallocation. But it does make programming a lot easier and less prone to bugs. And for most real-world programs, rapid development, lack of bugs, and easy maintenance are more important features than raw speed or memory efficiency.

14.3.5.2. Putting the Trash Out

What garbage collection means for your programs is that when you are done with an object, you can just forget about it—the garbage collector finds it and takes care of it. Example 14.13 shows an example.

EXAMPLE 14.13. *Leaving an object out for garbage collection.*

```
String processString(String s)
{
    // Create a StringBuffer object to process the string in.
    StringBuffer b = new StringBuffer(s);

    // Process it somehow...

    // Return it as a String. Just forget about the StringBuffer
    // object: it will be automatically garbage collected.
    return b.toString();
}
```

If you're a C or C++ programmer, conditioned to allocating and deallocating your own dynamic memory, you may at first feel a nagging sense of misgiving when you write procedures that allocate and then forget objects. You'll get used to it, though, and even learn to love it!

There is an instance where you may want to take some action to help the garbage collection process along by "forgetting quickly." Example 14.14 explains.

EXAMPLE 14.14. *Forced forgetting of an object.*

```
public static void main(String argv[])
{
    int big_array[] = new int[100000];

    // Do some computations with big_array and get a result.
    int result = compute(big_array);

    // We no longer need big_array.
    // It will get garbage collected when
    // there are no more references.
    // Since big_array is a local variable,
    // it refers to the array until this method returns.
    // But this method doesn't return. So we've got to
    // get rid of the reference
    // ourselves, just to help out the garbage collector.
    big_array = null;

    // Loop forever, handling the user's input.
    for(;;) handle_input();
}
```

14.3.5.3. Object Finalization

Just as a constructor method performs initialization for an object, a Java *finalizer* method performs finalization for an object.

Garbage collection automatically frees up the memory resources used by objects. But objects may hold other kinds of resources, such as file descriptors or sockets, as well. The garbage collector can't free these resources up for you, so you should write a finalizer method that takes care of things like closing open files, terminating network connections, and so on.

Example 14.15 shows the finalizer method from the Java `FileOutputStream` class.

Note that a finalizer is an instance method (i.e., non-`static`), takes no arguments, returns no value (i.e., `void`), and must be named `finalize()`.[18]

EXAMPLE 14.15. *A finalizer method.*

```
/**
 * Closes the stream when garbage is collected.
 * Checks the file descriptor to make sure it is not already closed.
 */
protected void finalize() throws IOException {
    if (fd != null) close();
}
```

There are some additional things to be aware of about finalizers:

- If an object has a finalizer, that method is invoked before the system garbage collects the object.
- The Java interpreter may exit without garbage collecting all outstanding objects, so some finalizers may never be invoked. In this case, though, any outstanding resources are usually freed by the operating system.
- Java makes no guarantees about when garbage collection will occur, or what order objects will be collected in. Therefore, Java can make no guarantees about when a finalizer will be invoked, or in what order finalizers will be invoked, or what thread will execute finalizers.

[18]C++ programmers, take note! Although Java constructor methods are named like C++ constructors, Java finalization methods are not named like C++ destructor methods.

- After a finalizer is invoked, objects are not freed right away. This is because a finalizer method may "resurrect" an object by storing the `this` pointer somewhere, so that the object once again has references. Thus, after `finalize()` is called, an object must once again be determined to be unreferenced before it can actually be garbage collected. Even if an object is "resurrected," the finalizer method is never invoked more than once. Note that resurrecting an object is never a useful thing to do—just a strange quirk of object finalization.
- The finalizer shown in Example 14.15 declares that it may throw an exception (exceptions are described in detail earlier). If an uncaught exception actually occurs in a finalizer method, however, the exception is ignored by the system.

14.3.6. Subclasses and Inheritance

The `Circle` class we've defined is good for abstract mathematical manipulation. For some applications this is exactly what we need. For other applications, we want to be able to manipulate circles and draw them on the screen. This means we need a new class, `GraphicCircle`, that has all the functionality of `Circle`, but also has the ability to be drawn.

We want to implement `GraphicCircle` so that it can make use of the code we've already written for `Circle`. One way to do that is the following:

```
public class GraphicCircle {
    // Here is the mathematical circle
    public Circle c;
    // Here are the old methods
    public double area() { return c.area(); }
    public double circumference() { return c.circumference(); }

    // The new graphic variables and methods go here
    public Color outline, fill;
    public void draw(DrawWindow dw) { /* code omitted */ }
}
```

This approach would work, but it is not particularly elegant. The problem is that we have to write stubs for methods like `area()` and `circumference()` that have nothing to do with drawing circles. It would be nice if we didn't have to do this.

14.3.6.1. Extending a Class

In fact, we don't have to do it this way. Java allows us to define `GraphicCircle` as an extension, or *subclass* of `Circle`. Example 14.16 shows how. Note that this example assumes we have two other classes of objects defined: `Color`, which represents a color, and `DrawWindow`, a class that has the window into which drawing is done and that defines the primitive methods to do the drawing.

EXAMPLE 14.16. *Subclassing a class.*

```
public class GraphicCircle extends Circle {
    // We automatically inherit the variables and methods of
    // Circle, so we only have to put the new stuff here.
    // We've omitted the GraphicCircle constructor, for now.
    Color outline, fill;
    public void draw(DrawWindow dw) {
        dw.drawCircle(x, y, r, outline, fill);
    }
}
```

The `extends` keyword tells Java that `GraphicCircle` is a subclass of `Circle`, and that it *inherits* the fields and methods of that class.[19] The definition of the `draw()` method shows variable inheritance—this method uses the `Circle` variables `x`, `y`, and `r` as if they were defined right in `GraphicCircle` itself.

`GraphicCircle` also inherits the methods of `Circle`. Thus, if we have a `GraphicCircle` object referred to by variable `gc`, we can say:

```
double area = gc.area();
```

This works just as if the `area()` method were defined in `GraphicCircle` itself.

Another feature of subclassing is that every `GraphicCircle` object is also a perfectly legal `Circle` object. Thus, if `gc` refers to a `GraphicCircle` object, we can assign it to a `Circle` variable, and we can forget all about its extra graphic capabilities: `Circle c = gc;`.

14.3.6.2. Final Classes

When a class is declared with the `final` modifier, it means that it cannot be extended or subclassed. `java.lang.System` is an example of a `final` class. Declaring a class `final` prevents unwanted extensions to the class. But it also allows the compiler to make some optimizations when invoking the methods of a class. We'll explore this in more detail when we talk about method overriding later in this section.

---

[19]Except for `private` fields and methods. We'll discuss `private` members of a class later. C++ programmers note that `extends` is the Java equivalent of the `:` operator in C++—both indicate the superclass of a class.

14.3.6.3. Superclasses, Object, and the Class Hierarchy

In our example, `GraphicCircle` is a subclass of `Circle`. We can also say that `Circle` is the *superclass* of `GraphicCircle`. The superclass of a class is specified in its `extends` clause:

```
public class GraphicCircle extends Circle { ... }
```

Every class you define has a superclass. If you do not specify the superclass with an `extends` clause, the superclass is the class `Object`. `Object` is a special class for a couple of reasons:

- It is the only class that does not have a superclass.
- The methods defined by `Object` can be called by any Java object.

Because every class has a superclass, classes in Java form a *class hierarchy*, which can be represented as a tree with `Object` at its root. Figure 14.3 shows a class hierarchy diagram which includes our `Circle` and `GraphicCircle` classes, as well as some of the standard classes from the Java API.

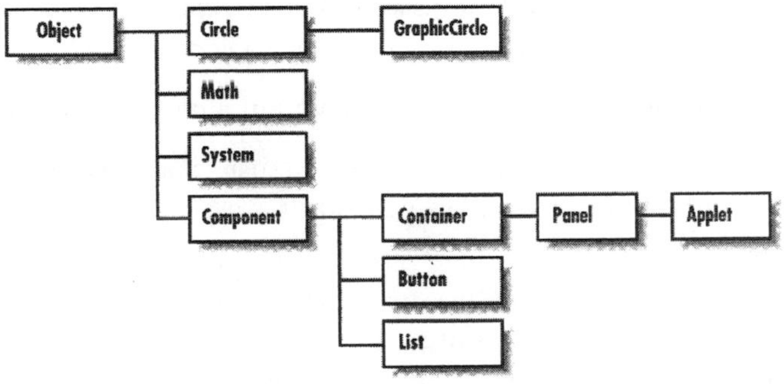

FIGURE 14.3. *A class hierarchy diagram.*

14.3.6.4. Subclass Constructors

In Example 14.10, we left out the constructor method for our new `GraphicCircle` class. Let's implement that now. Here's one way:

```
public GraphicCircle(double x, double y, double r,
                                  Color outline, Color fill)
{
     this.x = x;
     this.y = y;
     this.r = r;
     this.outline = outline;
     this.fill = fill;
}
```

This constructor relies on the fact that `GraphicCircle` inherits all of the variables of `Circle` and simply initializes those variables itself. But this duplicates the code of the `Circle` constructor, and if `Circle` did more elaborate initialization, it could become quite wasteful. Furthermore, if the `Circle` class had internal `private` fields (discussed later), we wouldn't be able to initialize them like this. What we need is a way of calling a `Circle` constructor from within our `GraphicCircle` constructor. Example 14.17 shows how we can do this.

EXAMPLE 14.17. *Invoking a superclass's constructor.*

```
public GraphicCircle(double x, double y, double r,
                             Color outline, Color fill)
{
     super(x, y, r);
     this.outline = outline;
     this.fill = fill;
}
```

`super` is a reserved word in Java. One of its uses is that shown in the example—to invoke the constructor method of a superclass. Its use is analogous to the use of the `this` keyword to invoke one constructor method of a class from within another. Using `super` to invoke a constructor is subject to the same restrictions as using `this` to invoke a constructor:

- `super` may only be used in this way within a constructor method.
- The call to the superclass constructor must appear as the first statement within the constructor method. It must appear even before variable declarations.

14.3.6.5. Constructor Chaining

When you define a class, Java guarantees that the class's constructor method is called whenever an instance of that class is created. It also guarantees that the constructor is called when an instance of any subclass is created. In order to guarantee this second point, Java must ensure that every constructor method calls its superclass constructor method. If the first statement in a constructor is not an explicit call to a constructor of the superclass with the `super` keyword, then Java implicitly inserts the call `super()`—that is, it calls the superclass constructor with no arguments. If the superclass does not have a constructor that takes no arguments, this causes a compilation error.

There is one exception to the rule that Java invokes `super()` implicitly if you do not do so explicitly. If the first line of a constructor, `C1`, uses the `this()` syntax to invoke another constructor, `c2`, of the class, Java relies on `c2` to invoke the superclass constructor, and does not insert a call to `super()` into `c1`. Of course, if `c2` itself uses `this()` to invoke a third constructor, `c2` does not call `super()` either, but somewhere along the chain, a constructor either explicitly or implicitly invokes the superclass constructor, which is what is required.

Consider what happens when we create a new instance of the `GraphicCircle` class. First, the `GraphicCircle` constructor shown in Example 14.17 is invoked. This constructor explicitly invokes a `Circle` constructor and that `Circle` constructor implicitly calls `super()` to invoke the constructor of its superclass, `Object`. The body of the `Object` constructor runs first, followed by the body of the `Circle` constructor, and finally followed by the body of the `GraphicCircle` constructor.

What this all means is that constructor calls are "chained"—any time an object is created, a sequence of constructor methods are invoked, from subclass to superclass on up to `Object` at the root of the class hierarchy. Because a superclass constructor is always invoked as the first statement of its subclass constructor, the body of the `Object` constructor always runs first, followed by the body of its subclass, and on down the class hierarchy to the class that is being instantiated.

14.3.6.6. The Default Constructor

There is one missing piece in the description of constructor chaining above. If a constructor does not invoke a superclass constructor, Java does so implicitly. But what if a class is declared without any constructor at all? In this case, Java implicitly adds a constructor to the class. This default constructor does nothing but invoke the superclass constructor.

For example, if we did not declare a constructor for the `GraphicCircle` class, Java would have implicitly inserted this constructor:

```
public GraphicCircle() { super(); }
```

Note that if the superclass, `Circle()`, did not declare a no-argument constructor, then this automatically inserted default constructor would cause a compilation error. If a class does not define a no-argument constructor, then all of its subclasses must define constructors that explicitly invoke the superclass constructor with the necessary arguments.

It can be confusing when Java implicitly calls a constructor or inserts a constructor definition into a class—something is happening that does not appear in your code! Therefore, it is good coding style, whenever you rely on an implicit superclass constructor call or on a default constructor, to insert a comment noting this fact. Your comments might look like those in the following example:

```
class A {
    int i;
    public A() {
        // Implicit call to super(); here.
        i = 3;
    }
}

class B extends A {
    // Default constructor: public B() { super(); }
}
```

If a class does not declare any constructor, it is given a `public` constructor by default. Classes that do not want to be publically instantiated should declare a `protected` constructor to prevent the insertion of this `public` constructor. Classes that never want to be instantiated at all should define a `private` constructor.

14.3.6.7. Finalizer Chaining?

You might assume that since Java chains constructor methods that it also automatically chains the finalizer methods for an object. In other words, you may think that the finalizer method of a class automatically invokes the finalizer of its superclass. In fact, Java does not do this. In practice, finalizer methods are relatively rare, and the need for finalizer chaining rarely arises. If a class `B` with a finalizer method is a subclass of a class `A` with its own finalizer method, then `B`'s finalizer should be sure to invoke `A`'s finalizer, explicitly creating a chain of finalizers. This is a little tricky, since finalizers always have the same name (`finalize()`), and we haven't yet learned how to invoke a method in the superclass when that method is also defined in the subclass. We'll return to the issue of finalizer chaining when we learn how.

14.3.6.8. Shadowed Variables

Suppose that our `GraphicCircle` class has a new variable that specifies the resolution, in dots per inch, of the `DrawWindow` object in which it is going to be drawn. And further, suppose that it names that new variable `r`:

```
public class GraphicCircle extends Circle {
    Color outline, fill;
    float r;  // New variable. Resolution in dots-per-inch.
    public GraphicCircle(double x, double y,
        double rad, Color o, Color f) {
        super(x, y, rad); outline = o; fill = f;
    }
```

```
        public void setResolution(float resolution) { r = resolution; }
        public void draw(DrawWindow dw)
            { dw.drawCircle(x, y, r, outline, fill); }
    }
```

Now, with this resolution variable declared, when we use the variable `r` in the `GraphicCircle` class, we are no longer referring to the radius of the circle. The resolution variable `r` in `GraphicCircle` *shadows* the radius variable `r` in `Circle`.[20]

So, how can we refer to the radius variable defined in the `Circle` class when we need it? Recall that using a variable, such as `r`, in the class in which it is defined is shorthand for:

```
this.r  // Refers to the GraphicCircle resolution variable.
```

As you might guess, you can refer to a variable `r` defined in the superclass like this:

```
super.r  // Refers to the Circle radius variable.
```

Another way you can do this is to cast this to the appropriate class and then access the variable:

```
((Circle) this).r
```

This cast is exactly what the `super` keyword does when used like this. You can use this casting technique when you need to refer to a shadowed variable defined in a class that is not the immediate superclass. For example, if `C` is a subclass of `B`, which is a subclass of `A`, and class `C` shadows a variable `x` that is also defined in classes `A` and `B`, then you can refer to these different variables from class `C` as follows:

```
x                  // Variable x in class C
this.x             // Variable x in class C
super.x            // Variable x in class B
((B)this).x        // Variable x in class B
((A)this).x        // Variable x in class A
super.super.x      // Illegal; does not refer to x in class A.
```

Note that you cannot refer to a shadowed variable `x` in the superclass of a superclass with `super.super.x`. Java does not recognize this syntax.

[20]This is a contrived example, of course—we could simply rename the variable and avoid the issue. Typically, we would rename the variable: Variable shadowing is a necessary part of Java syntax, but is not a useful programming technique. Your code will be easier to understand if you avoid shadowed variables.

14.3.6.9. Shadowed Methods?

Just as a variable defined in one class can shadow a variable with the same name in a superclass, you might expect that a method in one class could shadow a method with the same name (and same arguments) in a superclass. In a sense, they do: "Shadowed" methods are called overridden methods. But method overriding is significantly different than variable shadowing; it is discussed in the sections that follow.

14.3.7. Overriding Methods

When a class defines a method using the same name, return type, and arguments as a method in its superclass, the method in the class overrides the method in the superclass. When the method is invoked for an object of the class, it is the new definition of the method that is called, not the superclass's old definition.

Method overriding is an important and useful technique in object-oriented programming. Suppose we define a subclass `Ellipse` of our `Circle` class.[21] Then it would be important for `Ellipse` to override the `area()` and `circumference()` methods of `Circle`. `Ellipse` would have to implement new versions of these functions because the formulas that apply to circles don't work for ellipses.

Before we go any further with the discussion of method overriding, be sure that you understand the difference between method overriding and method overloading, which we discussed earlier. As you probably recall, method overloading refers to the practice of defining multiple methods (in the same class) with the same name but with differing argument lists. This is very different from method overriding, and it is important not to get them confused!

14.3.7.1. Overriding Is Not Shadowing

Although Java treats the variables and methods of a class analogously in many ways, method overriding is not like variable shadowing at all: You can refer to shadowed variables simply by casting an object to the appropriate type. You cannot invoke overridden methods with this technique, however. Example 14.18 illustrates this crucial difference.

---

[21]This is admittedly a strange thing to do, since, mathematically, a circle is a kind of ellipse, and it is customary to derive a more specific class from a more general one. Nevertheless, it is a useful example here.

EXAMPLE 14.18. *Method overriding versus variable shadowing.*

```
class A {
    int i = 1;
    int f() { return i; }
}

class B extends A {
    int i = 2;
    // Shadows variable i in class A.
    int f() { return -i; }
    // Overrides method f in class A.
}

public class override_test {
    public static void main(String args[]) {
        B b = new B();
        System.out.println(b.i);
        // Refers to B.i; prints 2.
        System.out.println(b.f());
        // Refers to B.f(); prints -2.

        A a = (A) b;
        // Cast b to an instance of class A.
        System.out.println(a.i);
        // Now refers to A.i; prints 1;
        System.out.println(a.f());
        // Still refers to B.f(); prints -2;
    }
}
```

While this difference between method overriding and variable shadowing may seem surprising at first, a little thought makes the purpose clear. Suppose we have a bunch of `Circle` and `Ellipse` (a subclass of `Circle`) objects that we are manipulating. To keep track of the circles and ellipses, we store them in an array of type `Circle[]`, casting all the `Ellipse` objects to `Circle` objects before we store them. Then, when we loop through the elements of this array, we don't have to know or care whether the element is actually a `Circle` or an `Ellipse`. What we do care very much about, however, is that the correct value is computed when we invoke the `area()` method of any element of the array. That is, we don't want to use the formula for the area of a circle when the object is actually an ellipse!

Seen in this context, it is not surprising at all that method overriding is handled differently by Java than variable shadowing.

14.3.7.2. `final` Methods

If a method is declared `final`, it means that the method declaration is the "final" one—that it cannot be overridden. `static` methods and `private` methods (which we haven't learned about yet) cannot be overridden either, nor can the methods of a `final` class. If a method cannot be overridden, the compiler may perform certain optimizations on it, as we'll see below.

14.3.7.3. Dynamic Method Lookup

If we have an array of `Circle` and `Ellipse` objects, how does the compiler know to call the `Circle area()` method or the `Ellipse area()` method for any given item in the array? The compiler does not know this; it can't. The compiler knows that it does not know, however, and produces code that uses "dynamic method lookup" at runtime. When the interpreter runs the code, it looks up the appropriate `area()` method to call for each of the objects. That is, when the interpreter interprets the expression `s.area()`, it dynamically looks for an `area()` method associated with the particular object referred to by the variable `s`. It does not simply use the `area()` method that is statically associated with the type of the variable `s`.[22]

Dynamic method lookup is fast, but it is not as fast as invoking a method directly. Fortunately, there are a number of cases in which Java does not need to use dynamic method lookup. `static` methods cannot be overridden, so they are always invoked directly. `private` methods (which we haven't learned about yet) are not inherited by subclasses and so cannot be overridden by subclasses; this means the Java compiler can safely invoke them without dynamic method lookup as well. `final` methods are invoked directly for the same reason: They cannot be overridden. Finally, when a method of a `final` class is invoked through an instance of the class, then it, too, can be invoked without the overhead of dynamic lookup. These `static`, `final`, and `private` methods that can be invoked directly are also candidates for inlining—i.e., if the methods are short, the compiler may simply insert the method body into the code rather than inserting a call to the method.

14.3.7.4. Invoking an Overridden Method

We've seen the important differences between method overriding and variable shadowing. Nevertheless, the Java syntax for invoking an overridden method is very similar to the syntax for accessing a shadowed variable: Both use the `super` keyword. Example 14.19 illustrates this.

---

[22]C++ programmers should note that dynamic method lookup is what C++ does for `virtual` functions. An important difference between Java and C++ is that Java does not have a `virtual` keyword; methods in Java are "virtual" by default.

EXAMPLE 14.19. *Invoking an overridden method.*

```
class A {
    int i = 1;
    int f() { return i; }           // A very simple method.
}
class B extends A {
    int i;                          // This variable shadows i in A.
    int f() {                       // This method overrides f() in A.
        i = super.i + 1;            // It retrieves A.i this way.
        return super.f() + i;       // And it invokes A.f() this way.
    }
}
```

Recall that when you use `super` to refer to a shadowed variable, it is the same as casting `this` to the superclass type and accessing the variable through that. On the other hand, using `super` to invoke an overridden method is not the same as casting `this`. In this case, `super` has the special purpose of turning off dynamic method lookup and invoking the specific method that the superclass defines or inherits.

In Example 14.19, we use `super` to invoke an overridden method that is actually defined in the immediate superclass. `super` also works perfectly well to invoke overridden methods that are defined further up the class hierarchy. This is because the overridden method is inherited by the immediate superclass, and so the `super` syntax does in fact refer to the correct method.

To make this more concrete, suppose class `A` defines method `f`, and that `B` is a subclass of `A`, and that `C` is a subclass of `B` that overrides method `f`. Then you can still use:

```
super.f()
```

to invoke the overridden method from within class `C`. This is because class `B` inherits method `f` from class `A`. If classes `A`, `B`, and `C` all define method `f`, however, then calling `super.f()` in class `C` invokes class `B`'s definition of the method. In this case, there is no way to invoke `A.f()` from within class `C`. `super.super.f()` is not legal Java syntax!

It is important to note that `super` can only be used to invoke overridden methods from within the class that does the overriding. With our `Circle` and `Ellipse` classes, for example, there is no way to write a program (with or without `super`) that invokes the `Circle area()` method on an object of type `Ellipse`. The only way to do this is to use `super` in a method within the `Ellipse` class.

Finally, note that this form of `super` does not have to occur in the first statement in a method, as it does when used to invoke a superclass constructor method.

14.3.7.5. Finalizer Chaining Revisited

Now that we've discussed method overriding and how to invoke an overridden method, we can return to the issue of the finalizer method that we left dangling earlier on.

In Java, constructor methods are automatically chained, but finalizer methods are not. If you define a `finalize()` method to free resources allocated by your class, you may be overriding a `finalize()` method in a superclass that frees resources allocated by that class. If your finalizer method does not invoke the superclass finalizer, the superclass finalizer never gets called, and resources are not deallocated when they should be.

To prevent this, you should be sure to invoke the superclass `finalize()` method. The best time to do this is usually after your `finalize()` method has done all of its deallocation. It is a good idea to add the following call:

```
super.finalize();
```

as the last line of all your finalizer methods. You should do this even if you know that none of your class's superclasses have finalizer methods, because future implementations of the class may include one.

14.3.8. Data Hiding and Encapsulation

We started this section by describing a class as "a collection of data and methods." One of the important object-oriented techniques that we haven't discussed so far is hiding the data within the class, and making it available only through the methods. This technique is often known as *encapsulation*, because it seals the class's data (and internal methods) safely inside the "capsule" of the class, where it can be accessed only by trusted users—i.e., by the methods of the class.

Why would you want to do this? The most important reason is to hide the internal implementation details of your class. If you prevent programmers from relying on those details, then you can safely modify the implementation without worrying that you will break existing code that uses the class.

Another reason for encapsulation is to protect your class against accidental or willful stupidity. A class often contains a number of variables that are interdependent and must be in a consistent state. If you allow a programmer (this may be you yourself) to manipulate those variables directly, she may change one variable without changing important related variables, thus leaving the class in an inconsistent state. If, instead, she had to call a method to change the variable, that method can be sure to do everything necessary to keep the state consistent.

Here's another way to think about encapsulation: When all of a class's variables are hidden, the class's methods define the only possible operations that can be performed on objects of that class. Once you have carefully tested and debugged your methods, you can be confident that the class will work as expected. On the other hand, if all the variables can be directly manipulated, the number of possibilities you have to test becomes unmanageable.

There are other reasons to hide data, too:

- Internal variables that are visible externally to the class just clutter up your class's API. Keeping visible variables to a minimum keeps your class tidy and elegant.
- If a variable is visible in your class, you have to document it. Save time by hiding it instead!

14.3.8.1. Visibility Modifiers

In most of our examples so far, you've probably noticed the `public` keyword being used. When applied to a class, it means that the class is visible everywhere. When applied to a method or variable, it means that the method or variable is visible everywhere.

To hide variables (or methods, for that matter), you just have to declare them `private`:

```
public class Laundromat {
     // People can use this class.
     private Laundry[] dirty;
     // They can't see this internal variable,
     public void wash() { ... }
     // but they can use these public methods
     public void dry() { ... }
     // to manipulate the internal variable.
}
```

A `private` field of a class is visible only in methods defined within that class. (Or, in Java 1.1, in classes defined within the class.) Similarly, a `private` method may only be invoked by methods within the class (or methods of classes within the class). Private members are not visible within subclasses, and are not inherited by subclasses as other members are.[23] Of course, non-`private` methods that invoke private methods internally are inherited and may be invoked by subclasses.

Besides `public` and `private`, Java has two other visibility levels: `protected` and the default visibility level, "package visibility," which applies if none of the `public`, `private`, and `protected` keywords are used.

A `protected` member of a class is visible within the class where it is defined, of course, and within all subclasses of the class, and also within all classes that are in the same package as that class. You should use `protected` visibility when you want to hide fields and methods from code that uses your class, but want those fields and methods to be fully accessible to code that extends your class.

The default package visibility is more restrictive than `protected`, but less restrictive than `private`. If a class member is not declared with any of the `public`, `private`, or `protected` keywords, then it is visible only within the class that defines it and within classes that are part of the same package. It is not visible to subclasses unless those subclasses are part of the same package.

A note about packages: A package is a group of related and possibly cooperating classes. All non-`private` members of all classes in the package are visible to all other classes in the package. This is okay because the classes are assumed to know about, and trust, each other.[24] The only time difficulty arises is when you write programs without a `package` statement. These classes are thrown into a default package with other `package`-less classes, and all their non-`private` members are visible throughout the package. (The default package usually consists of all classes in the current working directory.)

---

[23]Every object does, of course, have its own copy of all fields of all superclasses, including the private fields. The methods defined by the object can never refer to or use the private fields of superclasses, however, and so we say that those fields are not inherited.

[24]If you're a C++ programmer, you can say that classes within the same package are `friendly` to each other.

There is an important point to make about subclass access to `protected` members. A subclass inherits the `protected` members of its superclass, but it can only access those members through instances of itself, not directly in instances of the superclass. Suppose, for example, that `A`, `B`, and `C` are public classes, each defined in a different package, and that `a`, `b`, and `c` are instances of those classes. Let `B` be a subclass of `A`, and `C` be a subclass of `B`. Now, if `A` has a protected field `x`, then the class `B` inherits that field, and its methods can use `this.x`, `b.x`, and `c.x`. But it cannot access `a.x`. Similarly, if `A` has a protected method `f()`, then the methods of class `B` can invoke `this.f()`, `b.f()`, and `c.f()`, but they cannot invoke `a.f()`.

Table 14.4 shows the circumstances under which class members of the various visibility types are accessible to other classes.

TABLE 14.4. *Class member accessibility.*

	Member Visibility			
Accessible To	`public`	`protected`	`package`	`private`
Same class	Yes	Yes	Yes	Yes
Class in same package	Yes	Yes	Yes	No
Subclass in different package	Yes	Yes	No	No
Non-subclass, different package	Yes	No	No	No

The details of member visibility in Java can become quite confusing. Here are some simple rules of thumb for using visibility modifiers:

- Use `public` only for methods and constants that form part of the public API of the class. Certain very important or very frequently used fields may also be `public`, but it is common practice to make fields non-`public` and encapsulate them with `public` accessor methods.
- Use `protected` for fields and methods that aren't necessary to use the class, but that may be of interest to anyone creating a subclass as part of a different package.
- Use the default package visibility for fields and methods that you want to be hidden outside of the package, but which you want cooperating classes within the same package to have access to.
- Use `private` for fields and methods that are only used inside the class and should be hidden everywhere else.

Note that you can't take advantage of package visibility unless you use the `package` statement to group your related classes into packages.

14.3.8.2. Data Access Methods

In the `Circle` example we've been using, we've declared the circle position and radius to be `public` fields. In fact, the `Circle` class is one where it may well make sense to keep those visible—it is a simple enough class, with no dependencies between the variables.

On the other hand, suppose we wanted to impose a maximum radius on objects of the `Circle` class. Then it would be better to hide the `r` variable so that it could not be set directly. Instead of a visible `r` variable, we'd implement a `setRadius()` method that verifies that the specified radius isn't too large and then sets the `r` variable internally. Example 14.20 shows how we might implement `Circle` with encapsulated data and a restriction on radius size. For convenience, we use `protected` fields for the radius and position variables. This means that subclasses of `Circle`, or cooperating classes within the `shapes` package are able to access these variables directly. To any other classes, however, the variables are hidden. Also, note the `private` constant and method used to check whether a specified radius is legal. And finally, notice the `public` methods that allow you to set and query the values of the instance variables.

EXAMPLE 14.20. *Hiding variables in the Circle class.*

```
package shapes;
    // Specify a package for the class.

public class Circle {
    // Note that the class is still public!
    protected double x, y;
    // Position is hidden, but visible to subclasses.
    protected double r;
    // Radius is hidden, but visible to subclasses.
    private static final double MAXR = 100.0;
    // Maximum radius (constant).
    private boolean check_radius(double r) { return (r <= MAXR); }

    // Public constructors
    public Circle(double x, double y, double r) {
        this.x = x; this.y = y;
        if (check_radius(r)) this.r = r;
        else this.r = MAXR;
    }
    public Circle(double r) { this(0.0, 0.0, r); }
    public Circle() { this(0.0, 0.0, 1.0); }

    // Public data access methods
    public void moveto(double x, double y) { this.x = x; this.y = y;}
    public void move(double dx, double dy) { x += dx;  y += dy; }
    public void setRadius(double r)
        { this.r = (check_radius(r))?r:MAXR; }
```

```
    // Declare these trivial methods final so we don't get dynamic
    // method lookup and so that they can be inlined by the compiler.
    public final double getX() { return x; };
    public final double getY() { return y; };
    public final double getRadius() { return r; };
}
```

14.3.9. Abstract Classes and Interfaces

In Example 14.20, we declared our `Circle` class to be part of a package named `shapes`. Suppose we plan to implement a number of shape classes: `Rectangle`, `Square`, `Ellipse`, `Triangle`, and so on. We'll give all of these shape classes our two basic `area()` and `circumference()` methods. Now, to make it easy to work with an array of shapes, it would be helpful if all our shape classes have a common superclass, `Shape`. We want `Shape` to encapsulate whatever features all our shapes have in common. In this case, what they have in common is the `area()` and `circumference()` methods. But our generic `Shape` class can't actually implement these methods, since it doesn't represent any actual shape. Java handles this case with abstract methods.

14.3.9.1. Abstract Methods

Java lets us define a method without implementing it by making the method `abstract`. An `abstract` method has no body; it simply has a signature definition followed by a semicolon.[25] Here are the rules about `abstract` methods, and the `abstract` classes that contain them:

- Any class with an `abstract` method is automatically `abstract` itself, and must be declared as such.
- A class may be declared `abstract` even if it has no `abstract` methods. This prevents it from being instantiated.
- An `abstract` class cannot be instantiated.
- A subclass of an `abstract` class can be instantiated if it overrides each of the `abstract` methods of its superclass and provides an implementation (i.e., a method body) for all of them.
- If a subclass of an `abstract` class does not implement all of the `abstract` methods it inherits, that subclass is itself `abstract`.

[25] An `abstract` method in Java is something like a "pure virtual function" in C++ (i.e., a virtual function that is declared `= 0`). In C++, a class that contains a pure virtual function is called an "abstract class" and may not be instantiated. The same is true of Java classes that contain `abstract` methods.

That description of the abstract keyword was pretty abstract! Example 14.21 is more concrete. It shows an abstract Shape class and two non-abstract subclasses of it.

EXAMPLE 14.21. *An* Abstract *class and subclasses.*

```
public abstract class Shape {
    public abstract double area();
    public abstract double circumference();
}

class Circle extends Shape {
    protected double r;
    protected static final double PI = 3.14159265358979323846;
    public Circle() { r = 1.0; }
    public Circle(double r) { this.r = r; }
    public double area() { return PI * r * r; }
    public double circumference() { return 2 * PI * r; }
    public double getRadius() { return r; }
}

class Rectangle extends Shape {
    protected double w, h;
    public Rectangle() { w = 0.0; h = 0.0; }
    public Rectangle(double w, double h) { this.w = w;  this.h = h; }
    public double area() { return w * h; }
    public double circumference() { return 2 * (w + h); }
    public double getWidth() { return w; }
    public double getHeight() { return h; }
}
```

Note that the abstract methods in Shape have a semicolon right after their parentheses. There are no curly braces, and no method body is defined. Using the classes defined in Example 14.21, we can now write code like this:

```
Shape[] shapes = new Shape[3];
    // Create an array to hold shapes.
shapes[0] = new Circle(2.0);
    // Fill in the array...
shapes[1] = new Rectangle(1.0, 3.0);
shapes[2] = new Rectangle(4.0, 2.0);

double total_area = 0;
for(int i = 0; i < shapes.length; i++)
    total_area += shapes[i].area();
    // Compute the area of the shapes.
```

There are two important points to notice here:

- Subclasses of Shape can be assigned to elements of an array of Shape. No cast is necessary.

- You can invoke the `area()` and `circumference()` methods for `Shape` objects, even though `Shape` does not define a body for these methods, because `Shape` declared them `abstract`. If `Shape` did not declare them at all, the code would cause a compilation error.

14.3.9.2. Interfaces

Let's extend our `shapes` package further. Suppose we now want to implement a number of shapes that can be drawn on the screen. We could define an abstract `DrawableShape` class, and then implement various subclasses of it, such as `DrawableCircle`, `DrawableRectangle`, and so on. This would work fine.

But suppose we want our drawable shape types to support the `area()` and `circumference()` methods. We don't want to have to re-implement these methods, so we'd like to make `DrawableCircle` a subclass of `Circle`, for example, and `DrawableRectangle` a subclass of `Rectangle`. But classes in Java can only have one superclass. If `DrawableCircle` extends `Circle`, then it cannot also extend `DrawableShape`![26]

Java's solution to this problem is called an *interface*. An interface looks a lot like an abstract class, except that it uses the keyword `interface` instead of the words `abstract` and `class`. Example 14.22 shows an interface named `Drawable`.

EXAMPLE 14.22. *An interface definition.*

```
public interface Drawable {
     public void setColor(Color c);
     public void setPosition(double x, double y);
     public void draw(DrawWindow dw);
}
```

While an `abstract` class may define some `abstract` methods and some non-`abstract` methods, all the methods defined within an interface are implicitly `abstract`. We've omitted the `abstract` keyword in this example, but it is perfectly legal to use it if you want to belabor the abstractness of interface methods. A further restriction on interfaces is that any variables declared in an interface must be `static` and `final`—that is, they must be constants.

[26]C++ allows classes to have more than one superclass, using a technique known as "multiple inheritance." Multiple inheritance opens up a can of worms, so Java replaces it with what many believe is a more elegant solution.

So what can we do with an interface? Just as a class `extends` its superclass, it also optionally `implements` an interface. `implements` is a Java keyword that can appear in a class declaration following the `extends` clause. `implements` should be followed by the name of the interface that the class implements. In order to implement an interface, a class must first declare the interface in an `implements` clause, and then it must provide an implementation (i.e., a body) for all of the `abstract` methods of the interface.[27]

Example 14.23 shows how we can define a `DrawableRectangle` class that extends our `Rectangle` class and implements the `Drawable` interface we defined in Example 14.22. The example assumes that a `Color` class and a `DrawWindow` class are defined elsewhere, and that `DrawWindow` knows how to convert floating-point coordinates to pixel coordinates and knows how to draw primitive shapes.

EXAMPLE 14.23. *Implementing an interface.*

```
public class DrawableRectangle extends Rectangle
        implements Drawable {
    // New instance variables
    private Color c;
    private double x, y;

    // A constructor
    public DrawableRectangle(double w, double h)
        { super(w, h); }

    // Here are implementations of the Drawable methods.
    // We also inherit all the public methods of Rectangle.
    public void setColor(Color c) { this.c = c; }
    public void setPosition(double x, double y)
        { this.x = x; this.y = y; }
    public void draw(DrawWindow dw) {
        dw.drawRect(x, y, w, h, c);
    }
}
```

14.3.9.3. Using Interfaces

Suppose we implement `DrawableCircle` and `DrawableSquare` just as we implemented `DrawableRectangle` in Example 14.23. As we saw earlier, instances of these classes can be treated as instances of the abstract `Shape` class. They can also be treated as instances of the `Drawable` interface. Example 14.24 demonstrates this.

---

[27]This is the real difference between multiple inheritance in C++ and interfaces in Java. In C++, a class can inherit method implementations from more than one superclass. In Java, a class can inherit actual implementations only from one superclass. It can inherit additional `abstract` methods from interfaces, but it must provide its own implementation of those methods. It is rare, however, to actually be able to use C++ multiple inheritance to inherit useful, non-trivial implementations from more than one class. The elegance and simplicity of Java's interface more than compensate for the inability to inherit implementations from more than one class.

EXAMPLE 14.24. *Casting objects to their interface type.*

```
Shape[] shapes = new Shape[3];
     // Create an array to hold shapes
Drawable[] drawables = new Drawable[3];
     // and an array to hold drawables.

// Create some drawable shapes.
DrawableCircle dc = new DrawableCircle(1.1);
DrawableSquare ds = new DrawableSquare(2.5);
DrawableRectangle dr = new DrawableRectangle(2.3, 4.5);

// The shapes can be assigned to both arrays.
shapes[0] = dc;   drawables[0] = dc;
shapes[1] = ds;   drawables[1] = ds;
shapes[2] = dr;   drawables[2] = dr;

// Compute total area and draw the shapes by invoking
// the Shape and the Drawable abstract methods.
double total_area = 0;
for(int i = 0; i < shapes.length; i++) {
     total_area += shapes[i].area();
     // Compute the area of the shapes
     drawables[i].setPosition(i*10.0, i*10.0);
     drawables[i].draw(draw_window);
     // Assume draw_window defined somewhere
}
```

What this example demonstrates is that interfaces are data types in Java, just as classes are, and that when a class implements an interface, instances of that class can be assigned to variables of the interface type. Don't interpret this example to imply that you must assign a `DrawableRectangle` object to a `Drawable` variable before you can invoke the `draw()` method or that you must assign it to a `Shape` variable before you can invoke the `area()` method. `DrawableRectangle` defines `draw()` and inherits `area()` from its `Rectangle` superclass, and so you can always invoke these methods.

14.3.9.4. Implementing Multiple Interfaces

Suppose we wanted shapes that could be scaled to be larger or smaller. One way we could do this is by defining a `Scalable` interface and implementing subclasses of `DrawableRectangle` and the other classes. To do this, though, the new subclass would have to implement both the `Drawable` interface and the `Scalable` interface. This is no problem. You may specify a list of comma-separated interfaces in the `implements` clause of any class:

```
public class DrawableScalableRectangle extends DrawableRectangle
                  implements Drawable, Scalable {
   // The methods of the Scalable interface must be implemented here.
}
```

When a class implements more than one interface, it means simply that it must provide an implementation for all of the abstract methods in all of its interfaces.

14.3.9.5. Constants in Interfaces

As we noted above, constants may appear in interface definitions. What does it mean to implement an interface that contains constants? It simply means that the class that implements the interface "inherits" the constants (in a sense) and can use them as if they were defined directly in the class. There is no need to prefix them with the name of the interface, and there is no need to provide an "implementation" of the constants:

```
class A { static final int CONSTANT1 = 3; }
interface B { static final int CONSTANT2 = 4; }
class C implements B {
    void f() {
        int i = A.CONSTANT1;  // Have to use the class name here.
        int j = CONSTANT2;
    // No class name here, because we implement
    }
    // the interface that defines this constant.
}
```

When you have a set of constants used by more than one class within a package (for example, a port number and other protocol constants used by a client and server), it is convenient to define them in an interface that contains no abstract `methods`. Then, any class that wants to use those constants needs only to declare that it implements the interface.

14.3.9.6. Extending Interfaces

Interfaces can have sub-interfaces, just like classes can have subclasses. A sub-interface inherits all the abstract methods and constants of its super-interface, and may define new abstract methods and constants. Interfaces are different from classes in one very important way, however.

An interface can extend more than one interface at a time:

```
public interface Transformable extends Scalable,
    Rotateable, Reflectable { }
public interface DrawingObject extends Drawable, Transformable { }
public class Shape implements DrawingObject { ... }
```

An interface that extends more than one interface inherits all the abstract methods and constants from each of those interfaces, and may define its own additional abstract methods and constants. A class that implements such an interface must implement the abstract methods defined in the interface itself as well as all the abstract methods inherited from all of the super-interfaces.

14.3.9.7. Marker Interfaces

Another technique that is sometimes useful is to define an interface that is entirely empty. A class can implement this interface to provide additional information about itself. The `Cloneable` interface in `java.lang` is an example of this type of "marker interface." It defines no methods, but serves simply to identify the class as one that will allow its internal state to be cloned by the `clone()` method of the `Object` class. In Java 1.1, `java.io.Serializable` is another such marker interface. You can test whether a class implements a marker interface (or any interface) using the `instanceof` operator.

14.3.10. C++ Features Not Found in Java

Throughout this section, we've noted similarities and differences between Java and C++ in footnotes. Java shares enough concepts and features with C++ to make it an easy language for C++ programmers to pick up. There are several features of C++ that have no parallel in Java, however. In general, Java does not adopt those features of C++ that make the language significantly more complicated. These omissions from Java (or simplifications of C++) are described below.

C++ supports "multiple inheritance" of method implementations from more than one superclass at a time. While this seems like a very useful feature, adding it to the language actually turns out to introduce many complexities. The Java language designers chose to avoid the added complexity by using interfaces instead. Thus, a class in Java can only inherit method implementations from a single superclass, but it can inherit method declarations from any number of interfaces. In practice, this is not any particular hardship.

C++ supports (though not yet in a very standardized way) templates that allow you, for example, to implement a `Stack` class and then instantiate it as `Stack<int>` or `Stack<double>` to produce two separate types: a stack of integers and a stack of floating-point values. Java has no such facility. However, the fact that every class in Java is a subclass of `Object` means that every object can be cast to an instance of `Object`. Thus, in Java, it is often sufficient to define a data structure (such as a `Stack` class) that operates on `Object` values—the objects can be cast back to their actual type whenever necessary.

C++ allows you to define operators that perform arbitrary operations on instances of your classes. In effect, it allows you to extend the syntax of the language. This is a nifty feature, called operator overloading, that makes for very elegant examples. In practice, however, it tends to make code hard to understand. After much debate, the Java language designers decided to omit such "operator overloading" from the language. Note, though, that the use of the `+` operator for string concatenation in Java is at least reminiscent of operator overloading.

C++ allows you to define "conversion functions" for a class that automatically invokes an appropriate constructor method when a value is assigned to a variable of that class. This is simply a syntactic shortcut (similar to overriding the assignment operator) and is not included in Java.

In C++, objects are by default manipulated by value; you must use `&` to specify a variable or function argument that is automatically manipulated by reference. In Java, all objects are manipulated by reference, so there is no need for this `&` syntax.

14.3.11. Summary

This has been a long and detailed section. The following list summarizes the most important points to remember. This summary is not intended to simplify the complex material we've covered, but it may allow you to test your comprehension of the material now, and to help jog your memory later:

- A class is a collection of data and methods that operate on that data.
- An object is a particular instance of a class.
- Object members (fields and methods) are accessed with a dot between the object name and the member name.
- Instance (non-static) variables occur in each instance of a class.
- Class (static) variables are associated with the class. There is one copy of a class variable regardless of the number of instances of a class.
- Instance (non-static) methods of a class are passed an implicit `this` argument that identifies the object being operated on.
- Class (static) methods are not passed a `this` argument and therefore do not have a current instance of the class that can be used to implicitly refer to instance variables or invoke instance methods.
- Objects are created with the `new` keyword, which invokes a class constructor method with a list of arguments.

- Objects are not explicitly freed or destroyed in any way. The Java garbage collector automatically reclaims objects that are no longer being used.
- If the first line of a constructor method does not invoke another constructor with a `this()` call, or a superclass constructor with a `super()` call, Java automatically inserts a call to the superclass constructor that takes no arguments. This enforces "constructor chaining."
- If a class does not define a constructor, Java provides a default constructor.
- A class may inherit the non-`private` methods and variables of another class by "subclassing"—i.e., by declaring that class in its `extends` clause.
- `java.lang.Object` is the default superclass for a class. It is the root of the Java class hierarchy and has no superclass itself. All Java classes inherit the methods defined by `Object`.
- Method overloading is the practice of defining multiple methods which have the same name but have different argument lists.
- Method overriding occurs when a class redefines a method inherited from its superclass.
- Dynamic method lookup ensures that the correct method is invoked for an object, even when the object is an instance of a class that has overridden the method.
- `static`, `private`, and `final` methods cannot be overridden and are not subject to dynamic method lookup. This allows compiler optimizations such as inlining.
- From a subclass, you can explicitly invoke an overridden method of a superclass with the `super` keyword.
- You can explicitly refer to a shadowed variable with the `super` keyword.
- Data and methods may be hidden or encapsulated within a class by specifying the `private` or `protected` visibility modifiers. Members declared `public` are visible everywhere. Members with no visibility modifiers are visible only within the package.

- An abstract method has no method body (i.e., no implementation).
- An abstract class contains abstract methods. The methods must be implemented in a subclass before the subclass can be instantiated.
- An interface is a collection of abstract methods and constants (`static final` variables). Declaring an interface creates a new data type.
- A class implements an interface by declaring the interface in its `implements` clause and by providing a method body for each of the abstract methods in the interface.

14.4. What's New in Java 1.1

Java 1.1 is a huge new release. The number of packages in the API has increased from 8 in Java 1.0 to 23 in Java 1.1, and the number of classes has more than doubled from 211 to 503. On top of these changes to the core Java class libraries, there have been some important changes to the language itself. Also, the JDK—the Java Development Kit from Sun—includes a number of new tools in version 1.1.

The new features of Java 1.1 include:

Inner classes—Changes to the Java language itself to allow classes to be nested within each other, and within blocks of code.

Java beans—A framework for defining reusable modular software components.

Internationalization—A variety of new features that make it possible to write programs that run around the globe.

New event model—A new model for handling events in graphical user interfaces that should make it easier to create those interfaces.

Other new AWT features—The Java 1.1 AWT includes support for printing, cut-and-paste, popup menus, menu shortcuts, and focus traversal. It has improved support for colors, fonts, cursors, scrolling, image manipulation, and clipping.

Applets—JAR files allow all of an applet's files to be grouped into a single archive. Digital signatures allow trusted applets to run with fewer security restrictions. The HTML <APPLET> tag has new features.

Object serialization—Objects can now be easily "serialized" and sent over the network or written to disk for persistent storage.

Reflection—Java programs can now "reflect" upon themselves or upon an arbitrary class to determine the methods and fields defined by the class, the arguments passed to a method, and so on. The Reflection API also allows the invocation of methods specified by name.

Security—Java 1.1 includes a new package that supports digital signatures, message digests, key management, and access control lists.

Java Database Connectivity (JDBC)—A new package that allows Java programs to send SQL queries to database servers. It includes a "bridge" that allows it to inter-operate with existing ODBC database servers.

Remote Method Invocation (RMI)—An interface that supports distributed Java applications in which a program running on one computer can invoke methods of Java objects that exist on a different computer.

These and other new features are summarized in the sections below. Many of them are also described in more detail elsewhere in this chapter.

14.4.1. Java 1.1 Package-by-Package

The packages and classes of the Java class library are interlinked and interdependent. Many of the major new features of Java 1.1 rely on classes from multiple packages in the Java API. Before we examine those new features in detail, therefore, we need to understand the big picture of Java 1.1. The paragraphs below discuss each of the 23 packages that constitute the core API for Java 1.1; they introduce the new packages and explain the changes to existing packages.

`java.applet`—Despite the introduction of JAR files, digitally signed applets, and new attributes of the `<APPLET>` tag, the `java.applet` package has not changed in any significant way.

`java.awt`—The `java.awt` package contains new classes and interfaces to support printing, popup menus, and menu shortcuts and to improve support for layout management, cursors, scrolling, colors, and clipping. Several classes provide support for the new AWT event model, but most event support is contained in one of several new subpackages of `java.awt`.

`java.awt.datatransfer`—The classes and interfaces in this package define a generic framework for inter-application (and intra-application) data transfer. This package also includes classes to support a clipboard-based cut-and-paste data transfer model. In the future, this package may be extended to include support for data transfer through a drag-and-drop metaphor. One of the two underlying data transfer mechanisms supported by this package relies on the Object Serialization API of the `java.io` package.

`java.awt.event`—This package defines the classes and interfaces of the new AWT event handling model. The classes and interfaces of this package fall into three categories:

- Event classes—The classes that actually represent events.
- Event "listeners"—Interfaces that define methods that must be implemented by objects interested in being notified when an event of a particular type occurs.
- Event "adaptors"—Trivial no-op implementations of the event listener interfaces that are suitable for easy subclassing.

All the events and event listeners defined in this package extend the `Event\%Object` class or the `EventListener` interface defined in `java.util`.

`java.awt.image`—This package has two new image filter classes that implement improved image scaling. Changes have also been made to the `MemoryImageSource` and `Pixel\%Grabber` classes.

`java.awt.peer`—The changes to this package for the most part simply reflect changes to `java.awt`. There are new interfaces that represent a platform-dependent popup menu and scrolling area, for example.

`java.beans`—This package constitutes the much-touted JavaBeans API for creating and using embeddable, reusable software components. The classes and interfaces in this package can be used at three different levels:

- To create application builder tools that programmers (or even non-programmers) can use to compose applications out of individual Java beans.
- To develop Java beans for use in such application builders.
- To develop applications (without using a builder tool) that use Java beans.

Most of the classes and interfaces of the package are for use by application builders or by developers of advanced beans. Programmers using beans or writing simple beans do not need to be familiar with most of the package.

Application builders that manipulate beans rely on the Reflection API defined in `java.lang.reflect`, and many beans take advantage of the Object Serialization API defined in the `java.io` package. The JavaBeans API uses the same event model that the Java 1.1 AWT does, and event-related classes and interfaces in this package are extensions of a class and an interface defined in `java.util`.

`java.io`—The `java.io` package has become by far the largest of the core Java packages. This is because Java 1.1 adds

- A complete suite of new "character stream" classes to complement most of the existing "byte stream" input and output classes. These new "reader" and "writer" streams offer improved efficiency and support internationalization for textual input and output.
- New classes and interfaces to support object serialization.
- A number of new `IOException` types.

`java.lang`—This package has several new `Exception` and `Error` types, as well as new `Byte`, `Short`, and `Void` classes. With the addition of these new classes, all primitive Java data types (including the `void` type) have corresponding object types. This is important for the `java.lang.reflect` package, which defines the new Reflection API. In addition, the `Class` class has been greatly enhanced for use with the Reflection API. `Class` and `ClassLoader` have methods to locate "resources" associated with a class, such as images, audio files, `Properties` files, and so on. Resources are important for internationalization in Java 1.1.

`java.lang.reflect`—This new package enables a Java program to examine the structure of Java classes and to "reflect upon" its own structure. `java.lang.reflect` contains classes that represent the fields, methods, and constructors of a class, and enable a program to obtain complete information about any object, array, method, constructor, or field. The `java.beans` package relies heavily upon this package.

`java.math`—This new package contains only two classes, which support arithmetic on arbitrary-size integers and arbitrary-precision floating-point numbers. The `BigInteger` class also defines methods for modular arithmetic, primality testing, and other features required for cryptography.

`java.net`—The changes to the `java.net` package are quite low-level. They include the addition of multicast sockets, UNIX-style socket options, and new exception types that provide finer granularity when handling networking exceptions.

`java.rmi`—This package defines the fundamental classes and interfaces used for Remote Method Invocation. Most of the classes in this package are exception types. Subpackages of `java.rmi` provide additional, more specialized functionality. When objects must be passed as arguments to remote methods, RMI relies on the object serialization functionality provided in the `java.io` package.

`java.rmi.dgc`—This small package defines the classes and interfaces required for distributed garbage collection (DGC).

`java.rmi.registry`—This is another small package that defines the classes and interfaces required for a Java client to look up a remote object by name or for a Java server to advertise the service it provides.

`java.rmi.server`—This package is the largest of the RMI packages and is at the heart of Remote Method Invocation. It defines the classes and interface that allow a Java program to create an object that can be used remotely by other Java programs.

`java.security`—This package contains the classes and interfaces that represent the fundamental abstractions of cryptographic security: public and private keys, certificates, message digests, and digital signatures. This package does not provide implementations of these abstractions; by design, the Java Security API is implementation independent. Java 1.1 does include a default implementation, but vendor-specific implementations may also be used in conjunction with this package. The default security implementation relies on the `BigInteger` class defined in the `java.math` package.

`java.security.acl`—This package defines high-level interfaces, and some exceptions, for manipulating access control lists.

`java.security.interfaces`—This package defines a few interfaces that are required for the Java Security API's implementation-independent design.

`java.sql`—This package is the Java Database Connectivity (JDBC) API. The classes and interfaces it contains allow Java programs to send SQL queries to databases and retrieve the results of those queries.

`java.text`—The classes and interfaces in this package are used for internationalization. The package includes classes for formatting dates, times, numbers, and textual messages in a manner appropriate for the default locale or for any specified locale. It also includes classes for collating strings according to the rules of a given locale and iterating through the characters, words, and sentences of a string in a locale-specific manner.

`java.util`—As its name indicates, the `java.util` package contains miscellaneous utility classes. In Java 1.1, new classes have been added to this package to support the AWT and Java beans event model, to define "locales" and "resource bundles" used for internationalization, and to manipulate dates, times, and time zones.

`java.util.zip`—This package implements classes for computing checksums on streams of data, and for compressing and archiving (and uncompressing and unarchiving) streams of data, using ZLIB compression library and ZIP and GZIP file formats.

14.4.2. Inner Classes

While the bulk of the changes in Java 1.1 are additions to the core Java API, there has also been a major addition to the language itself. The language has been extended to allow class definitions to be nested within other classes, and even to be defined locally, within blocks of code. Altogether, there are four new types of classes that can be defined in Java 1.1; these four new types are sometimes loosely referred to as "inner classes."

As we'll see, inner classes are useful primarily for defining simple "helper" or "adaptor" classes that serve a very specific function at a particular place in a program, and are not intended to be general-purpose "top-level" classes. By using inner classes nested within other classes, you can place the definition of these special-purpose helper classes closer to where they are actually used in your programs. This makes your code clearer, and also prevents you from cluttering up the package namespace with small special purpose classes that are not of interest to programmers using your package. We'll also see that inner classes are particularly useful in conjunction with the new AWT event model in Java 1.1.

One important feature of inner classes is that no changes to the Java Virtual Machine are required to support them. When a Java 1.1 compiler encounters an inner class, it transforms the Java 1.1 source code in a way that converts the nested class to a regular top-level class. Once that transformation has been performed, the code can be compiled just as it would have been in Java 1.0.

14.4.3. The New AWT Event Model

The Java 1.1 change that will probably affect Java programmers the most is the new event processing model adopted for the AWT windowing and graphical user interface (GUI) toolkit. If you created applets or GUIs with Java 1.0, you know that it was necessary to subclass GUI components in order to handle events. This model worked okay for simple programs, but proved increasingly awkward as programs became more complex. Furthermore, with the development of the JavaBeans API, the AWT package needed an event model that would allow AWT GUI components to serve as beans. For these reasons, Java 1.1 defines a new model for dispatching and handling events.

The new event handling model is essentially a "callback" model. When you create a GUI component, you tell it what method or methods it should invoke when a particular event occurs on it (e.g., when the user clicks on a button or selects an item from a list). This model is very easy to use in C and C++ because those languages allow you to manipulate method pointers—to specify a callback, all you need to do is pass a pointer to the appropriate function. In Java, however, methods are not data and cannot be manipulated in this way. Only objects can be passed like this in Java, so to define a Java callback, you must define a class that implements some particular interface. Then, you can pass an instance of that class to a GUI component as a way of specifying the callback. When the desired event occurs, the GUI component invokes the appropriate method of the object you have specified.

As you might imagine, this new event handling model can lead to the creation of many small helper classes. (Sometimes these helper classes are known as "adaptor classes" because they serve as the interface between the body of an application and the GUI for that application. They are the "adaptors" that allow the GUI to be "plugged in" to the application.) This proliferation of small classes could become quite a burden, were it not for the introduction of inner classes, which, as noted above, allows this kind of special-purpose class to be nested and defined exactly where it is needed within your program.

Despite the major AWT event-handling changes, Java 1.1 does retain backwards compatibility with the event-handling model of Java 1.0. It is an all-or-nothing type of backwards compatibility, however—the two models are so different from each other that it is not really possible to mix them within the same application.

14.4.4. Deprecated Features

Although you can use the old AWT event model in Java 1.1, it has been officially "deprecated," and its use in new software is discouraged. When you compile code that uses the 1.0 event model, you'll be made aware of this by the "deprecation warning" that the `javac` compiler issues. This warning notifies you that your code relies on methods or classes in the Java API that have been superseded by newer, preferred alternatives. If you compile using the `-deprecation` flag, `javac` provides a detailed warning about each use of a deprecated feature. You can simply ignore these warnings, but when time permits, the better approach is to update your code so that it no longer relies on deprecated features of the Java API. While it is not strictly true to say that deprecated features are "unsupported," they will almost certainly receive far less support in practice than the features that replace them.

The reason that the compiler is able to issue deprecation warnings at all is the addition of a new `@deprecated` tag to the documentation-comment syntax of Java 1.1. As you may be aware, comments that begin with the `/**` character sequence are treated specially in Java, and are used by the `javadoc` tool to automatically generate online documentation for packages, classes, methods, and fields. Prior to Java 1.1, the compiler ignored the contents of documentation comments. In Java 1.1, however, it scans these comments for the `@deprecated` tag. If it is found, the compiler marks the class, interface, constructor, method, or field following the comment as deprecated, and issues a warning when the deprecated feature is used.

The old AWT event-handling model is not the only Java 1.0 feature that has been deprecated in Java 1.1; merely the one you are most likely to encounter first. A number of common AWT component methods have been renamed, to follow a more regular naming scheme that fits the JavaBeans naming conventions. These methods can be invoked by the old name or the new, but if you use the old name, you'll be rewarded with a deprecation warning. Fortunately, in simple cases like this, it is trivial to write a script or program to mechanically convert from the old name to the new. Other areas of the Java API have been deprecated as well. You'll notice that a few of the input and output stream classes in the `java.io` package have been deprecated and superseded by `Reader` and `Writer` stream classes, for example.

14.4.5. Other AWT Improvements

In addition to the major change in the AWT event model, there have been quite a few other improvements to the AWT. These improvements are summarized in the sections below.

14.4.5.1. Printing

Printing in Java 1.1 is implemented through the new `PrintJob` class and `PrintGraphics` interface. The `PrintJob` class represents a print request. When a `PrintJob` object is created, the user is prompted with a platform-dependent print dialog, which allows her to specify options such as which printer to use.

The `getGraphics()` method of a `PrintJob` object returns a `Graphics` object that can be used for printing. This object is an instance of a subclass of `Graphics` that knows how to print in a platform-dependent way. The object also implements the `PrintGraphics` interface. To print a component, you simply pass this `Graphics` object to the component's `print()` method. If the component does not define this method, the default implementation simply invokes the `paint()` method, which usually does the right thing. When you want to print a component and all of its subcomponents, you can simply pass the `Graphics` object to the `printAll()` method of the component.

Printing multiple pages is more complex, of course. The application is responsible for pagination of the output, and in order to draw the output on the page the application may also need to query the `PrintJob` object to determine the page size (in pixels) and page resolution (in pixels per inch).

For security reasons, applets are not allowed to initiate print jobs; if they were, you could expect to see applets on the Net that automatically printed hardcopy advertisements to your printer! Note, however, that this does not mean that applets cannot print themselves when the browser or applet viewer initiates the print request object and invokes the `printAll()` method of the applet.

14.4.5.2. Cut-and-Paste

Data transfer via the cut-and-paste metaphor is supported in Java 1.1 by the classes and interfaces in the `java.awt.datatransfer` package. One half of this package provides generic data-transfer functionality, and the other half provides the classes and interfaces needed for clipboard-based cut-and-paste. In future versions of the JDK, we can expect to see support for the drag-and-drop data transfer metaphor added to this package.

For the purposes of data transfer, the `DataFlavor` class represents the notion of a data type or data format. A `DataFlavor` consists of a human-readable name for the flavor and one of two possible machine-readable format definitions. The first of the machine-readable descriptions is a `String` that specifies a MIME type for the transferred data. The second is a `Class` object that represents a Java class. When a `DataFlavor` is specified with a `Class` object, it is an instance of this class that is passed when data transfer actually occurs.

Any value that can be transferred through the Java 1.1 data transfer mechanism must be represented by a class that implements the `Transferable` interface. This interface defines methods to query the data flavors that the class supports, and it defines a method that the data transfer mechanism calls to convert the transferable value into the appropriate form for a given `DataFlavor`.

While the `DataFlavor` class and the `Transferable` interface define the fundamental data transfer mechanism, they, by themselves, are not enough to initiate or perform data transfer. For this purpose, `java.awt.datatransfer` also defines the `Clipboard` class and the `ClipboardOwner` interface. Together, they support a cut-and-paste metaphor for data transfer. Because strings are often transferred between applications, `java.awt.datatransfer` provides the `StringSelection` class. This class implements both the `Transferable` and the `ClipboardOwner` interfaces and makes it very easy to transfer textual data through cut-and-paste.

Inter-application data transfer is performed through the system clipboard. It is also possible to perform intra-application transfers through a private clipboard that an application creates for itself. Note that untrusted applets are not allowed to access the system clipboard—there could be sensitive information contained on it that untrusted code should not have access to. This means that applets cannot participate in inter-application cut-and-paste.

14.4.5.3. Popup Menus and Menu Shortcuts

Java 1.1 adds support for popup menus to the AWT. The `PopupMenu` class is a subclass of `Menu`; menu items are added to it just as they are added to regular pulldown menus. A popup menu can be attached to an arbitrary AWT component, using the new `add()` method of the `Component` class. And, finally, a popup menu can be "popped up" by calling its `show()` method. (The menu pops itself down automatically.)

An application typically displays a popup menu when the user clicks a certain mouse button over the component that the menu is attached to. However, different platforms traditionally use different mouse buttons to display popup menus. You can use the new `isPopupTrigger()` method of `MouseEvent` to determine whether a given mouse click has the appropriate modifiers set to trigger the popup menu for the current platform.

Java 1.1 also adds support for menu shortcut keys. The new `MenuShortcut` class represents a menu shortcut key. An instance of this class may optionally be specified whenever you create a `MenuItem` object. Again, different platforms use different modifier keys to invoke menu shortcuts, so when you create a `MenuShortcut` object, you specify only the key in question (plus, optionally, the Shift key). The system translates this into a platform-dependent shortcut using Ctrl, Alt, or some other modifier key.

14.4.5.4. Keyboard Focus Traversal

The ability to operate a GUI without using the mouse is an important feature of any windowing toolkit. The addition of menu shortcuts in Java 1.1 is an important step in this direction. Java 1.1 also adds rudimentary facilities for keyboard focus traversal (i.e., moving keyboard focus among the individual components in a window) using the Tab and Shift-Tab keys.

Under the new focus traversal scheme, components within a container are traversed in the order in which they were added to the container. (Note, however, that it is possible to override this order by specifying an explicit position within the container's component list for a new component as it is added to the container with the `add()` method.) Beyond adding components to their container in the order desired for traversal, nothing else is required of the programmer in order to make keyboard focus traversal work.

If you are creating a custom component that can accept keyboard focus, you should override the `isFocusTraversable()` method to return `true`. The component should call the `requestFocus()` method it inherits from `Component` when the user clicks on it or otherwise activates it. Finally, when a component receives focus, (i.e., when its `processFocusEvent()` method is invoked), it should provide some sort of visual indication, such as a highlighted border, that it has the focus.

14.4.5.5. Miscellaneous Improvements

The `SystemColor` class represents a color used by the desktop system. On some platforms, these colors may be dynamically updated while the system is running. The `SystemColor` class also implements quite a few constants that represent system colors for various GUI components. Thus, if you want your GUIs to match the desktop color scheme, you might create them using colors such as `SystemColor.menu` (the background color for menus) and `SystemColor.menuText` (foreground color for menus), for example.

The treatment of fonts has been changed and improved somewhat in Java 1.1. The use of the font names TimesRoman, Helvetica, and Courier is now discouraged. Instead, you should use serif, sansserif, and monospaced—these names convey the essential style of the font face, without specifying the exact font to be used. The font names Dialog and DialogInput are still supported in Java 1.1. An important reason for switching to generic font names is that Java can now display any Unicode character for which there is an appropriate font installed on the host system. The names serif and sansserif have meaning even when applied to non-Latin character sets, such as Japanese Kanji characters; the names TimesRoman and Helvetica clearly do not. Another result of this fuller Unicode support is that the use of the ZapfDingbats font is also discouraged. Instead, regardless of what font you are using, you can simply encode these graphical symbols using Unicode characters between `\u2700` and `\u27ff`. This improved support for Unicode makes it much easier to write internationalized programs in Java.

In Java 1.0, mouse cursors could only be specified for a `Frame`. In Java 1.1, every component can have its own cursor, represented by the new `Cursor` object. There are new methods of `Component` for setting and querying the cursor. This change does not add any new predefined cursor images, nor does it add the ability to create custom cursors; it merely allows you to specify a cursor for any arbitrary component, and to do so in a more logical fashion.

The `ScrollPane` class is new in Java 1.1. It is a `Container` that makes it very easy to scroll a large component or GUI within a smaller visible area. Doing this in Java 1.0 required a custom container, and suffered from some serious performance problems.

Another new feature is the ability to create "lightweight components." These are components and containers that do not have a native window of their own. In Java 1.0, custom components and containers had to be subclassed from `Canvas` or `Panel`. In Java 1.1, however, you can subclass `Component` and `Container` directly. Doing so creates a simpler component or container, without the overhead of a native window. It also allows you to create partially transparent components that appear non-rectangular.

Java 1.1 also includes several miscellaneous changes to clipping and image manipulation:

- The `Graphics` class defines a method to set an arbitrary clipping rectangle, even to one that is larger than the current clipping region. There is also a new method to query the current clipping region.
- `Graphics` also defines two new `drawImage()` methods that are more flexible than the existing `drawImage()` methods. These new methods allow arbitrary image cropping, scaling, and flipping.
- There are two new classes, `ReplicateScaleFilter` and `AreaAveragingScale\%Filter`, that can be used to scale an image as it is loaded, and a new convenience method, `Image.getScaledInstance()`, to obtain a new `Image` object that contains a scaled version of some other `Image`.
- New methods have been added to the `MemoryImageSource` class that allow images generated from memory to be dynamically and efficiently updated, allowing a kind of image animation.
- New methods have been added to the `PixelGrabber` class to make it more efficient and flexible to use.

14.4.6. Internationalization

Internationalization[28] is the process of enabling a program to run internationally. That is, an internationalized program has the flexibility to run correctly in any country. Once a program has been internationalized, enabling it to run in a particular country and/or language is merely a matter of "localizing" it for that country and language, or *locale*.

You might think that the main task of localization is the matter of translating a program's user-visible text into a local language. While this is an important task, it is not by any means the only one. Other concerns include displaying dates and times in the customary format for the locale, displaying number and currency values in the customary format for the locale, and sorting strings in the customary order for the locale.

Underlying all these localization issues is the even more fundamental issue of character encodings. Almost every useful program must perform input and output of text, and before we can even think about textual I/O, we must be able to work with the local character encoding standard. This hurdle to internationalization lurks slightly below the surface, and is not very "programmer-visible." Nevertheless, it is one of the most important and difficult issues in internationalization.

Java 1.1 provides facilities that address all of these internationalization issues. If you write programs that correctly make use of these facilities, the task of localizing your program for a new country really does boil down to the relatively simple matter of hiring a translator to convert your program's messages. With the expansion of the global economy, and particularly of the global Internet, writing internationalized programs is going to become more and more important, and you should begin to take advantage of Java's internationalization capabilities right away.

There are several distinct pieces to the problem of internationalization, and Java's solution to this problem also comes in distinct pieces. The first issue in internationalization is the matter of knowing what locale a program is running in. A locale is typically defined as a political, geographical, or cultural region that has a distinct language or distinct conventions for things such as date and time formats. The notion of a locale is encapsulated in Java 1.1 by the `Locale` class, which is part of the `java.util` package. Every Java program has a default locale, which is inherited from the

[28]This word is sometimes abbreviated I18N, because there are 18 letters between the first I and the last N.

operating system (where it may be set by the user). A program can simply rely on this default, or it can change the default. Additionally, all Java methods that rely on the default locale also have variants that allow you to explicitly specify a locale. Typically, though, using the default locale is exactly what you want to do.

Once a program knows what locale it is running in, the most fundamental internationalization issue, as noted above, is the ability to read and write localized text. Since Java uses the Unicode encoding for its characters and strings, any character of any commonly used modern written language is representable in a Java program, which puts Java at a huge advantage over older languages such as C and C++. Thus, working with localized text is merely a matter of converting from the local character encoding to Unicode when reading text, such as a file or input from the user, and converting from Unicode to the local encoding when writing text. Java's solution to this problem is in the `java.io` package, in the form of a new suite of character-based input and output streams (known as "readers" and "writers") that complement the existing byte-based input and output streams.

The `FileReader` class, for example, is a character-based input stream used to read characters (which are not the same as bytes in all languages) from a file. The `FileReader` class assumes that the specified file is encoded using the default character encoding for the default locale, so it converts characters from the local encoding to Unicode characters as it reads them. In most cases, this assumption is a good one, so all you need to do to internationalize the character set handling of your program is to switch from a `FileInputStream` to a `FileReader` object, and make similar switches for text output as well. On the other hand, if you need to read a file that is encoded using some character set other than the default character set of the default locale, you can use a `FileInputStream` to read the bytes of the file, and then use an `InputStreamReader` to convert the stream of bytes to a stream of characters. When you create an `InputStreamReader`, you specify the name of the encoding in use, and it performs the appropriate conversion automatically.

As you can see, internationalizing the character set of your programs is a simple matter of switching from byte I/O streams to character I/O streams. Internationalizing other aspects of your program requires a little more effort. The classes in the `java.text` package are designed to allow you to internationalize your handling of numbers, dates, times, string comparisons, and so on. `NumberFormat` is used to convert numbers, monetary amounts, and percentages to an appropriate textual format for a locale. Similarly, the `DateFormat` class, along with the `Calendar` and `TimeZone` classes from the `java.util` package, are used to display dates and times in a locale-specific way. The `Collator` class is used to compare strings according to the alphabetization rules of a given locale, and the `BreakIterator` class is used to locate word, line, and sentence boundaries.

The final major problem of internationalization is making your program flexible enough to display messages (or any type of user-visible text, such as the labels on GUI buttons) to the user in an appropriate language for the current locale. Typically, this means that the program cannot use hard-coded messages and must instead read in a set of messages at runtime, based on the locale setting. Java provides an easy way to do this. You define your messages as key/value pairs in a `ResourceBundle` subclass. Then, you create a subclass of `ResourceBundle` for each language or locale your application supports, naming each class following a convention that includes the locale name. At runtime, you can use the `ResourceBundle.getBundle()` method to load the appropriate `ResourceBundle` class for the current locale. The `ResourceBundle` contains the messages your application uses, each associated with a key, that serves as the message name. Using this technique, your application can look up a locale-dependent message translation based on a locale-independent message name. Note that this technique is useful for things other than textual messages. It can be used to internationalize icons, or any other locale-dependent object used by your application.

There is one final twist to this problem of internationalizing messages. Often, we want to output messages such as "Error at line 5 of file `hello.java`." where parts of the message are static, and parts are dynamically generated at runtime (such as the line number and filename above). This is further complicated by the fact that when we translate such messages, the values we substitute in at runtime may appear in a different order. For example, in some different English, speaking locale, we might want to display the line above as: "hello.java: error at line 5". The `MessageFormat` class of the `java.text` package allows you to substitute dynamic values into static messages in a very flexible way and helps tremendously with this situation, particularly when used in conjunction with resource bundles.

14.4.7. Object Serialization

Object serialization is one of the major new features of Java 1.1. It refers to the ability to write the complete state of an object (including any objects it refers to) to an output stream, and then recreate that object at some later time by reading its serialized state from an input stream. You can serialize an object simply by passing it to the `writeObject()` method of an `ObjectOutputStream`. Similarly, you can create an object from a serialized object stream by calling the `readObject()` method of an `ObjectInputStream`. Both of these new object stream types are part of the `java.io` package.

Typically, object serialization is as simple as calling `writeObject()` and `read\%Object()`. There are a few additional twists, however, that are worth mentioning here. First, only objects that subclass the `Serializable` (or `Externalizable`) interface can be serialized. The `Serializable` interface does not define any methods, but merely acts as a marker that indicates whether serialization is allowed on a given object. Second, fields of a class declared `transient` are not serialized as part of an object's state. The `transient` modifier was legal in Java 1.0, but had no defined behavior. Third, some objects may need to implement custom serialization or de-serialization behavior. They can do this by implementing special `readObject()` and `writeObject()` methods.

Despite the fact that only a few classes and interfaces are part of the Object Serialization API, serialization is a very important technology and is used in several places in Java 1.1. It is used as the basis for transferring objects via cut-and-paste. It is used to transfer objects between a client and a server for remote method invocation. It is used by the JavaBeans API; beans are often provided as pre-initialized, serialized objects, rather than merely as class files. Java 1.1 also adds the capability for applets to be loaded into an applet viewer or browser as serialized objects. One common use we are likely to see for object serialization is as a way to save user preferences and other application state—a serialized object is an instant file format that works for any application. Another use that should be popular with GUI builder tools is saving the complete `Component` hierarchy of an application's GUI as a serialized object, and then later loading in that object in order to automatically recreate the GUI.

14.4.8. Reflection

Reflection in Java 1.1 refers to the ability of Java classes to reflect upon themselves, or to "look inside themselves." The `java.lang.Class` class has been greatly enhanced in Java 1.1. It now includes methods that return the fields, methods, and constructors defined by a class. These items are returned as objects of type `Field`, `Method`, and `Constructor`, respectively. These new classes are part of the new `java.lang.reflect` package, and they each provide methods to obtain complete information about the field, method, or constructor they represent. For example, the `Method` object has methods to query the name, the parameter types, and the return type of the method it represents.

Besides allowing a program to inspect the members of a class, the `java.lang.reflect` package also allows a program to manipulate these fields and methods. The `Field` class defines methods that get and set the value of the represented field for any given object of the appropriate type. Similarly, the `Method` object defines an `invoke()` method that allows the represented method to be invoked, and the `Constructor` class defines a `newInstance()` method that creates a new object and invokes the represented constructor on it. `java.lang.reflect` also defines an `Array` class. It does not represent a specific array, but defines static methods that read and write array elements and dynamically create new arrays.

With the addition of reflection, the `Class` class has been expanded to represent not just Java classes, but any Java type, including primitive types and array types. There is a special `Class` object that represents each of the eight Java primitive types, and another special `Class` object that represents the `void` type. These special `Class` objects are available as constants in the wrapper objects for the primitive types. `Integer.TYPE` is a `Class` object that represents the `int` type, for example, and `Void.TYPE` is a `Class` object that represents the `void` type.

Finally, new Java language syntax makes it easier to obtain a `Class` object that represents a Java class. If you follow the name of a class, interface, or other type with `.class`, Java evaluates that expression and returns the corresponding `Class` object. So, for example, the following two expressions are equivalent:

```
String.class
Class.forName("java.lang.String")
```

Note that this syntax also works with primitive type names: You can write `short.class`, for example, which returns the same value as `Short.TYPE`.

14.4.9. Java Beans

JavaBeans is a "software component model" for Java that has generated quite a lot of interest from many quarters. The JavaBeans API specification defines "beans" as follows: "A Java bean is a reusable software component that can be manipulated visually in a builder tool." The `java.beans` package defines classes and interfaces designed to work with beans at three distinct levels, described below.

Much of the JavaBeans API is intended for use only by those few people who are writing interface builder tools that manipulate beans. The main thing that a builder tool needs to be able to do with beans is "introspect" on them—i.e., to determine what properties are exposed by a bean, what methods it exports, and what events it can generate. This is information that a builder tool must be able to display to the programmer who is using the tool. The JavaBeans API defines a set of naming conventions for the methods that a bean defines. If a bean follows these conventions, a builder tool can use the new Reflection API to determine what properties, methods, and events the bean supports. The `Introspector` class uses reflection to obtain information about a bean and presents it to the builder tool in the form of a `BeanInfo` object, which itself contains various `FeatureDescriptor` objects describing the properties, methods, and events of the bean.

At the second level, the JavaBeans API contains classes and interfaces intended for use by programmers who are creating beans for others to use. One of the surprising features of the JavaBeans API is that there is no `Bean` class that all beans must extend. A bean can be of any class; however, as we've seen, beans should follow certain naming conventions. The `java.beans` classes that a bean creator uses are generally auxiliary classes, used not by the bean, but by the builder tool that manipulates the bean. These auxiliary classes are shipped with a bean, and provide additional information or methods that a builder tool may use with the bean. These classes are not included in finished software built with the bean.

For example, one of the auxiliary classes a bean may define is a custom `BeanInfo` class to provide information to the builder tool that is not available through the Reflection API. This information might include a human-readable description of the bean's properties, methods, and events, for example. Or, if a bean does not follow the standard naming conventions, this custom `BeanInfo` class must also provide more basic information about the bean's properties, methods, and events.

Besides a `BeanInfo` class, complex beans may also provide a `Customizer` class and one or more `PropertyEditor` classes. A `Customizer` class is a kind of configuration tool or "wizard" for a bean. It is instantiated by the builder tool in order to guide the user through bean customization. A `PropertyEditor` class is used to allow the user to edit the value of bean properties of a particular class. Builder tools have built-in property editors for common types such as strings, colors, and fonts, but a bean that has properties of some unusual or custom type may want to provide a `PropertyEditor` subclass to allow the user to easily specify values for those properties.

The third level at which the JavaBeans API can be used is by programmers who are assembling an application using beans. Some programmers may do this through a builder tool, while others may do it "by hand," the old-fashioned way. Programmers using beans do not typically have to use the `java.beans` package. At this level, it is more a matter of reading the documentation for the particular beans being used and following those instructions. Nevertheless, a programmer using beans does need to be familiar with the event model used by beans, which is the same as the Java 1.1 event model for AWT. Also, programmers using beans "by hand" should be familiar with the naming conventions for bean properties, methods, and events, in order to more easily understand how a given bean can be used. In Java 1.1, all AWT components are beans and follow these naming conventions.

14.4.10. Enterprise APIs: JDBC, RMI, and Security

Java 1.1 provides a number of important new features that are loosely grouped under the name "Enterprise APIs." These include JDBC (Java Database Connectivity), RMI (Remote Method Invocation), and Java Security. With Release 1.1, Java has grown too big for all of it to be documented, even in quick-reference format, in a single volume. Note, however, that while this volume does not cover the Java Security API, it does cover applet security, signed applets, and the `javakey` program that is used to create digital signatures, generate key pairs, and manage a database of entities and their keys.

14.4.11. Applet Changes

There are several new features in Java 1.1 that affect applets. The first is the introduction of JAR files. "JAR" stands for Java ARchive, and a JAR file is just that: an archive of files used by a Java applet. An applet often requires multiple class files, as well as images, sounds, and other resources, to be loaded over the the network. Prior to Java 1.1, each of these files was loaded through a separate HTTP request, which is fairly inefficient. With Java 1.1, all (or many) of the files an applet needs can be combined into a single JAR file, which an applet viewer or Web browser can download with a single HTTP request.

JAR files are stored in the ZIP file format. A JAR archive can be created with the `jar` tool shipped with the JDK. Once you have created a JAR file, you refer to it in an `<APPLET>` tag with the `ARCHIVE` attribute. This `ARCHIVE` attribute may actually be set to a comma-separated list of archive files to be downloaded. Note that specifying an `ARCHIVE` attribute simply tells the applet viewer or browser the name of a JAR file or files to load; it does not tell the browser the name of the applet that is to be run. Thus, you still must specify the `CODE` attribute (or the new `OBJECT` attribute, as we'll see below). For example, you might use an <APPLET> tag like the following to tell the browser to download the animation.jar file and start the applet contained in the file Animator.class:

```
<APPLET CODE="Animator.class" ARCHIVE="animation.jar"
    WIDTH=500 HEIGHT=200>
</APPLET>
```

There is another advantage to the use of JAR files. Every JAR file contains a "manifest" file, which you either specify explicitly when you create the archive, or which is created for you by the jar tool. The manifest is stored in a file named META-INF/MANIFEST.MF and contains meta-information about the files in the archive. By default, the jar tool creates a manifest file that contains MD5 and SHA message digests for each file in the archive. This information can be used by the applet viewer or Web browser to verify that the files in the archive have not been corrupted since the JAR file was created.

The main reason to include message digests in the manifest file, however, is so that a JAR file can have digital signatures added to it. An archive can be signed with the javakey tool. What a digital signature allows you to do is verify that the files in a JAR file have not been modified since the digital signature was added to the archive. If you trust the person or entity who signed the file, then you ought to trust the applet contained in the JAR file. (The javakey tool allows you to specify whether or not you trust any given entity.)

In JDK 1.1, the appletviewer tool understands digitally signed JAR files. When it loads an applet that has been signed by a trusted entity, it runs that applet without subjecting it to the usual security restrictions—the applet can read and write files, and do anything that a stand-alone Java application can do. Common Web browsers are likely to follow suit and give special privileges to trusted applets. One refinement we may see in the future is the ability to specify varying levels of trust, and to assign different sets of privileges to applets at those varying trust levels.

Besides the introduction of JAR files and trusted applets, Java 1.1 also supports "serialized applets." In an <APPLET> tag, you can specify the OBJECT attribute instead of the CODE attribute. If you do this, the value of the OBJECT attribute should be the name of a file that contains a serialized representation of the applet to be run. Graphical application-builder tools may prefer to output applets as pre-initialized object trees, rather than generating custom Java code to perform the initializations.

14.4.12. New JDK Utilities

JDK 1.1 includes a number of new tools. In the discussion of applets above, we've already seen `jar` for creating JAR archives and `javakey` for adding digital signatures to JAR archives. In fact, `javakey` can do much more that that—it is a very flexible tool for managing a database of entities, generating keys and certificates, and generating digital signatures.

`serialver` is a new tool used in conjunction with object serialization. When an object is deserialized, it is important to verify that the version of the class file for that object matches the version that was used to serialize it. This is done by computing a unique identifier for the class and encoding it in a private variable of the class. When an incompatible change is made to the class, a new unique identifier is computed, and the new value is stored in the private variable. It is the `serialver` tool that is used to compute this unique identifier.

`native2ascii` is a tool for programmers who program in a locale that uses a non-ASCII file encoding. The `javac` compiler can only compile files encoded in ASCII, with all Unicode characters converted to the `\uxxxx` format. What `native2ascii` does is to convert its input file to Unicode, and then output that Unicode version as an ASCII file that uses the `\u` escape for all non-ASCII Unicode characters. After you process a locally encoded file with `native2ascii`, `javac` can compile it.

In addition to the tools described here, JDK 1.1 also includes two new programs, `rmic` and `rmiregistry`, that are used in conjunction with Remote Method Invocation.

INDEX

Symbols

A

B

C

E

F

G

H

J

K

L

N

O

P

Q-R

S

T

W

X-Z